COMMENTARY ON THE DOCUMENTS OF VATICAN II

COMMENTARY
ON THE DOCUMENTS OF VATICAN II

GENERAL EDITOR:

Herbert Vorgrimler

EDITORIAL COMMITTEE:

Heinrich Suso Brechter
Bernhard Häring
Josef Höfer
Hubert Jedin
Josef Andreas Jungmann
Klaus Mörsdorf
Karl Rahner
Joseph Ratzinger
Karlheinz Schmidthüs
Johannes Wagner

COMMENTARY
ON THE DOCUMENTS
OF
VATICAN II

Volume II

DECREE ON ECUMENISM
DECREE ON THE BISHOPS' PASTORAL OFFICE IN THE CHURCH
DECREE ON THE APPROPRIATE RENEWAL
OF THE RELIGIOUS LIFE
DECREE ON PRIESTLY FORMATION

HERDER AND HERDER

1968

HERDER AND HERDER NEW YORK
232 Madison Avenue, New York, N. Y. 10016

BURNS & OATES LIMITED
25 Ashley Place, London S. W. 1

Original edition:
"Das Zweite Vatikanische Konzil, Dokumente und Kommentare",
Part II, Herder, Freiburg, 1967 (pp. 1–355)

Translated by
William Glen-Doepel, Hilda Graef, Richard Strachen, Ronald Walls and R. A. Wilson

Library of Congress Catalog Card No. 67-22928
First published in West Germany, © 1968, Herder KG
Printed in West Germany by Herder

CONTENTS

PUBLISHER'S NOTE

The publishers have not given the text of the Council documents in this book, as separate text editions, both in Latin and English, are easily available. All quotations from the English translation of the Council texts in this volume have been taken from *The Documents of Vatican II* (Walter M. Abbott, S. J., General Editor; Joseph Gallagher, Translation Editor), © America Press, published in New York, 1966, by Guild Press, Herder and Herder, and Association Press, and in London, 1966, by Geoffrey Chapman Ltd. Grateful acknowledgment is made herewith for permission to quote from these texts.

ABBREVIATIONS

AAS	*Acta Apostolicae Sedis*
AKK	*Archiv für Katholisches Kirchenrecht*
Baraúna	G. Baraúna, ed., *De Ecclesia* (1966)
CIC	*Codex Iuris Canonici*
CIO	*Codex Iuris Canonici Orientalis* (Unless stated otherwise, the references are to the law relating to persons.)
Denzinger	H. Denzinger, *Enchiridion Symbolorum* (32nd edition, 1963)
Denzinger-Schönmetzer	H. Denzinger and A. Schönmetzer, *Enchiridion Symbolorum* (33rd ed., 1965)
LTK	J. Höfer and Karl Rahner, eds., *Lexikon für Theologie und Kirche*, 10 vols. and an index vol. (2nd edition, 1957–67)
Mansi	J. D. Mansi, *Sacrorum Conciliorum Nova et Amplissima Collectio*, 31 vols. (1757–98), new edition and continuation ed. by L. Petit and J. B. Martin in 60 vols. (1899–1927)
Modi Ep	*Schema Decreti de pastorali Episcoporum munere in Ecclesia, Textus recognitus et Modi a Commissione conciliari de Episcopis ac de diocesium regimini examinati* (1965)
MTZ	*Münchener Theologische Zeitschrift*
NRT	*Nouvelle Revue Théologique*
PG	J.-P. Migne, ed., *Patrologia Graeca*, 161 vols. (1857 ff.)
PL	J.-P. Migne, ed., *Patrologia Latina*, 217 vols. and 4 index vols. (1878–90)
RGG	K. Galling, ed., *Die Religion in Geschichte und Gegenwart*, 6 vols. and an index vol. (3rd edition, 1957–65)
Vaticanum Secundum	O. Müller, ed., *Vaticanum Secundum* (1963)

Decree on Ecumenism

History of the Decree

by
*Werner Becker**

When a solemn vote was taken on the Decree on Ecumenism in the Council on 21 November 1964, and it was promulgated by Paul VI the same day, it did not find the Catholic Church unprepared. A long series of events preceded it. The ecumenical movement does not originate merely in theology, but in attentiveness to the will of God on the part of the whole Church. "Work for unity has always gone beyond the official limits of the ecumenical movement."[1] Among Catholics, it was in France and Belgium, at the beginning of the century, that men "who were concerned for the cause of unity" first began to work to achieve it. Following this, the *Una Sancta* movement became increasingly widespread.[2] In Germany it was aided by what R. Guardini has called the "awakening of the Church in the soul",[3] and on the theological level by the restoration of ecclesiology.

The ecumenical movement which came into being among non-Catholics sought to bring into contact with each other not merely Christians who were concerned for unity, but also Churches and ecclesial communities; but it failed at first to include the Catholic Church. The influence of the irenical approach of Pope Leo XIII, particularly towards the Eastern Churches, was still felt in Rome, but setbacks followed, both in the form of the encyclical *Mortalium Animos* (1928),[4] and also in 1948 and 1954, when Catholic observers were forbidden to take part in the assemblies of the World Council of Churches at Amster-

* *Translated by R. A. Wilson*
[1] Cf. Y. M.-J. Congar, "Ökumenische Bewegung", *LTK*, VII, col. 1174.
[2] Cf. J. Höfer, "Una-Sancta-Bewegung", *LTK*, X, cols. 463–6.
[3] Cf. R. Guardini, *Vom Sinn der Kirche* (1922), p. 1.
[4] Cf. M. Pribilla, *Um kirchliche Einheit, Stockholm–Lausanne–Rom* (1929), pp. 123–34; 202–40. According to a statement by F. Siegmund-Schultze, Catholic clergy took part as guests in the assembly of the World Council of Churches at Lausanne in 1927, with the agreement of the Swiss Bishop M. Besson. Cf. F. Siegmund-Schultze, "Max Josef Metzger, Martyrer der Una-Sancta" in G. Gloede and others, ed., *Ökumenische Profile. Brückenbauer der Einen Kirche* (1961), p. 361. The author also tells here of the success of his visit to the Vatican in the course of the preparation for the Edinburgh Conference on Faith and Order (p. 363).

dam and Evanston. But the instruction *Ecclesia Catholica*[5] must be regarded as the turning point in the attitude of the Catholic Church to the ecumenical movement. Its wording was still dominated by the tendency to admonish and warn, but it did recognize the working of the Holy Spirit in the non-Catholic ecumenical movement. Contacts and dialogues in which Catholics and non-Catholics could meet as equals *(par cum pari)* "to set forth the teachings of their faith as their own view" were placed under the supervision of the bishops or of the Holy See, but for the first time their encouragement was regarded and recommended as the task of the whole Church.

The accession of John XXIII brought to the See of Peter a Pope who for several decades had had personal experience of divided Christianity in the Balkans. His repeated invitation to unity was rightly understood, and given a surprisingly friendly reception, in many quarters. It lacked any trace of the desire on the part of the Church of Rome to "absorb" other Churches and communities. Hopes that Pope John had planned his Council as a Council of union were soon disappointed. His real motive was a concern for the condition and the missionary power of the Church, and indeed for the Christian gospel as a whole. This was the source of his appeal to the Church's spirit of fellowship, in confidence in the effective activity of the Holy Spirit in Christianity. An important part was played here from the first by his conviction that the idea of the Church was also awakened in the soul of non-Catholic Christians.[6] The setting up of the Secretariat for Promoting Christian Unity showed the world the Pope's true intention.

By the motu proprio *Superno Dei Nutu* of 5 June 1960[7] the task of the Secretariat was laid down. It was intended not merely to be a point of contact for separated brethren with regard to the Council, but was also intended to aid them "to find more easily the way to attain the unity for which Jesus Christ implored his heavenly Father in fervent prayer". Like the other preparatory commissions, the Secretariat had the task "of studying and submitting to scholarly inquiry, taking into account the proposals of the pastoral leaders of the Church and the indications and material proposed for discussion by the authorities of the Roman Curia", the subjects chosen by the Pope for the Council.[8] According to an early utterance by Cardinal Bea[9] the specific task of the Secretariat during the prepa-

---

[5] *AAS* 42 (1950), pp. 142–7.

[6] In his opening address to the second session of the Council on 29 September 1963 Paul VI declared: "What attitude will the Council adopt towards the vast number of brethren separated from us . . . what will it do? The question is quite clear. This Council itself was also called for this reason" (cf. *Vaticanum Secundum*, II, p. 69). The statement of W. Visser 't Hooft in his last report to the Central Committee of the World Council of Churches in Geneva says similarly that "the existence of the ecumenical movement was one of the reasons for the holding of the Council" (*Die Zeichen der Zeit* 20 [1966], p. 197).

[7] *AAS* 52 (1960), pp. 433–7.

[8] Cf. *Herder-Korrespondenz* 14 (1959/60), p. 514.

[9] In an interview at a press conference on 7 June 1960 in New York. Cf. Augustin Cardinal Bea, *Die Einheit der Christen* (1963), pp. 199–203.

rations for the Council was not only to provide information to separated Christians concerning the Council, and to receive their wishes and suggestions, but also to carry out an independent theological review of the themes discussed by the Council, from the ecumenical point of view. The Secretariat shared a responsibility for seeing that the whole Council expressed "the truth, unity and love present in the Catholic Church" in a way which would also be comprehensible to separated brethren. It was to make known to the Council in an appropriate way the results of its efforts towards a better knowledge of the Church's doctrine and the situation in different countries, as well as of the condition of the ecumenical movement, in a constant awareness that "the Holy Spirit, who is the Spirit of unity, is capable of far more than man".

On 14 November 1960 the Secretariat took up its task under the leadership of Cardinal Bea,[10] and went on to set up first ten and later fifteen sub-committees on a wide group of theological and practical themes in order to give an ecumenical dimension to the coming Council.[11]

When Bishop Hermann Volk later argued in a highly regarded speech in the Council[12] that Catholic theology must be ecumenical in all its branches, beginning with a dynamic understanding of the catholicity of the Church, and when he spoke of the duty of the Church to strive for a true universality in its doctrine and its life, he expressed ideas[13] which had already been brought to maturity in

---

[10] He was assisted by the Secretary of the Secretariat, Mgr. J. G. M. Willebrands, who had been the director of the "Catholic Conference for Ecumenical Questions" since 1952.

[11] For the earlier history of the Secretariat for Christian Unity cf. J. G. M. Willebrands in his introduction to Augustin Cardinal Bea and W. Visser 't Hooft, *Friede zwischen Christen* (1966), pp. 10 ff. On the task and composition of the Secretariat cf. J. F. Arrighi, "Le Secretariat du Concile pour l'Unité", *Ecclesia* 154 (Jan. 1962), pp. 193–201; also W. Becker, "Das Konzil und die Einheit der Christen", *Vaticanum Secundum,* I, pp. 133–88, especially 144 ff. The latter also contains a list of the sub-committees in so far as they were known at that time (p. 158). Cf. also *Herder-Korrespondenz* 17 (1962/63), pp. 274 ff. Cardinal Bea later stated: "The Secretariat is a channel of communication set up by papal authority and a means to assist the realization of full unity through all conceivable forms of co-operation." Cf. Augustin Cardinal Bea, *Einheit in Freiheit* (1965), p. 208. A full catalogue of the members and advisers of the Secretariat for Christian Unity *(Secretariatus ad christianorum unitatem fovendam),* which still exists today as an organ of the Roman Curia, has been given since 1963 in the *Annuario Pontificio,* Città del Vaticano; in the 1967 edition 45 members and 17 advisers are listed besides the 3 honorary members from the College of Cardinals and the permanent members of the Bureau in Rome (pp. 1132 ff.).

[12] On 21 Nov. 1963. Text in J. C. Hampe, *Ende der Gegenreformation?* (1964), pp. 322–6; cf. also the comments on the speech of Bishop E. De Smedts in *Vaticanum Secundum,* I, pp. 166 f., 333 f.

[13] Paul VI's first understanding of the matter was similar, when, at the time when he was still a cardinal, he spoke, at the requiem for John XXIII in Milan Cathedral on 7 June 1963, of the "universality of the Catholic faith", and the "ecumenism of the Roman Church" (cf. Augustin Cardinal Bea, *Einheit in Freiheit,* p. 208). For him the "inner *oikumene* of catholicity" meant unity in diversity, with great possibilities of development in a new phase of Church history. Thus in the opening address quoted in note 9 he said: "The Council is striving, as is often said, towards a full and all-embracing ecumenicity; in desire at least, in prayer at least, and in preparation at least."

early discussions in the Secretariat. The substance of these was that through the Council and in obedience to the gospel, the Catholic Church should manifest its true universality and catholicity in such a way that it would be comprehensible even to separated brethren. The issues which particularly concerned the separated brethren must be studied anew, not merely with the methods of the Counter-Reformation, but through the active consciousness in contemporary Catholic theology that a new beginning was being made, and taking into account the central problems which the ecumenical movement had encountered.

This meant that the sub-committees dealt with numerous themes in the sphere of the concept of the Church and the doctrine of the word of God. Some of the sub-committees had themes which they shared with the Theological Commission: the hierarchical structure of the Church, the universal priesthood and the mission of the laity, non-Catholic Christians in their relationship to the Church, and also the significance and pre-eminence of the word of God, the sources of revelation, etc.[14] Direct ecumenical importance attached to the sub-committees for the study of the ecumenical movement among separated brethren, especially those dealing with the concept of the unity of the Church, as seen by the World Council of Churches in Geneva, with prayer for Christian unity, with religious freedom and with mixed marriages. Two further sub-committees were explicitly concerned with Catholic ecumenism. These dealt with the nature and distinctive features of ecumenical work, with its distinction from the pastoral task of winning and caring for converts, and also with the practical realization of ecumenism in the Catholic Church. The question of the invitation of non-Catholic observers to the Council, raised by Cardinal Tardini in the presence of reporters on 30 October 1959,[15] and which was finally decided in a positive sense by the Central Commission,[16] was also one of the functions of the Secretariat.[17]

Here we are primarily interested in the contribution of the preliminary work of the Secretariat to the formulation of the Decree on Ecumenism.

In the programme laid down by the Secretariat for its work, the theme "Catholic ecumenism" had a dominant place from the beginning. The first reports were submitted to the full session of the Secretariat for Promoting Christian Unity at the end of August 1961.

---

[14] There was also, at the express wish of Pope John XXIII, a sub-commission on *Quaestiones de Iudaeis*. For liturgical questions and for the ecumenical aspect of the Eastern Churches joint commissions were proposed (with the *Commissio Sacrae Liturgiae* and the *Commissio pro Ecclesiis Orientalibus*).

[15] Cf. *Herder-Korrespondenz* 14 (1959/60), pp. 103 ff.

[16] At the request of the Pope, as the first object of discussion at the session of the Central Commission from 7 to 17 November 1961. (Cf. *Herder-Korrespondenz* 16 [1961/62], pp. 152 and 154.) The *relatio* of Cardinal Bea *(Quaestiones de non catholicis invitandis ad Concilium Vaticanum II)* appeared at the same time.

[17] A statute for the observers prepared by the Secretariat was included in the *Ordo Concilii Vaticani Secundi celebrandi*.

In December 1961 the members of the Secretariat received the following documents, which were passed on to the Central Commission as suggestions for the work of the coming Council:

1. *Votum de ecclesiae oecumenicitate*
2. *Pro decreto doctrinali elaborando de oecumenicitate suggestiones*
3. *Votum de oecumenismo catholico*

By the ecumenicity of the Church is understood a particular form of its catholicity, in the sense that with regard to its rites, its spiritual life, its theological systems, and the form of Christian life which it practises, as well as with regard to its ecclesiastical usages, the Church is not restricted to any particularism or uniformity, but on the contrary can accept in unity, and is bound to integrate into a unity, plurality and diversity.

With regard to other Christian communities a real recognition of the Christian inheritance of separated brethren is necessary. This means taking into account all "traces" or "elements" of the Church, which by the grace of God have persisted and are alive amongst separated brethren; this is how — albeit to an extent which can vary — they already really, although incompletely and imperfectly, belong to the Church.

Even in this early stage in the preliminary work the immediate aim of the ecumenical movement, that separated Christians should live a better life together in peace and in truth, was distinguished from the ultimate aim, that of the restoration of unity: "We must learn to know and love each other better."

The starting point for all these considerations was the instruction of 1949, which recognized the effective presence of the Holy Spirit even in the brethren separated from us, and affirmed the possibility of a dialogue conducted between equal partners *par cum pari*. Ecumenical dialogue assumes this equality between partners, not as something objective and ontological, but from the subjective and psychological point of view. Thus those who take part in the dialogue both learn and teach at the same time. There was also a recognition of the necessity that a conciliar document on the subject should not be written in a warning and censorious tone, but should have the aim of encouraging and strengthening this movement, which in our own time has seized the imagination of Christians.

In dealing with this question, the Secretariat found itself in accord with many of the desires which had been uttered by bishops and theologians throughout the world in the very earliest stages of preparation for the Council. Two hundred and ninety-nine proposals have been counted, which were made on the theme of ecumenism during the period. These mentioned the means and the ways to obtain unity, the special problems of the Orthodox, Anglicans and Protestants, the question of *communicatio in sacris,* and also the question of the invitation of non-Catholic observers to the Council — frequently also from the point of view of avoiding the dangers which an ecumenical opening of the Council could bring with it. Many other requests sent in by the bishops displayed concern for the relationship between the mystical body of Christ and non-Catholic Christians, and for the question of membership of the Church and the possibility of salvation outside the Church. Altogether, the Secretariat for Unity presented five draft statements to the Central Commission: 1. On the necessity of prayer for unity of Christians, especially at the present time (8 pages); 2. On the Word of God (8 pages); 3. On Catholic ecumenism (16 pages); 4. On the Jews (8 pages); 5. On religious freedom (20 pages).[18] Part of this material was discussed at the seventh session of the Central Commission, from 12 to 20 June 1962, and referred back to the Secretariat for revision.

There is little indication that at this time the Central Preparatory Commission for the Council concerned itself with these precise questions. They are not amongst the themes which this commission passed on to the Theological Commission.[19] However, two of the schemata proposed by the Commission for the Eastern Churches were allowed to go forward: on *communicatio in sacris* with non-Catholic Eastern Christians, and on the problem of the "reconciliation of Eastern dissidents". In accordance with this, the latter commission drew up texts "On the Unity of the Church, *Ut omnes unum sint*", and on *communicatio in sacris* with non-Catholic Eastern Christians.

The first of these two drafts formed one of the seven schemata which Pope John chose from the seventy-nine proposals for the Council passed by the Central Commission, to be dealt with during the first session of the Council. In the meantime, the Theological Commission had also drawn up, as Chapter XI of its schema for a Constitution on the Church, a section of sixteen pages on ecumenism, but this was only given to the Council Fathers towards the end of the first session.

In the fourth general congregation of the Council on 22 October 1962, the Pope's decision was announced that the Secretariat for Christian Unity, with all its members and consultors, should be made of equal rank to the other ten commissions of the Council. In fact this decision meant that the Secretariat had a special status by comparison with the other commissions. There was no need for a new choice of members to be made in this case, but only for it to be enlarged by eight bishops, in order for the complement of thirty bishops laid down for all the commissions to be attained.[20] It was possible for the work previously begun to be continued, with the co-operation of bishops and priests, so special care had been taken here to ensure that the continuity of the work which had preceded the Council with that which took place during the Council. The Secretariat was now able to bring the schemata it had drawn up before the

---

[18] Cf. G. Caprile, "L'iter del Decreto", *Osservatore della Domenica,* Special edition, "Concilio Vaticano II" (1965), p. 71.

[19] Bishop De Smedt declared in his speech on 19 November 1962: "The Pope has given our Secretariat the task of advising other commissions with regard to the ecumenical aspect of the draft they have prepared. But the Theological Commission has rejected our co-operation." (Cf. *Herder-Korrespondenz* 17 [1962/63], p. 197.)

[20] See above note 11.

Council on its own responsibility. However, during the first session the Secretariat for Unity never got as far as this. Within its own sphere of work, the only text still before the Council was that already mentioned, prepared by the commission for the Eastern Churches: *Ut omnes unum sint*.

The content of the schema *De Ecclesiae* *Unitate "Ut omnes unum sint"*

After a short introduction, the unity of the Church is derived from the unity of its government by the hierarchy, and more precisely by the Pope (§ 3). As a visible and invisible communion, the Church possesses "a double status". So far as it is the Church in time, it must necessarily "use the structure of a human society". Just as sinews and tendons are necessary to hold together the body, there must also be "authority and jurisdiction, hierarchy, the inequality of superiors and subjects, laws and punishments" in the Church (§ 4). Thus Christ himself built his Church upon the foundation of the apostles[21] and gave it an hierarchical order. The apostles instituted successors, the bishops, because the Church upon earth cannot exist without authority. In this respect Christ is in every way and from every point of view the true head of the Church, and both its lawgiver and judge;[22] Peter is only his deputy on the order of jurisdiction. The successor of Peter, who relies like all the faithful upon the grace of God, and like all priests is Christ's instrument, also acts in the name of Christ (§ 6). His governing authority takes in spiritual matters, in so far as they belong to the temporal order, e.g. the sacraments — the use of the power of consecration is subject to his jurisdiction — and also includes the proclamation of doctrine, the infallible teaching office which he exercises either alone or together with the college of bishops. This is the unity desired by Christ: a unity realized in visible form, and articulated through the bishops and their head, the successor of Peter.

In the next paragraph (§ 7) divisions and schisms are discussed. Through "human weakness", disputes, mutual ignorance and alienation came about within the flock of Jesus Christ, so that parts of the Church broke away and set themselves up as independent groups. The Church of Christ has been cruelly mutilated by this. Because the Church can only be one, there is, apart from the Church ruled by the successor of Peter, "no other Church, which can profess itself to be the true and only Church". No Church separated from the See of Peter belongs in the same way to that same Church, which is both visible and heavenly. § 8 goes on to emphasize that the necessary unity with the head does not exclude diversity within the body. Too great a uniformity would mar the beauty of the body. Hence the importance of distinctive traditions, especially amongst the venerable Churches of the East. But the more room that is made for differences, the greater the need for a single authority.

---

[21] Eph 2:20 is quoted, but without any mention of the prophetic element.
[22] Jn 5:17 and Jas 4:12 are given as references.

Anyone who in good faith lives in a separated Church is not regarded as a stranger by the true Church (§ 9). But he lacks very many means of salvation, and especially that of guidance by the teaching magisterium, which helps to maintain the wholeness of faith and morality. Division damages the inward and outer growth of the family of Christ. Consequently it is the wish of the Council that all "dissidents" should be concerned for the perfect unity of the flock of Christ, and come together in one fold (§ 10). Here, however, the common heritage must always be taken into account, and so must the spiritual link which still exists: "We have remained brethren."

The next paragraph emphasizes the constant effort of the Church to restore communion among all who believe in Christ: the Church has appealed for prayer for unity, summoned Councils, and given doctrinal decisions which are meant to illuminate what has been obscure; the Popes too have repeatedly uttered exhortations and invitations to unity. The intention of the Council is to lead all Christians to pray for the unity which Christ besought for his Church, and at the same time to use all appropriate means to remove what still hinders that unity.

In part II of the schema the means which can prepare the way for unity are dealt with in detail. Theological, liturgical, juridical, psychological and practical means are listed here. Supernatural means are discussed first (§ 13). Prayer, accompanied by invincible faith, is omnipotent, even in what from the human point of view seems a desperate situation.[23] In praying for unity public prayers should also be instituted, especially in the period before Pentecost, and during the week of prayer in January (§ 15), with the invocation of the help of the Virgin Mary, who in fact enjoys a special veneration in the East (§ 16): the mother of all will take care that Christians become one people who are brothers. As a pre-condition for the answering of prayer for unity, the renewal of Christian life in humility and love is required (§ 17).

In the next paragraph a change in the atmosphere between the Churches in the East and the West is demanded as a psychological necessity (§ 18). Here great transformations are possible and are required. A much greater respect than hitherto must be shown to the spirit of the East. One has no right to impose one's own mode of thought upon others, and it is wholly unnecessary to defend firmly and obstinately certain expressions which have been used hitherto (§ 19). What can help here is a return to the sources, to the holy Scriptures and to the Fathers of the Church, which are the common heritage of all (§ 20).

Here a positive method is necessary, not mere apologetics or even polemics. In particular, in the exposition of ecclesiology the ecumenical point of view must be maintained. In doing this, Catholic truth must be precisely distinguished

---

[23] In § 14 it becomes obvious that in spite of a title worded in general terms, the schema has unity with Eastern Christians particularly in mind.

from the theological theses of different systems and schools (§ 21). There is no place for false irenicism and accommodation at the expense of the purity of doctrine (§ 22).

The liturgy is also an important means towards unity. It is at this very point that diversity is the common heritage of the whole Church (§ 23).[24] Amongst Eastern Christians, it is in fact the oldest form which is the best. That which has come down from ancient times should be particularly cherished,[25] and false innovations should not be sought. In their "return to the Catholic Church" the Eastern Churches should find their own house ready for them, and not a strange dwelling.

In the sphere of canon law the Eastern Churches have the right to rule themselves according to their own discipline (§ 27). A better mutual knowledge, coming from love, is required.

Once again, the psychological factor is underlined (§ 29). Catholics of the West should show more respect and love to their separated brethren. They should be spoken to in simple and direct terms, and in an irenical spirit.[26] A special warning is given against all injurious zeal. Even what are apparently only trifling offensive expressions should be eliminated, although they may have been in use for a long time (§ 30).

Since the documents of the history of the Church's schism contain much that is contrary to love, a public confession of guilt is urged upon the Council. The petition of the Lord's Prayer "forgive us our trespasses", must also be applied to sins against unity.[27] After referring to the attitude of the tax collector in the gospel and to the Lord's warning in the story of the woman taken in adultery (Jn 8:7), the text reads: "As a consequence of the errors of the past, committed by both sides, the brethren of the Christian people have separated and taken opposite sides; their ways have parted. In the spirit of penitence and reconciliation on the part of all Christians, the final outcome will be that all are united in the one house of the Father" (§ 31).

With reference to Eph 4:5 it is emphasized that unity should only be sought in what is necessary (§ 32).

By mutual dialogue between experts, and with earnestness and love, the setting aside of mutual understandings and the restoration of trust should be sought (§ 33). These dialogues should be encouraged in particular by bishops, who are responsible for the sheep who are wandering outside the fold. To these can also be added common works in the practical sphere, especially in social

---

[24] Here the Council of Florence and the defence by Leo XIII of the maintenance of the Eastern rites is referred to.

[25] Here too is found the statement, which many found offensive, that in Orthodox rites everything should be retained which is not contrary to faith or morals.

[26] Express mention is made here of the necessity of revising history books.

[27] In this very extensive paragraph, the warning in 1 Jn 1:10 is also mentioned, and this also occurs in the final text of the Decree on Ecumenism.

life. Christians should form a common front against the inroads of atheism and communism (§ 35).

Once again mention is made of what the Church owes to Eastern Christians, right back to the earliest period of the Church. They are called the Churches of the seven Councils which took place in the East. The great Church Fathers of the East are mentioned by name (§ 37). Another practical means is that of drawing on the longing of Christians for unity, which is continually increasing at the present day (§ 38). In all this, the patriarchs who are united with Rome have assisted by their good example (§ 39).

For this to be carried out in practice, a commission of experts should be set up in every diocese (§ 40). Students of theology should be instructed as to what forms the right method of ecumenical action, and obtain a sound knowledge of the problem of the Eastern Churches (§ 41). In Rome and other places institutes should be set up, in which theology is conducted in the spirit and according to the methods of the Eastern Churches (§ 42). Care must be taken that Eastern Christians are provided with sufficient places for studying at Catholic universities.

All Christians must co-operate in this concern, in word, act and prayer, for the return of separated brethren to Catholic unity.

Part III of the schema deals with even more practical matters; it lays down the conditions for reconciliation and calls Eastern Christians to observe them (§ 43). It recommends *dies pro Oriente* (§ 44). The associations which have been founded for the restoration of unity are praised. The canonization of all who have fought for unity should be hastened (§ 45). In order to advance the unity of the Church, a sacred *consilium* or a congregation of experts in this matter should be set up at the Holy See (§ 46).

Once again special recognition is given to the Eastern Catholic Churches. They should also be given more part in the government of the Church. Nuncios should also be chosen from the Eastern Catholic Churches. All parts of the Church, being equal in value, should grow together under the one head, who is neither Eastern nor Western, but the father of all (§ 47).[28]

In the next paragraph concrete conditions for reunion are laid down, and the way to it is described. Eastern Christians should know that if they return to unity and take their place once again, no more will be asked of them on their return than what is necessary in order to become a member of the Church (§ 48). They would have to make the confession of faith, which includes the profession of the unity of the Church, without the renunciation of errors, and in a simple form. The right of Eastern Churches to maintain their own discipline is acknowledged (§ 50). Their orders are valid and can continue to be exercised (§ 51).

Those who return should not regard the present condition of the Church as

---

[28] It is notable that the words *Caput* and *Pater Communis* are written with initial capitals, although it is clear that it is not Christ but the Pope who is meant.

unalterable. Much can be improved, and must be, with regard to their return. The discipline of the Church and its hierarchical order can be altered on the basis of a necessity approved by the Pope, into a fuller form, which is more appropriate to the new circumstances and to the dignity and importance of the Eastern Churches (§ 32).

The document closes with a prayer from the Liturgy of Basil the Great for the return of those in error to the Catholic and Apostolic Church.

The debate in the Council

Fifty Fathers, including eleven cardinals and patriarchs, spoke in the debate on the schema from 26 to 30 November 1962. The report was made by Cardinal Cicognani and Fr. Athanasius Welykyi. Cardinal Liénart at once spoke very critically of the schema, which with its juridical language could only serve as a hindrance to the progress of reunion. Three other cardinals defended the schema. During the following day of the debate it became clear that the dominant note was that of rejection, especially amongst the Eastern patriarchs and bishops. The contributions of the Melchite Patriarch Maximos IV and the bishops of his synod were of particular note. The Patriarch declared[29] that the schema under discussion would in fact embitter those of good will among the Orthodox, rather than attract them. The historical outline underlying the document was typically Roman, and concealed the mutual responsibility for the schism of Christianity. In his own words: "The Eastern Churches are apostolic Churches, founded by the apostles. They are not derivative Churches, for they have existed from the very first. The schema does not show how Peter came to have his leading position in the college of bishops. It is necessary to lay more emphasis on the collegiality of the government of the Church, and the papacy would then be manifested as the foundation of this collegiality." The schema is headed "The Unity of the Church" and yet it deals only with our attitude to the Orthodox. As a matter of fact the Orthodox are much closer to us Catholics than are the Protestants. The only question which still divides us is that of the Roman primacy. "For us Eastern Catholics this separation from our Eastern brethren is a fearful torment, which strikes our inmost heart. Reunion is our greatest desire, and we are prepared for the utmost sacrifice to achieve it. They and we are *one* family, and consequently we desire to forget the dissension of the past and human considerations, and to unite ourselves with them in Christ, in order to realize his prayer: 'That they may be one'".[30]

Archbishop E. Zoghby declared: "Although the Eastern Church has always recognized the primacy of the Bishop of Rome in some form, it was never part of the Latin Church. It does not trace its descent from the latter and does not

---

[29] Patriarch Maximos IV Saigh of Antioch and two other bishops from the Arab region spoke in French.

[30] Cf. X. Rynne's book on the first session of the Second Vatican Council.

owe its existence to it. Its dogmatic and disciplinary development is independent of that of the Latin Church. Thus the Church of the East is a Church independent in origin, just like the Latin Church in the West. Its dogma is identical in substance, but its theology is different. This difference in tradition, thought and discipline is reflected in the difference of rites, which has always been recognized by Rome. One must now apply this principle constantly, and recognize the legitimate differences of discipline and theology . . .

"The Catholic Church today, united as it is in the Council, which is under God's blessing, appears to be universal and ecumenical as far as its territorial representation is concerned. It looks forward to the day when Orthodoxy with its two hundred million believers will be represented in it with regard to the legacy which the Fathers of its Church, the great Doctors of the Church and the holy monks have left, and through which it unceasingly nourishes and enriches the Churches of the East and the West. It has been said that this Council is no reunion Council. That may be. But in as much as Christians are separate, no Council inspired by the spirit of Jesus Christ can show itself to be uninterested in unity."

Archbishop N. Edelby of Edessa expressed a view which had already been heard outside the general congregation: the rejection of the dogmatic preamble of the schema, the main part of which, concerning the means for furthering unity, he accepted, albeit on the condition that certain changes were introduced into it. He was of the opinion that the Catholic Church had not done as much for unity in the past as the schema asserted. He also demanded that the title "Churches" should also be used for the separated Eastern Churches, on the grounds that they were of apostolic origin.

A. G. Vuccino, formerly Archbishop of the Latin rite in Corfù, argued along the same line: "We are very grateful that on a single subject not only one but three different drafts have been drawn up, the result of the work of the Theological Commission, the Commission for the Eastern Churches, and the Secretariat for Unity. One might, however, ask what is the reason for such a multiplicity of schemata and texts? May the reason not be the lack of co-operation between the commissions mentioned? I do not know whether I am making too bold a judgment. Apart from this, however, one must also ask for what reason the Fathers of the Council are now obliged to go to the trouble of filling substantial gaps, which could have been avoided if the commissions mentioned had gone to the trouble of coming to an agreement to work together. Let us therefore continue to work in peace, patiently prepared to listen to long speeches upon a single theme which has very unfortunately been broken up. What is the purpose of this waste of our precious time? We might suggest that under the heading 'The Unity of the Church' there should be four chapters, dealing first with the Catholic teaching on the unity of the Church, and then with the teaching of the Eastern Churches on the subject, and then with that of the Churches which have come into being through the Reformation. In Chapter IV ecumenism should be dealt with, as it is being realized at the present day by all Christian Churches, whether Catholic or not. It is desirable that a wholly new schema should be prepared along the lines suggested, but this time through the co-operation of the three commissions mentioned, or more simply, on the basis of the co-operation of the Commission for the Eastern Churches and the Secretariat for Unity . . .''

On the content of the schema he said, "If one disregards the first three paragraphs, one must affirm that in the rest only the purely juridical or institutional aspect of the unity of the Church is dealt with, a unity which is nowadays called social or structural. In fact in these few pages mention is made more than twelve times of concepts such as authority and jurisdiction, and of the juridical, governing and restrictive authority which is accorded to the Church and to the supreme head of the Church. Without doubt all this is necessary, but according to the will of Christ these things are all merely means meant to serve the sanctification of the members of the mystical body of Christ. One may also ask, not without an anxious concern, to what extent a purely juridical description of the unity of the Church can contribute anything at all to the dialogue with our Orthodox and Protestant brethren. It is my most profound conviction that the first part of the decree, instead of contributing to the setting up of an ecumenical dialogue, rather represents a serious hindrance to it, and is wholly alien to the orientation which the Council should have.

"Let me go into more detail. After spending more than thirty years on a peninsula in the Balkans, where I have been able to get to know our beloved brethren, the Orthodox, I wish to say that the description of the unity of the Church presented in the decree before us at the moment is not only incapable of arousing the slightest goodwill among our Orthodox brethren, but instead would provoke an almost instinctive rejection. We must be perfectly clear: we are concerned not with a modification of doctrine, but with the way to present it to our brethren. We Latins, heirs of the doctrine of the Council of Trent, have become used to giving pre-eminence, with a very special emphasis, and sometimes in too rigorous concepts, to the authority and power of the Catholic Church, and especially of its supreme head. In striving to encourage union among Christians we should guard against using such language, and go instead to the gospel, from which the authentic truth shines out.

"When Christ spoke of himself, he said, 'I am the good shepherd . . .' (cf. Jn 10:9–16). The task of the good shepherd is in the first instance constituted by what is called *diakonia,* service, the service of the care of souls, which proceeds from the heart of the good shepherd, that is, from love for his sheep. It is Christ who put to Peter the question: 'Simon, son of John, do you love me?' And after Peter had said that he did, Christ said to him 'Feed my sheep' (Jn 21:16f.). Let us therefore speak to our brethren in this language of the gospel, which they understand and which touches them. If we tell them that the primacy of Peter is in the first instance a *diakonia,* a pastoral task, a service, which the leader of the apostles received from Christ not in order to exercise power to rule, but to feed

13

the flock of Christ, then ultimately the juridical authority of Peter is related to his pastoral task . . . This *diakonia,* which proceeds from the heart of the sovereign shepherd, is poured out through the bond of the communion of the Holy Spirit upon the soul of his representative, to enable him to exercise his pastoral task with firmness and tenderness. And finally it is love, the bond of perfection, which rules everyone and everything in the Church of Christ, and draws everything, including juridical authority, into the building up of the body of Christ. This is the true image of the sovereign shepherd in the Church, which in its own distinctive way exercises its power of attraction upon separated brethren, who can only be led by love with a firm hand to the one fold of Christ, which is the Catholic Church."[31]

There were also Eastern bishops, including Cardinal Tappouni and the Chaldaean Patriarch Paul II Cheikho from Babylon, both of whom came from the world of thought represented by the Commission for the Eastern Churches, who approved the schema, while other Fathers even felt that it went too far in its irenical approach. All recognized the importance of the issue, and desired that the text should manifest the spirit of love which would flow out everywhere. A few emphasized that it was not always Rome that should be saying *mea culpa* (Cardinal Ruffini and Bishop Khoury of Tyre in Lebanon, who was of the Maronite rite). Two things were decisive: first, that the pattern of the debate was determined by the active participation of the Uniat bishops,[32] and second, that a new understanding of the ecumenical scope of the Council was surprisingly evident in this debate. When a few days earlier (19 November) Bishop De Smedt had called, during the debate on the schema on Revelation, and on behalf of the Secretariat for Unity, for the Council Fathers to be prepared for an ecumenical dialogue, and to open the conventional understanding of the faith to ecumenical love, and fullness, he had been vigorously applauded. Now many bishops demanded that the schema should contain "a comprehensive view of Church unity".[33] In no case should efforts on behalf of unity in the East be seen in isolation from the other historical divisions of Christianity. The conviction expressed by Bishop De Smedt, that it was not enough, if Christians were to draw closer to one another and be reconciled, simply to present Catholic doctrine clearly in conventional terminology, was taken up by several bishops, and applied in particular to the opening paragraphs of the schema, with their harsh presentation of the relationship between the Pope and the bishops.

The Ukrainian Archbishop Hermaniuk referred directly to the connection between the emphasis on the collegial structure of the universal episcopate, and the possibility of closer relations with the Orthodox Churches. The unity of the

---

[31] Texts from the French, given in R. Laurentin, *L'enjeu du concile. Bilan de la première session* (1963), pp. 114–17 (shortened).

[32] They formed a minority of 138 Fathers out of the 2160 who were present.

[33] Cf. *Herder-Korrespondenz* 17 (1962/63), p. 197.

Church is in no sense limited "solely to unity in Peter and his successors".[34] As Archbishop (now Cardinal) Heenan pointed out, what is decisive is that the Churches of the East and West are not separated by doctrine as such, but by the problem of authority.

Bishop Coadjutor A. Ancel of Lyons[35] declared that Catholics needed to have true humility, and ought to understand that they are "not the lords, but the servants of the truth". It is true that Catholics could joyfully profess that truth had always been present in the Church, but they should be sad that they had not always borne faithful witness to this truth. "We have no right to condemn those who have gone astray, especially where Catholics have frequently, to put it mildly, been the cause of misunderstandings and difficulties. Now is the time to do due penance for these wrongs. If we confess before God and man that we have contributed to these divisions through our incomprehension and errors — we ourselves, and not merely our predecessors — then we can hope that we may bring an end to the continuing errors and mistakes which even today prevent reunion. Just as in his own time the Apostle Paul had to prevent circumcision and Jewish dietary laws from being forced upon his new Gentile converts, so the Catholic Church at the present day should not force the issue, where the truth of faith is not at stake. And in general we should not judge our brethren, but ourselves." The Philippine Bishop A. Olalia recommended, in the interests of reunion, the dissolution of the Congregation for the Eastern Churches, instead of which the different Churches should be represented in the Roman Congregations.

Cardinal Bea also spoke during the discussion and declared that the demands of the modern age in which we were living were not taken into account in the schema. He also declared that it was necessary for the three present schemata, which at the moment dealt with different aspects of the question, to be combined into one.[36]

The content of Chapter XI of the schema *De Ecclesia*

Whereas the schema of the Secretariat for Unity mentioned by Cardinal Bea and several bishops was still unknown to the bishops, since it had not received the approbation of the Central Preparatory Commission, Chapter XI of the schema on the Church formed part of the text presented on 23 October 1962 in the full Council. This schema showed very little trace of the ecclesiological advance which was now becoming increasingly evident as the true purpose of the Council. No account was taken in it of recent theology, and least of all of the vision of the Church as historical reality; neither the inner significance of its structure nor

---

[34] Cf. O. Müller, "Das Schema 'Ut omnes unum sint'", in *Vaticanum Secundum,* I, pp. 386–9 (quotation from p. 387).
[35] Cf. X. Rynne, *op. cit.*
[36] Cf. also H. Helbing, *Das zweite Vatikanische Konzil. Ein Bericht* (1966), pp. 54 f.

its relationship to the Kingdom of God and to the gifts of the Holy Spirit were treated in it. The German bishops also advanced the view that as a whole it was too negative in its conception and neither pastoral nor ecumenical.[37] The weakness of this schema was manifested particularly in the concluding chapter on ecumenism. This chapter was divided into the following sections: 1. Introduction. 2. The links that still exist and the unity desired by Christ. 3. The relationship of the Catholic Church to individual separated Christians. 4. The relationship of the Catholic Church to separated Christian communities. 5. The relationship of the Catholic Church to the ecumenical movement outside the Church. 6. The aim of the ecumenical movement within the Catholic Church, and the dangers to be avoided with regard to it. 7. *Communicatio in sacris*. 8. The co-operation of Catholics with separated Christians.

The introduction says with regard to the divisions of Christianity, by which the manifestation of the unity asserted of it is to some extent obscured in the eyes of the world, that it is part of the missionary task of the Council to proclaim more effectively to those who glory in the name of Christ, and also to non-Christians, the true faith and the true doctrine of unity. The Council has to show the true aim of the desire for unity with which God has nowadays everywhere inspired the separated communities of Christians: that is, the Church as the only saving institution for all.

The next paragraph (§ 49) speaks of what is still held in common: especially the profession of Christ as God and Saviour, and the testimony to Christ before the world. With regard to Orthodox Christians, mention is made of the Holy Eucharist, which they too have as the sign and source of unity.[38]

But the recognition of the links which still exist seems only to provide in the course of the argument an excuse to emphasize how profound are the differences which exist in the conception of the one Church. "Only those who are in communion under a bishop who is linked to the Pope and confess the whole faith are admitted to the Holy Eucharist."

The next section (§ 50) makes an appeal to all individual Christians to follow the invitation of Mother Church. The presence of elements of the Church among them is only seen as a call to accede to the unity of the Catholic Church. This is particularly true of the holy Scriptures and the sacraments, which belong to the Church of Christ and are means towards unity. Christians

---

[37] In a very critical opinion put forward by the conference of German-speaking bishops in Munich on 6 February 1963 (cf. vol. I of this commentary, p. 175).

[38] A note states that the Eucharist is central to the Orthodox, who in part associate with it a "universalist ecclesiology" in the sense of the organized Church. The same is true of the High Church tendency in Protestantism. The Lutherans demand unity in the confession of faith, but not in the profession of adherence to the communion of the Church. The World Council of Churches has not yet come to any agreement about intercommunion. It is therefore necessary to set out the dogmatic and biblical basis, especially with regard to the relationship between unity in worship and institutional unity — also because some Catholics are not clear on the matter.

16

are not regarded here as merely individuals, but also as "united in their communities".[39]

Where the fullness of revelation is lacking, the elements of the Church which have been preserved themselves serve as the basis of the division of the inheritance of Christ, "although these elements bring salvation, and although a fruitful Christian spiritual life can grow from them". It is this which gives a special urgency to the invitation to the "fullness of the inheritance of Christ and of revelation", which has been maintained by the Catholic Church alone; and all Catholics are required to co-operate in this through their word and example (§ 51).

The next two paragraphs (52 and 53) deal with the ecumenical movement, but the theme is not that of its unity. The Holy Spirit is at work in the ecumenical movement. But everyone "who wishes to obey the will of Christ in his whole heart and grow in the degree of his ecumenicity must advance under the guidance of the Spirit of Christ more and more towards that Church, which is the one house of God with different dwelling places, in unity of faith, government and fellowship under the Vicar of Christ", the Roman Pope.

The growth of the ecumenical movement, which has also become an active force within the Catholic Church through prayer and theological and pastoral work, should increasingly show the Church to all Christians, and also to separated Christian communities, as their Father's house. Then mention is made of the dangers which can easily arise here, especially those of indifferentism and interdenominationalism. The bishops are recommended to encourage the movement under the supervision of the Pope.

The next paragraph (§ 54), which forms almost the half of the whole schema, deals with liturgical prayer in common.[40] Prayer in common with the Orthodox is not impossible — in fact the Church wishes that separated brethren should partake as far as possible and according to their needs, in the blessings of grace. With the purpose of restricting this, there now follow theological statements concerning the unity of the Church in worship. Because of this unity active participation is in itself also a profession of faith. A general permission would be a contradiction of this unity and an obscuring of the sign. Nevertheless, there can be exceptions, which the Church must define. The greatest difficulty arises in the active participation of Catholics in the worship of a Christian community which has not preserved the sacramental priesthood. They may not give an inner assent to this worship. They must never receive a "fugitive sacrament", because such a rite in itself is an affront to the Catholic truth. But even in the case of the Orthodox, their worship, being carried out in separation from the Church, contradicts the unity of the sign which the Church possesses in its worship, and

[39] A note is added, stating that it is also usual in official ecclesiastical documents to refer to the separated communities in the East as "Churches" (in the text they are not called "Churches").
[40] A note states that on this subject no less than 62 suggestions had been put forward by bishops and theologians, especially from among the Eastern Catholic Churches, who had been asked to submit their views before the Council.

is not carried out legitimately. *Communicatio in sacris* essentially implies an assent to the faith of the community concerned. This is particularly true of the reception of the Eucharist, but also of worship in which no sacrament is received. In the case of extreme spiritual need or even of great advantage, the dominant issue is whether or not the sacraments concerned are those which properly belong to the Church and are celebrated in an objectively true worship. These considerations do not apply to mere presence at the worship of other denominations. With regard to sacramentals, prayers, funerals and so forth, where the doctrine of the unity of the Church does not imply any hindrance to common worship, the point of view which becomes dominant is that of the advantage for the soul, including the non-Catholics concerned.

The concluding summary reads: "Thus one cannot regard true *communicatio in sacris* as a means which can generally be applied and which can lead to the restoration of the unity of all Christians in the one Church of Christ."[41] But this does not exclude the manifestation in prayer of the consciousness of our many links with separated Christians, so long as the principles mentioned above are maintained and the approval of those in authority has been obtained for each individual case.

Practical co-operation in defending the principles of the Christian religion, and of the natural law, particularly in social and cultural matters, is permitted (§ 55) and in some circumstances prescribed as a duty. This is also to the advantage of the Church, because mutual prejudices are overcome as a result. Here Catholics must have in mind the divine revelation, and, among other things, also the social doctrine of the Church, and must subject their undertakings to the supervision of ecclesiastical authority.

The conclusion declares that what this chapter intends must take a growing place among the tasks of pastoral care. An appeal is made for common prayer for unity, and the declaration repeated that the faith of Catholics, realized in moral life, is the most effective means of preparing the way for separated Christians to recognize the true Church of Christ and to enter it.

The vote on 1 December 1962

If this text had even been discussed by the whole Council, the voices of the bishops would have been raised to an even greater degree against its basic tendency to regard the ecumenical task as merely that of the invitation to return to the jurisdiction of the Catholic Church. But during the first session, on the basis of the discussion on the schema *Ut omnes unum sint,* the conviction became widespread that only one text should be produced on ecumenical problems. On 1 December 1962, therefore, a vote was taken on a resolution which recognized the precision of the doctrine and the irenical intention of this schema, but also

---

[41] This is one of the few sentences which found its way almost unchanged into the later versions of the schema.

put forward the demand that "... on the basis of the observations and suggestions heard in the Council, the decree, together with the Decree on Ecumenism prepared by the Secretariat for Christian Unity and Chapter XI, 'On Ecumenism', in the schema for a Dogmatic Constitution on the Church, will form a single document". By the almost unanimous acceptance of this resolution (2068 against 36, with 8 invalid votes) the Fathers affirmed the true ecumenical purpose of the Council, and also expressed with surprising unanimity their trust in the Secretariat for Unity, the proposed text of which was in fact still unknown to them.

The composition of the first version of the Decree on Ecumenism
and the petitions of the bishops concerning it

In the meantime, the Secretariat for Unity had taken up the suggestions of the Central Commission, and before and during the first session of the Council had worked out a new draft of its schema, with the provisional title, "Schema of a Decree on the Fostering of Unity among Christians". It already included the three chapters contained in the final decree, divided into 38 paragraphs, and provided with copious footnotes. This text, of 19 pages, was now, in accordance with the wishes of the Council, handed to a joint commission under the direction of Cardinal Cicognani and Cardinal Bea; but in practice the revision was undertaken by the Secretariat, which took into account the two other texts discussed above.[42]

Under the heading *De Oecumenismo,* the new texts contained three chapters with 24 paragraphs. In March 1963 it was discussed by a full meeting of the Secretariat, and on 22 April 1963 it was authorized by John XXIII. As soon as it came into the hands of the bishops[43] a lively debate began, many of the Fathers sending in written submissions, which, in spite of numerous objections, supported this text as a whole, and also in virtually all important details. Sixty bishops, whose opinions were frequently given in the name of their episcopal conferences, took part in this debate. The written submissions ran to approximately a hundred pages. During the third session these proposals were dealt with by the Secretariat, and the result was given to the Fathers in printed form on 18 November 1963.[44]

The content of the schema of 1963

The schema has no introduction, and begins with a dogmatic presentation of the principles of the unity and unicity of the Church (Chapter I). This unity is derived

---

[42] Cardinal Lorenz Jaeger (*Das Konzilsdekret "Über den Ökumenismus". Sein Werden, sein Inhalt und seine Bedeutung,* 1965, pp. 19f.) wrote on this: "The schema *De Oecumenismo* owes its original form more to French- and Dutch-speaking theologians than those from German-speaking regions, whose preparatory work, predominantly in the field of controversial theology, was of more significance in providing its underlying assumptions."

[43] The full title is *Schemata Constitutionum et Decretorum de quibus disceptabitur in Concilii sessionibus. Schema Decreti de Oecumenismo* (Typ. polygl. Vat., 1963).

[44] *Emendationes a Concilii Patribus scripto exhibitae super schema Decreti de Oecumenismo* (Typ. polygl. Vat., 1963), 32 pages.

from the saving will of God, which comprehends the whole of mankind, in order that it may be redeemed by Christ and drawn together in unity. At the very beginning mention is made of the Eucharist as the sacrament of unity, and of the activity of the Holy Spirit, in whom Christ calls the people of God to a unity of faith, hope and love. The offices of the Church's ministry are not derived here from the sociological necessities of a human society, but from their character as a ministry effected by the Spirit for the sanctification of the members of the people of God.[45] These members grow towards unity in faith, hope and love, in the sacrament of baptism and in the ministry of service (Eph 4:4–5, 16). No longer only the apostles, but also prophets in the sense of Eph 2:20 are named as the foundation of the Church. Thus here, with reference to the entire gospel message, everything was subordinated to the scriptural goal of the Church — even before the decisive turning point in ecclesiology had come about through the revision of the schema on the Church. With regard to the question of the holder of the universal office of teaching, governing and sanctifying, the college of the Twelve is mentioned first, followed by its president, St. Peter, with his commission to strengthen individuals in the faith and to tend the whole flock in perfect unity, Jesus Christ always remaining the highest cornerstone. The Holy Spirit is also at work in their successors, who have to proclaim the gospel and administer the sacraments, and this he does in such a way as to bring about the profession of the one faith, common participation in divine worship, and brotherly harmony in the government of the Church.[46] The Church is seen as a Church of pilgrimage to its true native land, and the exemplar and source of the deepest mystery of the Church is seen in the Holy Trinity.

The next paragraph deals with the relationship of separated brethren to the Catholic Church (§ 2). In the course of history schisms and divisions have come about within the Church, and Christianity today presents a picture of numerous Christian communities, living their life in separation from the Catholic Church. But the division among those who believe in Christ is only partial. What is lacking is the "perfect" communion of the Church,[47] which sees its sons in all the baptized. But beyond its frontiers the gifts of the Holy Spirit are present, and also visible elements, by which the unity of the Church is still manifested. The schema sees those who are separated from us not as individuals, but as

[45] This demand was also made by Archbishop A. Vuccino (cf. above p. 12).

[46] Bishop L. Carli later commented on this passage that Christ had built the Church on Peter, taken on his own, and that the text should not be silent on this. The expression *in regiminis fraterna concordia* also failed to satisfy some bishops as a reference to the hierarchal structure of the Church — they said that it ought to be replaced by the formula *in unitate magisterii et regiminis*.

[47] Thus at this point the important distinction between "complete" and "incomplete" membership of the Church was introduced (cf. vol. I of this commentary, pp. 168–77). John XXIII had also spoken of the separated brethren in this way, as "brethren who do not yet participate completely in the unity which the Lord willed and instituted", and of the visible unity and truth which the great Christian family "has not yet reached in completion and perfection" (cf. his opening address on 11 October 1962, quoted in *Vaticanum Secundum,* I, p. 213).

members of Churches and communities, which in themselves are of significance for salvation, and are actually used by the Spirit of Christ as means of salvation.[48]

The third paragraph, headed "Ecumenism", leads to the definition of the word ecumenism as "the movement and organized activity for the fostering of that unity among Christians, which Jesus Christ besought of the heavenly Father with fervent prayer". The unity of the Church is no longer described here within the limits of a "Catholic ecumenism", but as the fulfilment of the Christian inheritance, which ought to be manifested in the world ever more perfectly. Everywhere in the world at the present day the knowledge and the longing for this unity which Christ wills is growing, and Catholics are called to take a full part in this movement. To this belongs the desire for the renewal of the Catholic Church on the basis of the knowledge that through the guilt of so many of her members the fact of the Church appears deformed in her encounter with separated brethren.

The demand for unity in essentials does not mean that a legitimate diversity and true freedom in everything which is not really of the doctrine of faith is excluded, or that charity may not prevail in all things. Catholics are faced with the task, which is never completed, of manifesting more fully from day to day a catholicity which is regarded as dynamic and universal and is deserving of this name. Once again, mention is made of the truly Christian blessings which are to be found outside the Catholic Church, from all of which we too can learn. It is a consequence of the division of Christianity that the realization of Catholic fullness is made difficult for the Church of the present day, and is poorly expressed in her life. Catholics should avoid everything which encourages existing prejudices and conflicts with a mutual relationship of respect and co-operation. Under the guidance of the bishops this ecumenical attitude and action should henceforth become increasingly widespread among Catholics.

It is obvious that Chapter I, with the dogmatic foundation it provided for the unity of the Church and its definition of ecumenism, sought to adopt a mediating position between two extremes. The concept of the Church in the decree was certainly far more open than that in the first draft of the Constitution on the Church, in which the doctrine of the people of God did not yet occupy a dominant position. But the schema avoided making the membership of all the baptized in the body of Christ the basis of its discussion.

Chapter II deals with the practice of ecumenism. A short introduction makes a concern for unity the task of all Catholics, so that the already existing bond of brotherhood may be more clearly manifested, and strengthened in the direction of the perfect unity which God desires.[49]

---

[48] A note on this passage (cf. above p. 17) refers to the fact that in the Church's tradition the name "Churches" was always accorded to Orthodox communities in the East, as by Pius XII in 1952 in his encyclical *Orientales Ecclesiae* (*AAS* 45 [1953], p. 5).

[49] In the judgment of one bishop this chapter is so constructed that it is able to eliminate in the minds of non-Catholics every suspicion of a Roman "imperialism" which would now like to

Here again the theme is the inner renewal of the Church[50] (§ 4). It consists in an increased fidelity to her own calling. But this calling is not seen as that of exclusiveness towards what is outside the Church, but as something dynamic, which grows in fact in dialogue with separated brethren. A pledge of this dynamism is to be found in the movements which have previously arisen in the Catholic Church, and are now to be found in every part of her: the biblical and liturgical movements, together with the efforts for the renewal of the preaching of the word of God, the fostering of the apostolate of the laity, the renewal of the religious life and of married life; the social teaching and social activity of the Church, are also mentioned at this point. Two paragraphs (5 and 6), which were later combined into one, deal with the change of heart and sanctity of life. Self-denial, humility and patience in brotherly service are named as gifts of the Holy Spirit; above all, those who hold office in the ministry of the Church are reminded of the attitude of Christ who served. It is in this that the right answer is seen to the longing for unity, which the Holy Spirit has poured into the hearts of all Christians at the present time.

Conversion to a holy life in the sense of the gospel demands mutual brotherliness, and is necessary to repair the scandal caused to separated brethren by the lukewarmness and the sinful life of so many Catholics.

The passage which follows, on prayer in common, speaks almost exclusively of special prayer for unity. It is a form of the "spiritual ecumenism"[51] which should be regarded as the soul of the whole ecumenical movement. This fellowship in prayer is recommended, so long as it does not mean sharing official worship in common. The celebration of the holy Eucharist in common is wholly excluded, since liturgical prayer must always be a testimony to a unity and community already present, and the bond of this communion, which exists only in part and imperfectly, does not go so far as to allow such common acts of worship. Here the arguments in Chapter XI of the first draft of the schema on the Church evidently provided a landmark beyond which no one dared to go.

A further task is that of better mutual understanding among brethren. This is particularly to be achieved by serious study, which should also extend to the non-theological factors in the separation, and to all the distinctive doctrines of

"fish" for them and conquer them by the method of ecumenism. E. Schlink has also declared that the directions on the practical realization of ecumenism "could equally be regarded as valid by other Churches in all essentials" (cf. *Kirche und Dienst* 10 [1964], pp. 164–91).

[50] Here Innocent III (*PL*, CCXVII, 674) and the Fifth Lateran Council (*Conciliorum Oecumenicorum Decreta* [1962], 626, 39) are quoted. In his opening address to the second session of the Council Paul VI ascribed to the Church "the constant necessity of continuous reform . . . in so far as it is a human and earthly institution" (cf. *Vaticanum Secundum*, II [1964], pp. 59 ff., especially pp. 67 f.).

[51] The expression goes back to Fr. Paul Couturier (1881–1953), as does the formulation of the ultimate aim of the ecumenical movement so often used in the Council, and also by Paul VI, of attaining to unity, "as Christ willed it and in the way in which he willed it" (cf. G. Curtis, "P. Couturier", in *Ökumenische Profile,* I, pp. 347–53).

separated brethren. Common theological meetings, held by those who are truly competent, and under the supervision of their own Church authorities, are strongly recommended. A special aspect of this task is the ecumenical pattern of the formation of theologians in the seminary. And in particular, future missionaries must also be educated and instructed in the significance which ecumenism has for their apostolate.

A special paragraph (§ 10) is devoted to the manner and order in which the doctrine of faith should be presented. It should be equally remote from a false conciliatory approach and from a lapse into polemic, which would obstruct the way to the understanding of what is meant by each partner in the dialogue. Next, co-operation in different spheres of practical life, which are listed in detail, is recommended (§ 11). A reference to the importance of common witness to Christian faith before unbelievers, which distinguishes the co-operation of Christians with one another from brotherly co-operation with all men of good will, which is likewise required, is still lacking.

Chapter III, which in the draft bears the heading "Christians Separated from the Catholic Church" begins, like the original schema of the Commission for Eastern Churches, with a reference to the particular closeness of the Eastern Churches to the Catholic Church. But here the recognition accorded to the Eastern Churches is no longer set in the framework of a demand to return to the Catholic Church. The explicit subject here is the "character of the relationship which obtained between the Eastern Churches and the Roman See before the separation". It is notable that in Chapter III the "communities which have come into being since the 16th century", are only briefly discussed, as it were as an addendum.

In the lengthier first section, "A Special Consideration of the Eastern Churches", it had been possible to draw on the draft of the Commission for the Eastern Churches, which in fact had dealt with this theme as a whole. What was laid down there as a means of preparation for a return, respect for the common heritage and the spiritual bonds which have remained in spite of the separation, becomes here the object of a positive treatment. Dissensions and mutual alienation are not derived merely from historical wrongs and human weaknesses: "The different forms and ways in which the apostolic heritage was received" are now ascribed to a "difference in spiritual attitude" which is a historical fact.

The next paragraph (§ 13), with the title "The Distinctive Spirit and Peculiar History of Eastern Christians", mentions the long period during which both cultures "went their own way" and nevertheless "persevered in a communion of faith and sacramental life", in which in particular cases the Roman See "with general consent" was the decisive arbiter. Emphasis is placed on the apostolic origin of many local Churches (still without the mention of the concept of the patriarchate and the continuing brotherly harmony of the Orthodox Churches, which indeed actually regard each other as autocephalous Churches. The fact that the early Ecumenical Councils all took place in the East is also emphasized.

Particular notice is to be taken in the ecumenical dialogue of the fact that their dogmatic tradition is an original one.

In § 15 the liturgical and spiritual tradition of Eastern Christians is described. Their liturgical devotion is portrayed in its special richness, and special emphasis is placed on the importance of holy Scripture. Their liturgical veneration of Mary is also an example to all Christians. One of the riches of the East is monasticism, which had its origin there, as well as other forms of contemplative life.

With regard to the question of Church order and discipline, more attention should be given to the truly Catholic principle of diversity in unity than has been the case in the past.[52]

Whereas the first draft stated that Catholic truth must be distinguished from the theological theses of different systems, the schema now discusses at length the different ways of presenting theological doctrines in the East and in the West. The theological method of the East was acknowledged to have the advantage that it was particularly rooted in holy Scripture, was closely related to liturgical and spiritual life and to contemplation, and was nourished by the works of the Eastern Church Fathers.

The chapter which in the first draft discussed the conditions for the restoration of the unity of the Church is reduced in the new version to a single paragraph, inserted into the conclusion. It lacks, however, any direct appeal to return. There is an explicit statement that it is necessary to take into account the nature of the relationships which existed before the schism between the Eastern Churches and the Roman See, and this provides a standard by which the present Catholic Church, with its Latin Church law, must be measured. The right and task of the Roman See "to take precedence in love" is stressed. The inward aspiration to break down through the grace of God the wall which separates the two Churches, is formulated in such a way that Eastern Christians can also make it their own. The goal is that of the "one dwelling, firmly established on the corner stone, Christ", who will make both one.

The notable feature of the second section of the chapter, on the "Communities which have come into being since the sixteenth century", is the attempt, which was later abandoned, to characterize the distinctive theological features of the communities which came into being in the crisis at the beginning of the modern period. The draft states that these communities were endeavouring above all to emphasize the transcendence of the revelation of God which has taken place in Christ, in which man can only participate by grace. This principle was so strongly emphasized that the result was "the denial of the essential mediation of the Church". This refers to the diminishing of the saving reality of Christ by a radical understanding of the principles of *sola fide* and *sola gratia*. But this did not destroy the communion which is created by the name of Christ and the

---

[52] It is notable that the opportunity of including at this point as impressive a confession of guilt as was uttered in § 31 of the schema *Ut omnes unum sint* (cf. above p. 9) was not yet taken in this draft.

sacrament of baptism, nor are the separated brethren deprived of the love of Christ and the gifts of the Holy Spirit. The conclusion of this section explicitly emphasizes that there are also separated communities in the West which have preserved a valid priesthood and the means of salvation associated therewith.

An important factor in the communion which remains and the link that still exists is the "basis" of the ecumenical movement, which is now quoted in the next paragraph, according to the formula of New Delhi (§ 20, with note 9). The passage which deals with the confession of Christ as the characteristic feature of these separated communities takes into account the ecumenical movement with its burning longing for unity in Christ and the insight, dominating everything else, of the necessity to bear witness through faith in Christ.

The next paragraph (§ 21) emphasizes that holy Scripture is the common possession of the whole of Christianity, and is specially studied and held in honour by these communities. In it they "find Christ, who speaks to them", and holy Scripture can be the starting point of dialogue with them. It is "the instrument in the mighty hand of God for attaining that unity which the Saviour holds out to all men".

It is said of the sacrament of baptism (§ 22) that through it "a man becomes truly incorporated into the crucified and glorified Christ and is reborn to a sharing of the divine life". Baptism is seen as oriented toward the fullness of life in Christ, a complete profession of faith, and a complete incorporation into the system of salvation such as Christ himself willed it to be, as complete participation in eucharistic communion.

A special section then deals with the way of life of these communities, which, in the power of baptism and in the spirit of holy Scripture, is truly "a life with Christ". Mention is made of the spirit of prayer, of the virtues that belong to the life of society, and of institutions for the practice of neighbourly charity.

That the authors of the text were eager not to ignore any spiritual reality in the realm of the Churches and communities of the Reformation is shown by the concluding section of this paragraph, which was later omitted. Even in the communities which have not preserved the sacramental reality of baptism, the profession of faith in Christ and love for him has remained, and a spiritual life nourished by the Scriptures and true neighbourly love is present.

In conclusion, a further appeal is made to the responsibility of Catholics to take part in a right spirit in the dialogue which has already begun among Christians, and to respond by action to the urging of the Holy Spirit, who has inspired in men's souls a longing for unity.

The *emendationes*

The written submissions, which, as we have mentioned, were sent in during the summer of 1963, displayed a wide variety of points of view. Only a few of the Fathers were of the opinion that the schema was not in accord with traditional

Catholic theology, and went too far in its approach to non-Catholics. The suggestion was made in various ways that the danger of a growing indifferentism, especially among less instructed Catholics, was not sufficiently guarded against. The difficulty was noted of composing a conciliar text which was appropriate both to the universal Church and to the quite different situations in individual countries. The form which the ecumenical task would take in practice, it was suggested, must be left to be set out in a general directory which the bishops could each adapt to the situation in their own area. Only very few bishops disapproved of the fact that the aspect of the invitation to separated brethren to return was allowed in the present text to fall into the background, or was transformed in the direction of the ultimate goal of the ecumenical movement.

However, the tendency of most of the proposals made by the Fathers was towards a strengthening of the ecumenical statements, and in particular many bishops demanded a humble confession of the guilt which also lies upon Catholics for the separation of Christians.[53] The distinction between the ecumenical purpose and the task of guiding individual Christians towards conversion should be set out more clearly. Already one of the Council Fathers raised the point that in setting out the Catholic faith account should be taken of the true hierarchy of Christian values, according to which not every truth of faith possessed the same rank in the Christian life. The most widely criticized paragraph was that concerning *communicatio in sacris*. Whereas a few Fathers stressed the danger of indifferentism, against any recommendation of prayer in common, all the other Fathers with views on this point demanded a redrafting of this paragraph in an ecumenical spirit, which should also take into account usages which were already in force among a number of Eastern Catholic Churches with regard to common prayer with the Orthodox. There a general realization that a far too narrow concept peculiar to Western theology had not yet been overcome here. The exclusion of any *communicatio in sacris* in official worship seemed to go much too far. A distinction must be made at least between the sacramental worship of the Orthodox Churches and the Communion liturgy of the Reformation Churches.

The discussion in the Council concerning the title of "Churches" and "ecclesial communities" given to communities separated from the Catholic Church was also anticipated in these written submissions. If it is true that by schism and heresy the Church itself "is divided into many different parts" (*Denzinger*, 873a), then this must also be expressed in the language used and in the titles given to other Churches. The expression *communitas* was to be preferred to the word *communio*, which had become widespread, particularly in France, as the rendering of the biblical term κοινωνία.

Has not the Church repeatedly declared that all the baptized are "members

---

[53] This attitude was given decisive support at the beginning of the second session of the Council by the confession of guilt which the Pope made in his opening address of 29 September 1963 (cf. *Vaticanum Secundum*, II, p. 63).

of Christ, belonging to the body of the Church" (cf. *Denzinger*, 696)? From the other point of view, the demand was made that an introduction should speak in clear scholastic language of the unity and unicity of the Church, and that the concept of ecumenism should also be distinguished as "Catholic ecumenism", by contrast with the understanding of the present day ecumenical movement (Bishop Carli). Again, from a different point of view, the demand was made that the argument should proceed from that which in these concepts was common to Christianity at the present day. One bishop wrote that in the effort to lead brethren who thought differently towards unity with the successor of Peter, everything must be avoided which could provoke an impression of pride and arrogance. For this reason a separate section at the beginning of the schema should state only what could be sure of the assent of all Christians at the present moment. All the baptized already form a communion in Christ. Catholics should also confess their guilt for schism, and beseech God to bring back his separated people in his own way to perfect unity. The absence of this confession of guilt was also noted as a deficiency by other Fathers. The explicit request was made that the schema should provide an answer to the question whether by a schism "merely a large number of former members of the Catholic Church became separated, while the Church remained perfect and undivided", or whether in this division, which has taken place against the will of God, the Church itself was divided in some sense".

Another important demand was that the whole complex of co-operation with separated brethren should be dealt with from the point of view of common witness to Christ.

With regard to the first section of Chapter III, dealing with the Eastern Churches, there was sometimes a demand for it to be closer to the original text, even to the point of appealing for a return to the Catholic Church. But this was balanced by the objections to the concluding paragraphs, where it was felt necessary to find more considerate and truly ecumenical language.

It was suggested that a new title should be found for the second part of the chapter, since Christian communities of this sort had already come into being before the sixteenth century. Both the historical presentation of the facts which led to the Reformation and also the attempt to find a common denominator for differences of doctrine were criticized. Many of the Council Fathers also made it clear that they were dissatisfied with the way in which the problem of how far validly baptized non-Catholics belonged to the Church was dealt with; most of them demanded here a clear statement that baptism was "a means of incorporation into the Church".

The *relationes*

The schema was brought before the Council for debate in three *relationes*, which in part already took into account the emendations that had been submitted, on 18 November 1963. It was certainly of significance for many Fathers that Cardinal A. G. Cicognani had been prevailed upon to be the first *relator*, dealing with the whole of the five chapters of the schema "On Ecumenism".[54] In a certain discrepancy between the arguments of Cardinal Cicognani and those of the other *relatores* we can once again perceive the way in which the desire for the unity of Christians came to be formulated in the Council. In giving his report, he emphasized first the continuity of the work, which towards the end of the first session had been handed over to a mixed commission. He went on to defend the word "ecumenism" in the title of the schema. As early as 1928 Pius XI accepted this concept in the sense of the non-Catholic ecumenical movement, and the encyclical *Orientales Ecclesiae* of Pius XII[55] also made use of this concept; the Cardinal also referred to the instruction of the Holy Office "On the Ecumenical Movement" of 1949.

Cardinal Cicognani saw nothing really new in ecumenism, except as a name for the constant endeavour of "almost all the Councils", to protect, advance or restore peace and unity among the sons of the Church. He made particular mention of the Councils of Union of Lyons (1274) and Florence (1439–45). Because at the present day the time is not yet ripe for a council of union ("under the present circumstances unity in faith cannot be attained"), it is even more necessary for something to happen which will help to bring about an honest unity of souls and set aside the obstacles and difficulties which hinder this. This is especially true, when in a period of unavoidable encounters between men of different religious convictions, these questions are becoming ever more urgent, and indications exist that paths and doors are being opened. Thus Cardinal Cicognani traced a line from the ecumenical enterprises and desires of Leo XIII to the most recent Popes. He mentioned the *Acta* and documents, almost 240 in number, which Leo XIII wrote to advance the apostolate of unity with the Eastern Church, and in which he repeatedly appealed to them to come closer and to unite. During his pontificate a Commission for Fostering the Unity of Christians was set up, which, however, did not long remain active at that time.

This defence of the wording of the title of the schema was followed by a definition of the nature of "true" and "good" ecumenism in relation to the pastoral task of the Council, as Cardinal Cicognani saw it: the saving mission of the Church, which according to the will of Christ is intended for the whole world, for Christians and non-Christians, must at the present day "be made more effective" and must be adapted to all men *(modo congruenti et consentaneo)*. Thus ecumenism is a new "form of the method" of this mission.

From this point of view he went on to give a brief description of all five chapters, always in relation to Christ's missionary command to teach all nations

---

[54] Cardinal Bea restricted himself to a *relatio* on the chapter concerning the problem of the Jews, which, moreover, was his special concern.
[55] Cf. above note 48.

(Mt 28:19). The necessity of belonging to the true and only Church is laid down in the first chapter, on Catholic Ecumenism, as a basic principle, and set out in a way which should overcome the difficulties and concern of separated brethren. The practice of a sound ecumenism should be guided by St. Paul's words "speaking the truth in love" (Eph 4:15), paying regard to fraternal affection and in the spirit of dialogue.

In his account of the third chapter, he emphasized the attitude taken towards the Eastern Churches; a high value is placed on the services they have given to the Church, the glory they have achieved, and also on their closeness and similarity to our Christian deposit of faith. The Cardinal took this opportunity of greeting the patriarchs and other bishops of the Eastern Churches united with Rome, who even now, in the Council, "are to a certain extent the represent-atives of separated brethren from these countries". With regard to the Churches of the Reformation, Cardinal Cicognani contented himself with a brief mention of the great and powerful bonds which link us with them, such as baptism, a love for holy Scripture, and love for Christ. The cordial welcome which he gave to the observers from these Churches formed a certain parallel to the previous mention of the Eastern Catholic Churches.

On Chapter IV, "On the Attitude of Catholics to Non-Christians and Especially to Jews", he laid strong emphasis on the purely religious purpose of the text, having in mind the attacks from outside the Council, and the concern expressed by many Eastern bishops.[56] The Catholic principles of religious freedom, which are dealt with in Chapter V, were regarded by the Cardinal from the point of view of the missionary command of Jesus Christ. In conclusion he spoke of the growing readiness of those outside the Church to form true ideas about Christ the Lord and his Church. The institutions which in many dioceses serve to provide such information and encourage such a dialogue were especially praised by him, and recommended to the bishops.

Admittedly, the loving and irenical attitude expressed in this *relatio* is still entirely in the realm of what Y. Congar, likewise with reference to Leo XIII, has called *un irénisme pré-œcuménique*.[57] It is the spirit of the schema *Ut omnes unum sint* of 1962, for which Cardinal Cicognani had accepted responsibility. And certainly this way of interpreting the new schema did not fail in its effect on the bishops of the minority, who still held the old point of view.

A decisive step forward was taken by the *relatio* which followed, and which was given by Archbishop J. M. Martin of Rouen, as spokesman of the Secretariat

[56] At this point Cardinal Cicognani, in reading his *relatio*, went beyond the printed text, saying (according to the present author's notes): "A different interpretation would be wholly alien to the Council. It is truth which is at issue. We hope that this intention of the Council is properly understood and accepted by all. What is at issue is the place which this people has within the mystery of salvation constituted by Christ himself, from which its relation to the Church's own proper mission is derived.

[57] Cf. *Vatican II, Le Concile au jour le jour* (1963), p. 83.

for Christian Unity, on the first three chapters of the schema *De Oecumenismo*. The most striking contradiction to the *relatio* given by Cardinal Cicognani lies in the following statement. Archbishop Martin said: "The problem of ecumenism is an entirely new one. No previous Council has ever dealt with it, and even in theology it has not been mentioned until modern times. Its urgency arises from a situation which has only come into being very recently." Not until today has the fact of the centuries-long division between Christians become evident to all men as a true scandal, as disobedience to the explicit will of Christ, and as an impediment which is virtually "paralysing" the missionary task of the Church. This is the situation in which the ecumenical movement has come into being, and it is therefore a task appropriate to the present age, and truly pastoral in nature, to instruct the faithful in the spirit and the providential significance of the ecumenical movement. In the course of his discussion of the matter, Archbishop Martin said that the relationship between Catholics and separated brethren at the present moment had reached a deadlock, which must ultimately be overcome. Here Martin distinguished between "the actual and immediate aim of ecumenical action" and the final goal of "ultimate unity", which "lies in the hand of God". The ecumenical movement is only concerned with the "preparation" of ways which ought ultimately to lead to the restoration of the unity of all Christians in the flock of Christ. Briefly summing up the contents of the chapter, he emphasized the proposals in the schema for the practical life of Catholics, which are put forward in the spirit of John XXIII. It is not sufficient to debate about ecumenism, and it must certainly not be regarded as a fashion of the present time. The schema is an appeal for a spiritual conversion and renewal of the heart, a matter for which all should pray in common and with one mind. Mutual understanding between brothers is bound to grow in love, and co-operation in works of love, which proceed from the spirit of the gospel, must be encouraged.

Taking up the themes of Chapter III, with its positive evaluation of non-Catholic Churches and communities, the *relatio* then dealt with a number of objections which had been made. Profound and serious doctrinal difficulties should not be treated lightly. The dialogue must be conducted from the very first soberly, and in a sound and irenical spirit, free from all Machiavellism. To this end it is first necessary to seek a common basis for dialogue, and the controversial questions which have been emphasized often enough in the past must be dealt with in a new perspective, and with a new and positive intellectual attitude. The method of dialogue which is now available to us today requires that both sides should listen to each other, understand each other and learn from each other. By this process no point of doctrine is concealed and no way left open for indifferentism. The aim and the method of dialogue between Christians separated from one another consists in "all understanding each other better and all receiving a deeper insight into the word of God".

Details should be reserved for the later production of a handbook *(directorium)* of ecumenical problems, and special "directories" should deal with the different circumstances of individual countries and dioceses. It is only in such practical "directories" that the special question of those individuals who have the desire to enter the Catholic Church as converts can be discussed more closely. It is sufficient for the schema to affirm that the two pastoral tasks, the apostolate of conversion and ecumenical action, are not opposed to one another.

The description of the Churches separated from Catholic unity does not contain inordinate praise, but simply gives due honour to the truth. As far as the Eastern Churches are concerned, Leo XIII established a custom in the Catholic Church by his recognition of their venerable traditions. With regard to the communities which have become separated from the Pope since the time of the Reformation, similar grounds exist for looking first at what is held in common, especially since they have led a common Christian life with us in the one Church for five hundred years longer than the Eastern Churches.

Finally, Archbishop Martin drew attention to two requirements which he believed would assist the positive acceptance of the schema by all the Council Fathers. The first was the Council's trust in the work of the commission it had set up, which had to carry out a task which was impossible for the Council as a whole: in this case, the commission concerned was the Secretariat for Christian Unity. Here, as Archbishop Martin says, under the guidance of the universally revered Cardinal Bea, its work had been carried out with the utmost care and "in a spirit of fraternal and friendly co-operation", in spite of all the differences between its members, while at the same time the friendship and trust which had arisen between the members of the Secretariat and the observers and guests had been an effective influence from the first.

The second requirement is that of trust in the efficacy of the Holy Spirit, which from the very first had been evident in the ecumenical movement. Here he made explicit mention of the World Council of Churches, but also referred to what had grown up in recent years in this respect within the Catholic Church itself. With regard to the intellectual struggles of our time, we must bear common witness to the fact that among the sons of the Christian family, through the grace of God, the first fruits of a future unity are already present. Although many fundamental questions between separated Christians are still unresolved, a change has already taken place in the attitude of minds and hearts. The true ecumenical dialogue has begun.

This *relatio* closed with a quotation from the address of Paul VI to the observers on 17 October 1963, concerning the end of the period of polemic and the beginning of the effective work of mutual love.[58]

In a third *relatio*, Archbishop-Coadjutor Bukatko of Belgrade spoke, on behalf of the Commission for the Eastern Churches, on the special issues in

---

[58] Compare the authentic text in the catalogue of *Observateurs-Délégués et Hôtes du Secrétariat pour l'unité des chrétiens au deuxième Concile Œcuménique du Vatican* (Typ. polygl. Vat., 1965), pp. 19–24.

Chapter III (1), which had been left out of the previous *relatio*. After referring to the new schema of the Commission for Eastern Catholic Churches, the *relator* first sought to explain who had been responsible for the schema *De Oecumenismo*. In the case of Chapter III (1) there had been "a certain co-operation" on the part of the Commission for the Eastern Churches, in accordance with the wish of the Council, which had accepted the schema *Ut omnes unum sint* as a basis of discussion. Thus in the text of the first part of Chapter III, which like the whole schema was laid before the Council on the responsibility of the Secretariat for Christian Unity itself, "some elements" of the earlier text had been incorporated.[59] The Commission for the Eastern Churches gave its approval to this text as a whole, but hoped for some improvements on the basis of the discussion by the full Council which was now to follow.[60]

The debate during the second session of the Council

On 18 November 1963, there began an exceedingly fruitful debate[61] on the schema *De Oecumenismo;* in the view of Cardinal Bea, "it was inspired by a genuine love and a great zeal for the unity of Christians". Its positive contribution to the three first chapters, which were discussed in general and in detail, was of great importance. When Cardinal Bea, in his summary on 2 December, derived the diversity of views put forward from the different circumstances in individual countries, this was certainly true in the further sense that each of the Fathers spoke from his own experience. That was the reason why the word "ecumenism" was disputed from the very first. Many bishops were only accustomed to thinking in the categories of a unity understood in static terms, such as formed the basis of the original schema *Ut omnes unum sint*. But the purpose of the decree was different, and the overwhelming majority of bishops became persuaded during the first two days of the debate that the way it posed the task was the right one. The concern of the decree was with the participation of Catholics in the ecumenical movement which had come into being among non-Catholics, and in every respect this was something new in the history of the Church. This was the reason for many of the objections, but as day followed day they formed an ever smaller minority.

Let us first note some of those speeches in the debate which regarded the schema as going too far. As in the original schema *Ut omnes unum sint*, its starting point was the doctrine of the Church. But this was deprived of its scholastic

---

[59] The original plan to combine the two texts was shown to be impracticable. Cf. vol. I of this commentary, p. 307.

[60] The text of these *relationes* can be found in *Vaticanum Secundum,* III/2 (1967).

[61] On this cf. E. Stakemeier, "Die Ergebnisse der Konzilsdiskussion über das Schema de Oecumenismo", in *Theologie und Glaube* 54 (1964), pp. 161–91. This study was also reprinted in *Vaticanum Secundum,* II, pp. 54–60, where the names of the bishops who took part were inserted in each case.

clothing, and a number of bishops already saw signs of a false irenicism in the way it began with the history of salvation. Bishop Carli demanded the elimination of what was (at that time) "the disputed and contentious" concept of the collegiality of the apostles. Some of the Fathers wanted to see an explicit mention of the necessity of the Catholic Church for salvation and of the infallibility of the Pope.[62] Was it sufficient to speak of the Church of Rome in patristic terminology as a communion of love, without taking into account the warnings of the encyclical *Mystici Corporis* against separating the "juridical Church" and "the Church of love"?[63] Was it right to see the Church as something dynamic, as a communion *(communio)*, in which there were different ways and levels of participation? The objection was also raised that the Holy Spirit could only be described as the soul of the Catholic Church in its concrete form, and could only be effective *per accidens* outside the frontiers of the Church. Although it was not denied that the Holy Spirit also used the non-Catholic Christian communities as means of salvation, it was necessary to state clearly that these did not come under his influence in so far as they were "separated bodies" but only with regard to what they had retained from the Catholic Church. Even the elements of the Church which they retained were in practice, in the view of some bishops, a manifestation rather of their separation than of a unity which still existed. Now as previously, the distinction between the immediate aim and the ultimate aim of the ecumenical movement presented difficulties to some of the Fathers. They expected the Council to make an appeal for the return of separated Christians, and many could find no good in the distinction, dealt with only briefly in the text, between the work of conversion and the task of ecumenism. Many bishops failed to trust the ecumenical movement, simply because they lacked knowledge of its recent development, and they asked whether it should be regarded as a unity at all. The text still spoke of a Catholic ecumenism in the heading of Chapter I, and this allowed them to demand that a sharper distinction should be made between the two forms of ecumenism. Was not the discussion of separated Christians "more than polite" (Cardinal Ruffini)? Are they all without exception of good faith? What is the purpose of this *laudatio protestantium*? Is not the recommendation of contact with non-Catholic Christians bound to result in a danger to faith, which the Church desires to guard against even by the Index of Prohibited Books?

As far as details are concerned, several objections were raised in particular against prayer in common. Could the prayer of a Catholic for unity ever mean anything but prayer for the conversion of brethren who are still separated? The concept of "spiritual ecumenism", mentioned in the text without further explanation, was strange to many who spoke.[64] The respectful mention of those

---

[62] Some of the observers, especially the Anglicans, stated at the time that they too saw the failure to mention the papal claims as a deficiency in the text in the direction of false irenicism.

[63] Cf. the 1947 Freiburg edition, pp. 66f.

[64] Cf. above note 51.

believers in Christ who have not retained the sacrament of baptism was rejected from various motives.

But these objections could not prevent the overwhelming impression that in the debate, to the surprise of many, a genuine breakthrough towards ecumenical thought became evident. Almost everyone saw the schema as constituting a great step forward from the theological, and especially from the ecclesiological and pastoral points of view. As Cardinal Léger declared, the acceptance and approbation of so many bishops represented a "true conversion". The readiness for an encounter conducted not in the spirit of contradiction, but in that of a true dialogue, was obvious. M. von Galli has rightly pointed out how many Spaniards revealed a genuine enthusiasm for the schema in their speeches.[65] Even in countries in which proselytism on the part of sects is a fact, there was a desire not to be satisfied with an admonition to caution, but to trust in the truth and true pastoral methods.

Thus in the speeches in the debate the Fathers who sought the strengthening of the tendency expressed in the schema formed a decisive majority. Among the requests which were intended as positive improvements to the schema was the demand that the connection between the ecclesiological statements of the schema and the schema "On the Church" should be more clearly expressed, but in terms of the concept of the people of God, which had been chosen as the new starting point of the latter. Secondly, there should be a fuller discussion on the Holy Spirit, and a more explicit statement on the holy Eucharist. One should not speak of the "traces" but of the "riches" of Christ, and acknowledge the "elements" of the Church in non-Catholic communities without qualification. Associated with this was the demand that separated Christian communities should be referred to as "Churches", or at least by the biblical term *communio*, κοινωνία. Cardinal König proposed that these communities should be referred to as a whole as "Churches and ecclesial communities" *(communitates ecclesiasticae)*.[66] The proposal was also made to relate the elements of the Church explicitly to Christ, in order to exclude a "quantifying"[67] understanding and cataloguing of these elements of the Church, to which in particular some of the observers had objected. Bishop Volk stated that the Church's inner catholicity as its ecumenical dimension must be made more manifest.

But the decree, it was stated, had as its aim the renewal of the Church, and not merely of individuals, and sought to begin a dialogue among Churches, and not between individual Christians. The Church should be more explicitly called

[65] Cf. M. von Galli and B. Moosbrugger, *Das Konzil, Kirche im Wandel. Zweiter Text- und Bild-bericht* (1963), p. 29.

[66] Because the term *ecclesiasticae* seemed to possess an already fixed meaning, it was decided to use the formula *communitates ecclesiales*, although the adjective is a neologism in Latin.

[67] The expression was used especially by E. Schlink in his talks at the German press centre in Rome on 23 October 1963 and October 1964, and his book *Nach dem Konzil* (1966), especially pp. 118 f.

upon to participate in the ecumenical movement, which in fact has already done so much for the growth of an ecumenical consciousness. There must be a clear declaration that the Catholic Church does not wish to set up an ecumenism of its own, parallel to the ecumenical movement.[68]

All it claimed to do was that which the declaration of Toronto (1950)[69] has accorded to all Churches: to take part in the work of the ecumenical movement according to the principles of its own ecclesiology. Consequently, a change in the title of Chapter I was suggested, so that it would no longer speak of "Catholic ecumenism". All this assumed a clearer distinction between the immediate aim and the ultimate aim of the ecumenical movement, the ultimate aim being that unity which cannot be brought about by man, but which, as Archbishop Martin had already said in his *relatio,* lies in the hand of God. On this basis too the distinction between the task of ecumenism and the apostolate of conversions should be made clearer. A few bishops were dissatisfied by the mention of the "basis" of the assembly of the World Council of Churches. The World Council of Churches should not be named merely in a note, as had been the case in one of the earlier texts, but should be explicitly mentioned in the text.[70] In general, the description of the nature of ecumenism in Chapter I of the schema should be more exact and more detailed.

Because the division between Christians involves both sides, one should not rest content with the expression "separated brethren", against which the observers had also raised objections, but one should at least say "brethren separated *from us*",[71] and the expression *fratres separati* should be replaced by *fratres seiuncti*.

In an important contribution Bishop Pangrazio criticized the way in which the nature of the Church was described in the schema. The aspect of the living dynamism present in the history of the Church, which also afforded room for hope for the longed for unity of separated Christians, was lacking. Proceeding from this point, the speaker asked that in the evaluation of the unity which still existed and the differences that were present "the hierarchical precedence

---

[68] The same view was expressed by Cardinal König, who at first had clung to the expression "Catholic ecumenism", in his speech on 19 November 1963. Cf. also O. Müller, "Katholischer Ökumenismus", in W. Becker, ed., *Aufbruch zur Einheit der Christen* (1965), pp. 169–88.

[69] At the session of the Central Committee of the World Council of Churches which took place in 1950 at Toronto, a theological declaration on "the Church, the Churches and the World Council of Churches" was resolved, which sought to unite "dialectically" a respect for the obligation of members of individual constituent Churches of the World Council to their own Churches and their specific ecclesiology, with a conviction of the essential oneness of the Church of Christ. Cf. H. H. Walz, "Ökumenischer Rat der Kirchen", in *Weltkirchenlexikon* (1960), pp. 1056–64.

[70] Protestant observers put forward another objection: this was not the right place to mention the "basis" where only the Reformation Churches are being discussed, since the Orthodox Churches are members of the World Council. This view has been taken into account by the mention of the common basis in the introduction.

[71] "They are separated from us and we from them" (Patriarch Maximos).

among the revealed truths and ecclesiastical elements" on which the Church is based, should always be borne in mind. The difference is that between the ultimate end, with regard to which unity already largely exists, and the means of salvation. This led him to the conclusion that in this respect "all Christians are already united as one family in the primary truths of the Christian religion".[72]

With regard to the account of the practice of the ecumenical movement in Chapter II, this task should be more clearly presented as the concern of the whole Church in all its ranks, even though a number of speakers declared that the greatest responsibility for carrying it out in practice lay in the hands of bishops and episcopal conferences (Archbishop Conway). With regard to the renewal of the Church, there should be no hesitation in using the expressions "reform" and "reformation", following the precedents of the medieval Councils, and in particular an explicit confession of guilt should not be omitted. The limitation of prayer in common by the exclusion of *communicatio* "in official worship" was criticized by many of the Fathers, especially from the area of the Eastern Churches. Attention should be directed more towards ways of participating in different forms of divine worship, a participation which should never be merely passive, but which finds its limit in the prohibition of participation in a non-sacramental eucharistic service. The co-operation of Christians should not be limited merely to practical activities, but, as German bishops in particular proposed, should have the character of a common testimony to Christ. The concern for individual needs of the age should be made more precise by a lengthier discussion in the schema.

A considerable number of Fathers expressed dissatisfaction with Chapter III, which a few even wanted to be rejected entirely. The Indonesian bishops had pointed out that the principle by which the chapter was divided into two parts, and the different treatment of the Churches and communities of the East and of the West, was neither necessary for practical reasons, nor in accord with the tendency followed by the work of the World Council of Churches. In any case everything must be done to avoid the appearance that by this division of the chapter into two parts a wedge was being driven between the Eastern and the Western member Churches of the World Council. On the other hand, the views expressed by many bishops showed that from the Catholic point of view great differences existed between these two groups, to the extent that some of them would have preferred them to be dealt with in two different chapters.

Many of the speeches posed once again the question of the title both of the whole chapter and of the two sections, with the intention of giving better expression to the similarities and differences between the situation in the East and that in other parts of the world. It was suggested that instead of "Christians separated from the Catholic Church", the title should be "Christian brethren, who have some measure of communion with the Catholic Church".

[72] For the text of this speech cf. *Vaticanum Secundum*, II, pp. 612f.

In the case of the Eastern Churches, there ought to be a stronger emphasis on the continuation of the apostolic succession, the activity of the Holy Spirit, and the validity of the celebration of the Eucharist. In dogmatic questions there ought to be a clearer expression of the way in which a predominantly Western theology needs to be complemented.

With regard to the second section of the chapter, a more precise distinction between Churches and sects was sought, as well as a rejection of the proselytism of many sects.

In the submissions which they made to the Secretariat, the observers declared that they felt that the description of the principles of the Reformation did not show a proper understanding of their position. They, and also individual Catholic bishops, proposed that special account should be taken of the Lord's Supper among the ecclesial communities of the Reformation.

Cardinal Bea spoke twice during the debate, to make clear the intention of the schema and to defend it against misunderstanding. At the conclusion of the debate the Cardinal laid special emphasis on the importance of the bishops in leading Catholics to co-operate with the ecumenical movement. He promised that all suggestions and objections would be carefully dealt with, since even in the view of the Secretariat the schema "was still in need of improvement in many respects". A number of the suggestions for improvement could be taken into account in the proposed *directorium* for ecumenical work.

The production of the final version of the text

In the early months of 1964, the Secretariat for Christian Unity worked on the new version of the text, in co-operation with experts from the Theological Commission and also from the Commission for the Eastern Churches. There were now no less than 471 opinions put forward by the Fathers, in addition to the previous submissions; on the basis of these a new version of the schema was prepared and presented to a full session of the Secretariat, which sat from 25 February to March 1964. Having received unanimous approval here, after a few changes, the text followed the usual course to the Co-ordinating Commission, and on 27 April 1964 it also received the approbation of Paul VI. In this version, which was subsequently altered in relatively few passages, the schema was circulated to the Fathers in May and June, while in July they also received an extensive *relatio* from the Secretariat. Including the notes, the text covered twenty-six pages.[73]

A comparison of the two versions of the text, of 1963 and 27 April 1964, shows the progress that had been achieved. At the sessions of the Secretariat at the beginning of 1964, the question of the whole schema was raised once again.

[73] The volume bears the title *Schema Decreti de Oecumenismo*; an appendix contains the "Declaratio prior" *De Libertate religiosa*.

Instead of unfamiliar words like "ecumenical movement" or "ecumenism", which sounded strange in many countries many bishops would have preferred another title.[74] But it was intended to give prominence in the title itself to the ecumenical movement, which was something new to most Catholics, as well as to the name which it has come to bear everywhere, and therefore the previous title was retained.

Many submissions deplored the lack of a preface, in which the aim of the schema would be set out in accordance with the situation and tasks of the present age. The Secretariat now proposed such a preface. Here too the starting point is the foundation of the one and only Church by Christ. The situation of discord in which Christianity finds itself today contradicts the will of Christ, provides a stumbling block to the whole world, and inflicts damage on the effectiveness of the Church's mission. But in recent years the ecumenical movement has come into being among our separated brethren. This movement is briefly characterized by a reference to the "basis" of the World Council of Churches.[75] A positive view is also taken of the final goal of this whole movement: it claims to be content not merely with an invisible Church, but longs "that there may be one visible Church of God", a Church which is "truly universal", and which will thereby fulfil its missionary office, of being sent forth to the whole world, to bring salvation to all men. The schema then goes on to declare its intention of setting out in the following three chapters the ways and methods in which Catholics too can take a fruitful part in this movement.[76]

Chapter I: Catholic Principles of Ecumenism

The title of the chapter in the first version had been "Principles of Catholic Ecumenism". That the concept "Catholic ecumenism" is no longer used in the new draft is of great importance. It is not the intention of the schema to contrast two different concepts of ecumenism. If this were not so, there would be a danger that two blocs would be formed in the great ecumenical movement, in which both sides would court the adherence of the Orthodox. This was how the encyclical *Mortalium Animos*[77] had seen the ecumenical situation, and the new title is a clear rejection of this point of view. The preface acknowledges that the ecumenical movement first came into being outside the Catholic Church, and that the Catholic Church wishes to participate in it on the basis of its own

---

[74] For example, *De unitate christianorum fovenda*.

[75] The shortened formula contains only two of the principal ideas in the formula of the "basis", as it was enlarged in 1961 in New Delhi (*qui Deum Trinum invocant atque Iesum confitentur Dominum et Salvatorem*).

[76] The schema is consequently "not an ecumenical programme for the whole of Christianity, nor a manifesto of union, nor a demand for an appeal to non-Catholic Christians, but a pastoral instruction, the purpose of which is to inspire and prepare ecumenical thought and action in the Catholic Church" (Cardinal Jaeger, *op. cit.*, p. 27).

[77] Cf. above p. 1.

principles. Chapter I now presents a more detailed account of the nature of this movement. Glancing over the whole of Chapter I, one can see that on the basis of the debate in the Council, the following themes are dealt with more fully than before:

1. Repentance and confession of guilt.[78]
2. The imperfections in the Church, which as a society of men is not free from spots and wrinkles.[79]
3. The aspect of unity in diversity.
4. The significance of the holy Eucharist for unity.
5. The significance of the Holy Spirit for unity, and his work in the life of the people of God.[80]
6. The catholicity of the Church and its claim upon all men (a section on this is added in § 4).
7. The missionary dimension of ecumenism (which is mentioned in the preface and in Chapter III).
8. The dynamics of the history of salvation.[81]
9. The commandment of love is explicitly mentioned in the new text.[82]
10. The shame and the scandal of separation, which contradicts the will of Christ, is emphasized more strongly than before (in the preface).
11. Following the wish of some of the Fathers, the ecumenical movement required to be described more accurately and in more dynamic terms. This is done in § 4 and at the conclusion of the whole schema.

In order to emphasize that the separation is mutual in many passages the expression "separated brethren" is replaced by "brethren separated from us".

Some of the bishops had demanded that the doctrine of the people of God should be more clearly predominant in the exposition. This would make possible a concept of unity which was stressed more in terms of the Spirit and was more existential, a theology of *communio,* and at the same time a theology of schism, and it would also be possible to point out more clearly that by the sacrament of baptism man becomes a member of the mystical body of Christ. But since the decree was intended to be a pastoral and not a dogmatic document, these suggestions were not followed.

The Secretariat could not agree with the view of some bishops, who wished to see everything theological removed from this pastoral decree. With the avoidance of any false irenicism, § 2 gives a brief account of the Catholic doctrine of the unity of the Church under the heading "On the Unity and Unicity of the

---

[78] Apart from a reference to this in § 4, the new text contains a separate section in Chapter II on this subject.

[79] Cf. the closing sentence of § 3.

[80] Cf. the second section and the closing sentence of § 3.

[81] This is set at the beginning of Chapter I, and also at the end of § 3, with reference to Gal 3:27–29 and Eph 4:12.

[82] At the end of the first section of Chapter I.

Church". This is derived from God's plan of salvation, from the activity of the Holy Spirit as the invisible principle of the unity of the Church, and from the significance of the Eucharist for unity. Because the schema, as is stated in the preface, can assume the dogmatic teaching of the constitution *De Ecclesia,* the doctrine of the unity with which Christ has endowed his Church is only set out here in summary form.[83]

With regard to the question of the visibility of the Church desired by God, a method of formulation was sought which remained very close to the wording of holy Scripture. Here it was necessary to ignore questions still disputed by exegetes, e.g., the question of the time when Peter was chosen and given his commission. The structure of the section is as follows:

1. Christ has already established his Church for his present age. Thus it is not something which belongs to the world to come.
2. The task of teaching, ruling and sanctifying was entrusted by him to the college of the Twelve.
3. Christ built his Church upon Peter, to whom he entrusted the office of shepherding all in the Church in perfect unity.
4. Peter fulfilled his office in the name of Christ, who for ever remains the chief cornerstone of the whole building.

The expression criticized by many of the Fathers, "in fraternal unity of government", is enlarged to read "in fraternal harmony under the rule of the shepherds".

In § 3 ("The Relationship of Separated Brethren to the Catholic Church") the exposition proceeds from the present situation of Christianity, and from the schisms and division in the one and only Church of God, "developments for which, at times, men of both sides were to blame". At present Christians live from birth in different communities. Although profound differences in doctrine and discipline are present, yet they are in "a certain, though imperfect, communion with the Catholic Church". The significance of baptism is described more precisely in the new text. By baptism "they are incorporated into Christ",[84] and have a right to be honoured by the title of Christian, and are properly regarded as brothers by the Catholic faithful.

The saving function of non-Catholic ecclesial communities is clearly expressed, as was in fact the case in previous texts.[85] Furthermore, the decree emphasizes

---

[83] This demand had been made, for example, by Cardinal Frings on 28 November 1963 in the Council.

[84] Just as in the Constitution on the Church, the word *membrum* is avoided here; the formula *Christo incorporantur* has been chosen; it occurs, as is mentioned in a note, in the statements of the Council of Florence (Sess. VIII [1439], Decree *Exsultate Deo;* see Mansi, XXXI, 1055 A). This formulation goes beyond that of the encyclical *Mystici Corporis,* but cannot be regarded without qualification as the equivalent of a direct statement concerning membership of the mystical body.

[85] The statement that the Spirit of Christ uses separated ecclesial communities as a means of salvation is formulated in the text in negative terms: *Spiritus Christi . . . uti non renuit.* When one

the necessity for all who already belong in any way to God's people to be fully incorporated into the body of Christ on earth. The people of God is described in its state of pilgrimage, and the dynamic aspect of growth in Christ up to the fullness of glory in the heavenly Jerusalem is emphasized.

§ 4 ("Ecumenism") once again states the theme of the decree: the appeal to participate in the ecumenical movement, which is inspired by the Holy Spirit. This is followed by a description and definition of this movement, with special emphasis on dialogue and prayer in common. In this way all Christians will be led to "renewal and reform", and finally to the unity which Christ bestowed on his Church from the beginning, a unity which already dwells in the Catholic Church, but which should increase from day to day.

The new version places a special value on the distinction between the apostolate of conversions and the ecumenical movement, which has another purpose and a different formal principle. In this regard it is also of significance that § 4 begins with a description and definition of ecumenism on the basis of the actual activities which at the present day have developed both among Catholics and even more among separated brethren. This leads to the special task which Catholics have within and with regard to this movement. It is Catholics who should "take the first steps" here.

Thus the Church must repeatedly purify and renew itself. Unity will grow in freedom and love, and emphasis is placed upon the possibility of a diversity of forms, both in the sphere of liturgy and spirituality, and also in the theological exposition of revealed truth. In this way the Catholic faithful themselves will give an ever richer expression to the authentic catholicity and apostolicity of the Church. They must recognize the riches of Christ and the gifts of the Holy Spirit in the lives of others who are bearing witness to Christ, sometimes even to the shedding of their blood. The continuance of divisions makes it more difficult for the Church to express in her life her full catholicity.

Chapter II: The Practice of Ecumenism

The opening paragraph emphasizes more clearly than before that a concern for restoring unity pertains to the whole Church in its different spheres. Here the decisive theme is the renewal of the Catholic Church. In the new version the expression "summoned to a continual reformation" occurs not merely in a note, but in the text, and this necessity is worked out as a consequence of the historical nature of the Church. She is the Church on her pilgrim way, and the necessity of "reformation" affects not merely details but also Church discipline and the formulation of doctrine. Here the document refers in a note to papal utterances,

Council Father objected, the Secretariat explained that this stylistic formulation did not imply any weakening of the statement. It is perhaps notable that the encyclical *Mystici Corporis* uses the same wording (*Denzinger-Schönmetzer* 3808) when it denies the indwelling of the Holy Spirit with regard to those who are wholly separated from the mystical body of Christ.

including some of recent date.[86] The admission that in each of the three aspects mentioned, the word of Christ has previously "not been preserved closely enough" is new.[87]

The two paragraphs on the conversion of the heart and holiness of life are combined into one (§ 7). At the request of many bishops a confession of guilt for the sins which have been committed against unity is introduced here as a separate section.

The following paragraph (§ 8) strongly emphasizes the importance of prayer for the unity of Christians in close association with this spirit of repentance in the heart, as "spiritual ecumenism". In certain circumstances this prayer in common with separated brethren is not merely "allowable" but wholly "desirable". True *communicatio in sacris* is now more clearly distinguished from this than before. Two principles are advanced concerning the latter, which complement each other: the principle of the unity of the Church, which should be outwardly manifested and to which witness should be borne in worship in the proper way, and the principle of sharing in the means of grace, from the point of view of pastoral care. This means that as far as the course to be adopted is concerned, and in view of the great variations in circumstances, different forms of worship in common are possible, and this is entrusted to the decision of the bishops.

§ 9, which deals with the necessity of mutual understanding between brethren, once again stresses that Catholics must be adequately prepared for this task. It was here that several bishops had raised objections, because this outlook was quite new to their faithful. In the demand for an ecumenical formation of future priests, explicit mention is now made of historical studies (§ 10). In the discussion of the manner and order in which Catholic belief should be expressed and explained (§ 11), emphasis is placed at the very beginning on the responsibility of those who teach it for seeing that it does not become an obstacle to dialogue with our brethren. Every more profound and precise explanation of Catholic belief, which must take place without obscuring its sense, will be of service to mutual understanding. What is new in this text is that it opens the way for common study on the part of Catholic and non-Catholic Christians, so that they may better reveal the riches of Christ to all.

In the paragraph on practical co-operation with our separated brethren (§ 12) the possibility and necessity of a common witness to Christ before the world is emphasized at the very beginning. The number of tasks which should be carried out in common is now extended and put in more concrete terms; work for peace in the world now comes first, and mention is also made of co-operation in science and art.

[86] The reference to the encyclical of John XXIII *Ad Petri Cathedram* (*AAS* 51 [1959], p. 511) is no longer to be found in the final text.
[87] At the end of the first section of § 6.

Chapter III: Churches and Ecclesial Communities
Separated from the Roman Apostolic See

The new wording of the title of Chapter III expresses the fact that consideration has been given here not to "separated Christians" but to the communities in which they lead their Christian life. They are called separated "Churches and ecclesial communities". A newly added preface proceeds from the fact that in the course of its discussions the Council came to realize in a completely new way that the ecumenical movement has grown together from two great streams of tradition. The divisions which have damaged the seamless robe of Christ can be divided into two groups, which are now not set in their historical order, but geographically: the first occurred in the East, and the second in the West. They are very different in their nature, especially from the point of view of faith and ecclesiastical structure. The Council gives consideration both to the differences between them as well as to what they have in common. This is the reason why both are dealt with in the same chapter, albeit in two different sections, and in a different way; thus the fundamental unity of the ecumenical movement is preserved, from the point of view also of the work for unity of the World Council of Churches.

When these texts are compared with their predecessors, it is evident that the account of the Eastern Churches has been considerably enlarged. Emphasis is placed on what is held in common: the existence of patriarchates, the apostolic succession, the validity of their sacraments; while the Eucharist, as an effective factor in the building up of the Church, is given special mention. On the other hand, there is reference to the difference between the Eastern and Western traditions. The constancy of Eastern Christians in maintaining and defending the Christian faith is specially stressed. For many bishops it was of great importance that there is no contradiction between true catholicity and the maintenance of the distinctive characteristics of the East, such as had led to a demand for a change in ecclesiastical discipline and structure in the Catholic Church.

The special section on the Eastern Churches separated from the Apostolic See[88] begins with § 14, on the spirit and history of the Eastern Churches. First of all, the situation of the still united Church of the first millenium is described, with the inclusion of a reference to the relations which obtained at that time between the Eastern Churches and the Roman See.[89] The leading position of the latter was based upon common consent, and was manifested in its acting as a moderator in disagreements. The reason for the origin of the schism is given as a failure in mutual understanding and charity, "added to external causes" — the implication, therefore, is that the blame was on both sides. Only by giving due consideration to the special aspects of the origin and growth of the Churches of

[88] Throughout the decree this term refers both to the true "Orthodox" Churches that have come into being since 1054, and also to the non-Chalcedonian Churches.
[89] The more precise characterization *cuius est praesidere in caritate* has now been removed.

43

the East, and to the character of the relations which obtained between them and the Roman See before the separation, is it possible to form a correct evaluation of the facts. The aim of this whole process is explicitly mentioned here: it is that of dialogue, a genuine exchange of ideas among Christian Churches. In the three paragraphs that follow the particular heritage of Eastern Christians is described, and first place is given to their liturgical and spiritual tradition. In the new text, more space is given first to the holy Eucharist, in which the believing Christian enters into communion with the most holy Trinity. Through this celebration, in each individual Church, the Church of God is built up and grows in stature. Special mention is made of the form of concelebration which is characteristic of the East.

Here the close relationship of these Churches with the Catholic Church, based upon the apostolic succession, is made evident. The conviction of many bishops, that without in any way giving rise to the danger of indifferentism, this closeness demanded a wider extension of *communicatio in sacris,* including its extension to mixed marriages,[90] was taken into account in the new text to a considerable extent. In the same context the liturgical veneration of the Virgin Mary and the other saints, especially the Fathers of the universal Church, is mentioned.

Among the traditions of the East special mention is made of monasticism, which began in the East.

All these are riches of Christ, which are of the utmost importance for the fullness of Christian tradition, its faithful maintenance, and the ultimate reconciliation of Eastern and Western Christians.

Secondly, the specific discipline of Eastern Churches is explicitly acknowledged (§ 16). They have "the right and duty to govern themselves according to their own disciplines, . . . for the good of souls". This freedom of the Eastern Churches has always been acknowledged on principle, but has frequently not been adequately honoured by the Catholic Church in practice. But following this admission of guilt, it is named as a necessary prerequisite for any restoration of unity.

The exposition then turns to the forms of the theological expression of doctrine (§ 17). Here too variety is declared to be legitimate, and described in its positive aspect. Once again, attention must be paid to what is mutually complementary, rather than to the discrepancies which exist. A newly inserted section emphasizes that the entire heritage of spirituality and liturgy, of discipline and theology, in the different traditions, belongs to the full catholic and apostolic character of the Church.

This is also the place in which the Catholic Eastern Churches are mentioned and praised. In fact most of the chapter contains arguments which apply equally

---

[90] In the present decree the question of mixed marriage is not really dealt with, but in the Decree on Eastern Catholic Churches a decision was taken in the sense that marriage with a baptized Eastern non-Catholic carried out before a *minister sacer* is valid (cf. vol. I of this commentary, p. 326).

to the Eastern Churches separated from Rome and to those united with Rome. They have the same characteristics and the same history.

A concluding summary (§ 18) looks forward solemnly, but in cautious terms, to the final communion and unity, which can only be attained gradually, and which depends upon prayer, fraternal dialogue, and readiness to be of help, especially towards Eastern Christians who have emigrated. When the wall dividing the Eastern and Western Church is one day removed — it is Christ who can make both one — then one must "impose no burden beyond what is indispensable" (Acts 15:28).

Many of the Fathers had shown themselves dissatisfied with the second section of Chapter III. Some had even voiced the impression that after the careful treatment of the Eastern Churches, this part was an inevitable anti-climax, and might produce the effect of having been added as an afterthought. Is it in any case the task of the Catholic Church and the Council to describe other communities and to pass judgment on historical events such as the Reformation? This description, which suffered from many over-simplifications, and did not give adequate expression to the differences between individual communities in the West,[91] was in any case not to be an end in itself. Its aim should not be the return of the separated brethren, but the ecumenical dialogue.

The whole text was now recast with the requirements of this dialogue in mind. It continued to be divided according to the four spheres in which the elements of the Church which have been maintained by these communities have particularly taken shape: the confession of Christ, zeal for holy Scripture, the sacrament of baptism as the entrance to sacramental life as a whole, and life in fellowship with Christ and for Christ's sake. In each case what is held in common is mentioned first, and then follows a reference to the profound differences which manifest themselves in the very midst of what is held in common, but which are not of such a nature as to make dialogue impossible. The purpose of the whole is that the ecumenical dialogue may be more easily undertaken, on the basis of the affirmation of the riches of Christ, and the recognition of the honest concern to be found among other Christians.

The title of this passage had previously spoken of "communities". But as the decree recognizes,[92] it is dealing here not simply with human forms of community but with Christian communities, and in fact with a genuine *communio* of believers, in which something of a Church is manifest. Ought one as a consequence call them "Churches" in the strict theological sense? On the other hand, there are also Protestant communities, which are themselves member Churches of the World Council, which refuse to apply the name "Church" to themselves. It was therefore decided to introduce the term *communitates ecclesiales*, "ecclesial

[91] The Protestant observers had also clearly expressed their view on this passage to the Secretariat. Their criticism and especially that of Lukas Vischer, certainly contributed to the new version.
[92] Cf. above p. 40.

communities". The new title "The Separated Churches and Ecclesial Communities in the West" also expresses the fact that not all of these owe their origin to the Reformation, such as, for example, the Waldensians, which are older than the Reformation, and the Old Catholics, who first came into existence after 1870. Thus at the beginning of the exposition (§ 19) mention is made of the origin of the new ecclesial communities "at the end of the Middle Ages, or during later times".

This paragraph goes on to make an explicit renunciation of the attempt to reduce the differences which exist to a common denominator, in view of the difficulties of this task, which had frequently been mentioned in the debate in the Council.

A few bishops had drawn attention to the fact that the ecumenical movement is not yet so far advanced in every country as to exclude anti-Catholic proselytism. This difficulty is now explicitly mentioned. But at the same time the hope is expressed of a gradual increase and strengthening of ecumenism. The passage that follows is also new; it refers to the fact that the Churches are divided not only by non-theological factors, but also by weighty differences in the interpretation of revealed truth. The recognition of the profundity of these differences is the pre-requisite for any realistic ecumenism and dialogue. In the spirit of "sound irenicism" it is now proposed to specify the common ground, as well as dogmatic differences.

The confession of Christ by Western Churches and ecclesial communities is once again referred to in the words of the "basis", which the Assembly of the World Council of Churches accepted in New Delhi,[93] though a shorter form is given here. As was several times suggested in the Council, the words that follow speak explicitly of Christ as the source and unifying centre of ecclesiastical communion among Protestants. So extensive an accord can only be a reason for great rejoicing. But at the same time differences in the interpretation of revelation concerning the doctrines of God's incarnate Word and his work of redemption, as well as about the consequences for the mystery of the Church, and for its ministry, are referred to here. The next paragraph testifies that the brethren separated from us affirm the divine authority of holy Scripture, and, in the words of a brief addition, "at the prompting of the Holy Spirit" they find God in holy Scripture, who speaks to them in Christ. The expression that Scripture is the most precious "medium" for ecumenical dialogue, was left out at the request of a French bishop, on the grounds that it requires interpretation, and only its true, authentic sense can form such a medium. Different views on the relationship between the Scriptures and the Church, and especially her teaching office, form a serious difficulty for dialogue, but it is a difficulty which can be overcome by the mighty hand of God, who in this dialogue uses the Scriptures as an instrument.

[93] Cf. above p. 25.

Few observations were made in the debate on the paragraph (§ 22) which follows, on sacramental life. Of significance here is the demand of the Scandinavian bishops that the expression *homo vere Christo incorporatur* should be strengthened, and that explicit reference should be made to the membership of the mystical body of Christ, constituted by baptism. One bishop demanded that the sacrament of marriage, which the baptized administer to each other, should be mentioned as a common heritage of all.

Of these requests for additions, the only one which was granted was the addition of a section on the celebration of the Lord's Supper in the Protestant Churches, which follows the thesis that baptism of its nature is intended to bring "a complete participation in eucharistic communion". The new version mentions first the consequences which follow especially from the lack of the sacrament of orders in the case of the celebrant of the Protestant Lord's Supper; the ecclesial communities separated from us have "not preserved the *plena realitas* of the Eucharist". But it goes on to say that when they commemorate the Lord's death and resurrection in the Holy Supper, they too profess that it signifies life in communion with Christ, and that they await his coming in glory. This is regarded as a positive starting point for dialogue.

In the next paragraph (§ 23), "On Life with Christ", a section is added which refers to the existing differences of judgment in moral matters. But as the text says, this does not prevent the ecumenical dialogue from being rekindled again and again by a genuine readiness to obey Christ and to do everything in the name of Christ.

The arguments in § 24, the conclusion of the whole schema, appear in the new text in a strengthened and extended form. The intention is to bring to the forefront once again the importance of the ecumenical movement and ecumenical activity, and especially to strengthen the awareness that so great a task exceeds human powers, and can only be undertaken in Christian hope and in trust in God. Here again it is emphasized that ecumenical activity in the true sense of the word is Catholic, and is loyal to the received truth and in harmony with the faith of the Catholic Church. This is particularly true if there is no Catholic ecumenism, in contrast to a Protestant or Orthodox ecumenism, and if all initiatives in this field, as the new text says, "should be joined with those of the separated brethren". The Council's greatest concern must be not to obstruct the ways of divine providence, which is at work here, but to leave the way open for what the Holy Spirit will bring about in the future, and for the hopes which the ecumenical awakening of our times both justifies and makes a duty.

The *relationes* at the third session of the Council

On 5 October 1964 began the reading of *relationes* on individual chapters of the new schema by representatives of the Secretariat for Christian Unity.

Archbishop Martin of Rouen reported upon the new text of the first chapter of the schema. He gave an assurance that the Secretariat was concerned to express exactly the opinion of the Council Fathers, and that no attempt had been made to force its own view upon the general congregation. By means of intensive and detailed work the submissions of the Fathers had first been analysed by small commissions of theologians, and then by all the members of the Secretariat. The same was true of the submissions which were not made until after the printing of the text. He referred to four particularly important changes in Chapter I.

1. The first point concerns the preface, which was asked for by a number of Fathers, so that at the very beginning of the decree its meaning and object might be clearly expressed. This preface was formulated with special regard for our separated brethren. It is also meant to establish the connection between the Decree on Ecumenism and the Constitution on the Church.

2. The title of Chapter I was altered, in order to exclude the mistake that there is a specifically Catholic ecumenism. There is only one ecumenism, and Catholics are invited to take part in this ecumenical movement in loyalty to their own Catholic principles.

3. The activity of the Holy Spirit in the ecumenical movement is more thoroughly emphasized than before.

4. The description and definition of ecumenism is also new, and is considerably longer than in the first version, in order to make it clear that this is a movement inspired by the Holy Spirit, and not something static, and in order to take into account future development, which cannot be laid down in advance, since "the Spirit blows where he will".

The *relator* then declared that from the Council impulses had gone out which were in accordance with ecumenical thought and action, and which could even now be seen at work. There was now a more sensitive and more painful awareness of the wounds of separation. In many cases the thinking of Catholics was increasingly concerned with the cause of unity, and the attempt was being made in prayer to attain to what is the will of Christ in this matter. Here he also mentioned the conversations with the observers, which had not merely led to a close personal acquaintance, but to an altogether new kind of relationship and mutual trust among Christians. Great hopes were rightly placed in this, especially if such contacts were to help both sides to work under the influence of the Holy Spirit to renew themselves.

The *relator* also mentioned the pilgrimage of Paul VI to Jerusalem, and the kiss of peace "at that happy meeting, worthy of remembrance for centuries", as the Patriarch Athenagoras called it. He concluded with a few words concerning the aim and intention of the decree. The difficulties which still exist cannot simply be overlooked. But as Paul VI said in his encyclical *Ecclesiam Suam,* the time has now come, to lay more emphasis on "that which is common to us", rather than on "that which separates us".[94] It is this which is the intention of the schema.

[94] See *AAS* 10 (1964), pp. 609 ff.

"We still stand at the beginning of the way. What has been divided for centuries cannot be restored to unity in a few days. What is certain is that as long as ignorance and mutual mistrust predominate, nothing will be done to restore unity, while everything becomes possible, through the grace of God, where the spirit of understanding, good will and brotherly love reigns." The report closed with an expression of the hope, shared by so many today, that in accordance with the will of God the moment of the restoration of unity may already be near, and with a call for unanimity on the part of the Fathers.

Bishop Helmsing of Kansas City gave a short report on Chapter II of the schema. Since the wishes of the Fathers with regard to this chapter only affected a few individual points, he proceeded by drawing the attention of the bishops once again to the content of individual paragraphs.

He particularly emphasized to confession of guilt with regard to unity, and the strengthening of the call to repentance and public admission of guilt, directed towards each individual, which had been included in § 7 of the schema.

With regard to the question of prayer for unity, especially in fraternal participation with the Orthodox and Protestants, account had been taken of the wishes of many Fathers, by setting out in the schema a positive principle for common prayer and participation in the worship of other Christian Churches or ecclesial communities. With regard to the differences in the situation in different areas, it had been decided to lay down a principle in very general terms, and for the rest to leave the individual cases to the judgment of the bishops. This combines two basic ideas which, in the words of the *relator*, "are in dialectic tension": the witness to unity and the regard for grace required by pastoral care.

The next four paragraphs of the chapter were to be voted on separately by the Fathers. These dealt with mutual understanding, dialogue, the ecumenical formation of the clergy and the laity, and practical co-operation with all Christians in the service of the common good and of peace. In dialogue truth should be expressed in love, so that both false irenicism and also the hardening of the heart and intellectual pride are avoided.

In conclusion he emphasized the importance of this chapter for the renewal of the Church. It must be made clear that the ecumenical movement has an intimate relationship with the life of Holy Mother Church, so that the bishops are encouraged everywhere to take under their care the fostering of ecumenical activity.

The ecumenical "directory" desired by so many would be considered by the Secretariat for publication in the near future. Here again suggestions were expected from the Fathers.[95]

[95] This directory was approved by Pope Paul VI on 14 May 1967 and published by Cardinal Bea as president of the Secretariat for Promoting Christian Unity (*Directorium ad ea quae a Concilio Vaticano secundo de re oecumenica promulgata sunt exequenda* [Typ. polygl. Vat., 1967]). The second half of the directory is yet to appear.

Archbishop Maximos Hermaniuk, Metropolitan of the Eastern rite for Ukrainians in Canada, gave a report on the section specially devoted to the Eastern Churches (Chapter III, 1). He discussed the way in which this part of the schema makes evident to all Catholics "the unity of the Church in the East and in the West", which according to Paul VI was one of the principal tasks of the Council.[96] It is the desire of the Church to declare to everyone clearly and authoritatively that both in the objective study of the reasons for the grievous division between the East and the West, as well as in any attempt to restore the previous unity, the East and the West — in almost every case — only diverge from each other in the different way in which they express the same dogmatic truth, while their liturgical practice is identical and their Church discipline similar. As long as this fact remains unknown or is not put into practice, the effect on the whole Church life of Christians can only be most harmful, resulting in dissensions, bitter accusations, and sometimes in mutual condemnation. The *relator* mentioned here the events of the year 1054, when the Papal Legate, Cardinal Humbert, accused the Patriarch and his adherents of all the heresies which existed at that time in the Church, and excommunicated them on that account, although, as historical study has now confirmed, no doubt was cast on a single dogmatic truth in this whole dispute.

Thus the Secretariat had set itself the task of directing the special attention of all to the Eastern Churches, and of clearly showing to all Christians their mentality, history, liturgical traditions, spiritual life, ecclesiastical discipline and distinctive theology.

He next dealt with a number of objections. One of the Fathers had objected to the statement in the schema that by the Eucharist celebrated in the Eastern Churches "the Church of God is built up and grows in stature".[97] But wherever it is validly celebrated, the holy Eucharist is the source of the life of the Church, brings the increase of the grace of Christ, the head of the mystical body, in the soul, and is the pledge of future glory.

Archbishops Hermaniuk dealt in greater detail with the question of why no mention was made at this point in the schema of the special ecumenical task of the Eastern Churches united with Rome. His reply was that in many places tensions existed between Catholic and Orthodox Eastern Churches, which sometimes led the Orthodox to demand the abolition of these Uniat Churches. By contrast with this view, and looking at the matter from the ecumenical aspect, he saw it as the special task of these Churches to persevere in their double loyalty, that is, to maintain perfect loyalty to the successor of Peter, and also to their own Eastern traditions, which are a visible sign of the catholicity of

[96] Cf. the opening address of 14 September 1964: the Council ought "to show how similar the conception of the constitution of the Church is in the East and in the West, although expressed in different ways".

[97] As is remarked in the note, this wording derives from John Chrysostom (*In Ioannem Homilia,* XLVI; see *PG,* LIX, 260 ff.

the Church. Perhaps by this double loyalty it may be made easier to open the way to dialogue with separated brethren in the East.

The Secretariat had accepted with real joy the proposals of many Eastern Fathers, that under certain circumstances common worship with separated brethren should be specially recommended and encouraged, with regard to the Orthodox Church.

The report on the second part of Chapter III was given by Archbishop (now Cardinal) J. C. Heenan of Westminster. He first gave the reason for the change in the title, which had been made at the request of the Fathers. The very title is meant to give the impression that the communities which have come into being in the West as a result of the separation do not simply represent agglomerations of individual Christians, but are constituted by elements of ecclesiastical communion, which preserve the common Christian heritage and truly belong to the nature of the Church. The title "Churches and ecclesial communities" includes all who "are adorned by the name of a Christian". No attempt is made to answer the question as to which elements are necessary before a Christian community can be called a Church in theological terms. The new title, in accordance with historical truth, is no longer derived from a date, the time of the Reformation, but refers to a place.

At the request of many of the Fathers, a new form of exposition had been chosen for the text, though no structural changes had been undertaken. All attempts to describe the communities had been given up. The text is restricted to four points: the profession of Christ, the study of holy Scripture, sacramental life and life in fellowship with Christ. In all these cases we are dealing on the one hand with elements which are common to all Christians and provide a basis for dialogue; on the other hand, on each of these points there are clearly doctrines concerning which agreement is still lacking. The dialogue has already begun by the bringing to light of these disagreements, and the wishes of some have been satisfied by the avoidance on the one hand of any kind of proselytism, and on the other hand of false irenicism.

In the closing paragraphs, which are intended as the conclusion of the whole schema, the principles from which the whole work of ecumenism derives its inspiration are once again named: loyalty to the Catholic faith which has been handed down to us by the Church, and loyalty to the influence of the Holy Spirit, who is leading all Christians to attain the unity willed by Christ. In conclusion the *relator* said that priests and Catholic laity, as well as non-Catholic Christians, and in fact the whole world, were awaiting the result of this vote. Here was the opportunity of showing by a unanimous approval that Christians could be recognized today, as in the times of the apostles, by their brotherly love.

The votes in the third session.
The evaluation of the *modi* and the nineteen alterations

It was intended that during the third session of the Council there should be no discussion of the improved schema, but only the voting introduced by the four *relationes* discussed above. The paragraphs were put to the vote either singly or in groups of a few at a time. Then whole chapters were voted on, although it was also possible to express a reservation by voting *juxta modum*. In the voting on 5 October 1964 there were votes against every one of the paragraphs of Chapter I: § 1 received 16 votes against, § 2 = 30, § 3 = 57, and § 4 = 50 votes against. In the voting on the whole chapter, the votes against were reduced to 30, but 209 *modi* were submitted. In the case of Chapter II, the *non placet* votes were more numerous. On §§ 5–6, 46 Fathers voted against, on § 7, 92, on § 8, 292, and on §§ 9–12, 62. When this chapter was voted upon as a whole, there were 564 *modi*, while only 32 *non placet* votes were recorded. On Chapter III the difference in the case of the *non placet* votes was smaller. On the three votes on §§ 13–24, the number of negative votes was 21, 39, and 43 respectively, while in the final vote on the whole chapter on 8 October 1964, 24 *non placet* votes and 296 *modi* were recorded. Consequently, many *modi* were submitted by bishops who had previously voted *non placet*.

The Secretariat now had the task of working on an evaluation of the *modi* which had been submitted — and since many of the Fathers made several suggestions on a single vote, their total reached almost two thousand. In the second week of November, a report on this work was printed in the form of three stout volumes, and was submitted to the vote of the Fathers on 10 November.[98] Because the *modi* were often verbally identical, it had been possible to reduce them to about 400. The majority of the reservations made by the Fathers were rejected, and only 28 were accepted by the Secretariat. (12 in the preface and in Chapter I, 5 in Chapter II, and 3 in Chapter III.) The reason for this procedure is given in the *relatio* of the Secretariat on Chapter III: many of the reservations could not be reconciled with the spirit of the text, the integral form of which had already been decided by the Fathers' acceptance.[99] Although the *periti* of the Secretariat had attempted to do justice to everything that had been put forward, they had only accepted relatively few *modi*, after lengthy discussion in the sessions of the Secretariat. Changes and transpositions had only been accepted when they led to a clearer and better expressed text. The catalogue of *modi* contained in each case a brief summary

[98] The first volume, entitled *Schema Decreti de Oecumenismo. Modi a Patribus Conciliaribus propositi a Secretariatu ad christianorum unitatem fovendam examinati,* was distributed on 9 November; from 11 to 14 November followed the notes on the treatment of the *modi* on Chapters II and III.
[99] The feeling had come to prevail in the Council that such *modi* as could be called a form of concealed *non placet,* were inadmissible once the schema had already been approved by a vote on its substance.

of the reasons submitted with each individual *modus,* and the answer of the Secretariat.

In the preface, which in the vote on 5 October had been accepted with only 16 votes against, there were two statements in particular concerning the ecumenical movement with which some of the Fathers disagreed. Firstly, the activity of the Holy Spirit was recognized in this movement, which had come into being among non-Catholics; this recognition had already been made by the instruction of the Holy Office in 1949. *Modi* which were directed against this statement because only a "vague Christianity" was being given expression in it, were not accepted by the Secretariat for Promoting Christian Unity. The other thesis expressed a positive judgment on the whole situation of the ecumenical movement, that it had reached a point in which there was no longer satisfaction with an invisible Church, but a longing for the visible and at the same time "truly universal" Church, which would be in the position to fulfil its missionary task towards the whole world through its universality. The text reads *quae sit vere universalis,* in order to point to the fact that what is meant here is not the concrete Catholic Church, but a Church of the future. Here the *modi,* which wished the subjunctive to be replaced by the indicative *est,* had been rejected, in order to retain the meaning of the text already accepted by the Fathers.

The same is true of the individual requests made for a return to the earlier version of the title of Chapter I, and to the expression "Catholic ecumenism".

In some of the *modi* the problem of proselytism was raised once again. The work of conversion must also be carried out in an ecumenical spirit, in a spirit of mutual trust between Churches and ecclesial communities, and with the avoidance of any kind of proselytism. But in the view of the Secretariat, the overcoming of proselytism was a theme which belonged properly to the Declaration on Religious Freedom. Thus the wish of many bishops who in their dioceses suffered from the proselytism of many sects, that proselytism should be condemned, perhaps at the conclusion of the decree, was not fulfilled. The "directory" on ecumenical practice promised by the Secretariat would also have to deal with this question. The theological clarification of the distinction between ecclesial communities and sects, which was repeatedly asked for, was nowhere attempted in the resolutions of the Council. The Secretariat expressed the hope that the spread of the ecumenical movement, which in New Delhi had attacked the proselytism of a number of particular sects in a declaration of its own, would gradually lead to a decline in such unworthy missionary tactics.

Among the *modi* accepted by the Secretariat, only a few were of any great importance: the mention of the bishops with the successor of Peter as their head; the addition of the special section on the "hierarchy" of the truths of Catholic doctrine; a more exact distinction between the work of conversion and the ecumenical task; the introduction of a mention of the patriarchal Churches in the text of Chapter III; and finally, in the discussion of the Lord's

Supper in the ecclesial communities of the Reformation, the extension of the expression "full reality of the Eucharist" by the term *mysterium*.[100]

Since both the *modi* accepted by the Secretariat and those rejected by it are discussed in the commentary on the individual passages of the text concerned, there is no need to go into them at this point.

We might make special mention here of a passage which many of the Fathers seemed to find objectionable, and which caused the Secretariat great difficulties in dealing with the *modi*. So many *modi* had been submitted on the newly inserted passage on the importance of the Lord's Supper among the Churches of the Reformation (17 *modi* with 335 signatures) that an alteration in the text seemed necessary here, so long as it was borne in mind that the positive evaluation of the Protestant Lord's Supper, already accepted by the Council, could not be withdrawn. But the emendation did not deal with the objections of those Fathers who had argued against the gradation implied in the text between a "total" and less total reality of the sacraments; it only added the concept *mysterium* — instead of *plenam realitatem Eucharistiae* it now read *plenam realitatem Mysterii eucharistici* —, with the intention of setting aside any ambiguity with regard to the Real Presence in the sacrament of the Eucharist.

Moreover, the Fathers had not treated this evaluation of the Protestant Lord's Supper as a reason for voting *non placet* in the vote on 8 October — there had been only 43 *non placet* votes on this section of Chapter III. On the vote on the *expensio modorum* on each of the three chapters there were 2068 *placet* votes against 47 *non placet,* with 4 invalid votes, on 10 November; 2021 *placet* against 85 *non placet,* with 3 invalid votes, on 11 November; and on 14 November there were 1870 *placet*, against 82 *non placet* and 11 invalid votes; thus there were fewer *non placet* votes on Chapter III than on Chapter II.

Thus the Council had expressed its trust in and assent to the work of the Secretariat by an overwhelming majority, and the schema went to the printers in this form, in order to be voted upon a few days later (on 20 November) as the final text.

But the opposition was not yet content with this text, and in the final days of the session, when Paul VI had already given way to a certain extent to the wishes of the minority in the questions of the college of bishops, and freedom of religion, similar requests were submitted to him with regard to this text. That here again the Pope had the intention of satisfying the wishes of the minority as far as possible, was known at first neither to the Secretariat for Unity nor to the Council. Not until 19 November, when introducing the final vote, did Archbishop Felici announce that the printed text was not yet the final one. At the last moment, *ad maiorem claritatem textus,* nineteen further changes had been introduced on the basis of "well-intentioned and authoritatively expressed suggestions"; and after they had been read they were handed out

---

[100] Cf. above p. 47.

to the bishops on a duplicated sheet. It has come to be known that these changes were only part of a much larger body of proposals.[101] More than forty changes had been handed to Cardinal Bea and his closest colleagues only the day before, as *suggestiones benevolae* of the Pope, at too late an hour for any further session of the Secretariat to be possible. Of these proposals for alterations, nineteen were then accepted by Cardinal Bea and his colleagues.[102]

One may suppose that these forty points went back for the most part to the *modi,* for the rejection of which the Secretariat had received the *placet* of the Council in the votes from 10 to 14 November. G. Caprile has recently carried out a comparison of some of the nineteen alterations with the rejected *modi.*[103] It is possible to extend this comparison.[104] In some passages requests were taken into account which had only been contained in written submissions by the Fathers.

If one considers the nineteen alterations as a whole from this point of view, it is possible to resolve the confused questions which are still being asked up to the present time.[105] Evidently Paul VI wanted to take into account the misgivings of the minority, the strength of which was only evident to him after the vote. He did, in fact, defer his decision, due to the demands on his time during the preceding weeks, to the last minute, but trusted the Secretariat to find a way which still lay within the rules of the Council. The representatives of the Secretariat, called together at so late an hour, had the freedom to choose from the forty points only those which they were convinced could not be interpreted in the sense of the substance of the text. The Secretariat for Unity had come to be so highly trusted by the overwhelming majority of the Fathers that scarcely a single voice was heard which attributed to Cardinal Bea the responsibility for the changes in the text, although they were given out in the name of the Secretariat. In reality Cardinal Bea had helped the Pope to attain his purpose of overcoming the genuine conscientious doubts of certain theologians and of gaining their votes for the text.[106]

---

[101] These statements are taken from a report in the journal *Irénikon* 37 (1964), pp. 50 ff.

[102] Cf. G. Thils, *Le décret sur l'Œcuménisme, commentaire doctrinal* (1966), pp. 23 f.

[103] Cf. *Il Concilio Vaticano II. Cronache del Concilio Vaticano II edite de "La Civiltà Cattolica",* a cura di G. Caprile SJ, *Terzo Periodo 1964–1965,* Vol. IV (1965), p. 480.

[104] The author discusses these questions in greater detail in *Vaticanum Secundum,* III/2 (1967), pp. 587–97. That volume contains (pp. 557–97) a more detailed version of this history of the Decree on Ecumenism.

[105] G. Thils has asked, "What did the authors really desire in the large number of proposals for changes which they put forward? Did they wish at the last moment to obtain from the Pope a postponement of the promulgation of the decree — as had in fact been done in the case of the Declaration on Religious Freedom? Or was a papal intervention, with so many changes in a text which had already been voted upon, intended so to anger the Fathers that a considerable group of *non placet* votes would be drawn from the majority to the minority, so that the whole schema would ultimately fall?" According to Thils, such questions were seriously posed *(op. cit.).*

[106] After the promulgation of the decree, Paul VI, in his general audience on 20 February 1965, referred to the decree as a "significant, outspoken and reliable" *(fiducioso)* document, which would certainly bear rich fruit.

That the reading of the nineteen alterations on that "black Thursday" produced a real crisis in the Council, the effect of which extended to the beginning of the fourth session, must also be attributed to psychological factors. As we have said, many things were combined. The adjournment of the Declaration on Religious Freedom, which later proved to be valuable, had had the effect of an earthquake. The bishops and the Pope himself were overburdened and overtired. The date of the conclusion of the session was already fixed by the Pope's journey to Bombay. If there had only been three days' interval to interpret what had taken place, it would have been possible for the Pope to make his intention clear to the bishops and also to the observers.

It is necessary to express thanks to the non-Catholic observers, who, mostly only after overcoming their own first shock, helped us to see the positive possibilities which were provided by the genuine resolution of such a crisis in the Council. The text as a whole was not essentially altered, and while in the vote on 20 November, 64 Fathers (evidently from very different motives) had voted against the decree (11 votes were invalid), in the final vote on 21 November there were 2137 *placet* against only 11 *non placet* votes. Scarcely anyone at the beginning of the Council would have regarded such a unaminous agreement on so novel a schema as possible.

The growth of the text from its modest beginnings also bears witness to the way in which the members of the Secretariat grew in stature to deal with the task committed to them. They became more and more bold in breaking new ground. The Church has now made the intentions of the ecumenical movement its own, whereas only a few years ago in many countries it seemed to be the affair of only a few pioneers. The pangs of birth through which this new thinking came to be accepted by the Council will be forgotten, especially as that which must have given the impression of being offensive has already been forgiven in Christian brotherly love. What remains is "this great and beautiful text".[107]

---

[107] Cf. Y. M.-J. Congar, *Documents conciliaires* (1965), p. 165.

Commentary on the Decree

by

*Johannes Feiner**

Title. The description of this document as a "decree" expresses the fact that like other Council documents referred to as decrees, it consists largely of instructions for the practical attitude of Catholics, derived from the doctrinal teaching of the Council. As can be seen from the final passage of Article 1, the Dogmatic Constitution on the Church is meant to provide the main doctrinal basis for the decree. At the same time, its doctrinal content is not insignificant: it carries into effect the doctrinal teaching on the Church in detail, and adds certain emphases which are worthy of note. Thus while one must affirm that the Decree on Ecumenism should be interpreted by means of the doctrine of the Constitution on the Church, the reverse is also true: the doctrine of the Constitution on the Church must be read in the light of this decree.[1]

The term "ecumenism" was not accepted at the Council without certain objections from German-speaking members of the Council. It is true that the words "ecumenical" (*ökumenisch*; used in a different sense from the traditional meaning which it had always had in Catholic usage in such expressions as "ecumenical councils") and *Ökumene* had been taken into German Catholic usage from non-Catholics long before the Second Vatican Council, to refer to movements aiming at the union of Christianity. In this sense Pius XI and Pius XII had already used the word. But the noun "ecumenism" had not been in use before the Council in the German-speaking area, either among Catholics or among non-Catholics. There was unhappiness about the introduction of this new expression "ecumenism" on the grounds of the feel of the German language, in which an "-ism" (the word in German is *Ökumenismus*) has a pejorative significance. Among French-speaking people, the term "ecumenism" had gradually come into use before the Council, after Y. Congar had introduced it in his epoch-making work *Chrétiens désunis. Principes d'un œcuménisme catholique*

---

* *Translated by R. A. Wilson*

[1] Thus, for example, the recognition of the significance for salvation of the Churches and ecclesial communities separated from us, which is contained only implicitly in the Constitution on the Church (Article 15), is explicitly stated in the Decree on Ecumenism (Article 3, paragraph 3).

57

(1st ed., 1937). In his doctoral thesis *Catholic Ecumenism* (Catholic University of America, Washington 1953), E. F. Hanahoe, S. A., adopted the expression in an English form, and so contributed to its naturalization among English-speaking people. In the documents of the Council it appears for the first time in the schema *De Ecclesia,* which the Preparatory Theological Commission had draw up: Chapter IX bore the title *De oecumenismo.* At first, the Secretariat for Christian Unity did not use the term for the title of its text, but afterwards accepted it. Henceforth it defended it on several occasions against objections during the debates in the Council. Since then it has come to be widely used by German speakers.

Introduction: **Article 1.** The introduction, which in the final version was placed at the beginning of the text at the justifiable request of several of the Council Fathers, briefly presents the starting-point and introduces the theme of the decree, as is the purpose of an introduction. It refers to the aim of the Council, to the fact of the division of Christianity, the urgent impulse of the Lord towards unity, and the efforts of Christianity at the present day for the restoration of unity. This is followed by an appeal to Catholics to take part in ecumenical efforts according to the directives that follow.

The two opening words *Unitatis redintegratio,* by which the decree has henceforth been known, were moved during the Council by the Secretariat for Unity from the middle of the first sentence, where they previously stood, to the beginning, in order to characterize not merely one of the aims of the Council, but also the goal of this decree and of ecumenism in general. In the *modi,* the expression was contested by individual Fathers, who asserted that the uniting of Christianity could not be described as the aim of a Council. The reply of the Secretariat was a two-fold one: first, that the sentence does not say that the restoration of unity is *the* aim, but one of the aims of the Council; secondly, the wording is not that the restoration of unity itself is the task of the Council, but the promoting of the restoration of unity *(redintegratio ... promovenda).* In other words, the restoration of unity is not the immediate aim, but is certainly the ultimate aim of the Council, which it is its immediate task to promote. That the Council has been given as one of its tasks the work of uniting Christianity had been emphasized by Pope John XXIII when he first announced the Council on 25 January 1959. He repeated this in the motu proprio *Superno Dei nutu* of 5 June 1960, with which he opened the preparatory phase of the Council (*AAS* 52 [1960], p. 433), in the apostolic constitution *Humanae salutis* of 25 December 1961, by which the beginning of the Council was announced (*Oecumen. Conc. Vat. II Constitutiones, Decreta, Declarationes,* 1960, p. 845) and in his address of 11 October 1962 at the opening of the first session of the Council *(ibid.,* p. 868). Numerous acts of the Pope, and especially the appointing of the Secretariat for Christian Unity and the invitation of non-Catholic observers to the Council, confirmed this aim. Pope Paul VI affirmed the intention of his predecessor from the very first. In his address at the opening of the second session of the Council (29 September 1963) he explicitly referred to the reuniting of all Christians as one of the four main aims of the Council (*ibid.*, pp. 914–19). A majority of the Fathers also constantly concerned themselves with the ecumenical alignment of the Council, as can be seen in fact from the documents of the Council in general.

With regard to the formula "promoting the restoration of unity among all Christians" in the first sentence of the decree, we may further note that it does not speak of the restoration of the unity of *the Church*; thus the division of Christianity is assumed, but the question is left open, whether one can also speak of a division of the Church.

A brief confession of the unity and unicity of the Church desired by Christ, which is taken up later in the text of the decree, is followed by a reference to the division of Christianity: all Christians confess Christ as their Lord and assert in their thinking and their lives that they wish to follow his will; thus by their own confession they seek to be united in a single community; but in reality there are numerous communities, differing from each other in their thought and action, each of which claims to be in accord with the will of Christ. Thus the text does not state here what is not conceded by all Christians, that only the Catholic Church represents the true heritage of Jesus Christ, while the other Christian communities have been unfaithful to this heritage. It simply affirms the fact, acknowledged by all Christians, of the separation of the disciples of Jesus, which ought not to exist. All Christian believers agree that this fact contradicts the will of Christ. The recognition that the lack of unity of Christianity contradicts the will of Christ is fundamental: efforts towards unity are concerned in the first instance with fulfilling the will of Christ. Again, all are agreed about the consequences which follow from the division, which the text goes on to mention: the separation is a stumbling block to the world and seriously damages the preaching of the gospel, which the disciples of Jesus have been commanded to carry out. The context and wording of this statement (especially when statements later in the text concerning the witness to Christ made by other Churches are borne in mind) show that the damage referred to does not signify that other Churches draw numerous believers away from the Catholic Church by their missions. Rather, it has in mind the decreased credibility of the preaching of the gospel caused by the division within Christianity, regardless of which Church is carrying it out. It is significant that the beginning of the ecumenical movement was an appeal from missionaries who had become conscious from their own experience of the damage done to evangelization by the disunity of the Churches (the Protestant Missionary Congress of Edinburgh, 1910). At the Second Vatican Council two cardinals from missionary countries (the Japanese Cardinal Tatsuo Doi and the African Cardinal Rugambwa) spoke with great urgency on the scandal of separation and the damage done to the spread of the faith.

The whole of the second section of the introduction is devoted to an evaluation of the ecumenical movement in Christianity at large. The content and tone of this evaluation are in marked contrast to the encyclical *Mortalium Animos* of Pius XI (6 January 1928); but it is also more positive than the instruction *Ecclesia Catholica* of 20 December 1949, which was the beginning of a change in the attitude of the Catholic Church.[2] The decree begins by looking at the whole of Christianity, including Catholic and non-Catholic Christians, and affirms that the movement for unity in our own time has undergone a remarkable strengthening and extension. This process is seen as the work of the Spirit, and indeed as a repentance ("on behalf of us sinners", "remorse over their divisions", "grace"), and so themes are introduced which are later worked out more fully. It must be noted that this passage does not merely record a visible historical process, but makes an assertion of faith, that in this whole process God is at work through his grace. This statement is repeated with clear emphasis when the text turns to the movement for unity among non-Catholic Christians:[3] this movement, to which the usual term "ecumenical movement" is applied, has come into being "fostered by the grace of the Holy Spirit". One may ask whether it would not have been appropriate to mention in this context the World Council of Churches. In any case, there can be no doubt that this passage refers to the world-wide fellowship in which most non-Catholic Churches and ecclesial communities are joined, and that its immense and world-wide efforts for the restoration of the unity of all Christians are thankfully acknowledged. Apart from the vote in the Council on this matter, the reference to the trinitarian and christological "basis" of the World Council of Churches ("who invoke the Triune God and confess Jesus as Lord and Saviour") makes this clear.[4] That express mention is made here of this basic formula demonstrates the great interest on the part of the Catholic Church in the fact that the Churches of the World Council know that they are joined together in the confession of the two basic Christian truths which the Catholic Church also professes as the foundation of its faith. This common basic confession of faith, however, is not sufficient either in the view of the Council, nor according to the opinion of the World

---

[2] A brief and sound account of the historical development of the ecumenical idea in the Catholic Church is given by G. Tavard, *Two Centuries of Ecumenism* (1960).

[3] The most complete historical account of the ecumenical movement outside the Catholic Church (which includes all the official statements of the Catholic Church on the subject since 1910) is given by Ruth Rouse and Stephen Neill, eds., *History of the Ecumenical Movement, 1517–1948* (1954); cf. also G. Thils, *Histoire doctrinale du mouvement œcuménique* (2nd ed., 1963).

[4] The constitution of the World Council of Churches defines that body in the following words: "The World Council of Churches is a fellowship of Churches which confess the Lord Jesus Christ as God and Saviour according to the Scriptures and therefore seek to fulfil together their common calling to the glory of the one God, Father, Son and Holy Spirit" (W. A. Visser 't Hooft, ed., *New Delhi Report. Third Assembly of the World Council of Churches* (1961), pp. 152 and 426. Regarding membership the constitution lays down that all Churches which express their assent to the basis upon which the World Council is founded, and which are in accordance with the standards determined by the General Assembly or the Central Committee, may be elected as members of the World Council of Churches.

Council of Churches, to make these member Churches into a universal Church or "super-Church".[5] The text of the decree shows this by speaking of the communities which each of their believers regard as "his Church, and, indeed, God's". But we must look also at the positive side of this, the fact that the decree does not merely concern itself with individual Christians separated from the Catholic Church, but also the "corporate groups in which they have heard the gospel". This important change to a positive vision of non-Catholic Christian communities and an evaluation of their significance for the salvation of their members, which is clearly expressed later in Chapter I (Article 3), is already unmistakable in the introduction. Without this positive evaluation of non-Catholic communities it would not be possible to speak of ecumenism in the modern sense, for the object of the ecumenical dialogue is not individual believers, but Christian communities as such. Concerning the Christian belief of the non-Catholic ecumenical movement, the final sentence of this passage states that they (at least "almost every one") longs for one visible Church of God, which would be truly universal and sent forth to the whole world. This is a reference to the fact which is of decisive importance for the ecumenical movement, that the Churches of the World Council have come to recognize clearly that an invisible unity is not sufficient, and that they must rather strive for a visible unity of the Churches.[6] In the relative clause which mentions the universality of the Church, the subjunctive *sit*[7] ("would be") should be noted: it does not emphasize the universality of the Catholic Church, or assert that non-Catholic Churches are striving towards the Catholic Church which is in fact universal, but describes the ecumenical movement according to the understanding of non-Catholic Christianity, which regards the catholicity and universality of the Church not as something which simply exists, but as the goal of a developing process.

The rejoicing of the Council, in accordance with its belief that the ecumenical

[5] In Toronto (1950) the Central Committee of the World Council of Churches declared that the World Council of Churches was not a Super-Church, and ought never to become so; it was not the universal Church; it was not the *Una Sancta* of which the creeds speak. It added that this misunderstanding constantly recurred, although it was rejected as clearly as possible in the official declaration of the World Council. Cf. W. A. Visser 't Hooft, "The Super-Church and the Ecumenical Movement", in *The Ecumenical Review*, 10 (1958), pp. 365–85.

[6] Cf., for example, the report of the sub-committee on unity of the Assembly of the World Council of Churches in New Delhi, 1961, published in *New Delhi Reports* (see above note 4). Unity is described there both as the gift of God and the task of men. The visible unity which is already present must be made visible. The sub-committee expressed the belief that the unity which is at the same time God's will and his gift to his Church is made visible by all in every place who are baptized into Jesus Christ and confess him as Lord and Saviour, being led by the Holy Spirit into a communion which is fully binding upon them, which professes the one apostolic faith, which preaches the one gospel, which breaks the one bread, which unites in common prayer and which leads a common life directed towards all men in witness and service.

[7] Unfortunately the meaning of this word *sit* is not expressed clearly in most of the translations of the Council texts.

movement is the work of the Holy Spirit, and which can be perceived even in that part of the text which has so far been discussed, is explicitly affirmed at the beginning of the final paragraph of the introduction. The decree goes on to refer to the Constitution on the Church, the doctrine of which is to be regarded as the basis for what the decree proposed. In fact in many passages it is possible to trace the lines leading from the Constitution on the Church to the Decree on Ecumenism. But here we must note that in the process of composing the two texts during the Council, the text on ecumenism preceded the Constitution on the Church in various points, and several statements were first taken into the latter after they had already been included in earlier versions of the text on ecumenism.

Catholic Principles of Ecumenism

In the schema which was laid before the second session of the Council the title of Chapter I was "The Principles of Catholic Ecumenism". The alteration, requested by several Council Fathers, into the definitive title "Catholic Principles of Ecumenism", which in the Latin text required only the addition of a single letter *s* *(De catholicis oecumenismi principiis)* is of fundamental importance. The earlier formula spoke of a Catholic ecumenism, and implied thereby that there were several or at least two ecumenical movements. Could not such a formula perhaps even provoke the impression that Rome now sought to set up its own ecumenical movement alongside that of "Geneva"? In reality there is only a single ecumenical movement, the goal of which is the union of Christianity. The Catholic Church found this movement already in existence, when it decided at the Council to join it and to co-operate within it (albeit — at least for the time being — without becoming a member of the World Council of Churches). It is taken for granted that the Catholic Church takes part in ecumenical efforts on the basis of the principles of its own faith, and in particular according to the principles of its ecclesiology. The member Churches of the World Council also take part in these efforts in accordance with their own ecclesiological principles, and in this very way make their own contribution to the ecumenical dialogue. This whole situation is now expressed in the final title of the chapter, according to which Chapter I deals with the specifically Catholic principles of ecumenism, as the conditions required by the Catholic faith for participation in the ecumenical movement.

Article 2. All six paragraphs of this article are concerned with describing the unity and unicity of the Church. This theme has to be dealt with at the beginning because of the nature of the subject. If the Catholic Church is to participate in efforts for the union of Christianity it must first confess its own vision of the unity of the Church, and set out what according to its belief are the essential factors of the unity of the Church. On this basis, the relationship of separated brethren to the Catholic Church is then defined (Article 3) and the ecumenical movement is described more closely (Article 4). The presentation of the Church and its unity in this article is based entirely on the Bible and the history of salvation, and is therefore, as in the Constitution on the Church, not static but dynamic. The text begins with the sending of the Son, as a sending to unite the human race through grace, and proceeds to the sending of the Holy Spirit, through whom the Lord carries out the unifying of mankind in history, as the image of the fundamental pattern of unity which is that of the Father, the Son and the Holy Spirit.[8] If one compares the whole account of the Church and its unity with the formulae used so often in the course of the Church's history: *Ubi Spiritus, ibi Ecclesia; Ubi Eucharistia, ibi Ecclesia;* and *Ubi Petrus, ibi Ecclesia,* it is easy to recognize that the statements of the article as a whole cannot be reduced to any of these three formulae, and that the text is rather concerned to give due value to different aspects of all three formulae. The doctrine of the Church underlying the whole account can be described as a *communio* ecclesiology. What this means is explained by G. Thils in the following words: "This means an ecclesiology which defines the Church as an organic whole composed of spiritual bonds (faith, hope and charity), and of visible structural forms (the profession of faith, the sacramental economy, the pastoral ministry), and which culminates in the eucharistic mystery, the source and expression of the unity of the Church, or rather of the one Church. This ecclesiology obviously makes use of the essence of the constitutive elements of the Church — the Holy Spirit, theological activity, its ministerial structure, the papacy — but each of these 'elements' is considered in so far as it promotes, conditions, realizes or brings about the 'communion' which is the Church."[9]

The first paragraph of this article is a brief summary of New Testament passages (1 Jn 4:9; Col 1:18–20; Jn 11:52; 13:34; 17:21; 16:7) which present the event of Christ as the revelation of the love of God, with the intention of drawing the human race, in need of redemption, into unity through grace. The incarnation, the cross, the prayer of Christ, the institution of the Eucharist, the commandment of love, and the promise of the Spirit who would abide with the disciples, are therefore presented as saving acts of the Father, the Son and the Spirit in order to create the unity of the communion which is the Church. The Church is not presented as a society brought into being by men, but as a *communio* brought about by God. Particular emphasis is laid on the function of the Eucharist in bringing about unity. Thus here, as in the Constitution on the Church (Article 26) and in the Constitution on the Liturgy (Articles 2, 47 and 48), the Eucharist is seen in its social and ecclesiological aspect, as the symbol and effective cause of the unity of the Church *(mirabile sacramentum, . . . quo unitas ecclesiae et significatur et efficitur).* This is wholly in accordance with patristic tradition, both for the Eastern and the Latin Fathers.

[8] Cf. H. Mühlen, "Das Verhältnis zwischen Inkarnation und Kirche in den Aussagen des Vatikanum II", in *Theologie und Glaube* 55 (1965), pp. 171–99.
[9] *Le Décret sur l'Œcuménisme du deuxième Concile du Vatican* (1966), p. 38; J. Hamer, *L'Église est une communion* (1962).

The second paragraph describes the role of the Holy Spirit in the Church as the people of God of the New Covenant, and so brings to the fore the pneumatological aspect of the Church. The Holy Spirit is the principle of unity implanted in the Church by Christ, joining the faithful with each other and with Christ. In the faithful he creates the various supernatural gifts, especially the "theological virtues" of faith, hope and love, and also brings into being the different offices through which he builds up the single body of Christ from the multiplicity of believers. Here the New Testament doctrine of the Holy Spirit as the principle of the life and unity of the Church, newly brought to the fore in the encyclical *Mystici Corporis* of Pius XII, is briefly set forth; it is also set out in the constitution *Lumen Gentium* (Articles 4, 7 and 13). The text of the decree does not do much more than gather and summarize the New Testament texts. Of the explanatory concepts which go beyond the mere adducing of texts, particular attention should be paid to two: the Holy Spirit is called *Ecclesiae unitatis principium* and the Church is described as *unitas fidei, spei et caritatis* (in the Constitution on the Church it is described as *communitas fidei, spei et caritatis,* Article 8), and as *communio fidelium*. It is noteworthy that the Spirit as the principle of unity is discussed before the ministry as a unifying factor (in the next paragraph), and that the Church is presented as a communion of faith, hope and charity before the structure of the Church as a society is discussed. Thus both in the Decree on Ecumenism and the Constitution on the Church, there is an expression of the primacy of the Spirit over the ministry, and the pre-eminence of the communion of grace over the aspect of the Church as a society, something which is not always made clear in Catholic preaching. The ministry is the instrument which the Spirit uses, and the Church as a visible society is the servant of the supernatural communion in grace. This emphasis on the activity of the Holy Spirit in creating unity is unquestionably of great importance from the ecumenical point of view. The text of the decree is in this respect wholly in accord with the statements of the World Council of Churches at the Assemblies in Evanston (1954)[10] and New Delhi (1961).[11] The statements of the Decree on Ecumenism concerning the Holy Spirit as the creator of the Church's communion of faith,

---

[10] Cf. the report of the first sub-committee on "Our unity in Christ and our Disunity as Church", which states that by the indwelling of the Spirit, the Comforter, who leads the Church into all truth, the unity of the Church is already a foretaste of the fullness which will be present, because it is so already. The report adds that Christ has given his Spirit as the bond of peace and love, and to lead us into all truth.

[11] According to the New Delhi Assembly, it is the unity which is given to his people through his Spirit and all the gifts of the Spirit, which vivifies, builds and strengthens the new humanity in Christ. The Church exists in space and time through the power of the Holy Spirit, who is at work in all the elements of her life which compose her unity, her witness and her service. It is the gift of the Father in the name of Jesus Christ, in order to build up the Church and to lead her to the freedom and fellowship which form her peace and her joy. For every step forward to a fuller unity than is now visible we are wholly dependent upon the presence and the guidance of the Holy Spirit. See *New Delhi Report* (cited above in note 4).

hope and charity, provide (in association with the one baptism, which is referred to in the quotation from Eph: 4:4–5) the basis for the recognition of the reality of non-Catholic Churches as Churches, and for the statement concerning individual members of these Churches, that in them the Church (from this more fundamental point of view) is more fully realized than in individual members of the Catholic Church, in so far as faith, hope and charity are more lively in the former than in the latter.

The third and fourth paragraphs describe the hierarchical structure of the Church, the third its foundation in the apostolate of the Twelve, and the fourth its continuation in the post-apostolic Church. In both passages the authority of the Church, in accordance with the theme of the whole article, is described above all with regard to its function of creating unity. Thus the decree does not omit to give an account of the specifically Catholic elements of the doctrine of the visible structure and unity of the Church; at the request of some of the Fathers this is set forth in a more precise form in this final version, by a clearer emphasis on the primacy of Peter, than in the earlier versions of the text.

The third section again seems at first sight to be only a brief summary of familiar New Testament passages concerning the commission to the twelve apostles and to Peter in particular (Mt 28:18–20 and Jn 20:21–23 for the Twelve; Mt 16:19; Lk 22:32; Jn 21:15–17 for Peter). But on a closer examination a number of interpretative clarifications can be seen. Among these is the fact that the whole body of the apostles is named at the beginning, before Peter is mentioned, and that this body is described as a college. Peter is not intended to be seen separately from the college of the Twelve, but as one of the college, to whom a special position is accorded in it. This is the reason for the expression "among their number he chose Peter". It is clear that this reflects the teaching of the Constitution on the Church concerning the collegiality of the apostles. A further interpretative phrase is the explicit naming of the familiar threefold office of the ministry (*munus docendi, regendi et sanctificandi,* again on the pattern of the Constitution on the Church: cf. Articles 20, 25, 26 and 27), and there is also the explicit mention of the meaning and purpose of the apostolic ministry (*ad ... Ecclesiam stabiliendam*): to confirm, to hold together the believing community. This statement of the purpose of the apostolic ministry is implied by the theme of the whole article. This is particularly true of the definition of the significance of the Petrine office: it serves to confirm and unite the disciples of Christ (*universas oves in fide confirmandas et in perfecta unitate pascendas.* Lk 22:32, *confirma fratres tuos,* is not quoted word for word here, in order not to decide the question of whether the *fratres* there are only the apostles or all believers). The reference to Peter's profession of love is intended to show the spirit in which his ministry is exercised. Finally, an important elucidation of the doctrine of the Church's ministry is given in the last statement in the paragraph, that Christ himself for ever remains the chief cornerstone (Eph 2:20) and shepherd of our souls (1 Pet 2:25). The Church's ministry, even the ministry of Peter, is not on the same level as that of Christ, and is not a substitute for Christ, but is wholly at the service of the Lord of the Church who is constantly present and active in his congregation (quite apart from the fact that the ministry of the Church is only meaningful during the period of the Church's earthly pilgrimage and comes to an end with the present age, whereas Christ's mediation of salvation continues in the aeon to come). This fresh emphasis upon the unique and irreplaceable position of Christ, directly after the mention of the Petrine office, is evidently based upon the ecumenical desire to avoid giving the false impression that the Catholic Church regards the bearer of the Petrine office as a head of the Church alongside Christ, or in place of Christ.

Whereas what is said in the third paragraph concerning the apostles and Peter, and as an immediate consequence of this, concerning the primitive Church, is largely accepted by non-Catholic Christianity as well, the fourth paragraph goes on to discuss the specific characteristics of the Catholic view of the ministry. This paragraph speaks of the bishops as the successors of the apostles, and of the successor of Peter as their head (the expression "head" was added later at the request of a number of Fathers, who desired to see explicit mention made of the primacy of the successor of Peter). Here again, the threefold function of the Church's ministry is mentioned, though in different terms from those of the third paragraph, and in a different order *(Evangelii praedicationem, sacramentorum administrationem . . . gubernationem in dilectione)*. The accent is once again on the unifying function of the Church's ministry. But it must be noted that the creating of the unity of the Church's *communio* is ascribed to Christ himself and to the Holy Spirit *(Spiritu Sancto operante);* the Church's ministry is their servant, if it is exercised in love, as the text mentions. The threefold unifying function of the ministry corresponds to the threefold unity of the Church mentioned at the conclusion of the paragraph: the preaching of the gospel corresponds to the confession of the one faith, the administration of the sacraments to the common celebration of divine worship, and the exercise of authority to the fraternal harmony of the family of God. The words *unius (fidei), communis (celebratio), fraterna concordia* are a fine expression of the unity of the Church as a *communio*. It may also be noted that the description of the Church as *familia Dei* was used at the request of African bishops (in place of the previous *regiminis pastorum,* which emphasized only the unity of the clergy), since this image of the Church has a particular appeal for Africans. But it also meant that a particularly beautiful appellation of the Church is included in the text, one which is used in the Canon and in other prayers of the Roman Mass.

In the fifth paragraph all that strictly belongs to the theme of the article is the emphasis on the unicity of the Church. What has always been implied in the previous passage is here explicitly stated in the image of God's one flock *(unicus Dei grex):* there are not several Churches of God, but only the one Church, which God brings into being in history through the sending of the Son and the Holy Spirit. This of course raises the question, to which the decree later proposes an answer, how the many differing and separated Churches are related to the one Church of Christ.

The other three statements of this paragraph briefly take up ideas which are particularly emphasized in the Constitution on the Church: the pilgrim state of the Church on earth, its function as a sign, and its nature as a servant, and expresses at the same time the way in which it is bound to the form of this world, as well as its openness towards the world. The emphasis on the eschatological character of the Church illuminates the institutional elements of the Church which have just been discussed, and in particular the ministry, concerning which the Churches are in disagreement; although these elements are essential to the Church in its pilgrim state, they are destined to cease in the final communion towards which the Church strives.

Finally, the last paragraph expresses the character of the unity of the Church as a mystery, and refers to the triune God as the exemplar of the unity of the Church. The unusual formula *in Spiritu Sancto* characterizes the Spirit as the bond of love between the Father and the Son, just as he also "brings about that marvellous communion of the faithful and joins them together so intimately in Christ that he is the principle of the Church's unity" (second paragraph). Just as the Church as a whole is a mystery of faith (cf. *Lumen Gentium,* Chapter I), so in particular is its unity. As the visible cohesion of the faithful, the unity of the Church possesses an aspect which every one can see for himself, but it does not consist of this alone, for it reaches down into depths which only faith can plumb, just as only faith can know that the unity of the Church is an image of the mysterious unity of the divine Trinity.

In looking back upon the whole article one may make special mention of the fact that the text never speaks explicitly of the *Catholic* Church. It always speaks explicitly of the Church of Jesus Christ, and mentions the inner and the outward visible elements which according to the doctrine of the Catholic Church constitute the unity of the Church of Christ. But since the text clearly states that the Church makes its way through the ages in the unity desired by Christ, and vouchsafed in particular through the successors of Peter, it leaves no doubt that according to the Catholic faith the Church of Christ is in fact realized in the Catholic Church, which itself displays the visible elements of unity which have been mentioned. It is nevertheless of decisive importance for the passages that follow that the Church of Christ and the Catholic Church are not simply identified here, and that "Catholic Church" is not simply used in place of "the Church of Christ". Thus the question (which is answered later in the text) remains open, whether the Church of Christ is not also present in some way in other Christian communities. If the Church is seen as in this article as a *communio,* that is, as a complex reality in the form of a communion, the unity of which has been brought about by numerous and various factors, the possibility remains open that constituent elements of the Church may be present even in Christian communities outside the Catholic Church, and may give these communities the nature of a

Church. Thus the one Church of Christ can also be present outside the Catholic Church, and it is present, and also, indeed, visible, in so far as factors and elements which create unity and therefore the Church are effective here. If the Church were described here only in terms of the juridical concept of a *societas (perfecta)*, as has been done to an excessive and one-sided degree in Catholic theology for centuries, then the Church would cease once the limits of the Catholic community had been reached, and outside that, there would only be the "non-Church". But if instead the Church is seen as a *communio*, the unity of which is produced by the working together of different factors, then even one who affirms in faith the full (albeit imperfect) realization of the Church of Christ in the Catholic Church can also comprehend the reality of the Church outside the Catholic Church. This vision is in accordance with the substitution of the word *subsistit* in the Constitution on the Church for the earlier *est* (*Haec Ecclesia ... subsistit in Ecclesia catholica,* Article 8). This important phrase in the Constitution on the Church, which avoids a straightforward identification of the Church of Christ and the Catholic Church, makes possible the recognition that non-Catholic Christian communities possess the character of a Church.

Article 3. The text now passes from the description of the unity of the Church to a definition of the relationship of separated brethren to the Catholic Church. If a reorientation of the attitude of Catholics to their fellow-Christians is to take place, such as the decree is striving for, the relationship which exists between non-Catholic Christianity and the Catholic Church must first be redefined in theological terms. Here the picture of the Church and its unity set out in the previous article is applied, and makes possible statements which have never previously been known from the Church's magisterium. This is true not merely of the way in which the statements are made, their note of brotherly love, but even more of the new content of the statements. The obvious purpose of the text is to see non-Catholic communities in as positive a way as seems possible from the point of view of Catholic faith; it seeks to affirm all the elements of the Church which are maintained in them, and also to emphasize thereby their links with the Catholic Church. It must be noted that although most of the passage speaks of non-Catholic Christians rather than of their communities, they are not seen as isolated individuals, but in fact as members of their community; furthermore, direct and decisive statements are also made concerning non-Catholic communities.

The transition from the account of the unity of the Church to the definition of the relationship of separated brethren to the Catholic Church is naturally provided by the mention of the divisions which of course form the background to the whole question. The main reason why reference is made to the rifts mentioned in the text, which according to 1 Cor 11:18–19; Gal 1:6–9; 1 Jn 2:18–19 (and other passages could also be quoted) already arose among the faithful in the primitive Church, is because of the censure which Paul passed upon them, and which is naturally even more true of the much more profound divisions which appeared in later centuries. A true irenicism does not conceal the human guilt which lies at the origin of every division in the Church. Whereas the differences of opinion and disagreements in the primitive Church did not lead to the formation of separate *communities,* the later disagreements of which the decree is now speaking led to the separating of quite large communities *(Communitates haud exiguae).* The decree does not attempt an extended account of the historical events and facts concerned, because it is not meant to be dealing with Church history and with the judgment of individual events. The brief reference to the historical facts is solely intended to bring about an awareness of the actual situation which has led to the posing of the question of the relationship which other Christians have to the Catholic Church. In the brief theological description of schism in the Church which is provided by the first sentence of this paragraph, three expressions are characteristic of the vision of the Decree on Ecumenism. It must first be noted that it does not speak of the division of the one Church of Christ into several Churches, but of the separation of quite large communities from the Catholic Church. This is in accordance with the conviction of the Catholic faith that the Church of Christ, in spite of the divisions, has not ceased to have a continued existence in the Catholic Church, as the concrete form of its existence. But separation from the Catholic Church does not signify that separated communities simply cease to be Churches, as is made clear from the articles that follow in the text.

In the second place, the words "separated from *full* communion with the Catholic Church" *(a plena communione Ecclesiae catholicae seiunctae)* are of great importance. The text of 1963 still spoke simply of a separation "from the communion of the Catholic Church". The final text states that these divisions do not involve a complete and total separation from the Catholic Church. The separation is not total, and unity is not radically destroyed, but a certain link between the separated communities and the Catholic Church persists. Such statements, however, can only be made on the basis of the dogmatic concept of *communio* set out previously. Anyone who conceives of the Church only in terms of the normal canonical and juridical concept of *communio* cannot speak of a greater or lesser degree of *communio* with the Catholic Church: either one is in communion with the Church or one is not in communion with it. A few of the Council Fathers in fact put forward, on the basis of a purely juridical concept of communion, the view that one could not be *plene* or *non plene* in communion with the Church. On the basis of its dogmatic concept of *communio* the decree affirms the possibility of an incomplete communion with the Catholic Church (the expression *communio non perfecta* is explicitly used in the next sentence but one). The participle *seiunctae,* which was consciously used instead of *separatae,* also implies an incomplete separation: *seiungere* expresses a less profound separation than *separare.* In English (as in German), however, the nuance is difficult to reproduce.

Thirdly, attention must be paid to the way in which the question of guilt is expressed at the conclusion of the first sentence. What is at issue here is not the question whether the present state of separation, the fact of being separated, implies guilt at the present moment on one side or the other, or on both sides, but rather the origin of the present situation, which from the point of view of the gospel is undoubtedly an anomaly and an evil. According to the text of the decree, human guilt lies at the origin of this separation. The language used is intentionally unspecific; there is no intention here of putting history on trial, so that individual cases are not examined. At times, says the text, the blame lay on both sides. This recognizes that the guilt is not merely to be sought on the side of those who separated themselves from the Catholic Church, but, sometimes at least, also on the Catholic side. Nor does the wording of the decree in fact require the acceptance of the view that those who separated themselves from the Catholic Church were always and necessarily to blame. The text in fact explicitly reads "*men* of both sides were to blame". This avoids the basic question whether one can also speak of guilt on the part of the *Church*. This question is a disputed one in Catholic theology, and the Council had no reason to decide on it in one direction or the other. What is certain is that it is both possible and necessary to speak of the guilt of men in the Church. With regard to the concrete case of the breach between Constantinople and Rome in 1054, the Ukrainian Archbishop Hermaniuk (of Winnipeg; a member of the Secretariat for Unity) spoke very clearly in the Council of the errors committed by the representatives of the Pope, and which were undoubtedly partly to blame for the breach. As far as the divisions of the Western Church in the 16th century are concerned, Catholic historical scholarship agrees at the present day that the state of the Church, which lasted beyond the early stages of the Reformation, shared in the blame for the separation.

The assurance which now follows in the decree, that those who are born in separated communities and are instilled therein with Christ's faith are in any case not to blame for the separation, would be expressing a mere commonplace if the separation it speaks of referred to the parting of the ways at the origin of the schism. The only reasonable meaning which can be placed upon separation here is that of continued separation, the state of being separated at the present day. If one considers that thought and language on the Catholic side have for the most part for far too long implied that non-Catholic Christians in general remain separated *mala fide* from the Catholic Church, there is clearly good reason for the Council here to refer to the good faith of separated Christians, to speak explicitly of their faith in Christ, which is mediated to them within their communities, and to describe them as brothers to whom the Catholic Church owes respect and affection. Faith in Christ, wherever it is present (even if in its doctrinal development it differs from the doctrine of the Catholic Church), and baptism are stated in the next sentence to be the fundamental facts which already create a true communion with the Catholic Church. They are, of course, not capable of bringing about a full but only an imperfect communion *(communio non perfecta)*. Undoubtedly a decisive step forward would be taken – even though it would be far from achieving the goal of ecumenism — if the consciousness of all Catholics and all Christians of the bond that joins them on the basis of faith in Christ and baptism became living and effective, if the whole of Christianity understood more clearly that the decisive boundary lay not between the Churches, but between baptized and unbaptized mankind, and if Christianity was thereby more clearly manifested in the eyes of the world as a communion of faith in Christ and in baptism.

The distinction between full and imperfect communion, which the Decree on Ecumenism postulates here, is based, moreover, on the doctrine of the Constitution *Lumen Gentium,* which in Chapter II, Article 14, gives the following description of full incorporation into the Church: "They are fully *(plene)* incorporated into the communion of the Church who, possessing the Spirit of Christ, accept her entire system and all the means of salvation given to her, and through union with her visible structure are joined to Christ, who rules her through the Supreme Pontiff and the bishops. This joining is effected by the bonds of professed faith, of the sacraments, of ecclesiastical government, and of communion." One can only speak meaningfully of a *communio plena* if one takes into account the possibility of a *communio non plena* or *imperfecta*. But on the basis of the account given in the Constitution on the Church, such a possibility exists not only because believing and baptized Christians do not acknowledge certain institutional elements in the Church, such as some of the sacraments, or the office of the Pope, but also because some Catholics who recognize all the institutional elements of the Church do not possess the "spirit of Christ", that is, do not live in the "state of grace". Thus even within the Catholic community there is an important degree of variation in the extent to which individuals are in communion. The next sentence provides a brief answer to the question, which obstacles prevent the full communion (here again the concept of *plena ecclesiastica communio* appears) of non-Catholic Christians with the Catholic Church. These are the various differences in matters of doctrine, discipline and the structure of the Church which are dealt with more fully in Chapter III. In this context the goal of the ecumenical movement is seen not as the return of other Christians to the Catholic Church, but rather the restoration of full communion with the Catholic Church by the overcoming of the obstacles mentioned. It is not merely that a different term is being used for what is meant by "return", but rather that the thought here is quite different. The text of the decree later makes it clear that one can only think of a union of the Church if the Catholic Church also changes. It is particularly stressed in the last sentence of this paragraph that the obstacles which hinder full communion do not prevent incorporation into the body of Christ: even outside the Catholic Church one is not merely justified by faith in baptism (*ex fide in baptismate:* baptism as the sacrament of faith) but also incorporated into the body of Christ.

The Latin text does not in fact use the expression *corpus Christi,* but says (in equally Pauline terms) *Christo incorporantur,* the concept of the body being retained in the verb. The translation "they are incorporated into the body of Christ" is as much in accord with the meaning as the rendering "they are incorporated into *Christ*". Special mention is made of this here, because it raises the question of the identity of the (mystical) body of Christ. The encyclical *Mystici Corporis* of Pius XII (1943) opposed views which did not sufficiently maintain the unity of the mystical body of Christ as an invisible reality and the Catholic Church as a visible and social reality;[12] it used the very strongly worded formula: "The mystical body of Christ *is* the Catholic Church." If this formula is not understood in its historical context, and the identity of the body of Christ as the Catholic Church is pressed, justice cannot be done to the reality of the Church outside the Catholic Church.

The Second Vatican Council recognized that it was possible to speak in a more complex way of the relationship between the body of Christ and the Catholic Church. Thus the Constitution on the Church makes the following carefully balanced statement: "The society furnished with hierarchical agencies and the mystical body of Christ are not to be considered as two realities, nor are the visible assembly and the spiritual community, nor the earthly Church and the Church enriched with heavenly things. Rather they form one interlocked reality which is comprised of a divine and a human element" (Article 8). The statement of the Decree on Ecumenism is based upon a vision which on the one hand does not regard the body of Christ and the Catholic Church as two separate entities, but on the other hand does not regard them as simply identical. Those who outside the communion of the Catholic Church are brought to faith in Christ and are baptized, are incorporated into the mystical body of Christ; thus while they do not belong to the Catholic Church as this clearly defined community of faith with the ordered structure of a society, nevertheless they are fundamentally in communion with it through faith and baptism. Here again note must be taken of the fact that the Decree on Ecumenism (like the Constitution on the Church) does not make use, in defining the link between non-Catholic Christians and the Catholic Church, of the problematic concept of the *membrum Ecclesiae in voto,* by means of which it was earlier intended to express that non-Catholic Christians are on the one hand not members *(membra actu)* of the Catholic Church, and on the other hand are not simply non-members. The image of a member, unlike the concept of *communio,* scarcely permits varying degrees. Nor does the decree use the distinction, which was often previously used, between the body and the soul of the Church, by means of which the statement could be made that non-Catholic baptized Christians belonged to the soul of the Church, but not to its body. This did not take into account the fact that baptism, as a visible and pal-

---

[12] For the historical context in which the encyclical *Mystici Corporis* is to be seen, cf. C. Lialine, "Une étape en ecclésiologie", in *Irénikon* 19 (1946), pp. 129–52, 283–317; 20 (1947), pp. 34–54.

pable element of the Church, belongs to the nature of the Church as a body, and makes the Church visible in the person who receives it. Outside the Catholic Church, not only the "soul" but also the "body" of the Church is present.

The second and third paragraphs of the article now emphasize the constitutive elements of the Church which also exist in the communities separated from the Catholic Church. Here the application to these bodies of the term Churches and ecclesial communities in the fourth paragraph, and in Chapter III, is given a theological foundation. The decree proceeds from the view that the form and body of the Church is built up from a complex whole of invisible and visible endowments, which Christ has bestowed upon his Church and effects within it. In the wholeness (not perfection) accorded by Christ to his Church these endowments are found, according to the Catholic belief, only in the Catholic Church. But they are to be found also in varying, reduced degrees in other Christian communities, and still possess their power to create and maintain communion. These endowments, values and realities, which are essential constituents of the Church, are referred to in the second paragraph of this article as (ecclesial) elements. This term is also used in documents of the World Council of Churches. Even someone who does not regard this term as the best, will find it difficult to find one which is more appropriate. In any case, it is more appropriate than the term *vestigia Ecclesiae* which has often been used hitherto both in Catholic and in Protestant theology, and which Calvin already uses in his *Institutio Religionis Christianae* (lib. IV, cap. 2, nn. 11 and 12). The Decree on Ecumenism recognizes in non-Catholic communities more than Calvin does in the papal Church, more than mere scanty "vestiges" or miserable "relics"; it sees in them essential structural elements of the Church. And in such communities it even recognizes "very many of the most significant elements". The decree makes no attempt to give a full list of these elements; this makes it all the more important that it makes specific mention of the written word of God and then of the life of grace, of faith, hope and charity. The word of God which we encounter in holy Scripture is the fundamental "element" which constitutes the Church, and which first of all, before its interpretation separates individual ecclesial communities from one another, unites them all with one another by faith in salvation in Christ. The holy Scripture is the "institutional element" through which Christianity is constantly led to recognize its calling to the communion of the Church, and by which its recognition of other constitutive elements of the Church willed by Christ, such as the sacraments and the ministry, is maintained. And the life of grace, consisting of faith, hope and charity, which the decree mentions, forms the primary inner gift of grace, which links Christians with one another in the communion of the Church, and which all outward elements of the Church ultimately exist to serve. With the observation that all (visible and invisible) elements lead back to Christ, as they also come from him, the decree points both to their dynamic character and also to their unity of purpose. In the final observation in the second paragraph, that all these endowments "belong by right to the one Church of Christ", one must not overlook the fact that the wording is not "to the *Catholic Church*", but "to the one *Church of Christ*". The Catholic Church has no intention of arrogating to itself and claiming as its own property the values which exist outside its visible limits. But in so far as these endowments are the same as can also be found in the Catholic Church, they are not the basis of division, and do not serve to build up communities as Churches separate from the Catholic Church, but make present the very same Church of Christ, which according to Catholic belief possesses its concrete mode of existence in the Catholic Church. In other words, the same elements which within the limits of the Catholic community build up the Church of Christ, also serve outside these limits to build up the very same Church of Christ.

The third paragraph of the article speaks in particular of the liturgical actions which are carried out amongst separated brethren. Of course they belong to the visible elements which have already been mentioned, but are particularly stressed here because they provide the basis of a statement which from the ecumenical point of view is of great importance, that of their power to effect grace and their significance for salvation for the believers of a non-Catholic community. It is the sacramental actions in the strict sense, the sacraments, to which the term *actiones sacrae* naturally refers in the first instance, but the term also includes other liturgical actions such as, for example, the preaching of the word of God, blessings, etc. The phrase "in ways that vary according to the condition of each Church or community" are above all a general reference to the fact that the situation with regard to the sacraments is different in individual Churches and communities. Whereas the Orthodox Churches maintain all the seven sacraments which are recognized by the Catholic Church, and the Catholic Church acknowledges the validity of all the sacraments of the Orthodox Churches, most of the Reformation Churches only recognize baptism and the Lord's Supper. This is the reason why the Catholic Church, for example, regards the Eucharist of the Orthodox Church in a different light from the Lord's Supper of the Protestant Churches, as is made clear in Chapter III of the decree. This does not mean that the Catholic Church denies the effectiveness for grace of the Protestant Lord's Supper — as indeed it also considers marriage between Protestant Christians as a sacrament effecting grace, even though the Reformation Churches do not share this conviction without qualifications. But the statement made in this paragraph ought not to be limited to sacramental actions in the strict sense. Preaching, blessings and other liturgical actions affect grace and create access to the communion of salvation, albeit in a different way from the sacraments.

Whereas the third paragraph spoke of the ecclesial endowments which are also found among separated brethren, the fourth paragraph speaks in formal terms of the non-Catholic communities themselves, in which the one Church of Christ is present through these ecclesial elements. The basic statement that is made here undoubtedly represents a decisive step forward in the ecumenical thought of the Catholic Church: the non-Catholic Christian communities, are, as communities, means which the Spirit of Christ uses to lead their members to salvation. Thus it is not sufficient to say, in accordance with the usual thinking hitherto, that non-Catholics can attain salvation, *although* they live outside the Catholic Church. Rather, one must say that Christ gives them salvation through the reality of non-Catholic communities, albeit not in so far as these are separated from the Catholic Church, but in so far as within them the effect is present of the elements of the Church through which Christ effects the salvation of the faithful in the Catholic Church also. Thus these communities possess "significance and importance in the mystery of salvation", as the decree says. They are instruments in the hand of Christ, through which the word of God is proclaimed and forgiveness and grace vouchsafed to the faithful, through which the faithful are led to the worship of God and obedience towards God, and to Christian service towards their neighbour, and through which they are sanctified and redeemed.

If such language is used concerning the status and function of non-Catholic Christian communities in the history of salvation, then the question naturally arises, whether these communities should not be termed Churches. There is naturally no question that each of these communities may be another Church of Christ; the text of the decree excludes this itself in emphasizing the uniqueness of the Church of Christ. But are they not to be regarded as individual Churches, in which the one Church of Christ is visibly present? Just as in the primitive Church each individual Church (Ephesus, Thessalonica, Corinth, etc.) was regarded as the realization of the one Church of Christ at a particular place ("to the Church of God in Corinth", 1 Cor 1:2; 2 Cor 1:1), so that it was possible to speak of "Churches" in the plural, so also the dioceses of the Catholic Church are not merely administrative districts of the one universal Church, but the concrete presence of the one Church in a particular place, so that one can speak of (particular or local) Churches in the plural (the Church of Paris, the Church of Cologne, the Catholic Eastern Churches). Should not the non-Catholic Christian communities be regarded in a similar way as different realizations and different kinds of presence of the one Church of Christ, and therefore be known as (particular) Churches? This is not possible on the basis of the invisible gift of grace which is undoubtedly given to them also, but possibly on the basis of the visible ecclesial elements by which they are built up.

Cardinal König of Vienna proposed in the debate in the Council that these communities should be termed *communitates ecclesiales*. By this, recognition was given on the hand to the fact that they possess the character of Churches, and that they fulfil the task of the Church for their faithful, while on the other hand it expresses the fact that these communities, according to Catholic belief, lack to varying degrees constitutive elements necessary for them to be Churches in the full sense. Other Fathers went further and expressed the wish that non-Catholic communities should also be termed *ecclesiae,* not merely as it were from politeness, because they call themselves Churches, but also for the theological reasons given. At the same time, it was emphasized that the concept "Church" was being used here in an analogical sense. There was no difficulty in using the term Church for the Orthodox communities, since this corresponds to the traditional terminology of the Catholic Church and had its practical basis in the fact that through the episcopal ministry in the apostolic succession, and all the valid sacraments, these communities possess the essential ecclesial elements which constitute them as individual Churches, and lack only the relationship uniting them with the bearer of the Petrine office as the hierarchical factor of the unity of all individual Churches. The Secretariat for Unity was also able to adduce in the footnotes to the drafts of the text a large number of documents of Popes and Councils in which the separated Eastern Churches are referred to as *ecclesiae.*[13] The situation was different with regard to the communities separated from Rome in the West, since it was not possible here to state in general terms that they are constituted as individual Churches in the full sense of the word by the episcopal office with the apostolic succession and by the full range of sacraments. This could be said with certainty, in the same sense as of the Orthodox Churches, only of the Old Catholic Churches. Whether the concept "Church", in the theological sense, can also be applied if the episcopal ministry with apostolic succession is not (or not certainly) present, and where only some of the sacraments are recognized, as in the case in the Reformation Churches, was the subject of a difference of opinion among the Council Fathers.[14] In addition, a number of Reformation communities do not wish to refer to themselves as Churches.

In order to do justice to this whole complex situation and to obtain the assent of the majority of the Council, the Secretariat for Unity suggested that where reference was being made to the separated Eastern Churches, the term *ecclesiae* should always be used (cf. Articles 14–18), but where the reference was to the separated communities (of the East and West) on the whole, or to the non-Catholic communities produced by the divisions in the Western Church, the twofold expression *ecclesiae et communitates* (or *communitates ecclesiales,* cf. Article 19) should be used. In accepting this form of appellation the Council made clear that among the separated communities of the West there are also those which should be regarded as Churches, but left open, or referred to theologians, the

---

[13] Y. Congar, *Chrétiens désunis* (1937; 2nd unchanged ed., 1964), pp. 381–2, and *Irénikon* 23 (1950), pp. 22–24, provide a collection of numerous official texts of the Catholic Church which use the term *Ecclesiae* for the separated Eastern Churches.

[14] On this question cf. G. Baum, "The Ecclesiastical Reality of the Other Churches", in *Concilium* 4 (1965), pp. 34–46. One may ask how far conclusions can be drawn from the repeated *O Ecclesiae* of Pope Paul VI in his opening address to the third session of the Council; see *Sacrosanctum Oecumenicum Concilium Vaticanum II. Constitutiones, Decreta, Declarationes* (1966), p. 965.

question which communities were intended by this in concrete terms. Moreover, the constitution *Lumen Gentium* uses the same twofold expression as the Decree on Ecumenism, with the sole difference that instead of the neologism *ecclesiales* the usual form *ecclesiasticae* is used (cf. Article 15). Because the normal form *ecclesiasticae* has hitherto almost invariably been used only of communities, laws and customs within the Catholic Church, and in order to avoid the juridical associations of the usual form, the Secretariat for Unity decided upon a neologism in Latin, but one which in the judgment of an authority on Latin in Rome was wholly in accordance with the spirit of the Latin language. The Secretariat also preferred, instead of the term *communitas*, which can also have a secular sense, the purely religious term *communio,* which draws a very full meaning from a long theological tradition.[15] But since *communio* was to be used to refer to the bond that links all Christians to each other, and non-Catholic Christians to the Catholic Church, it was not possible to use it in another sense. The whole context shows that *communitas* is always used here in a religious and Christian sense.

While the previous paragraph spoke of the communities which on the basis of "elements" of the Church present in them, are means of salvation and bring people into the *communio* of the Church, but which, because they lack some of the elements of the Church, can only create a *communio non plena*, the final paragraph turns to the Church in which the full range of essential constituent elements of the Church are to be found, and which is therefore able to create a *plena communio*. The point of view from which the Catholic Church is regarded here in comparison with non-Catholic Churches, is that of the visible unity accorded by Christ to his Church, as his mystical body, which is the central aim of the ecumenical movement. The word *credimus*, which is strongly emphasized in the third sentence of this paragraph, characterizes all its statements as confessions of faith: the unity of the Church is a mystery of faith, as has already been asserted in Article 2. The Catholic Church proposes itself to Catholic faith as the "all-embracing means of salvation". The expression *generale auxilium salutis* is taken from the letter of the Holy Office to Archbishop Cushing (1949) concerning the necessity of membership of the Church for salvation (*Denzinger–Schönmetzer* 3869–71), where it both distinguishes the Church as an all-embracing institution in contrast to the sacraments of the Church as individual institutions (*generale* in the sense of "total" by contrast to *particulare*), and also characterizes it as a saving institution meant for all men and binding upon all men (*generale* in the sense of "all-embracing, universal", as it is rendered in the translation of the letter mentioned and of this decree). This point of view is in accordance with the use of the concept "sacrament" of the Church as a whole in the Constitution on the Church: "by her relationship with Christ, the Church

[15] Y. Congar, "Note sur les mots 'Confession', 'Église' et 'Communion'", in *Chrétiens en dialogue* (1964), pp. 211–42.

78

is a kind of sacrament or sign of intimate union with God, and of the unity of all mankind" (Article 1).

Thus at this point in the text of the Decree on Ecumenism, the Church is regarded not as the "fruit of salvation", that is, not as a society of men to whom the grace of salvation itself has in fact been given, but as a "means of salvation" *(auxilium salutis)* which assists in obtaining the grace of salvation. Thus the Catholic Church is looked at and evaluated here as an institution, just as the other Churches are only evaluated from their institutional aspect. This must be carefully noted if the text is to be rightly understood. That is why the text speaks not of the fullness of salvation, but of the fullness of the *means* of salvation *(salutarium mediorum plenitudo)*. The text does not say that all Catholics avail themselves of the means of salvation given in the Church, nor that the grace of salvation is found in all Catholics in accordance with them. Nor does it say that the grace of salvation is not imparted to non-Catholic Christians, or is imparted to them in a lesser degree. The decree compares the Catholic Church to non-Catholic Churches and communities from an institutional point of view, and emphasizes the importance of the institutional elements of the Church for the unity of the Church and for the building up of the (visible) body of Christ. It is from this point of view that "fullness" is predicated of the Catholic Church: in it alone are the means of salvation willed by Christ available in their totality, and consequently it is through the Catholic Church alone that full incorporation into the body of Christ can take place *(plene incorporantur),* in so far as the latter is essentially a visible body, and only through the Catholic Church that the whole unity of the Church is vouchsafed. *Plenitudo* in no sense signifies the perfection of the Church's institutions, far less a perfect equivalence between the visible institution and either the inner, spiritual gifts of salvation, or the Church's state of grace and sanctity. Other passages in the decree, and indeed the Council as a whole, in fact clearly point to the need for a reform of the institutional aspect of the Catholic Church, and the necessity of spiritual renewal within it; and the last sentence of this article explicitly refers to the sinfulness of the pilgrim Church in its members. The fullness of the means of salvation assists the growing in stature of the Church, which finds its consummation in the "fullness of eternal glory" only when it reaches the "heavenly Jerusalem".

The *plenitudo* which the decree accords to the Catholic Church therefore signifies wholeness, totality, the "whole gamut", completeness (of the visible elements of the Church), but the expression avoids the excessively quantitative tone which these terms carry with them. When the text says that "all the blessings of the New Covenant" are entrusted to the Catholic Church as the Church in which the apostolic ministry, with Peter as its head, still endures, the term also refers of course to the inward gifts of grace, but the decree makes no comparison between the Catholic Church and the other Churches with regard to the non-institutional "level of endowment" of "actual" inner and charismatic gifts;

for such a comparison is not possible, even though the inward blessings of the life of grace, of faith, hope and charity, as well as the special charismata, never remain purely inward, but are manifested in Christian life. But the comparison on the level of sacramental and institutional life leads Catholic Christians to the realization that non-Catholic Churches and communities lack elements of the Church to varying degrees, so that their adherents, although they "already belong in some way to God's People", are not fully *(non plene)* incorporated by them into the body of Christ, and the separated brethren do not enjoy the full unity of the Church, as has been said at the beginning of the paragraph. In these statements the idea of belonging to the people of God and of incorporation into the body of Christ on several different levels is found once again. Full membership is realized on a double level, on an inward and spiritual level, and on an outward and visible level.

Even though the visible, institutional sphere is related to the inward and spiritual sphere as its sign and instrumental cause, no kind of mechanical or automatic correspondence exists between the two. On the one hand, the visible sign, outward membership of the Church, can become for an individual person through his own guilt a *sacramentum validum, sed informe*; and on the other hand, membership of the Church and incorporation into the body of Christ on the inward level, what is signified, can be fully realized even though the sacramental and institutional sign, membership of the Church on the visible level, is incomplete. Thus while the decree accepts that non-Catholic Christians *non plene incorporantur* because of a lack in the sacramental and institutional sphere, it must be borne in mind that the Council recognizes a much more grave *non plene incorporantur* for Catholics. The Constitution on the Church, the ecclesiology of which is applied in the Decree on Ecumenism, similarly mentions as the first condition for full membership of the body of Christ the "possession of the Spirit of Christ" and goes on to say: "He is not saved, however, who, though he is part of the body of the Church does not persevere in charity. He remains indeed in the bosom of the Church, but, as it were, only in a 'bodily' manner and not 'in his heart'" (Article 14). Membership of the body of Christ is not an indivisible reality, not even within the Catholic Church. Nor is it a static condition, since on both levels it can either grow or decrease, both within and without the Catholic Church.

This "ecclesiology of elements" which is applied in the Decree on Ecumenism has frequently been criticized, particularly on the Protestant side. It is alleged that it represents a "quantitative mode of thought", and makes the Church far too much the juxtaposing or conglomeration of different elements, so failing to regard in their indivisible wholeness other Churches, which, it implies, if they were to add to what they possess in the institutional sphere, could be Churches in the full sense. The particular objection is made that this "ecclesiology of elements" ultimately makes the Church something man can control and manipulate, so overlooking the fact that the Church is an occurrence freely created by

God's sovereign word.[16] We cannot deal here with these objections (at which we have only hinted), and they must certainly be taken seriously by Catholic ecclesiology in developing further the starting points laid down in the Decree on Ecumenism. It was not possible, nor was there any intention, that the brief statement of the Decree should be the last word on the Catholic side, or anything more than the contribution to the ecumenical dialogue which was possible at that particular moment. They were naturally drawn up in full awareness that the Catholic understanding of the Church differs from that of other denominations principally in its evaluation of the visible, sacramental and institutional aspects of the Church, the level of "signs", "means", "ways", and the Church as an institution. What is of decisive importance is the question whether by firmly holding to the institutional elements which it regards as constituting the Church on earth, the Catholic Church is submitting itself to the word of God, or trying to control it.

Article 4. After setting out the ecclesiological principles which govern the participation of the Catholics in the ecumenical movement, the decree now turns to discuss the ecumenical movement itself. The first paragraph forms a transition to the following paragraphs of the article. The reference to the ecumenical efforts which are being carried out in many parts of the world at the present day is repeated, and they are once again seen as brought about the Spirit of God.

This shows the meaning of the reference to the "signs of the times" (an expression which also occurs in other Council documents), which Catholics are exhorted to recognize as the call of God.[17] In accordance with the previous discussion concerning *incorporatio non plena* and *plena* the final aim of ecumenical movement is referred to as *plenitudo unitatis*. The addition of the words "which Jesus Christ desires" recalls the well-known expression formulated by Abbé Couturier, the French pioneer of "spiritual ecumenism" (cf. Article 8), in the prayer for Christian unity. If one recalls the tendency to uniformity which has long prevailed in the Catholic Church, and which derives from a misunderstanding of true unity, it is clear that the appeal to strive for "that fullness of unity which Jesus Christ desires" does not only mean that Catholics should help other Christians in the search for full unity, but that a change of heart is also required on the part of Catholics.

The second paragraph gives an account of the ecumenical movement. The first version of the text proceeded by first listing different ecumenical activities, and then concluding with the words: "All this is the meaning of the ecumenical movement." Following a number of written submissions by Council Fathers

---

[16] An example of a critical Protestant attitude to the "elements ecclesiology" is provided by W. Dantine, "Die kontroverstheologische Problematik der sogenannten 'Ekklesialen Elemente' im Blick auf das ökumenische Gespräch", in J. Lell, ed., *Erneuerung der Einen Kirche. Arbeiten aus Kirchengeschichte und Konfessionskunde* (1966), pp. 140–54.

[17] Cf. M.-D. Chenu, "Les signes des temps", in *Nouvelle Revue Théologique* 87 (1965), pp. 29–39.

who did not find this account sufficiently clear, the Secretariat for Unity altered the arrangement so that the paragraph now begins, perhaps in a somewhat didactic way, "The 'ecumenical movement' means . . ." Thus the whole passage forms a kind of definition. A brief synthesis sums up the activities and enterprises which are described in greater detail in Chapter II. Since we discuss each individual kind of activity more fully in the following chapter a few brief remarks will suffice here. According to the text of the decree, ecumenism first consists of an honest self-control on the part of Catholics, who must ask themselves whether their thoughts and judgments upon other Christians, and their whole attitude towards them, satisfy the demands of fairness and truth. This sentence has in mind not so much a consciously unjust and unloving attitude, which is exercised in bad faith and can be recognized at once as culpable, but rather judgments and attitudes which have been unconsciously and thoughtlessly taken over from an era of polemic, which are certainly not required by the assertions of the Catholic faith, which even to Catholics are recognizably not in accord with the actual facts, and which are therefore bound to be felt by non-Catholic Christians as unjust and wounding. Just as in general the mere fact that other people are different can lead unconsciously to a negative attitude towards them, so it is particularly easy for this to happen in the religious sphere. Furthermore, even legitimate apologetics tends to regard other Christians as opponents, and to present their characteristics in such a way that they can be more easily "refuted". What the Decree on Ecumenism and the Constitution on the Church state concerning the standing of separated brethren as Christians, and the ecclesiological status of their communities, can and must lead Catholics to reconsider their attitude to other Christians. There is no doubt that self-control and self-criticism on the part of Catholics, such as the decree demands here, is in itself an important contribution to the overcoming of the centuries-old alienation between Christians of different denominations, to the amelioration of their relations with one another, and to the creation of a new climate among Christians.

Emphasizing the key word "dialogue", the text continues its descriptions of ecumenism, and so turns to a central but difficult issue in the ecumenical movement. By dialogue between Christians of different denominations, which long before the Council had been begun by small groups, but which is here recognized and recommended by the highest ecclesiastical authority as the appropriate method of encounter and of seeking full unity, the centuries-long era of monologue on the part of individual Churches, and of polemic between Churches, is officially concluded. This turning point is also clearly marked by the encyclical *Ecclesiam Suam* of Pope Paul VI, and by the lengthy passage on dialogue in the second part of the Ecumenical Directory prepared by the Secretariat for Unity. The text of the decree only gives an anticipatory summary here, while a fuller discussion follows in Chapter II (Articles 9 and 10). The text understands dialogue here not in the broader sense, as discussion on religious questions between any Christians of different denominations, but in the narrower sense as dialogue between competent experts *(inter peritos)*. Since what is meant is not an academic religious discussion or an existential personal involvement, but a committed discussion on matters of faith, it is certainly in order for the decree to refer to the spiritual atmosphere *(in spiritu religioso ordinatis)* with which such meetings for dialogue should be imbued. The decree describes here only the first stage of the dialogue, in which those who take part try to give such an account of the doctrine of their own communities that their partners in the dialogue can better appreciate the deeper meaning of the doctrine of the other denominations, and more justly evaluate the particular Church life of the other communities. It is rightly accepted here that in the effort to bring separate denominations closer together the first and fundamental condition is an exact knowledge of the opposite point of view. This is the only way in which to establish accurately the points of fundamental agreement, and the real substance of the differences that divide the denominations.

It is quite evident at the present day that to establish these precise points is not as easy as is often supposed. Thus even for the *periti* the decree does not accept that their mutual knowledge is already sufficient. It is clear that this is even less true of Christians in general. The mutual alienation of Christians of different denominations is mainly due to an insufficient knowledge on all sides of the way in which others understand and live their faith. Numerous misunderstandings are due to the fact that in different communities, during the period in which they have been divided, different modes of thought and different languages have been developed. Often the same thing is described in different words and concepts, or alternatively the same words can refer to different things. Thus the problem of language plays a decisive role. The decree also rightly accepts that the best people to give a correct account of the doctrine and life of one community to representatives of another are those who themselves live in the former community. The living exchange of question and answer, statement and response, through which each partner in the dialogue can also attain to a more precise understanding of his own position, and to a more reflective understanding of himself, through listening attentively to the other, is a surer way than any other of ensuring that each party can make itself understood to the other, and each can understand the real intention of the other.

The decree in no way regards dialogue as a method of convincing the non-Catholic partner of the rightness of Catholic doctrine, that is, as an attempt at conversion, but as a means of mutual understanding. It expects as the first fruit of the dialogue "a truer knowledge and more just appreciation of the teaching and religious life of both Communions". But the decree also expresses the hope that this better mutual understanding and evaluation will lead to common action in the world. Here we see the important desire for common witness through action, which recurs in other passages of the decree, and in several other documents of the Council; even though the union of the Church is not possible, yet on the basis of common belief in Christ, the co-operation of all Christians is possible, and more necessary than ever at the present day. It must begin with a common commitment to an ordering of the way men live together, and of human society, which can be satisfying to the Christian conscience (*in quibusvis officiis ad bonum commune ab omni conscientia Christiana postulatis*). The demands of justice, humanity and love are not limited to individual Churches, but common to all. Human society poses all Christian Churches the same questions, problems and tasks, and for the most part their solutions are to be found not in what separates the Churches, but in their common Christian basis of faith.

A further fruit of dialogue, according to the decree, is that the division of the Church is not so profound that not even prayer in common is possible. Common Christian faith makes possible, and the concern for the spiritual growing together of all Christians actually demands, Christian prayer in common. This prayer is dealt with more fully in Article 8, where the limitations implied by the qualification "where this is permitted" are explained. Finally, a fruit of dialogue which is of decisive importance, and which is mentioned at the end of this second paragraph, is the question which is necessarily posed to all who take part in the dialogue, including Catholics of course: Are we faithful in everything to the will of Christ, with regard to what he expects of his Church? Thus the decree anticipates as a positive result of the encounter with representatives of other communities, a genuine questioning of the Catholic Church as well, and in fact accepts the inevitable corollary that in the case of the Catholic Church it is also impossible to speak of complete faithfulness, for otherwise Catholics, to whom the decree is directly addressed, could not be required without qualification to undertake the "task of renewal and reform" (*opus renovationis et reformationis*). The theme of the renewal of the Church is taken up at the beginning of Chapter II (Article 8).

It is true that the second paragraph of this article directly mentions only individual Christians of different denominations who are concerned for the ecumenical movement, but the whole context clearly shows that they are not seen as isolated individuals, but as members of these Churches. The passage is dealing with the encounter of different Churches and communities, but this encounter is carried out by individuals. The decree is quite clearly thinking of Christians who are rooted in their own communities and who genuinely represent them to other communities. But it likewise clearly expects that these Christians, including Catholics, should not complacently assume that in their own community the will of Christ is perfectly fulfilled. Consequently, it rightly refers at the beginning of the paragraph to ecumenism as a "movement". The foundation and guiding factors of ecumenism are of course definite dogmatic principles, but as such it is a movement, that is, a complex of activities, enterprises and efforts, all of which aim at bringing closer together and finally uniting all Christians. Naturally, it consists not of a series of activities which are related only outwardly, but of efforts which proceed from a spirit that is constantly renewed. Consequently, the ecumenical movement cannot bind itself to a plan of action which is fixed once for all, but must always be open to further developments called forth by the spirit which inspires it.

In the third paragraph the decree first mentions the immediate aims of the ecumenical movement, which even now can and must be attained, before the ultimate goal can be seen. We cannot dispense ourselves from ecumenical effort on the grounds that it is not possible to see how the union of the Church can ever take place. If we do not set out upon the way which alone leads to full unity, "the obstacles to perfect ecclesiastical communion" remain. Even if we must be prepared for the union of the Church to be impossible before the end of time, we must recognize and acknowledge that the unity of Christians, which in fact has never been fully destroyed, can even now grow and must do so. There is no doubt a long and painful way to be followed before all the obstacles are overcome by the "blessings of justice and truth (in the sense of the true assessment and true evaluation of other Churches, and a growth on one's own part in the knowledge of the truth), of concord (as opposed to the centuries-old discord) and collaboration (by contrast to the isolated activity of each Church that has taken place hitherto), as well as of the spirit of brotherly love and unity" (which should naturally obtain among members of a family, and which is in contrast to a previous un-Christian alienation). The decree therefore rightly points to the necessity of prudence (not in the sense of a tactical cunning, but in the sense of the biblical requirement) and patience. Both can be termed specifically "ecumenical virtues".

The decree then turns with a hopeful outlook from the indirect aims to the lofty ultimate aim which in accordance with the statements of Article 3 is described as *perfecta ecclesiastica communio*. This full unity must be expressed in the common celebration of the Eucharist on the part of all Christians, because the Church is essentially a eucharistic table fellowship. There follows here in the text of the decree a statement which is once again explicitly characterized as a statement of faith *(credimus)*: the unity which Christ bestowed upon his Church is not lost (to varying degrees) from every Church, but "dwells" in the Catholic Church and by God's grace is something she can never lose *(inadmissibilem)*. The expression used here, *in Ecclesia catholica subsistere* is adopted from the Constitution on the Church (Article 8); the latter says of the Church of Christ that it subsists in the Catholic Church, while the same is said here of the unity given by Christ. The *relatio* on the Constitution on the Church says concerning this passage: *Dicitur subsistit ut expressio melius concordet cum affirmatione de elementis ecclesialibus, quae alibi adsunt.* The same can be said of the Decree on Ecumenism: it uses the term *subsistit* in order to express the fact that "very many of the most significant elements" (cf. Article 3, para. 2) of unity are also to be found in other communities. The Catholic Church owes it to other Churches to make this confession of faith, according to which a unity bestowed by Christ is realized in itself, at least with regard to the essentials of this unity. The Catholic Church knows that this represents the greatest difficulty for the union of other Churches with itself, but rightly sees therein no obstacle to its genuine participation in the ecumenical movement. Nor would this conviction of faith hinder its entry into the World Council of Churches, for according to the Toronto Declaration of the World Council of Churches, each member Church can remain faithful to its own ecclesiology.[18] The Catholic Church would in fact not be the only Church to regard the essentials of the unity desired by Christ as realized in itself. But the final observation of the paragraph shows that it does not regard its unity as perfect, for this states that unity can grow even within the Catholic Church, and that its perfection is an eschatological entity.

The whole passage shows, moreover, that the decree does not think of the union of the Churches as the "return" of other Churches to the Catholic Church. The expression "return" is consciously avoided in the text. Nor is it a return that is actually meant; the reason is rather that this concept is not appropriate to what the passage intends. A return would presume that non-Catholic Christians of the present day had left the Catholic Church, which is obviously not the case. Moreover, there are great non-Catholic communities, as for example the Methodists, which have come into being not by departing from the Catholic Church, but by separating from the traditional Churches of the Reformation. The concept of a return would also not do justice to the fact that non-Catholic Christians, as the Council explicitly acknowledges, already belong to the people of God, and that in their communities the Church of Christ is already present in various ways. Finally, a "return" would imply that the union of other communities with the Catholic Church in its present form was expected. The Catholic Church would wait, unchanged, until those who are separated came back to her, and at best would pray for their conversion, while the separated Churches would have to deny their whole past when they united. But in fact the Catholic Church, as is shown by the Decree on Ecumenism and the whole Council, is thinking not merely of a movement on the part of others, but is undertaking a reform itself, even from the institutional point of view. It must undergo a change of form in many respects, in the spirit of the gospel. But what its future concrete form will be, when it has carried out the reconsideration and reform of itself which has only just begun, it is not yet possible to tell at present, even though Catholic faith is certain that this form should always be characterized by the ministry of the successors of the apostles and the Petrine office. Thus the aim of the ecumenical movement can be described, as is done in the decree,

[18] At the session in Toronto (1950) the Central Committee of the World Council of Churches said among other things that if a Church is a member of the World Council of Churches, this does not mean that it regards its own view of the Church as merely relative or that it thereby accepts a particular doctrine concerning the nature of the unity of the Church, or that it either accepts or rejects the doctrine that the unity of the Church consists of the unity of the invisible Church.

as the setting up of perfect ecclesiastical union between non-Catholic Churches and communities and the Catholic Church, as the gathering of all Christians to the unity of the one and only Church.

The fourth paragraph, which deals with the problem of "conversions", forms a kind of aside in the argument of Article 4, which inevitably intrudes itself as a consequence of the preceding discussion, and which serves to clarify what has been said. Ecumenical work may appear to many Catholics as a new method of working for conversions, whereas others may gain the impression that the conversion of individuals to the Catholic Church has now become meaningless, since we are now concerned with the union of Churches as such. In this regard the decree seeks to make the position clear in two respects. In the first place, it clearly states that a concern for non-Catholics who wish to be received into the Catholic Church is of its nature distinct from ecumenical action. This makes it clear that ecumenical work is not a method of obtaining conversions; it is not concerned with the adherence of individual non-Catholic Churches to the Catholic community, but with the drawing closer and the union of Christian communities as such. On the other hand, as the decree goes on to emphasize, ecumenical work does not exclude the reception of individual non-Catholic Christians into the Catholic Church. The grace of God is not at work only in the ecumenical movement, but also where the conversion of the individual non-Catholic Christians to the Catholic Church takes place for reasons of conscience. Certainly individual conversions from one Church to another raise their own problems, and form a burden in the relationship between the Churches.[19] But no Church would disagree that every believer has to follow his conscience, and no non-Catholic Church, for example, rejects the acceptance of Catholics into its communion. What is rightly rejected is proselytizing propaganda among the believers of another Christian community.

The decree does not speak at all of propaganda or of an apostolate, but only of the "work of preparing (which means in general the necessary religious instruction) and reconciling those individuals who wish for full Catholic communion" (and who according to what has been said already enjoy a certain communion with the Catholic Church). It would certainly be wrong to see a proselytizing tendency in the statements of this paragraph. Moreover, the term "conversion", which was hitherto usual, is intentionally and rightly avoided (it is also used by non-Catholic Churches for those who leave another community for their own). For the biblical expression *conversio* (corresponding to the Greek *metanoia*) means the turning of a person formerly apart from God, to God in Jesus Christ, that is conversion to Christian faith as such. In its true sense, the process never ends in this life, and every believer in every Church must constantly strive for *conversio cordis* (cf. Article 7). As a term for adherence to the Catholic Church by a believing Christian, something which does not

[19] K. Rahner, "On Conversions to the Church", in *Theological Investigations,* III (1967), pp. 373–84.

mean the acceptance of the Christian faith as such, but the recognition of the sacramental and hierarchical structure of the Church, and of doctrines which are rejected by other Churches, *conversio* is certainly inappropriate. Its use derives from a time in which Christians of other confessions were regarded from the Catholic point of view as formal heretics, or were equated in practice with unbelievers. The decree uses the word *reconciliatio,* which expresses the situation better, but cannot itself be regarded as the most appropriate term, for reconciliation implies a previous discord. The best expression would probably be "acceptance".

The fifth paragraph once again turns to the description of ecumenical work. It is intended to make Catholics aware of what their first aim must be. The statements earlier in the decree, that all the essential elements of the Church are to be found in the Catholic Church, while certain constitutive elements are lacking in other Churches and communities, might lead to the view that the ecumenical activity of Catholics should be mainly concerned with other Churches. This is specifically denied in the present paragraph. The primary duty *(in primis)* of Catholics is with their own Church. Certainly they should also think of separated Christians and carry out Christian service towards them, such as will contribute to their mutual reconciliation. They should include them in their prayers, "keep them informed about the Church" in dialogue and by exchanging ideas, and make the first approaches towards them *(primos gressus ad illos movendo),* wherever an opportunity for encounter offers. But the decree sees the ecumenical task of Catholics wholly in the spirit of Pope John XXIII, who regarded the self-renewal of the Catholic Church as the most urgent Catholic contribution to the reconciliation and union of the Churches. Catholics should not complacently persist in the view that their Church possesses the full truth and all the institutions willed by Christ. The presence of all institutional means is no guarantee that the essential reality, which the institutions are only meant to serve, is present to the same degree. Moreover, the "institutions" *(instituta)* willed by Christ are not anything in themselves, and do not work in a mechanical or automatic way. They are there for the sake of the Christian life of the whole community. Even "pure doctrine" is meant to contribute to the life lived by faith, which is not identical with mere orthodoxy. All the external practices of the Church avoid becoming empty routine, and become worthy of belief, only when the faithful really consent to God's offer of grace, and make the meaning of the "outward means" visible through a life lived by grace. Consequently, the decree demands of Catholics, for the sake of their ecumenical task in particular, that in the first place the testimony that they bear to the doctrine and the institutions that have been given to them should be more faithful, and therefore more worthy of belief.

In the next paragraph the decree once again speaks of the Catholic Church as "endowed with all divinely revealed truth and with all means of grace", so emphasizing the fullness of the institutional elements it possesses. But it does this only in order to admit that the life of Catholics falls short of the demands made by this rich endowment. What matters here is the sanctification of the Church as a demonstration of its apostolicity. There is no room here for triumphalism. Nor is any reference made, as in apologetics, to the great saints who have always been present in the Catholic Church, and who unquestionably form the most convincing testimony to the Catholic Church, but who are an insignificant minority among the vast number of the faithful. Seen from such a point of view, the endowment "with all divinely revealed truth and with all means of grace" would constitute in reality a demand for a Christian elite, for the pre-eminence of the whole Catholic community over all the rest of Christianity. This is obviously not the case. The face of the Church, the radiance which is consequently insufficient, is not the "image" presented by ecclesiastical institutions visible to all, but the spirit of sanctity, faith, hope and love, manifested in the Christian life of the faithful. It is only through this that the Catholic Church becomes worthy of belief in the eyes of other Christians and of the whole world. What matters is not the apotheosis of the Catholic Church, but the kingdom of God, which is meant to grow in the world, and the growth of which is constantly retarded *(retardetur)* by the guilt of the members of the Church; what matters is the praise of the grace of God in accordance with the Lord's saying: "Let your light so shine before men, that they may see your good works and give glory to your Father who is in heaven" (Mt 5:16).

This paragraph is not concerned with the reform of the Church's institutions, but with the spiritual purification and renewal of the Church, which is something that can only take place through the spiritual renewal of the members of the Church. This is also shown by the demand, associated with a reference to Jas 1:4 and Rom 12:1–2, to all Catholics to aim at Christian perfection. The Church will of course never reach a perfectly immaculate and glorious state in the present age, for that will be given by Christ at the end of this aeon. The sentence beginning *Donec* shows that it is an eschatological reality. The Apostle Paul's description of the Church as "without spot or wrinkle" (Eph 5:27) is no longer referred to the historical structure of the Church, as was done in the encyclical *Ad Petri Cathedram* of John XXIII, almost in terms of enthusiastic millenarianism (1959). The striving for perfection discussed in this paragraph echoes Chapter V of the Constitution on the Church ("The Call of the Whole Church to Holiness"), from the particular point of view of the testimony to the truth of the Church, while the reference to "the humility and dying of Jesus", which the Church has to bear in her own body, recalls Article 8 of Chapter I of *Lumen Gentium,* where it is emphasized that the Church must not seek earthly glory, but in following the path of Christ should give the world an example of humility and sacrifice.

The seventh paragraph passes from the sanctity of the Church to another characteristic of the Church, which is also of decisive importance from the ecumenical point of view, that of its catholicity. Catholicity is not understood here in the sense of geographical universality, that is, in a "quantitative" sense, as the extension of the Church to all countries and people. Apologetics in the modern period has emphasized this aspect of the Church's Catholicity above all. The present paragraph does not deal at all with this point of view, which in view of the world-wide extension of other Churches has come to present difficulties, but discusses exclusively the inner, "qualitative" catholicity, the multiplicity within the unity of the Church, and its unity in diversity, which derive both from the multiple potentialities of man as a created being, and also from the fullness of Christ's gifts of grace.[20] The text does not state explicitly here, as in the case of the Church's sanctity, that the Catholic Church has previously been lacking in this respect. But this idea is clearly assumed by the demands made in this paragraph. In fact one cannot overlook the fact, which has frequently been stressed in connection with the Council, that centuries of over-emphasis on unity within the Catholic Church have prevented the development of the diversity which belongs to full catholicity. The unity essential to the Church was widely equated with uniformity. The ideal was the introduction of one and the same Roman and Latin liturgy and one and the same Roman canon law throughout the Catholic Church, and the supervision and control of all areas of Church life, as far as possible, by the central authorities in Rome. The efforts to latinize the Catholic Eastern Churches, which persisted until very recently, were characteristic of this tendency to uniformity. In so far as these Churches were allowed to retain any characteristics of their own, it was regarded as an unavoidable concession.

That this uniformist and centralizing practice damaged the true catholicity of the Church was not realized until very recently.[21] But at the Second Vatican Council this awareness was powerfully asserted. The reaction against previous practice took place in the name of a fuller realization of the catholicity of the Church, from the conviction that the practical, and not merely theoretical, recognition of the multiplicity and diversity which derives from the creation and the fullness of the grace of Christ, and is manifested between nations, groups of persons, and individuals, does not mean a lessening of the true unity of the Church, but the realization of the fullness vouchsafed to it. The frequent celebration of non-Roman liturgies during the Council by bishops of the Catholic Eastern Churches, and the pleas of these Fathers on behalf of the distinctive nature of their own Churches, undoubtedly made a considerable contribution to the creation of a more Catholic consciousness. The process of a more determined universalizing of thought and action in the different spheres of the Church's life, which was begun by the Council, is also of decisive importance for the future of the ecumenical movement. The union of the Churches by means of the levelling out of the legitimate characteristics and independence of individual Churches is unthinkable.

[20] Cf. on this Y. Congar, *Mystery of the Church* (1960).
[21] "Consequently, uniformity in all things is not the ideal of catholicity, but a caricature." See J. L. Witte, "Die Katholizität der Kirche: Eine neue Interpretation nach alter Tradition", in *Gregorianum* 42 (1961), pp. 239f.

The observations of this paragraph concerning the catholicity of the Church reflect the more universalist thinking which came to prevail at the Council. They are consequently of the utmost importance for the ecumenical orientation of Catholics. The principle stated at the beginning, that of *unitas in necessariis,* is fundamental. Where something inessential is at issue, freedom should prevail. The expression *in variis formis* is a direct contradiction of the principle of uniformity. The affirmation not only of variety in spirituality, in the outward forms of Church life, and in the liturgy, but also of diversity in "the theological elaborations of revealed truth" is certainly not in accord with the thought that prevailed in Roman Catholicism until very recently, but cannot be overestimated in its value to the ecumenical movement. If the faithful give "richer expression" to the catholicity of the Church in this way, so, at the same time, the apostolicity of the Church will also be more fully realized, as the text points out. The basic principle of the "Apostolic Council", "to lay upon you no greater a burden than these necessary things" (Acts 15:28), the recognition of diverse charismata, the readiness of the Apostle Paul to become a Jew to the Jews and one outside the law to those outside the law (1 Cor 9:20f.), are characteristic of the attitude of the apostolic Church. Uniformity and centralism are certainly ill fitted to demonstrate the identity of the present day Church with the apostolic Church.

The next paragraph draws the attention of the Catholics to their separated brethren. These statements mark a change of thought towards non-Catholic Christians. Merely to affirm the lack of elements of the Church in their Churches would be a purely negative approach. An open ecumenical outlook joyfully recognizes the positive Christian values which are found in other Christian communities as a common heritage. It is necessary to do this not merely out of benevolent condescension, or in order to please other Christians, but in order to praise the grace of God, which is not limited to the Catholic Church, but works its miracles in all who believe in Christ and are ready to bear witness for his sake. Such an open outlook recognizes in other Christians not merely scattered vestiges of Christianity, but the "riches of Christ". It sees in the *martyrium* of other Christians not the fanaticism of heresy, but a genuine witness to Christ, which is only possible through the power of the grace of God. Here we may recall that on 18 October 1964, a month before the promulgation of the Decree on Ecumenism, Pope Paul VI, in an address on the occasion of the canonization of the twenty-two Catholic martyrs of Uganda, said of the Anglican martyrs who suffered at the same time that they too died in the name of Christ.[22] The purpose of the observations in this paragraph is clearly to strengthen the awareness of Catholics of their links through grace with other Christians, and to help them to overcome the centuries of alienation among Christians. They will also play their part in overcoming one-sided "institutional thinking" among

---

[22] Cf. the address of Pope Paul VI on the occasion of the canonization of the martyrs of Uganda on 18 October 1964.

Catholics, and in accustoming them to the idea of the free activity of the grace of God, who is not restricted to any instrument he uses, and will help them to judge other Christian communities in a way which is not determined by the consideration of institutional elements of the Church.

In the next paragraph, the decree goes a step further: Catholics should not only rejoice at the Christian endowments which they find among other Christians. It is not simply a case of recognizing among their separated brethren only such Christian values as are already in existence and alive in the life of the Catholic community. Rather, they should remember that in the life and the teaching of non-Catholic communities, aspects of what is Christian have developed, which in Catholicism have been manifested either inadequately or not at all. It is possible that Catholics have rejected much that they see among non-Catholic Christians, simply because things are different within the Catholic Church, whereas in reality they are genuinely Christian and in no sense conflict "with the genuine interests of the faith". Consequently, Catholics should regard such values as an enrichment of their own life in faith, and should allow them to contribute to their own edification by bringing to realization aspects of Church life and Christian understanding within Catholicism which were not previously developed. A positive evaluation of the form taken by Christian faith in other Churches can lead in this way, within the Catholic community, to a better understanding and realization of the fullness contained in the mystery of Christ and the Church.

The statements of this paragraph are the product of the understanding which led even before the Council to a dialogue with Protestant and Orthodox theology, and to contact with the life of non-Catholic Churches, and which then came to prevail at the Council itself; that is, the realization that in the Catholic Church, not least as a consequence of a polemical reaction to one-sided emphases in the doctrine and life of the non-Catholic Churches and theologians, numerous one-sided developments have taken place in the understanding of the faith and in Church life, and that many aspects of Christian revealed truth have been suppressed from the consciousness of the Catholic faith and are inadequately realized in the life of the Church. The Council's rebuke of numerous false emphases and correction of many one-sided attitudes in the Catholic presentation of doctrine by complementary statements, and its restoration of many forms of Church life, was certainly due in part, if not solely, to the example of the Churches which were represented at the Council by observers. Examples of this, to which it would be easy to add, are the stronger emphasis on the work of the Holy Spirit and the freely given gifts of the Spirit, the emphasis on the significance of the word of God and its power to bestow grace, and on the unique position of holy Scripture in the life of the Church, the revival of the doctrine of the universal priesthood of all believers, and the renewal of the liturgy through its simplification, through the clarification of its nature as a community action, and by the introduction of the vernacular and the chalice for the laity. If, following the example of the Council, Catholics welcome, in the course of the ecumenical encounter, "whatever is wrought by the grace of the Holy Spirit in the hearts of our separated brethren", this does not mean a "protestantizing" of the Catholic Church, as many Catholics have wrongly understood it to be, but a more ample realization of the fullness of the mystery of Christ and the Church, and therefore of the Catholicity of the Church.

The last paragraph but one now points out that as long as the divisions of the Church endure, it is not possible to bring into being the fullness of catholicity proper to the Church, for two reasons. It is not possible in the first place because the separation prevents all the institutional means of salvation, which are essential constituents of the Church of Christ and which are given as *salutarium mediorum plenitudo* to the Catholic Church (cf. Article 3) from being effective among separated Christians, who are nevertheless related to this fullness by baptism. This statement follows naturally from what has been said earlier. But a change from previous Catholic thought is found in the second statement, that as a consequence of the divisions it is also scarcely possible for the Catholic Church to express in its actual life all aspects of the catholicity of the Church. This statement now recognizes in principle that for true catholicity a diversity of Christian forms of life, of Christian spirituality, of liturgical forms, of ecclesiastical discipline, of theological thought and of types of doctrine are necessary, and there is no doubt that in the future a much greater variety will develop in many respects in the Catholic Church. But so long as large parts of Christianity, with their own characteristic features, are separated from the Catholic Church, it will be hardly possible for all these legitimate expressions of Christianity and each type of Church (in the sense of particular Churches) to develop to the full within Catholicism, and it is only these which would bring about a manifestation of the full catholicity of the Church "in actual life".

The chapter concludes with an admonition to the faithful and the bishops. By the calling of the Council, and by its evident ecumenical orientation, ecumenical efforts within the Catholic Church received a powerful impetus, and became much more widespread among Catholics; in fact too much was expected. The Council here encourages the faithful by expressing its joy at the growth of ecumenical efforts among Catholics. The recommendation to the bishops, which aims at the realization of the ecumenical movement everywhere in the world, was also expressed in the Decree on the Bishops' Pastoral Office (Articles 11 and 16). The Ecumenical Directory prepared by the Secretariat for Unity is intended to be above all a help to the bishops in responding to the task of skilfully promoting and prudently guiding the ecumenical task which is here given to their faithful by the Decree on Ecumenism, in as meaningful a way as possible, according to the circumstances of their countries. The various national and diocesan ecumenical commissions, which since then have been set up by national episcopal conferences and individual bishops, show that this demand of the Council has not remained a dead letter.

The Practice of Ecumenism

In Chapter II, the decree passes from the account of fundamental doctrinal principles set out in Chapter I to the presentation of a programme for ecumenical practice, which clearly represents the results of decades of experience on the part of Catholic ecumenism. But from the nature of the subject it was not possible to divide the material strictly between the setting out of principles on the one hand (Chapter I) and the discussion of the practical realization of ecumenism on the other (Chapter II). Article 4 in Chapter I has already mentioned ecumenical practice, while Chapter II extends in many respects the ideas of Chapter I on the Catholic principles of ecumenism.

Article 5. Ecumenism is essentially "concern for restoring unity". This concern must be actively exercised by all the faithful. Consequently, in this introduction to Chapter II, the decree emphasizes first the universal duty to take part in ecumenical work. Ecumenism is not merely the affair of specialists but that of all the faithful, of whatever rank in the Church. Nor is it a matter simply of extraordinary enterprises but rather of "daily Christian living", of the whole orientation of the life and the activity of the Church. If the Catholic Church is to contribute to the union of Christians, above all by its self-renewal and if, as Article 4 stresses, the "Church's face" is to be more radiant and the Catholic Church more Catholic, all in whom the Church is present because of baptism are called to the ecumenical task. It would consequently also be false to regard the duty of an ecumenical orientation and ecumenical action as limited to Catholics who live in countries where there is more than one denomination. Even though Catholics in traditionally Catholic countries are unlikely to come into personal contact with non-Catholic Christians, yet their attitude and behaviour play an essential part in deciding the form taken by the Catholic Church, and so decisively influence the judgment of non-Catholic Christianity upon the Catholic Church. One has only to think of the influence which Catholic Spain has exercised upon the judgment of the Catholic Church by the Protestant world through its attitude to the question of religious freedom, in spite of its tiny Protestant minority. Secondly, this introductory paragraph makes special mention of a fundamental understanding which determines the whole argument of Chapter II: the ecumenical movement is essentially concerned with the better manifestation of the bond of brotherhood and unity which already exists among all Christians. The arguments of Article 3 already stress an awareness of the unity which even now exists between the Churches on the basis of the different elements of the Church which are present in them, and what follows is intended to show how this unity can and ought to be more clearly manifested, so that it may continue to grow, and that there may be hope of its consummation through the grace of God.

Article 6. At the head of its programme for ecumenical activity in the Catholic Church the decree places the renewal of the Church, which in the same paragraph is referred to as a *renovatio* and a *reformatio*.[23] In its efforts for the restoration of unity the Catholic Church must not think in the first instance of other communities, but must take stock of itself. A concern for the reuniting of the Churches demands that the Church should test her "fidelity to her own calling", because if this faithfulness is lessened, the union of the Churches is necessarily hindered. The decree thereby recognizes and accepts the ecumenical programme which Pope John XXIII gave to the Council in numerous statements, and which Pope Paul VI confirmed and made more specific from the very beginning of his pontificate: the growing together and final unity of the Churches, through the self-renewal of the Church. Although the text does not go so far as to express its hope for the renewal on the part of the non-Catholic Churches, this hope on the part of the Catholic Church is nevertheless a fact. The growth of faithfulness towards the Church's own calling, which is how the decree regards renewal, means nothing less than an effort to fulfil more faithfully the demands of the gospel, efforts which the Reformation Churches have always professed in the principle *Ecclesia semper reformanda*. When the decree says here of the Church on her pilgrim way, as the Constitution on the Church describes the Catholic Church (Articles 6, 8, etc., also Chapter VII), that it is called by Christ to a *perennis reformatio,* this is equivalent to the profession of the principle *Ecclesia semper reformanda*. The consciousness that this was in fact an ancient Catholic idea was revived only in the years preceding the Council. Many Catholics find the application of the term *reformatio* to the Catholic Church unfamiliar, but it derives from an ancient Catholic tradition. Popes, Councils, and churchmen of the

[23] "*Reformatio* and *renovatio* were indeed not specially distinguished in the decree, but there is nevertheless a difference between the two expressions, which can be seen in the doctrine of the Council and in the testimony of the Church's tradition. *Reformatio* means a restoration on the pattern of the previous age, which has been deformed through human weakness and sin. This is the sense in which the Catholic reform of the 16th century used the word, and the pattern to which it referred was that of the Church of the patristic age, though it did not thereby call into question the legitimate development since that period. By contrast, *renovatio* means a more faithful and more profound attitude to all areas of Christian life, based upon the spirit of the gospel." E. Stakemeier, "Kirche und Kirchen nach der Lehre des Zweiten Vatikanischen Konzils", in R. Bäumer and H. Dolch, eds., *Volk Gottes. Zum Kirchenverständnis der katholischen, evangelischen und anglikanischen Theologie* (1967), p. 513.

Middle Ages and the Reformation period used the expression quite naturally for the Catholic Church, and so did the Council of Trent *(Decreta et Canones super reformatione)*.

At the Second Vatican Council the recognition of the Church's need of reform which the decree mentions here *(qua . . . perpetuo indiget)* and the will to reform, became so clear, that Karl Barth could write of this Council, "If it was anything, it was a reforming Council."[24] The Church's need for reform, as the text says, applies to the Church "in so far as she is an institution of men here on earth". Thus it applies to the historical form of the Church, in so far as it is determined by the thought and action of the members of the Church, by contrast to that which is effected and determined in the Church by God. It must be borne in mind that this essential nature of the Church, desired and effected by God, never exists on its own, but always in a particular historical form determined by the thought, action, and behaviour of men in the Church. Since the thought and behaviour of the members of the Church at all levels, and also the concrete historical form in which the Church is manifested, are also determined by innumerable historical factors, including the spirit and the corruptions of a particular period, the Church must constantly ask how far this historical form is in accordance with the spirit and demands of the gospel, and must make constantly renewed efforts to order itself according to the gospel. It is impossible to determine precisely at any given historical moment how profoundly this concrete form can and must be changed. The Second Vatican Council became more aware of the historical relativity of different aspects of the Church's life, institutions and structures, than any previous Council. This is shown, for example, by the demands made in the Council, and in the context of the Council, that the Church must overcome the effects of the "era of Constantine", the Middle Ages, the Baroque period, the Counter-Reformation, etc., all of which have played a large part in giving it its present form. The word coined by Pope John XXIII and often quoted at the Council, *aggiornamento* (although it was often misunderstood as a demand for the mere "modernization" of the Church) certainly helped to restore this awareness. If the Decree on Ecumenism speaks here of the necessity of a reform from an ecumenical point of view, it does so from the conviction that since the historically conditioned *(pro rerum temporum-que adiunctis)* form of the Church in many respects prevents non-Catholic Christianity from understanding that the Church of Christ *subsistit in Ecclesia catholica*. The demand for a renewal of conduct, which the text places first, has never been omitted from the preaching of the Catholic Church, but is urged here from an ecumenical point of view. The following references to the necessary renewal of Church discipline and of the formulation of doctrine show that this reform is not to be understood purely in the moral sense, but is also intended to be an institutional reform. The demand for a reform of Church discipline *(in*

---

[24] K. Barth, *Ad Limina Apostolorum* (1967), p. 59.

96

ecclesiastica disciplina) is in the first instance a demand that Catholics should be more loyal to existing Church order. But it also includes a demand for those who hold authority in the Church (Article 5 specifically addressed "the clergy"), to concern themselves with a renewal of Church order and legislation, ecclesiastical institutions and structures, through which the Church can attain to a greater "fidelity to her own calling".

The demand for a renewal "in the formulation of doctrine", which is also of the utmost ecumenical significance, introduces the theme which is dealt with further in Article 11. As the documents of the Council show, the Council itself introduced a many-sided renewal *in doctrinae enuntiandae modo* by its pastoral language, much more closely based upon the holy Scripture, by many changes in emphasis which it introduced in doctrine, by removing much that was one-sided, and by rediscovering neglected aspects of revealed truth. A living acceptance of this renewed doctrine by the whole Church would at once bring with it a profound renewal of the proclamation of doctrine. The particular demand made here by the Decree on Ecumenism for the renewal of the formulation of doctrine signifies that dogmatic and pastoral theology should regard the work of the Council not as the conclusion but as the beginning of a reform, which must be continued in the spirit of the Council. The comment in the decree that the nature of the formulation of doctrine must be distinguished from the *depositum fidei* itself is in accordance with the distinction required by Pope John XXIII between the inalterable substance and the formulation, in need of renewal, of doctrine.[25] The necessary reformulation and reinterpretation must not go so far as to explain away doctrine which the Church has declared to be binding. Nevertheless, in view of the close connection between the content and the form of revealed doctrine, the distinction between its substance and its formulation, the way in which doctrine is propounded and the deposit of faith, will in practice constantly pose serious questions (this is the hermeneutic problem of the interpretation of the Church's doctrinal statements.)

That the renewal of the Church is intended to go further than what the Council has specifically required is also made clear in the second paragraph of the article. The movements already present for many years in the Church, which the decree mentions without claiming to list them in full, are not only noted with satisfaction, but explicitly described as "favourable pledges and signs" for the future of the ecumenical movement. Thus they are seen here not merely as gratifying expressions of the active life of the Church, but are evaluated from the particular point of view of their significance for the growing together and uniting of the Church. It is no accident that mention is made first of the movement for biblical renewal.

[25] Address at the opening of the first session: "The substance of the ancient doctrine of deposit of faith is one thing, and the way in which it is presented is another. And it is the latter that must be taken into great consideration with patience if necessary, everything being measured in the forms and proportions of a magisterium which is predominantly pastoral in character." See W. M. Abbott and J. Gallagher, eds., *The Documents of Vatican II* (1966), p. 715.

Its effects can be seen in every sphere of the Church's life. The closer use made of holy Scripture by Catholic theology has already led at the Council to a change in doctrine which is of great importance from the ecumenical point of view. It has brought Catholic theology into a fruitful dialogue with theologians of other denominations. To this is due the realization, very important for ecumenism, that not only do the Church's dogmas interpret Scripture, but Scripture in turn interprets dogma. The direct contact (not merely mediated by the Church's doctrine) of the faithful with the Bible, as the sacred book common to all Christians, has already done much to advance their awareness of belonging and being linked to all who believe in Christ, and if it spreads and grows more profound, it will continue to contribute to the promotion of common thinking among Christians. The co-operation, which has already begun, of the Catholic Church with the international Bible societies to produce and distribute translations of the Bible is both a fruit of the awareness that all Christians are linked by holy Scripture, and a contribution to the strengthening and spread of that awareness. Common Bible reading in ecumenical groups and the celebration of common biblical worship by all the congregations of a neighbourhood make the faithful much more conscious of the common basis of Christian faith than was possible at a time when the main emphasis was on differences of doctrine.

The ecumenical significance of the movement for liturgical renewal, which the decree mentions next, is also clear. The simplification that has already taken place, the reintroduction of the vernacular, the reduction of elements which serve mainly to increase the differences that mark Catholic worship as something apart, and the greater participation of the people in the liturgy as a realization of the universal priesthood, by contrast with a one-sided emphasis on the ministerial priesthood in the earlier liturgy, all help to make the common basis of all Christian worship more clearly visible, thereby strengthening the awareness of the existing unity of all Churches, and making the faithful conscious of the fact that many differences between Churches are not dogmatic in nature, but are due to historical developments. It would be possible in the same way to show the ecumenical significance of the other movements of renewal mentioned in the decree.

Article 7. The text passes from renewal on the ecclesiastical level, which was the subject of the previous article, to the personal renewal of the individual believer. The demands of the gospel mentioned here are made to every Christian, quite apart from the divisions which exist between Churches, but they are set out here, in so far as their fulfilment is necessary to all efforts to bring Christians closer to each other and to unite them. Ecumenism appears here as a movement which in its innermost essence is spiritual. It is only as such that it is preserved from purely outward activity and routine. The driving force of the institutional renewal of the Church comes from a spiritual renewal, without which it would lose its meaning and its value: the opening words of this paragraph state very definitely that "there can be no ecumenism worthy of the name without a change of heart". It uses the fundamental biblical concept *conversio (metanoia)* in the sense of an ever more decisive turning away from human egotism and self love, a more radical turning to God and readiness to fulfil his will, the conversion and change of heart which even in the baptized is constantly necessary and never completed. The expression drawn from Eph 4:33, *novitas mentis,* refers to the fact that this involves not merely a "moral" attitude, but a fundamentally new kind of thought, a new vision and judgment of things through faith, a constant transformation of thought and understanding. With its powerful emphasis on self-denial and humility, the text is a clear rejection of all self-righteousness and superiority, every kind of "triumphalism", and also of the self-assured and opinionated apologetics which says nothing about the deficiencies and failings in its own Church but expatiates all the more on those of other Churches. The spirit of brotherly love and service is stressed in many documents of the Council, but an urgent exhortation thereto could not be omitted from this paragraph, for it is a spirit which is more than the mere avoidance of mutual hatred, and more than just leaving each other in peace, and it creates a new climate in Christianity (as the shining example of John XXIII demonstrated in outstanding fashion to the whole world), produces a desire for unity, and alone makes possible a true encounter and fruitful dialogue among Christians of different denominations. But the spirit of inward renewal is a gift of God's grace, and therefore, as the decree states, it must be sought in prayer. This call to prayer again makes it clear that ecumenical efforts should not stop short at outward activity.

It is easy to understand why the decree, like other Council documents, addresses its exhortation to humility, love and service, above all to the clergy. For on the one hand, the ministry brings to those who bear it the danger that they may forget the fact that the character of their office is one of service, while on the other hand, an example of true service given by the clergy is of particular value because of their standing, and is very influential in forming the countenance of the Church.

An essential element in conversion is the recognition of one's own guilt, and repentance. If conversion is to be seen from the point of view of the union of separated Christians, attention must also be paid to sin against the unity of Christianity. Consequently, the second paragraph of this article takes up the theme of guilt for the divisions among Christians, which has already been mentioned in the preface to the decree, and discusses it here from the point of view of the change of heart which is essential for ecumenism. In the first drafts of the text the Secretariat for Unity did not yet dare to include in the decree a confession of guilt. The realization that the blame for the coming into being and the continuance of separation was also to be sought on the Catholic side had not become sufficiently established, and for the most part it was only the guilt of others which was perceived. The instruction *Ecclesia catholica,* 1949, of the Holy Office did speak of *defectus Catholicorum,* but of *culpae Reformatorum.*[26] At ecumenical

---

[26] *AAS* 42 (1950), p. 144.

conferences of non-Catholic Churches the guilt of all Churches for separation had long been expressed, in 1920 at the Lambeth Conference, in 1927 at the Faith and Order Conference in Lausanne, in 1948 at the World Church Conference in Amsterdam, and in 1953 at the second Assembly of the World Council of Churches at Evanston. At the Second Vatican Council, the previous situation on the Catholic side was rapidly changed by the confession of guilt and the request for forgiveness which Pope Paul VI uttered in his opening address to the second session on 29 September 1963.[27] In his address to the observers on 17 October 1963 the Pope returned to this theme in the following words: "In our address of 29 September, we dared to have recourse first of all to Christian forgiveness, mutual if possible. *Veniam damus petimusque vicissim.* Our minds need this calm, if they are going to begin friendly relationships, calm conversations."[28]

This made it possible for the Secretariat for Unity to include a confession of guilt, a request for forgiveness and an offer of forgiveness in the text. It was possible for it to refer to the Pope's statements, when 133 Fathers in the submission of *modi* requested the omission of this passage, and 25 others that its wording should be less sharp. The great majority of the Fathers approved the statement and several spoke in the Council debate on exactly the same lines. Like the confession of guilt uttered by the Pope, that of the conciliar decree was also welcomed on the non-Catholic side. It is clearly uttered in the spirit of the gospel, and recalls the parable of Jesus in Luke 18, with its warning not to imitate the self-righteous Pharisee, but the tax-collector who was aware of his guilt, and who prayed, "Lord, be merciful to me a sinner". The confession of guilt is expressed in the decree by applying the general statements of John 1:10 to the sin against unity. It is a long way from the unworthy and insincere behaviour of those Catholics who have never finished smelling out and holding up for inspection the faults of the Catholic Church and its hierarchy in particular. It also takes into account guilt on the non-Catholic side, but in a way that cannot wound: in the form of a brief declaration of readiness to forgive, taken from the Lord's Prayer. Thus the evident intention of the passage is to encourage in Catholics a simple, evangelical honesty and truthfulness.

Like the introduction, this passage avoids the question disputed among Catholics, whether it can be said of the Church as such that it is sinful. Many theologians dispute this, saying that the subject of sin can only be an individual person, and that even if each individual member of the Church were a sinner, the Church as such could not be called sinful, since as a supra-individual and transcendent personality it is more than the sum of Christian individuals (as which it is regarded for the most part in Protestant theology). So Charles Journet says: "The Church, which is not without sinners, is nevertheless without sin."[29]

[27] *Constitutiones, Decreta, Declarationes* (see above, note 14), p. 916.
[28] *Osservatore Romano,* 19 October 1963.
[29] *L'Église du Verbe Incarné,* II. *Sa structure interne et son unité catholique* (1951), p. 904.

Y. Congar sums up this view as follows: "In this concrete sense (that is, as a particular community of saints, governed by the bishops and the Pope, but also in the sense of its ruling élite, its intellectuals, etc.) one can ascribe to the Church acts of meanness, reaction, and omission, historical failings in short; but it should be noted that in so far as it is a matter of sins of commission or omission, as sins in the moral sense these must be ascribed to the persons who commit them, and not to the Church, which cannot be the subject of these sins."[30] Other Catholic theologians come closer to the view held in Protestant theology, and see the Church as *simul justa et peccatrix*.[31] In his study entitled *Casta Meretrix* H. U. von Balthasar produces numerous testimonies from the patristic period and the Middle Ages which show that at these periods the Church (as a concrete community of sinful believers) was widely regarded as holy and sinful at the same time.[32] The Constitution on the Church of the Second Vatican Council contains a statement which approaches this view, saying of the Church, and not merely of individual believers: "The Church . . . is at the same time holy and always in need of being purified, and incessantly pursues the path of penance and renewal" (Article 8).[33]

There are many who will not find it easy to understand how Catholics ascribe good actions to the Church without question, when its representatives resolve and act in a way which is morally good, while there is hesitation in postulating the guilt of the Church when its representatives act sinfully. The whole question is admittedly largely theoretical. What is decisive for the confession of guilt in the Decree on Ecumenism is that it says comprehensively that *we* also share the guilt for the scandal of division, and *we* beseech God and our separated brethren for forgiveness. Again, whereas Article 3 spoke of guilt for the origin of the divisions, this passage refers to the sins which contribute to the continued separation, maintain alienation, and hinder a brotherly relationship among Christians and the growing together of the Churches: unloving and unjust judgment upon fellow Christians and their communities, the imputation of unworthy motives, a hostile arrogance and wounding attitude to other Christians, self-righteous obduracy, intolerance, the lack of a will to understand and of readiness to make atonement, sins of omission, oversights, and neglect of the effort to obtain mutual understanding, contact and co-operation.

The final paragraph of this article sees "the call of the whole Church to holiness", with which Chapter 5 of the Constitution on the Church deals, in the light of efforts for the unity of Christians. The striving to live "purely . . . according to the gospel" as the text puts it here, is not merely a concern for one's own salvation, but essentially a growth in one's relationship with one's own brethren.

---

[30] See *Mystery of the Church* (1960).
[31] Cf. K. Rahner, "Kirche der Sünder", in *Schriften zur Theologie*, VI (1965), pp. 301–20.
[32] H. U. von Balthasar, *Sponsa Verbi. Skizzen zur Theologie*, II (1960), pp. 203–305.
[33] Cf. K. Rahner, "Sündige Kirche nach den Dekreten des Zweiten Vatikanischen Konzils", in *Schriften zur Theologie*, VI (1965), pp. 321–45.

Institutional elements in the Church are there to help the faithful to live according to the gospel; consequently, the renewal of the Church's institutions would be in vain, if it were not accompanied by a more intensive striving on the part of the faithful for holiness of life, a striving which consists essentially of the promotion and practice of unity and brotherly love among all who believe in Christ. This striving makes it possible to see and believe in the Church as what it is in its nature, a community of brethren. The text goes on to mention the profoundest fruit of Christian life, communion with the triune God, which is also the ultimate basis of the unity of the Church, the highest exemplar and source of the mystery of unity, in the words of Article 2. The growth through grace in the bond with the divine exemplar and source of communion among men also leads to a closer link among those who believe in the Father, the Word and the Spirit.

Article 8. The new term *oecumenismus spiritualis,* which is used in the first paragraph of this article, is a translation of the French expression *œcuménisme spirituelle,*[34] which was coined by Paul Couturier of Lyons (1881–1953).[35] Couturier was one of the Catholic pioneers of the ecumenical movement, a charismatic personality who for decades worked above all to make ecumenical efforts spiritually more profound. The Catholic Ecumenical Association derived from him, as does the centre *Unité Chrétienne* in Lyons, which has continued to work in his spirit and is in close contact with the World Council of Churches in Geneva (especially in drawing up common texts for the World Week of Prayer) and which from the very first was represented in the Vatican Secretariat for Unity. Couturier was guided by the conviction that at their profoundest level the divisions between the Churches consist not of differences on the level of theological understanding, but of a breach in the spiritual bond of fraternal communion, which damages the manifestation, willed by Christ, of the mystery of the unity of the Church. Consequently, he emphasized the fundamental significance of spiritual values in the ecumenical effort, and as the decree here expresses it, saw the soul of the whole ecumenical movement in a change of heart, expressed in a life lived according to the gospel and in prayer for unity. It is the intention of the decree, in the face of the danger of a one-sided emphasis on academic efforts for theological understanding and on activity in the organizational sphere, to bring to prominence the religious spirit which must sustain and penetrate all ecumenical efforts. The unity of the Church is a mystery of grace, which in the first instance is effected by the Holy Spirit, and can only come to perfection in its visible form if those who believe in this mystery accept in their innermost being God's offer of grace.[36]

[34] Cf. P. Michalon, *Œcuménisme Spirituel,* Pages documentaires V (1960).
[35] Cf. M. Villain, *L'Abbé Paul Couturier* (1957); P. Michalon, *L'Abbé Paul Couturier et l'unité chrétienne* (1962).
[36] A brief historical account of the different movements of "religious ecumenism" is provided by G. Tavard, *Two Centuries of Ecumenism* (1960).

The second and third paragraphs are concerned with common prayer for the unity of the Church. The first of these speaks of the prayer for unity which is carried out among Catholics, while the next speaks of the common prayer in which Catholics join with non-Catholics. The assumption and foundation of the prayer of believing Christians for unity is the prayer of Christ for the unity of the disciples (Jn 17:11, 21–23). The formulation of the intention of the prayer of Catholics which is given in the text is a conscious testimony to a change in Catholic thought. Whereas prayer was offered in the past for the return of all separated Christians to the one flock of Peter, the text of the decree speaks of the prayer for the unity of the Church, which Christ himself besought of his Father. Here too the idea of a return is consciously avoided, and not merely in order to avoid shocking other Christians or in order to have a formula of prayer in which non-Catholic Christians can also participate. The decisive reason lies rather in a change of ecclesiological outlook; the unity of the Church is a mystery which on the one hand is already realized, but on the other hand must be more perfectly realized: non-Catholic Christians are not simply outside the community of the Church, but should grow further into this unity, just as Catholics in their own way must grow further into the unity of the Church. Thus the new formulation of prayer for unity is a reflection of the ecclesiology which is found in the Constitution on the Church and the Decree on Ecumenism. The nature of the change involved can be seen if one compares the form of prayer used by the founder of the Week of Prayer for Unity, P. J. F. Wattson (1863–1940), with that introduced by Abbé Couturier. Wattson, a High Church Anglican clergyman in the U.S.A., who in 1909 joined the Catholic Church together with the Anglican Brotherhood and Sisterhood of the Atonement which he had founded, had already begun, in 1908, the World Octave of Prayer (18–25 January) with a number of Anglican and Catholic parishes. This was later approved and encouraged by the Popes, and spread in the whole Catholic Church (and with a different phrasing of its intentions, also in the other Christian Churches throughout the world). The intention of the prayers formulated by Wattson was based on the idea of the return of all separated Christians into the one fold of Peter. The intentions for each day of the Octave concerned the return of all separated Christians to the Catholic Church, the return of Eastern Christians, Anglicans, the Protestants of Europe, the Protestants of America, the return of non-practising Catholics to the practice of religion, the conversion of the Jews, and the conversion of the whole world. Père Couturier changed the "World Octave of Prayer for the Unity of the Church" into the "World Week of Prayer (because "octave" is an exclusively Catholic term) of Christians for Christian Unity" and proposed, instead of the word "return", a formula which could be accepted not only by Catholics, but by all Christians: the prayer was to be "that the visible unity of the kingdom of God may come, as Christ willed it and through the means which he willed". The intentions of each day were to be: the unity of all Christians, the sanctification of Catholics, of the Orthodox, of Anglicans, of Protestants, of Jews, of non-Christians, and the unity of all men in the love and the truth of Christ. Thus it became possible for Christians of all denominations to unite in prayer with the same intention.

The third paragraph is not content with merely proposing the same intention for the prayer of all Christians, but also recommends common prayer on the part of Catholics with their separated brethren. The occasions which the text suggests — prayers "for unity" (this refers particularly to the World Week of Prayer) and ecumenical gatherings — are intended only to be examples. Even when the intention of the prayer is not the unity of Christians, the common prayer of Catholics with other Christians is desirable, because common prayer as such already binds them together. The decree turns here to a basic idea which it has often emphasized already, that there still exists a real unity among all Christians, and that this must be made visible. But common prayer itself is an effective testimony to the existing unity, and one which in its turn strengthens these bonds. Mention is made of the ultimate basis of this unity, Christ, who is present wherever two or three gather together in his name (Mt 18:20). Yet constant objections were raised, even in the Council, against common prayer on the part of Christians of different denominations: the different interpretations which individual denominations give to the same prayers prevent them from being uttered in common. Thus at first there were reservations on the Catholic side even against saying the Lord's Prayer in common with Protestants. After this had been conceded by the instruction of the Holy Office in 1949, it was believed that one ought not to say the Creed in common, since in particular the clause concerning the "One, Holy, Catholic and Apostolic Church" was differently understood by different denominations.

But since then, numerous prayers have come into common use besides the Lord's Prayer and the Creed. Representatives of the Faith and Order department of the World Council of Churches of Geneva and of the Catholic Centre at Lyons have produced for many years a common booklet of prayers for every World Week of Prayer, containing scriptural texts, meditations, prayers and petitions, which is used at the present day not merely within individual denominations, but often also in common services of readings and prayers by Christians of different denominations. It is easy to multiply examples. These activities were encouraged by the example of Paul VI, who with many of the Council Fathers held a common service of lessons and prayers with the non-Catholic observers at the end of the last session of the Council (3 December 1965) in the Basilica of St. Paul, consisting of scriptural readings, addresses, and hymns and prayers in common. There are undoubtedly prayers which express the specific beliefs of a particular Church and in which Christians of other denominations cannot take part (e.g., Catholic prayers to Mary and the saints). But there are also prayers, the statements of which are understood by all Churches in essentially the same sense. As far as prayers are concerned which are said in the same words by different denominations, but where individual Churches understand their statement, at least partly in a different sense, one ought first to ask whether the different interpretations are such as to divide the Church, or merely represent a difference in theology. When it is a question of a different dogmatic under-standing of the statements of prayer, there is always a basic common theme which is also present, and which can be expressed in common prayer (thus, for example, when Catholics and Protestants speak of grace while praying in common). If one examines from this point of view the common texts used for the World Week of Prayer, one can find in them numerous truths of Christian revelation which Christians of different denominations can profess in common in prayer; for prayer is not in fact theology, but an adoring, praising, thanking, trusting, beseeching and interceding address to God.

Thus G. Thils rightly states: "Together, we can worship the Father, the Word, and the Spirit, the source of all unity. Together we can believe and hope in the city of God, gathering together in glory all the elect of the Father. Together we can proclaim that Jesus Christ, God and Saviour, is the Alpha and Omega of all unity. Together we can thank God for the reception of the good news of his word, the gospel of peace. Together we rejoice to be united in baptism. Together we can reject the sins we have committed against unity. Together we can adore the ways of the Lord and ask him to make us sensitive to his impulses with regard to unity."[37] Thus it is natural that the Ecumenical Directory published by the Secretariat for Unity contains a far-reaching recommendation of prayer in common by Catholics and other Christians (*Pars prima*, no. 32–37, Rome, 1967).

There is, however, a form of the Church's prayer in which communion between denominations is excluded, or is only possible in special cases. This is discussed in the next paragraph of this article, which deals with what is known as *communicatio in sacris*. This concept, the main role of which has hitherto been in canon law and moral theology, is not defined more closely in the Decree on Ecumenism. We may adopt here the definitions given in the Ecumenical Directory. *Communicatio in sacris* is a *species* included in the *genus* of *communicatio in spiritualibus,* which is therefore the wider concept. The Directory says of the latter: "Communion in spiritual matters *(communicatio in spiritualibus)* means all prayers offered in common, the common use of sacred things or places, and all liturgical communion, *communicatio in sacris* in the true and proper sense." What is recommended in the third paragraph of Article 8 of the Decree on Ecumenism falls within the concept of *communicatio in spiritualibus,* without being *communicatio in sacris.* The Directory says of the latter: "*Communicatio in sacris* takes place, when anyone takes part in any act of liturgical worship or in the sacraments of (another) Church or ecclesial community." It adds the following further explanation: "By 'liturgical worship' *(cultus liturgicus)* is

---

[37] *Le Décret sur l'œcuménisme du deuxième Concile du Vatican* (1965), pp. 107 f. Cf. also G. Thils, *Histoire doctrinale du mouvement œcuménique* (2nd ed., 1963), pp. 322–4.

meant worship ordered according to the books, rules, or usages of any Church or community, which is conducted by a minister or other person authorized by this Church or community, in so far as he is carrying out his ministry."

Of their nature the divisions of the Church have always brought about the breakdown of the worshipping community, so that the members of one community were excluded from the worship and sacramental action of the other. But it is natural that in the course of the ecumenical movement the question has constantly recurred, whether, under what conditions, and to what degree communion in worship and the sacraments could be restored between separated Churches. The scandal of separation is constantly manifested in its most blatant form in separate worship. In the conferences and assemblies of the World Council of Churches, the problem of intercommunion has been vehemently discussed. As is well known, many member Churches of the World Council do not have any liturgical or sacramental communion with one another. But in the course of time, such a communion has been brought about between individual Churches to varying degrees. Since the third Faith and Order Conference in Lund (1952)[38] a whole scale of concepts has come into use: full eucharistic communion between different Churches; intercommunion and intercelebration (where ordained clergy have the right to minister at the altar of other denominations); intercommunion (without intercelebration; on the basis of an agreement between the denominations concerned, members of different denominations have a mutual right to Communion); open communion (the members of other denominations are admitted to the Eucharist by a given denomination); mutual open communion (mutual admission to the Eucharist is permitted without a formal agreement by the denominations concerned); limited open communion (mutual admission to the Eucharist under certain conditions, and in a limited context); closed communion (only members of a particular Church are admitted to Communion in it).

The practice which obtained in the Catholic Church up to Vatican II was very strict: anyone who did not share the full faith of the Catholic Church and was not in communion with the Pope and the episcopate of the Catholic Church, could not take an active part in Catholic worship, and was not admitted to Communion and the other sacraments, while in turn Catholics were not permitted to take part in the worship of other denominations and to receive the sacraments in other communities. This strict attitude, which was laid down in canon law (cf. e.g., *CIC,* can. 732, § 2, and can. 1258; marriage before a non-Catholic minister was punished by excommunication: can. 2319, § 1), was based on an

---

[38] The report on intercommunion of the Third World Conference of Faith and Order in Lund (15–28 August 1952) expressed its awareness of the fundamental and complicated questions of faith and order involved in attempting greater unity at the Lord's Table. The report stated that it was not merely a question of human pride or narrow-mindedness: the difficulties derived from more profound differences of conviction concerning the nature of the Church and the sacraments, and these differences were a cause of great perplexity.

ecclesiology which still did not recognize that other Christian communities possess the character of Churches. It was particularly remarkable with regard to the Orthodox Churches, where the Catholic Church had always recognized the validity of the sacraments and their episcopal and priestly ministry. This former strict attitude could not be reconciled with the new ecclesiological outlook which came in with the Council. This change is expressed in the present article in the Decree on Ecumenism. The undiscriminating view which is sometimes put forward that *communicatio in sacris* (the Latin technical term is more exact than a rendering such as "common worship") is an appropriate means for the restoration of Christian unity is of course rightly rejected. Against such a view it is firmly emphasized that a distinction must be made (by contrast with a practice carried out *indiscriminatim*): the general participation in the worship and sacraments of other Churches, permitted with regard to all other Churches and in all cases, is not possible, but in some cases it is nevertheless permitted and even recommended.

As the Ecumenical Directory makes clear, the distinction demanded is principally that which must be made between the separated Eastern Churches with their valid sacraments and valid priesthood, and other separated communities. The Decree on Eastern Catholic Churches recommends a less strict practice with regard to the separated Eastern Churches (Articles 26–29), and its provisions were taken even further in the broad interpretation put upon them in the Ecumenical Directory of the Secretariat for Unity (Part 1, Articles 39–54). Here the basic principle is emphasized that the practice should be mutual (Article 43) and it is laid down that care should be taken to avoid any suspicion of proselytism (Article 46). A general permission is given, under certain conditions, for the mutual reception of the sacraments of penance, holy Communion, and holy unction, and participation in the sacred liturgy. The Ecumenical Directory provides for a much more restricted *communicatio in sacris* with regard to other separated brethren. This is dealt with in Articles 55–63. Permission is given to administer to a separated fellow-Christian in danger of death or in great distress (persecution, imprisonment) the sacraments of holy Communion, penance and unction, "if the separated brother cannot go to a minister of his own community, and of his own accord requests the sacraments from the Catholic priest, and in so far as he expresses a belief, with regard to these sacraments alone, in accordance with the faith of the Church, and has the right inner disposition. In other cases of urgent need, the ordinary or the episcopal conference is to decide" (Article 55). The distinction which is made with regard to the Eastern Churches is expressed above all in the following provision: "But a Catholic, who finds himself in the same position, may only request the sacraments from a minister who has validly received priestly ordination" (*ibid.* One may think in particular here of the Old Catholic Church). A relaxation of previous practice is found in the provision in the Directory that in certain cases Catholics may take part in the common responses, hymns and acts in the worship of other communities, although the reception of the Eucharist is always excluded. "The same is true in turn of the way in which separated brethren may take part in worship in Catholic churches" (Article 59).

The Decree on Ecumenism, which does not go into details of practice, provides the doctrinal basis for this new practice, by putting forward two principles which are decisive for the whole question. The first principle is that liturgical worship and the sacraments are signs of the (already existing) unity of the Church. This is true above all of the Eucharist: those who go to Communion together are bearing witness to the fact that they are one in faith. The Constitution on the Church says of the Eucharist: "Strengthened anew at the Holy Table by the Body of Christ, they (the faithful) manifest in a practical way that unity of God's People which is suitably signified and wondrously brought about by this most awesome sacrament" (Article 11). The second principle is that liturgical worship and the sacraments are means of grace for the faithful. Here it must be borne in mind that worship and the sacraments, in so far as they impart grace and so strengthen the bond with God, also serve to promote the unity of the Church, and are therefore means for the growth of unity. The attitude of the Church to the question of *communicatio in sacris* is determined by these two principles. If one considers the first principle, it follows that in most cases *(plerumque)* common worship is not possible, because the necessary unity of faith does not exist between the Catholic Church and other Churches. A sacramental communion set up without qualification would give the illusion of a unity which does not exist. But the word *plerumque* refers to a case in which, according to the Catholic view, unity is already sufficiently realized for *communicatio in sacris* to be possible in certain circumstances and under particular conditions, that of the Orthodox Churches. The Decree on Eastern Catholic Churches and the Ecumenical Directory define the circumstances and conditions more precisely. But one may also think of the Old Catholic Church with its valid priesthood and seven valid sacraments. When one considers the second principle, it follows that in particular cases (more precisely defined in the Ecumenical Directory) liturgical and sacramental communion is also possible and desirable between the Catholic Church and those Churches which have a less close communion of belief with the Catholic Church than the Eastern Churches, and with regard to whom the first principle would in itself prevent common worship (the Churches of the Reformation). Thus from these two principles the concrete attitude cannot in fact be determined so unambiguously that there is no need for the Church authorities to order it in more precise detail according to the circumstances of the time, the place and the persons concerned. But in the practical ordering of the matter, which is mentioned at the end of the article, centralism is avoided: the diocesan bishops are competent and responsible in the matter, in so far as particular provisions are not issued by the episcopal conference, or by the Holy See.

Article 9. The text passes from the sphere of spirituality to that of the intellect, to a demand for a better understanding of the outlook of separated brethren. The demand is addressed to Catholics, but the whole text reveals a desire that non-Catholic Christians may in their turn achieve a similar better understanding of the Catholic Church. Thus the intention is for better mutual understanding. In reading these appeals, one must constantly bear in mind that the demand made by this article (like other demands in Chapter II) is made with the desire that the already existing unity of the Church may be more clearly manifested and at the same time advanced. A better mutual understanding will also make Christians aware of how they are joined together, and will help to increase the fraternal bond between them. The first sentence is addressed to the Catholic faithful in general, whereas the rest of the passage, indirectly at least, is addressed to experts who are in a position to make a more profound study. It is characteristic that in the very first sentence the text does not say that one must learn to know the doctrine of other Christians, as might have been said at an earlier period. What is said is much more than this, that there should be a better understanding of the *animus* of others; the rich conceptual content of this word is hard to translate. The demand for a better understanding of the *animus* of others, which at a period when Christians of different denominations were opposed or simply practised their faith in indifference to each other, was not possible, and is lacking or inadequate among most Catholics even at the present day, asks a great deal, and requires an effort going further than mere knowledge of doctrine, though even the latter requires more effort at the present day than in the past. Most Catholics are not in a position to carry out the fundamental and extensive study which is demanded further on in the text. Apart from the knowledge which they can obtain themselves by meetings, dialogue, occasional attendance at the worship of others, by reading and in other ways, a better understanding of "the outlook of our separated brethren" must be mediated to them by those who are properly prepared for this study *(debito modo preparati)* and who possess the necessary academic ability for dialogue with representatives of other Churches.

The description of the study of other Churches and dialogue with their representatives which this article gives from the second sentence on (continuing the discussion of the nature of this dialogue in Article 4) obviously reflects the experiences and understanding of Catholic ecumenists who have devoted themselves for several decades to this study and dialogue. It is very characteristic of the change from the period of polemic controversy to that of ecumenical dialogue. Study must be carried out not merely in accordance with the truth, but with that loving spirit of goodwill, without which the personal truth which is at issue here cannot be truly apprehended. *Veritatem facientes in caritate* (Eph 4:15). Particularly characteristic is the description of the object of study. This is not merely the doctrine of other Churches, even though that is undoubtedly of fundamental importance. But a Church is more than merely doctrine, and doctrine is not the whole concrete reality of the being and life of a Church.

Rather, the object of study is everything in which the *animus* of other Christians is expressed, and by which it is formed: doctrine and history, spiritual and liturgical life, religious psychology and cultural background. Thus what must be sought is a comprehensive understanding of the total concrete reality of other Churches, for this is the only way in which the study of another Church can be conducted *secundum veritatem*. Again, the principle emphasized in the text, *par cum pari agat,* is of great value for the ecumenical meetings which are particularly recommended for this study: dialogue must be conducted on a level where each can deal with the other on an equal footing. This principle, the observance of which is essential to ecumenical dialogue, had already been laid down in the instruction of the Holy Office on 20 December 1949. Consequently the Secretariat for Unity could introduce it into the conciliar text without difficulty by appealing to this Instruction.

The principle naturally does not mean that those who take part in a dialogue should regard the view and interpretations of the faith held by all Churches in a relativist and indifferentist fashion, as though all were equally true and of equal value, for an ecumenical dialogue would be meaningless if everyone who took part did not firmly profess the faith of his own Church. Rather, what the principle states is that with regard to this dialogue, the same status must be accorded to all who take part, and that no one should be allowed any privileges over the others. The situation must not be that some come as *beati possidentes* and as teachers, while the others are there only to hear and to learn; instead, all have the same right to speak and the same duty to listen. This is the only way to obtain a real insight into the point of view of another. The mention in the text of "authoritative guidance" from Church authority obviously does not mean constant surveillance, authoritarian direction and continual intervention on the part of Church authority, but a contact between the leaders of the Church and other members of the Church, which is obviously necessary for responsible action. It must also be noted that the decree requires from those who take part a thorough knowledge of the matter and true competence *(vere periti sint)*. This is a protection against the dilettante approach which easily arises when something which is good in itself becomes fashionable. Unlike the instruction of 1949, the decree rightly does not specify priests as the experts concerned, for in the first place there are at the present day an increasing number of lay theologians, who are no less competent at theology than priests, and secondly, the subject of interdenominational discussions need not necessarily be theological problems, for they may also deal with other matters with which the different Churches are concerned, such as non-theological factors in their separation, the sociological situation of Christianity at the present day, the legal status of the Churches in the state, questions of charitable work and Christian education, and any sphere where theological training does not give the necessary competence. Thus competence here cannot simply be equated with an adequate ability in theology.

When the last sentence of the article mentions as the fruit of dialogue that the partners on one side obtain a better understanding of the mode of thought and belief of the other, one might regret the absence of a statement that we Catholics can better learn to understand our own faith through such dialogue, and obtain a more profound understanding of revealed truth. But this statement is contained, if not sufficiently clearly, in that of the last sentence but one, which emphasizes that by dialogue "the true posture *(condicio)* of the Catholic Church" will emerge still more clearly. This does not mean that only those who take part on the other side in the dialogue will understand this *condicio* more clearly: it is undoubtedly possible for this to be recognized more clearly by the Catholic partners as well, through the confrontation which takes place in the dialogue with the *condicio* of the other Church. The Latin word *condicio* signifies not merely the outward "situation" of the Catholic Church in the present world, but primarily its inner condition, its own internal disposition, and the whole way in which it is constituted. Thus, for example, the dialogue can lead to the Catholic participants becoming aware, or at least becoming more clearly aware, that the usual Catholic presentation of doctrine is one-sided in one respect or other, and must be supplemented by aspects which are given greater prominence in another Church, and that some institutional elements of the Catholic Church are conditioned by history, are not sufficiently in accordance with the demands of the gospel, and must therefore undergo a change, etc. It is possible to give many concrete examples of the way in which the results of ecumenical dialogue have assisted Catholics to understand themselves in this way. We may also note that Part II of the Ecumenical Directory deals with the ecumenical dialogue in a significantly more detailed and more fundamental way than was possible in the Decree on Ecumenism.

Article 10. If an ecumenical outlook is to pervade the whole communion of the Church and if all the faithful are to be seized by a desire for the growing closer together and the union of the Church, the first concern must be for ecumenical orientation in the training of the Church's ministry. Article 10 of the decree is devoted to this end. "It is upon the formation which priests receive that the necessary instruction and spiritual formation of the faithful and of religious depend so very greatly" (second paragraph). The preaching and teaching activity of the clergy, the way in which they present Catholic doctrine and speak about the other Christians with whom innumerable Catholics must live and work together every day, and the example of their own attitude towards non-Catholics, are of decisive importance to the attitude of Catholics towards their non-Catholic fellow Christians, and for their knowledge and judgment about other Churches. It is consequently of the greatest importance to the future of the ecumenical movement in the Catholic Church, that from the first the theological formation of "future bishops and priests" in the seminaries, at the theological faculties of the universities, and in other places where their formation takes place, should be carried out entirely in an ecumenical spirit. This does not

111

mean in the first instance that a distinct department of "ecumenical studies" should be set in each of these institutions, but rather that an ecumenical spirit must pervade all theological disciplines: exegesis, dogmatics, moral theology, Church history, canon law, pastoral theology, and the theology of the spiritual life. What is at issue is the "ecumenical dimension" of the whole of Catholic theology. This means that in every department of study, its relationship to the mystery of the unity of the Church must be borne in mind and made clear, and that in every sphere of theology serious attention must be paid to the understanding expressed in the Decree on Ecumenism and in the Constitution on the Church, that genuine Christian endowments and Christian life are also to be found in other Christian communities, and that the one Church of Christ is also present in them.

Thus Catholic theology must bear constantly in mind the whole of Christianity, and must participate in the thought of other Christians in order to discover what the testimony of their doctrine and life has to tell to us Catholics. Catholic theology must discover and set forth the Christian heritage of truth and spirituality which is common to all Christian Churches, and must create an awareness of the doctrinal richness and spiritual endowments which are characteristic of other Christian communities, and which can lead to a deeper understanding of the true catholicity of the Church. Those who are preparing for the priesthood must learn to pay attention to the "hierarchy" of the truths of revelation, must be protected against the spirit of uniformity, and must be made familiar with the idea that a justifiable diversity is possible in the way in which Christianity is expressed and in the form taken by the Church, and that there is also a justifiable and desirable diversity possible in theology, which enriches the Church and theology and protects it from a narrow-mindedness which impoverishes it. A fundamental aspect of the ecumenical outlook in theology is a firmer biblical and patristic orientation, a determined recourse to the sources common to the whole of Christianity *(ressourcement)*. The Constitution on Revelation states: "Sacred theology rests on the written word of God, together with sacred tradition, as its primary and perpetual foundation. By scrutinizing in the light of faith all truth stored up in the mystery of Christ, theology is most powerfully strengthened and constantly rejuvenated by that word. For the sacred Scriptures contain the word of God and, since they are inspired, really are the word of God; and so the study of the sacred page is, as it were, the soul of sacred theology" (Article 24). That decree says the same of the formation of priests (Article 16). The Decree on Ecumenism is certainly justified in stressing especially that the teaching of history should also be carried out from an ecumenical point of view. The nature and characteristics of different Churches can only be understood from their origins and historical development. A polemical and apologetic Catholic historiography has often led to a one-sided and unjust presentation of what took place at the moment of division between Churches, and to a purely negative judgment upon those who initiated the movement which led to the separation. That is why the decree demands historical instruction which "may more accurately correspond to the facts of the case" and which, for example, clearly sets forth the genuine intentions of the Eastern Churches in their separation from Rome, the genuinely Christian impulses at the Reformation and the religious character of the Reformers, and does not omit to describe the faults committed on the Catholic side. The text of the decree specifically rejects theology which is conducted polemically *(non polemice)*. This naturally does not imply the blurring of doctrinal differences or of the errors which according to Catholic conviction are to be found in other Churches; rather, it is meant as a warning against considering the representatives of other communities merely as *adversarii,* oversimplifying and schematizing their views in such a way that they can be refuted as easily as possible, and overlooking their more profound intentions and the questions which they have to pose to Catholic theology.

The demands made in the Decree on Ecumenism are also reflected in the Decree on Priestly Formation, which states in Article 16: "According to an opportune evaluation of the conditions of various regions, students should be led to a more adequate understanding of the Churches and ecclesial communities separated from the Roman Apostolic See. Thus the students can contribute to the restoration of unity among all Christians according to the directives of this sacred Synod." Part II of the Ecumenical Directory of the Secretariat for Unity gives a more extensive presentation of the ideas of this article; it deals with the spiritual and intellectual formation of candidates for the priesthood, and describes the ecumenical aspects of individual branches of theology. It also recommends a special course in ecumenical studies, which should include instruction in the knowledge of history of the ecumenical movement, its doctrinal principles, its aims and its methods, and the particular problems it presents, and should also give an introduction to the knowledge of different Christian Churches. But the main accent is placed upon the "ecumenical dimension" of the whole of theology.

The second paragraph of the article refers to the particular importance of an ecumenical orientation of Catholics who are engaged in missionary work. This reference must be seen in the light of the renewed awareness brought about by the Council that missionary work is not a secondary or supplementary task of the Church, but belongs so much to the essence of the Church, that it is impossible to separate the Church and its mission from each other. But if the Church as a whole is essentially missionary in character, that is, if it is sent to preach the gospel and to bear witness to that part of humanity which is not yet Christian, then the questions of the fragmentation of Christianity and of the unity of the Church, the questions of ecumenism, are posed with special urgency with regard to missions. As the sacrament of unity, the Church has the task of leading men to unity in Christ. But if the Christians who have to carry out this task — that is, not merely Catholic Christians, but Christians of all denominations, since the one Church is present in all of them — are separated from each other, then fundamental damage is done to the fulfilment of the unifying task

113

of the Church as the sacrament of unity. Christianity ought to be manifested as a unity above all in the missions, if the mission it has from God is to be understood by non-Christian nations. The effect of the divisions in Christianity is particularly catastrophic in the missionary work of the Church. For the sake of its missionary vocation, the Church must therefore regard itself as particularly constrained to create an awareness of the unity which already exists among Christians, and to promote it with all its might. If the inseparable link between the mission and the unity of the Church is perceived, it becomes evident that at the Council, in association with the renewal of the Church's understanding of itself, the problems of ecumenism and the missions were necessarily posed as central questions. The unity of ecumenism and the Church's mission was recognized from the very first in the ecumenical movement outside the Catholic Church, and was ultimately given organizational expression by the incorporation of the International Missionary Council into the World Council of Churches, at New Delhi in 1961. Against this background, the specific reference made in the Decree on Ecumenism to Catholics engaged in missionary work is seen in its true light. It is a demand that the idea of competition and the rivalries between missionary Churches should be overcome in an ecumenical spirit, that the importance of non-Catholic missions for the evangelization of non-Christian nations should be recognized, that witness should be borne to solidarity with them by fraternal co-operation, and that the unity of Christians should be promoted with the missionary field, with its own special interest in unity particularly in mind.

Article 11. The text once again takes up the idea of the dialogue between Catholic and non-Catholic Christians, and discusses the question how the Catholic partners in this dialogue should express their own faith. The statement distinguishes between faith itself and the way in which it is formulated, which is of decisive importance for mutual understanding. For centuries too little attention has been paid to the importance of the form of doctrinal statements, so that those who were addressing each other have completely failed to make themselves understood. Bishop E. J. De Smedt referred to this fact in his famous speech of 19 November 1962 concerning ecumenical dialogue (during the debate on the schema on the Sources of Revelation): "For centuries we Catholics believed that it was sufficient to give a straightforward explanation of our own faith. On both sides Christians formulated their doctrine in their own language and from their own point of view. This made it difficult for non-Catholics to understand what Catholics were saying, and we could not understand what the others meant. The method of 'clearly affirming the truth' could bring no progress in the direction of a reconciliation. On the contrary, prejudices, accusations, mistrust, quarrels and polemic disputes became increasingly numerous on both sides."[39] Bishop De Smedt said concerning the

[39] Quoted from J. C. Hampe, *Ende der Gegenreformation? Das Konzil. Dokumente und Deutung* (1964), pp. 283 f.

method of ecumenical dialogue: "The distinctive feature of this method is that it is not limited to a simple affirmation of the truth, but that it also gives some thought to how a truth of faith can be so presented that others may understand it. Christians of different denominations help each other in this dialogue to obtain an increasingly better understanding of doctrines which are not their own." The beginning of this article refers to these facts when it states: "The manner and order in which Catholic belief is expressed should in no way become an obstacle to dialogue with our brethren." The sentences of the first paragraph which follow demand that the whole of Catholic doctrine should be clearly presented, and warn against a false irenicism. This warning against false irenicism was constantly and rightly repeated at the Council. Non-Catholic ecumenists also constantly warn against the mistaken view that the ecumenical dialogue demands that the doctrines which divide the Church should be concealed and kept in the background "for the sake of peace and quiet". In fact ill service is rendered to the cause of ecumenism by the concealing, blurring over or blunting of the significance which the Church gives to a doctrine. Otherwise dialogue would become superficial and disloyal, and lead to illusory agreement. The differences must be taken seriously. The non-Catholic partners in dialogue have the right to hear the whole of Catholic doctrine put forward by the Catholic partners, just as we Catholics expect of other Christians that they do not hide any of their doctrine from us. In the speech quoted above Bishop De Smedt said on this subject: "Above all, any trace of indifferentism must be excluded. An ecumenical statement should contain the whole and complete Catholic doctrine in a particular field, in loyalty to the truth. For how are non-Catholics to know what the Catholic faith really teaches if the doctrine which we proclaim is presented incompletely, or in a distorted or confused way? It has been asserted that to speak ecumenically prevents a full profession of the truth. Anyone who asserts this understands nothing about the true nature of ecumenical dialogue. This dialogue is not undertaken in order that both sides may deceive each other."[40]

The true ecumenical attitude was characterized by the then General Secretary of the World Council of Churches, W. Visser 't Hooft, when he received Cardinal Bea in Geneva on 18 February 1965: "We are not watering down our disagreements. We do not see how we can be reconciled with each other. The ecumenical movement is not based upon the impression that the disagreements are in the process of disappearing. It is based on the conviction that in spite of the differences we can talk together, and where possible work together."[41] While there is a warning against a false irenicism, there is also a true, genuine and necessary irenicism.

The whole Decree on Ecumenism is pervaded by this true irenical spirit, which avoids polemic, practises brotherly love in word and act, recognizes what

[40] *Ibid.*, p. 284.
[41] Quoted from *Herder-Korrespondenz* 19 (1965), p. 313.

is good and true wherever it is to be found, and constantly recognizes and emphasizes what it held in common. If the partners in the dialogue are to have a right understanding of Catholic doctrine, it must not only be set forth fully, but, in the words of the second paragraph, more profoundly *(profundius)*, more correctly and more precisely *(rectius)*, and explained, unfolded *(explicanda)* and set forth in a language which the partners in dialogue can understand. These statements once again reflect the experience of ecumenists who for decades have carried on a theological dialogue with representatives of other denominations; the dialogue repeatedly forced the partners on both sides to undertake a more fundamental reflection upon their own point of view, to make more precise statements with clearer distinctions, to use more comprehensible language, and in short, to speak, in the words of the text of the decree, *profundius, rectius, comprehensibiliter.* *Profundius* means that a superfical presentation cannot reveal the true and deeper sense of a doctrine of the Church. The mere repetition and piling up of conciliar definitions and papal doctrinal utterances ("Denzinger theology") and the normal presentation of theological text-books is of no value to ecumenical dialogue. The questions are more complex than appears at first. The historical situation in which doctrinal statements were formulated must be examined, a study must be made of the ultimate intentions of the magisterium in formulating dogma (and the questions at issue at the present day must not be projected back into a previous age), and the deeper links between individual doctrines, and their connection with the central concern of Christian revelation must be demonstrated. Here it must be borne in mind once again that the dogmas formulated by the Councils and Popes, which were mostly defined in opposition to errors, and for this very reason do not set forth all aspects of revealed truth, do not contain the whole of Catholic doctrine, and therefore do not exhaust its deeper meaning, and that the definitions must be supplemented, constantly thought out anew and interpreted on the basis of other testimonies to tradition and above all on the basis of holy Scripture. The Second Vatican Council in many respects undertook a more profound presentation of Catholic doctrine in this way, especially in the Dogmatic Constitutions on the Church and on Divine Revelation.

Rectius signifies that ecumenical dialogue demands more careful distinctions in thought and a more precise expression than has been found in popular presentations of Catholic doctrine. For example, too broad an interpretation of the axiom *extra ecclesiam nulla salus* does not properly reflect the sense of Catholic doctrine. The presentation of theological questions in a journalistic way may be ingenious and stimulating, and justified in its place, but lacks the necessary precision for a serious dialogue between denominations. A correct and precise presentation of Catholic doctrine must renounce antithetical slogans and glib schematizations ("here is the Church of the sacrament and of tradition — there is the Church of the word and holy Scripture"). It must distinguish between ultimately binding doctrinal decisions, doctrinal statements of less authority, and theological opinions; between the enduring content of a doctrine and the form it takes, which depends upon the time at which it was formulated. The example of the dispute concerning Scripture and tradition at the Council has shown that failure to pay attention to historical circumstances, together with an interpretation of doctrinal statements which has become traditional, and which makes use of theological formulae which have become habitual *(duo fontes revelationis, partim — partim)*, does not provide a proper representation of the true doctrine of the Church (the unique status of holy Scripture in the life of the Church). A more exact presentation of the Church's true doctrine can often remove misunderstandings on the part of the other partners in the dialogue, and may perhaps show that the lines of demarcation are not so firmly drawn, and the disagreements not so deep as has hitherto been supposed (e.g., in the doctrine of justification or in the doctrine of the sufficiency or insufficiency of holy Scripture).

Sermone comprehensibili: the problem of language and therefore that of mutual understanding has not been clearly perceived until recently. The ecumenical dialogue has shown that in different denominations and in the theologies they profess different languages and different terminologies can be developed, which make mutual understanding difficult. Concepts are used which are not familiar to the others, the same words are used with a different meaning, or different concepts are used with the same meaning. Mutual understanding requires a "translation" into the other "language", although the same terms are being used. "We must look to see whether our way of speaking does not contain assertions and formulations which are difficult for non-Catholics to understand. Here I might emphasize that the scholastic language and doctrinal method which is still in use in many theological schools provides a serious difficulty to non-Catholics, and only too often provokes errors and prejudices on their part. The same is true of our abstract and purely intellectual style, which Eastern Christians cannot understand. On the other hand, many difficulties, prejudices and confusions would be avoided if we preferred the language of the Bible and the Fathers of the Church" (Bishop De Smedt in the speech quoted above).[42] Naturally, it is not simply a question of returning to the language of the Bible, but rather of a closer orientation to the thought and language of holy Scripture.

The third paragraph begins by describing true ecumenism: loyalty to the doctrine of the Church, love for truth, charity and humility must characterize those that take part in ecumenical dialogue. We must not overlook the observation that this dialogue means inquiring, together with separated brethren, into the truth of revelation *(una cum fratribus seiunctis)*. This represents a new view by comparison with the period in which the theologians of one denomination never thought of relying on the co-operation of theologians of other denomina-

---

[42] Quoted from J. G. Hampe, *op. cit.,* p. 285.

tions or of being able to attain with their help "to a deeper realization and a clearer expression of the unfathomable riches of Christ".[43]

The statement which follows, that "in Catholic teaching there exists an order or 'hierarchy' of truths", is of great importance.[44] The Council's profession of this fact, which was included in this paragraph only in the final redaction of the text, is the most important of all the changes and additions made on the basis of the *modi*, and was very well received on the non-Catholic side, and greeted with great satisfaction. In fact the picture of the Catholic Church as seen by non-Catholic Christians is largely determined by "secondary" and "tertiary" features of Catholic doctrine and similarly of Catholic practice, e.g., by the doctrine and practice of the veneration of the saints, or of indulgences (especially in the form which has been in use since the Middle Ages). A one-sided emphasis on the formal aspects of doctrines in opposition to the denial that they are in fact truths of revelation, could help to give the impression that for the Catholic Church all doctrines, or the realities which they express, are on the same level, with the result that the central issue of revelation is obscured and neglected. One should not wonder that it is difficult for non-Catholics to see that the main issue and a proper balance has been maintained in the doctrine and practice of the Catholic Church if, for example, the invoking of the saints leaves little room for prayer to God through Christ, or when Mariological literature grows apace and fills whole libraries, while christological and soteriological questions are neglected. Perhaps the observation of Suffragan Bishop S. A. Leven of San Antonio (USA) in a speech in the Council may be a rhetorical exaggeration: "There are Fathers who speak as though the sole text in holy Scripture was v. 18 of Chapter 16 of the Gospel of Matthew, 'You are Peter, and on this rock I will build my church'";[45] but it points to a false emphasis which exists within the Catholic Church and which has a decisive effect on the judgment of non-Catholic Christians upon the Catholic Church. The statement

---

[43] For the possibility and necessity of ecumenical dialogue cf., for example, the views expressed by the Reformed theologian J. L. Leuba, "Das ökumenische Gespräch als theologisches Problem", in J. Lell, ed., *Erneuerung der Einen Kirche* (1966), pp. 115–26. Cf. also K. Goldammer, "Zur Idee des Dialoges und des dialogischen Denkens in den interkonfessionellen und interreligiösen Beziehungen und Erwägungen", *ibid.*, pp. 127–39; Y. Congar, "Vorschläge für den Dialog", in *Kerygma und Dogma* 12 (1966), pp. 181–6.

[44] The idea of the hierarchical ordering of revealed truths was heard for the first time at the Council in the speech which the then Bishop of Gorizia, A. Pangrazio, made on 25 November 1963 during the discussion on the schema *De oecumenismo*. "In order that the unity which already exists among Christians, and at the same time the differences which still endure, may be rightly distinguished, it seems important to me to pay careful attention to the *hierarchical order* of the revealed truths through which the mystery of Christ is expressed, and of the ecclesial elements on which the Church is founded. If all revealed truths are to be believed with the same divine faith and all constitutive elements of the Church maintained with the same loyalty, they nevertheless do not all claim or possess the same status" (Y. Congar, H. Küng and D. O'Hanlon, *Konzilsreden* [1964], pp. 142 f.).

[45] *Ibid.*, pp. 114 f.

in the decree concerning the hierarchy of truths is in any case a demand (addressed in the first instance to partners in dialogue, but ultimately to all Catholics), not to think, with regard to the truths taught by the Church, only of the formal element common to them all, that they are revealed, but also to bear in mind the significance of their content.[46] This is wholly in accord with the ancient practice of the Church of including only those truths of faith ("articles of faith") which were the most important in content in the Creed. Thus the awareness of a hierarchy of truths, based upon their contents, had always been present in the Church. There is no doubt, for example, that the doctrine of indulgences (even when it is purged of all elements that derive from the views of a particular period) is not of the same rank as the doctrine of the Trinity, and therefore plays a less decisive role than the latter in the understanding of the faith, and the life of faith, of Catholics. In spite of its great importance, the doctrine of the ministerial structure of the Church is not of the same rank as the doctrine of the incarnation of God and of salvation through Christ.[47]

This hierarchy, of course, must not be arbitrarily determined. The decree itself gives the criterion: the order of doctrines in this hierarchy depends on "their relationship to the foundation of the Christian faith". Thus the importance of a doctrine is not determined by the degree to which it is theologically binding, as though a defined doctrine belonged to the first rank of truths solely on the basis of the fact that it had been defined, while a non-defined truth of revelation was *eo ipso* of a lower rank. The criterion is rather the closeness to the mystery of Christ, which of course includes the mystery of the Trinity. The statements of faith which are direct utterances upon the foundation (or one could use a simpler metaphor and speak of the "centre") of the Christian faith, always possess the first rank in the "hierarchy" of truths. Naturally, the decree has no intention of despising or neglecting truths of faith of the second or third rank, but it lays down that the fact that not all truths of faith possess the same status and value in the faith as a whole should always be borne in mind, that attention should be paid in the first instance to the foundation and centre of the Christian

---

[46] The distinction made here is not in contradiction to the teaching of the encyclical *Mortalium Animos* of Pius XI (1928), according to which all revealed truths are to be maintained with the same act of faith. But the formal aspect of Catholic doctrine emphasized there is not its only aspect.

[47] "Theological writing, preaching and catechetics should be concerned with the 'hierarchy' of truths in Catholic doctrine, for a belief has greater or less consequence in the measure in which it relates to the foundation of the Christian faith. Grace has more importance than sin, sanctifying grace more than actual grace, the Holy Spirit more than Our Lady, the resurrection of Christ more than his childhood, the mystical aspect of the Church more than its juridical, the Church's liturgy more than private devotions: baptism more than penance, the Eucharist more than the anointing of the sick. And what is most important, this hierarchy of values must be expressed in Christian living as well as Christian teaching" (T. Stransky, "The Separated Churches and Ecclesial Communities", in M. Adams, ed., *Vatican II on Ecumenism* (2nd ed., 1967), p. 55.

faith, and that all other truths should be seen and evaluated in the light of the fundamental and central truths of faith.[48]

It is important to observe this hierarchy, particularly for the sake of ecumenical dialogue, in order that unity concerning Christian truths of the first rank should not be overlooked as a result of controversies in matters of the second and third rank. The strict enjoining of the basic principle of the "hierarchy" of truths in the Decree on Ecumenism is ultimately addressed, however, to all Catholics. A general and more conscious awareness of this basic principle would effect a transformation in the thought and life of the faithful which could so alter the face of the Catholic Church as seen by non-Catholic Christianity, that the consciousness of the mutual links between the two would be strengthened. Catholics must be more clearly aware that not all truths of Catholic doctrine are such as "relate us directly to eternal life" (*Summa Theologica*, II, II, q. 6, a. 1), that there are numerous truths which belong not to "the order of the end" but to the "order of the means",[49] and that the greater part of believing Christianity is one

[48] On the whole matter cf. H. Mühlen, "Die Lehre des Vaticanum II über die 'hierarchia veritatum' und ihre Bedeutung für den ökumenischen Dialog", in *Theologie und Glaube* 56 (1966), pp. 303–35. "In order to understand these statements, it is important to refer to the *modus* on the basis of which the statement concerning the *hierarchia veritatum doctrinae catholicae* was introduced into the text. As a justification for this insertion it states: 'It seems to be of the utmost importance for ecumenical dialogue that both the truths on which Christians are agreed, as well as the truths about which they disagree, should be *weighed* rather than *enumerated (potius ponderentur quam numerentur)*. Although there is no doubt that all revealed truths are to be maintained with the same divine faith, their significance and their weight *(momentum et 'pondus' earum)* differ according to the degree to which they are related to the history of salvation and the mystery of Christ.' Thus in ecumenical dialogue the truths of faith should not simply be quantitatively enumerated, so that the main object of the dialogue is simply the quantitative fullness and completeness of the truths maintained in the Catholic Church; rather, these truths should be 'weighed' and should be the object of dialogue, in accordance with the weight and importance of each. This 'weight' and this importance of individual truths of faith is measured according to the degree to which each is related to the history of salvation and to the mystery of Christ, although all revealed truths are to be believed with the same faith which is due to God. We shall have to look more closely, later on, into the question whether this homogeneity of *fides divina,* which also applies to the formal structure of faith, includes at the same time a similar equal degree of *intensity in the exercise of faith*. For if it is possible to speak of more or less important truths of faith, and if moreover the assent of faith is not a purely intellectual act, but an act which involves the whole person, then one may ask whether the degree of personal involvement in the exercise of faith, which is in fact a relationship between one person and another, may also be measured according to the weight of the truth of faith, which in a given case is the content of the personal exercise of faith" *(ibid.,* pp. 304 f.).

[49] "There are truths which belong to the *order of the end,* such as the mystery of the Most Holy Trinity, the incarnation of the word, the redemption, divine love and grace towards sinful mankind, eternal life in the perfection of the kingdom of God, and others. But there are other truths which belong to the *order of the means of salvation,* such as the truth that there are seven sacraments, the hierarchical structure of the Church, the apostolic succession, etc. These truths concern the means which Christ has bestowed upon his Church for its earthly pilgrimage; but thereafter they cease. It is a fact that the differences in doctrine between Christians concern not so much

in its faith in the Christian truths of the first rank concerning the triune God and salvation in Christ. (The question must also be posed whether divergencies in the interpretation of basic Christian truths are genuinely such as to divide the Church, and are not for the most part merely differences in theology.) This would also make Catholics more fully aware that the primary division lies between the totality of those who believe in Christ and that part of humanity which does not yet believe or no longer believes in Christ; and that by contrast with these, the divisions between denominations are secondary. For Christian witness in a non-Christian world (in the missions and in so-called Christian countries) to be effective, it is of decisive importance that Christianity should appear as a unity in the face of non-Christian humanity. There must consequently be a more lively awareness that a common witness, above all with regard to the fundamental and central truths of the Christian gospel, is even today, before the union of the Churches can be expected, both largely possible and also necessary.

Article 12. This article speaks first of the common witness mentioned above, and then turns to co-operation among all Christians. The two groups of statements — those concerning common witness in the first sentence, and those concerning co-operation in the sentences that follow — are not unrelated to each other. Rather, co-operation is seen as a realization of common witness. In the whole article, common witness is the ruling concept. This witness is realized in concrete terms by the common profession of faith mentioned in the first sentence, and by the co-operation of Christians, described in the rest of the article. The two basic New Testament terms "testimony" and "service" have rightly been brought into the foreground by the ecumenical movement. They constantly recur in the documents of the World Council of Churches, and also play a decisive part in the teaching of the Council. The mission of the apostles, which consists of *martyria* for Christ (leading to *martyrion* in the narrower sense of the word) and of *diakonia* according to Christ's example, is continued in the Church. The text first mentions the witness which is to be borne before the world by the common profession of faith, that is by the word (of preaching and of prayer), and then of the witness which should be borne through co-operation, that is, by the common carrying out of service to mankind. As the text makes clear, the common profession of faith is limited in content: as the content of the faith common to all Christians, the text names the mystery of

those truths which belong to the order of the *end,* but rather those which belong to the order of the *means,* and are undoubtedly subordinate to the former. One can say that unity in fact exists among Christians in their common faith and profession of those truths which belong to the order of the end. If this distinction concerning the hierarchy of truths and elements is explicitly stated, then in my view the unity which already exists between all Christians will be better manifested, by which all Christians are already united as a family in the primary truths of the Christian religion" (Archbishop Pangrazio in the speech in the Council quoted above; see Congar, Küng and O'Hanlon, *op. cit.,* p. 143).

God the Three in One, the mystery of the incarnation of the Son of God, and the life of the world to come, towards which Christian hope is directed. The allusion to the trinitarian and Christological "basis" of the World Council of Churches, which has already been made in the introduction, and which also expresses the faith of the Catholic Church, is also unmistakable at this point. But whereas on the one hand there are few truths of revelation which all Christians can profess and to which they can bear witness in common, one must not overlook on the other hand that these are truths of which the "relationship to the foundation of the Christian faith" is the most close, and which therefore hold the first rank in the "hierarchy" of truths.

The common basis of faith held by all Christians makes possible, and their common calling to bear witness demands, a particularly close co-operation on the part of all Christians in the service of mankind. It is true that there is also a general human basis which imposes upon all men, whatever their conviction and view of the world, a duty to co-operate, and this co-operation already exists, as the text states with regard to social matters. For those who believe in God the summons is stronger. But Christians of all denominations have in addition to this a specific vocation on the basis of their common faith in Christ. All Christians have the mission to make "the features of Christ the servant" visible in history through their service, based on Christian faith. They fulfil this mission better if they carry out this service to humanity not separately, according to their denominations, but wherever possible in co-operation between Christians of all denominations (for the concept of the servant of God, cf. particularly the *ebed Yahweh* songs of Deutero-Isaiah: Is 42:1–7; 49:1–9a; 50:4–9; 52:13–53:12, and the New Testament passages where Jesus is described as the servant of God: Mt 12:18; Acts 3:13, 26; 4:27, 30. The text of the decree seems to be directly influenced by the saying of Jesus in Lk 22:27, "I am among you as one who serves", and by the account in Jn 13:4–15 concerning the washing of the disciples' feet). Two basic New Testament ideas expressed in the Council, the Church as a community bearing witness to Christ and as a community of service in the imitation of Christ, are brought into association here with the ecumenical desire frequently expressed in the decree, that "the bond which already unites them (Christians)" may be vividly expressed. The decree expects from this co-operation in the spirit of the gospel that Christians may understand each other better and esteem each other more, and grow in unity (cf. the conclusion of the article).

As a particularly appropriate theme for practical co-operation the decree sees the sphere of social, charitable and humanitarian work, but also (following a suggestion by the Japanese Cardinal Tatsuo Doi) the sphere of the arts and sciences. Both with regard to this field of co-operation, and also with regard to the hope awaited from it, the decree is in agreement with the Life and Work Movement (for practical Christianity) outside the Catholic Church, the efforts of which, going back to the period of the First World War, led, on the initiative of the Swedish Archbishop Nathan Søderblom, to the World Conference for Practical Christianity at Stockholm in 1925. By contrast to the Faith and Order Movement, which was concerned with closer doctrinal agreement, its aim was to unite separated Christianity by a love and concern for social justice. The Continuing Committee of the Stockholm Conference constituted itself from 1930 on into a standing body which at the second World Conference in Oxford (1937), on the theme "Church, People and State", made a social and ethical declaration against the totalitarian State and in favour of a responsible society. In 1938 plans were made to unite the Life and Work Movement with the Faith and Order Movement, to form the World Council of Churches. From 1948 on, the Life and Work Committee has formed a separate branch ("Church and Society") of the Department of Studies of the World Council of Churches. In the mixed working party which has since been formed by Rome and Geneva, the main discussion has been upon questions of practical co-operation which the Decree on Ecumenism mentions here, and which are studied by the "Church and Society" department in Geneva.

One may perhaps regret that the decree does not mention co-operation in such an important Christian field as that of the biblical movement (co-operation in Bible translations and in the distribution of the holy Scriptures). A reference to translations carried out in common is made in the Constitution on Divine Revelation (Articles 22). Several conciliar documents recommend co-operation between Catholic and non-Catholic Christians in various fields, such as the Decree on the Apostolate of the Laity (Article 27), the Decree on the Missionary Activity of the Church (Articles 15 and 41) and the Pastoral Constitution on the Church in the Modern World (Articles 88 and 90).

Churches and Ecclesial Communities
Separated from the Roman Apostolic See

Where the first two chapters set out in general terms the principles, the attitudes and the way in which the Catholic Church desires to take part in the ecumenical movement, Chapter III of the decree discusses the two main groups of separated communities, those in the East and those in the West, in order to show in more concrete terms how ecumenical work must be carried out in accordance with the characteristics of the two groups.

This purpose means that the chapter has a distinctive structure. The preface (Article 13), which covers both the sections which follow, is followed by the first section, which deals with the special position of the Eastern Churches (Articles 14–18). The second section then deals with the separated Churches and ecclesial communities in the West (Articles 19–23). At the end comes the concluding article of the whole decree (Article 24). In order to specify the groups of Churches which were meant, a point of view had to be chosen which best corresponded to what was meant. It was not possible to base the distinction between the two groups on the particular moment when the separation took place. Thus it was not possible to say, for example, in the case of the Eastern Churches, "The Churches which separated themselves from the Papal See in the 11th century". For among the separated Eastern Churches there were some which had separated from Rome as early as the 5th century. Nor, in the case of the Churches of the West, was it possible to say, "The Churches which separated from the Roman See in the 16th century". For the Waldensians trace their origin back to the Middle Ages, and it could scarcely be said of the communities which came into being later, by breaking away from the original Reformation Churches, that they separated from Rome in the 16th century (quite apart from the Old Catholic Churches, which separated from Rome in the 17th century — the Church of Utrecht — or in the 19th century). After various attempts to find a satisfactory terminology, the Secretariat for Unity decided upon the geographical point of view and spoke of the Churches of the East and the Churches of the West, although of course this refers only to the place of their origin, for since then Eastern Churches have come into existence in the West as well, and throughout the world, and Western Churches in the East and in every part of the earth.

The wording of the main title of this chapter likewise caused the Secretariat for Unity certain difficulties. What was meant in concrete terms was clear; the whole of non-Catholic Christianity, including the Eastern and the Western Churches. But how was this best to be expressed? The wording of the first title was "The Christians Separated from the Catholic Church". But this was unsatisfactory for two reasons. Firstly, because it failed to express the fact that the decree was not discussing individual non-Catholic Christians, but their communities as such. The result of the debate in the Council was that these communities came to be known as "Churches and ecclesial communities" (cf. above, pp. 76–78). Secondly, it was not in accordance with the ecclesiology set forth in the decree for these communities to be described as separated from the Catholic Church, for the decree insists on the fact that in spite of the separation a certain communion still persists; and the awareness of this had long been growing much more clear, especially with regard to the Eastern Churches. Consequently, the fact of their separation from the Roman Apostolic See, the jurisdiction of which is rejected by all non-Catholic Churches, was used to characterize them all.

Article 13. The text of this article provides an introduction to the two main sections which follow. It does not speak of two divisions, but of two particular categories of division, since in fact both in the East and in the West there were several divisions on various occasions, although of course the Eastern and Western Churches which arose from the divisions each possessed a particular affinity among themselves.

The second section of the preface discusses the divisions in the East, first those of the 5th century, then those of the 11th century. The first are the divisions in the Church which followed the Christological disputes. At the Council of Ephesus (431) one Christological extreme was condemned, the doctrine of two persons in Christ. As a result of the rejection of the credal formula of Ephesus and also through various non-theological factors, Nestorianism came into being as a distinct form of Christianity. It was strengthened particularly by the official adherence to it of the East Syrian Church of Persia. From this starting point, Nestorianism developed an extensive missionary activity reaching India, North Arabia, Turkestan, and ultimately China. After the numerous persecutions which the Nestorian Church has suffered, there are at the present day only about 80,000 Nestorians in Iraq, Iran and Syria, about 5,000 in India and 25,000 in America. At the Council of Chalcedon (451) the other Christological extreme was condemned, the doctrine of a single nature in Christ. Monophysitism, which rejected the doctrine of two natures in Christ, proclaimed at Chalcedon, became very widespread in Armenia, in Syria and Mesopotomia, and in Egypt and Ethiopia. At the present day the so-called Syrian Jacobite Church numbers about 80,000 members, the Armenian, in spite of severe

125

persecutions, about 2,300,000, and the Coptic Churches in Egypt and Ethiopia together about 7,000,000 (the majority being in Ethiopia). There is also the Syrian Church of Malabar in India, which in the 17th century adhered to the Syrian Monophysite Church, and which numbers about 220,000. The Nestorian and Monophysite Churches are known as pre-Chalcedonian Churches. As it is understood at the present day, at least, their Christology differs only verbally from that of the Orthodox and the Catholic Churches. Today they are often referred, together with the separated Byzantine Churches, as Orthodox Churches.

After the schisms of the 5th century, the second paragraph of the article mentions the great schism[50] which is usually dated in the year 1054, the year in which on 17 July the Papal Legate Humbert of Silva Candida deposited the bull of excommunication against the Patriarch Michael Cerularius on the altar of Hagia Sophia in Constantinople, to which Michael responded by the excommunication of the papal legates. But a long history lay behind this separation. After the division of the Roman Empire into Eastern and Western parts, which finally took place at the end of the 4th century, the East and West grew increasingly apart. Political factors, the different cultural development of Eastern and Western Christianity, their different spirit and mode of thought, and the differences in their ecclesiastical discipline and legal development, led to an increasingly greater alienation, so that the final breach with Rome must be regarded as merely the final point in a long process. With the patriarchate of Constantinople, the other patriarchates of the East separated from Rome, as did the nations which had been evangelized from Byzantium. The Crusades, the conquest of Constantinople, and the setting up of a Latin Empire in the East helped to drive the separated Eastern Churches even further from the Latin Church.

The term Eastern Churches refers to the Churches of the Eastern half of the Roman Empire (east of the line running through present day Yugoslavia), as well as the communities which were founded in dependence upon the Churches of the Eastern half of the Empire. Even in Christian antiquity the status of principal Churches — later known as patriarchates — was attained by the Churches of Alexandria, Antioch, Constantinople and Jerusalem. Constantinople soon came to dominate the whole East. In the five original Eastern Churches of Alexandria, Antioch, Constantinople (within the frontiers of the Empire), Persia and Armenia (outside the frontiers of the Empire) arose the five oriental rites: the Alexandrine, Antiochene (West Syrian), Byzantine, Chaldean (East Syrian) and Armenian rites. It was the Byzantine rite which became the most widespread, since in the course of the centuries numerous other Churches were founded by Constantinople, particularly among the Slavs. All the Eastern Churches which exist at the present day derive historically from one of the five original Churches mentioned. The Chalcedonian Churches, separated from

[50] Cf. Y. Congar, *After Nine Hundred Years* (1959).

126

Rome, which in accordance with their own understanding of themselves refer to themselves as Orthodox Churches, all acknowledge the same doctrine, possess the same sacramental and hierarchical structure, and maintain a close relationship *(koinonia)* with each other. After the Catholic Church, Orthodox Christianity forms by far the largest unified non-Catholic community. It is estimated that at the present day it numbers 95 million faithful, of whom 6 million are in Western Europe, America, etc. It is not possible to give a more precise figure for Orthodoxy as a whole. The Patriarch of Constantinople, whose own jurisdiction is a great deal smaller than it used to be is accorded a primacy of honour as "Ecumenical Patriarch" within Orthodoxy as a whole. In general a certain precedence is accorded to the Bishop of Rome, but his primacy of jurisdiction is denied. The particularly close relationship which the Catholic Church feels that it has with the Eastern Churches, and the fact that Chapter III of the Decree on Ecumenism speaks of them first, is natural in view of the extensive agreement in doctrine and in their sacramental and hierarchical structure.

Small parts of Eastern Christianity have reunited once again in the course of time with the Catholic Church (Uniat Eastern Churches). They have maintained their Eastern characteristics, especially in their rite, but to a varying degree have suffered a certain "Latinization", against which a particularly firm stand was taken at the Second Vatican Council. These unions were not regarded with favour by the Orthodox Churches. The Decree on Ecumenism did not deal with these Uniat Eastern Churches, which are the subject of the conciliar Decree on the Eastern Catholic Churches.

The third paragraph of the article then turns to the divisions in Western Christianity brought about by the 16th century Reformation. By contrast to the Eastern schism, the Western division did not bring about a single type of Church with a number of particular Churches agreeing in doctrine, and forming together a single sacramental and hierarchical *communio*. Rather, from the very first, Churches distinct in doctrine and structure were formed, from which in the course of time numerous further Churches and communities derived, differing from their parent body and from each other in doctrine, order and the characteristics of their Church life. Thus the concept of Protestantism in no sense forms a parallel to that of Orthodoxy. The differences of belief within Protestantism are so considerable that to a large extent eucharistic communion does not exist between the Churches and communities of the Reformation. By the expression "national and denominational communions", however, the text points to the fact that the national Churches of the Reformation are not closed in on themselves, but are in communion with the Churches who hold the same confession of faith.

A number of speeches made in the Council drew attention to the special characteristics of the Anglican Church: the suggestion was even made that a special section should be devoted to the Anglican Church, as to the Eastern

Churches. The Secretariat for Unity did not go as far as this, but included in the text a special mention of the Anglican Communion. As the wording shows, the assertion is not made that "some Catholic traditions and institutions continue to exist" only in the Anglican Communion. There are other examples of this, such as the Lutheran Churches with their episcopal Church order and liturgical forms handed down from the Middle Ages. The "special place" of which the text speaks is accorded to the Anglican Communion (the text does not speak of the "Church of England" but of the *Communio Anglicana*), not only because it has spread throughout the world, but even more because of its mode of thought and attitude which comprehends ("comprehensiveness" rather than "uniformity") and reconciles differences and contradictions, which makes it able to act as a "bridge Church" between the Catholic Church and the Protestant Churches.

The fourth paragraph contains two basic ideas concerning the Churches separated from Rome which derive from the Eastern and Western divisions. Reference is first made to those differences between them which are purely historical in origin ("by reason of their source, location and age") and which are easily understood in historical terms, are justified in themselves, and present no insuperable difficulties to the growing together and union of the Church. But attention is then drawn to differences in faith and in Church order, which represent the really great obstacles to efforts to achieve unity.

As the final paragraph states, the Council understands the "differences between the various Christian bodies", and therefore does not look at them in a uniform way; yet it does not forget that despite the divisions bonds continue to exist among all Christians. But because the ultimate aim of ecumenical efforts is the full communion and unity of Christians, it seeks to show Catholics in the articles that follow how they should participate in ecumenical efforts with regard to the two main groups of separated Churches.

The Special Position of the Eastern Churches

The whole of the first section of Chapter III presents an extremely detailed description of the Eastern Churches, in which the prudent work of the experts on the Eastern Churches in the Secretariat for Unity, as well as the specialists in the Commission for the Eastern Churches, can easily be recognized. It must be borne in mind that this description is meant in the first instance for Catholics, by far the greatest part of whom belong to the Western Church, and who mostly have no proper conception of the special nature of the Eastern Churches, or who even regard them as an oddity which from a strict Catholic point of view one may still tolerate, but which is not fully in accord with the "ideal of unity". Thus the intention is to lead Catholics to a knowledge of the Eastern Churches which will fill them with a high regard and a love for these Churches. In particular, the account seeks to persuade them to give up the desire to see all alike, to cease to equate unity with uniformity, and to accept a legitimate diversity in the one Church. But the account is also intended as a testimony to Eastern Christianity of the high regard and love which the Catholic Church has for Eastern Churches, and to show them that the Catholic Church does not think of union as the levelling out and reducing to uniformity of all distinctions and that it regards the existence of distinct Churches in the community of the one Church rather as an enrichment and an increase of the catholicity of the Church. A further sign of the acknowledgment of this diversity in the one Church is the new evaluation made of the Catholic Eastern Churches by the Council, which is expressed in the Decree on the Catholic Eastern Churches. The representatives of the Catholic Eastern Churches, especially the Melchite Patriarch Maximos IV Saigh, advocated with determination and success the preservation and restoration of the independent position of their churches.

Article 14. The first article of this first section begins the description of the Eastern Churches by looking back in history to the time when Eastern Christianity, in spite of its different nature, and in spite of the increasingly marked separate development of the Eastern and Western Churches ("for many centuries" they "went their own ways"), were nevertheless still united with Western Christianity in a single universal Church, and were bound together with the West in "a brotherly communion of faith and sacramental life". In this communion "the Roman See acted by common consent as moderator". The decree here refrains from anachronistically projecting back into the period before the separation, later concepts and later practice with regard to the government of the Church by the Bishop of Rome.[51] It does not speak of a primacy of jurisdiction, but of a *moderari communi consensu,* a role as moderator acknowledged by all. That this does not mean a centralized government is shown by two statements in the text. The first is found in the words "if disagreements in belief and discipline arose among them". Thus it was a matter of an occasional intervention on the part of the Bishop of Rome, when the unity and purity of the faith were threatened, and when there was a crisis in Church order; that is, of a "subsidiary" function of the Petrine office which became actual when the work of other organs of the Church were insufficient. One might speak of a ministry as guardian and arbitrator on the part of the Bishop of Rome, for the sake of unity, order and peace in the Church.

The second indication in the text is given by the special mention of the patriarchal Churches in the same paragraph, where the separate origins and relative independence of the patriarchates are mentioned, a theme which is expressed even more clearly in Article 16. The value placed upon the patriarchs of the Catholic Eastern Churches by the Second Vatican Council (cf. the Decree on Catholic Eastern Churches, Articles 7–9) points in the same direction. Some of the local Churches of early Christianity achieved a special importance and

51 Cf. F. Dvornik, *Byzantium and the Roman Primacy* (1965).

precedence at a very early period, because of their foundation by an apostle or disciple of the apostles, their great influence upon a particular region, the political rank of their city and the regard in which they were held by the whole of Christianity (e.g., Antioch as a missionary centre, as early as the apostolic period). Their bishops came to be known as patriarchs, and their status among the local Churches which had a special link with them was gradually given more precise legal definition. The early Councils recognized the particular status of the five classical patriarchates (later known as the Pentarchy) in the following order of precedence: Rome, Constantinople, Alexandria, Antioch, Jerusalem. In the West, particularly because of the increasing influence of the authority of the Bishop of Rome, no other episcopal see attained the rank of a patriarchate. The bestowing of the title of patriarch (for example, to the Bishop of Aquileia in the 6th century, transferred in 1451 to Venice) signifies merely a title of honour. The increasing importance of the primacy meant that the ıunction of the Bishop of Rome as Patriarch of the West fell completely into the background, so that it ceased to form part of the consciousness of Western Christianity. (In the *Annuario Pontificio,* among the titles of the Bishop of Rome, that of "Patriarch of the West" is still found. Similarly, as a consequence of the separation of the Eastern Churches and the vast expansion of the Latin Church, Latin Christianity lost its awareness of the fact that the Western Church, like any individual Catholic Eastern Church, is a particular Church. A reminder of this was given at the Council by representatives of the Catholic Eastern Churches.) In the Eastern Churches the patriarch (who is also a local bishop) possesses not only a primacy of honour but a genuine legal status with certain powers: he is the head and father of his patriarchate. The patriarchates are institutions of canon law, but the principle of the patriarchate has proved itself to be a valuable means for joining together a region of the Church with its own history and culture, an assurance of the distinctive nature and (relative) independence which it has obtained, and therefore a balancing force against an excessive centralization within the universal Church. Thus the maintenance of the institution contributes to the genuine catholicity of the Church. In addition, the ancient patriarchates were added to in the Orthodox Churches by further patriarchates set up in more recent times (Moscow, Belgrade, Bucharest, Sofia).

The text of the decree draws particular attention to the fact that a number of Eastern Churches were founded by apostles or disciples of the apostles, whereas in Latin Christendom this can only be said of the Roman local Church. Representatives of the Eastern Churches particularly emphasize that the Christian faith was not brought to their Churches through Rome, but rather that they received it in a direct line from the apostles.

The final sentence of the paragraph refers to the close "horizontal" associations between individual Churches, which have always been particularly cherished in the Eastern Churches (the principle of *koinonia*), and which manifest the Church as a *communio* in faith and in love. The description of local Churches linked with each other in this way as sister Churches *(sorores)* shows how the Church is a family, in which individual Churches preserve both their "individual personalities" and the bonds that join them together. The whole passage recalls another in the Constitution on the Church: "Within the Church, particular Churches hold a rightful place. These Churches retain their own traditions, without in any way lessening the primacy of the Chair of Peter. This Chair presides over the whole assembly of charity and protects legitimate differences, while at the same time it sees that such differences do not hinder unity but rather contribute toward it" (Article 13). A Catholic must also bear in mind that in spite of their separation from Rome, and largely on the basis of their mutual links, the Orthodox Churches have retained one and the same faith, the sacraments and their hierarchical structure without anyone having authority and jurisdiction over them all, and that therefore they cannot see the guarantee of the unity of the faith in the papacy alone.

The third paragraph points to the historical facts which make evident the importance of the Eastern Church for Western Christianity itself, and for which the latter should show thankfulness and reverence towards the East. The Latin Church owes much to the East in the fields of liturgy, spirituality and Church order. (The decree goes into greater detail concerning the liturgical and spiritual riches of the Eastern Church in Article 15, while Article 16 deals with Church discipline.) The East is the cradle of Christianity, and after Christianity had left its place of origin and gone out into the world, the whole pattern of its life was formed by the East. The elements of the Christian liturgy deriving from Jesus and the apostles were first developed in the Eastern Churches, and much was taken over from the Roman Church, as for example the eucharistic liturgy, the hours of prayer, and the liturgical feasts. The first Christian literature and the first monasticism arose in the Eastern Churches and excercised their influence upon the Church of the West. The canons of the first Councils, all of which took place in the East, laid down the pattern of Church law, and also applied to the Western Church. The legislation of Byzantine emperors, as for example the *Corpus* of Justinian I, was also of importance for the law of the Roman Church.

Secondly, the decree refers to the fact that all the Ecumenical Councils before the schism took place in the East. Pope Gregory the Great compares the first four Councils, to which the greatest significance is accorded, to the four gospels. It is to the bishops of the Eastern Church that we owe the great intellectual achievement of the formulation of the basic Christological and trinitarian dogmas of the Christian faith (at the Council of Nicaea in 325, only five of the 250 Fathers were from the West).

Finally, the text mentions the oppressions and persecutions which the Eastern Church has suffered in the past, and which many are still suffering at the present day. Thus the Nestorians were persecuted by the Sassanids (6th–7th centuries), degraded under Moslem rule, submitted to a particularly bloody persecution by Tamerlane (1380), and largely exterminated during the First World War by the Turks. A large part of the Eastern Church had to suffer for centuries under Islam. The Orthodox Greeks of Asia Minor were persecuted in the years following the First World War and occasionally later by the Turks, and are once again exposed to oppression at the present day. The Armenian people have had a history of suffering which is reminiscent of the fate of the Jewish people under the Nazis. In the last decades of the 19th century numerous Armenians were slaughtered every year by the Turks with the toleration of the "Christian" Great Powers. From 1894 to 1896 alone, 100,000 Armenians, including 190 priests, were murdered, and 1,500 cities and villages plundered. At Christmas 1895, 1,200 Armenians were burned alive in the Cathedral of Urfa. Many Armenians displayed the courage of heroic martyrs when they were faced during the First World War by the Young Turks with the choice of accepting Islam or suffering death; only a few defected, while all the rest suffered a cruel martyrdom. Almost all the Armenian inhabitants of Asiatic Turkey were carried off from their homes; they were allegedly to be resettled in Mesopotamia, but were mostly murdered on the way by the Turkish soldiery (more than 1,000,000). The faithfulness of Christians of the Eastern Churches, who have often lived for centuries as a small minority in their countries, and for the most part have been subject to constant oppression, can only arouse reverence and admiration among other Christians.

While elsewhere the Decree on Ecumenism emphasizes that the historically determined differences in the form taken by Christianity are not an obstacle to the unity of the Church, it finds it necessary to refer in the third paragraph of this article to the fact that together with external (especially political) reasons, they provided the occasion for the separation between Eastern and Western Christianity. But the differences in the life and thought of the Church were only the occasion of a separation, while the schism itself would not have come about if understanding and love for a different pattern of Christianity had not been lacking on both sides. Here the decree returns to the theme of the guilt which is present at the beginning of every schism. In the final paragraph the Council therefore expresses the wish that Catholics may make an effort to obtain an understanding which is a prerequisite for a fruitful dialogue, and which was deficient at the time of the schism. The articles that follow go more closely into the special characteristics of the Eastern Churches.

Article 15. It is no accident that the decree begins its characterization of the Eastern Churches with their liturgy, for the religious life of Eastern Churches has always been wholly concentrated upon the liturgy and nourished by it, more strongly for the most part than has been the case in general, and for centuries at least, among Latin Christians. This is largely connected with the fact that the Eastern rites are more in accord with the character of the people, that they ensure a fuller active participation on the part of the people, and that (at least in most of the Eastern rites) a greater place is given to the vernacular than was the case in the Latin Church before the reform of the liturgy. Through the liturgy Eastern Christians become familiar with holy Scripture; the rich treasury of prayer in the liturgy, penetrated and formed as it is by the Church's doctrines of the Trinity, Christology and the Holy Spirit, keeps alive in them their faith in the basic Christian truths, and provides the essential orientation of their understanding of the faith. The liturgy is a constant living instruction in the faith. In the beauty and magnificence of liturgical worship they experience an anticipation of the glory that is to come. Liturgical worship allows them to experience what the Church is, and constantly strengthens the communion of the Church. The description of the conception which the Eastern Churches have of the celebration of the Eucharist, as the decree describes it, no longer appears strange, as would have been the case in the past, to a Catholic who is in sympathy with the liturgical renewal in the Catholic Church, and who is aware of the teaching of the Constitution on the Liturgy and the Constitution on the Church. The present teaching and practice of the Catholic Church has in fact been powerfully influenced by this concept of the liturgy in the Eastern Churches. Thus the restored Catholic liturgy can increase awareness of the bond with the Eastern Churches. It will suffice here to give a series of headings, summing up the characteristic features of the liturgy of the Eastern Churches mentioned in the decree, and especially of the celebration of the Eucharist: its eschatological character, unity with the local bishop, its orientation towards the doctrines of the Trinity, Christology, and the doctrine of the Holy Spirit; the divinization of man (a fundamental principle in the theology of the Eastern Churches);[52] its ecclesiological character; communion between individual Churches through concelebration on the part of bishops and priests.

The second paragraph recalls a characteristic of the Eastern Churches by which they are linked in a special way with the Catholic Church (by contrast with Protestantism): the veneration of Mary and of the saints. Here, however, mention is deliberately only made of the two basic Mariological truths which were made dogma before the separation, and which are constantly mentioned in the Eastern liturgies: that Mary is Mother of God and ever Virgin. The Catholic dogmas of the Immaculate Conception and the Bodily Assumption of Mary are generally rejected by Eastern Christians, not because they are not convinced of the truths which they express but because they are wary of the dogmatic formulation of mysteries which they are convinced should be uttered only in the form of prayer and praise, and because these dogmas were defined by the Pope alone without the participation of the Eastern Churches. The Eastern Churches also emphasize that Mary should not be regarded in isolation, but always in relation to the mystery of the Incarnation. This view is expressed in iconography by the fact that Mary is always (with very few excep-

---

[52] Cf. Y. Congar, "La déification dans la tradition spirituelle de l'Orient", in *Chrétiens en dialogue. Contributions catholiques à l'Œcuménisme* (1964), pp. 257–72.

tions) represented with the divine child in her arms. As far as the veneration of the saints is concerned, the reference in the decree to the veneration of the "Fathers" of the universal Church, which means, apart from the apostles and the disciples of the apostles, such as Mark and Timothy, the Doctors of the Church and the Church Fathers, is not meant to be exclusive: there are a large number of other saints from the period before the separation who are venerated both by the Eastern Churches and by the Latin Church. The use of the expression *Patres universalis Ecclesiae* shows, however, that the *universalis Ecclesia* is no longer equated with the Latin Church, as was usual in the past. More recently, the question has been posed whether the Catholic Church might also recognize saints of the Eastern Church who lived or were canonized after the separation. In view of the positive acknowledgment and high regard given to the elements of the Church, the sanctity, the worship, the traditions, the juridical autonomy, etc., of the Eastern Churches, which has been expressed by the Catholic Church, the question must be presumably answered in the affirmative.[53]

In further describing the blessings which are held in common, the third paragraph mentions the sacraments, especially the Eucharist and the priesthood. Particularly since the time of Leo XIII, the Popes have frequently recognized the validity of the sacraments of the Eastern Church. By this, the Catholic Church knows that it is linked in a very close relationship *(arctissima necessitudine)* with the Eastern Churches. That the central position is given to the Eucharist follows from its special ecclesiological significance. It is again no accident that it is mentioned in association with the priesthood, which is valid because of the apostolic succession: the Eucharist is valid, because a validly ordained bishop or priest presides over the worshipping community. In the case of the Protestant Lord's Supper the problem with regard to the validity of the Eucharist does not derive from the outward form of the action (matter and form), but from the ministry, i.e., from the apostolic succession. Because the Catholic Church recognizes the apostolic succession of the hierarchy of the Eastern Churches, and therefore also the validity of the priesthood in the Eastern Churches, it also affirms the full validity of the Eucharist in these Churches. On the basis of this sacramental bond with the Eastern Churches, the text now draws the practical consequences from the principles set out in Article 8: "Given suitable circumstances and the approval of Church authority, some worship in common *(communicatio in sacris)* is not merely possible but is recommended." Here what has been laid down in principle in Article 8, without any particular Church being named, is applied in concrete terms to the Eastern Churches. (On *communicatio in sacris* with the Eastern Churches in accordance with the Decree on the Catholic Eastern Churches and the Ecumenical Directory, cf. above pp. 107f.) The question of the validity of sacramental absolution given by priests of the separated Eastern Churches in the sacrament of penance has been

[53] Cf. id., "À propos des saints canonisés dans les Églises orthodoxes", *loc. cit.,* pp. 289–311.

posed in the past by Catholic theologians. The doubt arose on the basis of the distinction between a purely material and a formal succession: only the first was present in the separated Eastern Churches, while the latter was lacking; since the power of absolution also assumes a jurisdiction, which is only present in the case of a formal apostolic succession, the question arose whether priests of the Eastern Churches could give valid absolution, and if so, how this was to be explained (possibly by a passive according of the power of jurisdiction by the Pope). The view taken of these questions at the present day is probably different. In practice any doubt is removed by the fact that the Council does not exclude the sacrament of penance in acknowledging the validity of the sacraments of the Eastern Churches, and recommends that Catholics should receive the sacrament of penance under certain circumstances in the Eastern Churches.

In the fourth paragraph the decree speaks of the spiritual riches of the Eastern Churches, and in particular of monasticism, in which Eastern spirituality has developed in a distinctive way, and through which it has illuminated the whole of Christianity from the early centuries up to the present time, through the example of the life of the monks, wholly based upon the evangelical counsels, by their numerous spiritual and theological writings, by the spiritual advice and guidance which faithful, even laymen in high office, and priests sought from the monks, and by the bishops, who were chosen from the ranks of the monks. Eremitic monasticism (hermits and anchorites), which was anticipated by the asceticism of the first two centuries, came into being in the 3rd century, when ascetics withdrew from the life of the world and retired into the deserts of Egypt, to lead a life in special closeness to God. St. Paul of Thebes is regarded as the "first hermit". The greatest representative of the ancient eremetical life is St. Anthony the Great, who replaced the life of the solitary by communities of hermits, and exercised an extraordinary influence upon his generation and the period which followed. The *Life of St. Anthony,* composed by St. Athanasius, exercised a great effect. Thousands withdrew as hermits into the deserts of Egypt, and monks travelled from all parts to Egypt, to learn about monasticism. St. Pachomius formed genuine monastic (coenobitic) communities of monks, for which he also composed the first monastic rule. The rules of St. Basil the Great, through which monasticism was led from the desert into a closer contact with the world, were particularly well known. Monasticism soon spread towards Palestine and Syria, and finally throughout the whole East. In 563, there were seventy-three monasteries in Constantinople. Many monasteries, such as those of Sinai and Athos, attained an extraordinary importance and a widespread influence. From the East monasticism also penetrated the Western Church. St. Athanasius brought it to the West, when in 335 he took two monks with him to Trier, where he was exiled. As early as the 4th century, monasteries were founded in Italy, Africa, Spain, and France. John Cassian, who lived for a long time in a monastery in Bethlehem, and after that spent ten years amongst the monks of the Sketic and Nitriote deserts, described the experiences of monasticism in his spiritual writings, and so mediated the spirituality of the East to the West. He exercised a decisive influence on the piety of the Middle Ages. The rules of Eastern monks (Pachomius, Basil) are among the sources of the Rule of the patriarch of Western monasticism, St. Benedict.

The spiritual riches contained in the numerous writings of the Eastern Church Fathers, all of whom were monks, or had close association with monasticism, are certainly too little known to the faithful of the Latin Church. Consequently, the decree rightly recommends Catholics to make themselves more familiar with them.

Although not all Catholics can devote themselves to the study of the liturgical and spiritual heritage of Eastern Christians, nevertheless all, as the final paragraph states, should be conscious of the importance of the knowledge, veneration, maintenance and preservation of this heritage. Without the heritage of the East, the tradition of the Church lacks its fullness. These statements on the part of the Council are signs of a decisive change in the Catholic Church by comparison with previous centuries, during which Latin missionaries in the East, filled with an automatic consciousness of superiority and often completely despising the Eastern rites and everything Eastern, saw nothing but errors and abuses everywhere, and showed no understanding or regard for the distinctive nature of Eastern Churches. They imposed upon Eastern Christians Latin forms of worship and Western devotions, Latin theology and spirituality, as though they were the only ones that were correct, often tore up and burned their books, and sought to replace all their previous literature by new material on the Latin pattern. Boys in colleges directed by Latin missionaries had to learn the Latin language and were educated in an entirely Latin spirit.[54] These attempts to Latinize the East were brought to an end for good by the Second Vatican Council — a necessary prerequisite for a reconciliation with the Eastern Churches.

Article 16. If what the decree states on principle, concerning unity in essentials, freedom in the form taken by Church life, and the catholicity of the Church which is to be realized thereby (cf. Article 4) is not to remain abstract theory, and if the words of praise with which the particular Churches of the East are mentioned, the special emphasis placed on the Eastern patriarchates and the protestation in Article 14 of the high regard in which the heritage and tradition of the Eastern Churches are held are not to be compliments which commit no one, then not only must these assurances be given, but also the independent Church order and independent discipline of the Eastern Churches must be given serious attention in concrete terms. This the Council does in the present article, with remarkable solemnity: "Sacra Synodus, ad omne dubium tollendum (the Roman tendency to centralization, and especially the earlier practice of the

---

[54] Cf. W. de Vries, "Die geistige Latinisierung des Ostens", in *Rom und die Patriarchate des Ostens* (1963), pp. 318–27.

Catholic Church towards the Catholic Eastern Churches, gave Eastern Christians reasons for doubt) declarat . . ." Applying the principle already affirmed of unity in diversity and variety, the Council now lays down the principle of autonomy in canon law in the framework of the order desired by Christ, applying it to the Eastern Churches: "The Churches of the East, while keeping in mind the necessary unity of the whole Church, have the power to govern themselves according to their own disciplines, since these are better suited to the temperament of their faithful and better adapted to foster the good of souls."

Here two fundamental views are uttered, which must determine any concrete Church order and discipline: a regard for the distinctive nature of one part of Christianity, which has come into being through historical causes, and the fostering of the salvation of souls. It must be noted that nothing is said of privileges which are guaranteed or recognized, or of exceptions which are tolerated. Eastern Council Fathers spoke in very decided terms at the Council against the conception normally held in the past of the gracious granting of privileges and the retrospective toleration of peculiarities and uncomfortable exceptions, which was based on an inveterate urge for uniformity and a consciousness of superiority on the part of the Latins.[55] In fact these views have now changed: what is now recognized is the *facultas,* or as the text stated before the nineteen "papal changes" (of which more in the appendix) a *ius et officium* of the Eastern Church. That *facultas* is to be understood not merely as a right, but also as a duty, was explained by Cardinal Bea in an interview given to the Greek newspaper *To Vima* on 12 May 1965.[56] This follows from the Decree on Catholic Eastern Churches, which declares in Article 5: "This sacred Synod, therefore, not only honours this ecclesiastical and spiritual heritage with merited esteem and rightful praise, but also unhesitatingly looks upon it as the heritage of Christ's universal Church. For this reason, it solemnly declares that the Churches of the East, as much as those of the West, fully enjoy the right, and are in duty bound *(iure pollere et officio teneri),* to rule themselves. Each should do so according to its proper and individual procedures, inasmuch as practices sanctioned by a noble antiquity harmonize better with the customs of the faithful and are seen as more likely to foster the good of souls" (cf. also the statements in Article 6 of the same decree). With regard to the change from *ius et officium* into *facultas* in the Decree on Ecumenism, for which no official explanation was given by "higher authority", the following considerations may be useful. The Decree on Eastern Catholic Churches is directly addressed only to the Eastern

---

[55] The Eastern Fathers also decisively rejected the proposal for a unified *Codex* for all Churches. Thus the Melchite Patriarchal Vicar J. Tawil said in a speech in the Council on 25 November 1963: "To demand a unification of the *Codex* for the two Churches of the East and the West, or a unification of jurisdiction, would be to block every path of the ecumenical movement, to shut oneself off in a fatal isolation, and to form a real obstacle to unity for the whole Church" (Congar, Küng and O'Hanlon, *op. cit.,* p. 146).

[56] *La Documentation catholique,* 18 July 1965, col. 1303.

Christians united with Rome; as far as they are concerned, the Council, at which representatives of these Churches also took part, can speak of a duty. But the Decree on Ecumenism speaks of Eastern Churches in general (the paragraph twice uses the expression "The Churches of the East"), and therefore of both the separated and the Uniat Eastern Churches, and in fact its direct reference is to the separated Eastern Churches. But to impose a duty upon them is presumably not the business of a Roman Catholic Council, even if it is convinced that this duty exists.

That the statements of this paragraph have in mind the patriarchal structure of Eastern Churches, although explicit mention is not made here of the patriarchates, is immediately obvious; for they form an essential part of the Church order characteristic of the Eastern Churches. (Cf. the statements concerning the patriarchates in the Decree on the Eastern Churches, Articles 7–11.) The high status there accorded to the Catholic patriarchate has an important function as a testimony to the separated Eastern Churches. It is clear that in a union with separated Eastern Churches, the boundaries between the Orthodox Churches and the minority Catholic Eastern Churches would disappear, and no more reason would remain for keeping in being separate patriarchates for the previous minority, alongside those of the majority of Christians; the former would be absorbed by the latter. This solemn declaration of the Council concerning the recognition of the independent Church discipline of the Eastern Churches takes further a line of thought which is already to be found in earlier Roman doctrines, and has recently come to the fore since the time of Leo XIII.[57] In the course of the centuries, the promises of the Popes to respect the rites of the Eastern Churches, and especially of the patriarchs, were frequently not kept, and the resistance of the Roman Curia constantly played an important part in this. The recognition in the decree that the principle present in tradition "has not always been honoured" is in accord with the historical facts. After the solemn declarations of the Second Vatican Council the epigram of the Russian Pobedostsev, "Le Pape passe, la curie romaine reste" ("The Pope passes, the Roman Curia remains"),[58] is no longer of the same significance as before.

It should finally be noted that the statements of the decree concerning the (relative) autonomy of the Eastern Churches are also significant as a testimony to the other separated Churches, and therefore have a general ecumenical importance; a union of separated Churches can only be thought of as a union of different "types of Church" which, within the unity sought by Christ, would preserve their own distinctive nature and their "canonical" autonomy.

Article 17. In conclusion, the decree applies the principle of diversity in

---

[57] Cf. W. de Vries, *op. cit.,* pp. 223–46, "Die Haltung Roms gegenüber der Disziplin der Orientalen"; pp. 247–300, "Die Haltung Roms gegenüber der Autonomie der Patriarchate im zweiten Jahrtausend".
[58] Quoted *ibid.,* p. 297.

unity to another important sphere, that of theology. On the basis of a consciously historical understanding, and since different modes of theological thought and language have begun to develop even within Western Catholic theology, it has already become obvious to many theologians of the Latin Church that there should be no uniformity in theology, and that for example scholastic methods, modes of thought, concepts and language, however justified they may be, do not constitute the whole of the apparatus of Catholic theology. But this was not always a natural assumption in the Catholic Church, and since at the Second Vatican Council bishops had to defend this realization, it is obviously not a natural assumption to all Catholics even at the present day. The decree, however, seeks to make Catholics aware, and to testify and give an assurance to Eastern Christians, that the Catholic Church does not hold the view that there is only one method and mode of procedure in theology and only one possible way of formulating revelation. Revelation, with the study of which theology is concerned, does not consist of a compendium of firmly established statements, but of the mystery of God, revealed in historical events, but incomprehensible and unfathomable by the human mind. A person's mind, which approaches and applies itself to this mystery in faith, is always determined by historical conditions, by those of the history, the culture, and the tradition of his people, all of which form his thought, and prescribe for it certain limits, certain questions and a particular language; by the period in which he lives and which determines his interests; and by his personal temperament and individual talents. The transcendence of the mystery of God on the one hand, and the historical nature of human thought on the other hand, make possible a diversity of theological reflection and theological language concerning the revelation of God. Even in holy Scripture, which is not the revelation, but a testimony to the revelation which has taken place, and the outcome of human reflection upon the event of revelation, different "theologies" can be distinguished, which cannot easily be reconciled at every point. Much has been written about the difference between Hebrew and Greek thought. But there are differences in the thinking of Latin and Greek Church Fathers concerning the same revealed truth and the formulation of the same truth. Scholasticism developed its methods, categories of thought and language, on the basis of the Aristotelian concept of knowledge.

The Council does not intend, as was often done automatically in the past, to impose upon Eastern Christians the Latin scholastic mode of theology, and it does not regard the Eastern mode of theological thought as a theology of a lower rank. Western theology can be enriched by the theology of the East, firmly rooted as it is in holy Scripture and in apostolic tradition, and can be made aware by it of aspects of the truth which have been more clearly set out in Eastern theology. The reference of the decree to the possibility that the formulation of Eastern and Western theology may complement each other is important. This does not mean that all divergent theological statements are to be understood as complementing each other, but it must be borne in mind that often *(non raro)* they are to be considered not as conflicting *(opponi)*, but as understandings and statements which are complementary *(inter se compleri)*. The classic example of the way in which divergent statements of the Eastern Church and the Latin Church complement each other, as is now solemnly recognized by the magisterium, and in this case not merely in theology but in Church dogma, is provided by the expressions *ex Patre* (or *ex Patre per Filium*) and the *ex Patre Filioque,* for the procession of the Holy Spirit (the Council of Florence, in the bull *Laetentur Caeli* of 6th July 1439).[59] The affirmation of the possibility of various types of theology by the Decree on Ecumenism is of importance not merely for the relationship between the Catholic Church and the Eastern Churches, but for the ecumenical movement in general, and ultimately also for the Church's missionary work.

In summing up, the Council now returns to the thought that the integration of the whole spiritual, liturgical, disciplinary and theological heritage of the Eastern Churches, with its varied tradition, is essential to the catholicity and apostolicity of the Church. Thus what is at issue is not the permitting of a number of exotic marginal manifestations, but the realization of the fuller catholicity and apostolicity of the Church: the Catholic Church must become more Catholic and apostolic. To some extent, however, the values of the Eastern Church are present within the Catholic Church through the Eastern Churches united with Rome, which have come into being through the adherence of small sections of the different separated Eastern Churches to the Catholic Church, with the maintenance of their traditional rites, their liturgical language and their hierarchy. But until recently, this presence within the Catholic Church was not very effective, because Latin Catholics had scarcely any knowledge of these Eastern Churches, on account of the relatively small number of their faithful; because they were able to manifest their Eastern heritage only inadequately, as a result of the Latinization mentioned above, and were scarcely able to make the Latin Church conscious of it; and because of the precarious situation in which they existed.

This has largely changed as a result of the Council. Through the frequent celebration of their own liturgy in the Council, and above all the bold intervention of many Eastern Fathers on behalf of the recognition of the legitimate characteristics and the significance of Eastern Christianity, not only was the influence of the Catholic Eastern Churches strengthened, but to some extent the separated Eastern Churches were also made present at the Council (apart from their presence through observer delegates). Patriarch Athenagoras of Constantinople and other personalities of the Orthodox Church explicitly acknowledged that the Eastern Catholics (otherwise not favourably regarded by the Orthodox,

[59] *Concilium Oecumenicorum Decreta,* published by Centro di Documentazione, Istituto per le Scienze Religiose, Bologna (1962), pp. 501–3.

and disparagingly referred to as "Uniats") had represented Orthodoxy at the Council. The concluding sentence of this article, which calls for the "delatinizing" and "re-easternizing" of the Eastern Catholic Christians, is (together with the separate Decree on the Eastern Catholic Churches) a reflection of this process. The Eastern Churches united with Rome are thereby accorded a mediating role in the effort for union with the separated Eastern Churches.

It is worthwhile here to give some brief details concerning these Eastern Catholic Churches. The sole form of Eastern Catholic Christianity which is a unity in itself (and has no equivalent among separated Eastern Churches) is that of the Maronites, who for the most part live in the Republic of Lebanon, with a smaller number in Syria, Palestine, Cyprus, Egypt and North and South America. There is a Maronite patriarchate of Antioch, and the union with Rome took place in 1181. Numerous groups derive from Orthodoxy, and are therefore of the Byzantine rite. There have been various unions since the 15th century: the Melchites in the Near East (the Melchite patriarchate of Antioch), and in Europe the Ruthenians (now mostly known as Ukrainians, many of whom have emigrated to America), the Catholic Greeks, Rumanians, Bulgarians, Italo-Albanians (in Sicily), and the diocese of Presov (Slovakia), Kreutz (Yugoslavia) and Hajdudorog (Hungary). From Nestorianism come the Catholic Chaldaeans, throughout the Near East, and especially in Iraq, with their patriarchate of Babylon (united since 1553, with intervals); and the St. Thomas Christians on the Malabar coast of India. From Monophysitism come the Catholic Armenians, with the patriarchate of Sis in Cilicia (Turkey), who have been united since 1742, the Catholic Copts in Egypt, with the Coptic patriarchate of Alexandria, who have been united since 1895, the Catholic Syrians with the Syrian patriarchate of Antioch, who have been united since 1663, with intervals, and the Catholic Ethiopians, in the 19th century. The total number of faithful of all Eastern Catholic Churches amounts to approximately 10 million.

Article 18. The final statement of the decree concerning the relationship between the Catholic Church and the separated Eastern Churches contains a number of directions and observations which are of special note. In the first place, there is a reminder of the efforts of previous Councils and Popes to obtain union with the Eastern Churches. These took place above all at the Second Council of Lyons (1274) and the Council of Ferrara-Florence (1438–39). At Lyons a union was achieved with the Greeks. The ambassadors of the Greek Emperor Michael VIII Palaeologus put forward in his name a confession of faith, the decisive points of which were the *Filioque,* and the doctrines of purgatory, of the seven sacraments and of the primacy of the Pope.[60] But the union was not enduring, largely because it derived only from the emergency with which the Emperor Michael was faced. At the Council of Ferrara-Florence unions were

[60] Text of the *Professio fidei Michaelis Palaeologi* in *Denzinger* 461–6.

141

made with the Greeks[61] (the large delegation was led by the Patriarch Joseph II of Constantinople, the Procurators of Alexandria, Antioch and Jerusalem, and the Emperor John VIII Palaeologus. The principal spokesmen were the determined advocates of the union, Bessarion, Archbishop of Nicaea, later appointed Cardinal and Patriarch of Constantinople, and the opponent of union, Mark Eugenicus, Metropolitan of Ephesus, who did not sign the decree of union, and fought against the union after its return), with the Armenians[62] and the Egyptian Copts,[63] and, after the Council had been moved to Rome, also with the Syrians[64] and with certain Chaldaeans and Maronites in Cyprus.[65] These unions too did not last long. Both the union of Lyons and the unions of Florence and Rome were ultimately doomed to failure, because they were not prepared for by a gradual growing together of the separated Churches, nor firmly rooted in the people and the clergy.

The statements and procedure of the Second Vatican Council were based on this historical experience. The decree speaks as a result of a "gradual" *(paulatim)* realization of unity. A true union cannot simply be decreed "from above" but must grow up "from below". Unity does not exist *in indivisibili,* but has various stages (even within the Catholic community). For the growth of unity a change is necessary "in the various organizations and living activities of the Church", that is, in the institutional sphere, which also includes *communicatio in sacris;* but even more necessary is prayer, a change of attitude and co-operation. But a change of attitude and intellectual willingness are not sufficient; there is also a need for the clarification of theological and pastoral problems; consequently the decree specially recommends dialogue on these problems. Concerning the declarations of previous Popes on the question of union cf. what was said above on Article 16.[66] Nor does the decree overlook the Churches which exist among those who have emigrated. In recent years considerable groups of Christians from the Orthodox and pre-Chalcedonian Churches have emigrated to Western Europe, North and South America and other continents. For most Catholics, their personal contact with Eastern Christianity is provided by these emigrants. The close bond of brotherhood which exists should be clearly manifested to them, and this particularly includes help in social matters.

The decree gives a special warning against a spirit of "quarrelsome rivalry" *(secluso omni spiritu contentiosae aemulationis)*. Here one may think in particular of what is known in the ecumenical movement as proselytism. From the purely

---

[61] Bull *Laetentur caeli,* in *Concil. Oec. Decreta* (see above, note 59), pp. 499–504.

[62] Bull of Union, *ibid.,* pp. 510–35.

[63] Bull of Union, *ibid.,* pp. 543–59.

[64] Bull of Union, *ibid.,* pp. 562–5.

[65] Bull of Union, *ibid.,* pp. 565–7.

[66] Cf. the entire second part ("Roms Haltung zur Eigenart des Ostens") of the work of W. de Vries, *Rom und die Patriarchate des Ostens* (1963), pp. 183–393.

etymological point of view, the word can have a good sense, but within the ecumenical movement it is understood in a pejorative sense. The World Council of Churches has frequently discussed the problem of proselytism. It describes proselytism in the following terms: "Proselytism is a caricature of witness. Christian witness is caricatured, when, secretly or openly, the arts of persuasion, bribery, unjustified pressure or intimidation are used to obtain an apparent conversion; when we subordinate the glory of Christ to the success of our Church; when we carry out the dishonest practice of comparing the ideal image of our Church with the reality of another; when we seek to gain advantage for our own cause by a false testimony about another Church; when genuine love for the individual with whom we are dealing is replaced by a personal or group ambition. Such a caricature of Christian witness points to a lack of trust in the power of the Holy Spirit, a lack of respect for human nature, and a failure to recognize the true nature of the gospel."[67]

There is a passage in the Declaration on Religious Freedom which implies a condemnation of proselytism: "In spreading religious faith and in introducing religious practices, everyone ought at all times to refrain from any manner of action which might seem to carry a hint of coercion or of a kind of persuasion that would be dishonourable or unworthy, especially when dealing with poor or uneducated people. Such a manner of action would have to be considered an abuse of one's own right and a violation of the right of others" (Article 4).

Essential to the ecumenical attitude of the Catholic Church towards the Eastern Churches is the profession uttered in the first sentence of the article in the words of the so-called Apostolic Council, which states that for the restoration or preservation of communion and unity it is necessary "to impose no burden beyond what is indispensable" (Acts 15:28), a principle which is naturally also true for union with other non-Catholic Churches. This is once again a statement of the fact that Catholic efforts towards union do not mean that the Catholic Church is proposing to other Churches that they should accept everything in the form taken by the Catholic Church, which is due purely to historical causes, or that it thinks of union as the adoption of uniformity, in such a way as to require other Churches to accept more than what is required by the will of Christ.

The article concludes with the fine image of the pulling down of the wall dividing the two Churches, which is drawn from the bull of union *Laetentur Caeli* of the Council of Florence (6 July 1439), and according to which the Church is presented as a single dwelling containing both West and East, in which the two Churches form, in anticipation of this, two dwellings separated by a wall. The New Testament image of the cornerstone (1 Pet 2:7) Jesus Christ, who breaks down the dividing wall between Jews and Gentiles (Eph 2:14), in order

---

[67] See report of the commission on Christian witness, proselytism and freedom of belief, approved by the Central Committee of the World Council of Churches at St. Andrews (1960).

to unite them in the single house of the Church, is here applied to the relationship between the Catholic Church and the Eastern Churches.

The Separated Churches and Ecclesial Communities in the West

For the title of this second section of Chapter III, see the discussion of *Ecclesiae et Communitates Ecclesiales* on Article 3 (above pp. 76–78) and that concerning the sub-division of Chapter III (above pp. 124 f.).

Article 19. The first article of the section provides an introduction to the discussion which follows. The quite justifiable desire of the Co-ordinating Commission of the Council to follow the description of the separated Eastern Churches in Chapter III of the Decree on Ecumenism by a similar account of the Christian communities of the West in the second section presented the Secretariat for Unity with considerable difficulties. The Churches of the East, united in their faith and structure, provide a contrast to the almost incalculable diversity of the Western communities and groups, which differ a great deal in their doctrine and structure. The original attempts of the Secretariat for Unity to characterize the faith and structure of the Reformation communities by describing characteristics common to them all were a failure. Whereas it was relatively simple to describe the ecclesiological status of the Eastern Churches, it proved impossible to achieve anything similar for the Western communities.

The renunciation of a description of this kind is reflected in the second paragraph of this article. It soon became clear that it was necessary to proceed differently here and to adopt a different style from that of the first section. Therefore a number of principal themes were chosen, which made it possible to state what was essential concerning the main concrete intentions and the Christian and Church life of the Reformation Churches and communities: their confession of Christ, the study of holy Scripture, their sacramental life and their life in Christ. In an ecumenical spirit, the decree strives to state as much as possible which is positive which unites these communities with the Catholic Church. But no service would have been done to the ecumenical movement — as several Protestant observers emphasized to the Secretariat for Unity — if nothing had been said concerning the differences and the divisive factors by contrast with the Catholic Church and Catholic teaching. So in each theme specific mention is made of differences of doctrine, and, again wholly in the spirit of ecumenism, there is an emphatic statement that these doctrinal differences should be the object of ecumenical dialogue between the Catholic Church and the Churches of the Reformation.

In order to state in concrete terms who the partners in the dialogue are, there is a brief and schematic summary of the most important Reformation denominations and communions, whose faithful number in all 246 million (or according to other estimates 263 million, against 548 or 493 million Catholics): Protestant Christians of the Lutheran Confession (75 million): Protestant Christians who are Calvinist or Zwinglian in outlook: Reformed Church, Presbyterians, Congregationalists (46 million in all), Methodists (41 million), Baptists (24 million), various other communities (10 million), Anglicans (50 million).

In addition to this there are a number of other autonomous national ecclesial communities which are separate from Rome and which do not derive from the Reformation; these number about 5 million faithful, and among them special mention should be made of the Old Catholic Churches of the "Utrecht Union".[68]

As already mentioned (cf. above pp. 76–78), the decree does not decide which of these communities should be called Churches in the theological sense from the point of view of the Catholic faith. No one on the Catholic side disputed that this term could apply to the Old Catholic Church with its apostolic succession, its valid priesthood and completely valid Eucharist. As far as the Anglican Communion is concerned, the question of the validity of Anglican orders has been reopened by some Catholic theologians.[69] But the question is complicated once again as a result of the union which the Anglican Communion is seeking with other communities who hitherto have had no episcopate (e.g., the Methodists). In South India these efforts have already been successful (the United Church of South India). Many Catholic theologians would prefer to see the criterion by which a community was judged to be of the nature of a Church less in an apostolicity and ministerial succession understood in a too "material" sense, and are consequently ready to accord the title Church (in the theological sense) much more extensively.

With regard to the complexity of the processes which led to the Reformation, and the event of the Reformation itself, it is natural that the decree does not attempt a description. In the first paragraph of this article, it does no more than speak in general terms of the very serious crisis *(gravissimo illo rerum discrimine)* and states that this was already beginning at the end of the Middle Ages. Doctrinal attitudes and demands which are characteristic of the Reformers are already to be found among a number of predecessors of the Reformation, especially John Wycliffe (d. 1384) in England and John Huss (d. 1415) and the Hussites in Bohemia. In order to emphasize the special links of Catholics (the Latin Church at least) with Christians of the communities which proceeded from the division in the West, the text points to the common religious history of the whole of Western Christianity. Numerous common factors of a historical, cultural, psychological, linguistic and ethnic nature have determined the thought and action of the Western Churches in a similar way, and in spite of the great differences which exist, have given the whole of Western Christianity certain common features *(peculiari affinitate ac necessitudine iunguntur),* so that their unity may seem greater to someone outside them than can be seen from within. Thus Orthodox

[68] Statistical details given from the *Handatlas des Neuen Herder* (1966), p. 11. The figures refer to the year 1960.
[69] The decision of Leo XIII (which was not an *ex cathedra* dogmatization) is contained in his letter "Apostolicae Curae", 13 September 1896; see *Denzinger* 1963–6.

theologians have already expressed the view that the gulf between Orthodoxy and the whole of Western Christianity, including the Catholic Church, seems greater to an Orthodox Christian than the gulf between the Catholic Church and the other Churches of the West (which is certainly not the case in regard to dogma).

The third paragraph of the article expresses in cautious terms a reserve which seems wholly appropriate in view of facts which are obvious. It was South American Fathers in particular who referred to saddening experiences in their own countries, where "Protestantism" was present in the form of numerous sects, which with their proselytism and an often intolerant attitude still showed scarcely anything of an ecumenical outlook. Furthermore, numerous Reformation communities refuse to take part in the World Council of Churches and its ecumenical efforts, and among the member-Churches of the World Council not all are ready for dialogue with the Catholic Church to the same extent. (This is presumably one of the reasons why the entry of the Catholic Church into the World Council of Churches is not yet recommended.) In many cases, Reformation communities are still concerned that the ecumenical movement may gradually lead to an abandonment of the understanding and achievements of the Reformation, that the World Council of Churches may develop into a centralized and totalitarian authority, and that to engage in dialogue with the Catholic Church would lead to a betrayal of the Bible and the sole lordship of Christ. But the decree expresses the hope that the ecumenical outlook which in recent decades has attained an extent which could not previously have been thought possible, will in time prevail throughout Christianity and overcome the mistrust that is present.

That the Decree on Ecumenism does not stand for false irenicism is shown by the last paragraph of this article, which clearly points out that very weighty differences *(magni ponderis discrepantias)* exist between the Catholic Church and the Reformation communities. Even what are called non-theological factors of separation must not be underestimated, but it is the significant differences in the interpretation of revealed truth which are decisive. It is these very questions of doctrine, however, which should be the subject of dialogue between the Churches, which, because of the essential differences between Reformation communities, cannot in fact simply be between the Catholic Church and "Protestantism", but must be carried out with each particular denomination. The themes of this dialogue, which are stated in the following four articles, naturally do not claim to cover the whole field.[70]

Article 20. A concern for the recognition of the fundamental and central status of Jesus Christ in the faith and life of the Church, and a striving towards a thorough-going Christocentrism, was from the very first the fundamental

---

[70] On the whole section cf. A. Brandenburg, "Die Sicht des Reformatorischen im Dekret De Oecumenismo", in *Theologie und Glaube* 56 (1966), pp. 335–49.

characteristic of the Reformation movement. The decree is consequently right in beginning with the confession of Christ, which for the Churches of the Reformation, as for the Catholic Church, is the foundation and centre of the whole confession of faith. But because the understanding of faith in Christ is different among Reformation Christians themselves, the Council addresses itself in the first instance to those whose confession of Christ is in fundamental agreement with that of Catholics. The clear allusion to the Christological and trinitarian wording of the "basis" of the World Council of Churches, accepted in New Delhi in 1961, shows that the reference is to the Reformation Churches which have joined together to form the World Council of Churches. The World Council described itself in the following terms: "The World Council of Churches is a fellowship of Churches which confess the Lord Jesus Christ as God and Saviour according to the Scriptures and therefore seek to fulfil their common calling to the glory of the one God, Father, Son and Holy Spirit."[71] The progress this represents by contrast with the wording of the "basis" of the World Assembly at Amsterdam, 1948 ("The World Council of Churches is a fellowship of Churches which recognize our Lord Jesus Christ as God and Saviour") is joyfully recognized by the Second Vatican Council in the Decree on Ecumenism. This of course does not mean that the more precise interpretation of the wording of the basis by individual Churches of the World Council is identical with the understanding of the Catholic Church. Thus within Churches which belong to the World Council theological opinions exist which reject the Christological and trinitarian dogmas of the Councils of early Christianity, which the Catholic Church and many Reformation Churches maintain. Moreover, there have been for centuries within Protestantism Unitarian communities and tendencies, which in their denial of the Trinity and the divinity of Christ show a profound divergence from the confession of Christ made by the Catholic Church and the greater part of Protestant Christianity. In any case a fuller understanding of Christ, and therefore also of faith in redemption, must be the object of ecumenical dialogue.

The Secretariat for Unity was anxious to mention also the necessity of dialogue concerning the ecclesiological and Mariological questions which today, as in the past, form the main points of controversy. Since no article was planned on these two groups of questions alone, it seemed best to refer to them in the present article concerning the confession of Christ: the mystery and ministry of the Church and the work of Mary are in fact very closely related to the mystery of Christ and of redemption.

That the Church is impelled by its faith in and loyalty to Christ to seek a greater ecclesiastical unity and to bear witness to Christ in the world, as the final sentence of the article states, is also emphasized by the World Council of Churches.

---

[71] Quoted in W. A. Visser 't Hooft, ed., *New Delhi Report. Third Assembly of the World Council of Churches* (1961), pp. 152 and 426.

Article 21. In the Reformation and in the whole of Protestantism a thoroughgoing reliance on holy Scripture was from the very first as characteristic as their Christocentricism, and was intimately associated with it. The reaction of the Reformers against the way in which the Christian gospel had become overgrown with human traditions during the late Middle Ages led to a new value being placed on holy Scripture, with a radical concentration on the biblical testimony, which was expressed in the principle *scriptura sola*. But it was a misunderstanding of the conviction held by the Reformers, for Protestant orthodoxy, at a later period, to make the Bible into a "paper Pope", as though the Reformation was concerned with the Bible as such, and as though its very letters were themselves the evident word of God. There was a reaction within Protestantism itself against this misunderstanding of the scriptural principle of the Reformation, on the basis of a simple identification of Scripture with the word of God. "Scripture possesses this authority, because it is the primary testimony of the revelation of God in Jesus Christ. Both the Old and the New Testaments, both Christian doctrine and Christian faith, are concerned with this revelation. Jesus Christ comes to us through the testimony of the apostles; as that which underlies and creates our faith, this testimony has normative force for us . . . The truth is that the real norm is the revelation, Jesus Christ himself, who bears witness to himself for our sake through the Holy Spirit, but who makes use of the testimony of the apostles for this self-revelation. But while we are committed in an absolute sense to the medium, the means by which revelation is given, represented by the apostolic witness, we are committed only in the relative sense to the authority of this testimony. The absolute authority is Jesus Christ himself, whom we possess only through the account and the doctrine of the apostles; but he whom we possess only through them, is above them."[72] In this comment, Emil Brunner is professing his acceptance of Luther's statement that Christ is *rex et dominus scripturarum*. Here false faith in the letter of the Bible is rejected, and replaced by what the Decree on Ecumenism states in the second paragraph of this article concerning Protestants: "Calling upon the Holy Spirit, they seek in these sacred Scriptures God as he speaks to them in Christ, the One whom the prophets foretold, God's Word made flesh for us." The testimony of the apostles laid down in holy Scripture is the primary means through which the revelation, the word of God which is Jesus Christ himself, comes to us. The "love, veneration, and near cult of the sacred Scriptures" on the part of Protestants, which the decree mentions, is based on the conviction that God uses the Bible to speak to us through the Holy Spirit at every time and place concerning the word revealed in Jesus Christ, which brings salvation. It is not the book as such, but the word of God to which the book bears witness, the gospel, which is regarded as "the power of God for salvation to everyone who has faith", as the decree describes the Protestant conviction in the language of Rom 1:16.

[72] E. Brunner, *Dogmatik,* I (3rd ed., 1960), pp. 55–57.

Love for the Bible understood in this way is the precious heritage of the Reformation, which all Protestant communities guard vigilantly. The Christian life of the faithful and the life of the Church are therefore formed and are constantly put to the test on the basis of the Bible. Protestant theology understands itself as an effort to obtain a better and better understanding of the biblical message and to give it actuality for every age. It is this love for holy Scripture which has made possible the great achievements of Protestant exegetical scholarship, which are also of value to Catholic theology.

The first sentence of the second paragraph contains three changes from the text that existed before 19 November 1964, which will be discussed in the appendix.

The first sentence of the second paragraph describes the subjective religious attitude and intention of Protestants when they read holy Scripture, and when they concern themselves with the Bible: they seek in Scripture the word of God, and the reading of Scripture signifies for them an encounter with the living God, so that it is carried out in the spirit and the atmosphere of prayer. It is not possible for the decree to declare that in each individual case they actually find the word of God, for it would not be possible to say this even of Catholics, although the latter have at their disposal the help of the authentic teaching office of the Church (which is mentioned in the second paragraph). A biblicist Protestant in fact would himself not accept that a liberal Protestant finds the word of God in Scripture in every case, and the majority of Protestant theologians would themselves not assert that the fundamentalist always finds the word of God. But that this search for the word of God on the part of Protestants is not in vain, is implied by the whole section on the Protestant Churches, with all its positive statements concerning the faith of Protestant Christianity.

One might add to this that Protestants would not seek the word of God in Scripture if they had not already found God who speaks to them, and found him, moreover, in Scripture, which mediates revealed truth to them. The word *quasi* introduced into the first sentence on 19 November 1964 *(Deum . . . quasi sibi loquentem)* does not bear the same meaning as this word when it is used in modern languages ("as if", implying an idea of metaphor or even pretence), but rather possesses the same sense as, for example, in the Vulgate text of Jn 1:14 *(et vidimus gloriam eius, gloriam quasi unigeniti a Patre:* the glory of the Son as of the only-begotten of the Father, glory exactly as the only Son possesses it from the Father) and 1 Pet 1:14 *(perfecte sperate . . . quasi filii obedientiae:* as obedient children). The expression in the text is therefore identical with the Latin word *tamquam* and is properly to be translated: "God as he speaks to them in Christ" ("God, as he who is speaking to them in Christ"). The wording used for the object of this search (with reference to the Old Testament as well), and the whole second sentence of the paragraph, are intended to point to the Christocentricism of Protestants in this very matter of the reading and study of Scripture.

The third paragraph first emphasizes the fact that the Reformation Churches are in agreement with the Catholic Church in affirming the divine authority of holy Scripture. "The sacred Scriptures contain the word of God, and, since they are inspired, really are the word of God" (Constitution on Divine Revelation, Article 24). The importance of this fact, that one sacred book is common to all Christians, has for a long time been too little appreciated by Christians, by contrast with their partial divergence in interpreting it. Holy Scripture is the fundamental "element" which creates the Church's community, and which is a practical bond which in the first instance unites all Christians, before its interpretation divides them: by contrast to the non-Christian world, Christianity exists as a community which professes the Bible as a sacred book.

But the text of the decree then goes on to refer to the fact that the views of the Reformation Churches (views which differ in themselves) are also different from Catholic teaching. The wording of the text is characteristic of the changed situation both in Protestant and in Catholic theology. On the one hand, the text does not imply that in Reformation Churches the relationship between Scripture and the Church is not appreciated at all, while on the other hand it does not say, as was customary in the past, that the Catholic Church recognizes two sources of revelation, Scripture and tradition, and finds in tradition revealed truths to which Scripture does not bear witness. In Protestant theology at the present day, the principle of *scriptura sola* is in fact interpreted with many more distinctions and qualifications than has long been the case, and there is a general understanding of the importance which the Church possesses as the vehicle and mediator of the Scriptures, and of the importance of its tradition for the interpretation and understanding of Scripture. Thus Scripture is not seen in isolation from the life and thought of the Church.[73]

Again, on the Catholic side, the unique significance of holy Scripture is more clearly seen. The Council refused to speak of two sources of revelation, and also, not least through the efforts of the Secretariat for Unity, tolerated the view of many Catholic theologians that the whole of revealed truth is found in holy Scripture (although in part only implicitly), while tradition has an interpretative function with regard to Scripture. Through the revaluation of tradition on the Protestant side and the revaluation of Scripture on the Catholic side, the two points of view have grown closer together.

As the text of the decree rightly emphasizes, the decisive issue is that of the magisterium and its function in the interpretation of holy Scripture. According to Catholic faith, and by contrast to the Protestant view, there is in the Church an authentic teaching office, which "plays a special role in the explanation and proclamation of the written word of God". This, of course, does not mean that without this teaching office it is impossible to derive revealed truth from

[73] Cf., for example, the report of Section II of the Fourth World Council for Faith and Order at Montreal (12–26 July 1963) on Scripture, tradition and traditions. Cf. also the contributions by several Protestants and an Orthodox theologian in K. E. Skydsgaard and L. Vischer, ed., *Schrift und Tradition. Untersuchung einer theologischen Kommission* (1963).

Scripture, or that the magisterium gives a Catholic binding information about details of scriptural interpretation. According to Catholic belief, the magisterium is a tool which God uses in a special way to protect the believing community from misinterpretation of the essential content of scriptural revelation, and to ensure that it possesses a proper understanding of the fundamental biblical truths of revelation. Here the question is not whether God can act in this way, but whether he has in fact chosen this way for the Holy Spirit to work. Catholic faith affirms this on the basis, moreover, of the testimony of holy Scripture itself.

A passage from the Constitution on Divine Revelation may serve here to characterize the Catholic view: "This teaching office is not above the word of God, but serves it, teaching only what has been handed on, listening to it devoutly, guarding it scrupulously, and explaining it faithfully by divine commission and with the help of the Holy Spirit; it draws from this one deposit of faith everything which it presents for belief as divinely revealed. It is clear, therefore, that sacred tradition, sacred Scripture, and the teaching authority of the Church, in accord with God's most wise design, are so linked and joined together that one cannot stand without the others, and that all together and each in its own way under the action of the one Holy Spirit contribute effectively to the salvation of souls" (Article 10). Because according to both Reformation and Catholic belief, God himself speaks to us through Scripture, so, as was stated in the previous paragraph, when attention is paid in dialogue to the word to which holy Scripture bears witness, progress is made towards the unity of the Church desired by Christ. For it is not the word of God which divides the Church, but the interpretation of the word of God, which is affected by many human factors.

Article 22. In this article the decree considers the sacraments, which are of particular ecclesiological importance. Here, however, it cannot simply state, as in the case of the separated Eastern Churches, that in the Reformation Churches all the sacraments are validly celebrated. Yet the two sacramental actions which are carried out by the Reformation Churches and recognized by them as sacraments, baptism and the Eucharist, are those to which the testimony of the New Testament is the most clear and on which its emphasis is the most definite; it is these to which the Catholic Church also accords the first place among all the sacraments, and which, by comparison with the other sacraments, possess a particular ecclesiological and ecumenical importance.

The first and second paragraphs of the article deal with baptism as the basic Christian sacrament. By its universal recognition in the first paragraph that baptism is fully effective for grace, when it is "properly (*rite,* i.e. with the action and words required on the basis of the New Testament) conferred in the way the Lord determined, and received with the appropriate dispositions of soul", the decree recognizes on principle the validity and effectiveness for grace ("fruitfulness") of the baptism carried out in the Reformation Churches. Under the conditions mentioned (which apply also, of course, to baptism carried out in the Catholic Church), it has the saving effects mentioned in the text, incorporation into Christ (or into the body of Christ, which is the Church) and rebirth into divine life.

The practice of the conditional baptism of Protestants who have become Catholics, which for a long time has been almost universal in the Catholic Church, was not based upon a doubt about the possibility on principle of a valid and saving baptism in Protestantism — the decision which was made in antiquity against the African practice (Cyprian) of the rebaptism of schismatics and heretics had never been forgotten —, but upon a doubt whether Protestant baptismal practice fulfilled the required conditions for validity. This doubt was provoked by the baptismal practice of a number of Reformation Churches, which arose in part under the influence of liberal theology, and could involve either the mere sprinkling or touching of the forehead of the baptized person with water, baptism with a non-trinitarian formula, and sometimes a baptism without the use of water. This doubt, which in many individual cases was justified, led to the almost universal practice of the conditional baptism of Protestants who became Catholics. The result was to give the unavoidable impression that the Catholic Church did not take seriously the baptism conferred in the Reformation Churches, and likewise did not take seriously its own doctrine concerning the validity of baptism administered outside the Catholic community. The revision of Catholic practice which is now being carried out is made easier by the restoration of baptismal practice in individual Protestant Churches (thus certain Churches which, for example, previously permitted baptism "in the name of Jesus" have come to insist upon the trinitarian formula). It would also be made easier if some Churches expressed less ambiguously the symbolism of washing with water in the act of baptism.

Part I of the Ecumenical Directory published by the Secretariat for Unity contains a lengthy section headed "The Validity of the Baptism Conferred by Ministers of Churches and Ecclesial Communities Separated from Us", which in twelve articles (Articles 9–20) lays down the principles and rules for a practice which is better in accordance with the high value placed on the sacrament of baptism and the recognition of the baptism conferred in other communities. The Directory does not dispute the fact that there are cases where doubt is justified concerning the validity of baptism conferred in Protestant Churches, but lays down the following principle: "The practice of conditionally baptizing without distinction all those who seek full communion with the Catholic Church cannot be approved. For the sacrament of baptism may not be repeated (cf. *CIC*, can. 732, § 1). Consequently, it is not permitted to repeat baptism conditionally, if there is no justifiable doubt either concerning the fact of the validity of the baptism which has already been administered (cf. the Council of Trent, Session VII, can. 4; *CIC*, can. 733, § 2). If there exists a justifiable doubt concerning the validity of a baptism, a careful inquiry must be carried out" (Article 15). "The whole question of the theology and practice of baptism ought to be discussed in the dialogue between the Catholic Church and separated Churches or communities" (Article 16).[74]

The Council was very concerned to assert the bond between all Christians on the basis of their one baptism. Consequently, the first sentence of the second paragraph of this article states: "Baptism, therefore, constitutes a sacramental bond of unity *(vinculum unitatis sacramentale)* linking all who have been reborn by means of it." The Ecumenical Directory expands this, saying, "It follows from this that baptism is the sacramental bond of unity, and indeed the basis of communion among all Christians" (Article 11). The bond that links all the baptized is also emphasized in the Constitution on the Church: "The Church recognizes that in many ways she is linked with those who, being baptized, are honoured with the name of Christian, though they do not profess the faith in its entirety or do not preserve unity of communion with the successor of Peter" (Article 15).

In the statements made in the text of the Decree on Ecumenism concerning baptism, three points must be specially noted. The first point is that baptism, as is shown by the reference in the text to the necessary disposition of the baptized person, and the quotation of Col 2:12, is not to be understood in isolation from faith. Baptism and faith must be seen in their unity. Baptism is not a way to salvation which is an alternative to faith, but is the continuation of faith into its sacramental form, and is the sacramental realization of the salvation received in faith. Baptism is itself the fundamental profession of faith. Secondly, baptism is not a purely individual action which a person receives as an isolated individual person, but belongs of its nature to the communion of the Church: The Church accepts a person into its visible sacramental communion of faith. Baptism is essentially incorporation into the Church. Thirdly, from both the points of view mentioned, both as the sacrament of faith and as the sacrament of incorporation into the Church, baptism is only a beginning, a point of departure; it is not yet something complete, but is a beginning in which an inner dynamic, leading to completion, is inherent *(initium et exordium est, quippe qui totus in acquirendam tendit plenitudinem vitae in Christo)*. On the basis of baptism, the baptized person should grow increasingly into the full knowledge of the reality of the Church and into the whole communion of the Church, and his faith, which is founded in baptism, should attain to the full profession of faith *(ad integram fidei professionem)* and participation in eucharistic communion *(ad integram denique in communionem eucharisticam insertionem)*. Because the Church is essentially *communio fidei* and *communio eucharistica*, *plena incorporatio* and *integra insertio* into the visible communion of the Church only exist when there is a "complete profession of

---

[74] G. Baum puts forward the thesis that the validity of the baptism administered in Protestant Churches does not depend upon its being in accordance with the mode of baptism laid down in the Catholic Church, but upon its being in accordance with the rite prescribed in the Church concerned. See his article, "Baptism in Protestant Churches", in *The Ecumenist* 5 (1967), pp. 49–52.

faith" and therefore the recognition of all the institutional "elements" of the Church (all the sacraments, and the hierarchical structure of the Church), and above all, the reception of the sacrament of unity in the highest sense, the Eucharist.

Although on the one hand the decree recognizes the validity and effectiveness for grace of baptism in the Protestant Churches, and emphasizes the bond between Protestants and the Catholic Church on the basis of baptism, it must also affirm (at the beginning of the third paragraph) that between the Reformation communities and the Catholic Church the full unity conferred in baptism does not yet exist. As a result of the differences in doctrine, the rejection of certain sacraments and of the hierarchical structure of the Church, the unity remains incomplete.

Consequently, the decree turns to the second sacramental action which is recognized and celebrated by the Churches of the Reformation as a New Testament sacrament: the Eucharist, or, in Protestant terminology, the Lord's Supper; and in association with this, it also briefly discusses the question of the Church's ministry. The text first emphasizes — here again, the statement is a judgment based upon faith *(quamvis credimus)* — that in the Reformation Churches "the genuine and total reality of the Eucharistic mystery" *(genuinam et integram substantiam Mysterii eucharistici)* has not been preserved. Before 19 November 1964, the expression read: *plenam realitatem Mysterii eucharistici non servasse.* The meaning of the expression has undergone no change as a result of the replacement of *plenam* by *genuinam et integram* and the addition of *substantia,* and the sole purpose is to express more clearly what is meant. The expression points to the fact that in the Protestant Lord's Supper the specific sacramental presence of Christ which is described in the Catholic Church by the dogma of the Real Presence of Christ and of Transubstantiation is not brought about. The decree mentions as the principal reason for this the lack of the sacrament of order *(propter Sacramenti Ordinis defectum).* According to Catholic teaching, it is not sufficient at the celebration of the Eucharist for bread and wine to be used, and the words of institution to be spoken; rather, the ordained minister, who, *personam Christi gerens,* carries out the actions, also belongs to the full sacramental sign.

Even though a number of Catholic theologians have tried to demonstrate that Protestant ordained ministers possess the apostolic succession and therefore the power of consecration, it is nevertheless the general Catholic view that this is not the case. This is not to deny that in congregations which are celebrating the Protestant Lord's Supper Christ is present. If it is true in general that "where two or three are gathered in my name, there am I in the midst of them" (Mt 18:20), it is even more true of the eucharistic assembly. The definitive text of the decree replaces the term *Eucharistia,* in earlier versions of the text, by the well-chosen expression *Mysterium eucharisticum.* Here the attention is not fixed upon the sacramental Real Presence, or on Transubstantiation, but instead expression is

154

given to the fact that the Eucharist manifests various aspects and dimensions. Thus the decree can do more than merely refer to a deficiency, and can also — in spite of the lack of agreement within Protestantism concerning the meaning and significance of the Eucharist — emphasize common and essential positive aspects of the Protestant Lord's Supper. It is a commemoration of the Lord's death and resurrection, a sign of life in communion with Christ, and an expectation and anticipation of the parousia of Christ. Whenever a congregation gathers together to celebrate the Eucharist in faith, hope, eschatological expectation and love, this celebration will effect grace in the faithful and strengthen their bond with Christ. Thus even a Catholic may not regard the Protestant Lord's Supper as a mere ineffective sign.

Neither the Reformation Churches nor the Catholic Church may regard the present state of their understanding in the field of the sacraments as something final and complete. Consequently, the last sentence of the article stresses the necessity of dialogue between the Churches on this subject, in the hope that it will lead on both sides to a more profound understanding of faith and to the drawing together of the Churches. The new ideas present in Catholic sacramental theology (the sacraments and the word, the sacraments and faith, the sacraments and the Church, the hierarchy of the sacraments, etc.) and a widespread revaluation of the sacraments and the liturgy in various Protestant communities suggest that this hope is justified.

Article 23. That the Decree on Ecumenism does not judge the Reformation Churches on the basis of a one-sided sacramentalism is shown by the last article devoted to them, which deals with the Christian life of Protestantism. Here the decree applies to Protestants what it stated in Article 4 concerning separated brethren in general: "It is right and salutary to recognize the riches of Christ and virtuous works in the lives of others who are bearing witness to Christ, sometimes even to the shedding of their blood. For God is always wonderful in his works and worthy of admiration." In the present article so much that is positive is stated concerning Protestant Christianity that one is reminded of the statement of St. Thomas: "Deus virtutem suam non alligavit sacramentis, quin possit sine sacramentis effectum sacramentorum conferre" (*Summa Theologica,* III, q. 64, a. 7c).

One must recall, moreover, that the decree says of separated Churches that they are not without significance and importance in the mystery of salvation. "For the Spirit of Christ has not refrained from using them as means of salvation" (Article 3). For their members, the Reformation Churches are the "total sacrament", which indeed is not articulated in all the seven individual sacraments as recognized by the Catholic Church, but which God uses to bring about the riches of Christian life and action in the individual and social fields which the decree mentions here. Baptism, which is conferred and received in these Churches, meditation on holy Scripture, the proclamation of the word of God, the celebration of worship (which "sometimes displays notable features of an ancient, common liturgy", as the text emphasizes — one may think, for example, of the liturgy of the Anglican and Lutheran Churches) bear rich fruit on the basis of a living faith, in the individual life, in the family and in the whole of human society. The decree here is not pursuing an apologetic which recognizes the fruitfulness of grace in the Catholic Church alone, but is taking seriously its recognition that the one Church of Christ is effectively present in other communities. The text leaves no doubt that the endowments which are found in Protestant communities are not "natural virtues" but the fruits of Christian faith and of grace. When the decree speaks in the second paragraph of an *operosa fides,* this is naturally not meant in a polemic sense, as if, in spite of Protestant teaching, a "righteousness of works" was being ascribed to Protestants. The remark can rather serve to draw the attention of Catholics to the fact that the Reformation Churches do not understand the doctrine of justification by faith alone *(sola fide)* in such a way as to suggest that faith need not also bear fruit in a life lived by faith.

Although the decree recognizes and places a high value on the seriousness with which Protestant Christianity strives for a life in accordance with the demands of the gospel, it does not conceal the fact that in the sphere of ethics there are disagreements between the Reformation Churches and the Catholic Church. It is true that Protestants, like Catholics, wish to "cling to Christ's word as the source of Christian virtue" and to do everything in the name of Christ, but their interpretation of the basic ethical demands of the gospel, which in any case is not a volume of concrete prescriptions for all situations in Christian life, differs on many issues from the moral teaching of the Catholic Church. But on the common basis of the gospel, dialogue can lead to a more profound understanding on both sides.

Article 24. The basic idea which dominates the concluding article of the Decree on Ecumenism is that of looking forward in hope to the future, an outlook characteristic of all ecumenical efforts. The Council is undoubtedly justified here in uttering certain warnings to Catholics. The ecumenical movement is in danger of becoming a fashion. The unexpected and intense upsurge of interest in ecumenism which was brought about by the Council could arouse unjustified hopes which would obscure the great obstacles which hinder the union of Christianity, and could permit an underestimation of the difficulties which must be overcome. The cause of ecumenism is damaged not merely by indolence and apathy, but also by unenlightened zeal. The Council gives a particular warning against the false view that ecumenism means a reduced loyalty to the Catholic faith. The movement which has been brought into the Church by the Council, the new idea which has been put forward at the Council, particularly with regard to other Christian communities, may give rise among many Catholics to the misunderstanding that the Catholic Church is seeking a compromise with other Churches, in order to achieve the union of Christianity. Against this, the Council emphasizes that true ecumenism demands of Catholics faithfulness to the truth inherited from the apostles and the Fathers and taught in the Catholic Church.

But this is only to express one aspect of a proper ecumenical attitude. Faithfulness to the Catholic faith does not signify a complacent satisfaction with one's own inherited possession. Not merely the abandonment of the truth received in faith, but also an immovable rigidity is unecumenical. Now that the Council, especially in the Constitution on the Church and the Decree on Ecumenism, has so clearly described the pilgrim state of the Church on earth, Catholics must be aware that even with regard to the knowledge of revealed truth the Church is always moving, and that it is essential for the progress of the ecumenical movement in particular that the Catholic community should always strive for "that fullness with which our Lord wants his body to be endowed in the course of time". Here what Y. Congar wrote as early as the eve of the Assembly of the World Council of Churches at Amsterdam (1948) is true: "As Catholics, we must preserve a true loyalty to what the dogma of our own Church affirms, that unity and apostolicity have been given, and given in this Church. Loyalty to Catholic dogma, which for us is the truth. But there may be two dimensions to loyalty, because the Catholic truth itself has two dimensions. And Catholic truth has two dimensions because it is a living truth, subject to development. There is a simple loyalty to the form taken by the truth at any given moment of its development, and there is fidelity to the truth in the movement by which it develops, in so far as it contains possibilities not reached at the present moment."[75] What Congar was not allowed to publish at that time, can and must be stated openly at the present day: in many respects, even with regard to the understanding of truth, what is given in the Catholic Church still needs to be developed.

The second paragraph of the conclusion contains a number of statements which are of decisive importance for the future of ecumenical activity in the Catholic Church, because they show the outlook and basic attitude with which the Catholic Church desires to take part in the ecumenical movement. The warning of the Council to Catholics to place no obstacles in the ways of divine providence and not to prejudge the future inspiration of the Holy Spirit, implies an important understanding; the ecumenical movement is not a purely human undertaking, for within it, in the first instance, the Spirit of God is at work through his grace. The faithful must co-operate with the divine dynamic which pervades the history of the Church, and not obstruct it by a closed system. They must take into account the divine event which can burst upon the Church, incalculable, unexpected, and beyond human control, and hold themselves ready to receive it. The ecumenical movement demands from the faithful a constant readiness and availability towards the action of God's grace.

---

[75] "L'Église catholique et le mouvement œcuménique à la veille de la Conférence d'Amsterdam", in *Chrétiens en dialogue* (1964), p. 64.

Archbishop A. Pangrazio of Gorizia, in his speech in the Council on 25 November 1963, referred to the mystery of the Church's history, which is characterized by divine intervention: "In the history of the Church, through the operation of the Holy Spirit, and with the co-operation or with the resistance of man, events often occur in a wholly unprecedented and unexpected way, which we cannot predict or understand through any theological system ... This consideration of the mysterious property of Church history seems to me to be of great importance for Catholic ecumenism. For just as in the Old Covenant the people of God learnt of God's merciful purpose through revelation, and were always able to hope that God would transform and set to rights, through unexpected events, the history of the people, when it was oppressed by misfortune, so it is possible and right for the people of the New Testament to cherish in the same way the hope that through his merciful grace, God will lead his Church, in ways still unknown to us, along paths which none of us can foresee or predict." It is in the ecumenical movement above all that the divine dynamic at work in history must be borne in mind, "through which God can bring about, not merely in separate communities, but also in the Catholic Church, events, developments and changes which cannot be foreseen by the present generation or by our Council. Because of these facts, God can make possible the unity of separated Christianity which we long for, and which still appears impossible today, if only all Christians would follow the impulses of divine grace."[76]

Just as only a few decades ago no one could have foreseen the ecumenical attitude adopted by the Catholic Church at the present day, so today, no one can predict future developments. Consequently, the statements of the Decree on Ecumenism cannot have the character of a programme laid down once and for all; they are what the Catholic Church is able to say on the basis of its present understanding.

Finally, fundamental importance is to be accorded to the understanding and profession of the Council that the reunion of all Christians in the one and only Church of Christ, although requiring human effort, is ultimately not the work of man, but the work of God alone. An ecumenical attitude excludes all triumphalism, and demands the humble admission of human inability. The unity of Christianity cannot be brought about by human action, but is the gift of God's grace. Consequently, the decree wisely concludes with an expression of the Christian hope, which is not based on human powers, abilities and calculations, but proceeds from faith in the love of the Father, the prayer of the Son and the power of the Holy Spirit.

[76] Congar, Küng and O'Hanlon, *op. cit.*, pp. 141 f.

APPENDIX

The nineteen changes inserted into the text of the Decree on Ecumenism at the request of Pope Paul VI on 19 November 1964

Since the commentary above discusses only a few of the nineteen changes in the text concerning which Pope Paul instructed the Secretariat for Christian Unity on 19 November 1964, these alterations are set out in full and briefly discussed here. In order to make more clear what the changes consist of, the individual passages in the text are set out side by side, first in the version before 19 November 1964, and then with the changes. The words added are placed in italics.

			Version before 19 Nov. 1964	*Version inserted on 19 Nov. 1964*
1.	1	1	discipuli Domini diversa sentiunt et per diversas ...	discipuli[1] *quidem* Domini *omnes se esse profitentur ac*[2] diversa sentiunt ...
2.	1	2	Omnes tamen ...	*Fere* omnes tamen ...
3.	3	2	ad unicam Christi Ecclesiam pertinent.	ad unicam Christi Ecclesiam *iure* pertinent.
4.	3	4	quae Ecclesiae concredita est	quae Ecclesiae *catholicae* concredita est
5.	3	5	Qui populus ... , quamvis peccato obnoxius remaneat, ...	Qui populus ... , quamvis *in membris suis* peccato obnoxius remaneat ...
6.	4	1	Spiritu Sancto afflante, ...	afflante Spiritus Sancti *gratia* ...
7.	4	4	cum utrumque ex actione Spiritus Sancti procedat.	cum utrumque *ex Dei mirabili dispositione* procedat.
8.	4	8	Divitias Christi et dona Spiritus Sancti ...	Divitias Christi et *virtutum opera* ...

[1] The sheet handed out to the Council Fathers says here *discipuli*. For grammatical reasons, this had later to be changed into *discipulos*.

[2] In accordance with the sense, the word *ac* in the sheet mentioned was later altered into *at*.

9.	4	9	quaecumque a Spiritu Sancto in fratribus seiunctis effici- untur . . .	quaecumque *Spiritus Sancti gratia* in fratribus seiunctis efficiuntur . . .
10.	13	3	in ipsa occidentali Ecclesia ortae sunt . . .	in *Occidente* ortae sunt . . .
11.	14	1	ab ipsis Apostolis originem ducunt	ab ipsis Apostolis *ortum habere gloriantur*
12.	14	2	ex Virgine Deipara incarnato . . .	ex Virgine *Maria* incarnato
13.	14	3	propter defectum mutuae comprehensionis . . .	propter defectum *etiam* mutuae comprehensionis . . .
14.	14	4	plenae communionis inter . . .	plenae communionis *optatae* inter . . .
15.	15	3	ut Catholici accedant ad has . . .	ut Catholici *frequentius* accedant ad has . . .
16.	16		ius et officium habere . . .	*facultatem* habere . . .
17.	17	1	formulae potius inter se compleri	formulae *non raro* potius inter se compleri . . .
18.	21	2	Spiritu Sancto movente in ipsis Sacris Scripturis Deum inveniunt sibi loquentem in Christo, . . .	Spiritum Sanctum *invocantes* in ipsis Sacris Scripturis Deum *inquirunt quasi* sibi loquentem in Christo, . . .
19.	22	3	plenam realitatem Mysterii eucharistici . . .	*genuinam atque integram substantiam Mysterii eucharistici*

The paper distributed to the Fathers in the general congregation of the Council on 19 November 1964, which in view of the required haste had been duplicated in the office of the Secretariat for Unity, contained the following introduction to the nineteen alterations in the text: "Praeter emendationes iam introductas iuxta modos a Patribus Conciliaribus acceptos, etiam quae sequuntur introducta sunt ad maiorem claritatem textus, a Secretariatu ad christianorum unitatem fovendam, qui hoc modo excepit suggestiones benevolas auctoritative expressas." ("Apart from the changes already introduced in accordance with the *modi* accepted by the Council Fathers, those which follow have also been introduced, to make the text clearer, by the Secretariat for Christian Unity, which has taken up in this way the kind suggestions authoritatively put forward.") The words *a Secretariatu ad christianorum unitatem fovendam* might give the false impression that the changes were accepted by the whole Secretariat for Unity. In reality they were accepted by the President and the Secretary of the Secretariat after a number of discussions with representatives of the Pope on the evening of 18 November. It was no longer possible to call together the bishops and the theologians of the Secretariat. With regard to the words *auctoritative expressas*, many observed that the fact that the changes had been desired by Pope Paul VI should have been explicitly stated.

a) On the changes in general

Most of the changes are clearly unimportant. No alteration at all was introduced into the text of Chapter II. It is at once obvious that some of the changes were justified. If an essential change in the whole orientation of the decree had been intended, the objections that followed would have been much greater. Many passages in the text provide an opportunity for essential changes, which in fact remained unaltered. There can in any case be no question of the conscious adoption of an attitude opposed to non-Catholic Christians or to the ecumenical movement. Non-Catholic observers also expressed the view that if the text had from the very first read as it did after the nineteen changes, the passages at issue would scarcely have occasioned any special notice. It was above all the way in which the changes in the text were made which caused the sensation.

Since no official explanation of the changes was given, the meaning and significance of the individual modifications must be produced from a comparison of the two forms of the text and the context, as well as from the wishes of the minority at the Council, which the Pope wished to take into account.

b) The individual changes

1. The change in the text is clearly intended only to affirm what can be affirmed in human terms, that is, that Christians profess themselves to be disciples of the Lord, and to leave to God the judgment whether they are so in Christ. At the same time, the change in the text makes more clear the contrast between the profession which Christians make and the scandal of their divisions.

2. The word *fere* which is introduced, brings with it a precision which may probably be justified in view of the fact that it cannot be asserted that all who take part in some way in the ecumenical movement are working towards a single visible Church of God.

3. The introduction of the word *iure* is intended to emphasize that the ecclesial elements mentioned are accorded to non-Catholic communities not in so far as they are separated from the Catholic Church, but in so far as the same Church of Christ, which possesses its concrete form of existence in the Catholic Church, is present in the same way in them. This is in accordance with the doctrine expressed elsewhere in the decree.

4. The word *catholicae* added to the word *Ecclesiae* is evidently intended to avoid an abstract concept of the Church and to make more clear the fact that according to Catholic faith, the Catholic Church is the concrete form of existence of the Church of Christ.

5. The insertion of the words *in membris suis* is intended to avoid a decision on the question which is disputed in Catholic theology, whether the Church itself (the people of God) can be termed sinful. No one, on the other hand, denies that the Church is sinful in its members.

6. The replacement of *Spiritu Sancto afflante* by *afflante Spiritus Sancti gratia* is an allusion to the wording used in the instruction of the Holy Office concerning the ecumenical movement in the year 1949 (*AAS* 42 [1950], p. 142). Nothing of substance is altered by this in the text.

7. The statement in the altered text that both the acceptance of individual non-Catholic Christians into the Catholic Church, and also ecumenical work, proceed from God's providence, instead of from the action of the Holy Spirit, as in the earlier text, presents a different point of view, without contesting the previous point of view. The preface has already derived the ecumenical movement from the work of the Holy Spirit.

8. The earlier expression *dona Spiritus Sancti* has presumably been replaced by *virtutum opera* because "gifts of the Holy Spirit" has a particular theological sense in scholastic theology (alluding to Is 11:1), which is not intended here. That the *virtutum opera* mentioned are understood as the action of the Holy Spirit is shown by the whole context.

9. The replacement of *a Spiritu Sancto* by *Spiritus Sancti gratia* should presumably be understood as an assimilation to the wording mentioned under (6). Here again, no change in substance can be perceived.

10. The change introduced avoids the question whether it is possible to speak of a division of the Church through the Reformation (which those who advocated the change in the text no doubt denied) or only a division in Christianity (or the separation of part of Christianity from the Church which remained undivided).

11. The new wording is evidently intended to avoid the historical question whether all the particular Churches of the East which claim apostolic origin are in fact really of apostolic origin.

12. The new wording, which makes no alteration in substance, introduces the word *ex Maria Virgine* from the Nicene-Constantinopolitan Creed. Perhaps this was due in part to the desire to see the name of the Mother of God mentioned.

13. The word *etiam* introduced in the new text seeks to make clear that there is no intention of giving a full list of the occasions of separation. Thus it is justified, and makes the text more clear.

14. The addition of the adjective *optatae* to the noun *communionis* does no more than specify more precisely the aim of ecumenical efforts.

15. The word *frequentius* added here also makes a justified precision: it cannot be asserted that there has previously been no concern at all on the Catholic side for the riches of the Eastern Fathers.

16. The change from *ius et officium* to *facultatem* cannot mean that the Eastern Church does not also have the duty to rule itself according to its own discipline. Otherwise, the expression *iure pollere et officio teneri* in the Decree on Eastern Catholic Churches (Article 5) would have had to be altered, which did not in fact take place. Since the Decree on Ecumenism is speaking directly of the separated Eastern Churches, it was presumably inappropriate for the Council to place a duty upon them (which was quite possible in the case of the Eastern

Catholic Churches). Thus here the intention is simply to emphasize the legitimate canonical autonomy of the Eastern Churches.

17. The insertion of the words *non raro* once again brings a justified precision. One cannot exclude the possibility that the varying theological formulae of the East and West may in some cases express a real opposition, and cannot be regarded as simply complementary statements.

18. This was the most important of all the nineteen changes in the text, and it was also that to which most attention was paid, and which provoked the greatest stir. Looking back upon it, it does not seem to be as grave as at the moment when it was announced. If it is more closely examined, three separate changes can be seen. The first is that instead of the previous expression *Spiritu Sancto movente,* the text now states concerning Protestants that they read holy Scripture *Spiritum Sanctum invocantes.* Thus a statement concerning the "objective" side of the process is replaced by a statement concerning the subjective side. It is not being disputed that the Holy Spirit is at work, but this is not stated explicitly, as in the earlier text. All that is now stated is what is directly ascertainable by human knowledge. Two observations are in order here. In the first place, the other statements of this section repeatedly express the fact that God's grace is at work in the Christian activity of Protestants and bears fruit. Secondly, in describing the personal reading of Scripture by Catholics, one would have to demur from the statement that this always takes place at the inspiration of the Holy Spirit, because the Church can only describe the outward process, but cannot give any judgment upon God's action in concrete cases. This does not mean that the earlier wording was unjustified, because of course it was not to be understood of the activity of the Holy Spirit in every individual case.

As for the second change, the new version no longer says that Protestants find God in holy Scripture, but only that they seek him. Here again, the earlier statement is made subjective. Again, it is not disputed that those who read holy Scripture also find God. The other statements of this whole section make it sufficiently clear that such a finding is recognized by the Council. Again, however, it cannot be said of Catholics that in every case they find the word of God when they read Scripture. It is to be supposed that those who advocated the change were thinking above all of the liberal tendency in Protestantism, and also believed that they should guard against the misunderstanding that the personal reading of Scripture was sufficient, and that the teaching office was not also necessary. What we have said, however, does not imply that the two first parts of the change do not bring with them a certain weakening of the previous text.

This cannot be said, however, about the third change. For the word *quasi* which has been introduced cannot be translated "as if", as might be supposed from the use of *quasi* in modern languages. For if this were the meaning of the change in the text, the Latin would have to continue *quasi sibi loqueretur.* Rather, *quasi* has the same meaning as the word *tamquam*, as is also the case elsewhere in Church Latin (cf. Jn 1:14), *gloriam quasi unigeniti a Patre*, and 1 Pet 1:14, *quasi filii obedientiae*.

19. By replacing the previous wording *plenam realitatem Mysterii eucharistici* by the new wording *genuinam atque integram substantiam Mysterii eucharistici* no change in substance has been introduced. The latter more scholastic expression avoids the non-classical word *realitas* and at the same time states more clearly what is meant: as a result of lack of the sacrament of orders on the part of Protestant ministers, at the Protestant Lord's Supper, according to the Catholic view, the sacramental presence of Christ as described in the dogmas of the Real Presence and of Transubstantiation does not come about (which does not mean that Christ is not present at all or that the celebration of the Lord's Supper does not possess any effectiveness for grace). The word *substantia*, which in classical Latin means "permanence", "actual existence", may have been chosen as an allusion to the word *transsubstantiatio*.

Decree on the Bishops' Pastoral Office in the Church

by
Klaus Mörsdorf

History of the Decree*

The Decree on the Bishops' Pastoral Office in the Church is based on two different documents, the schema "On Bishops and Diocesan Government", which was discussed at the second session of the Council in connection with the schema of a dogmatic constitution of the Church, and the schema "On the Care of Souls" which failed to come up for a general discussion because of lack of time. During the second session the Fathers began to realize that they would have to limit the material before them if the Council was to be brought to a happy conclusion in the foreseeable future. Only two documents had reached the final stage, and fifteen more were waiting to be discussed. Hence restrictions were imposed after the second session; among them was the proposal to produce a new document which would integrate the more important parts of the schema "On the Care of Souls" into that "On Bishops and Diocesan Goverment". This accorded with wishes frequently expressed in the Council hall. The commission responsible for both schemata (*Commissio conciliaris de Episcopis ac de dioecesium regimine,* here either called simply the Commission, or Commission for Bishops, if it is to be distinguished from other commissions) went to work at once and gave the new draft the title: "On the Bishops' Pastoral Office in the Church". Thus the decree under discussion has developed from the two schemata "On Bishops and Diocesan Government" and "On the Care of Souls".

I. THE SCHEMA "ON BISHOPS AND DIOCESAN GOVERNMENT"

From the beginning the subject of the bishops, and especially their relation to the Pope, was one of the main themes to be discussed by the Council. As it belongs to the sphere of doctrine as well as to canon law, the Theological Commission dealt with the former, the Commission for Bishops with the latter aspect of the problem, while it was clear that the theological concept of the

* *Translated by Hilda Graef*

bishop was the basis of the legal position. The changes made in the schema on the Constitution of the Church regarding the bishops naturally affected the work of the Commission for Bishops, so that the development of the schema on the bishops is intimately connected with that of Chapter III of the Constitution on the Church. This connection was repeatedly pointed out in the Council hall, and the speakers emphasized that the legal order presupposes the theology of the episcopal office. They were, however, scarcely conscious of the fact that the "theological" statement about the bishops is already a legal statement, and that both are actually distinguished only in that one is the foundation of the other and provides the norm for further legal elaboration.

1. The working out of the draft

While the preparations for the Council were going on, the higher superiors of the religious orders, the dicasteria of the Roman Curia and the Catholic universities had made many suggestions on the subject of the bishops. By and large these were concerned not so much with the theological basis of the episcopal office as with practical questions, especially with giving the bishops greater powers and increasing the position of titular bishops, particularly in their capacity as coadjutors or auxiliary bishops. Taking into account the various suggestions, the Preparatory Commission produced five schemata which corresponded to the five chapters of the schema "On Bishops and Diocesan Government". This was made accessible to the Council Fathers in the third series of the "Schemata constitutionum et decretorum ex quibus argumenta in Concilio disceptanda seligentur" of the year 1962 (pp. 67–90). Having examined the schemata submitted to it in the spring of 1962, the Central Commission returned them to the Commission for Bishops with a number of proposed changes. After further alterations the schemata were submitted to a subcommission of the Central Commission "for the emendation of the schemata" and from there to the cardinalitial subcommission "on mixed matters". After further repeated examination this latter combined the two, handing the resulting document over to the General Secretariat on 6 December 1962, and directing it to be discussed in the Council hall after the Constitution on the Church. In the meantime the Conciliar Commission for Bishops had been formed; its president was Cardinal Paolo Marella, and about half of it consisted of members and advisers of the former Preparatory Commission. The Commission received the document on 12 December 1962. Some of the *periti* residing in Rome produced explanations of the various chapters, as had been requested by the mixed commission. In January 1963 the schema was submitted to the Co-ordinating Commission; Cardinal Julius Döpfner was to report on it. As there was little time left to make it ready for discussion by the Council, work on it was intensive. The Co-ordinating Commission suggested many alterations and ordered the various episcopal faculties to be taken out of the text and placed in an appendix, which was not to be discussed in the Council hall. This interfered considerably with the external form of the draft; it was meant to obviate the danger of a lengthy discussion of the various powers in which the bishops were very interested. This measure proved to be very fortunate, since it turned the attention away from the manifold powers, concentrating it rather on the main concerns of the schema.

On 31 January 1963 the decision of the Co-ordinating Commission was communicated to the president of the Commission for Bishops, the changes in the draft having to be completed by 10 March. For time was running short. A rump commission, consisting of several members and *periti* resident in or near Rome, produced the new text of the draft, including also proposals recently suggested by other members of the Commission. This new text was to be communicated to the Co-ordinating Commission on 20 March and the Bishops Commission was to decide on it at a plenary meeting to be called for 30 April. The Co-ordinating Commission, however, approved the draft on 26 March, and, considering a discussion by the Commission for Bishops unnecessary, had the new text distributed to all the Council Fathers. This was done by the Cardinal Secretary of State on 22 April. According to Bishop Carli's report some passages could still be improved during the printing; this was due to the co-operation of Commission members of several nationalities who happened to be in Rome at the time. Later this procedure was sharply attacked during the discussion in the Council hall. However, the exclusion of the Commission for Bishops cannot be attributed to ill will, but only to the pressure of time. It had, in fact, no bearing on the further course of the discussions, because the basic question of the episcopate, which belonged to the Constitution on the Church, had not yet been treated.

The schema destined for discussion by the Council gave a short introduction (n. 1) and was divided into five chapters, each with its own preface; several chapters were further subdivided into sections.

Chapter 1: The Relations between the Bishops and the Sacred Congregations of the Roman Curia (nn. 2–5).

I. The Powers of the Bishops (n. 3).

II. The Practice of the Sacred Congregations concerning the Bishops (nn. 4 and 5).

Chapter 2: The Coadjutor and Auxiliary Bishops (nn. 6–16).

Chapter 3: The National Episcopal Conference (nn. 17–25).

I. The Establishment of the Conference (n. 18).

II. The Direction of the Conference (nn. 19–21).

III. The Decisions of the Conference (nn. 22–24).

IV. The Relations between Episcopal Conferences of Several Nations (n. 25).

Chapter 4: The Suitable Boundaries of the Dioceses and Ecclesiastical Provinces (nn. 26–32).

Chapter 5: The Erection of Parishes and their Suitable Boundaries (nn. 33–37).

There followed two Appendices. The first Appendix contained the ordinary faculties to be given to the bishops in virtue of their office; a distinction was made between the diocesans, who were to be given twenty-nine faculties in all, and all the bishops, including the titular ones, who were to be given four faculties. In the latter case all bishops were to have faculties to hear confessions everywhere and to be able to absolve also from reserved sins and corrective punishments, to preach and to reserve the Blessed Sacrament in their own domestic chapels. The faculties suggested for the diocesan bishops were assembled according to the order of the *CIC* and aimed at a considerable decentralization of the ecclesiastical administration.

The second Appendix was devoted to the practice of the Cardinals' Congregations and their relation to the bishops. It took account of certain suggestions concerning the responsibilities and methods of the various Sacred Congregations, the reports of bishops to the Apostolic See, their early information about the measures of the Sacred Congregations and the abolition of taxes on sales of ecclesiastical property as well as church debts. It was proposed, for example, that the responsibilities of the individual congregations should be simplified and that matters of minor importance as well as those concerning only the dioceses of one nation should be left to the bishops or the episcopal conferences. Questions, for which several dicasteries are responsible should be dealt with by a mixed commission; the methods of the Cardinals' Congregations should be better adapted to the spirit of the times and a clear distinction should be made between administrative and judiciary methods. Furthermore, the manner of reporting to the Apostolic See should be simplified, and the bishops should be informed about measures of the Roman Curia before these were made publicly known. All these wishes concerned the reform of the Roman Curia, which is the responsibility of the Pope, and hence could not be carried out directly by the Council.

This draft differed considerably from the schema of 1962. The division into five chapters had remained the same, only the headings of Chapters II and IV were better adapted to their contents. Nevertheless, the overall picture was quite different. The lengthy preface had been radically shortened; instead, each chapter had been given its own preface. The two appendices on the faculties of the bishops and the practice of the Cardinals' Congregations allowed Chapter I to be limited to some principles, though these were unsatisfactory, since they were based on a conception of the episcopal office that had to be changed. The unity of diocesan government was more or less secured by the proposals in the second chapter, which dealt with coadjutor and auxiliary bishops. The third chapter removed the intervention of papal nuncios and delegates and suggested a compromise solution of the main question whether and in how far the bishops' conference was to become a hierarchical institution with authority to make legally binding decisions within its boundaries. The solution proposed gave it at least a general authority in some important spheres. Chapter IV, on the boundaries of dioceses and ecclesiastical provinces, was considerably shortened, which was a great advantage. Chapter V, on the erection and boundaries of parishes, was also shortened, but, like the draft, was far from treating adequately the difficult question of parish organization. On the whole, the patient work on the draft had resulted in a schema that compared favourably with others because of its brevity and relevance.

2. The discussion in the Council hall

The discussion began in the 60th (24th) general congregation on 5 November 1963 and was concluded in the 68th (32nd) general congregation on 15 November. In the general debate which occupied two sessions thirty Fathers spoke on the schema, opinions on which were divided. However, those who were against it as well as those who were for it accepted it as a suitable basis for discussion. For when, on 11 November, the question was put to the vote, 1610 Fathers voted for and 477 against it, 13 votes being invalid. In the same session Patriarch Maximos IV Saigh opened the detailed discussion with a report on Chapter I which attracted much attention. During the discussion of Chapter II the Moderators became convinced that a discussion of Chapter V could be dispensed with, not only because of the purely legal contents of the chapter, but also because the draft was jejune and time was running short. On 12 November the general congregation accepted the proposal of the Moderators, according to which Chapter V was not to be discussed but was to be transferred to the commission for the revision of the *CIC*, while the Fathers were free to make suggestions in writing.

Though the general debate was not meant to be concerned with details, the Fathers nevertheless considered such questions as the relation between Pope and bishops (Chapter I) and the episcopal conference (Chapter III). On the other hand, several Fathers made suggestions concerning the whole schema in individual debates. Hence we shall report on the discussions not chronologically, but systematically, also because there was no genuine dialogue. This had also been the case in the discussion of the same problems in the schema on the Church, though in both cases a true dialogue would have been urgently necessary. To understand the actual situation it should also be remembered that the discussion of our schema followed on the discussion of the schema on the Church and that the voting on the so-called test questions (cf. vol. I of this commentary, p. 116) had taken place on 30 October 1963, when the principle of collegiality had indeed been approved by a large majority, but had not yet been legally established. During the discussion of the schema on the Church both friends and enemies of the principle of collegiality had fought each other for three weeks; now, when this principle was to be applied in practice by the schema on the bishops they had once more an opportunity to air their views. This was especially important for the defenders of the principle of collegiality, because the schema under consideration was still based on different presuppositions.

a) Inclusion of the principle of collegiality

The criticism of the whole schema envisaged especially the question of collegiality. This was to be the leading idea of the whole schema (Garrone), which should even be expressed by a new heading, "The Practice of Collegiality" (Marty). The French Fathers made original suggestions for a new structure of the schema which was to be determined by the principle of collegiality. Thus Cardinal Richaud proposed to begin with a chapter dealing with the local Church (= diocese) and to go on from there to chapters on the relation of the diocese to the ecclesiastical province, to the episcopal conference and finally to the Apostolic See. Other Fathers made similar suggestions, advising a graded co-operation of the college of bishops, hence also its graded composition (Marty), or pointing out the fact that the ancient idea of *koinonia* was effective also in the relations between sections of the Church (Guerry). These considerations corresponded to criticism made by the representatives of the Eastern Churches, who objected that the schema took no account of their constitutional laws (Patriarch Maximos IV Saigh, Amadouni, Coderre). However, many Fathers also praised the structure of the schema, especially the proposals on the relation between the bishops and the Curia and on the episcopal conferences (Cardinal Gracias). The opponents of the principle of collegiality (among others Cardinals Ruffini, Ottaviani, Browne, and especially the sagacious bishop Carli) emphasized that nothing had yet been decided about the doctrine of the collegiality of bishops, the representatives of which might be suspected of wanting to limit the papal primacy at least in practice (Cardinal Ottaviani). Considering the as yet undecided question of collegiality a detailed discussion of the schema was regarded as premature (Veuillot). Moreover, the schema was said to lack a theological foundation and to offer no basis for approaching such important subjects as the relation between the bishops and the Roman Curia or the episcopal conferences. Hence the Fathers should wait for the final version of the schema on the Church.

b) Pastoral orientation

The schema was frequently criticized for being too interested in administration (Cardinal McIntyre), too legalistic in spirit and expression (de Bazelaire), too dry (Ruotolo), etc. It was therefore suggested to combine some parts of the schema with those on the care of souls and the training of priests to form a new comprehensive draft; thus the schema on the bishops would be less legalistic and more in line with the pastoral intention of the Council (Fernandes, Master General of the Order of Preachers). At the same time it was suggested to say more on the pastoral aims of the episcopal office.

c) Subsidiary principle

The whole debate was governed by the demand for restoring the original rights of bishops. Moreover, the German and Austrian Council Fathers (Cardinals König and Bea, Archbishop Schäufele for the German bishops and Bishops Gargitter and especially Schoiswohl) asked that the subsidiary principle should be recognized also in the Church. They knew well, of course, that this is a purely formal principle which does not suffice to establish concrete relations, and that there are barriers in the Church, erected by divine law, which cannot be abolished. But within these limits there are many differences, so that it was sensible to demand that the subsidiary principle should be valid also in the Church, a fact which, according to Archbishop Schäufele, had also been recognized several times by Pius XII. The main emphasis was on establishing a new relationship between the Pope or the Roman Curia and the diocesan bishops; while the critical observer noticed that the problem of the direct primatial authority of the Pope had not been mentioned. The Council Fathers admitted the right of the Pope to reserve certain matters to himself or to another authority, but they asked that this right should only be exercised when the unity of the Church demanded it. The same principle was to apply to the relation between the bishop and the diocesan authorities subject to him (Schoiswohl). Since the Council had revived the idea that all members of the People of God participate in the work of the Church, Cardinal Bea said that it was not the business of authority to do what the individual members could do themselves, but only to supplement what they could not do, to support them and to assure that their activities were well-ordered and directed towards the common good. The same principle should apply to the relation between lower and higher authorities.

d) Participation of the bishops in the direction of the whole Church

The question of the co-operation of the bishops in the direction of the whole Church played an important part in the new ordering of the relations between Pope and bishops. Since the Council could not continue for ever, the latter wanted to create a separate council of bishops which was to aid the Pope in the government of the universal Church. Even during the preparation of Vatican II such a council had been discussed, but the relevant schema had not envisaged it, but had only proposed to make diocesan bishops members or consultants of individual Congregations. Nevertheless, in his allocution to members of the Roman Curia of 21 September 1963, and again when opening the second session on 29 September, the Pope had declared himself prepared, if the Council wished, to create a council of bishops, consisting mostly of diocesans, which was to assist him in dealing with special questions of Church government. Cardinal Liénart, who was the first to speak on the schema of bishops, proposed to submit to the Pope a petition of the Council Fathers dealing with this suggestion.

The proposal, however, was pursued no further, probably because the wish of the Council Fathers was in any case generally known, and also because opinions on the task and legal form of a council of bishops differed to such an extent that it would have been almost impossible to draw up an acceptable document.

Patriarch Maximos IV Saigh produced a theologically as well as historically well-founded criticism of the schema. He said that, apart from the diffident attempt of making diocesan bishops collaborators of the Roman Congregations, the only bodies to assist the Pope in the government of the Church visualized by the schema were those that had emanated from the ecclesiastical government of the city of Rome. The difference between the direction of the universal Church and that of the Church of Rome was completely obscured. Instead of an ecumenical Church outsiders saw only a Church, which, owing to historical circumstances, was a highly developed particular Church. He demanded that the duties of the Pope as supreme pastor of the Church should be clearly distinguished from those he has to fulfill as the Patriarch of the Latin Church, the Primate of Italy and Bishop of Rome, the latter having to take second place. In the government of the universal Church the Pope as the successor of St. Peter ought to be joined by the bishops, the successors of the apostles, but not by the clerics of the city of Rome. To reflect the co-operation of "Peter with the apostles" in the government of the universal Church, it was proposed to establish a sacred college of the universal Church consisting of the resident apostolic patriarchs such as had been recognized by the first Ecumenical Councils, of those Cardinals who were resident archbishops and of bishops to be elected by the regional bishops' conferences. This council was to meet at regular intervals and as often as seemed necessary for discussing general questions. Furthermore, a Supreme Council of the Church *(Supremum Ecclesiae Consilium)* was to be created after the pattern of the permanent Synod of the Eastern Churches. This was to be a permanent institution to assist the Pope, to which all Roman institutions were to be subject. The relation between the Pope and these two commissions was not determined more exactly, but was probably to operate according to the formula *"una cum"*. These suggestions were based on a patriarchal and synodal administrative structure, while fully recognizing the papal primacy; but in the course of the discussion hardly any attention was paid to them. This is probably to be explained by the fact that a special decree on the Eastern Churches had been prepared. Hence the Council Fathers thought it unnecessary to integrate the characteristics of the constitutions of these Churches into the organization of the universal Church.

Cardinal Alfrink distinguished very strictly between the college of bishops and the council of bishops. According to him the council, whatever its composition, was neither the same as the college of bishops nor its so-called parliamentary representation, because the members of the council had no mandates from all the other bishops. Following up a suggestion of Archbishop Baudoux, Cardinal Alfrink regarded the council of bishops as a sign of the collegial leadership of the whole Church and moreover also as an instrument of carrying out this leadership, which would express the collegial character of the supreme government of the Church also apart from the Ecumenical Council. By emphasizing the unity of the Church this council of bishops would also in a way centralize ecclesiastical government, which was not unimportant in view of a certain decentralization brought about by the episcopal conferences.

A proposal made by Archbishop Schäufele in the name of the German episcopate suggested the creation of an apostolic council summoned by the Pope, in which resident bishops were to represent the episcopate of the whole world. Bishop van der Burgt, representing thirty bishops of Indonesia, proposed the creation of a senate, the majority of whose members were to be elected by the episcopal conferences. Many reasons were given for the necessity of such a senate, which was to be created while the Council was still in session, so that part of the Council material could be transferred to it and the bishops need not be kept much longer away from their flocks.

Even opponents of the as yet undefined doctrine of the college of bishops as the exponent of the supreme authority in the Church, e.g., Cardinal Ruffini, favoured the institution of a council of bishops according to the suggestion of the Pope, i.e., in agreement with the doctrine of the Church and canon law. It was also pointed out that such a council would be no novelty, since the Pope already had a council in the college of cardinals (M. Lefebvre).

e) The reform of the Curia

The discussion of the creation of a council of bishops was related to that of the reform of the Roman Curia. Evidently trying to effect a compromise Archbishop Florit proposed not to create a council of bishops but a central congregation within the framework of the Roman Curia. This was to be superior to all other congregations, to deal with matters as directed by the Pope and to be ultimately dependent on him. Several bishops, especially diocesans, were to be members of this congregation, so that the principle of collegiality was applied. Cardinal Lercaro, on the other hand, stated that no divine law prevented the Pope from according the body of bishops a more frequent or constant exercise of authority, at least through a truly representative body, if only the last decision on its suitability and activity always remained with the Pope. The Cardinal added that the institution of such a body was nothing new but corresponded to the earliest practice of the Holy See which had been continued till the 16th century. From the 12th century until the establishment of the Cardinals' Congregations by Sixtus V, the Sacred Consistory, which met three times a week, had been superior to all departments of the Roman Curia. Concerning the problem of curial reform Cardinal Lercaro said that today the Curia had no such general co-ordinating body, which he regarded as its greatest defect. He rejected Florit's proposal to create a central congregation, because a thirteenth congregation of the same structure as the others could not be *magis suprema,* especially as the Holy Office was already the highest congregation. He then turned briefly to the problems of curial reform such as the relation of the College of Cardinals to an organization representing the bishops and the distinction between an organization of general co-ordination and the specialized commissions, and stated that none of these problems could be solved by itself and that their solution was beyond the competence of the Council. Cardinal Spellman agreed, adding that the Curia was a papal organization, so that it could not be the task of the Council to determine its competences and institutions. Other Fathers, however, were concerned to emphasize that the college of bishops was superior to the Curia. Cardinal Alfrink especially stated that the Curia was not placed between the Pope and the bishops but that it served the college of bishops. The order in the Church was not first the Pope, then the Curia and after that the bishops, but first the college of bishops, i.e., the Pope with the other bishops, and then the Curia as the executive instrument of the college of bishops though also of the Pope. Others, however (e.g., Costantini), emphasized that the Roman Curia did not claim a special rank in the hierarchical structure of the Church, but was only an instrument of the Pope who alone had the right to determine its activities just as every other bishop with his Curia; hence the Roman Curia had no direct relation to the college of bishops. These utterances show how confused the constitutional problems of the college of bishops still were, especially as regards the relation of individual bishops to the Pope and the college of bishops as well as of the Pope and the episcopal college as bearers of the highest ecclesiastical authority. One Father (Simons) blamed the Curia for often being not simply an instrument of the Pope but governing according to their own ideas and raising, as it were, a wall between Pope and bishops. This may have confirmed the misgivings of many Fathers based on personal experiences with curial authorities.

As regards the officials of the Roman Curia, Cardinal Frings asked that fewer bishops and priests and more laymen should be employed. No one was consecrated a bishop only to honour his person or office, for being a bishop was itself an office, not an honour to be added to another office. If someone was consecrated, this was in order to make him a bishop and nothing else. In the same way ordination as a priest was not meant to honour anyone but to make him a pastor of the Lord's flock. The wish to internationalize the Curia was again expressed (by Gargitter among others). The idea of the draft to make bishops of various nationalities members or consultants of the Cardinals' Congregations was criticized (by Cardinals Lercaro and Rugambwa among others) because the problems of curial reform could not be solved in this way.

Questions of procedure were broached by Cardinal Frings. He suggested combining the essential statements of the second appendix, which dealt with the curial practice in relations with the bishops, with the schema itself, because otherwise it would remain too general and equivocal. The reform of the law of procedure was particularly important, especially the distinction between administrative and legal procedure in all Congregations including the Holy Office, the methods of which were frequently not in harmony with contemporary thought, were harmful to the Church and scandalized non-Catholics. Though well aware of the difficult work of the Holy Office, Cardinal Frings asked that no accused person should be judged or condemned before he and his bishop had been heard, been told why he or his writings were impugned and given the opportunity of amendment. The criticism of the methods of the Holy Office implied in these demands was vehemently rejected by Cardinal Ottaviani, who did not, however, offer an objective rebuttal. Nevertheless, the sometimes rather strong criticism of the Roman Curia was not wholly unemotional; hence other Fathers (Patriarch Batanian among others) felt impelled to praise its work and to declare these public criticisms a scandal.

f) The diocesan bishop

The draft provided that, apart from cases reserved to the Pope, the diocesan bishops were to have all the powers necessary for the proper exercise of their ordinary and direct authority under the Pope. Hence the powers they already had were to be increased and they were, among others, to have these enumerated in the first appendix. As was explained in a note, no legal titles for their faculties were given, since this was a theological question which was to be treated in the Constitution on the Church. But the Fathers (e.g., Mendes) were not satisfied with the will to give more power to the diocesans, for here the legal position of the bishops was at stake, and its definite clarification could no longer be postponed. In the general debate Archbishop Schäufele, representing the German bishops, demanded the restoration of the original episcopal law and proposed that because of his episcopal office the diocesan should have all the faculties due to him as the ordinary, the Pope always retaining the authority to intervene. In future there ought not to be a list of faculties but rather one of reservations. Other Fathers made similar demands on the Council floor, and a great number expressed their wishes in writing in order to avoid endless repetition. Some Fathers seemed to be annoyed by the very term "faculties", because this suggested the idea of a condescending grant (Cardinal Alfrink) or delegated powers which in legal terminology are regarded as privileges *praeter ius* (van Zuylen). Cardinal Ritter admitted that the change from the system of concessions to one of reservations would involve difficult legislation, hence he felt that this change could be made only together with the revision of the code of canon law.

One Father (Kalwa) criticized the draft for not defining the jurisdiction of a diocesan bishop more clearly and for only dealing with his relation to others without explaining how the diocesan bishop becomes what he is and how he can lose his episcopal position (Ferreira). An auxiliary bishop (Granados Garcia) suggested that here the bishop was not considered as a member of the episcopal college but as the head of his diocese; as such he was the bearer of Christ's salvation, the spiritual father of the faithful, the origin and centre of unity and at the same time the mediator of catholicity, because the universal Church is not only composed of individual Churches but subsists in them. Proposals for a new statement about the episcopal office made, among others, by French and South American bishops, were mostly concerned with the tasks of the diocesan bishop.

The question of the appointment of bishops concerned especially the abolition of the nomination rights of secular authorities (Ferreira, Attipetty). While this was discussed only rarely, the question of an age-limit provoked a lively debate. For in Chapter II, "On Coadjutors and Auxiliary Bishops", the diocesan bishops and others in an equal position were asked to resign voluntarily if permanent illness, old age or other grave reasons made this advisable. A note suggested that seventy-five was generally to be considered as the proper age-limit. Several Fathers opposed this, basing themselves on the early Christian idea of the spiritual marriage between a bishop and his diocese which is symbolized by his ring. Others regarded this as a no longer relevant mystical view, and Cardinal Suenens caused amusement when, referring to the present frequent translation of bishops, he suggested that the Council hall was full of bishops who had been divorced two or three times. The idea of the bishops' spiritual fatherhood ought not to be exaggerated, the most important matter was the salvation of souls. Many Fathers, including Cardinal Confalonieri, preferred voluntary to compulsory resignation. The views on the right date for retirement differed. Most Fathers were in favour of seventy-five, others of eighty years (Olaechea, Melas), and an African bishop wanted the age-limit for African bishops to be sixty years, because of the physical strains to which they were subjected. The economic objections of several Fathers aroused sympathy, for according to de Vito many bishops who had resigned their office were living in pitiful conditions. Hence Cardinal Cento suggested a pension fund to which all bishops were to contribute, thus giving an effective proof of episcopal collegiality. Representing many Indian and Asian bishops, the Coadjutor-Archbishop of Delhi, A. Fernandes, spoke of a realistic and an idealistic view of resignation. On the one hand sufficient provision should be made to prevent a bishop from fearing resignation for material reasons, for example by creating old age homes through the agency of the episcopal conferences, on the other retired bishops ought to give up the rights accorded to them by the draft. Abandoning all external splendour was the best preparation for a holy death.

g) Coadjutor and auxiliary bishops

The schema used a new terminology, according to which the coadjutor has always the right of succession, which the auxiliary bishop has not (n. 7). The latter is always the assistant of the diocesan, no matter whether his appointment is due to the needs of the diocesan or of the diocese.

From the beginning the legal position of the coadjutors and the auxiliary bishops belonged to the most controversial points of the schema on the bishops. The draft before the Council provided that the coadjutor bishop, in virtue of his office, should have the powers of a vicar general, while his diocesan could reserve nothing to himself, and that the Holy See or his diocesan could give him further faculties. The rights and duties of the auxiliary bishop, however, were to be determined in the apostolic decree of nomination; if this had not been done, the diocesan bishop was to give him necessary and suitable faculties not only to perform pontifical actions but also to serve in the diocesan administration. Thus the draft provided an office in the legal sense only for the coadjutor bishop, though even in this case the relation between the coadjutor and the vicar general appointed by the diocesan was not satisfactorily determined. That a real compromise had not been achieved could be gathered for example from the fact that the auxiliary bishops might be given further faculties by the Holy See or the diocesan bishop. Logically this presupposes that this extension of faculties is preceded by another, which is not delegated but exists in virtue of the office. Thus a statement had been retained which corresponded to an earlier conception but no longer made sense. The necessity of coadjutor bishops was widely questioned. This is proved by the fact that many Fathers favoured the retirement of diocesans at a certain age, for in this case coadjutors with the right to succession would no longer be necessary. Thus one coadjutor bishop (Anoveros) said that if the question of retirement were to be legally solved there would no longer be a reason for retaining the office of coadjutor. The proposal to invest the coadjutor with the rights of a vicar general by virtue of his office was rejected, because this might endanger the unity of diocesan government (Archbishop Schäufele). In order to avoid this danger it was also proposed to follow the practice common in the case of coadjutor abbots, according to which the coadjutor has all the rights and duties of an abbot, while the abbot himself retains only the honorary rights and may be consulted only in the most important matters (Gavazzi). Cardinal Confalonieri said that it was the experience of the Curia that the powers of a coadjutor bishop were frequently inadequate and had to be supplemented through the Holy See giving him the faculties of a diocesan; in some cases there might even have to be an Apostolic Administrator *sede plena*. The Fathers were probably unanimous in holding that the appointment of a coadjutor was to take place only in exceptional cases.

While the question of the coadjutor is solved by the death of the diocesan, the auxiliary bishop has become a constant institution, at least in the larger dioceses. The need for auxiliary bishops arises either from the size of the diocese or the number of the faithful, hence it coincides with the problem of diocesan organization. Only in exceptional cases will the appointment of an auxiliary bishop be due to the personal needs of a bishop. Hence it was criticized that the auxiliary bishop was not to be attached to the diocese but to its bishop (Stein). Cardinal Döpfner felt that more than one bishop in the same diocese conflicted with the principle of unity based on the bishop as head of the diocese. Hence overlarge

177

dioceses should be divided and an auxiliary bishop should be asked for only if no other measure would meet the need. Since auxiliary bishops were mostly required for administering the sacrament of confirmation, Cardinal Döpfner and Bishop Volk suggested to change the relevant rules so that the diocesan bishop could appoint a priest in a superior position to administer this sacrament. The representatives of the African Churches (Tchidimbo, Busimba) also demanded the abolition of auxiliary bishops; they argued that the idea of more than one bishop was foreign to African tribal mentality which recognized only one chief; Africans did not understand why a ceremonially consecrated bishop should have no authority afterwards, and what he could do better than a good and energetic priest, apart from administering confirmation and ordination. Others (Wehr and Stein) thought that large dioceses should be retained, but that they should be governed collegially "with and under the bishop" by a council of bishops to which the vicar general was to belong. According to this proposal all auxiliary bishops were to have the faculties of a vicar general.

Opinions were very divided on the powers of an auxiliary bishop, owing to the confusion regarding the relation between episcopal consecration and episcopal office in the legal sense of the term. Representatives of the auxiliary bishops asked which powers an auxiliary bishop had through his consecration, especially as the powers of a diocesan, too, resulted from his consecration. They pointed out that because of their consecration the auxiliary bishops were members of the episcopal college and thus participated at least in the basic tasks and powers of a bishop, within the diocese as well as outside it. This view, very popular on the Council floor, was opposed by Bishop Volk among others, who emphasized that the episcopal office had not yet been clarified theologically. Such a definition would have to start from the idea of the bishop as the head of an individual Church who not only led his faithful as their pastor, but also represented them at the Council as well as in the daily exercise of his office. The combination of consecrating and pastoral powers was based on the idea that the bishop should be responsible for a certain diocese. It was further said that in the Latin Church, which now had more titular than diocesan bishops, the proportion between a rule and its exceptions was reversed. Facts could indeed show what was possible, but not necessarily what was good.

Cardinal Döpfner opposed those who wanted to furnish auxiliary bishops with a legally defined office with certain duties and faculties. He considered this impossible, owing to the different conditions in the various dioceses; the auxiliary bishop was meant to assist the diocesan, who must decide how much assistance he needed. Apart from assisting at pontifical functions and representing the bishop on solemn occasions, many tasks might be assigned to the auxiliary bishop according to the needs of the diocese without damaging the unity of episcopal government. The auxiliary bishop might be appointed vicar general for the whole or part of the diocese; this would commend itself especially if part of the diocese seemed likely to have to be separated and erected into a new diocese in the near future. He might be given a post in the cathedral chapter or in the diocesan curia, if possible one closely connected with the visitation of the diocese, because here the auxiliary was the most important assistant of the diocesan bishop.

Bishop Pohlschneider opposed the proposal of the draft to entrust the auxiliary bishop with duties of government, because this might endanger the unity of diocesan government. The unity of diocesan administration depended on the vicar general; though in certain places it was customary to appoint several vicars general, it would be better to retain the principle of appointing only one, because otherwise the burden of co-ordination would fall back on the diocesan. Nor would it be suitable to appoint an auxiliary bishop the only vicar general, because the task of the former was mostly to assist the diocesan in preaching as well as in pontifical duties, especially in the visitation of parishes.

In order to increase the status of the auxiliary bishop the draft suggested that in the case of *sede vacante* an auxiliary bishop should be elected vicar capitular if this was possible. Cardinal Döpfner and Archbishop Schäufele, among others, opposed this in order to preserve the freedom of the chapter as well as to prevent a possible lessening of esteem if he were passed over. It would serve the auxiliary bishop's authority better if he were to be freely elected by the chapter without such an order.

The auxiliary bishop shares his unsatisfactory situation with every other so-called titular bishop; but in his case it is aggravated by the fact that he has real episcopal functions even if only in an assisting capacity, but is consecrated to a title which always reminds him that he is a shepherd without a flock. In order to obviate such feelings many Fathers (Caillot, Wehr, Stein, among others) asked that the practice of consecrating titular bishops to a no longer existing see should be given up, because it was a mere fiction and, moreover, was not acceptable from an ecumenical point of view. Some Fathers proposed to consecrate coadjutor and auxiliary bishops to the service of the diocese to which they were to be attached, and to assign to a diocesan who had resigned his bishopric not, as has been the custom, an extinct diocese but the honorary title of a bishop emeritus of his diocese. Titular bishops called to other duties, for example to the Roman Curia, might be consecrated to their special service.

h) The episcopal conference

The national conference of bishops had become an institution established by custom in many Western countries, but as yet without any legislative powers. According to the proposal of the draft it was to become a hierarchical intermediary between Pope and bishops, empowered to make legally binding decisions for its own region in a strictly circumscribed sphere. Against all expectations this proposal was severely criticized. It was generally accepted only that the episcopal conference had come to stay, that it was a useful institution and that the Council had to give it a basic legal form to be further developed by the individual conferences. Only few Fathers accepted the draft proposal, and even they only with certain proposed emendations, among them Archbishop Schäufele for the German and Cardinal M. Browne for the Irish bishops. The experiences with episcopal conferences in the United States, Germany and Poland were proudly presented by Cardinals Spellman, Frings and Wyszynski respectively, but, as Cardinal König pointed out, they were at the same time to prove that their development into a hierarchical body was not to be favoured. Beside the danger of a legal confusion, Cardinal Ruffini feared that the papal jurisdiction might be imperilled, because the Pope could hardly deny the decisions of an episcopal conference his consent.

Cardinal Spellman stated that if the episcopal conference were to be given legislative powers it would be superior to the General Council, because, unlike the latter, it would not be directed by a papal legate. There was also talk of the dangers of creating national Churches and an oligarchy of bishops (Olaechea) as well as a national curia (Franić). Cardinal Siri, among others, pointed out emphatically that the freedom of individual diocesan bishops must be preserved. Hence the criticism of the draft was twofold: on the one hand the Fathers feared a reduction of the rights of the Pope, on the other a diminished independence of the diocesans. The episcopal conference had, as it were, fallen between two stools. It is one of the oddities of the Council that the collegial element in the constitution of the Church was indeed approved for the whole Church, but not within individual churches. The Fathers affirmed the principle of collegiality in their relation to the Pope, but denied it for the relation of the bishops of one region to one another. This proved clearly that the doctrine of the episcopal college had been treated in too abstract a manner without regard to the fact that the principle of collegiality had first been applied in individual Churches.

Nevertheless, many French and Eastern Fathers also pointed out the connection between the episcopal conference and the rightly understood collegiality of the bishops. The episcopal conference was said to be a form of exercising collegiality (Cardinal Richaud), its absolute necessity for co-ordinating the work of the bishops was emphasized (Garrone) as well as its integration in a graduated structure of the episcopal college, with its own offices and general secretariates (Marty). The idea of the *koinonia,* the fraternal union of the individual Churches such as it existed in the first Christian centuries, which is founded on Scripture and tradition, was said to be one of the theological bases of the episcopal conference (Guerry). Another Father (Ancel) emphasized the responsibility that transcended one's own diocese and included the collegial support of others, a responsibility that preceded episcopal jurisdiction and was based on the apostolic vocation. An Eastern Father (Zoghbi) drew the parallel to diocesan synods and mentioned the synodal elements in both East and West, asking as a condition of the dialogue with the Eastern Churches that the episcopal conference should have legislative powers.

Bishop Carli opposed the idea that the episcopal conference was based by divine right on the principle of episcopal collegiality. Though not rejecting the common responsibility of the bishops in the horizontal sphere, he denied the idea for theological, legal and historical reasons and said further that no member of the Bishops' Commission had ever thought of it when working on the schema. He invited the diocesan bishops to consider the principle of episcopal collegiality with regard to the implications of the episcopal conference. Cardinal Alfrink, evidently trying to reconcile the opposing opinions, also rejected the view which regarded the episcopal conference as the realization of the collegiality of the bishops. According to him this referred always and essentially to the whole body of bishops and their work for the universal Church. He conceded, however, that the idea of collegiality was also in some way realized in the episcopal conference, but not as a participation in the power and authority of the episcopal college, and he sought to derive the authority of the episcopal conference from two different sources, first from the authority and power which each bishop has in his own diocese, so that the power of the episcopal conference does not transcend that of the individual diocesans, and secondly from faculties granted by the highest authority. For the decrees and constitutions of the Council provided for certain tasks to be transferred to the episcopal conferences in order to make the exercise of the highest ecclesiastical authority more effective and to arrive at a certain decentralization. Hence participation in the highest ecclesiastical authority, though by way of delegation! This contradiction shows that the theological basis and the nature of the episcopal conference have remained confused.

This confusion in the sphere of principles naturally affected the question of organization, especially the rights of membership and voting. Many titular bishops considered it self-contradictory that they should belong to the college of bishops by virtue of their consecration, but could participate and vote in the episcopal conference only by invitation. They demanded that titular bishops who had official duties should be members of the national episcopal conference by right with full voting powers, occupying at least the same position as in an Ecumenical Council; moreover, they should not be referred to as "mere titular bishops", since consecration was the decisive factor (McDevitt). The schema had suggested a two-thirds majority for decisions to be legally binding; several Fathers regarded this as insufficient and wanted unanimity (Bianchi); but this would have prevented the episcopal conference from acting as a hierarchical body.

i) Boundaries of dioceses and ecclesiastical provinces

The discussion on the subject dealt mainly with dioceses which were too large either in territory or because of the number of the faithful. These might be divided, or sections of them could be removed, whereas dioceses which were too small could be abolished or united with others. In the preface of Chapter IV the authors of the schema had tried to give directions for the right size of dioceses. On the one hand they should remain manageable, so that the bishop could frequently visit parishes and get to know his priests personally, on the other they had to be large enough to have a sufficient number of priests to care for the faithful and to establish and support all the institutions necessary for orderly government. Apart from the size of the diocese, the diversity of rites and nationalities, spiritual as well as geographical, social, economic and historical factors and secular frontiers would also have to be taken into account. Several Fathers thought these criteria were too general and feared that everything would remain as it was unless more concrete proposals could be worked out. One Father (Jop) suggested a limit of at most 500,000, but in Europe not less than 200,000 faithful, but this was not followed up.

The Fathers differed considerably even in their basic ideas about the size and the function of the diocese within the whole of the Church. One of them (László) admitted that the proposals were indeed new, but objected that they were still in the line of the present canon law and based on a too individualistic approach. The diocese was too self-contained, a part of the Church completely separated from other parts, with its own bishop who was responsible only for his territory and completely excluded any other bishop. Statistics proved that there were enormous differences in the relation between priests and faithful, hence a mere new definition of limits would be of no use; rather should the collegial spirit of the bishops be increased so that each diocesan would feel himself responsible also for other parts of the Church. The critical observer was struck by the fact that the problems of organization which would result from the combination of dioceses and ecclesiastical provinces were not even broached. The union of several ecclesiastical provinces in an "ecclesiastical region" suggested in the draft was rejected on the grounds that the regional needs were sufficiently catered for by the episcopal conference (Stein).

The practice of the first Christian centuries was adduced in defence of the small diocese, in which the bishop could really be the shepherd of his flock (Massimiliani), small dioceses ought at least not to be abolished but united with others (Renard). Other Fathers emphasized that the Church was a living organism; true, it protected tradition, but it was not a collector of antiques. They (Urtasun, Sorrentino) demanded that small dioceses should be abolished or combined, obviously referring to the nearly three hundred Italian dioceses, many of which had no more than ten to thirty parishes with about ten to thirty thousand faithful. Others mentioned the basic principle according to which the bishop ought to know those entrusted to him and vice versa, hence it was his pastoral duty to meet the faithful, and too large dioceses, in which the bishop appeared as a great prince rather than as a good shepherd should be divided. The only criterion of the boundaries of a diocese was its pastoral efficiency, not social or economic considerations, which reminded one of spiritual racialism (Soárez de Resende).

If too large dioceses could not be divided, the diocesan should form a local college together with his auxiliary bishops, and each should be given legally defined duties (Renard). Bishop Wehr of Trier and his auxiliary bishops Stein and Schmidt defended the principle of dividing large dioceses only if effective pastoral care could not be assured even by auxiliary bishops; they had in mind something like collegial government under and with the diocesan. Others pointed out that it would be much better if certain institutions required in principle by present canon law for every diocese, such as seminaries and law courts, were to be assigned to several dioceses or to the ecclesiastical province (Soárez de Resende). Another Father (Peralto) pointed out that the growth of the large cities was partly responsible for the apostasy of the masses; hence he suggested dividing these sees into zones to be presided over by their own resident bishops and to leave the title of diocesan to the bishop of the city centre, who would also be the superior of the other bishops and direct activities common to all with their advice.

According to Cardinal Feltin "personal dioceses", suggested by the draft for the care of the faithful of another rite, should be generally permitted where certain groups of the faithful could not be sufficiently cared for by the local authorities. The care of exiles and emigrants was mentioned in this connection. Communities for Catholics of different language and nationality were to be established on the parochial as well as on the diocesan level (Velasco). A representative of the Eastern Churches (Khoreiche) demanded equal rights for all rites. While the Latin rite had territorial dioceses everywhere, the Eastern rites had no territory of their own even in the East. One territory had several jurisdictions, not only Eastern ones but also a Latin one, all of which considered themselves with equal right as territorial. Therefore some Fathers demanded that only one territorial jurisdiction should exist in each region and as many personal jurisdictions should be established as would be necessary to care for the faithful of the various rites.

The draft had proposed to create a permanent episcopal commission in each nation which was to examine the limits of dioceses and ecclesiastical provinces and make suitable recommendations to the Holy See. But this proposal was rightly rejected, because it was not concerned with a permanent task but only with long-term measures of organization (Renard).

3. The motu proprio *Pastorale Munus* of 30 November 1963[1]

On 30 November 1963, a few days before the close of the second session, Pope Paul had issued the motu proprio *Pastorale Munus,* which granted the diocesan bishops a large number of new powers and to all bishops several privileges.

[1] Cf. L. Buijs, *Facultates et privilegia Episcoporum concessa Motu proprio "Pastorale munus" cum commentario* (1964), and K. Mörsdorf, "Neue Vollmachten und Privilegien der Bischöfe", in *Abhandlungen für das katholische Kirchenrecht* 133 (1964), pp. 82–101.

These were the powers which had been mentioned in the first appendix of the draft with the direction that they were not to be discussed. The motu proprio was drawn up in haste, hence certain imperfections which were partly removed when it was later published in the *AAS* (56 [1964], pp. 5–12).[2] The Council Fathers could regard the papal document which was delivered to them in the Council hall as the first fruits of their efforts to restore the episcopal rights. Though the motu proprio did not yet clear up the basic principles, the granting of forty faculties was nevertheless of great practical importance, because many matters which till then had to be submitted to the Holy See could now be settled by the bishops. The measure of the decentralization thus achieved may be gauged from the fact that in 1964 the work of the Congregation of the Sacraments was almost halved.

The motu proprio is divided into two parts, the first dealing with the new faculties of the diocesan bishops, the second with the privileges due to all, including the titular bishops. The division was the same as in the appendix of the schema, though this did not distinguish between faculties and privileges, but used the word faculties in both cases. Part I of the motu proprio is headed: *Faculties due to the diocesan bishop from the moment he takes possession of his diocese, which he cannot, however, delegate except to the coadjutor, the auxiliary bishops and the vicar general, unless something different is explicitly stated in the faculties.* The faculties are due to the diocesan by law *(iure)*, i.e., they are connected with the office of the diocesan by papal law and hence have the character of ordinary faculties which are acquired with the episcopal office and cease with its loss. But the diocesan is restricted in the delegation of these faculties, which differ in this from the faculties connected with his office according to the *CIC,* an effect of the way in which the former were conferred. Thus he can delegate them only to his coadjutor (the expressions of the motu proprio presuppose that in future the term coadjutor bishop will be reserved to the *Coadiutor cum iure successionis*), to his auxiliary bishops and to his vicar general. This limitation of the right to delegate powers contradicts the principle that the ordinary powers may be delegated to others either wholly or partly; this principle, however, allows of exceptions (can. 199, para. 1), so that the limitation of delegating powers can not be used to dispute that the diocesans' new faculties have the character of ordinary

---

[2] The following are the alterations in the *AAS*: n. 13 of the original was left out, because this faculty was already contained in ordinary canon law. In order to rectify the disturbed enumeration, n. 11 of the original was divided into two (11 and 12), and the original n. 12 became n. 13. In n. 14 the words "in singulis casibus" were eliminated and the words "clerici in sacris constituti" were replaced by "sacerdotes", because this passage concerned only priests. A new enumeration begins with the privileges. Here the words "in actu sacramentalis confessionis" in n. 3 are left out, because they are superfluous; in n. 4 the words "clerici in sacris constituti" are replaced by "sacerdotes". The privilege provided in n. 8, which was superfluous, was replaced by another one. The Pope ordered also that the powers granted in the motu proprio *Pastorale Munus* might be used from 8 December 1963, that is, before the document was published in the *AAS*.

authority. It should not be overlooked, however, that in the case of the quin-quennial faculties it is sometimes stated that they may be exercised only by the diocesan personally, hence cannot be delegated to others. This practice has evidently influenced the limitation of delegating powers, as perhaps also the wish to remind the bishops that these faculties were given by the Pope. Thus it has not yet been realized that the diocesan bishop has a divine right to all the powers needed for properly carrying out his episcopal duties, though it must be admitted that the exact determination of these powers must be left to the highest authority of the Church.

The introduction of the motu proprio states explicitly that the faculties due to the diocesans by law belong also to the vicars and prefects apostolic, the per-manent apostolic administrators and the exempt abbots and prelates according to the existing law. These latter enjoy the same rights and faculties as the residen-tial bishops in their dioceses. The vicars and prefects apostolic who could not appoint a vicar general could delegate the faculties to their vicar delegate who holds practically the position of a vicar general.

Part two is entitled: *Privileges which, apart from others enumerated in the CIC, belong to all, the resident as well as the titular bishops, as soon as they are authentically informed of their canonical institution.* These privileges are also faculties which belong to those who hold them by right, though there is no mention of a *iure.* They differ, however, from those granted to the diocesan and bishops in the same position as the latter in that they are exceptional and do not belong to the ordinary episcopal office. The most important privileges are faculties to preach and hear confessions everywhere. Here the authority of the local superior, even if he is not a bishop, is preserved because these faculties cannot be used if the local superior explicitly forbids it. This, too, shows the exceptional character of the faculties described as privileges.

II. THE SCHEMA "ON THE CARE OF SOULS"

From the beginning the Commission on Bishops had also to deal with the more important questions of the care of souls. Owing to the many different pastoral and theological problems involved it is understandable that the Commission had to make many attempts to come to grips with them. The members of the Commission produced no fewer than eight drafts, eighteen expert opinions and fifty written answers. The Central Commission was handed a draft in three versions, one of eighty, one of fifty and the shortest of thirty pages, not counting the notes. The last was divided into two sections, the first of which dealt with pastoral care in general, the second with particular cases. The first chapter of part one discussed the theological foundation of pastoral work, the second the selection and appointment of the collaborators of the bishop, his threefold office and his responsibility for the whole Church. Part two provided practical norms for certain sections of the Catholic population which often lacked proper pastoral care because of their circumstances, such as emigrants, naval and air personnel, migrants, tourists and faithful endangered by the errors of materialism. The Central Commission ordered the draft to be shortened and combined with other drafts on similar subjects.

For this purpose the Commission on Bishops enlisted the co-operation of secretaries and experts of other commissions, especially the commission for the discipline of clergy and faithful and that for religious. The draft resulting from this co-operation was referred to the central subcommission "on mixed matters", which shortened it, combined it with other drafts and produced a new schema with the title "On the Bishops' Pastoral Office and the Care of Souls". This was divided into two parts of four and eight chapters respectively. Part I dealt with 1) the tasks of the bishops, 2) the relations between bishops and parish priests as well as the rights and duties of the latter, 3) the appointment of parish priests and their permanent residence, their removal or transfer, 4) the relations between bishops and religious, especially in view of the works of the apostolate. Part II treated of 1) the catechetical instruction of the Christian people, 2) the pastoral care of the workers, 3–7) the care of emigrants, naval and air personnel, migrants and tourists, and 8) of the defence against materialistic errors. This draft existed in two versions, one of ninety, the other of sixty pages. The shorter version was published in the third series of "Schemata constitutionum et decretorum ex quibus argumenta in Concilio disceptanda seligentur" (pp. 91–180) under the title *De cura animarum* in 1962.

In January 1963 this draft was referred to the Co-ordinating Commission and Cardinal Julius Döpfner was to report on it. On 31 January the Co-ordinating Commission gave orders to leave certain parts to the revision of the *CIC* and to form others into a directory or pastoral manual. As regards the discussions in the Council, a shortened draft on matters of principle was to be made and the parts left for the revision of the *CIC* and for the directories were to go into an appendix. At the same time the Commission ordered that these parts were not to be discussed in the general congregation. The new draft was prepared by a subcommission consisting of members and experts of the Commission on Bishops, and was submitted on 20 March and approved by the Co-ordinating Commission on 26 March 1963. It was delivered to the Council Fathers on 22 April.

A general Preface referred briefly to the saving work of Christ and showed what parts the Pope, bishops, priests, religious and laity had to play in the apostolate of the Church. The draft itself was divided into five chapters:

    I. The Bishops' Pastoral Office (nn. 7–12).

    II. The Pastoral Office of the Parish Priests (nn. 13–18).

    III. The Relations between Bishops and Religious, especially concerning the
        Works of the Apostolate (nn. 19–46).

        1. General principles (nn. 20–22).

2. Norms on the religious being subject to the local superiors in the performance of external works (nn. 23–27).
3. Entrusting religious with the external works of the apostolate (nn. 28–35).
4. Giving the office of parish priest to religious (nn. 36, 37).
5. The proper co-ordination of the works of the apostolate (nn. 38–46).
IV. The Pastoral Care of Special Sections of the Faithful (nn. 47–52).
V. The Catechetical Instruction of the Christian People (nn. 53–60).

There followed seven appendices dealing with those matters which were left to the revision of the *CIC* or were to be included in a directory. Chapters I and II had each two appendices on the pastoral work of bishops and parish priests respectively, the other three chapters had only one, hence seven altogether. Together with the notes the whole draft comprised 123 pages, without the notes 43. Probably no other schema had undergone so many changes, and even the last version could not claim to be fit for the Council. Towards the end of the second session the Council was ever more pressed for time, and so it seemed better to give up the schema "On the Care of Souls", but to include some of its more important matter in the schema on the bishops and to produce a new draft combining the two. Several Fathers had also suggested this in the discussion of the schema on the bishops.

On 29 November 1963, the Co-ordinating Commission asked the Commission on Bishops to shorten its schema and, in accordance with the pastoral object of the Council to leave the legal questions to the forthcoming reform of the *CIC*. On 23 January 1964 the Co-ordinating Commission ordered the basic principles of the schema "On the Care of Souls" to be included in the schema "On the Bishops and the Government of Dioceses", the former being removed from the list of schemas.

III. THE SCHEMA "ON THE BISHOPS' PASTORAL OFFICE IN THE CHURCH"

1. The working out of the schema

Towards the end of the second session the Commission on Bishops began to organize work on the new schema on bishops. On 2 December 1963 it created five subcommissions, the first of which had to draw up its basic outline, while the other four were to examine the individual chapters. From 27 to 30 January 1964, a small committee of *relatores* and secretaries of the five subcommissions chosen from the *periti* met in Rome in order to produce a new draft according to the directions of the Co-ordinating Commission of 23 January. This received the title "On the Bishops' Pastoral Office in the Church" and consisted of a Preface and three chapters on the episcopal activity in the universal Church, in the particular Churches and for the common good of several Churches. Thus a new basic conception had been found so as to do justice to the oral and written suggestions of the Council Fathers. This draft was submitted to the members and several *periti* of the Commission on Bishops, which met in Rome in the first half of March. The subcommissions worked from 2 to 5 March and produced an amended version of the draft which was submitted to the plenary meeting of the Commission; there the draft was discussed from 6 to 12 March and approved after some alterations and the inclusion of some supplementary material. The voting produced unanimity or very great majorities. After the new draft had been approved by the Co-ordinating Commission the Pope directed on 27 April 1964 that it should be sent to the Council Fathers. The following are its contents:

Preface (nn. 1–3).

Chapter 1: The Relationship of Bishops to the Universal Church (nn. 4–10).

    I. The Role of the Bishops in the Universal Church (nn. 4–7).

    II. Bishops and the Apostolic See (nn. 8–10).

Chapter 2: Bishops and their Particular Churches or Dioceses (nn. 11–33).

    I. Diocesan Bishops (nn. 11–19).

    II. Diocesan Boundaries (nn. 20–22).

    III. Those who Co-operate with the Diocesan Bishop in his Pastoral Task.

        1. Coadjutor and Auxiliary Bishops (nn. 23–24).

        2. Diocesan Curia and Diocesan Councils (n. 25).

        3. The Diocesan Clergy (nn. 26–30).

        4. Religious (nn. 31–33).

Chapter 3: The Co-operation of Bishops for the Common Good of Many Churches (nn. 34–41).

    I. Synods, Councils, and Especially Episcopal Conferences (nn. 34–36).

    II. The Boundaries of Ecclesiastical Provinces and the Establishment of Ecclesiastical Regions (nn. 37–39).

    III. Bishops with an Interdiocesan Office (nn. 40–41).

General Directive (n. 44).

This division agrees with the decree passed by the Council. There is only a very minor change from n. 18 onwards, because in accordance with the Commission's decision of 16 September 1964 two new numbers were inserted in that place, dealing with the bishop's freedom in the exercise of his office (n. 18 bis) and with the freedom of the appointment of bishops (n. 18 ter).

2. Discussion in the Council hall

Only those parts of the new draft were put up for discussion which had been taken from the schema "On the care of souls" or had been added by the Commission. On 16 September the Council Fathers received a list of those parts of the draft which were to be discussed. Apart from the new Preface (nn. 1–3) these dealt with three subjects: 1) The notion of the diocese and the office of the diocesan bishop, divided into the teaching, priestly and pastoral office (nn. 11 to 18), 2) the diocesan curia, the creation of a pastoral council and the diocesan clergy, especially the parish priests (nn. 25–30), and 3) the relation of the bishop to the religious of his diocese (nn. 31–33). Thus the discussion dealt at least with the most important parts of the new draft, which had not yet been treated in connection with the schema "On bishops and the government of dioceses".

The discussion of the draft with Cardinal Döpfner as chairman needed only three general congregations (83–85 of 18, 21 and 22 September); two Fathers spoke afterwards in the 86th general congregation. During the discussion votes were taken on the schema on the Church, especially on Chapter III, which is the theological basis of the pastoral office of the bishops then under discussion. The discussion was introduced by a report on the work of the Commission on Bishops by its president, Cardinal Marella. Archbishop-Coadjutor Veuillot who had been chosen by the Commission to report on the draft explained it in detail. He pointed out three characteristics, namely the attempt at co-ordination, the basis in the theological doctrine of the episcopate and the emphasis on the pastoral duties of the bishop. He explained the division of the draft and particularly the new parts which were therefore put up for discussion.

a) General critical remarks

Not all Fathers obeyed the directive to discuss only the new parts of the draft. Cardinal Richaud, who spoke first, regretted that some important questions which ought to have been discussed at the Council had been referred to the commission for the reform of the *CIC*; he mentioned especially the removal and transfer of parish priests. The present procedure of a trial before the bishop and two priest consultors made too great demands on the latter and endangered the authority of the bishop, hence it should be replaced by a complaint before the metropolitan, and the system of benefices should be abolished, at least with regard to the parish priests. The episcopal conferences should be given at least some powers to decide less important cases without having to appeal to the Holy See. He regretted that the draft said nothing about some categories of priests worthy of a special mention such as professors and the directors of pastoral offices; he also pointed out that nothing was said about the metropolitan, who might co-ordinate the pastoral work of the ecclesiastical province and relieve the overworked Roman Curia in matters of minor importance.

Since nothing had as yet been decided about the theological foundations of the draft, these were once more called in question. Cardinal Browne opposed the idea that the authoritative office of teaching and governing was conferred by the episcopal consecration and that the episcopal college was the permanent bearer of the highest plenary power over the Church. Bishop Carli denied that the episcopate could share permanently in the highest governing authority apart from a Council or equivalent gatherings. He pointed out that the draft went beyond the schema on the Church because it granted the bishops membership of the Councils by virtue of their consecration, hence by divine law. He also attacked the view expressed in the Preface, according to which, contrary to the tradition dating from Ignatius of Antioch, the bishops belonged first and foremost to the whole Church and only in consequence of this and secondly to a particular Church.

A representative of the Eastern Churches (Ziadé) objected that the draft took too much account of the conditions in the Latin Church; he suggested that the present draft be combined with that on the Eastern Churches, so that the Council would finally produce a single document on the pastoral office of the bishops containing the general principles which were binding in East and West alike. This would provide a basis for a new *CIC* to be produced later, which would deal first with the general constitutional law of the Church and secondly with the particular law of the local, "Latin" as well as Oriental, Churches. Cardinal Léger sharply criticized the statements on the pastoral office of the bishop as timeless and too general. Contemporary man was critical and technological, he required authorities to be really competent and rejected all forms of paternalism. He made suggestions for the exercise of the teaching and pastoral office as needed in our time, he emphasized the necessity of permanent contact between bishops, faithful and priests and demanded a reform of the diocesan curia which would make it a vital instrument of the diocese. The cathedral chapter was to be completely reformed, and the bishops' councils should not be increased in number but united in one college. The outer appearance of the bishops should receive attention, and clothing, insignia, forms of address and general style of living which had often been mentioned in the Council hall should be reformed.

b) Questions of detail

Bishop and diocese. Though they admitted the progress that had been made, many Fathers still complained of a too legalistic (Ziadé) and too onesidedly institutional (Maziers) view of the subject. On the other hand, the episcopal office had been described too much in terms of service, while in some parts of the world the bishop's own authority had suffered in the estimation of both clergy and people (Corboy). Hence some speakers (Fares) reminded the Council that the teaching office also included the duty to protect the faithful from errors. It was emphatically demanded that the appointment of bishops should not only be free from the interference of secular authorities (Pildain), but that the relevant episcopal conference should take part in it and that the priests of the diocese and the opinion of laymen should also be consulted (González Moralejo).

Diocesan bishops and diocesan clergy. The French bishops made valuable suggestions about the relation of the diocesan bishop to his priests. They proposed to bring out more clearly the connection between the doctrines of the priesthood and the episcopate, especially with regard to the sacramentality and the collegiality of the latter, which had further consequences for the priesthood of the lower order. Moreover, the statements on the priesthood contained in several drafts should be harmonized in order to achieve a unified theological view (Guyot). Though the union of the clergy with their bishop was not on the same plane as episcopal collegiality, the latter should nevertheless be the image and pattern of the former, as well as of the mutual relations of the diocesan clergy with each other (Urtasun). Many Fathers emphasized the necessity of trusting collaboration and asked that the bishop should be accessible to all his priests and also accept criticism (Proano Villalba).

Bishop and religious. In the discussion of the relation between the diocesan and the religious orders the principle of exemption was vigorously defended. This had not actually been disputed, but some Fathers thought it was threatened because the draft had strongly emphasized the power of the bishop concerning the employment of religious in pastoral works. The spiritual life and the external apostolic activities of the religious could not be divided, and supra-diocesan and international tasks could not be accomplished without the practice of exemption (Corboy). According to Bishop McEleney a better co-operation between bishop and religious could be achieved not only by weakening exemption, which might involve a crisis of the religious life, but also by collaboration in the form of a mixed commission of bishops and religious, which might be given the right of issuing directives. The creation of such a permanent body was demanded especially in view of missionary experience (D'Souza). Since religious were at the disposal of the Pope and the college of bishops, the authority claimed by the diocesan ought not to hinder this disposability (Guilly). The principal problem to remain unsolved was the question whether and in how far the regular priests belong to the diocesan clergy and thus to the presbytery of a diocesan bishop. Since the draft was not clear on this, several Fathers (Guilly, Renard, Urtasun) urged the adoption of an unequivocal terminology.

The care of emigrants. From the many suggestions on problems of pastoral practice we would single out one serious matter, namely the care of emigrants, exiles, guest workers and others who are far from their homes whether for professional or other reasons. On this question, which had already been discussed during the preparations for the Council, the draft disappointed the hopes engendered by the universally recognized importance of the subject. The Fathers were touched by the votum of Archbishop Gawlina, lately dead, which he had composed as the representative of the bishops of Poland and Lithuania and which was read by Archbishop Baraniak. This mentioned among other things Pope John's insistence on the right of men to their homeland and to the protection of national minorities. The Archbishop asked that the care of emigrants should not be relegated to the future directory but be incorporated in the draft of the decree. This applied especially to the creation of an episcopal commission,

191

of diocesan and parish committees and generally to the right of emigrants and aliens to a suitable care of souls. As a last request it was suggested that apostolic visitors be appointed for emigrants of the Latin rite after the example of the special hierarchies established in many places for Oriental emigrants. This was to be done in any district where national minorities were strong enough to form a metropolis.

3. Voting on the amended text in the Council hall

The Commission on Bishops started immediately to work on the oral and written suggestions and to produce an amended text. The whole material was collected in two volumes. Until the beginning of the third session 31 Fathers had spoken on the draft, during this session 33 Fathers had spoken in the Council hall and 58 had made their suggestions in writing. 122 Fathers in all had remarked on the draft, suggesting about 400 alterations. Each votum was discussed in the Commission on Bishops first in the relevant subcommission and then at the plenary meeting. The amended text, comprising 102 printed pages, was handed to the Council Fathers on 30 October 1964.

The voting on the amended text took place in the general congregation (114–116; 35–37) from 4 to 6 November 1964. The spokesmen chosen by the Commission explained the text and also gave the reasons why certain proposals for alterations could not be admitted. Coadjutor-Archbishop Veuillot spoke on the draft as a whole and the Preface, Bishop Gargitter on Chapter I, Bishop Carli on Chapter II, Articles 1 and 2, Bishop Jubany on Article 3 of the same chapter and Archbishop Schäufele on Chapter III.

The voting on questions of detail referred mostly to several numbers, and only in more important cases, e.g., n. 8, to one number. These questions were to be answered either with yes *(placet)* or with no *(non placet)*; only the general questions, which concerned a whole chapter, might also be answered: Yes with reservations *(placet juxta modum)*. The first day already brought a great surprise: a large majority answered all detailed questions in the affirmative, but when the whole first chapter was put to the vote, 1030 of the 1965 Fathers present voted Yes, 77 No, and 852 Yes with reservations; 6 votes were invalid. Thus the individual articles had been accepted with a large majority, but as the whole chapter had not received the necessary two-thirds majority, it had not been approved — the first time such a paradoxical situation had developed during the Council.

Hence the question arises whether it makes sense to have a voting method which permits only a Yes or No on individual points, whereas a Yes with reservations together with proposed changes is allowed for the main subjects. As a rule the proposed alterations refer to individual statements and only rarely to the whole concept; hence it would be better to allow the three possibilities of voting for individual questions and the simple alternative of Yes or No for the whole complex. This method would have the further advantage that the number of affirmative and negative votes would show what importance to attach to the reservations on the decisive question whether someone makes the acceptance of the whole dependent on the acceptance of his proposed alteration. The awkward apparatus of an Ecumenical Council does not allow what would actually be the proper procedure, namely to vote on the individual chapters and on the whole draft only after the alterations suggested at the first reading have been dealt with. This reversal of the voting method would in any case ease the work of the commissions, because in the matter of alterations they would not have to rely only on their own judgment but would be guided by the votes of the general congregation. In our view even the second emended edition of the rules of Council procedure of 1963 *(Ordo Concilii Oecumenici Vaticani II cele-brandi)* would have needed a thorough revision in order to free the Council from tiring monologues and provide for real dialogue. Paul VI has shown a good way to achieve this in the additions to the rules of 2 July 1964 *(Addita-menta ad Ordinem Concilii Oecumenici Vaticani II celebrandi),* which should not be relegated to oblivion.

But to get back to the result of the voting on Chapter I. The average number of negative votes on the details was about 80, but increased to 225 in the case of n. 4, which dealt with the authority of the college of bishops. These negative votes came mostly from the titular bishops. They objected to the statement that, while all bishops who were members of the episcopal college had the right to attend the Ecumenical Council, they should at least be represented at it according to the principles laid down by the Pope. The *non placet* of the 225 was directed both against the possibility of representation and the fact that this was to be determined by the Pope. The proposed emendations showed that about 600 Fathers did not yet quite agree with the basic statement of the whole decree in n. 8 on the restoration of the original rights of the diocesan bishop. The large number of affirmative votes with reservations (852) was due especially to these proposals, with the result that the chapter in its then form was not approved.

The voting on Chapter II was on similar lines. The points of detail were put to the vote on 5 November 1964. Here the negative votes averaged between 8 and 57 except for nn. 33–35, where they reached 172, because the representatives of the religious feared for their independence. The whole of Chapter II was put to the vote only on the next day, and a positive result might confidently be expected. Nevertheless, the second chapter did not reach the necessary majority of votes either, for though there were 1219 positive and only 19 negative votes, 889 Fathers voted Yes with reservations. The reservations referred to many details, but especially to the relation between religious and diocesan bishops. Here changes were proposed by both sides, and thus the acceptance of the chapter was prevented. 570 Fathers demanded, for example, that the subordination in a certain sphere of both exempt and non-exempt religious to the diocesan should not be expressed by "are being subjected" *(subduntur)* but by "are subject" *(subsunt)*. This is a merely linguistic point which changed nothing in the existing subjection to the diocesan; but together with the other 255 to 297 proposed changes it led to the high figure of 889 votes with reservations and hence prevented the acceptance of Chapter II, though there was no genuine dissent.

The voting on Chapter III which took place on 6 November might have been expected to show greater opposition, especially on the questions of the composition of the episcopal conference and the voting rights, which had been hotly disputed and been solved by a compromise which could not satisfy everybody. Against all expectation the voting was successful. On questions of detail the negative votes remained between 11 and 27 and rose to 71 only on the question of the episcopal conference. When the whole chapter was put to the vote of the 2070 Fathers present 1582 voted Yes, 15 No, 469 Yes with reservation and four votes were invalid. Thus the necessary majority had been reached. The reservations referred mostly to the composition of the episcopal conference and the voting rights. On the grounds that all bishops were members of the episcopal college and of the Ecumenical Council 56 Fathers asked that auxiliary and other bishops of the region should have the same right to belong to the episcopal conference. On the other hand, 59 Fathers wanted this right to be limited to those auxiliary and other bishops who held a special pastoral office in the region of the conference, and 112 Fathers demanded that the right of auxiliary and certain other bishops to belong *(pertinent)* to the conference should be changed so that they might belong to it *(pertinere possunt)* according to the judgment of the conference. 9 Fathers wanted the nuncios and apostolic delegates excluded from the episcopal conference, while 151 suggested that they should be invited only after the conference had so decided. 62 Fathers demanded that all those who attended an episcopal conference should have a deciding vote. These proposed changes reflect the battle which had not been quite decided at the Council, but had been transferred to the sphere of the episcopal conference when the compromise formula had been agreed. Nevertheless, it was a great success for Archbishop Hermann Schäufele, who was the *relator* of the third chapter at the general congregation, that just this chapter which was expected to meet with the strongest opposition should have been the only one of the draft to be approved by the congregation.

4. The examination of the text and the passing of the decree

The Commission on Bishops had now to correct the text of the first two chapters in such a way that it would receive the necessary majority. This was no easy task, because the proposed changes were frequently opposed to each other and it was to be feared that if concessions were made in a certain question this might call forth the opposition of other Fathers. The Commission also included proposed changes for Chapter III, for it was anxious to produce a text which would do justice to the wishes of the Council Fathers as expressed in the voting. 33 changes *(modi)* had been proposed for the Preface and Chapter I, 196 for Chapter II and 47 for Chapter III. Since the third session was to end on 21 November, the Commission was hard pressed for time and did everything possible to get the schema passed before then. A small committee was working day and night and succeeded in producing the new text with the report on the suggested changes within about ten days. Nevertheless it could not be referred to the general congregation, because in the last days of the session the Council had to deal with too many other questions. In the last working session of 20 November the general secretary informed the Council that there was no more time to place the schema "On the Bishops' Pastoral Office in the Church" before the Fathers. They received it only a year later with the so-called *Textus recognitus* and the report on the proposed changes together with a supplement which gave the request of n. 5 for the creation of an episcopal council another form adapted to the new situation, for in the meantime Pope Paul VI had created the synod of bishops on 15 September 1965. Looking back, it is regrettable that those entrusted with producing the *Textus recognitus* were pressed for time and that later the intervening year was not used to polish the text still further and above all that its terminology was not completely harmonized with the constitution *Lumen Gentium,* which would also have meant the integration of the *nota explicativa praevia* of Chapter III of the Constitution on the Church. For this is concerned with legal questions which were neglected in the Constitution on the Church but ought not to have been left out of the Decree on the Bishops' Pastoral Office in the Church.

Coadjutor-Archbishop Veuillot reported on the textual alterations and the proposed changes of the Preface and Chapter I, Bishop Jubany on those of Chapter II, and Archbishop Schäufele on Chapter III. Voting took place from 29 September to 1 October 1965 in the general congregations 138–140 (11–13). The more important proposed changes of Chapters I and II were voted on separately, while the Fathers were asked if they approved the report of the Commission on the other proposed changes in each chapter, which for the greater part had not been accepted. The changes which the Commission had permitted for Chapter III were put to the vote together. The voting on questions of detail in Chapters I and II resulted generally in large majorities. In the questions on Chapter I the negative votes numbered between 8 and 54, on Chapter II between 5 and 185. In the case of the general questions the Preface and Chapter I received 15, Chapter II 76 and Chapter III 20 negative votes. There was no general voting on Chapters I and II though it ought to have taken place, because these chapters had not received the necessary majority of votes in the previous year. After the last results had been made known the general secretary of the Council declared that the whole schema had been accepted by the general congregation. Nevertheless the Moderators gave orders that the whole schema should be put to the vote. This voting took place on 6 October; of the 2181 Fathers present 2167 voted in favour and 14 against.

Thus the schema was ready to be finally passed in the Seventh Public Session of 28 October 1965. The long struggle was brought to a close with 2319 votes in favour and only 2 against the schema, one vote being invalid. Pope Paul promulgated the Council decree *Christus Dominus* with the formula that had been developed in the previous year and ordered that it should not come into force until 29 June 1966.

5. Directions for carrying the decree into effect and its passing into law

The post-conciliar Commission on Bishops *(Commissio post-conciliaris de Episcopis et de dioecesium regimine)* was established to work out the papal directions for carrying the decree into effect. This Commission was identical with the Conciliar Commission of the same name, except for the *periti* insofar as these were not re-appointed as consultors, but it was now functioning as an advisory body to the Pope. Since the decree *Presbyterorum Ordinis* of 7 December 1965 on the Ministry and Life of Priests treats of several questions also discussed in the decree *Christus Dominus* the post-conciliar Commission on Bishops was ordered to work out directions for both. The result of its work was to be communicated to the newly appointed Central Commission by the end of April. Owing to the short time allowed only the more important questions could be tackled insofar as they seemed capable of being solved within the framework of the directions. The Commission met for the first time between 17 and 19 February 1966, mapped out its work and established three subcommissions. The *relatores* and consultors of the subcommissions met between 21 and 25 March and worked out a draft first separately and in a final session together. A mixed commission, composed of members of the Commission for Bishops and the Commission for Religious, worked on questions regarding the relation of bishop and religious. The plenary meeting of the Commission on Bishops, in which five members of the former Conciliar Commission for the discipline of clergy and people took part, took place between 25 and 29 April and could pass the draft on time. Nevertheless, the directions could not be published, as had been hoped, before the decree was intended to come into force on 29 June. Hence the coming into force of "certain" Council decrees was postponed indefinitely by the motu proprio *Munus Apostolicum* of 10 June. One of the reasons given was that the Central Commission wanted to examine the drafts of the post-conciliar commissions still further and had also suggested to publish the directions on the various Council decrees gradually. In the same fascicle of the *AAS* (pp. 467–72) the motu proprio *De Episcoporum Muneribus* of 15 June 1966 was published, which regulated the power granted to the diocesan bishops in Article 8 of the decree *Christus Dominus* to dispense from general Church laws. This question was entrusted to the Consistorial Congregation. The directions for carrying out, among others, the Council decrees *Christus Dominus* and *Presbyterorum Ordinis* were given in the motu proprio *Ecclesiae Sanctae* of 6 August 1966 (*AAS* 58 [1966], pp. 757–82). These laws, to be observed experimentally *(ad experimentum)* until the promulgation of the new *Codex Iuris Canonici,* were to come into force on 11 October 1966. On this date the relevant Council decrees, too, came into force, though this was not expressly stated.

The Decree on the Bishops' Pastoral Office affects the legal order of the Church much more than any other document of the Council, especially as regards the Latin Church; hence it is understandable that it will become fully effective only with the reform of canon law. Pastoral questions will be treated in the directories, as originally intended.

The Relationship of Bishops to the Universal Church*

The title. *Decretum* is a broad technical term, in the canonical language of the Church, which may designate any act of jurisdiction, whether in the legislative, judicial, or administrative sphere.[1] It is difficult to make out any juridical distinction among *Constitutio, Decretum,* and *Declaratio* as used by the Second Vatican Council to entitle its documents. At times considerations that were non-canonical or even purely emotive determined a title, as in the case of the Pastoral Constitution on the Church in the Modern World. *Declaratio* means a statement on current questions which lays down no evident juridical norms; yet the Declaration on Christian Education lays down some distinctly juridical norms. These examples should suffice to show that the title of a document tells us nothing about its juridical weight. Nevertheless the conciliar documents do not all hold the same rank. By the nature of the case there is a difference between utterances on matters of dogma and those on the juridical order in the Church. Canon law presupposes and builds upon a theological understanding of the Church's nature and when we correctly grasp its ecclesiological role, is no less theological, where fundamental matters relating to the ecclesiastical constitution are concerned, than an explicit doctrinal exposition of the faith. Now our decree is a *law* which presupposes the constitution of the Church as set forth in the dogmatic constitution *Lumen Gentium* and explicitates it in certain fundamental respects; indeed foreshadows the structure of the episcopal office which may be expected to emerge from the revision of the *CIC*. So this decree can be considered a constitutional enactment, at any rate in its juridical provisions.

The title *De pastorali Episcoporum munere in Ecclesia* poses problems, because *munus pastorale* has various meanings. In the strict sense it means the office of governance as contrasted with the offices of teaching and sanctification in the doctrine of the three ecclesiastical "offices"; in a wider sense it transcends the three offices and means the whole range of the Church's work. In this latter

---

* *Translated by Richard Strachan*
[1] Klaus Mörsdorf, *Die Rechtsprache des Codex Iuris Canonici* (1937), pp. 62 f., 84 f., 347 ff.

sense Article 22, para. 1, speaks of *munera pastoralia* in the plural. Elsewhere *munus pastorale* becomes a synonym for *officium,* the episcopal office in the juridical sense, the office of presiding over a diocese (see Article 21). It would seem to have been preferable to speak of the bishops' *munus apostolicum,* especially since this expression is frequently used in the decree (see Article 6, para. 1, Article 11, para. 3, Article 19, para. 1, Article 20, para. 1) and would have made it unnecessary to add *in Ecclesia.* The English translation "pastoral office" attempts to avoid these difficulties.

The Preface. The purpose of the preface is to show how this decree fits in with the theological doctrine of the Church and why we have the division into three section. We need not weigh every word of it, for the object is not to say anything new or special. On the contrary one cannot help noticing that the transformation undergone by the schema of the Constitution on the Church has had no effect on Articles 1 and 2, which are taken bodily from the schema *De cura animarum.*

Article 1, following the introduction to the encyclical *Mystici Corporis* of 29 June 1943, identifies the Church with the body of Christ. The Constitution *Lumen Gentium* made the idea of the People of God the leitmotiv of its doctrine on the Church, though not to the exclusion of the idea of the mystical body. It uses both terms but without working them into a harmony. Our decree might well have remedied the omission, since the biblical roots of the Church's hierarchical structure, which is here set forth, are to be found in the Pauline image of the mystical body.

Article 2 contrasts the mission and power of the Roman Pontiff as Peter's successor with that of the bishops as successors of the apostles in the traditional manner and without so much as hinting at the doctrine of the episcopal college, which is among the Council's major pronouncements on the Church. The omission, which was not deliberate, can only be explained by reference to the earlier text. This schema *De cura animarum,* in accordance with its frame of reference, described the Pope's supreme power as a power "for the cure of souls" *(in curam animarum)* — sound enough, but not a complete definition. The final version of the text defined the Pope's supreme power in more detail, adding the word "direct" *(immediata),* which was not really necessary since the following sentence treats quite fully of the Pope as shepherd of all the faithful. We may observe here that neither the Constitution on the Church nor our decree broach the problems involved in the immediacy of the supreme papal power,[2] although occasion to do so presented itself, particularly in setting forth the relation between Pope and diocesan bishop. In part the difficulty was not seen, and in part it was advisedly overlooked because the time did not seem ripe for a thorough clarification. As to the meaning of "pastor", let it be noted that the word is three times

---

[2] See Klaus Mörsdorf, "Die Unmittelbarkeit der päpstlichen Primatialgewalt im Lichte des kanonischen Rechtes", in *Einsicht und Glaube. Festschrift für G. Söhngen* (1962), pp. 464–78.

used in the wider sense, which embraces the office of teaching, sanctifying, and governance *(omnium fidelium pastor, animarum pastores, aeternus pastor)*, and only once to mean the shepherd as distinct from the teacher and the sanctifier. This twofold use is encountered throughout the decree.

Article 3 points out in paras. 1 and 2 the three sections of the decree, stressing the words *uniti in Collegio, singuli,* and *aliqui coniunctim.* Joined in their college, the bishops work for the whole Church (Chapter I); individually each works for the flock entrusted to him (Chapter II); and at times certain of them collaborate in attending to the needs of their several particular Churches. This brief indication of the three parts to the decree is the burden of the preface and should not be credited with any deeper significance. We may remark, however, that contrasting *uniti in Collegio* with *quandoque aliqui coniunctim* is hardly defensible, for at best it reflects the mistaken idea that episcopal collegiality is confined to work *in Collegio* for the universal Church[3] and that common action on behalf of several particular Churches (dioceses) is not collegiate but collective.[4]

As to the relationship between the episcopal college and the diocesan bishop, deletion of the word *quoque* in para. 2 *(Illud quoque exercent . . .)* left the matter undecided.[5] The words *ad magisterium et regimen quod attinet* in para. 1 were inserted in the final draft so that it should harmonize with *Lumen Gentium,* Article 22, para. 2. On the other hand, the opening sentence of para. 1*(Hoc*

---

[3] The commission which deliberated on the right to membership of episcopal conferences even refused to consider this right as analogous to the right of episcopal collegiality *(Schema Decreti de pastorali Episcoporum munere in Ecclesia, Textus recognitus et Modi a Commissione conciliari de Episcopis ac de dioecesium regimine examinati, 1965:* Caput III, Modus 12). But this view proved to be practically untenable. Caution still prevails in B. Botte, "La collégialité dans le NT et chez les Pères Apostoliques", in *Le Concile et les Conciles* (1960), p. 17; Y. Congar in *Le Concile et les Conciles,* p. 320; M. Bonet, "The Episcopal Conference", in *Concilium* 8, no. 1 (1965), pp. 26–30; N. Jubany, "Las conferencias episcopales y el Concilio Vaticano II", in *Ius Canonicum* 5 (1965), pp. 343–63. Bolder views are found in G. Dejaifve, "La 'Magna Charta' de Vatican II", in *NRT* 87 (1965), pp. 13f.; F. R. McManus, "The Juridical Power of the Bishop in the Constitution on the Sacred Liturgy", in *Concilium* 2, no. 1 (1965); J. Ratzinger, "The Pastoral Implications of Episcopal Collegiality", pp. 18–26; id., "Die bischöfliche Kollegialität, theologische Entfaltung", in *Baraúna,* II, pp. 56, 67; W. Aymans, *Das synodale Element in der Kirchenverfassung* (Dissertation, Univ. of Munich, 1967), pp. 280–300 (not yet published).

[4] This opinion was expressed in the *relatio super Schema Decreti "De pastorali Episcoporum munere in Ecclesia"* (1964), which says that Chapter III deals "tantum de exercitio collective potestatis propriae inhaerentis cuique Episcopo, quod caute distinguendum est ab exercitio collegialitatis".

[5] In the *relatio* on the *Textus emendatus* (1964), p. 11, Archbishop Veuillot said of the relationship between *Ecclesia universalis* and *Ecclesiae particulares* that Christ founded his Church, "i.e., universalem, in qua postea tantum consitutae sunt particulares Ecclesiae seu dioeceses". But the same *relatio* goes on to say: "Episcopo enim aequali ratione consecrantur ad bonum Ecclesiae universalis et bonum Ecclesiae particularis sibi commissae" (p. 12). *Lumen Gentium* clearly sets forth the mutual bond: "In and from such individual Churches there comes into being the one and only Catholic Church. For this reason each individual bishop represents his own Church, but all of them together in union with the Pope represent the entire Church joined in the bond of peace, love, and unity" (Article 23, paragraph 1).

suum episcopale munus, quod per consecrationem episcopalem susceperunt) was not brought into line with *Lumen Gentium,* Article 21, para. 2, although proposals to that effect were made and higher authority even intimated such a desire (on 30 September 1965) after the voting. If the text was still left unamended that was because *Lumen Gentium* requires it to be interpreted according to the *Nota praevia;* and besides, a preface cannot be expected to make a new pronouncement on so dificult a subject.

The principle, laid down in para. 1, that the bishops exercise their ministry for the universal Church in communion with and under the authority of the Pope, of course applies to para. 2 as well. Generally speaking, the clarity of the sense suffers because "the bishops" are the grammatical subject of what is said about all the types of episcopal work; one does not properly see the differences, in particular the special character of collegiate activity.

Chapter I treats of the bishops in relation to the universal Church and comprises two sections. The first section deals in general terms with the role of the bishops in the Church universal. It begins by describing how the episcopal college exercises power (Article 4); then, after a reference to the help which bishops will afford the Pope through the new episcopal synod (Article 5), it speaks of the responsibility for all the Churches which the bishops have as members of the episcopal college (Article 6), and of bishops who are persecuted for Christ's name. The second section discusses the relations between diocesan bishops and the Apostolic See. Because of this arrangement the fundamental declaration on the power of the diocesan bishop, which in itself forms part of the subject of Chapter II, was brought into Chapter I (Article 8). Even in the first section of Chapter I, what paras. 6 and 7 say does not refer to the universal Church as such but to the particular needs of individual Churches, as is clear from the separate title in one provisional draft: *Relationes Episcoporum cum aliis Collegii membris.* Thus Chapter I originally comprised three sections; but this arrangement having been dropped, one hardly notices now that apart from collegiate work for the whole Church and the local activities of the individual diocesan bishop there remains another sphere of episcopal work which is not subject to the juridical norms governing work for the Church universal but is in effect left to the free initiative of the bishops engaged in it.

Article 4 states 1) who belongs to the episcopal college, 2) that this college possesses supreme and full power over the Church, and 3) that the college solemnly exercises its power in an Ecumenical Council, and may do so as well outside a Council. One observes that these declarations are basically restricted to what has already been said on the subject in *Lumen Gentium.* The only new point made is that *all* bishops who are members of the episcopal college have the right to attend an Ecumenical Council, and nothing is said about the question of the titular bishops' right to vote. Henceforward they are regular members of an Ecumenical Council and by contrast with the law hitherto in force (*CIC,* can.

223, § 2; *CIO,* can. 168) must be invited, so that the open question of their voting might be answered as seemed fitting on each occassion. But presumably the forthcoming reform of the *CIC* will see the matter settled at common law. From the fact that all bishops are regular members of an Ecumenical Council one cannot automatically conclude that all members must be entitled to vote there.[6] The answer to that question depends on the hierarchical position which titular bishops hold in the episcopal college.[7] The principle which equates the episcopal college with an Ecumenical Council and contributed in no small measure to the vindication of the doctrine on that college and to recognition of its supreme power over the Church,[8] declares the power to be episcopal in character but does not give us the last word on the right to attend Ecumenical Councils.[9] Details of the new arrangements that will be necessary were intentionally kept out of the discussion; nor did anyone point out that under existing law some who are not bishops rank as regular members of an Ecumenical Council — abbots and prelates nullius and, unless the letter of convocation specifies otherwise, the abbot primate, the heads of other monastic orders, and the superiors general of exempt religious institutes for priests (*CIC,* can. 223, § 1, nn. 3, 4; *CIO,* can 168, § 1, nn. 3, 4). Our decree does not say whether the representatives of monastic orders will continue to be regular members of an Ecumenical Council. But assuredly they must do so, because the monastic orders play so important a part in Catholic life, above all in the missions, that no genuine representation of the Church is thinkable without them. At the same time the juridical title which these non-episcopal dignitaries have to attend an Ecumenical Council cannot be their membership of the episcopal college;[10] so that we may

---

[6] See W. Aymans, *op. cit.,* pp. 173–83. For the opposite view see for example W. Bertrams, *De relatione inter Episcopatum et Primatum. Principia philosophica et theologica quibus relatio iuridica fundatur inter officium episcopale et primatiale* (1963), p. 81; id., "Die Einheit von Papst und Bischofskollegium in der Ausübung der Hirtengewalt durch den Träger des Petrusamtes", in *Gregorianum* 48 (1967), p. 37.

[7] Insofar as *communio hierarchica* (*Lumen Gentium,* Article 21, para. 2, Article 22, para. 1), the root concept here, conveys anything about the nature of *communio,* it must not be understood solely of the relationship between Pope and bishops. Rather, calling *communio* "hierarchica" also means that each bishop has his own niche, in the structure of this *communio,* which gives him definite rights and duties, by no means all of a kind. On this matter see W. Aymans, *op. cit.,* pp. 167–88.

[8] See K. Mörsdorf, "Das synodale Element der Kirchenverfassung im Lichte des Zweiten Vatikanischen Konzils", in R. Bäumer and H. Dolch, eds., *Volk Gottes. Festschrift J. Höfer* (1967), pp. 578f.

[9] See W. Aymans, *op. cit.,* pp. 148–59, especially 155ff.

[10] It should be noted in this connection that when the Fathers asked whether abbots and prelates nullius enjoyed the rights, priveleges, and faculties mentioned in the schema of the Decree on the Bishops, the lapidary reply of the commission was: "Abbates et Praelati nullius in iure veniunt nomine Episcoporum (*CIC,* can. 215, § 2)". The query and reply are set under the heading *De Schemate in genere* and must therefore be taken to apply to the schema at large; see W. Aymans, *op. cit.,* pp. 155f.

not regard an Ecumenical Council as simply the assembled college of bishops.[11] This problem still awaits clarification.

As Article 4 largely consists of quotations from the constitution *Lumen Gentium,* one gathers that the Fathers were unable to agree on a text which would explain how the college exercises its power — the original purpose of this article. Nothing came of the attempts made in the earlier drafts, nor in particular of the schema providing that selected representatives might hold an Ecumenical Council, which reached the stage of being voted on.[12] The Council did not consider in what juridical forms the supreme power of the college might be exercised out of Council.[13] On the whole Article 4 fails to achieve its aim.

Originally **Article 5** envisaged the establishment of an episcopal council, to help the Pope more effectively and demonstrate at the same time that all the bishops share responsibility for the universal Church. Paul VI responded to this desire by setting up the Synod of Bishops — *Synodus Episcoporum* (motu proprio *Apostolica Sollicitudo,* 15 September 1965); and therefore Article 5 was recast, but without regard to the fact that not only bishops but also representatives of religious institutes are convoked to the Synod of Bishops. On the Synod of Bishops see Appendix I.

Article 6 deals with the solicitude of bishops for all the Churches. These duties do not follow from any juridical competence or power but from the responsibility each bishop has for the Church universal, which is composed of individual Churches. Diocesan bishops and other local ordinaries are those chiefly concerned, since they alone are in a position to discharge the duties here outlined. In particular they are to

1) foster the preaching of God's word in the missions and in areas where the faithful cannot be adequately cared for because of the lack of priests;

2) have their people support evangelization and other forms of the apostolate, especially helping to prepare priests, religious, and laymen for service on the missions and other apostolic work in areas suffering from a lack of clergy; they are exhorted to see that some of their priests go to such areas or to the missions, whether permanently or for a certain time; and

3) offer financial aid to other dioceses that are in need.

The instructions for carrying out Article 6 (and Article 10 of the Decree on Priestly Formation), promulgated in the motu proprio *Ecclesiae Sanctae,* 6 August

---

[11] See K. Mörsdorf, *Lehrbuch des Kirchenrechts,* I (11th ed., 1964), p. 354; id., "Das synodale Element der Kirchenverfassung", *loc. cit.,* pp. 577f.; W. Aymans, *op. cit.,* pp. 146–61; The other view is taken for example, by U. Betti, "Die Beziehungen zwischen dem Papst und den übrigen Gliedern des Bischofskollegiums", in *Baraúna,* II, p. 79, note 19.

[12] See Mörsdorf, "Primat und Kollegialität nach dem Konzil", in H. Gehrig, ed., *Das bischöfliche Amt* (1966), pp. 41f.; id., "Das synodale Element der Kirchenverfassung", *loc. cit.,* pp. 571f.; Karl Rahner takes a similar approach; see his "On the Divine Right of the Episcopate", in K. Rahner and J. Ratzinger, *The Episcopate and the Primacy* (1962).

[13] On the practical possibilities see W. Aymans, *op. cit.,* pp. 189–95.

1966, deal with the better distribution of the clergy (I, nn. 1–4) and financial help for needy dioceses (I, n. 5).

1. Better distribution of the clergy

It is proposed to have a special council at the Holy See lay down general principles for an evener distribution of the clergy (n. 1). Patriarchal synods and episcopal conferences are called on to make rules and regulations for the bishops, within the framework of the Holy See's prescriptions, so that a more suitable distribution of the clergy may be achieved in the dioceses of the conference and to the benefit of the missions and of areas under-supplied with priests. Each episcopal conference is to set up a commission of its own whose business it will be to examine the needs of the dioceses within the territory of the conference and the feasibility of sending clerics to other local Churches, to implement the decisions taken by the episcopal conference, passing on the appropriate instructions to the bishops concerned (n. 2). The principle that every cleric must be incardinated (*CIC*, can. 111)[14] is upheld but incardination is to be adapted to new conditions. Here is a straw in the wind as to the reform of the code (can. 111–117). In order to facilitate the transfer of a secular cleric from one diocese to another the following is laid down:

a) Readiness to serve the Church universal (I, n. 3, §§ 1, 3)

Seminary training shall be such that clerics may feel concern not only about the diocese for whose service they are to be ordained but also about the whole Church, and with the consent of their ordinaries may express a desire to enter the service of particular Churches which are hard-pressed (n. 3, § 1). Ordinaries shall see to it that clerics who intend to transfer from their own diocese to a diocese abroad are given an appropriate training for their future ministry, especially as regards the language of the place and an understanding of its institutions, social conditions, manners, and customs (n. 3, § 3).

b) New rules on transferring to another diocese (I, n. 3, §§ 2, 4, 5)

Except in the event of a real emergency in their own diocese, ordinaries may not withold the necessary permission from clerics who they know are willing, and believe are fit, to go to territories ill-supplied with priests and exercise their sacred ministry there, and must see that the rights and duties of these clerics are set down in a written agreement with the ordinary of the new diocese (n. 3, § 2). Without prejudice to the possibility of changing one's diocese by excardination and incardination (*CIC*, can. 112), ordinaries may authorize their clerics to

---

[14] See K. Mörsdorf, *Kirchenrecht* I, pp. 249 ff.

enter the service of another diocese for a certain period, which may be frequently extended, provided that such clerics remain incardinated in their own diocese and on their return shall enjoy whatever rights would have accrued to them had they been serving in their home diocese (n. 3, § 4). But a cleric who has lawfully gone from his own diocese to another is *ipso facto* incardinated in this diocese after the lapse of five years if he has given both the ordinary of the guest-diocese and his own ordinary written notice that such is his desire and if neither ordinary has intimated any objection in writing within four months (n. 3, § 5). The legal transfer here envisaged presupposes that the change to the other diocese was made lawfully, that is, with the permission of the priest's own ordinary, regardless of whether the permission was given for a set period or not (this latter is possible under can. 144 of the Code).

c) Erecting prelatures of secular clergy with special tasks (I, n. 4)

In order to provide for a more flexible deployment of the secular clergy, the motu proprio envisages the erection of prelatures staffed by seculars and designed to train and send out priests with special pastoral missions to particular territories or social groups. These prelatures are not dioceses but secular entities with special tasks and apart from their secular character bear a certain resemblance to centralized religious congregations. The prelature has its own statutes and articles, its own ordinary, and its members are affiliated to it. The prelate must set up and direct a national or international seminary to train clerics along suitable lines; he may incardinate these and present them to be ordained for the service of the prelature. Logically the right of incardination would extend to the case of a secular cleric incardinated in a diocese, who having secured his excardination asked to be incardinated in a prelature. The prelate must see to the spiritual life of his affiliated members, to the constant improvement of their special training, and to their deployment in the ministry, which will be regulated by written agreements with the ordinaries to whom these priests are sent. He must likewise arrange for their fitting support, whether by contract with the ordinary to whom the priest is sent, by the prelature's own means, or by other suitable aids; and provide for those who because of ill-health or other circumstances are unable to continue their appointed ministry. By contract with the prelature laymen, whether single or married, may enter the service of the prelature.

Erecting this type of prelature is the province of the Holy See, which is bound to consult the episcopal conferences of the area concerned beforehand, since the operation of such prelatures will affect the interests of the individual churches there. The sentence is the more difficult to understand because prelatures and episcopal conferences are spoken of in the plural. Since erection always concerns one particular prelature and none can foresee in what territories its work, designed to benefit the whole Church, will actually develop, we must assume that the episcopal conference to be heard before a prelature is erected is that of the area in which the prelature as such will operate — that is, where it has its seat. Great care must be taken that the work of the prelature respects the rights of the local ordinaries and is always carried on in close touch with the relevant episcopal conference. This is to be a guiding principle in all that is done by the prelature and the priests it sends out to the various dioceses: on no account must the autonomy of the prelature interfere with administrative arrangements in the individual Churches.

2. Financial help for needy dioceses (I, n. 5)

Patriarchal synods and episcopal conferences, although the needs of the dioceses in their territory have first claim to their attention, shall make appropriate arrangements for the use of Church funds, requiring the dioceses to contribute to apostolic and charitable works and to the relief of Churches which have a slender income or are in need because of special circumstances. Here the patriarchal synods and episcopal conferences have been given both a power and a duty because the bishops' responsibility for the universal Church includes helping individual Churches in distress; that is, they may exact certain payments from their dioceses and must do so, the financial position of the diocese permitting. This regulation is an initial step towards extending responsibility for the whole Church to the economic sphere. First there must be an equalization of burdens among the dioceses within the territory of each episcopal conference, their needs having first claim to consideration; then comes support for supradiocesan work, such as aid to needy Churches. The new right of the episcopal conference restricts the financial independence of the dioceses within the territory of the conference.

Article 7, admonishing the bishops to cherish those among their colleagues who are persecuted for the sake of Christ, is also meant to remind the world's conscience of the coercion to which Catholic bishops are subjected.

Article 8 deals with the power of the diocesan bishop and says two things, clearly distinguished under headings (a) and (b). Article 8 (a) makes the basic statement about the power "automatically enjoyed" by the diocesan bishop over the flock entrusted to him, and Article 8 (b) authorizes the diocesan bishop to dispense, within certain limits, from the general laws of the Church. Similarly the Pope's right to reserve cases to himself or some other authority is asserted *simpliciter* in (a) but in (b) only insofar as there have been special reservations.

Article 8 (a) defines the essential relationship between Pope and diocesan bishop. The old controversy over whether the diocesan bishop receives his power of jurisdiction directly from God or from the Pope[15] has been largely deactivated by the doctrine set forth in *Lumen Gentium* (Article 18) that a bishop's

---

[15] On this matter see K. Rahner, "Pastoral Theological Remarks on the Episcopate in the Teaching of Vatican II", in *Concilium,* 3, no. 1 (1965); C. Moeller, "Die Entstehung der Konstitution, ideengeschichtlich betrachtet", in *Baraúna,* I, p. 73.

power comes into being through episcopal consecration (Article 21) and becomes an exercisable power through canonical mission (Article 24), order and jurisdiction no longer being considered two separate powers but complimentary elements of the one ecclesiastical power.[16] Though certain diffculties await clarification, in substance the controversy has been settled: the bishops govern their particular Churches as the vicars and ambassadors of Christ, not as vicars of the Roman Pontiff (Article 27). Hence our decree draws the conclusion that as successors of the apostles the bishops automatically *(per se)* — that is, of right — have all the power necessary for carrying out their pastoral ministry. More particularly, the *per se* means that the power of the diocesan bishop does not derive from the power of the Pope but is a power of divine right, with an existence of its own apart from the papacy. That this power, as the decree specifies, is ordinary, proper, and immediate, is traditional doctrine;[17] but now

[16] In the Latin Church the distinction drawn since the 12th century between the power of order and the power of jurisdiction degenerated into a real sundering of the one ecclesiastical power and produced as real a sundering of the hierarchy into a hierarchy of order and a hierarchy of jurisdiction. More and more, the distinction was taken to mean that the power of order existed for dispensing the means of divine grace and the power of jurisdiction solely for the outward governance of the Church. Later this dichotomy was associated with a trichotomy of ecclesiastical power — deriving from the doctrine of the three offices of Christ (as teacher, priest, and king) and defended in the 19th century by the German canonists F. Walter (*Lehrbuch des Kirchenrechts* [10th ed., 1846], §§ 14–19) and G. Phillips (*Kirchenrecht*, I [1845], § 32) — in such a way that the *potestas sanctificandi* was identifid with the power of order while the *potestas docendi* and *potestas regendi* were assigned to the power of jurisdiction (see among others W. Bertrams, "De potestatis episcopalis exercitio personali et collegiali", in *Periodica de re morali, canonistica, liturgica*, 53 [1964], pp. 455 ff.). As a result juridical power was often contrasted with admittedly sacramental power, opening a baneful gulf between sacrament and law. The original sense of the distinction between the powers of order and jurisdiction became wholly obscured: their oneness, consisting in a polarity between order that cannot be lost and canonical mission that can, is ultimately meant to safeguard the exercise of the Church's mission against dangers arising in the personal sphere. By stressing the oneness of ecclesiastical power the Second Vatican Council has exploded the idea of the separation, although the pattern of thought which tries to combine the dichotomy of power with the trichotomy is still reflected in various of the Council's declarations. Since on the one hand this pattern of thought necessarily leads to splitting up power, and the Church herself, between a sacramental domain and a purely juridical one, and on the other hand the Council teaches that ecclesiastical power is *one*, specialists must scrutinize the interior structure of the single ecclesiastical power historically and systematically in order to arrive at a satisfactory clarification. See K. Mörsdorf, "Weihegewalt und Hirtengewalt in Abgrenzung und Bezug", in *Miscelánea Comillas* 16 (1951), pp. 95–110; id., "Die Entwicklung der Zweigliedrigkeit der kirchlichen Hierarchie", in *MTZ* 3 (1952), pp. 1–16; M. Kaiser, *Die Einheit der Kirchengewalt nach dem Zeugnis des Neuen Testamentes und der Apostolischen Väter* (1956); K. Nasilowski, *De distinctione potestatis in ordine in primaeva canonistarum doctrina* (1962) (not yet published); K. Mörsdorf, "Einheit in der Zweiheit — Der hierarchische Aufbau der Kirche", in *AKK* 134 (1965), pp. 80–88.

[17] Note the saving clause in Vatican I's decree: "Tantum autem abest, ut haec Summi Pontificis potestas officiat ordinariae ac immediatae illi episcopalis iurisdictionis potestati, qua Episcopi, qui positi a Spiritu Sancto (cf. Acts 20:28) in Apostolorum locum successerunt, tamquam veri pastores assignatos sibi greges singuli singulos pascunt et regunt" (*Denzinger* 1828); similarly the *CIC*

the fact that the bishop has his "own power" *(potestas propria)*[18] comes to mean that the local ordinary's jurisdiction is a power given him by God, even though he is appointed to his concrete office by the appropriate ecclesiastical authority — in the Latin Church by the Pope — and that authority is competent to withdraw the office from him according to law.[19]

We must observe that the various gradations of episcopal ministry must be based not on consecration but on office, for consecration must always produce the same effects. Pope, patriarch, metropolitan, and diocesan bishop are all in the same episcopal orders, but in respect of office they occupy different hierarchical levels which exist for the unity of God's people. Except for the papacy and the episcopal college, which exist in the concrete by divine institution, all other episcopal offices, relating as they do to particular communities within the Church universal, have to be given concrete existence by the appropriate ecclesiastical authority. Here we are dealing on the one hand with the establishment, by law or custom, of various kinds of episcopal office and on the other with the concrete erection of a particular office. In both respects the gradations of episcopal ministry are the work of the Church's constituent power, but the substance of each ministry remains of divine law because episcopal office is of divine law.[20] Thus the competent ecclesiastical authority enters into bestowal of this power as the instrumental cause; that is, giving nothing of its own it merely passes on the gift of Christ, in whose name the diocesan bishop wields his office[21] (see *Lumen Gentium,* Article 27, para. 1).

declares that diocesan bishops are "ordinarii et immediati pastores in dioecesibus sibi commissis" (can. 334, § 1). Though neither text speaks of a *potestas propria,* no proof is needed that canonists have always so described the power of local ordinaries, though it is true that the sense attached to the words has somewhat varied, as in the case of the other adjectives *(ordinaria, immediata).*
[18] On the use of the terms *potestas propria* and *vicaria* see K. Mörsdorf, *Kirchenrecht,* I, p. 309.
[19] See K. Rahner, "On the Divine Right of the Episcopate", in K. Rahner and J. Ratzinger, *The Episcopate and the Primacy* (1962); W. Bertrams, in his various articles on the subject, tries to establish the same idea by supposing that the totality of episcopal power is substantially, or ontologically, conferred by the sacrament of episcopal consecration, but that the power of jurisdiction has to be fitted into the social structure of the Church by a further juridical act (of the Pope) in order to become an exercisable power; see "De quaestione circa originem potestatis iurisdictionis episcoporum in concilio Tridentino non resoluta", in *Periodica* 52 (1963), pp. 458–76; id., *De relatione inter Episcopatum et Primatum* (1963), especially pp. 57–90; id., "De potestatis episcopalis exercitio personali et collegiali", in *Periodica* 53 (1964), pp. 455–81; id., *Papst und Bischofskollegium als Träger der kirchlichen Hirtengewalt* (1965), pp. 10–29; id., "Die Einheit von Papst und Bischofskollegium in der Ausübung der Hirtengewalt durch den Träger des Petrusamtes", in *Gregorianum* 48 (1967), pp. 34–36. J. Ratzinger (in *Theologische Revue* 62 [1966], pp. 320–2) and J. Lécuyer ("Das dreifache Amt des Bischofs", in *Baraúna,* II, pp. 181 ff.; and "Die Bischofsweihe als Sakrament", *ibid.,* pp. 35 f.) on the whole support this "theory of loosing". K. Mörsdorf is critical of it; see his "Die hierarchische Verfassung der Kirche, insbesondere der Episkopat", in *AKK* 134 (1965), pp. 93 ff.
[20] See K. Mörsdorf, "Bishop, IV (Canon Law)", in *Sacramentum Mundi,* I (1968).
[21] See W. Aymans, "Papst und Bischofskollegium als Träger der kirchlichen Hirtengewalt. Gedanken zu einer Schrift gleichen Titels von W. Bertrams", in *AKK* 135 (1966), pp. 138 f.

The diocesan bishop possesses *all power (omnis potestas)* that is requisite for exercising his pastoral ministry *(munus pastorale)* in his diocese, whether it relate to the office of teaching or of sanctifying or of governance. True, Article 27 of *Lumen Gentium* speaks of the office of governance as distinct from that of teaching and sanctifying, declaring that the bishop has the right and duty to promulgate laws for his subjects, to pass judgment on them, and regulate everything that has to do with ordering worship and the apostolate; but the power of the diocesan bishop which comes into play in legislative, judicial, and administrative work is not confined to the sphere of governance, it operates throughout that whole range of the Church's work which concerns the three offices of teaching, sanctifying, and governing. Here the Constitution still follows a schema of thought which it has superseded with its doctrine that ecclesiastical power is one.

With the declaration that the diocesan bishop — without prejudice to the Pope's right of reservation — has all power necessary for the exercise of his ministry, the former system of granting faculties to bishops (the system of concession) which the Council of Trent summed up in the juridical phrase *tamquam Sedis Apostolicae delegatus*[22], has been displaced by a system of papal reservations. The relationship between Pope and diocesan bishop has been radically changed: the latter is now presumed to have all power necessary to his ministry. Still this is not a revolutionary innovation, because canon law has kept intact a good measure of the bishop's original rights — for example, it recognizes that he has a legal claim to bestow all benefices within his diocese (*CIC*, can. 1432, § 1), so that there is a presumption in favour of the bishop's right against papal reservation.

We must also note that Article 8a lays down a principle but confers no immediately operative right. It remains to be seen in what technical canonical terms the broad decision of the Council will be embodied. There might be a list of all the domains and cases which the Pope reserves to himself or some other authority (patriarch, for instance, or episcopal conference). Although this procedure is suggested by the conciliar declaration, I do not feel that it would adequately define the power of the diocesan bishop. The diocesan bishop has his place in a hierarchical structure which stretches both above and below him; so not only must the Pope's prerogatives be safeguarded, the bishop's rule must not degenerate into arbitrary government. So even with the new relationship between Pope and bishop the ordinary must still be bound to rule his diocese *ad normam sacrorum canonum* (*CIC*, can. 335).[23] The office of diocesan

---

[22] See H. Jedin, "Delegatus Sedis Apostolicae und bischöfliche Gewalt auf dem Konzil von Trient", in *Die Kirche und ihre Ämter und Stände. Festschrift Joseph Kardinal Frings* (1960), pp. 462–75; id., *Kirche des Glaubens — Kirche der Geschichte. Ausgewählte Aufsätze und Vorträge*, 2 vols. (1966), pp. 414–28.

[23] The Constitution *Lumen Gentium,* Article 27, para. 1, rightly points out that the exercise of the diocesan bishop's power is ultimately regulated by the Church's supreme authority and can be circumscribed by certain limits for the advantage of the Church or the faithful.

bishop cannot be defined in purely negative terms; we must have some positive statement of its content, with which it will be quite in order to combine explicit reservations in favour of the Pope or some other authority, whether higher prelates (patriarch, metropolitan) or collegiate bodies (synods, episcopal conferences). Here let it be observed that the problem of delimiting a sphere of competence will often present one aspect to the legislator, who must lay down general norms binding on the whole Church or sections of it, and quite another to the judge or administrator, who must apply the norms or make binding regulations in a sphere for which the norms do not provide. Now the sphere of the diocesan bishop's activities is so vast that practically every canon relates to it, and therefore the principle enunciated in Article 8a cannot be implemented by "statutory rules and orders"[24] but only in the course of reforming canon law.

Article 8b empowers the diocesan bishop to dispense from the general laws of the Church within certain limits. This authorization indicates that although the (diocesan) bishop has "all" the power requisite for exercising his ministry he is nevertheless bound by law that takes precedence over him. The power of dispensation does not relate to particular matters and is therefore a general power; at the same time — apart from being limited by papal reservation of cases — it is limited by the proviso that the granting of a dispensation must be to the spiritual benefit of a member of the Church. Thus the spiritual benefit of a Christian chiefly determines the scope of the dispensing power. By the motu proprio *De Episcoporum muneribus*, 15 August 1966, Article 8b was applied to the Latin Church (see Appendix II).

Articles 9 and 10 aim at a reform of the Roman Curia. The Council did not wish to take this matter out of the Pope's hands, but offered some stimulus by making known its desires.

Article 9 deals with the work, juridical position, and organization of the Curia and in one sentence — added only in the final draft — mentions papal legates. The officials of the Curia are assistants of the Pope, working in his name and by his authority — that is, exercising duly delegated power. The Pope makes use of them in exercising his supreme jurisdiction over the universal Church, so that the work of these officials redounds to the good of individual Churches, in and of which the one Catholic Church consists (see *Lumen Gentium*, Article 23, para. 2), thus being of service to the shepherds of the individual Churches. Here there is no mention of the fact that the Bishop of Rome is not only supreme head of the Church on earth but also Patriarch of the Latin Church. That merging of his two competences, primatial and patriarchal, which has hitherto marked the organization of the Roman Curia and the development of canon law in the

---

[24] No regulations for implementing Article 8a have as yet been issued and presumably none can be expected. *Ecclesiae Sanctae*, I, n. 6, does say that regulations for implementing Article 8 have been promulgated by the motu proprio *De Episcoporum Muneribus;* but inaccurately, for the motu proprio only related to Article 8b.

Latin Church, obscures the image of the Pope's primacy of jurisdiction. Not least because of ecumenical considerations, it will be necessary to create special organs for each of the Pope's two spheres of duty, so that the Roman Curia will credibly body forth oneness in variety.[25] Then the organs having to do with the universal Church *(Curia Ecclesiae universalis)* must be separated from those having to do with the patriarchate of the West *(Curia Ecclesiae Latinae)*.

Acknowledging the outstanding services which the curial departments have rendered the Pope and the shepherds of the Church, the decree asks for them to be reorganized and adapted to the needs of the times and of the various regions (meaning the Latin Church in particular) and rites, especially as to their number, names, competence, methods of procedure, and the co-ordination of their work. These few words outline a very full programme.

The adaptation to the needs of the various rites here called for, can only be made by establishing one Curia for the universal Church and another Curia for the Latin Church. There is no proper place for a supreme authority in charge of Eastern Churches, like the present Oriental Congregation, in a body of officials which by reason of its origins and its work is essentially an organ of the Latin Church. Moreover, a whole series of activities concern the universal Church by their very nature (for example, upholding faith and morals, propagating the faith, governing the relations between rites, fostering links with non-Catholic Christian communities, non-Christian religions, unbelievers, and governments) and therefore should be seen to by organs of the universal Church, without prejudice to the autonomy of the rites. The first steps in this direction have already been taken with the setting up of permanent secretariats (1) for Christian unity, (2) for non-Christian religions, and (3) for unbelievers. When the Curia for the universal Church is a separate organization from the Curia for the Latin Church, the Pope will be unable to dispense with an organ standing in a special relationship to himself, as the Secretariat of State now does, to form a permanent bridge between the two Curias. Meantime the term "Secretariat of State", inherited from the days of the Papal States, should be abandoned and replaced by something like "Apostolic Chancery".

Reorganization of the Curia's *competence* involves two sets of problems: (1) delimiting the functions of the different rites and, within the Latin Church, of the diocesan bishops, the metropolitans, and the episcopal conferences as permanent organs of the ecclesiastical regions which are now contemplated;

---

[25] When all is said and done it is those same considerations which call for the creation of a fundamental law for the whole Church antecedent to the law of the individual rites. See K. Mörsdorf, "Streiflichter zur Reform des kanonischen Rechtes", in *AKK* 135 (1966), pp. 45 ff.; L. M. Orsy, "Towards a Theological Conception of Canon Law", in *Jurist* 24 (1964), p. 388; A. Gommenginger, "Verfassung und Strukturen in einem neuen Kirchenrecht", in *Orientierung* 31 (1967), pp. 27–28; more bibliography on this subject in P. J. M. Huizing, "Reform of Canon Law", in *Concilium* 8, no. 1 (1965).

and (2) distribution of labour within the Curia, where besides separating the work of the universal Church from that of the Latin Church there is an urgent need to sift judicial from administrative business, assigning the former to tribunals and the latter to administrative departments.[26]

A related concern is that procedure be reformed, ultimately so that judicial matters are dealt with by independent tribunals bound to act according to set rules, and administrative matters by administrative officials bound to act according to set rules. As far as possible the cognizance of administrative departments is to be so defined that the same department shall always deal with the same class of business, putting an end to the state of affairs where several organs might be competent in the same matter, which meant that conflicting decisions were likely to be given from time to time. Since overlapping cannot be avoided altogether, even when the functions of each department are better defined, the decree appeals for a co-ordination of work — hitherto altogether lacking — which can only be effected by a special organ staffed by representatives of the departments concerned.

The request that the function of papal legates be more precisely defined in view of the bishops' pastoral role, is meant to give effect to the diocesan bishop's native rights, recognized in principle by Article 8 a, vis-à-vis the Pope's legates as well. Obviously the provision of the *CIC* that papal legates may not interfere with the free exercise of the local ordinaries' jurisdiction (can. 269, § 1) has not sufficed to ease the relationship between nuncio and diocesan bishop. There is a long history behind the difficulties,[27] but under the present law these arise less from the nuncio's (apostolic delegate's) office than from the powers the pope gives him.

Article 10 expresses the desires of the Fathers as to the personnel of curial departments and the choice of papal legates. Drawing more of these men from different rites and from various regions of the Latin Church will help bring out the universal character of the curial organs. Still, this point must not be over-stressed, because such men are not easily come by for service in the Curia and because those who are recruited lose touch with their homeland in the course of time. Again, the Curia is not alone to blame if its personnel has heretofore left something to be desired.

If as requested, certain bishops, especially diocesan bishops, become members of curial departments — which can only mean collegiate organs of the administration, the congregations of cardinals —, then more thorough con-

---

[26] See K. Mörsdorf, *Rechtsprechung und Verwaltung im kanonischen Recht* (1941); P. J. M. Huizing, "Reform of Canon Law", *loc. cit.*; H. Schmitz, "Möglichkeit und Gestalt einer kirchlichen Gerichtsbarkeit über die Verwaltung", in *AKK* 135 (1966), pp. 18–38; A. Gommenginger, "Verfassung und Strukturen in einem neuen Kirchenrecht", in *Orientierung* 31 (1967), p. 267.

[27] On this subject see K. Walf, *Die Entwicklung des päpstlichen Gesandtschaftswesens in dem Zeitabschnitt zwischen Dekretalenrecht und Wiener Kongress, 1159–1815* (1966).

sultation will be possible. But this will not be feasible on a large scale, because a diocesan bishop is usually so overburdened that he could not regularly confer with the department. The desire to give laymen more of a hearing and assure them their due participation in Church affairs should not be thought a mere concession to the spirit of the age; it is a concern rooted in the nature of the Church.

The Synod of Bishops*

When at the solemn opening of the fourth session of the Second Vatican Council, on 14 September 1965, Pope Paul VI announced that a Synod of Bishops[1] would be established, all the Fathers broke into spontaneous applause. This happened not only because there was general surprise but also because the Fathers found themselves relieved of the concern they had felt, understandably enough at the beginning of the last session, about the future effectiveness of collegiality. On the very next day, 15 September 1965, the motu proprio *Apostolica Sollicitudo* was promulgated in the aula.[2] Without a word to anyone the Pope, who has it much at heart that the bishops shall co-operate as a college in the work of the universal Church, sought and found a means that gratified both friend and foe of collegiality. The new institution, which the Pope himself named the Synod of Bishops *(Synodus Episcoporum)*, is a response to the desire expressed in the draft decree *De pastorali Episcoporum munere in Ecclesia* for the setting up of a council of bishops to assist the Pope in exercising his supreme jurisdiction and at the same time demonstrate that all the bishops share responsibility for the whole Church.[3] As Paolo Cardinal Marella explained at a press conference on 25 October 1965,[4] the idea of enlisting the bishops' co-operation in the

---

* *Translated by Richard Strachan*

[1] See the following commentaries on it: C. Berutti in *Monumenta Ecclesiae* 90 (1965), pp. 531–46; W. Bertrams in *Periodica* 55 (1966), pp. 115–32; K. Mörsdorf, *Das synodale Element der Kirchenverfassung im Lichte des Zweiten Vatikanischen Konzils. Festschrift J. Höfer* (1967).

[2] A special edition of the motu proprio was distributed in the aula on 17 September 1965 and publication in the *AAS* followed on 30 September 1965: 57 (1965), pp. 775–80.

[3] The desire expressed in para. 5 of the draft text that a *consilium centrale* be established was advisedly put in such a way as to leave the structure of the council entirely to the Pope's discretion. The text read: "Cum universale Summi Pontificis munus maiores in dies auxilii et praesidii vires exposcat, Sacrosancti Concilii Patres magnopere exoptant ut aliqui Episcopi diversarum orbi regionum, modis tamen et rationibus ab Ipso opportune statuendis, etiam in Coetum seu Consilium quoddam convenientes, quo simul significari possit omnium Episcoporum universae Ecclesiae sollicitudini participatio."

[4] *L'Osservatore Romano,* no. 222, 26 September 1965.

government of the universal Church goes back to the days when the Second Vatican Council was in preparation. Such a proposal was made as early as 5 June 1960 by the Preparatory Commission *De Episcopis ac de Dioecesium regimine* and favourably received by the Preparatory Central Commission, some members of which went on to suggest the creation of a consultative episcopal assembly. Thus a bishops' council was in the air even before the Council began.

To give effect to the motu proprio *Apostolica Sollicitudo* Pope Paul VI issued rules of procedure for the Synod of Bishops *(Ordo Synodi Episcoporum Celebrandae)* through the Cardinal Secretary of State on 8 December 1966.[5] They consist of three parts. Part I sets forth the constitutional structure of the Synod in accordance with the motu proprio, Part II lays down general rules, and Part III deals with procedure.[6] The first Synod of Bishops was called for 29 September 1967.[7]

After the introduction the motu proprio *Apostolica Sollicitudo* says: "Nostra apostolica auctoritate erigimus ac constituimus hac in alma Urbe stabile Episcoporum consilium pro Ecclesia universa, Nostrae potestati directe atque immediate subjectum, quod nomine proprio Synodum Episcoporum appellamus." Read in conjunction with the statement in no. 1c that this entity is "natura sua perpetuum", these words might be taken to mean that the Synod of Bishops has been set up as a collegiate juridical person. But such is not the case at all, because the Synod of Bishops, unlike the episcopal college, is not a permanent college. It is a permanent institution only in the sense that the law sets it up, like other synods, for a period. The term *Synodus Episcoporum* is aptly chosen, as designating a group which operates only insofar as its members for the time being happen to foregather in one place for a certain period (no. 1d). While they are gathered there the members of the Synod form a college which in common counsels and takes decisions. The existence of a synod does not depend on how often it meets.

The Synod of Bishops is a central organ of the Church, called upon to represent the entire Catholic episcopate (no. Ia and b). One is struck by the fact that the motu proprio *Apostolica Sollicitudo* never mentions the episcopal college in this context — probably to counter any idea that the Synod of Bishops, as representative of the episcopal college, might claim the supreme authority proper to that college. In itself the Bishops' Synod is a purely advisory organ; but it can take decisions if the Pope empowers it to do so, in which case it is for him to approve such decisions. If we bear in mind that the Pope's assent is a constituent element of any collegiate act on the part of the episcopal college, then from the purely juridical point of view it seems to be largely a point of canonical etiquette

---

[5] *AAS* 59 (1967), pp. 91–103.
[6] It should be noted that matters of procedure also figure in Part II, for example, the method of voting.
[7] Its meetings embraced twenty-four sessions and lasted about a month. This excursus was written before the meeting of the Synod.

whether the Synod can only advise or also make decisions; for the Pope is not compelled by law to accept advice or agree with any decision that others have reached. These juridical bounds are set by the hierarchical framework of the Church's constitution and in no way detract from the weight properly attaching to collegiate advice offered by a body representative of the bishops.

The Synod of Bishops is immediately subject to the Pope, who ratifies the election of members, convokes the Synod, sets the agenda, and presides in person or through others (no. 3). Article 2 of the rules of procedure provides that a president delegate *(Praeses delegatus)* shall occupy the chair in the name and with the authority of the Pope. He is chosen by the Pope and his duties cease with the close of the meeting for which he was appointed. If the Pope names several presidents, they serve one after the other in the order determined by the Pope.

The Synod of Bishops may be convoked in three ways: 1) as a general meeting *(coetus generalis)*, 2) as an extraordinary meeting *(coetus extraordinarius)*, and 3) as a special meeting *(coetus specialis)* about a particular matter (no. 4). Some members will be chosen in a specified way and others in ways to be specified (nos. 5–10). Patriarchs, primates and metropolitans outside a patriarchate of the Eastern Catholic Churches are automatically members of the Bishops' Synod in all three of its forms, except that in the third form only those shall be members who have jurisdiction over the territory in question. Within the Latin Church the representatives of the episcopate for the Synod in its first and third form are chosen by the national episcopal conferences or, where there are no such, by an episcopal conference common to several countries; where a conference numbers no more than 25, 50, or 100, the number of representatives is 1, 2, or 3, respectively, while conferences with over 100 bishops have 4 representatives. In the second form of the Synod *(coetus extraordinarius)* the chairmen of the national episcopal conferences and of the conferences embracing several countries are the representatives of the episcopate. Religious to be chosen by the Roman Congregation of Superiors-General also belong to the Bishops' Synod in each form, with 10 representatives for the first form and 3 for the second form. No number is given for the third form (no. 7);[8] Article 6, § 2, n. 4, of the rules of procedure says "not more than two". Article 6, § 1, n. 2, and § 2, n. 1, provides that the elective members of the Synod shall be chosen in turn, each by separate ballot. The names of those elected may not be made known until the Pope has confirmed the election (rules of procedure, Article 6, § 3).

Cardinal Prefects of Congregations in the Roman Curia are also members of the Bishops' Synod in its first and second form (no. 5, sub-para. 2 and no.6, sub-para. 2); the rules of procedure say the same of the third form, but only in the case of Cardinal Prefects whose Congregations are concerned with the

---

[8] Reference to nos. 5 and 8 only reveals the number of episcopal representatives. The number of representatives for the religious is absolutely fixed at 10 for the general (meeting) and 3 for the extraordinary meeting. Neither rule allows for any proportional adjustment.

matter in hand (Article 5, § 3, n. 2). Since a clear-cut distinction between the legislative and the executive is the ideal within the Roman Curia as elsewhere, it may seem surprising to find that the heads of administrative departments are members of the Bishops' Synod which, though purely advisory, is chiefly occupied with work of a legislative nature. But one must remember that men hammering out legislation cannot dispense with the accumulated experience of senior administrators. The Bishops' Synod does not, like secular parliaments, reach its decisions by majority vote; and therefore it seems to me wise and necessary for the heads of curial departments to be among the members of the Synod. Moreover, the Pope reserves the right to increase the membership of the Bishops' Synod, in any of its forms, up to 15% of its canonical strength by convoking other bishops, representatives of religious communities, and clerical experts (no. 10). There is certainly no question here of strengthening the Pope's influence over the Synod through men who are in his confidence, but simply of making lawful provision for calling in acknowledged experts to the Synod, should the electors concerned have overlooked them. In electing representatives of the episcopate and the religious communities, not only a man's general suitability should be considered but also his special competence, both theoretical and practical, in the matters which happen to lie before the Bishops' Synod (no. 11). Although this principle can operate only insofar as members of the Synod are to be elected — that is, only within the Latin Church and here, as a rule, only within the first and third form of the Synod (in the case of religious, also with the second) —, it is clear that the Pope wants a Bishops' Synod which will really be able to stand by him in word and deed.

In Article 21 the rules of procedure provide that the matters a Synod of Bishops is to deal with shall be assiduously discussed by each episcopal conference, and in the Eastern Churches by a corresponding assembly of bishops; that each episcopate — that is, each episcopal conference or assembly — shall express its consensus in some way which seems suitable; and that the delegated members of the Bishops' Synod shall make known to it the views of their episcopate. These instructions apply *mutatis mutandis* to religious. Though each member of a Synod represents a particular group and must convey the common view of his group at the Synod, he is free to make his own decisions and is not bound by any instructions from his group, as is borne in on us by the nature and purpose of a synod.[9] When an assembly of the Bishops' Synod ends membership

---

[9] Article 35, § 1, of the rules of procedure seems to state the contrary in instructing individual members of the Synod once discussion is over, to present their opinion, according to the consensus of their group (Article 21, § 2), in the form of a written vote handed in to the secretary general. The words "mentem suam, de qua in art. 21 § 2, pandunt . . ." must be interpreted to mean that the individual members of the Synod shall form their opinion with due consideration of their group's consensus; otherwise they would not be members of a synod but simply postmen. Indeed the whole of Article 35 strikes me as ill-expressed. It distinguishes between casting a vote (§ 1) and taking a vote if the Pope gives instructions for one (§ 2), doubtless because in

of it expires, as do any tasks or functions which that assembly has assigned its individual members (no. 11); this norm, arising from the canonical nature of the Synod, shows beyond all doubt that the Synod of Bishops is not a permanent college. It does, however, have a permanent secretary general; and each assembly of the Synod has a special secretary who remains in office until the assembly closes (no. 12). The perpetuity[10] of the secretary general, we gather from the contrast drawn between him and the special secretary, means not only that the post of secretary general has been set up for more than a certain period but also that the post shall always be filled. Thus in a sense the secretary general remains the one constant factor as assemblies of the Bishops' Synod come and go. His perpetuity is different from that of the Synod, which as we have pointed out can only be considered an *institutum natura sua perpetuum* insofar as it is juridically set up from time to time. Unlike the Synod, which can be operative only as an assembled college, the secretary general is always operative.

In all its three forms the Bishops' Synod is a flexible organ, easily adaptable to the needs of any particular age. As a general assembly it looks very much like a future Ecumenical Council with a representative membership. As an extra-ordinary assembly the Bishops' Synod is available at practically any moment, since only three representatives of religious communities have to be elected to it. As an extraordinary assembly the Bishops' Synod has a multitude of uses — among others, acting as a representative synod of the Latin Church, a counterpart to the patriarchal synod in the Eastern Churches. Again the forthcoming reform of the Latin *Codex Iuris Canonici* might well be a task for such a synod.

In practice cardinals will represent a substantial part of the Bishops' Synod in any form; indeed they will so dominate the second form, even numerically, as to make it seem a meeting of cardinals. Here we encounter the problem of the relationship between the Bishops' Synod and the College of Cardinals, the more so as the reform introduced by John XXIII[11] and continued with gentle persistence by Paul VI[12] has laid the groundwork for a sacred college representative of the universal Church. An old aspiration, voiced by the Council

itself the Synod of Bishops is a purely advisory organ which the Pope may authorize, by way of exception, to make decisions (motu proprio, no. 2). But it overlooks the fact that the Synod as an advisory body does not exist in order to collect the opinions which individual members have formed with due consideration for the consensus of their group, but in order to form an opinion of the Synod through the common deliberations of its members — which in the nature of things can only be done by means of a vote.

[10] No. 12, para. 1, says that the Bishops' Synod has a *secretarium perpetuum seu generalem*. The word *seu* here can neither be disjunctive nor serve to define *perpetuus* by *generalis. Et* would be better than *seu,* and a relative clause stating what *perpetuus* means would be still better. Para. 2, on the secretary general, aptly describes his office.

[11] Motu proprio, 11 April 1962, *AAS* 54 (1962), pp. 253–6.

[12] Motu proprio, 26 February 1965, *AAS* 57 (1965), pp. 295–7.

of Basle[13] and taken up by the Council of Trent,[14] is now nearing fulfilment. At the same time there is an opportunity to revive the consistory, which originally inherited the tradition of the Roman Synods, became the supreme collegiate organ of the Roman Curia, but went into a decline with the creation of the congregations of cardinals, and nowadays can hardly be called a functioning organ in any of its three forms (secret, semi-public, and public consistory). During the lifetime of a Pope most business is not handled by the Sacred College but by individual cardinals who occupy a prominent position as prefects or members of administrative departments and tribunals and outside the Curia strengthen ties with the Sovereign Pontiff through their prestige and especially as chairmen of an episcopal conference. New thinking about the collegiate element in the ecclesiastical constitution offers the College of Cardinals an opportunity to become the Pope's real senate once again as a college gathered in consistory. Unlike the Bishops' Synod, which can only be convoked from time to time, the College of Cardinals, by nature a permanent college with a chairman — the dean — who is *primus inter pares,* has it in its power to hold regular meetings, ordinary and extraordinary, whenever there may be occasion. It can take the initiative and offer the Pope its help, which the Bishops' Synod can only do when assembled and to a limited extent. Were the consistory revived, the old formula that the Pope reaches his decisions *de fratrum nostrorum consilio* could become meaningful again. Not as though the consistory should "compete" with the Bishops' Synod. Rather the consistory should complement the Synod's work and with it ensure that the principle of collegiality is kept operative. The most important right of the College of Cardinals will always be the right to elect the Pope. Suggestions that this right should be transferred to the Bishops' Synod are impractical, given the present structure of the Synod, which is always constituted by a papal act.[15]

[13] Sess. XXIII: *De munere et qualitate cardinalium.*
[14] Sess. XXIV, can. 1 de ref.
[15] Such suggestions were made by some Fathers of the Council in connection with establishing a "council of bishops", and have sometimes been put forward since as a prospect for the Bishops' Synod. Although from the purely technical point of view it might seem feasible to alter the structure of the Synod — which presupposes a reigning Pope — for the special purpose of having it elect the Pope, in the long run it might feel that having made the Pope it was in some way his master. Such a danger should be forestalled, and that will best be done if the College of Cardinals is given a membership which can be considered representative of the whole Church. In any case there is very little difference in membership between the College of Cardinals and the Synod of Bishops in the form of its extraordinary assembly — the only one that would in practice be concerned with papal elections — and that slight difference will all but vanish in the near future.

The Diocesan Bishop's Power of Dispensation according to the Decree "Christus Dominus", Article 8 b*

On 15 June 1966 the motu proprio *De Episcoporum Muneribus* was published.[1] It gave effect in the Latin Church to the power of the diocesan bishop under Article 8 b, to dispense from general laws of the Church. This is a provisional decree, which came into force on 15 August 1966 and will become inoperative when the new *CIC* is promulgated. Understanding the regulations — graphic evidence of how difficult it is to get the feel of conciliar authority — is a good deal of a puzzle,[2] which one feels should not be so. After an introduction acknowledging the native power which the diocesan bishop has under Article 8 a to exercise his pastoral office, the motu proprio sets forth the norms for the dispensing power in nine articles:

1. Preliminary questions (Articles 1–3)

First comes a reminder that the *CIC* and ecclesiastical laws promulgated in accordance with it continue in force until revoked unless Vatican II has evidently abrogated them altogether or in part, or tacitly amended them in certain respects by making new laws on the subject concerned (Article 1). This reminder, superfluous in itself, is timely all the same because Catholics act on occasion as though the *CIC* and all other pre-conciliar legislation had more or less gone by the board. The reason is to be sought not only in a fanaticism, widespread today, which has declared war on all canon law, but also in the obscurity of legislative language. For we must admit that it is often very difficult to tell whether a pre-conciliar norm has been abrogated or amended by the Council or by papal laws issued since the Council. The Apostolic See, therefore, should be called on to

---

* *Translated by Richard Strachan*

[1] *AAS* 58 (1966), pp. 467–72.

[2] On this matter see L. Buijs, "De potestate Episcoporum dispensandi", in *Periodica* 56 (1967), pp. 88–115, and J. Lederer, "Die Neuordnung des Dispensrechtes", in *AKK* 135 (1966). It is little wonder if the two attempts at interpretation widely diverge. We cannot enter into particulars here.

bear in mind when legislating in future that the law must be certain and to specify, when changing the law in force, precisely which norms are affected.

It is then stated that Article 8 b of the Decree *Christus Dominus* only abrogates part of can. 81 in the Code (Article 2). Here the need for precise legislative language has been respected; only it does not appear what change has been made in can. 81 by the conciliar decree. The power granted by the Council fits effortlessly into the declaration of can. 81; it leaves intact the principle there enunciated that ordinaries beneath the Pope may not dispense from the general laws of the Church even in individual cases unless this power has been explicitly or implicitly conferred on them. The power *(facultas)* given in Article 8 b is a power *(potestas)* in terms of can. 81; the fact that it is not limited to particular matters and is therefore a general power makes no difference, because the *potestas* of can. 81 includes every kind of *facultas,* not excluding the general (can. 15 is an example). Nor does it matter whether the power is granted by law or by administrative act; for in either case the power remains one deriving from the authority of the legislator. So it cannot be said that the rule of can. 82 has been broadened by the power of dispensation under Article 8 b.

The conciliar norm itself has been broadened meantime by the provision of the motu proprio (Article 3) that the "bishops" on whom Article 8 b confers the dispensing power shall include not only diocesan bishops but also persons having the equivalent juridical status. The equality of rights as between diocesan bishops and these other dignitaries, the common foundation underlying their rights, and the necessity of seeing to the spiritual welfare of the faithful, are given as the reasons for the provision. Accordingly, the motu proprio states, the dispensing power shall also be enjoyed by vicars and prefects apostolic (can. 294, § 1), permanently appointed apostolic administrators (can. 315, § 1), and abbots and prelates nullius (can. 323, § 1). Now an enumeration is made in order to exclude other persons or things. But to take the enumeration in this motu proprio just as it stands would be an error. As in the motu proprio *Pastorale Munus* of 30 January 1963, which uses the same enumeration,[3] the legislator's evident intention is that all who preside over a diocese or a quasi-diocesan territorial entity, that is all local ordinaries, shall enjoy the power bestowed on the diocesan bishop. Hence there is no reason to doubt that the prefect of an independent mission *(missio sui iuris),* the vicar capitular, the vicar general *sede impedita,* and pro-vicars and pro-prefects as interim rulers of dioceses and quasi-diocesan territorial entities, likewise share the dispensing power of the diocesan bishop.

Although the power now acknowledged in the diocesan bishop and local ordinaries equated with him is one deriving from the supreme authority, it is an ordinary power — that is, a power attached to the office of a local ordinary, acquired along with the office and lost when the office is lost. Since no restric-

---

[3] See K. Mörsdorf, "Neue Vollmachten und Privilegien der Bischöfe", in *AKK* 133 (1964), pp. 82 ff.

tions of any kind are imposed on its exercise, it also belongs to the vicar general in virtue of his office; to the coadjutor, who in future must always be appointed vicar general; and to episcopal vicars whose office gives them the rights of the vicar general. The same is true of the vicar delegate, who in effect occupies the position of a vicar general. Moreover the dispensing power may be delegated to others, altogether or in part (can. 199, § 1).

2. General limits of the dispensing power (Articles 4–8)

The conciliar text says that the power to dispense from general laws of the Church in particular cases is subject to the bishop's judgment that a dispensation will be to the spiritual benefit of the faithful; whence it follows that the power does not apply wholesale to the Church's general laws but only to such as affect the spiritual good of the faithful. Such a limitation of the dispensing power would have been logical and to the point in any case. Twice the motu proprio applies it: when stating that the rules of judicial procedure cannot be dispensed from (Article 4, para. 3) and when stating that the spiritual good of the faithful is the lawful ground for granting a dispensation (Article 8). This basic thought behind the dispensing power bestowed by the Council does not emerge elsewhere. Instead there was an effort to confine the power within purely formal limits by examining it in terms of the concept of dispensation on the one hand, and in terms of certain kinds of law on the other. Each of the two problems is duly posed but separately, not in combination as a canonist would wish, so that no clear, practical solution is given to either.

As to the broad sense given the words *dispensare* and *dispensatio*,[4] it was necessary first of all to point out the technical meaning of dispensation in the *CIC* (can. 80), which says that to dispense is to suspend the obligation of an ecclesiastical law in a special case (Article 4, first sentence).[5] Moreover, Article 4, para. 2, states that the granting of a permission, a faculty, an indult, or an absolution does not come under the heading of a dispensation. True enough, although we must observe that when actually applying the law it is not always easy to distinguish between a dispensation and a permission and that indults are often mere dispensations. Obviously absolution — absolution, that is, from a vindictive penalty, especially that of excommunication, which by its nature excludes one from sacramental absolution and therefore from receiving Holy Communion — is not a dispensation in the technical sense; but looking at the matter in a somewhat less technical way one might have concluded that the power bestowed by the Council extends to absolving from vindictive penalties, because these always relate to the spiritual welfare of the faithful. Article 5 of the motu proprio says that general laws of the Church mean only *leges dis-*

---

[4] See J. Lederer, *Der Dispensbegriff des kanonischen Rechtes unter besonderer Berücksichtigung der Rechtssprache des CIC* (1957), pp. 127–209.
[5] *Ibid.*, pp. 44 ff.

ciplinares made by the supreme ecclesiastical authority, never the laws of God, whether natural or divine positive law. Thus a dispensation in the technical sense is distinguished from what is called an improper dispensation — of which dissolving the vinculum of an unconsummated marriage and dissolving a marriage by the *privilegium fidei* are cited as examples.[6] Trying to determine the scope of the dispensing power by analysis of the concept of dispensation, therefore, leads to the meagre conclusion that it is only a power to dispense from purely ecclesiastical laws *(leges disciplinares)*.[7]

As to which general laws of the Church fall under the dispensing power, the motu proprio establishes two points: 1) The power relates to laws which command and forbid *(leges praecipientes vel prohibentes)* but not to *leges constitutivae* (Article 4, para. 1, sentence 2). 2) Laws governing judicial procedure *(leges ad processus spectantes)* do not fall under the dispensing power because they are made to protect rights and excusing from their observance does not directly bear on the spiritual welfare of the faithful (Article 4, para. 3). The second statement is clear; the first is enigmatic. No such expression as *lex constitutiva* occurs in the *CIC*. Offhand one would suppose that *leges constitutivae* are legal rules whose observance is essential to a legal transaction; but not at all. It seems that *leges constitutivae* mean constitutional rules[8] — *leges constitutionales*, in the technical term — which one cannot, however, contrast as the motu proprio does, with laws that command and forbid, because constitutional rules — like any law, after all — also contain injunctions and prohibitions. So the effort to lay down general limits to the dispensing power has failed, and if dispensations are not to be handed out now at random, they can only be limited according to the mind of the Council on the basis of the spiritual good of the faithful.

That limitation is necessary in any case, since the spiritual good of the faithful is the lawful ground *(causa legitima)* for granting a dispensation (Article 8, sentence 2); that is, the power can be used only for the sake of some spiritual benefit to the faithful. All those general laws, then, which require or forbid the bishops and their fellow-workers to do given things are automatically excluded except insofar as they bear directly on the spiritual good of the faithful. The purpose of the dispensing power is not to emancipate bishops from the general law of the Church but to enable them to serve their Christian people even when these would suffer spiritual detriment by observing the general law

---

[6] In accordance with the doctrine which still finds general acceptance, the motu proprio assumes that the Pope dispenses in these cases by his vicarious authority; yet in neither case can there be any question of a real dispensation — that is, of suspending the obligation of a divine law. On this point see J. Lederer, *op. cit.,* pp. 85 ff.

[7] The expression has the same meaning here as in can. 6, no. 6, of the *CIC;* see K. Mörsdorf, *Lehrbuch des Kirchenrechts,* I, pp. 76 f.

[8] We find the term used in this sense — contrasted with *leges directivae* — to mean the subject matter of the constitution *(constitutio)* of a religious institute, in a decree of the Sacred Congregation for Religious, 6 March 1921, n. 22, i: *AAS* 13 (1921), p. 317.

of the Church in particular circumstances. Apart from the lawful grounds antecedently required for the valid and licit use of the dispensing power, there must be a just and reasonable *cause*, in estimating which it is also necessary to consider the gravity of the law that would be dispensed from (Article 8, sentence 1). Although the motu proprio does not expressly say so, here the sanction of can. 84, § 1, applies, that a dispensation granted by delegated authority without a just and reasonable cause is not only illicit but also invalid.

The dispensing power can be used in respect of the faithful over whom the bishop exercises authority, that is, jurisdiction, according to law; which means, the motu proprio says, all the faithful subject to the bishop on grounds of residence or any other legal title (Article 8). There is probably no intention of restricting the conciliar norm, as one might think was being done here since jurisdiction — especially where discretionary power *(iurisdictio voluntaria seu gratiosa)* is concerned, as in this case — can often be exercised over non-subjects. Including persons subject to the bishop on grounds other than residence covers cases of "subjection *ad hoc*", for the exercise of a concrete act of jurisdiction. So the general rules of cognizance apply to the use of discretionary power, particularly the exercise of the dispensing power.[9] Moreover, the dispensing power may be used not only in the case of the individual faithful but also in that of several physical persons who form a society in the strict sense (Article 6). This provision is brought in to explain the sense of *casus particularis* but it has another meaning. It is modelled on can. 1245, § 1, which specifies that not only the individual faithful but also particular families may be excused from the law of fasting, abstinence, and attendance at Mass on Sundays and holy days; so it must be interpreted to mean that whenever a situation which would justify granting a dispensation affects not only one person or another but several at once, all these can be dispensed by a single act if they are in some way permanently associated. This makes granting dispensations simpler.

In principle the faithful over whom the bishop exercises authority according to law include religious resident or working in the diocese. So logically the question of the bishop's power to dispense religious would come into Article 7, which defines the persons for whom the dispensing power can be used, and not, as has happened, into the list of papal reservations. That list reserves to the Pope: 1) dispensations from the general laws of the Church in favour of religious as religious, but not insofar as they are subject to the local ordinary at common law and particularly by the conciliar decree *Christus Dominus* (nos. 33–35), always saving the discipline of the institute and the rights of the superior; and 2) dispensations from other general laws, only in the case of an exempt clerical institute (Article 9, no. 4). It is not clear what is meant by *ceterae leges generales* in para. 2. The word *ceterae* refers to something that has not yet been

---

[9] See K. Mörsdorf, *Lehrbuch des Kirchenrechts,* I, pp. 169, 328 ff.

mentioned, and what follows has to be understood by contrast to what has been said before. The principle laid down in para. 1 is so broad that it seems to need no amplifying, but an amplification is necessary because the difference of status as between exempt and non-exempt religious has not yet been broached. Obviously para. 2 is meant to supply the omission. As to religious as religious, the autonomy of a religious institute varies according to whether it is of papal or episcopal right and an institute is exempt only insofar as the Pope has removed it from the jurisdiction of the local ordinary.

3. Catalogue of papal reservations (Article 9)

This list is introduced with a reservation of the powers "specially" bestowed on papal legates and ordinaries — which means that these powers are not affected by the papal reservations about to be detailed. There was no particular need to add a saving clause about the powers of papal legates and personal ordinaries since the motu proprio merely implements the dispensing power of diocesan bishops and other local ordinaries. Then the question arises what powers are to be regarded as "specially" bestowed. Doubtless these include the five-year faculties which the Consistorial Congregation is accustomed to grant, with certain variations for religious institutes, and the ten-year faculties for missionary ordinaries and faculties for particular territories, such as Latin America and the Philippines.[10] These are delegated powers; they are given to ordinaries as holding an office which entails jurisdiction, for the sake of such office but not through it. The formal canonical structure of these powers, which can be considered permanent powers since they are granted more or less automatically (see can. 166), lies just on the borderline between delegated and ordinary power. They have now been largely suspended by Pope Paul VI's motu proprio *Pastorale Munus* of 30 November 1963,[11] which sets forth a majestic catalogue of powers belonging to local ordinaries as of right *(iure)*; these, accordingly, attach to the bishop's office and are to be considered ordinary powers. Apart from the fact that these powers do not relate solely to dispensation, the question arises whether dispensing powers which the ordinary enjoys as of right can be looked on as "specially" conferred.[12] *Specialis* is a very elastic word in canonical language. In connection with *facultas dispensandi* it describes

[10] The text of these faculties is given in Vermeersch and Creusen, *Epitone Iuris Canonici*, I (8th ed., 1963), pp. 709 f.; see L. Buijs, *Facultates* (1963).

[11] *AAS* 56 (1964), pp. 5–12; see L. Buijs, *Facultates et privilegia Episcoporum concessa Motu proprio "Pastorale Munus" cum commentario* (1964), and K. Mörsdorf, "Neue Vollmachten und Privilegien der Bischöfe", in *AKK* 133 (1964), pp. 82–101.

[12] J. Lederer, in *AKK* 135 (1966), thinks that the powers under the motu proprio *Pastorale munus* cannot be reckoned as powers specially conferred, but admits that the opposite opinion would have desirable consequences. L. Buijs, in *Periodica* 56 (1967), p. 114, does not discuss the question at all and without hesitation sets the powers granted by *Pastorale Munus* under the heading of powers specially conferred.

a particular power granted according to circumstances as opposed to a general power.

Thus far there is no difficulty about considering the powers of *Pastorale Munus* to be conferred *specialiter*. But it would seem that the adverb *specialiter* relates not so much to the nature of the powers as to the manner of their bestowal; in which case the bare word does not establish whether we are dealing with delegated or with ordinary powers, much less whether powers bestowed by administrative act alone, or by law as well, can be withdrawn. So I think it is fair to hold that the ordinary powers conferred by the motu proprio *Pastorale Munus* fall within the saving clause; not least because when the Pope has anticipated the conciliar decree by granting certain powers he cannot be presumed to be withdrawing some of them, in the very act of implementing the conciliar decree,[13] unless he plainly says that this is what he is doing. Nor can there be any doubt that the dispensing power of local ordinaries which is built into the *CIC* — whether it be a general power (can. 15, 81) or a special one (as in can. 990, § 1, 998, § 1, 1028, 1043, 1044, 1245) — continues in force,[14] though here it would be much more difficult to speak of powers conferred *specialiter*.

To get down to particulars, the Pope reserves to himself the right to grant the following dispensations:

1. *Duties attached to an ecclesiastical state*

a) From the obligation of celibacy which binds deacons and priests even when they have lawfully returned, or been reduced, to the lay state (Article 9, para. 1, to be read with can. 132, § 1, and 213, § 2).[15]

b) From the law which forbids married men to exercise the priesthood if they have been ordained without a papal dispensation (Article 9, para. 2, to be read with Article 9, para. 9 c, and can. 132, § 3, and 987, no. 2).

c) From the laws which forbid clerks in holy orders (Article 9, para. 3) to practise medicine or surgery (can. 139, § 2),[16] to accept public offices that

---

[13] The list of reservations in the motu proprio *De Episcoporum Muneribus* coincides with the powers granted by the motu proprio *Pastorale Munus* at the following points: Article 9, § 4, with 1, nos. 35–37; Article 9, § 8, with 1, no. 17; Article 9, § 18c with 1, nos. 21 and 22; Article 9, § 20, with 1, no. 3.

[14] J. Lederer admits as much, in *AKK* 135 (1966), when he says à propos of the reserved dispensation from the canonical form of marriage (Article 9, para. 17) that the powers conferred by can. 1043 and 1044 remain intact.

[15] The words *aut regressi*, from can. 213, § 1, have been used without regard to the fact that deacons and priests cannot, like men in minor orders, leave the clerical state of their own accord (see can. 211, § 2) but can only be reduced to the lay state by an act of jurisdiction. In this matter, however, the Code itself speaks uncanonically of an *ad statum laicalem redire* (can. 212, § 2).

[16] Can. 139, § 2, says that one is freed from this prohibition by indult; which shows that indultum is also used in the sense of *dispensatio*.

involve exercising secular jurisdiction or administration, to become a senator or deputy in countries where such a papal prohibition is in force (can. 138, § 4).[17]

2. Sacramental law

a) Penance and the Eucharist

1) From the duty of denouncing a priest for soliciting in the confessional (Article 9, para. 5, to be read with can. 904).

2) From the time prescribed for the eucharistic fast (Article 9, para. 20); it does not appear why this reservation is made.[18]

b) Holy orders

1) From more than a year of the canonical age for ordination (Article 9, para. 6 and can. 975); when considering whether to dispense from canonical age, bishops are to remember the instructions given in the conciliar decree *Optatam totius*, Article 12.

2) From the order of studies in philosophy and theology, whether as to the time prescribed or the subjects (Article 9, para. 7); here too one wonders what purpose is served by a papal reservation.

3) From all irregularities that are before a judicial forum (Article 9, para. 8, to be read with can. 990, § 1).

4) From all irregularities and impediments that bar one from holy orders (Article 9, para. 9), namely a) birth out of wedlock in the case of *filii adulterini vel sacrilegi*,[19] physical defects, epilepsy, and mental illness, b) public defection from the faith and public adherence to heresy or schism (see can. 985, no. 3, d) murder and procuring abortion (can. 985, no. 4), and e) the impediment which prevents a married man's admission to the priesthood while his wife is alive (can. 987, no. 2).

5) From irregularities which prevent the exercise of orders already received (Article 9, para. 10) — bigamy (can. 985, no. 3) in public cases, murder and procuring abortion (can. 985, no. 4) also in private cases unless recourse to the Sacred Penitentiary is impossible, in which case the person dispensed remains bound to approach the Penitentiary as soon as that becomes possible.

---

[17] Can. 139, § 4, envisages the possibility of securing permission *(licentia)*.

[18] One notes that this reservation has got to the end of the list, which otherwise follows the order of the *CIC*.

[19] This reservation should be reconsidered in the spirit of the constitution *Gaudium et Spes*, Article 27, para. 2.

c) Marriage

1) From more than a year of the canonical age for marriage (Article 9, para. 11, to be read with can. 1067).

2) From the impediment to marriage arising out of diaconal and priestly orders and solemn religious profession (Article 9, para. 12, to be read with can. 1072, 1073).

3) From the impediment of crime specified in can. 1075, nos. 2 and 3 (Article 9, para. 13).

4) From consanguinity in the direct line, and in the collateral line as far as the second degree touching the first (Article 9, para. 14, to be read with can. 1076). This reservation should have been expressed with more care. Consanguinity in the first degree is generally held to be an impediment of divine law, one therefore that cannot be dispensed from. Whether the same is true of other degrees in the direct line is a subject of controversy. At any rate no one should expect a papal dispensation from consanguinity in these degrees. In practice only a relationship in the second degree touching the first might be dispensed from.

5) From affinity in the direct line (Article 9, para. 15, to be read with can. 1077, § 1).

6) From all impediments, in the case of mixed marriages, if the conditions required in no. 1 of the instruction on mixed marriages, 18 March 1966, cannot be satisfied (Article 9, para. 16). This reservation is based on the general principle of the law on dispensations that where several dispensations are sought the whole case must be referred to the superior who has all the necessary faculties. The chief aim is to ensure that there shall be no tampering with divine law.

7) From the form required for the validity of marriage (Article 9, para. 17, to be read with can. 1094), which in practice chiefly means that the bishops are powerless to allow mixed marriages unless these observe the canonical form of celebration.[20] The power to use an extraordinary form in danger of death, in accordance with can. 1043 and 1044, remains unchanged.

8) From the need to renew matrimonial consent for a sanation of marriage *(sanatio in radice)* (Article 9, para. 18) a) whenever a dispensation is required from an impediment reserved to the Apostolic See, b) whenever the impediment is one of natural or divine positive law and has ceased, and c) whenever the

---

[20] The decree *Orientalium Ecclesiarum,* Article 18, states that in mixed marriages between Catholic and non-Catholic Eastern Christians the canonical form is necessary for their legitimacy alone. For their validity the presence of a sacred minister suffices, so long as the other requirements of law are observed. A decree of the Oriental Congregation, 22 February 1967, extended this rule to cover marriages between a Catholic of the Latin rite and a non-Catholic Eastern Christian. At the same time the local ordinaries concerned were authorized to dispense from the need to observe the canonical form for the sake of legitimacy, when dispensing from disparity of worship, if they prudently think it advisable.

marriage is a mixed marriage which has not been contracted according to the requirements of no. 1 of the instruction on mixed marriages. This last reservation overlaps the powers for *sanatio in radice* which were granted by the motu proprio *Pastorale Munus*, Article 1, nos. 21 and 22, in response to an urgent pastoral concern. Those powers still exist, as we have noted above.

3. Penalties

Remission of a punitive penalty *(poena vindicativa)* at common law which the Apostolic See has declared or imposed is also reserved to the Pope (Article 9, para. 19). The remission of such a penalty is not a dispensation in the technical sense,[21] because it does not suspend the obligation of a law in a particular instance but quashes the penalty which has resulted from a law, whether automatically or by the sentence of a judge. This point is clearer in the latter case, where the penalty first comes into being through the sentence; whereas in the former case the penalty comes into being by the operation of law and a judge enters the picture only if it is necessary to determine when the penalty was incurred. By calling the remission of a punitive penalty *(poena vindicativa) dispensatio* and the remission of a corrective penalty (poena medicinalis) or censure *absolutio*, the canonical language of the Church (can. 2236, § 1) cannot disguise the fact that we are dealing in both cases with the remission of punishment, whatever differences there may be between the two sorts of punishment. In view of the fact that censures directly concern the spiritual good of the faithful, it would have been well to revise the list of reserved censures. That task should no longer be put off.

---

[21] See K. Mörsdorf, *Lehrbuch des Kirchenrechts,* III (10th ed.), pp. 354 ff., and J. Lederer, *Dispensbegriff,* pp. 113 ff.

Bishops and Their Particular Churches or Dioceses*

It is not quite clear from the heading of Chapter II that this treats chiefly of the bishop in the plenary sense of the word, that is to say, of the president of a particular Church or diocese.[1] The so-called titular bishops who act as co-adjutors or auxiliary bishops are mentioned only as co-operating in the running of the diocese. Futhermore, the term *Ecclesia particularis* is not used in the same sense throughout the documents of the Council. In our decree *Ecclesia particularis* means diocese, while in the Decree on the Eastern Catholic Churches it signifies the individual autonomous Churches of the East (*Ecclesiae particulares seu ritus*; cf. Article 2 of the Decree *Orientalium Ecclesiarum*), and in the Decree on the Missions all the Churches of a district of the same culture (*Ecclesiae novellae* = *novae Ecclesiae particulares*, Decree *Ad Gentes*, Article 22).

Chapter II is divided into three sections: 1) Diocesan Bishops (Articles 11–21), 2) Diocesan Boundaries (Articles 22–24) and 3) Those who Co-operate with the Diocesan Bishop in His Pastoral Task. This last section deals with Coadjutor and Auxiliary Bishops (25 f.), the Diocesan Curia and Councils (27), the Diocesan Clergy (28–32) and the Religious (33–35). This subdivision is merely the outer framework of what the Council meant to express; a comprehensive description of the tasks and organization of the diocese was not intended.

Article 11. According to the definition given in the first paragraph, "a diocese is that portion of God's people which is entrusted to a bishop to be shepherded by him with the co-operation of the presbytery". On the one hand this makes the essential point, because the diocese is not a district, but part of the people of God, that is a community of believers; the territorial element does not constitute, but merely determines the diocese. On the other hand the definition is too general, because it includes also those parts of the people of God who are entrusted to a bishop not *qua* bishop, but by reason of another

---

* *Translated by Hilda Graef*
[1] On the history see A. Scheuermann, "Diözese", in T. Klauser, ed., in *Reallexikon für Antike und Christentum* (1950 ff.), III, cols. 1053–62.

legal title, e.g., as an apostolic administrator. For greater clarity a statement from paragraph two must be added, according to which the bishop presiding over a particular Church is the proper, ordinary and immediate pastor who feeds his sheep in the name of the Lord. Here the most important characteristic is *proprius pastor*, so that we arrive at the following definition: The diocese is part of the people of God, over which the bishop presides as their proper pastor, representing the invisible Lord to the flock entrusted to him and, co-operating with his presbytery, unites the individual faithful in and to Christ in such a way that the one, holy, Catholic and Apostolic Church is truly active and present in this particular Church. Thus understood the particular Church is an essential element of the constitution of the Church.

The first sentence of paragraph two is similar to Article 8a, so that the reader may be referred to our remarks on that passage. The following passage demands that the diocesan bishops should acknowledge the rights which belong to patriarchs and other hierarchical authorities, including, apart from the metropolitan (cf. Article 40, nos. 1 and 2), especially collegial organs such as synods and episcopal conferences. Thus the diocesan bishop is placed within a hierarchical structure that contains not only a highest authority but also intermediate ones, while the office of the diocesan is the foundation of all further grades, because each head bishop such as a patriarch and a metropolitan, even the Pope himself, is always also the president of a diocese.

In para. 3 the apostolic office of the bishops is described in such general terms that the diocesan's special responsibility for the faithful entrusted to him is not made clear. Here it ought to have been mentioned that the diocesan bishop possesses a pastoral authority exercised through legislation, jurisdiction and administration.

Articles 12–16 treat of the diocesan bishop's duties in the teaching, priestly and pastoral spheres. This section is a concise summary of texts taken from the schema *De cura animarum*; but as the various dioceses differ in size, they are not equally applicable to all diocesan bishops. Taking into account all that is required of him, it can hardly be denied that the diocesan is overburdened, even if the Council document referred only to a medium-sized diocese. In smaller dioceses many organizational suggestions can not be realized, whereas in the very large ones it will be impossible to place the pastor sufficiently near his flock. Hence in practice modifications will have to be made in either direction.

The decree, being chiefly concerned with pastoral matters, describes the duties of the bishop as briefly and concretely as possible and makes suggestions for a comtemporary care of souls. Hence the legal questions arising in the doctrinal, priestly and pastoral spheres are rather neglected. But the Decree on Bishops ought to have clarified the legal aspects of the principles regarding the duties of bishops as stated in Articles 25–27 of the Constitution *Lumen Gentium* and have integrated them in the structure of the diocese.

The diocesan's duties are presented according to the doctrine of the *triplex munus*.[2] To place this presentation in its proper context it should be remembered that the Council did not accept the threefold division of the Church's authority into doctrinal, priestly and governing powers (*potestas docendi, sanctificandi* and *regendi*), on which the schema of the Constitution of the Church of 1963 had been based, but that it professed the unity of the sacred authority (*sacra potestas*) founded on holy orders, an authority determined by the canonical mission through which it may also be exercised.[3]

Article 12. The preaching of the gospel "is eminent among the chief duties of bishops"; this should not be taken to mean that the doctrinal office of the bishop ranks more highly than his priestly office. His duty is not so much to preach the word himself, as to arrange for it to be preached.

Article 13 mentions among other things the duty to guard Christian doctrine, though it does not say in so many words that the diocesan is to judge whether the teaching of an individual agrees with the doctrine of the Church, and to discipline those who teach a wrong doctrine.

Article 14 stresses the responsibility of bishops for the proper catechetical training of children as well as adults.

Article 15. It is surprising that the co-operation of the priests is mentioned only in connection with sanctification (that is, the priestly office); and even there it is only stated that the priests depend for the exercise of their authority on the bishops (*ab ipsis*). The plural does not make it clear that the priests do not depend on the bishops, but on their diocesan or possibly on a superior who has not been consecrated a bishop. The priests share in the doctrinal, priestly and pastoral office and "assume in part the bishop's duties and cares and carry the weight of them day by day" (Constitution *Lumen Gentium,* Article 28, para. 2; Decree *Christus Dominus*, Article 16, para. 3); hence the co-operation of the priests in the threefold duties of the bishop might have been mentioned. However, here as in many other statements it becomes clear that the triad of doctrinal, priestly and pastoral office is no adequate division.

Article 16. The exhortation that "in exercising his office of father and pastor, a bishop should stand in the midst of his people as one who serves" envisages all spheres of episcopal activity. For the sake of their office bishops have a God-given authority to which those entrusted to them should submit willingly. The article mentions their duty to set an example and their care for the priests, the faithful, the separated brethren and the non-Christians, these directions concerning the doctrinal, priestly and pastoral spheres. In the final redaction an important direction was added, asking the bishop that, "in exercising this pastoral care he should preserve for his faithful the share proper to them in Church affairs; he should also recognize their duty and right to collaborate actively in the building up of the Mystical Body of Christ". Hence the teaching only in connection with sanctification (that is, the priestly office); and even

[2] Cf. J. Fuchs, *Magisterium, Ministerium, Regimen* (1941).   [3] Cf. above p. 207, note 16.

this the laity "are in their own way made sharers in the priestly, prophetic and kingly functions of Christ. They carry out their own part in the mission of the whole Christian people with respect to the Church and the world."

Concerning the priests the following instructions were given by the motu proprio *Ecclesiae Sanctae* of 6 August 1966 for Article 16 and at the same time for Articles 19–21 of the Decree *Presbyterorum Ordinis:*

1. Further scholarly and pastoral education (I, n. 7)

The bishops — whether one or several together — are to see to it that 1) immediately after ordination the new priests attend a one year pastoral course even if they have already a post, and 2) that all other priests periodically attend courses in order to perfect their knowledge of pastoral methods, theology and especially morals and liturgy,[4] to strengthen their spiritual life and to exchange experiences with their brethren. The bishops are to take care that such courses are organized, whether on a diocesan or supra-diocesan plane, and that they are attended by their priests; the one-year courses for new priests will probably have to be made compulsory.

According to local needs the bishops or the episcopal conferences are also to see to it that one or more priests of sound knowledge and proved virtue are to be appointed as directors of studies of these pastoral and other courses needed for the scholarly and pastoral education of the priests of a district; the creation of centres of studies, of travelling libraries and conferences on catechetical, liturgical and similar questions is also suggested.

2. Adequate remuneration and social security (I, n. 8)

a) *Remuneration.* As regards remuneration, this should be the same for all priests in similar circumstances, taking into account the various forms of ministry and circumstances of place and time. It must be sufficient for the clergy to live decently and also to be able to help the poor.[5] The patriarchal synods and the episcopal conferences are to legislate either for individual dioceses or for the whole district in order to assure an adequate income both for the active and the

---

[4] The text gives the impression as if morals and liturgy were not to be regarded as theological subjects, and even if they were to be understood as such (cf. can. 131, para. 1), today such a statement is no longer sufficient, for it is absolutely necessary that a pastor should be made familiar with the latest results of theological research also in other subjects, for example in New Testament exegesis.

[5] The principle of "equal remuneration for equal work" is to be understood as a basic equality taking into account special circumstances. In *Presbyterorum ordinis,* Article 20, para. 3, it is defined as *fundamentaliter eadem sit* and in the motu proprio as *praecipue eadem.* The former passage also demands that the remuneration of priests should allow them to pay adequate wages for domestic help and to finance their own holidays. These statements are important, because they are the conditions for a *vita honesta* of the clergy.

retired clergy. The terms of reference for this legislation regarding particular Churches are intentionally vague, because local needs are so different; the responsibility for a just remuneration is placed with the episcopal conference — in the case of the Oriental Churches with the patriarchal synod — which is also empowered to legislate for a fixed order of salaries in its district.

The commission for the reform of the *CIC* is ordered to examine the system of benefices.[6] In the meantime, after consulting their councils of priests, the bishops are to organize an adequate financial distribution, including the income from benefices.

At least in those districts where the clergy are supported either entirely or partially by the contributions of the faithful the episcopal conferences are to create a special institute which is to receive all the gifts collected for this purpose. This is to be administered by the bishop who is to be assisted by priests and, where advisable, by laymen versed in economics.

b) *Social security.* The episcopal conferences are to establish organizations for one or more dioceses, or for the whole district served by the conference, which are to be responsible for the support of sick, disabled and aged priests. These organizations must conform to both ecclesiastical and national legislation under the supervision of the hierarchy.

c) *Funds.* The commission for the reform of the *CIC* is to legislate for the creation of another fund which is to be the property of the individual dioceses or districts. This is to enable the bishop to meet other obligations to servants of the Church and various needs of the diocese as well as those of poorer dioceses.

The directions of the motu proprio thus deal with the same problems that confront the laity, who, moreover, are not generally concerned only with the care of one individual but also of their families.

Article 17 deals in a general way with the apostolate, giving three directions: 1) Various forms of the apostolate should be encouraged and co-ordinated in a unified action under the direction of the diocesan (para. 1). 2) The laity have the

[6] The Council has directed that "the so-called benefice system should be abandoned or at least it should be reformed in such a way that the beneficiary aspect, that is, the right to revenues accruing to an endowed office, will be treated as secondary, and the main consideration in law will be accorded to the ecclesiastical office itself" (*Presbyterorum Ordinis,* Article 20, para. 5). The alternative here described forces an open door because the subordination of revenue to office has long been in force; for the principle *beneficium propter officium* is to be found already in the law of decretals (can. 15 in VI⁰ 1,3). In the meantime the system of benefices has become an empty shell, especially through economic changes, so that it may easily be suppressed. It should be remembered, however, that in the present canon law the benefice is more than its legal definition (can. 1409) and means especially the basic office (see K. Mörsdorf, *Kirchenrecht,* I [11th ed.], pp. 274f.), and also that the formation of a particular ecclesiastical community such as a diocese or parish necessitates a certain financial basis. Hence a basic office must imply a legal person, though it does not matter much whether the legal person is connected with the office or with the particular ecclesiastical community to which the office belongs.

duty of carrying on the apostolate and should be encouraged to join the various works of the lay apostolate (para. 2). 3) The forms of the apostolate should be adapted to current needs. This is not the place to discuss in detail the difficult problems of the apostolate. It should only be mentioned that the share of the religious in the apostolate of the Church is fully treated in Articles 33–35 of this decree and that a special decree of the Council deals with the participation of the laity in the apostolate of the Church.[7] The legal and organizational problems concerning the apostolic work of the religious have been solved satisfactorily. The laymen's share in the Church's apostolate, however, is still suffering from the distinction between hierarchical and lay apostolate, often felt to be opposed to each other. This distinction has contributed considerably to the present popular opposition of the official to the lay Church, which has taken the place of the former distinction between the legal Church and the Church of love. The distinction between the hierarchical and the lay apostolate gives rise to the idea that clergy and laity have their own circumscribed fields of apostolic activity, thus obscuring the definite teaching of the Council that all members of the people of God share in the Church's apostolate, even though in different ways.[8] Nor does this distinction help the practical realization of the fact that the laity share in their own way in the priestly, prophetic and royal office of Christ and "carry out their own part in the mission of the whole Christian people with respect to the Church and the world" (cf. *Lumen Gentium,* Article 31, para. 1). Despite the differences in the kinds and forms of the apostolate there is actually only *one apostolate,* in which all members of the new people of God share in their own way. This is one in its efficacy not only because of the mission of all members of the Church, but because of the hierarchical structure of the new people of God despite the differences of service. In order to make clear this unity also in the form of words, the distinction between hierarchical and lay apostolate should be given up, and the lay apostolate should be understood as the share of the laity in the apostolate of the Church.

Article 18. The pastoral questions arising from the greater mobility of modern man are so manifold that the Council had to content itself with some general suggestions. In paragraph 2 the episcopal conferences are told to pay energetic attention to the more pressing problems confronting the aforementioned groups and to promote their spiritual welfare by means of suitable methods and institutions. In order to carry out this demand the motu proprio *Ecclesiae Sanctae* laid down that a priest *(sacerdos delegatus)* or a special commission should be appointed to deal with everything concerning the spiritual care of these groups. This might look like an interim solution, but it makes clear that in this pastoral sphere it is most important to support local initiatives.

Article 19. From the point of view of the episcopal office the Council makes

[7] On this see the commentary to the decree *Apostolicam Actuositatem* on the apostolate of the laity.

[8] See the statements of principle in Article 2 in the decree *Apostolicam Actuositatem.*

a statement of principle about the relation between Church and state. This says nothing new, but makes it clear that even though the Church is prepared to enter on a dialogue with the world it cannot abrogate its demand to be independent[9] from any secular power. While the pastors devote themselves to the spiritual care of their flock, they are also in fact having regard for social and civil progress and prosperity. This passage reminds the state of the Church's contribution to its wellbeing, regardless of how the state treats the Church.

Article 20 attacks a problem burdened with a long history: the relation between Church and State.[10] It demands complete freedom of the competent ecclesiastical authority with regard to nominating and appointing[11] bishops. As this is a question of rights generally based on concordats, the demand of the Council was expressed in the form of a request addressed to the apostolic see on the one hand and the governments in question on the other. The apostolic see is expected no longer to concede to civil authorities the right to make legally binding proposals[12] for nominating and appointing bishops, and those civil authorities which by reason of a concordat or custom are still enjoying such rights are requested to renounce them voluntarily after having discussed the matter with the Holy See. The abolition of these rights has been going on for a long time, so that today it is only a question of removing the last instances especially in Spain, Portugal, and some South-American states, strangely enough also still in France (Strasbourg and Metz). It is incompatible with the deeper understanding of the relation between Church and State that a government should practically dispose of the bishoprics. The demand of the Council does not, however, envisage the present practice of consulting the civil authorities before appointing a bishop in case there should be political objections. This

---

[9] On this cf. K. Mörsdorf, *op. cit.,* pp. 52 ff.

[10] Cf. U. Stutz, *Über das Verfahren bei der Nomination auf Bischofsstühle* (1928); A. Kindermann, *Das landesfürstliche Ernennungsrecht* (1933).

[11] The phrase *ius nominandi et instituendi* is not meant to designate two different acts but to express all the forms — rather in the manner of a hendiadys — in which a diocesan bishop is appointed by the competent authority. Both expressions are not exactly well chosen, for apart from the papal appointment of a bishop which is the rule in the Latin Church (can. 329, § 2), *nominare* also describes the legally binding proposal of a secular government which is carried into effect by the *institutio* of the proposed person by the Pope. No mention is made of the election of bishops which is still the regular practice in the Catholic Churches of the Eastern rite, and, though obscured by the rights of nomination and presentation granted to secular princes, was the rule also in the West before the papal right of appointment was gradually taking its place. However, even today election is practised and even confirmed by concordats in certain places. Cf. K. Mörsdorf, *Das neue Besetzungsrecht der bischöflichen Stühle unter besonderer Berücksichtigung des Listenverfahrens* (1933).

[12] In order to make it as complete as possible there is mention of "iura aut privilegia electionis, nominationis, praesentationis vel designationis ad Episcopatus officium". The mention of election, especially in the first place, is odd, because the election of a bishop, as far as it is still practised, does not belong to the state but to an ecclesiastical organization such as a cathedral chapter or an electoral synod.

practice arose as a substitute for the earlier nomination rights; it is determined in detail in modern concordats, but may be followed also without a concordat, as is done for example in France.[13]

According to the motu proprio *Ecclesiae Sanctae* (I, n. 10) the episcopal conferences are to consider in secret every year which priests would be suitable candidates for bishoprics within their districts, according to the instructions of the Holy See, which is to be furnished with a list of names. This practice which has been in existence in many districts[14] has now been given its legal foundation.[15] A new feature is that in future the episcopal conferences are to consider the matter and to make proposals collegially; the special regulations hitherto in force are to be examined with this in view.

Article 21. The Council did not decide on the question whether a diocesan bishop should be appointed for life or whether there was to be an age-limit; but it was urgently requested that a bishop should resign his office if old age or another serious reason make it advisable. The motu proprio went further in that it laid down an age-limit for resigning. According to this all diocesan bishops and other superiors in the same position are asked to resign voluntarily after completing their seventy-fifth year at the latest. It is left to the discretion of the competent ecclesiastical authority after considering each individual case to decide whether the resignation is to be accepted or not. The possibility of another serious reason leading to resignation was not mentioned in *Ecclesiae Sanctae,* probably because it is both difficult and unnecessary to lay down details; for in such a case resignation may be invited.

A bishop whose resignation has been accepted may continue to reside in his diocese if he so wishes. The diocese has to support the retired bishop as befits his position, and it is the duty of the episcopal conference to determine by general directions how the dioceses have to carry this out. This regulation differs from Article 21, according to which the authority which has accepted the resignation will make provision for the suitable support of those who have resigned. This, however, did not mean that the Apostolic See, which is the relevant authority in the Latin Church, should itself undertake to support the retired bishops, but

[13] Cf. J. Kaiser, *Die politische Klausel der Konkordate* (1949).
[14] On this K. Mörsdorf, *Das neue Besetzungsrecht,* pp. 12 ff.
[15] This, however, applies only to the absolute, not to the relative system of lists; the latter refers to the appointment to a definite vacant see. The relative system has its origin in the fact that the election of a bishop was deprived of its legal force; it was increasingly abandoned in favour of the absolute system, because this seemed better to guarantee the actual freedom of the Apostolic See. The disadvantage of the absolute system is sought to be mitigated by mentioning which candidates are most suitable for which sees (cf. the decree of the SC Consist., of 25 July 1916 for the United States: *AAS* 8 [1916], pp. 400 ff.). According to diocesan law both systems are sometimes combined, for example in Germany, where in the case of a vacant see the cathedral chapter — formerly in Prussia also the bishops — must produce a list (*Bayerisches Konkordat,* Article 4, para. 1; *Preussisches Konkordat,* Article 6; *Badisches Konkordat,* Article 3, and *Reichskonkordat,* Article 14, para. 1).

that it should make suitable arrangements so that even the bishops of poorer dioceses would be able to resign without having to face financial distress. Hence episcopal collegiality might have been more strongly emphasized, at least as regards the episcopal conference. Nevertheless the decision to make the diocese of the retired bishop responsible for his support was the right one. Moreover, it would be desirable to abandon the present practice of giving a retired bishop the title of an extinct diocese and to assign to each bishop who has honourably resigned his diocese the title of an *Episcopus emeritus* of his see. This change in the title would express the permanent spiritual union of the bishop with his diocese and at the same time continue the ancient tradition according to which the bishop is espoused to his see in a kind of spiritual marriage.[16] Undoubtedly this proposed change would also make it easier for a bishop to resign his see as soon as he realizes that his strength no longer suffices to carry out his heavy duties.

Very few alterations were suggested at the discussion of the draft of Articles 22–24, which deal with diocesan boundaries.[17] This unanimity seems surprising, because it is well known that the examination of diocesan boundaries, which aimed especially at dividing very large and suppressing too small dioceses, was bound to meet with the opposition of many of the bishops concerned. This opposition can hardly be said to have been broken; but perhaps the desire for dioceses of the right size sufficiently helps both the small and the large dioceses to preserve their property. Moreover, it will take a long time until the principles expressed by the Council can be turned into concrete organizational measures.

The diocese is part of the people of God (cf. Article 11), hence it needs a clearer definition or circumscription of those forming it. The Latin technical term *circumscriptio* means not only "circumscribing" but also the authoritative act by which a diocese is erected and the legal creation that has come into existence. Basically, a diocese is territorially erected,[18] that is to say, those Christians living in an exactly defined area are formed into a community whose spiritual head is the bishop assigned to it. Thus the individual Christian is given his own pastor (so-called material territorial principle). As regards the relations between the bishops, the territorial limits also assure an orderly exercise of episcopal authority (so-called formal territorial principle). So-called personal dioceses may be erected by way of exception, particularly if a special hierarch seems to be needed to look after Christians belonging to another rite; but even here the delimitation within the relevant rite is territorially determined. Ecclesiastical communities resting on a purely personal foundation may be largely exempt from the authority of the ordinary, but they are not called dioceses.

---

[16] Cf. V. Fuchs, *Der Ordinationstitel von seiner Entstehung bis auf Innozenz III.* (1930), pp. 83 ff.

[17] In his general report Bishop N. Jubany says that only few remarks were made on this section so that the text could remain almost completely unchanged. In the report on suggested changes not a single one is mentioned for articles 22 to 24. See *Textus recognitus et Modi,* pp. 60 and 76.

[18] On this see K. Mörsdorf, *Kirchenrecht,* I, pp. 339 ff.

Article 22 is based on the leading idea that the nature of the Church must be clearly evident in the diocese (para. 1), from which follows the demand for a corresponding determination of the diocesan boundaries (para. 2) and for a prompt examination of the existing ones (para. 3).

The leading idea is not very well expressed; for the fulfilment of the proper purpose of the diocese[19] which is to show forth the nature of the Church is nothing other than that the bishops should be able to carry out their pastoral duties effectively and thus the welfare of the people of God be served.[20]

As the nature of the Church manifests itself in many different ways, its manifestation in the diocese might have been expected to have been more clearly defined (cf. the explanation of Article 11). Even though the leading idea aims at giving a general basis for the right size of the diocese, it cannot be overlooked that there are no set norms for it. All efforts to deduce such norms from the nature of the diocese and the episcopal office are futile, because both are decisively influenced by the ecclesiastical element which is subject to changing circumstances. The city *(civitas)* has always been the pattern on which dioceses were erected, "ne episcopi nomen et auctoritas vilipendatur" (Synod of Sardica, can. 6). Thus it will be no doubt also in the future; but in view of sociological changes the actual importance of a city for a region will have to be taken into consideration.

The leading idea demands "a proper determination of the boundaries of dioceses and a distribution of clergy and resources which is reasonable" (para. 2); This refers probably not only to the size of the territory but also to an adequate number of priests and sufficient financial resources, both of which are necessary for meeting the pastoral needs of the diocese, though they are not always available. Often a diocese may lack either one or the other, sometimes even both. This twofold need goes beyond the diocesan limits and has to be met by larger organizations such as the ecclesiastical province, the episcopal conference and the apostolic see.[21] Paragraph 2 continues that "all these things will truly benefit not only the clergy and Christian people directly involved, but also the entire Catholic Church". This makes it clear that the ideas about the size of the dioceses were determined solely by the relation between the dioceses and the Church as a whole, while any intermediate structures were deliberately overlooked. By and large this corresponds indeed to the constitution of the Church such as it has developed in the Latin Church, where the intermediate offices, especially that of the metropolitan, have become increasingly unimportant and the administration has been centralized in the Curia. Even though collegiality was referred too one-sidedly to the college of bishops and the Church as a whole,

---

[19] The phrase *in populo Dei ad ipsam dioecesim pertinente* means simply the diocese, which, according to the definition of Article 11, is part of the people of God.

[20] The connection of the two duties introduced by *ut* is obscured by the *denique*.

[21] First measures in this direction have been taken by the motu proprio *Ecclesiae Sanctae*, I, nn. 1-5; see the explanation of Article 6.

the Fathers of Vatican II nevertheless made decisive efforts to re-organize the intermediate sphere, for example by suggesting the establishment of episcopal conferences as hierarchical organizations of their territory. They further advised the creation of ecclesiastical regions which were to be co-ordinated to an episcopal conference comprising several ecclesiastical provinces, and they asked for an examination of the rights of the metropolitan, which meant a revaluation of this ancient office (cf. Article 40). Now questions of organization can be properly solved only in the context of the whole, hence it is essential to consider which tasks belong to the dioceses, which to the ecclesiastical province and which to a future ecclesiastical region. It is one of the indispensable duties of the diocese to guarantee that the saving mission of the bishop and his priests should be accomplished in orderly fashion, whereas the conditions of such pastoral activities, for example the training of priests, need not necessarily and normally be produced on the diocesan plane.

The diocesan boundaries are to be examined from the point of view of the good of souls *(animarum bonum)*; this should be understood to mean that the bishop with his priests and other collaborators must be able to guarantee the orderly accomplishment of his saving mission to the faithful entrusted to him. Wherever this cannot be done the boundaries of the diocese are to be changed according to the directions of Article 23. Too large dioceses, which the bishop cannot handle as necessary, are either to be divided into two or more new dioceses, or sections of their territory are to be assigned to one or more neighbouring dioceses. Too small dioceses, on the other hand, lacking in funds and personnel for their proper upkeep, are to be combined with another diocese or, what is not said in the text, are to be abolished and to be assigned to another diocese. The change of the diocesan boundaries comes under the notion of dismembering *(dismembratio)* and may happen to large as well as to small dioceses. The change of the episcopal see to a better placed city would normally occur only in large dioceses; this is necessary whenever the episcopal city has become so much less important than other cities of the diocese that the bishop can no longer administer his territory efficiently. This is so especially if a city has become the capital of a state. Dioceses which are composed of rather large cities are to be provided with a new internal organization, but nothing is said about its mode. This would be not so much a matter of externals as of a proper distribution of duties, while safeguarding the unity of administration indispensable for a large city. In the case of mammoth cities a division into several dioceses might be advisable, even though certain matters needing a central administration would have to remain the responsibility of the metropolitan. Finally, these problems do not only concern the organization of large cities but apply quite generally, because the individual dioceses depend on co-operation.

Nos. 1–3 of the first paragraph of Article 3 provide directions for examining the existing diocesan boundaries, while paragraphs 2 and 3 deal with the special provisions to be made for the faithful of a different rite or another language.

The directions given in paragraph 1 are based on the idea that, as regards personnel, officers and institutions, the diocese is to be an organic unity and a properly functioning body. Hence they provide, among other things, that 1) the territory of each diocese should be continuous; 2) the extent of the diocesan boundaries and the number of its inhabitants should be such that, on the one hand, the bishop can duly exercise his functions and, on the other, that the diocese can provide sufficient scope for his own energies and those of his clergy; 3) officers, institutions and organizations which are proper to the activities of a particular Church should be on hand or at least should be prudently foreseen. The remark that the needs of the Church at large are not to be over-looked (end of n. 2) makes it clear once more (cf. our comments on Article 22) that the directions on the size of the diocese envisage only the relation between the dioceses and the Church as a whole and, neglecting the indispensable intermediary organs, consider the diocese too much as an unalterable entity.

In any case, a diocese should be sufficiently manageable to safeguard the necessary presence of the bishop. Though no definite rules can be given, the bishop should at least be united to his priests, who "make him present in a certain sense in the individual local congregations . . . and take upon themselves, as far as they are able, his duties and concerns, discharging them with daily care" (*Lumen Gentium*, Article 28, para. 2), so that he can take responsibility for their activities. In my view it is important that there should be an adequate proportion between the necessary diocesan staff of priests and the parish priests having the care of souls. Starting from the few demands made for the erection of a diocese by the *CIC* the diocesan staff would comprise between 20 to 30 priests, while the parish priests would be ten or twenty times their number.

The remarks in paragraph 2 on the care of the faithful of a different rite cor-respond to the present law and practice. A merely formal difference is this that the newly created episcopal vicar (see commentary on Article 27) has been added to the vicar general provided in can. 366, para. 3, of the *CIC*.[22] In the case of an episcopal vicar, be he a priest or a bishop, as opposed to that of a vicar general, the diocesan bishop himself determines his duties. If a special hierarchy is to be established, for example in the form of a so-called personal diocese or any other substitute (e.g., an apostolic administrature) the persons belonging to the new hierarchy leave that part (or parts) of the people of God to which they had been attached and form a particular Church of their own.

The provisions for the care of members of another language differ from those

---

[22] From the fact that there is no mention of the appointment of a vicar general which is possible according to can. 366 it cannot be concluded that this possibility, which allows a more com-prehensive care of members of another rite, has been abolished. The appointment of a vicar general remains legally possible and should generally be preferable in practice, because the relevant tasks require an office the rights and duties of which are laid down by law. Nevertheless, the same purpose may be achieved also if the diocesan bishop confers all the rights of a vicar general on an episcopal vicar. But then it may be asked why he is not nominated vicar general.

made for the faithful of another rite merely by the fact that the erection of a special hierarchy has not been mentioned, at least not in so many words.[23] The reason for this is that it does not seem advisable to create dioceses differing only in language and nationality in one and the same territory. What is suitable in the sphere of the parish, where it is a matter of the daily care of souls, may in the diocesan sphere easily lead to divisions so that the always necessary duty to think and act also for others would be forgotten.

Article 24 considers it desirable that the episcopal conferences should examine the diocesan boundaries without prejudice to the discipline of the Oriental Churches.[24] The directions of the motu proprio *Ecclesiae Sanctae* (I, n. 12, para. 1) carry the matter a step further. They ask the episcopal conferences to examine the boundaries of the particular Churches in their territory and, if necessary, to appoint a commission for this task. The conditions of the diocese as regards territory, personnel and offices are to be duly investigated and not only the bishops directly concerned but also those of the whole ecclesiastical province or territory examined are to be heard, and experts, both clerical and lay, are to be consulted. Reasons making the alterations of boundaries advisable should be considered impartially, and all proposed changes should be submitted to the Holy See. If dioceses are to be divided or parts of their territory removed priests and seminarians should be suitably distributed according to the pastoral needs of the diocese as well as to their own circumstances and desires.

As regards the Oriental Churches the motu proprio wishes that the boundaries of the eparchies should be defined according to the localities in which the faithful of the same rite reside.

Most alterations in Chapter II were suggested for the third section dealing with "those who co-operate with the diocesan bishop in his pastoral task". They concern especially the legal position of the coadjutor and auxiliary bishops. This means that both diocesan bishops and their episcopal collaborators still wanted many changes, even though hardly any other draft had already been subjected to so many alterations. But the schema that was put to the vote had proposed a compromise acceptable to both sides, which might have been endangered only too easily by the acceptance of more changes. Hence, apart from one unimportant alteration, the Council kept the text of the schema as it stood.

Articles 25 and 26 which deal with co-adjutor and auxiliary bishops are without logical coherence. Both articles treat of the same questions: appointment, faculties and exercise of office, perhaps the only difference being that first these problems are approached rather theoretically and then from a more practical point of view. A new terminology is introduced only in Article 26. This lack of system may be due to the fact that the articles constitute a compromise. It is, however, not one that affirms and denies simultaneously; for though

---

[23] The article says that provision may also be made "in some other more appropriate way". This may suggest that in exceptional cases the creation of a special hierarchy is to be considered.
[24] This reservation refers to the different conditions of the Eastern Churches.

the solution is not completely satisfactory, it nevertheless provides a clear legal picture.

According to the new terminology the co-adjutor bishop (episcopus co-adjutor)[25] is distinguished from the auxiliary bishop *(episcopus auxiliaris)* in that the former always has the right of succession (Article 26, para. 4), which the latter has not (Article 26, para. 1). The new definition follows the canon law of the Eastern Church *(CIO,* can. 417, para. 2), but it does not, like the Oriental canon law, draw the logical conclusion, namely that the office of the auxiliary bishop expires with the death of the diocesan unless the nomination papers decree otherwise *(CIO,* can. 421, para. 2). Hitherto Latin canon law had distinguished between personal co-adjutors, attached to the person of the bishop with or without the right of succession, and diocesan co-adjutors who were appointed for the needs of the diocese *(CIC,* can. 350).[26] This is no merely linguistic matter,[27] since in the case of the auxiliary bishops of the new order it does not matter whether they were appointed because of the personal needs of the diocesan bishop or for the needs of the diocese.[28] Because of this simplified terminology the different duties of the auxiliary bishop arising from the different reasons for his nomination play no part in determining his legal position. The abandoning of the distinction hitherto in force will lead to difficulties especially if a newly appointed diocesan is confronted with an auxiliary bishop who had been assigned to his predecessor for personal reasons, but whom the new diocesan does not need, and whose faculties he cannot accept.

Article 25 deals first with the possible reasons for appointing an auxiliary or a coadjutor bishop. First, the appointment of one or more auxiliary bishops is advisable if the extent of the diocese or the number of the faithful is too large.[29] According to Articles 22–24 the same reasons require the partition of a diocese or at least the separation of some of its parts. Even though nothing is said as

---

[25] The *CIC,* however, uses the term *Coadiutores Episcoporum* (heading of can. 350),which seems more correct to me. For though the coadjutor is a bishop, his position is naturally related to the person to whom he is assigned, so that it is more accurate to speak of the coadjutor of the bishop.

[26] Larger dioceses have permanent auxiliaries; in Germany this is even laid down by concordat for several dioceses (cf. Prussian Concordat, Article 2, n. 10, concerning the archiepiscopal sees of Cologne, Breslau and Paderborn and the episcopal sees of Trier, Münster and Aachen).

[27] According to the terminology of the *CIC, Auxiliaris* is a co-adjutor given to the person of the diocesan bishop without right of succession (can. 350, § 3). Unlike the diocesan coadjutor, who also has no right of succession, the office of the auxiliary expires with that of the diocesan (can. 355, § 2), whereas the office of the diocesan coadjutor continues also during the vacancy of the see (can. 355, § 3).

[28] The Schema Decreti *De episcopis ac de dioecesium regimine* (1963), p. 12, a. 1, deals with coadjutors and auxiliaries. The coadjutor is appointed mainly, though not exclusively, to help the bishop if he is ill or aging, and resignation is not possible, while the auxiliary is appointed chiefly, though again not exclusively, to serve the diocese if it is too large but cannot be divided.

[29] Though the text mentions *incolae* = inhabitants, it only refers to those who belong to the people of God thus defined.

to which of the two measures (division of a diocese or appointment of an auxiliary) is to be preferred, there can be no doubt that preferably too large dioceses ought to be divided and that only if this seems impossible auxiliary bishops should be appointed. In too large dioceses auxiliary bishops are appointed chiefly because the diocesan cannot administer all the confirmations himself. The Council Fathers suggested several times that priests in superior positions should be delegated by the diocesan to administer confirmation, a measure which would make the appointment of auxiliary bishops largely unnecessary. A true need for them seems to me to exist whenever part of a diocese is in process of becoming itself a diocese. Here the desired separation could suitably be prepared by sending an auxiliary bishop. Apart from the needs arising from the size of a diocese special pastoral conditions may require the appointment of one or more auxiliary bishops. This is the case especially if the faithful of a different rite or language have to be cared for (cf. Article 23, paras. 2 and 3). Other reasons justifying the appointment of an auxiliary bishop would concern especially the personal situation of the diocesan. This would include not only support of a sick or aged bishop, if neither resignation nor the appointment of a coadjutor would seem feasible, but also of a bishop so overwhelmed with supra-diocesan tasks as to be unable fully to carry out his diocesan duties.

No particular reasons are given for the appointment of a coadjutor bishop, except that a special need sometimes requires it. This suggests the reasons given in Article 21 about the resignation of bishops. Here, too, nothing is said as to which way is to be preferred; but it can scarcely be doubted that resignation is to be preferred to the appointment of a co-adjutor, which seems rather a subsidiary measure. The reason for the appointment of a coadjutor — as opposed to that of an auxiliary bishop — is always to be found in the person of the diocesan.[30]

As regards *faculties,* co-adjutor and auxiliary bishops should be granted them in such a way that the unity of the diocesan administration and the authority of the diocesan bishop are always preserved and that at the same time their work is rendered more effective and their episcopal dignity is safeguarded. Among the principles to be observed when appointing auxiliary bishops the motu proprio *Ecclesiae Sanctae* also mentions the position due to them as members of the college of bishops. Nevertheless, no faculties can be deduced for them from their episcopal dignity and from their membership of the college of bishops, even though this has sometimes been attempted. The episcopal dignity is founded on the episcopal office, not the office on the dignity; only the share in the office determines the faculties. Membership of the episcopal college does not give the bishops any rights or powers apart from the college. Hence the Council has not granted the auxiliary bishops any legal powers. The measure of an auxiliary

[30] This applies so exclusively that it might almost be called a defining characteristic. But it should be noted that in exceptional cases an episcopal coadjutor may be appointed for other reasons, for example to prevent difficulties to be expected over the appointment of a new bishop.

bishop's powers can be properly determined only by the tasks entrusted to him.

The co-adjutor and auxiliary bishops should execute their office in agreement with the diocesan, to whom they are to give obedience and reverence, while he, "in turn, should have a fraternal love" for them and hold them in esteem. Thus the mutual relationship is made clear. The diocese is governed solely by its residential bishop, there can be no question of his episcopal collaborators forming "actually an episcopal senate" to which the cathedral chapter as the council and senate of the bishop (can. 361) and the pastoral council that is to be established would be subordinated.[31] On the contrary, the effort of establishing the idea of episcopal collegiality in the diocesan sphere must be considered to have failed.

Article 26 treats of auxiliary (paras. 1–3) and coadjutor bishops (para. 4) in greater detail.

If the salvation of souls requires it the diocesan bishop should not hesitate to ask for one or more auxiliary bishops (para. 1). The motu proprio *Ecclesiae Sanctae* (I, n. 13, para. 1) explains that it is necessary to appoint auxiliary bishops as soon as the needs of the diocesan apostolate truly require it. Since it lies with the diocesan to ask for one or more auxiliary bishops it is naturally his responsibility to decide on the necessity while taking into account the reasons given in Article 25, para. 1.

In accordance with his title the auxiliary bishop is to help the diocesan, who is chiefly responsible for judging the measure of the help he needs and for granting the necessary powers. In exceptional cases, especially if the diocesan is ill or very old, it may be advisable that the faculties required by the situation should be laid down in the nomination papers. If this has not been done, the diocesan is obliged[32] to nominate his auxiliary bishop(s), vicar general(s), or at least episcopal vicar(s) (see the commentary on Article 27, para. 2). If the auxiliary bishop is nominated vicar general he is given this office as defined by canon law,[33] the

---

[31] J. Neumann ("Weihe und Amt in der Lehre von der Kirchenverfassung des Zweiten Vatikanischen Konzils", in *AKK* 135 [1966], pp. 15 ff.) thinks that this may be deduced from the directions of Article 26, according to which the diocesan should consult his auxiliaries "in examining questions of major importance, especially of a pastoral nature" (para. 2), and that "the diocesan bishop and his coadjutor should not fail to consult with one another on matters of major importance" (para. 5). Quite apart from the fact that the relation of the diocesan to his coadjutor differs considerably from that to his auxiliaries, as is clear from the passages he quotes, Neumann has overlooked that in the case of the latter it is only a question of *consulere velit*. Hence the consultation of the auxiliaries is not a legal duty of any kind but is a request addressed to the diocesan.

[32] In order to avoid a possible misunderstanding the direction expressed by *constituat*, which might be interpreted as an "ought", has been expressed in the motu proprio *Ecclesiae Sanctae*, I, n. 13, § 2, in the words *constituere debet*, that is, as a "must".

[33] On this see E. V. Kienitz, *Generalvikar und Offizial auf Grund des CIC* (1931); K. Hofmann, *Die freiwillige Gerichtsbarkeit (iurisdictio voluntaria) im kanonischen Recht* (1929), pp. 87 ff.; K. Mörsdorf, *Rechtsprechung und Verwaltung im kanonischen Recht* (1941), pp. 66 ff.; id., *Kirchenrecht*, I, pp. 428 ff.

diocesan being free either to limit his legal tasks or to enlarge them if the special situation requires it (cf. *CIC*, can. 368, para. 1). If he is nominated episcopal vicar, his duties are left entirely to the diocesan; within the sphere of these duties the auxiliary has the powers of a vicar general. This regulation makes it clear that the auxiliary bishop as such has no office in the legal sense of the term; for he receives his faculties either by way of delegation through his nomination papers or through being given one of two other offices. Of these that of vicar general is established by canon law, whereas that of episcopal vicar has only the formal structure of an office, its content having to be determined by the diocesan. It should further be noted that an auxiliary bishop appointed vicar general may at any time be removed from this office by the diocesan, but in that case he must automatically be appointed episcopal vicar. In the same way a diocesan may define the duties of an auxiliary bishop appointed episcopal vicar, that means he may increase, restrict or take away his former activities, but in the last case he must assign other tasks to him, however humble. What is to be done if an auxiliary bishop is no longer able to carry out the duties assigned to him is laid down neither in the Council decree nor in the motu proprio.[34] Here a distinction must be made. A duty assigned to the auxiliary bishop in his nomination papers can be taken away from him only by the nominating authority; but in case of emergency the diocesan may order a temporary dismissal and must inform the higher authority. He may also revoke an appointment as vicar general or episcopal vicar, for his duty to appoint an auxiliary bishop at least an episcopal vicar naturally presupposes that the auxiliary bishop is able to carry out the necessary tasks.

Auxiliary bishops who have been appointed vicars general or episcopal vicars *depend only on the authority of the diocesan*.[35] This means that the auxiliary is directly

---

[34] The request for resignation expressed in Article 21 does not include the auxiliary bishops. This shows that the question of the incapacity of an auxiliary has not been considered as particularly important. In general such cases will be settled amicably; nevertheless this question requires to be settled by law, as an auxiliary may not have a sufficient understanding or may no longer be capable of exercising it.

[35] In the final version the words *ab ipso* were changed into *a sua auctoritate;* according to the report this made it clearer that the auxiliaries must always be under the authority of the diocesan bishop. It was further pointed out that this change did justice to the view of the Council Fathers who on the one hand had asked for greater powers for the auxiliaries and on the other for a clear affirmation of the sole authority of the diocesan (*Textus recognitus et Modi*, p. 60). Nevertheless, the change has achieved neither the one nor the other; it gives no powers to the auxiliary nor does it make the position of the diocesan any clearer. On the contrary, the formula *ab ipso* had clearly expressed the wish of the auxiliaries to have to obey only the diocesan, but not the vicar general, whereas the new formula *a sua auctoritate* may be understood as implying that the auxiliary bishop shall depend also on an authority acting in the name of the diocesan. But just this the new formula was not meant to say. One of the Council Fathers suggested replacing the words *ab ipso dumtaxat dependentes* by *ad nutum dumtaxat et ab ipso dependentes*. He was answered that his proposal was covered by the newly admitted text "a sua auctoritate dumtaxat dependentes" (*Modi Ep,* ch. II, *modus* 84). This answer, too, is unsatisfactory on both counts.

subject to the diocesan bishop and that no one else is allowed to give orders to the former, especially not a vicar general who is not normally a consecrated bishop. This rule is basically due to the fact that in view of their episcopal dignity the auxiliary bishops considered it unacceptable to take orders from a vicar general, who is usually a simple priest. But it has its drawbacks, especially in the larger dioceses, for because of this rule the bishop will give his auxiliaries only the less important tasks so as not to endanger the unity of the diocesan administration which is safeguarded by the vicar general as the alter ego of the diocesan. Otherwise the diocesan bishop would have to co-ordinate the administrative work himself, a burden he could not carry in the larger dioceses. This shows that the reversal of the relation between office and dignity cannot remain without its consequences.

According to the motu proprio *Ecclesiae Sanctae* (I, n. 13, para. 3)[36] the powers and faculties belonging to the auxiliary bishops according to paragraph 3 *a iure* are those due to him in his capacity as vicar general or episcopal vicar. According to canon law the office of the vicar general (as in principle also that of the episcopal vicar) expires when the episcopal see is vacant (*CIC*, can. 371). The auxiliary bishops, however, do not lose their powers as vicars general or episcopal vicars in such a case. But it must be asked whether the term *a iure* properly describes these powers. For *a iure* means "by rights"; in connection with the granting of powers it ought to express the fact that these are given by law in such a way as to belong to someone by right (law) and need not be specially conferred by an ecclesiastical authority *(ab homine)*.[37] The auxiliary bishops as such, however, have no powers which are in this sense *a iure*;[38] on the contrary, they receive the faculties needed by their duties through a special delegating act *(ab homine)* either from a higher authority or through being appointed vicar general (as provided by canon law) or at least through being made episcopal vicar by the diocesan.[39] Hence the term *a iure* is at least

---

[36] Potestas et facultates is a hendiadys; for both terms express the same thing. Leaving aside the emotional undercurrents the terms sometimes produce, there is a linguistic difference in that potestas in the singular does not usually signify a single power but an aggregate of powers, especially of those connected with a certain office.

[37] Canon law habitually distinguishes between *delegatio a iure* and *ab homine* (cf. E. Rösser, *Die gesetzliche Delegation (delegatio a iure)* [1937], pp. 52 ff.). The terms *poena a iure — ab homine* have a different sense. Here *poena a iure* means a definite punishment laid down in the law itself, so that until sentence is passed the punishment is *a iure tantum* and only afterwards *a iure simul et ab homine,* but in the latter case is regarded as *poena ab homine* (*CIC*, can. 2217, para. 1, n. 3; see Eichmann-Mörsdorf, *Kirchenrecht,* III [10th ed.], pp. 334f.). Here the *a iure* passes over into an *ab homine;* in a similar way this is true of the *a iure* in Article 26, para. 3. In any case the episcopal commission was fully agreed that the powers mentioned are those belonging to an auxiliary bishop when the office of a vicar general or an episcopal vicar is conferred on him.

[38] Together with the other titular bishops and the residential bishops they have well defined faculties *a iure* which are regarded as privileges because of their extraordinary character (cf. *CIC*, can. 349 and motu proprio *Pastorale Munus* of 30 November 1963, II).

[39] In order to make the problem of the *a iure* even clearer the reader should be reminded that the

open to misunderstanding; one might perhaps say that these are powers the conferment of which is prescribed in the law *(in iure)*. The powers given to an auxiliary bishop in his capacity of vicar general or episcopal vicar are ordinary powers, because they have been conferred by virtue of an office; in this respect the auxiliary bishop has a *potestas ordinaria vicaria*.

The Council document had asked that when the see was vacant "the office of ruling the diocese should be committed to the auxiliary bishop or, when there are more than one, to one of the auxiliaries". This was expressed only as a wish, so that the cathedral chapter as well as the diocesan council retain the freedom to nominate someone who is not an auxiliary bishop to be vicar capitular or vicar of the diocesan council.[40] An auxiliary bishop who has not been elected vicar capitular retains those faculties granted to him as vicar general or diocesan vicar during the vacancy of the see,[41] but he is obliged to exercise them in complete agreement with the vicar capitular as the president of the diocese (motu proprio *Ecclesiae Sanctae*, I, n. 13, para. 3). It follows that an auxiliary bishop is subject to the orders of a vicar capitular who is not a bishop.

Para. 4 lays down that the diocesan must always appoint his coadjutor

---

auxiliary bishops urged that they should have all the powers canon law assigns to the vicar general in virtue of their office, that is to say, as auxiliary bishops. A proposal on these lines was rejected on the grounds that it was difficult to understand that the auxiliary bishops should by right *(ipso iure)* have all the powers of the vicar general without his office (*Modi Ep,* Ch. II, *modus* 78). Another proposal made by one of the Fathers suggested leaving the granting of faculties to the auxiliary bishops more to the discretion of the diocesan. This was rejected because in the second session the almost unanimous view of the Fathers had been that the powers of the auxiliary bishops should be increased and defined by law *(in iure)* (*Modi Ep,* Ch. II, *modus* 83).

[40] The non-election of an auxiliary bishop may not only be a matter for regret to the person concerned but is hardly likely to safeguard the episcopal dignity which was the main object of the wish expressed. As their real aim could not be realized, it would have been in the true interest of the auxiliary bishops to abandon the wish expressed by the Council.

[41] The motu proprio *Ecclesiae Sanctae*, I, n. 13, § 3 lays down that an auxiliary bishop who is not elected vicar capitular retains his powers (as vicar general or episcopal vicar) until the new bishop has taken possession of his see; it follows that he loses them afterwards. This provision is only concerned with the auxiliary bishop who has not been elected vicar capitular and leaves it open whether an auxiliary bishop who has been elected vicar capitular regains the powers due to him before he was elected after the vacancy of the see has terminated. The question of the loss of faculties as vicar general or episcopal vicar ought to have been treated in the context of the statement that the auxiliary bishop does not lose his faculties when the see falls vacant. It goes without saying that the new bishop can determine the work of his auxiliaries; he can confirm them in their office, he can revoke their appointment as vicar general, though only while appointing them episcopal vicar, and he can assign new duties to the latter. In order to assure this, however, it is not at all necessary for the powers of the auxiliary bishops to expire automatically when the new bishop takes possession. In my view it would be better to seek a more flexible regulation which would allow the auxiliary bishops to continue their work for the time being and leave the new bishop time to make new arrangements for them. It would suffice if, after the arrangements for the episcopal official, it would be laid down that in their capacity of vicars general or episcopal vicars the auxiliaries need to be confirmed in their office *adveniente novo Episcopo* (cf. can 1573, para. 5).

bishop vicar general, which guarantees a minimum of faculties to the coadjutor. The point is not that the co-adjutor should take the place of the — normally — one vicar general, but that the diocesan must give him the powers of a vicar general which includes the legal possibility of limiting or enlarging the tasks of a vicar general. In special cases he may be granted greater powers; the competent authority is either the Apostolic See which may confer the necessary faculties either in the nomination decree or, if need be, also later, or the diocesan bishop himself, who may give his coadjutor faculties beyond those of a vicar general.

By laying down that "the diocesan bishop and his coadjutor should not fail to consult with one another on matters of major importance" the Council Fathers ask both for their close co-operation. Though this duty concerns both, it does not involve their legal position; for despite the duty of consultation the right of the diocesan bishop to give orders continues, unless the co-adjutor has been granted faculties by the higher authority which he can exercise independently of his diocesan. Nothing is said about the relation between the coadjutor and the "acting" vicar general. This problem may be solved in this way: that the acting vicar general, regardless of whether he is a priest or a bishop, has no right to give orders to a co-adjutor bishop, and that, on the other hand, a coadjutor has no such right with regard to the "acting" vicar general unless the competent authority has given him powers beyond those of a vicar general. The presence of two administrative heads would endanger the unity of the diocesan administration, though this remains legally assured, since the diocesan bishop can take the measures necessary for it.

Article 27 deals with several questions concerning the diocesan curia and councils, especially the introduction of episcopal vicars, the reform of the cathedral chapter and the creation of pastoral councils.

The statement that "the most important office in the diocesan curia is that of vicar general" (beginning of para. 1) recalls that this office had been under considerable stress, because the auxiliary bishops wanted to be both equal to and independent of the vicar general and have partly succeeded in this demand. Thus the declaration that the office of the vicar general is an *officium eminens* is no mere form of words, but means to emphasize that the vicar general will continue to be the most important official of the diocesan curia. The vicar general is the representative *(alter ego)* of the resident bishop in the general diocesan administration both in its voluntary and in its compulsory spheres. He is the head of the diocesan administration and thus bears a heavy burden of the episcopal office. The office of the vicar general has been highly successful, especially in the large dioceses; it is so conceived as to be easily adapted to different circumstances. On the one hand it is left to the diocesan whether he wants to appoint a vicar general (*CIC*, can. 366, para. 1), on the other the ordinary may also either narrow the legally determined duties of a vicar general or enlarge them by way of a special mandate (can. 368, para. 1). The vicar general is bound by the orders of his diocesan and may not exercise his powers against the opinion and will of the latter (can. 369). Normally only one vicar general may be appointed so as to preserve the unity of administration. If, however, the difference of rites or the size of the diocese make it necessary several may be nominated. In the first case the competence is defined personally, in the second objectively (according to spheres of action), or, more often, locally, so that each vicar general is responsible for a part of the diocese (can. 366, 3). The last possibility, however, is disputed.[42]

In order to assign adequate tasks and powers to the auxiliaries the council has introduced the office of episcopal vicar *(Vicarius Episcopalis)*. Though it was created for the auxiliary bishops, this office may also be entrusted to priests. The episcopal vicar is modelled on the vicar general; he is so to speak a "small" vicar general, because his duties are strictly circumscribed, whereas those of the vicar general are much more comprehensive; nevertheless, within his sphere of action he has the same powers as the vicar general. True, the new office was not actually needed, since that of the vicar general is so flexible that it might include also the duties of the newly created episcopal vicar. Nevertheless this is to be welcomed, because it is even more flexible than that of the vicar general and helps to preserve the principle that normally only one vicar general ought to be appointed, who represents the bishop throughout the diocese (can. 366, 1). The greater flexibility of the new office consists in this that the diocesan may determine the duties of an episcopal vicar according to his own ideas. There are three possibilities: 1) The episcopal vicar may be assigned for one part of the diocese; this would be advisable especially if this part were later to be separated and itself formed into a diocese. 2) The episcopal vicar may be assigned to a special department regardless of how large this is; even a very modest task would suffice, provided it belongs in some way to the diocesan administration, even though it might not belong to the diocesan curia but have to be carried out elsewhere, for example in the case of parish visitations. 3) The episcopal vicar may be given the care of certain groups of the faithful (of another rite or of immigrants).[43] In all three cases the diocesan is free to reserve certain matters to himself or to the vicar general, and he may also confer a special mandate on the episcopal vicar in matters for which canon law provides this (motu proprio *Ecclesiae Sanctae,* I, n. 2). Hence the new office has only the *formal structure* of an office, because it has no legally determined duties and receives the content necessary for an office in the legal sense only through the diocesan. But just the flexibility due to this formal structure makes the office of the episcopal vicar an excellent instrument for the diocesan.

The episcopal vicar is obliged to report to the bishop on all his activities

---

[42] See on this K. Mörsdorf, *Kirchenrecht,* I, pp. 428f.
[43] The motu proprio *Ecclesiae Sanctae,* I, n. 14, § 2, supplemented the legislation of the Council which envisaged only the faithful of a certain rite by laying down that it also applies to the care of another group *(seu coetus personarum).*

and plans and may never act against the latter's will. He must also frequently confer with the other collaborators of the bishop, especially with the vicar general, according to the directions of the diocesan, so that unity of discipline is preserved by clergy and people and the diocese flourishes (motu proprio, I, n. 14, § 3). These directions are evidently meant for an auxiliary bishop appointed episcopal vicar and neglect that a priest in the same position may be placed under the orders of the vicar general.

The unity of diocesan administration is endangered by the existence of several representatives of the diocesan with the powers of a vicar general directly under the bishop. So as to prevent one representative being played off against another the motu proprio *Ecclesiae Sanctae* (I, n. 14, para. 4, 1)[44] has ordered that a favour refused by a vicar general or an episcopal vicar may not legally be granted to another vicar of the same diocesan even if the vicar in question has given him the reasons for his refusal. As regards the relation between the vicars general and the episcopal vicars to the diocesan bishop the motu proprio takes over the rulings of canon 44, § 2, for the relation between the bishop and the vicar general. According to this a favour is invalid if it has been refused by a vicar general or an episcopal vicar and has later been obtained from the diocesan without mentioning the refusal; a favour refused by the diocesan, however, cannot validly be obtained from a vicar general or an episcopal vicar without the agreement of the diocesan even if the refusal has been mentioned (I, n. 14, para. 4, 2).

Episcopal vicars who are not auxiliary bishops are appointed for a certain period which is to be laid down in the nomination papers; they may be dismissed by the diocesan, and have to resign when the see is vacant. It is, however, to be recommended that the vicar capitular should delegate them so that the diocese may not suffer (motu proprio, I, n. 14, para. 5). The time limit prevents them from getting too old for their post and gives special chances to those episcopal vicars who are not auxiliary bishops, especially when their work requires a man in full possession of his powers.

Paragraph 2 demands that the diocesan councils, especially the cathedral chapters, should be adapted to present-day needs; but there are no suggestions as to what changes are to be made. However, the creation of new councils such as the priests' senate and the pastoral council makes it necessary for their tasks to be co-ordinated with those of the older institutions. Paragraph 5 recommends the creation of pastoral councils *(consilium pastorale)* presided over by the bishop "in which specially chosen clergy, religious, and lay people will participate. The function of this council will be to investigate and weigh matters which bear on pastoral activity, and to formulate practical conclusions regarding them." In order to guarantee the collaboration between the bishops and the priests, Article 7, para. 4, of the decree *Presbyterorum Ordinis* asks that "a group

---

[44] See Mörsdorf, *Kirchenrecht*, I, pp. 133 ff.

or senate of priests representing the presbytery should be established". This college, which was given the name "council of priests" *(consilium presbyterale)*[45] in the motu proprio *Ecclesiae Sanctae* (I, n. 5), is "by its counsel ... to give effective assistance to the bishop in his government of the diocese". It will not be easy to distinguish between the spheres of activity of both bodies, and it betrays an insufficient co-ordination of the work of the Council[46] that new diocesan councils should have been recommended or prescribed by two different decrees. The creation of a council of priests belongs to the questions dealt with by the decree *Christus Dominus.* As an organ of the presbytery the priests' council is closely related to the cathedral chapter which originated from the presbytery, as well as to the council of diocesan consultors which is entrusted with the duties of a bishops' senate where there is no cathedral chapter (*CIC,* can. 427). The new council of priests will be a serious competitor of these older institutions.[47] Though the pastoral councils are only recommended they will probably be established everywhere; hence it will be important to give them, too, a genuine function of their own.

The instructions given by the motu proprio *Ecclesiae Sanctae* (I, nn. 15f.) on the priests' and pastoral councils follow closely the texts of the Council documents and deal chiefly with questions of organization, while leaving much scope to the particular churches.

1. The priests' council *(consilium presbyterale)* is to be established in every diocese; its task is to advise the bishop in the government of the diocese. This duty is meant to express the union between the bishop and his priestly collabora-tors, but it seems to me that it may easily be interpreted as giving the latter a voice in the government, in accordance with the spirit of the age which has penetrated even into the Church. What is even more important, the creation of this council is inspired by the care for the priests themselves, for it is to be fashioned in such a way as to preserve and strengthen the bonds uniting the priests to the bishop as well as to each other (cf. the comment on Article 28). A well-ordered presbytery inspired by the spirit of the Lord is the most effiacious instrument of the bishop in the government of his diocese and at the same time a solid basis for the formation of the priests' council. This would have to be elected (perhaps for three years), subject to confirmation by the bishop, and consist of representatives of all groups such as parish priests, curates and other priests entrusted with special tasks. Members belonging to the council of priests by right would be: the coadjutor bishop and auxiliary bishops, the vicar general,

---

[45] Unfortunately this term does not express that according to the will of the Council it is an institution whose members represent the presbytery, or, to be more exact, by which the presbytery itself is represented. Hence it would be more correct to call it *Consilium Presbyterii.*

[46] Elsewhere, too, both decrees have occasionally dealt with the same questions; hence it was right to give common directions for both.

[47] This is already evident in the motu proprio *Ecclesiae Sanctae,* I, n. 21, §§ 2 and 3, where the coun-cil of priests is accorded the right to be heard in two important questions of parish organization.

the head of the cathedral chapter or of the council of diocesan consultors, the dean of the theological faculty where it exists and the regent of the seminary. Besides, the diocesan bishop might have the right to appoint several priests to this council so as to assure the co-operation of those with a particular knowledge in certain fields. Such a composition of the priests' council which is advisable especially in larger dioceses would be allowed by the motu proprio *Ecclesiae Sanctae* (I, n. 15, § 1) which lays down that the council is to established in such manner and forms as are to be determined by the diocesan. The motu proprio provides also for religious engaged in parishes or the works of the apostolate to be appointed to this council. This, of course, concerns only religious who are also priests. For though these do not belong to the diocesan presbytery, they may be represented in view of the services they render to the diocese.

In the priests' council the bishop is to listen to his priests, ask for their advice and talk with them about pastoral needs and matters concerning the well-being of the diocese (I, n. 15, § 1); this council, however, has only an advisory function (para. 3). It should be noted that such an organization has the duty of forming an opinion which must be made known to the person it is supposed to advise. Now a collegial organization forms an opinion by way of resolutions, regardless of whether it has a merely advisory or a decision-making function. Insofar as it is laid down by law that the priests' council has to be heard (e. g., motu proprio *Ecclesiae Sanctae*, I, n. 21, §§ 2 f.) the diocesan bishop can act lawfully only after hearing the priests' council (cf. *CIC*, can. 105, n. 1). Thus despite its close connection with the bishop the priests' council does not only afford opportunities for priests and bishop to meet and take counsel together, but it has a similar relation to the bishop as the cathedral chapter.

The cathedral chapter, however, governs the diocese as soon as the see is vacant (*CIC*, can. 431, § 1) and must elect a vicar capitular within eight days to govern in its place (can. 432, n. 1), whereas the priests' council ceases to exist when the see is vacant, except in the case of special circumstances which must be approved by the Holy See, when it is confirmed by the vicar capitular or by an apostolic administrator. The new bishop appoints a new council of priests (*Ecclesiae Sanctae*, I, n. 15, § 4). According to canon law this council thus depends entirely on the person of the diocesan bishop, whereas the presbytery which it represents is not affected by the vacancy of the see but continues to function also under the temporary government of the diocese. Hence the law that the priests' council ceases to exist with the vacancy of the see has no objective foundation but may be attributed to exaggerated caution. Hence we would suggest a change in the law according to which the priests' council would continue during the vacancy of the see and it would be left to the bishop to confirm it or to order new elections.[48]

---

[48] A further consideration of the problems arising from the existence of the two priestly councils, the cathedral chapter and the priests' council, as well as the desired reform of the former ought to justify this suggestion.

Even according to the directions of *Ecclesiae Sanctae* the pastoral council *(consilium pastorale)* is not decreed by law but only "strongly recommended". The function of this council is "to investigate and to weigh matters which bear on pastoral activity, and to formulate practical conclusions regarding them". The motu proprio (I, n. 16, § 1) explains that the life and activity of the people of God are to be furthered in harmony with the gospel. In order to fulfil its purpose the common activity of the council should be preceded by preparatory studies, if necessary also through institutions available for this purpose (I, n. 16, § 4). This suggests that the pastoral council is to be convoked only from time to time and after due preparation.

It is composed of priests, religious and laymen to be specially selected by the diocesan (I, n. 16, § 3). The religious may be priests or laymen and women. The fact that they are chosen by the bishop does not exclude some form of election, and as far as possible the people of the diocese should be adequately represented. The pastoral council has a merely advisory function and may be constituted in different ways (I, n. 16, § 2, first sentence). This means that it is left to the bishop how this council is to be formed and how it is to function. Sentence two says further: "Though of its nature it (i.e., the pastoral council) is a permanent institution, as regards its members and its activity it may be only temporary and function on occasion." Thus the structure of the pastoral council is formed on the model of the episcopal synod;[49] yet it would be quite wrong to relate both institutions to each other. That a council which is only "strongly recommended" should by its nature be a permanent institution is unintelligible and makes it clear that the model has been too closely applied. Nevertheless it should be noted that the structure of the pastoral council as described in the second sentence defines only its general form without prejudice to sentence one which lays down that the pastoral council may be constituted in different ways. In relation to sentence one the statement of sentence two is merely subsidiary. No matter how the pastoral council is constituted, it is left to the diocesan to convoke it as often as he considers advisable (sentence 3). Where there are hierarchies of different rites in the same territory the pastoral council should, if at all possible, consist of priests, religious and laymen of the different rites (I, n. 16, § 5). This is legally possible, since the pastoral council has only an advisory function; it should nevertheless be considered that an interritual pastoral council is nowhere at home[50] but hovers, as it were, above the various particular churches

---

[49] Cf. the motu proprio *Apostolica Sollicitudo,* I, according to which the episcopal synod is to be constituted in such a way that it is *natura sua perpetuum* (c) and *quoad structuram, ad tempus atque ex occasione munere suo perfungens* (d).

[50] The interritual principle mentioned leaves open many organizatorial questions, especially as regards the fact that every pastoral council is attached to a local bishop. A special legislation would be needed for such matters as its convocation, its presidency, the composition of committees and so forth. Since pastoral questions are different in every rite, pastoral councils of the same rite could hardly be dispensed with where there are special hierarchies; mutual consultation between these organizations would also be useful.

and is thus hampered in its work, because the recognized independence of the rites considerably limits the work of inter-ritual organizations in the diocesan sphere.[51] The other matters are left to the diocesan bishop, who must take note of the directions of n. 17 regarding the co-ordination of the diocesan councils.

3. As regards this co-ordination (I, n. 17) the bishops are advised to decide on the relation between priests' and pastoral councils and between these and the older councils of the bishop especially in the episcopal conferences, so that similar principles may be in force in all dioceses of the conference territory (para. 1, 1). This direction leaves much scope, extending from the unified principles laid down by the episcopal conference to the individual principles established by each diocesan; in the latter case the bishops have only to see to it that their principles are similar to each other. The bishops are also responsible for the proper co-ordination of all diocesan councils through exact definition of their competence, through mutual participation of their members, through common or successive sessions or in any other way (para. 1, 2). Thus it is clear that the directions have not solved the problems of organization arising from the number of diocesan councils. The suggestion of common sessions and of participation of the members of one council in the deliberations of another (e. g., of members of the priests' in those of the pastoral council) makes it only too evident that a clear definition of competence is still far away. It can hardly be hoped that the bishops will be able to co-ordinate all these activities satisfactorily, as suggested by the motu proprio, especially as they have no complete freedom to act; for at the moment the councils established by the present canon law, that is to say, the cathedral chapter and the diocesan consultants and other existing ones, retain their own office and comoetence (para. 2). Thus the final regulation of these difficult questions is left to the reform of the *CIC*.

Article 28 introduces the section on the diocesan clergy. It deals in general with the presbytery of a particular Church (para. 1), especially with the relationship between the bishop and his diocesan priests (para. 2) and the union of the diocesan priests among one another (para. 3). Paragraphs 1 and 3 also contain statements which do not really fit into the context, namely on the freedom of the bishop in assigning offices and benefices and the suppression of rights or privileges limiting this freedom (para. 1)[52] as well as the duty of the priests to "contribute generously according to their means to the material needs of the diocese" (para. 3). The directions concerning Article 28 deal only with the suppression of rights and privileges in assigning offices and benefices.

Paragraph 1 distinguishes between diocesan and religious priests: "All priests . . . participate in and exercise with the bishop the one priesthood of Christ and are thereby meant to be prudent co-operators of the episcopal order."

---

[51] On this question see comment on Article 38, § 2.

[52] This statement occurs first in the *Textus emendatus* of 1964; it is similar to what is said about the appointment of parish priests in Article 31, § 2; its origin can be traced to the *schema decreti* of 27 April 1964 (so-called *Textus prior*).

The last statement derives from the Preface of the ordination of priests[53] and might easily be misunderstood; for the priests are not attached to the bishops, but the individual priest is hierarchically co-ordinated to his particular bishop or another pastor in a similar position.[54] To other bishops the priest owes due reverence, but not obedience. The hierarchical co-ordination of the priest to his bishop is determined by the hierarchical order in which the individual priest is placed. Here the distinction between secular and regular priests is of fundamental importance. The decree under consideration does not use the term secular priests *(presbyteri saeculares)* but diocesan priests *(presbyteri dioecesani)*; thus it uses a new terminology which is not, however, without its difficulties. This is evident from another passage which says that in a certain genuine sense religious priests "must be said to belong to the clergy of the diocese[55] inasmuch as they share in the care of souls and in carrying out works of the apostolate under the authority of the sacred prelates" (cf. Article 34, 1). That religious priests should belong to the clergy of the diocese even though they must be distinguished from the diocesan priests leads to a linguistic confusion which ought to have been avoided, especially as the new terminology does not cover different facts.

The diocesan priests hold the first place in the care of souls. The reason given is that they are incardinated in a particular Church and dedicated to its service. This is true as a rule; but it leaves aside the fact that secular priests frequently serve a diocese in which they are not incardinated; hence the concept of the diocesan priest also fails to produce clarity about priests who are not regulars.

The diocesan priests are said to form one presbytery under the bishop as their father. This determines more exactly the general statement of the constitution *Lumen Gentium* (Article 28, 3) according to which the priests "constitute one

---

[53] *Sit providus cooperator ordinis nostri*, these words point unequivocally to the hierarchical relation to the ordaining bishop and are developed in the promise of obedience made by the newly ordained priest to him and his successors. These texts presuppose — what went without saying in the system of relative ordination — that the ordinand will join the presbytery of the ordaining bishop. In the constitution *Lumen Gentium*, Article 28, § 2, the words of the preface of consecration have been changed to *ordinis Episcopalis providi cooperatores*, on which the words of our decree are based. See also the decree *Presbyterorum Ordinis*, Article 7, § 1.

[54] Cf. also above, commentary on Article 15.

[55] The report on the *Textus emendatus* of 1964 (p. 72) states that the words *ad clerum dioecesanum* had been changed into *ad clerum dioecesis*, because this was more correct *(quod quidem verius est)*. This was meant to express, even though in not quite adequate terminology, that the relation of the regular clergy to the diocese and its bishop differs from that of the diocesan clergy, who had hitherto been called secular priests *(presbyteri saeculares)* in legal terminology, in order to distinguish them clearly from the regular clergy. The motu proprio *Ecclesiae Sanctae*, I, n. 5, § 4, 1, however, again speaks of the priests of the secular clergy *(presbyteri cleri saecularis)*, which is indeed necessary in the context, because here it is a question of priests who are neither incardinated in a particular Church (= diocese) nor in a religious institute but in a prelature, which is chiefly designed as a spiritual home of secular priests who work in various places.

priesthood with their bishop" — a statement[56] which will have to be more critically examined. But before making any criticism we would say that the revival of the idea of the presbytery, which had already been lost[57] to theological thought, is not one of the least fruits of the Council. But apart from the creation of a priests' council to represent the presbytery (see commentary of Article 27) the tasks given to the presbytery as such are not described, hence the problems of organization due to the difference in the size of dioceses are not discussed.

The question who belongs to the presbytery is answered by the statement that the diocesan priests form the presbytery. This evidently means that the priests incardinated in a particular Church are the presbytery. This certainly is essentially correct, for only those priests whose spirit home[58] is in a particular Church have the duty to serve it and its president. A secular priest who serves the Church outside his spiritual home does not cease to remain united to his own particular Church (cf. *CIC*, can. 144); on the grounds of another legal title, however, he is united to the particular Church which he serves in such a way that he may be considered to belong to the presbytery of this diocese. However much his legal position may differ from that of the priests whose spiritual home is in this particular Church, yet on account of the spiritual tasks proper to the presbytery it would be fully justified that secular priests whose home is elsewhere should be considered part of the presbytery. The regular priests are in a different position. As far as they are attached to a particular Church on a fulltime basis they should be given a proportionate share in the spiritual tasks of the presbytery. Nevertheless, they have their own spirituality which they should practise within their own conventual community. It this is impossible for practical reasons, especially in the case of regular priests attached to a particular Church without sufficient contact with their community, they, too, should have a spiritual home in the presbytery.

If the union of the priests presided over by their diocesan is not to remain an empty word the presbytery needs a suitable organization. If a presbytery is too large to assure contact of the bishop with his priests and of the priests with each other it should be divided into several chapters, so that the priests belong-

[56] Other Council decrees, too, speak of the presbytery, for example the decree *Presbyterorum Ordinis,* which orders the creation of priests' councils whose members represent the presbytery (Article 7, para. 1) and the decree *Ad Gentes,* according to which the local (that is to say the native) priests *(presbyteri locales)* form one presbytery together with the foreign missionaries under the authority of the bishops (Article 20, para. 3).

[57] In the second edition of LTK "presbyterium" (vol. VIII, col. 725) is defined only as a room in the church building. But in the Kirchenlexikon edited by Wetzer and Welte (vol. X, 1897, cols. 368 f.) the other meaning is also given, according to which even in the ancient Church "especially the permanent senate of the bishop, consisting of the presbyters and deacons of the episcopal city" was called thus.

[58] On the notion of the spiritual home, which is unknown in Latin legal terminology, see Mörsdorf, *Kirchenrecht,* I, pp. 249 ff.

ing to one chapter could, if possible, meet once a week or at least once a month and the bishop could join them at least once a year in order to preserve contact with those whose duty it is to make him present, as it were, at the place of their work (cf. *Lumen Gentium*, Article 28, para. 3). For this purpose the present division of the dioceses into deaneries might be changed, so that the latter would consist of chapters of the presbytery and the deanery (better to be called archipresbytery) would be presided over by an archpriest who would be elected by the chapter and confirmed by the bishop.

What is said in paragraphs 2 and 3 about the relations of the bishop to his priests, their union with each other and their obligation to the diocese comprises more or less the tasks of the presbytery in union with its bishop. This is expressed particularly in the demand that the bishop should discuss pastoral matters not only with individual priests but in common with his presbytery or its individual chapters, and this not only occasionally but if possible at regular intervals.

In the second sentence of paragraph 3 a subject is introduced which has nothing to do with the union of the priests. They are reminded that "the benefits which they receive by reason of their ecclesiastical office are closely bound up with their sacred work. Therefore, they should contribute generously according to their means to the material needs of the diocese as the bishop's programme provides for them." This does not mean limiting the freedom of the priests to dispose of their ecclesiastical income; for they are only asked to contribute to the needs of the diocese as made known by the bishop according to their means and freely. This is actually the old idea familiar from the law of benefices, according to which those whose income derives from the service of the Church are obliged to give the "superflua" to the poor or other pious works (cf. *CIC*, can. 1473).

The bishop's freedom in assigning offices is mentioned twice in the decree under discussion. According to Article 28, 1, rights and privileges limiting this freedom are to be suppressed, while Article 31, 2, decrees that, excepting the rights of religious, in the case of parishes "all rights whatsoever of presentation, nomination, reservation are to be suppressed, including any general or particular law of concursus". Though both passages differ formally in that one is of a general character while the other envisages only parishes, they nevertheless form a unity, so much so that the motu proprio *Ecclesiae Sanctae*, I, n. 18, treats both statements of the Council together in the directions for Article 28 without even mentioning Article 31. These directions are immediately applicable law. They give the following instructions:

1. Suppression of the papal rights of reservation

In future the Apostolic See does not reserve to itself the appointment to those ecclesiastical offices which are not consistorial benefices, whether these be benefices or not or pastoral offices or non-pastoral ones (n. 18, para. 1, 1). Thus the laws reserving certain minor benefices to the Pope (can. 396, para. 1, 1435) are no longer in force.

2. The abolition of the rights to elect and propose for non-consistorial offices

a) In future no conditions restricting the freedom of the bishop in conferring the benefice will be permitted when creating any benefice (n. 18, para. 1, 1).

b) *Privilegia non onerosa* which may have been granted to physical or legal persons are abolished, if they include the right to elect, nominate or present for any available non-consistorial office, whether it is beneficed or not (n. 18, para. 1, 1). Further: Customs and rights to nominate, elect, or present a priest to a parish are abolished. These customs and rights are privileges, that is exceptional rights which according to can. 63, para. 1, may be acquired from the competent authority (by law or administrative act) or by custom or usucaption. Hence the *consuetudines* and *iura* need not have been specially mentioned. It cannot be doubted that election and proposal rights which are connected with taxes (e.g., in the case of patronage) are not abolished even in the most usual case of parishes. It is surprising that the reservation in favour of religious (Article 31, 2, of the Council decree) has not been included in the motu proprio; but this may merely be due to an oversight.

c) The abolition of electoral and proposal rights of non-consistorial offices is to be discussed with the authorities concerned; the rights envisaged are based on an agreement between the Holy See and a government or physical or juridical persons. This regulation follows from the natural law: *pacta sunt servanda* (pacts must be observed); in this connection it may be noted that the right of patronage granted in recognition of services rendered (the so-called *privilegium remuneratorium*) is ultimately based on a contract (n. 18, para. 2).

d) As regards the so-called elections of the people, the episcopal conferences in whose territory these exist are asked to make suitable proposals to the Holy See for including them as far as possible (n. 18, para. 1, 2).

3. Granting of offices by competition (lex concursus)

This is abolished in those territories where it was still in force both as regards the most frequent case of parishes and also other, non-pastoral offices (n. 18, para. 1, 1).

Article 29 treats of those collaborating more closely with the bishop and charged with works of a supraparochial nature (para. 1), supradiocesan tasks (para. 2, second sentence) or apostolic work in schools and other institutions (para. 2, first sentence). The latter activities may take place on a parochial, supraparochial or supradiocesan level. The legal questions that might arise have not been broached; only those priests entrusted with supradiocesan works[59] are recommended to the special care of the bishop in whose diocese they reside. This recommendation is of no real help, because it leaves open the decisive questions of assigning duties and carrying them out. In principle it may be said that a supradiocesan activity may be engaged on either after agreement with the *local* bishops or on order of a supradiocesan authority, especially of the episcopal conference. In both cases it is possible that the individual bishop may not have the right to give orders. Finally, the rather awkward connection of the individual statements by two "etiams" and "quoque" shows that the Council only wants simply to make suggestions in order somehow to round off the activities of the priests.[60]

Article 30 is concerned with the parish priests (nn. 1 and 2) and the assistant priests (n. 3). The importance of the parish priests is expressed by the statement that they "co-operate with the bishop in a very special way, for as shepherds in their own right they are entrusted with the care of souls in a certain part of the diocese under the bishop's authority". The parish priest shares the dignity of being a shepherd in his own right (pastor proprius) with the bishop (see commentary of Article 11, para. 1); but he is distinguished from him by the fact that his pastoral office is only a share in that of the bishop and concerns part of the diocesan community which is itself part of the people of God. The parish priest is sent by the bishop and depends on him in the exercise of his office; yet he is not merely a kind of extension of the bishop distributing what the bishop gives. No, the service of the parish priest is a true representation of the invisible Lord, for which he is prepared sacramentally by ordination and receives powers from the bishop. He is the spiritual head of the parish to which he represents Christ, and it is his duty to unite the individual faithful in a community founded in and for Christ. Thus he belongs to those called to preside over a particular community within the structure of the Church, though dependent on his bishop, and it is his duty to safeguard by his daily labours the salvation of those entrusted to him.

In the first paragraph of n. 1 the parish priests are told so to "fulfil their duty of teaching, sanctifying, and governing that the individual parishioners and the parish communities will really feel that they are members of the diocese and of the universal Church". Here the theological meaning of the service of the parish is at least suggested. But more is needed than arousing and fostering a mere feeling of belonging to the diocese and the universal Church. What Article 28 of the Constitution *Lumen Gentium* says of the priests in general

[59] According to Article 30, n. 1, § 1, the parish priest is obliged to co-operate with those priests who have supraparochial duties.
[60] This is borne out by the genesis of this article. The present n. 1 which mentions works of a supraparochial nature is already to be found in the schema of 27 April 1964 (Article 27); para. 2, sentence 1, was added in the *Textus emendatus* of 1964 (Article 29, para. 2) and sentence 2 in the *Textus recognitus* of 1965.

concerns largely the parish priest, because he exercises not only some of the Church's saving functions but is called to accomplish the whole of its saving mission for the faithful entrusted to him. Hence it is true especially of the parish priest that he makes visible the whole Church to his flock under the authority of his bishop. This distinguishes him from the other collaborators of the bishop.

The parish priest must co-operate with the other parish priests and with those entrusted with a pastoral office in the district or with tasks of a supra-parochial nature. The legal relationship of the parish priests to those three categories of the bishop's collaborators differs according to the manner of their co-operation.

The motu proprio *Ecclesiae Sanctae*, I, n. 19, has issued directions regarding the office of vicar forane *(vicarius foraneus)*,[61] also called archpriest or deacon, and in the Eastern Church protopresbyter. He is mainly the bishop's local supervisor of the parishes belonging to his vicariate and has also the care of the parish priests (cf. *CIC*, can. 445–50).[62] The motu proprio provides for these vicars to further and direct the pastoral work in their district and to be furnished with the necessary faculties by the bishop. Besides, it recommends that they should be consulted by the bishop in the matter of the appointment, translation or removal of the parish priests of their district. These vicars should be priests excelling in sound doctrine and apostolic zeal. Their office is not tied to a particular parish, they are appointed for a certain period to be determined by the particular Church and may be removed at the discretion of the bishop.

The second paragraph of n. 1 concerns the missionary spirit with which the care of souls should always be infused, "so that it reaches out in the proper manner to everyone living within the parish boundaries" not only to the actual members of the parish (cf. Article 16, para. 6). The suggestion that if the parish priest cannot reach certain groups of people "he should seek the help of others, including laymen, who can assist him" seems still to derive from the idea that laymen should collaborate in the mission of the Church only by way of substitute.[63] Like the bishop (see comment on Article 16, para. 5) the parish priest is bound to give the laity their rightful share in matters concerning the Church.

N. 2 is a summary of the parish priest's duties in the teaching, priestly and pastoral spheres. It is a kind of "pastor's mirror" connected with the "bishop's mirror" of Articles 12–16.

N. 3 refers briefly to the assistant priests. As collaborators of the parish

---

[61] The vicar forane is here regarded as one of the priests holding a suprapastoral office. Hence the difference preserved in the Council document between the pastoral office in a district, of which the vicar forane is given as an example, and supraparochial work is disregarded.

[62] See K. Mörsdorf, *Kirchenrecht*, I, pp. 458 f.

[63] This view has definitely been abandoned with the proclamation of the doctrine of the new people of God, but it still turns up now and again, even in the preface of the decree on the lay apostolate.

priest they often have to carry the main burden of the day-to-day pastoral care, hence the Council Fathers wanted to give them the recognition due to them. They are under the authority of the parish priest (*CIC*, can. 476, § 7), but should be united to him in fraternal charity.

Article 31 received its present form only in the final redaction.[64] It deals with the conferment of the parish priest's office and with his stability in it.

The freedom of the bishop in the appointment of parish priests has already been discussed in the commentary on Article 28, para. 1. As far as the bishop is free in making this appointment, that is to say not bound by electoral or proposal rights, he must give the vacant parish to the priest he considers most suitable without respect of persons. On the question of how the bishop is to judge the suitability of a priest modern canon law has turned away from the Tridentine legislation, even though certain fragments have been preserved pending a different ruling by the Holy See (*CIC*, can. 459, § 4).[65] Vatican II marks the end of this development; but apart from the suppression of the concursus (motu proprio *Ecclesiae Sanctae*, I, n. 18, para. 1) no further rules have been laid down. But it may be expected that the parish examination for determining the qualifications for appointments to parochial office may be preserved and that the judgment on the suitability of a priest is freed from all formal juridical ties.

The stability of the parish priest is still confirmed in principle, but is considerably limited (para. 3). The benefices of secular priests, that is to say those offices to which seculars must be appointed, are conferred for life (cf. *CIC*, can. 1438); this principle remains in force, but the stability of the parish priest depends on the good of the souls entrusted to him. Thus on the one hand the parish priest is safe in his office so that he may fulfil his duties regardless of the favour or disfavour of the faithful, on the other he must leave his post if he is no longer equal to his tasks. The earlier idea of total stability derived from Germanic private law, which regarded the clerical office as an object to which the parish priest had a personal right; this has now been replaced by the view of public law, which allows the parish priest to be removed from office even if he has not incurred any guilt. This new conception goes back to the Council of Trent, was evolved by the Congregation of the Council, was first formulated in the decree *Maxima Cura* of 20 August 1910[66] and was included with some procedural alleviations in the *CIC* (can. 2142 ff.).[67] The reform desired by Vatican II aims at a further loosening of the law of procedure, so that a parish priest may be removed as soon as possible. The final solution of this difficult problem can be expected only in the course of the reform of canon law; it is to be hoped that

---

[64] Paras. 1 and 3 as well as the statement on the concursus in para. 2 were added in the *Textus recognitus* of 1965.

[65] See K. Mörsdorf, *Rechtsprechung und Verwaltung im kanonischen Recht* (1941), pp. 141 ff.

[66] *AAS* 2 (1910), pp. 636 ff.

[67] Cf. Eichmann and Mörsdorf, *Kirchenrecht*, III (10th ed.), pp. 268 ff.

the pastoral requirement of the stability of the parish priest will be harmonized with that of removing him when desirable. But in order to eliminate any arbitrary decisions it is indispensable to institute a legal enquiry which will give the parish priest concerned an adequate opportunity for defence.

The distinction hitherto in force between parish priests who cannot be removed and those who can has been abolished. According to canon law the former had up to now enjoyed the right to object and to demand a second trial before the bishop and two consultant assessors (cf. *CIC*, can. 2153). The motu proprio *Ecclesiae Sanctae* (I, n. 20, para. 1) provides that until canon law has been reformed the rules governing the removal of the latter are to be applied (*CIC*, can. 2157–61). The juridical reasons for instituting the process of removal (*CIC*, can. 2147), which in any case have not been enumerated exhaustively, remain in force, but they may be supplemented by a similar reason according to the judgment of the bishop. The canon law of the Eastern Church is not affected by this ruling.

Article 32 mentions very briefly the erection, suppression and changing of parishes, stating that the basis for these measures should be the concern for souls and that the bishop can institute them on his own authority. In view of the fact that these are the most important measures of ecclesiastical organization in the diocese the brevity of the statement is surprising. The schema of the decree *De episcopis ac de dioecesium regimine* of 1963 had devoted a special chapter to this question which, however, had not been discussed in the council hall because the draft had been too unsatisfactory. Nevertheless, what has been left of it in the brief statement of Article 32 is still very important, especially that the bishop may carry out these measures on his own authority. The mention of the bishop's authority at least implies that the original organizing powers of the bishop are fully recognized, also as regards the erection of personal parishes for the faithful of another language or nation, which had hitherto been reserved to the Holy See (*CIC*, can. 216, para. 4, and *CIO*, can. 160, para. 4).[68] This, by the way, is presupposed also in the relevant directions addressed to the diocesan (see commentary on Article 23, n. 3, 2 and 3).

The suppression of the distinction between parish priests who can be removed and those who cannot has also made the translation of a parish priest much easier. Hitherto the latter could be moved to another parish only as a penal measure (cf. *CIC*, can. 2298, n. 3) but not for administrative reasons.[69] The

---

[68] Cf. *ibid.,* pp. 279 ff.

[69] The motu proprio says: "... Episcopus debet ut translatio valide decernatur, eumdem modum procedendi in omnibus servare, de quo supra." This refers definitely to the procedure of removing a removable parish priest mentioned in para. 1 with reference to can. 2157–61. This may be an editorial mistake, because here it is a question not of removing, but of transferring a parish priest. Nevertheless the procedure for transferring a parish priest might have been mentioned (can. 2152–67), where only the special direction for the irremovable parish priest would have had to be excepted (can. 2163, § 1).

motu proprio *Ecclesiae Sanctae* (I, n. 20, para. 2) provides that a parish priest who administers his parish well may be moved to another parish or to any other ecclesiastical office if the good of souls or the needs of the Church demand it. If the parish priest refuses, the bishop must follow exactly the procedure prescribed for the removal of a pastor.[70]

Voluntary resignation is requested should increasing age or another serious reason prevent the parish priest from properly carrying out his duties (para. 4). As in the parallel case of the bishops the motu proprio (I, n. 20, para. 3) visualizes only resignation for reasons of age. All parish priests are requested voluntarily to tender their resignation to their bishop at the latest after completing their 75th year. Having weighed all local and personal circumstances the bishop may either accept or delay the resignation and is responsible for providing an adequate livelihood and dwelling.

1. Division and combination of parishes (para. 1)

If apostolic work is made difficult, whether on account of the large number of the faithful, the extent of their territory or for any other reason, parishes should be divided according to the prevailing needs or certain parts should be sliced off. In the same way parishes that are too small should be combined as far as necessary and circumstances permit. The decision if and when one of these reasons applies in a given case rests with the bishop. He will act according to his own view, while using in the best possible way the personnel as well as the material means available for a more intensive care of souls.

2. Abolition of the incorporation of parishes in cathedral and secular canons' chapters (para. 2)

Parishes are no longer to be completely incorporated into cathedral chapters or secular canons' chapters (of former monasteries).[71] Existing incorporations are to be abolished after consulting the chapter or priests' council concerned, and a parish priest is to be appointed who is to enjoy all the powers due to parish priests according to law, whether he be taken from members of the chapter or not. Though this is not directly related to Article 32, it is covered by the demand for reforming the cathedral chapters (see Article 27, 2) and may be interpreted as hinting that a legal person can no longer be a parish priest *(parochus habitua-*

---

[70] The schema for the decree *De Episcopis ac de Dioecesium regimine* of 1963 provided in Article 36 that the bishop could establish personal parishes for the faithful of another rite or nationality on his own authority, pointing out in a note that *CIC,* can. 216, § 4, and *CIO,* can. 160, § 4, are altered insofar as these measures no longer require the co-operation of the Apostolic See.

[71] The motu proprio speaks of the *Capitula canonicorum*; see K. Mörsdorf, *Kirchenrecht,* I, pp 438 ff.

lis) — an idea derived from the financial aspects of Latin law (cf. *CIC*, can. 451, 1).[72]

3. Erection, abolition and change of parishes (para. 3)

The diocesan bishop may on his own authority erect, suppress or in any way change parishes,[73] though with the proviso that possible impediments due to concordats or acquired rights of physical or legal persons have been removed by the competent authority. The bishop is obliged to hear the council of priests. The term *episcopus dioecesanus* who has this power comprises also all other local bishops, even the presidents of so-called personal dioceses, which within a certain circle of persons are ultimately territorially determined,[74] but not the vicar capitular nor the vicar general without special powers.

In the conclusion of section III dealing with the collaborators of the diocesan, Articles 33 to 35 treat of the religious.[75] They are mentioned in the last place simply because membership of a religious community involves particular legal problems. Furthermore, the general scheme of the decree[76] did not permit the position of the religious in the diocese in the Church as a whole to be treated in greater detail. This could only have been done adequately if the special character of religious life and activity, to which another Council decree is devoted,[77] would have been included in the presentation. When discussing the directions on the religious as collaborators of the diocesan laid down in the present decree, the implications of the religious life should always be taken into account. Article 33 mentions the vocation of all religious to the apostolate of the whole Church as well as of particular Churches. Article 34 treats of religious priests as co-operators of the bishop in general, while distinguishing between

[72] This opens an approach to the constitutional law of the Oriental Churches, which admits no partial but only the full incorporation, but not in the way that the legal person itself becomes a parish priest, because only a priest can be that (cf. *CIO,* can. 489, §§ 1 and 2, and 490, § 2, n. 2). The problem of a parish incorporated in a monastery has not yet been clarified; cf. on this K. Mörsdorf, *Kirchenrecht*, I, pp. 453 f.

[73] "Quoquo modo innovare" (I, n. 21, § 3) includes all changes regarding the parish as such (e.g., division etc.) but not changes within the parish (e.g., building a new church or presbytery). With regard to minor alterations such as assigning a house to a different parish it would hardly make sense if the priests' council would have to be heard as a matter of obligation.

[74] Cf. above, commentary on Article 11, 1.

[75] See L. Gutiérrez Martín, "De ratione inter episcopos et religiosos iuxta Concilium Vaticanum II', in *Commentarium pro Religiosis* 47 (1966), pp. 121–48.

[76] It should be remembered that the schema of the decree *De Episcopis ac de Dioecesium regimine* of 1963 which was discussed in the Council hall did not treat the relation between religious and diocesan at all. The relevant questions had been treated in the schema of the decree *De cura animarum* (ch. III: "De rationibus inter Episcopos et religiosos praesertim quoad apostolatus opera"); only the basic principles were included in the council decree.

[77] Decree *Perfectae Caritatis* of 28 October 1965.

them and those religious who are not priests. Article 35 establishes the principles for the collaboration between diocesan and religious.

The directions laid down in the motu proprio *Ecclesiae Sanctae* (I, nn. 22–40) for Articles 33 to 35 of the Council decree go far beyond the contents of the latter. With only a single exception (I, n. 39, § 1) they do not attempt to follow the decree, as would have been the normal procedure. The reason for this somewhat strange state of affairs is that the decree as well as the motu proprio are based on the same original, namely the schema of the decree *De cura animarum*. The directions of *Ecclesiae Sanctae* provide the material which did not find its way into the decree because this had to be fairly brief.[78] Hence the directions will be treated separately (see Excursus III: The Religious as Collaborators of the Diocesan Bishop).

Article 33. What will be said in the following Articles 33–35 of the religious applies correspondingly also to the members of other communities taking no religious vows but professing to live according to the evangelical counsels of chastity, poverty and obedience. These may either lead a common life and so approach fairly closely to the religious societies, (cf. *CIC*, can. 673–81) or be secular institutes.[79] They resemble the religious in that their way of life is recognized as a canonical state in which they strive for Christian perfection. They all are reminded of their duties towards the whole Church as well as to the particular Churches. The Council decree addresses the members rather than the congregations as such, a manner of speaking frequently used in the law regarding religious, but which includes also the orders themselves. For the special characteristic of these members of the new people of God is precisely that they wish to serve the Church within their communities. The Church places these associations as well as their members under its special protection and while confirming the special character of each expects that they will devote themselves more intensively to the external works of the apostolate without giving up their identity. The concept *externae apostolatus opera* is difficult to define. Every activity of the religious is always directed not only inwards, but also outwards, towards the sanctification of all men; this is basically true even of the purely contemplative communities. Leaving these latter out of account, it can be said that the concrete aims of all religious associations are in some way outward looking and thus directed towards the external works of the apostolate. In the present context, however, what is intended is rather that the societies in question should be prepared also beyond their narrower aims to undertake work both for the whole Church and for particular Churches as long as it is still compatible with their special character.

Article 34 deals with the relation of religious priests and other religious, both men and women, to a diocese. The former are said "in a certain genuine

---

[78] For further details see L. Gutiérrez Martín, "Criteria practica ad rationes inter Episcopos et religiosos componendas", in *Commentarium pro Religiosis* 48 (1967), pp. 19 ff.

[79] On this see K. Mörsdorf, *Kirchenrecht,* I, pp. 554 f.

sense . . . to belong to the clergy of the diocese", the latter to "belong in a special way to the diocesan family". Both statements show the desire to approach the associations themselves as well as their members more closely to the diocese and its bishop. These efforts, however, were not successful, since the ecclesiological problems had not been worked out. The Council had revived the idea that the one and only Catholic Church consists of particular Churches (cf. *Lumen Gentium*, Article 23, 1), but this cannot stop short before monastic and other religious societies. These belong to the Church and have high aims, but they are not particular Churches in which the saving mission of the Church is normally carried out (see explanation of Article 11). As far as they have a priestly character they are, so to speak, independent in the care for the salvation of their members, and insofar as these priestly societies are exempt, they have a superior governing his society or part of it with quasi-episcopal rights. But, however much they may approach the structures of the particular Church,[80] even the centrally organized religious societies cannot themselves be particular Churches. Hence all religious societies belong essentially to a certain particular Church, however, autonomous they may be. This is particularly clear in societies with *stabilitas loci* which have always been conscious of it. But despite the mobility of the centralized societies, these, too, have relations to the particular Churches based on the nature of the constitution of the Church, not only by working in the service of a particular Church but by the very fact that one of their houses or some of their members are placed in one. This is a basic relation which concerns the societies as well as their members and precedes all monastic autonomy even though it may take the form of a papal or patriarchal exemption. An infallible pointer to this ecclesiological fact is the principle preserved in canon law and hedged round with all possible safeguards, according to which the diocesan bishop has to be asked to ordain the members of a religious house situated in his diocese (cf. *CIC*, can. 965–7).[81]

Though it is true that the regular clergy must be regarded in a certain genuine sense as belonging to the clergy of the diocese inasmuch as they share in the care of souls and in carrying out works of the apostolate under the authority of the consecrated bishop (see explanation of Article 28, 1) it should nevertheless

---

[80] Through the rescript *Cum Admotae* of 6 November 1964 (*AAS* 59 [1967], pp. 374–8) the superiors of orders and congregations of priests of papal right have received a share in the enlarged ordinary powers granted to the diocesan bishops by the motu proprio *Pastorale Munus* of 30 November 1963. Those of the ordinary episcopal powers applicable to religious and several others have been delegated to the highest superiors of priestly associations as well as of monastic congregations. Most of these, which are very important for the relation to the bishop, may again be delegated to higher superiors. This assimilation regarding the powers of the diocesan is connected with a levelling of the differences between exempt and non exempt conventual associations of papal right and the non-conventual societies with or without a common life.

[81] In ecclesiastical practice, however, this norm has largely been nullified by the so-called *privilegia a quocumque*, which proves that the essential connection with the particular Church was no longer recognized.

not be overlooked that religious priests are not incardinated in the diocese but in a conventual association (*CIC*, can. 111). Thus as priests they belong to their own spiritual home association[82] presided over not by the bishop but by the constitutional religious superior. It follows from this that not the bishop, but only the competent superior or possibly the Pope (cf. can. 499, 1) can determine how they are to be employed. The same legal situation applies to non-conventual priestly associations of papal right whose priestly members are regarded as secular priests; this presupposes that they have their own spiritual home association. This is always the case where the superior has the right to arrange for the ordination of the members of his association by issuing letters testimonial.[83] The *CIC* retains that only the higher superiors of exempt conventual associations can issue these, hence it lays down that the ordination of other religious follows the law applying to seculars, according to which the diocesan or another local superior of equal position is competent to arrange for ordination (*CIC,* can. 964 with can. 956). This applies all the more to the members of non-conventual societies. Thus the *CIC* preserves an original episcopal right, which, however, has been completely voided in practice by a too general grant of letters testimonial. As the Council Fathers wanted to bring the regular clergy into closer relation to the diocese and its bishop, it would have been advisable to provide for an examination of these privileges,[84] especially as this legislation applies not only to the regular clergy but equally to secular priests who are also removed from the authority of the diocesan because they belong to an association of papal right. Moreover, the new secular institutes of priests, even though they are not yet under papal law, considerably limit the rights of the bishop to dispose of his clergy, certainly not less than the former rights to elect and propose persons for ecclesiastical offices.

Article 35 lays down principles for the apostolic work of religious in the dioceses, with a view to assuring the harmonious co-operation of all concerned as well as the unity of the diocese.

According to n. 1, para. 1, "religious should always attend upon bishops, as upon successors of the apostles, with devoted deference and reverence". In order to prevent misunderstandings due to the plural form it should be pointed out that the religious owes reverence to every bishop, but obedience only to his diocesan, and even in this case only within the limits imposed by conventual autonomy. The following sentence, introduced by *praeterea* (moreover) lays

---

[82] See K. Mörsdorf, *Kirchenrecht*, I, pp. 249 ff.

[83] See *ibid.*, II, pp. 99 ff.

[84] The recent legal development, however, has been in the opposite direction. The rescript *Cum Admotae,* I, n. 11, of 6 November 1964 (*AAS* 59 [1967], p. 376) gave the right to issue letters testimonial to all priestly orders of papal right which did not yet enjoy it according to can. 964, n. 2, of the *CIC*. Moreover, the same power was granted also to the non-conventual societies with common life (cf. *CIC*, can. 673–81) and to the priestly secular institutes of papal law, but to these only for the members not incardinated in a diocese (II, n. 2).

down that religious legitimately called to the works of the apostolate are subject to the diocesan. This makes it clear that the preceding sentence means they are hierarchically attached to the bishop, a fact presupposed by any diocesan duties. The term *legitimate*[85] states that the diocesan bishop can entrust a religious with apostolic activities only if the competent religious superior agrees.[86] In this case the religious association as represented by the superior is the partner of the bishop, not the individual religious. The conventual associations are expected willingly to grant the bishops' requests, and so as to gain a legal basis for this their constitutions are to be examined, where necessary, according to the directions laid down in this decree.[87]

N. 1, para. 2, emphasizes the urgent need for the religious to co-operate in the service of the diocese, laying down at the same time that "the particular character of each community should, however, be kept in mind".

N. 2 supplements n. 1. Religious engaged in external apostolic works remain subject to their religious superiors, and the bishops are told to impress this obligation upon them. This is meant to obviate the danger of one authority being played off against the other.

At the Council the subject of exemption[88] had been discussed but not seriously tackled. This is approached in n. 3 in a way that seems to leave everything as it was and to suggest no new departures. The Pope or another ecclesiastical authority (especially the oriental patriarchs) calls the religious to their service, thus withdrawing them from the jurisdiction of the bishops. According to paragraph 2, "this exemption, however, does not exclude religious in individual dioceses from the jurisdiction of the bishop in accordance with the norm of law *(ad normam iuris),* insofar as the performance of his pastoral office[89] and the right ordering of the care of souls require". This corresponds on the whole to the traditional notion of exemption, according to which the exempt religious are withdrawn from the jurisdiction of the local bishop except in cases laid down in the law *(CIC,* can. 615). The decree states further that exemption applies chiefly to the internal order of the community and that its purpose is that the Pope may make use of the religious for the good of the universal Church. These statements, too, correspond to the customary ideas on the meaning and

---

[85] This was added to the *Textus emendatus*; see the report of 1964 on it.

[86] The proposal to eliminate the word *legitime* was refused by the episcopal commission on the grounds that it was necessary: "Nempe significatur Religiosos advocari ab Episcopo non posse, nisi per legitimos Superiores et servatis de iure servandis" (*Modi Ep*, ch. II, *modus* 171).

[87] This will have to be done when the Constitutions are examined, as is also demanded by the decree *Perfectae Caritatis.*

[88] See A. Scheuermann, *Die Exemption nach geltendem kirchlichem Recht mit einem Überblick über die geschichtliche Entwicklung* (1938).

[89] The word *horum* relates not to the religious, but to the bishops to whom the religious are subject in the various dioceses. This is essential for the understanding of the text; for the limitations of exemption are to be measured by the pastoral office of the diocesan bishops, not by that assigned to the exempt religious.

purpose of exemption. Nevertheless the Council has intended a change which is at least implied in the report on the Textus emendatus which says that the words "ad normam iuris" do not apply to the present, but to the future canon law.[90]

Yet the text itself does not suggest this intention and gives no concrete directions regarding the new law. Those of the motu proprio (see Excursus III) which would have afforded the first opportunity to realize the intention of the Council follow the present law. It remains to be seen whether the reform of the *CIC* will integrate the new understanding of the constitutional law of the Church in the doctrine of exemption. The question boils down to this, whether the old idea is to be retained, according to which the exempt religious are removed from the jurisdiction of the local bishop in such a way that they are regarded as strangers in the particular Church,[91] or whether the point of departure is to be that they basically belong to the particular Churches[92] (see comment on Article 34) and their relations to the hierarchical intermediaries, especially the episcopal conference and in the Eastern Churches the patriarchal synod and the patriarch, and lastly to the supreme pontiff are to be determined from there. These fundamental questions of a new legislation on exemption belong to the problem of the supreme direct jurisdiction of the Pope[93] which has not been treated by the Council (see explanation of Article 2).

N. 4 concerns exempt and non-exempt religious. It defines in general those matters in which religious are subject to the authority of the local Ordinaries.[94]

---

[90] The so-called *Textus prior* did not contain these words; they were inserted in the *Textus emendatus,* on which the first voting in the Council hall was based. It was certainly realized that the words *ad normam iuris* limit the statement of the *Textus prior* which resembled a general clause, hence it was expressly stated that *ad normam iuris* relates to the *ius condendum,* not to the *ius conditum.* Cf. the report on the *Textus emendatus* of 1964. The proposal of 25 Fathers to suppress the words *ad normam iuris* was refused on the grounds that the suppression was unnecessary if the words were rightly understood, as had been explained in the earlier report. It was added: "Revere existere debet aliqua norma iuris: agitur tamen non de iure condito, sed de iure condendo" (*Modi Ep,* ch. II, *modus* 182).

[91] Cf. A. Scheuermann, *Exemption,* pp. 130 ff.

[92] A change proposed by 8 Fathers suggested that the subject of exemption should be treated in such a way that the subjection to the bishops should come first and the exemption from it afterwards. The commission replied that it was more logical to retain the reversed order of the text (*Modi Ep,* ch. II, *modus* 193). This reply seems too facile. For this is not a question of logical sequence, but whether individual members of the Church or ecclesiastical associations can exist within the Church without the basic membership of a particular Church.

[93] L. Gutiérrez Martín (*De ratione inter Episcopos et Religiosos,* p. 134) points out that the right of the bishop to direct the works of the apostolate in his diocese is not absolute and that the Pope has the right to decide whether it is suitable to exercise his own right together with the bishops. In former times the Popes had done this through the exempt religious, to whom they granted rights and privileges which were to be exercised quite — or almost — independently of the bishops of the dioceses. Today, however, it is the general rule that the Pope wants to be active in the apostolate of the Churches only in and through the bishops.

[94] On the suggestion of 570 Fathers the word *subduntur* was replaced by *subsunt.* In itself this is an unimportant nuance, nevertheless it was sufficiently important for so many Fathers to propose

This is merely a supplement to n. 3. For the enumeration of these matters is only a more detailed description of what was said in more general terms in n. 3, para. 2, about the jurisdiction of the bishop. That this applies also to the non-exempt religious goes without saying.

Nn. 5 and 6 give general directions for an orderly co-operation. Apart from the care of the Apostolic See for the universal Church and that of the bishops for their dioceses the decree mentions the patriarchal synods and the episcopal conferences which are competent to supervise this co-ordination for their respective territories. Thus it is clear that exemption does not concern only the relation between Pope and diocesan bishop, but also the union of particular Churches in the episcopal conference. This will offer new perspectives for legislation.

a change. This is meant to convey that the subjection to the local bishop belongs to the essence of the constitution of the Church, especially to the episcopal office and is not based on a papal concession.

The Religious as Collaborators of the Diocesan Bishop*

The directions laid down in the motu proprio *Ecclesiae Sanctae*, I, nn. 22–40,[1] for Articles 33–35 of the decree *Christus Dominus* are not arranged in systematical order. This is true not only of the sequence of statements in the individual numbers, but also sometimes for what is said in one and the same number (e. g., n. 25 and n. 39). Hence it seems best to disregard the sequence of the numbers and to seek to arrange the directions systematically.[2] But I want to emphasize that I am only concerned with the directions which, with few exceptions, hardly go beyond the present canon law.[3] No general presentation of the relation of the religious to the diocesan bishop is intended.

I. General remarks (nn. 22–24, 40)

The norms laid down in the motu proprio apply to all religious, both men and women, and to all rites, though they do not affect the rights of the Oriental patriarchs (n. 22). Since the directions of the Council in Articles 33–35 apply also to non-conventual associations practising the evangelical counsels the motu proprio applies to these, too.

With regard to interritual relations the following directions are laid down: If religious, including the exempt ones, work in places where there is only a rite different from their own or where the number of the faithful of such a rite is so large that this rite is regarded as the only one, the religious depend in all matters concerning their external works on the local bishop or the hierarch of this rite

---

* *Translated by Hilda Graef*
[1] See L. Gutiérrez Martín, "Criteria practica ad rationes inter Episcopos et religiosos componendas", in *Commentarium pro Religiosis* 48 (1967), pp. 19–31; A. Scheuermann, "Die Ausführungsbestimmungen zu den Konzilsweisungen für die Ordensleute", in *Ordenskorrespondenz* 8 (1967), pp. 113–41; J.-M.-R. Tillard, "Relations entre hiérarchie et supérieurs majeurs d'après les directives du Concile Vatican II, in *NRT* 99 (1967), pp. 561–81.
[2] I partly follow the system chosen by A. Scheuermann *(Konzilsweisungen)*.
[3] Cf. H. Hanstein, *Ordensrecht* (2nd ed., 1958).

and are subject to him according to the law (n. 23, § 1). Where, however, there are several local bishops or hierarchs, the religious are bound in the exercise of their service for the faithful of different rites by the norms these bishops and hierarchs have laid down after due consultation (n. 23, § 2).[4]

As regards the activity of religious in the missions their exemption within the legal sphere remains in force; but because of the special circumstances of their service in these places the particular precepts issued or ratified by the Holy See are to be obeyed. These regulate the relations between the local bishop and the religious superior, especially in a mission entrusted to a religious society (n. 24). The co-operation is to be achieved according to the decree *Ad Gentes*.[5]

Since the directions of the motu proprio envisage the apostolic activity of religious in a diocese, it is finally added that the laws governing the works to be done in the dioceses under the direction of the bishop are to be applied also to supradiocesan activities (n. 40). Here it has to be carefully distinguished between supradiocesan tasks in the strict sense and common efforts concerning several dioceses, but which are related to the service of one diocese in such a way that the authority of the individual ordinary cannot be questioned.

II. Hierarchical Co-ordination to the Diocesan Bishop by virtue of Belonging to a Particular Church
(nn. 25, paras. 25, 2a–d, 27, 34)

As described in Article 34, the conventual associations and their members are essentially related to the particular Churches, hence, as A. Scheuermann[6] rightly says, "even before embarking on any spiritual or apostolic activity they are subject to the bishop as the master of public ecclesiastical life by their very existence in the diocese". These are fundamental relations which precede conventual autonomy even if it appears as exemption. The following directions of the motu proprio are relevant to this:

1. Personal Relations (n. 25, para. 2a–d)

The religious are bound by the laws, directions and instructions of the local ordinaries and the episcopal conference in the following personal matters among others:[7]

a) Public use of all social means of communication according to Articles 20 and 21 of the decree *Inter mirifica*.

---

[4] Cf. *CIO,* can. 4, 5, 15, 195, para. 1, n. 4, and *CIO* (law for religious), can. 5, para. 1.
[5] According to Article 30 of this decree all missionaries including the exempt religious are under the jurisdiction of the bishop as regards the works of their sacred apostolate.
[6] A. Scheuermann, *Konzilsweisungen,* p. 129. See also Scheuermann, *Die Exemption,* pp. 126 ff.
[7] It goes without saying that the same applies to the norms laid down by other organs of particular Churches such as plenary and provincial councils.

b) Participation in public entertainments (cf. *CIC*, can. 140).

c) Membership or co-operation regarding societies or associations that should be avoided by order of the local bishop or the episcopal conference.

d) Clerical costume. The directions of canon law (*CIC*, can. 596, and *CIO*, can. 139) remain in force; further, the local bishop or the episcopal conference may forbid the wearing of lay clothes by both secular and regular clergy if it is apt to scandalize the faithful.

2. Collections (n. 27)

After hearing the views of the religious superiors concerned the episcopal conference of any nation may issue instructions concerning collections of money which have to be observed by all religious including those who, because of their constitution, are called mendicants, but with due regard to their rights as laid down in *CIC*, can. 621 (n. 27, § 1). Religious may not publicly organize collections without the consent of the local ordinaries in whose territory such collections are to be made (n. 27, § 2). These instructions contain nothing really new, but there is some progress in that the episcopal conference is enabled to give directions applying to its whole territory.

3. Abolition of religious houses (n. 34)

No religious house belonging to an exempt society can be suppressed without the consent of the Apostolic See and without consultation of the local bishop (n. 34, § 1). The last condition is an addition to the existing law (*CIC*, can. 498). The abolition of a religious house always affects the interests of the diocese. Since according to *CIC*, can. 497, § 1, the written consent of the local bishop is necessary for the erection of an exempt religious house it was only consistent at least to consult him before it is suppressed. In our time the suppression of religious houses is frequently necessary on account of the lack of postulants and it needs tact on both sides. Religious superiors who want to suppress a house or give up an activity for some reason or other ought not to act precipitously; they ought to consider that all religious are bound not only to co-operate in building up the whole mystical body of Christ, but also to promote the well-being of the particular Churches (n. 34, § 2). But if superiors want to give up either houses or activities, especially because of lack of personnel, the local bishop should favourably consider their wish, whether he has to give his consent in the case of non-exempt houses of papal right (cf. *CIC*, can. 498) or has to decide himself in the case of houses of episcopal right (n. 34, § 3).

III. Divine Service of the Religious (nn. 26, 37, 38)

1. General principle

The religious are bound by the laws and instructions of the local bishop according to canon law as regards their churches and their public and semi-public chapels, if the faithful have access to these, but in accordance with their own rite which the community lawfully uses and the order of choir service as well as the liturgical functions belonging to their order.

2. Participation in the pastoral work of the diocese (n. 37)

For all churches as well as for all public and semi-public chapels of the religious which are constantly open to the public the local bishop may prescribe that episcopal publications such as pastoral letters and fasting instructions should be publicly read, that catechetical instructions should take place and that special collections should be made for certain diocesan, national or general purposes and the proceeds faithfully sent to the episcopal curia.

3. Visitation (n. 38)

The right of visitation regarding the churches and chapels of religious, especially of the exempt,[8] has been considerably enlarged. The local ordinary has now the right to make a visitation of the churches as well as of the public and semi-public chapels of the religious, including the exempt, if the faithful have normally access to them. The right of visitation extends to the observance of the general laws and the episcopal directions regarding the divine service. If abuses are noticed, the religious superior will be requested to put an end to them; if he does not do so the local ordinary can correct them on his own authority. This extension of the visitation right is based on the fact that the bishop may direct the liturgy in his particular church in accordance with canon law.[9]

IV. The Apostolate of the Religious (nn. 25, § 1, 28–33, 35, 36, 39)

1. Principles of the relation between the diocesan bishop and the religious (nn. 25, § 1, 32, 39, § 2)

a) Fundamental rule (n. 25, § 1)

All religious including the exempt are bound to observe the laws, directions and instructions issued by the local ordinary regarding the various works which concern the exercise of the apostolate and a pastoral or social activity prescribed

[8] Cf. *CIC,* can. 615, 1171, 1261, para. 2. See Scheuermann, *Die Exemption,* pp. 107 f.
[9] See the Constitution on the Sacred Liturgy, *Sacrosanctum Concilium,* Article 22, para. 1, and the decree *Christus Dominus,* Article 15.

or recommended by him. This describes the whole sphere of activities beyond the divine service of the religious. The distinction between the apostolate and the pastoral and social activities prescribed or recommended should probably be understood as meaning that *sacri apostolatus exercitium* compromises every extra-liturgical activity requiring ecclesiastical jurisdiction, that is mainly pastoral work.

b) Visitation right (n. 39, § 2)

The local ordinary may inspect either himself or cause someone else to inspect, according to canon law, all schools and other educational institutions, nursing homes, children's homes, hospitals, orphanages and similar institutes of religious devoted to the worship of God or the corporal and spiritual works of mercy; the only exceptions are schools of religious orders attended only by the alumni of the order (n. 39, § 2). Strangely enough, this rule about the local ordinary's right of inspection follows that on the direction of Catholic schools; it embraces every institutional activity of religious, but there is no mention of the matters to which this right refers. These will probably be the same as in the present canon law.[10]

c) Dismissal of religious (n. 32)

A religious entrusted with an office or any service by an external authority is responsible to this authority for the faithful discharge of this duty but as a religious remains subject to his superior. In order to guarantee the necessary security to both sides the motu proprio lays down that every religious may freely be relieved of his office for a serious reason, both by the authority who has entrusted the duty to him and by his religious superior; in both cases the other authority has to be notified, though both have the same right to order the dismissal and do not need each other's assent. Neither need communicate the reason for his decision to the other let alone produce evidence for it. The possibility of lodging a complaint with the Holy See will not delay the carrying out of the decision.

2. General Remarks on the Works of the Apostolate
(nn. 28–31, 36)

a) The activities proper to a religious community to take first place
(nn. 28, 29, § 1)

The religious are to pursue zealously the activities proper to their society, that is to say those which, with the approval of the Apostolic See, have been laid down

---

[10] Cf. K. Mörsdorf, "Religiosis concredere", in *AKK* 123 (1948), pp. 60 ff.; id., *Kirchenrecht*, II, pp. 488 ff.

and regulated in their constitutions or other ordinances either when they were founded or by venerable traditions. The spiritual needs of the diocese are to be particularly considered, and brotherly harmony is to be preserved with the diocesan clergy and with other societies devoted to similar works (n. 28). Particular or special works carried out in the houses of the society including rented ones depend on the religious superiors directing these works according to their constitutions. But such works, too, are under the jurisdiction of the local bishop according to canon law (n. 29, § 1).

b) Apostolic works conferred by the bishop (nn. 29, §§ 2, 36)

The Council was most anxious that religious should be employed more than before in the apostolic works of the diocese. Leaving aside the purely contemplative communities, the special activities of a religious society do not make it impossible for the diocesan to enlist the help not only of regular priests but also of other members, whether men or women, while taking account of the character of each society and with the consent of the competent religious superior. This will be done especially in the case of urgent pastoral needs and when there is a lack of secular clergy, when religious can give effective assistance to the dioceses or ecclesiastical regions (n. 36, § 1). At the request of the local bishop the religious superiors are to grant this assistance wherever the former regards it as necessary or very useful for the manifold apostolic, charitable and pastoral works of the secular parishes or diocesan associations (n. 36, § 2). All activities, whether those proper to a religious society or those conferred by the local bishop are subject to the latter's jurisdiction and authority without prejudice to the right of the religious superiors to supervise the lives of their subjects and, together with the bishop, their duties laid upon them (n. 29, § 2).

aa) Those entrusted to a religious society (n. 30)

When the local bishop confers a work of the apostolate on a religious community in accordance with what is otherwise laid down by canon law, a contract must be drawn up in writing between him and the competent religious superior. All matters referring to the work in question, the religious to be assigned to it, and finance must be clarified in the contract (n. 30, § 1). Religious who are really suitable for the work are to be selected by the superior after consultation with the bishop. In the case of an ecclesiastical office they are to be appointed by the latter at the suggestion or at least with the consent of their own superior and for a certain period to be agreed upon by both parties (n. 30, § 2).

bb) Those entrusted to individual religious

If a bishop or an episcopal conference entrusts a religious with a special duty, this has to be done by written contract and with the consent of the religious superior (n. 31). The contract has to be drawn up between the competent superior and the authority wanting to employ the religious.

3. Special ways in which religious exercise the apostolate (nn. 33, 35, 39, § 1)

a) Parishes

The *CIC* mentions only two connections between a religious house and a parish; these are the cases of partial or whole incorporation mentioned in the law of benefices (can. 1425).[11] In recent times a new form has developed, especially in the large cities. This is the so-called simple entrustment by which a religious community is entrusted with a parish either permanently or for a certain time without any financial changes.[12] The following directions are given for such cases: With the consent of the competent religious superior the local bishop may, on his own authority, entrust a religious association with a parish; in this case a conventual church of the same order or congregation may also become a parish church. Whether this is done permanently or for a certain period, in both cases a contract must be drawn up in writing between the local bishop and the competent religious superior. This contract must carefully lay down whatever concerns the duties, the persons to be entrusted with them and the financial conditions (n. 33, § 1). With the permission of the superior a bishop may also appoint a religious parish priest of a parish not entrusted to a religious society, in which case there is also to be a contract between the bishop and the superior (n. 33, § 2).

b) Ecclesiastical societies (n. 35)

Ecclesiastical societies directed by a religious are subject to the diocesan bishop, even if they have been erected by the Apostolic See. The ordinary has the right and duty to do this in accordance with canon law (can. 690), so that the limitations with regard to those associations which exempt religious bodies have erected within their confines in virtue of apostolic privilege remain in force. If associations devote themselves to apostolic works or the promotion of divine service they must obey the relevant precepts of the ordinary or the episcopal conference.

c) Catholic schools (n. 39, § 1)

The apostolic work of the religious is especially concerned with schools. The Council took a great interest in co-ordinating all the work done in this field.

---

[11] Cf. *ibid.*, pp. 452 ff.

[12] In the legal terminology of the *CIC* the phrase *paroecia religiosis concredita* does not only mean the parish entrusted to them (can. 456) but also that which is totally incorporated (can. 472, n. 2) and that which is totally or half incorporated (can. 475, para. 1). Cf. K. Mörsdorf, *Religiosis concredere*, pp. 56 ff.

Referring to Article 35, n. 4, of the decree *Christus Dominus,* the motu proprio states that all Catholic schools should be suitably distributed within the diocese and should co-operate with one another. Catholic schools are just as capable as others to realize cultural and social aims. The right of the religious to direct their schools remains intact; but the directions given in Article 35, n. 5, of the decree about mutual consultations between the bishops and religious superiors are to be obeyed. No difference is made between schools belonging to religious orders and those entrusted to them. Nevertheless, this distinction is still important for the local bishop's right of supervision.

Concerning the Co-operation of Bishops for the Common Good of Many Churches*

The Title. Having dealt with the episcopal office in its relation to the whole Church in Chapter I and to the local Church in Chapter II, the decree now turns in Chapter III to those tasks in which the bishops[1] co-operate for the good of several particular Churches. The heading is so comprehensive that the chapter might be expected to cover the whole field of mutual relations between bishops or local Churches. Here the Council has limited itself considerably, probably because it only wanted to deal with some particularly important questions.[2] Hence the division of this chapter into three sections, a division which is not necessitated by the subject matter; the chapter simply discusses three points belonging to its theme.

Section I is concerned with the synodal element in the diocesan constitution of the Church. Both in the title of the section and in Article 36 the terms *synodus* and *concilium* are used side by side. This does not imply a difference in meaning but only the use of both Eastern and Western terminology.[3] There is, however, more than a shift of emphasis as regards the synodal element in the present decree if compared with its place in the *CIC* or in the *CIO*.[4] In the *CIC* and in the *CIO* patriarchs and metropolitans with their respective synods are regarded as sharing in the supreme power in accordance with ecclesiastical law, with the

---

* *Translated by Hilda Graef*

[1] It should be noted that *Episcopus* in the title is not to be understood in the narrow sense of diocesan bishop, but includes also those who share in the episcopal office through their consecration (titular bishops) or through their office (priests in similar positions to bishops).

[2] Several such themes had been mentioned in the constitution on the Church; cf. *Lumen Gentium*, Article 23, para. 4 (*relationes* to the missions, the neighbouring and the needier Churches) and para. 5 (Churches of Eastern and Western rites). Here, however, these tasks are seen as evolving from the collegiality of the bishops, hence under the aspect of the whole Church; they have therefore been treated in Chapter I of the present decree (cf. comments on Articles 6 and 7).

[3] Cf. W. Aymans, *Das synodale Element in der Kirchenverfassung*, pp. 18 ff.

[4] Motu proprio *Cleri Sanctitati* of 2 June 1957: *AAS* 49 (1957), pp. 433–603.

remark that what is involved here is participation by virtue of divine law.[5] Now even though the episcopal grades derive from ecclesiastical authority, nevertheless the office itself does not lose its foundation in divine right owing to the divine institution of the episcopate.[6] As the title of Chapter III makes clear, the synodal element in the sphere of the particular Churches is not a participation in the supreme power, but only a special form of the co-operation of the bishops for the common good of several Churches, even though the competence and thus the authority of the synods is not the sum of the authority of the bishops participating but an authority *sui generis*. This is a considerable gain for the understanding of the Church's constitution. On the one hand this conception does justice to the history of the synods of particular Churches, which originated in the spontaneous need of the bishops to tackle their common problems together,[7] on the other it corresponds to the ideas of the Council. This had limited the collegiality of the bishops materially to the sphere of the whole Church[8] and thus to the supreme power, hence it had strictly separated the supreme power from the power of particular Churches, but without formally denying the collegiality of the bishops in the sphere of particular Churches.[9] Thus the synodal element appears clearly as derived from the episcopal power and is not to be misunderstood as deriving from the primatial power. This, however, does not exclude that in future, too, the Pope reserves to himself the examination of synodal decisions of particular Churches; but it is evident that the papal co-operation as such does not change the legal character of such decisions into papal laws.[10]

Articles 36–38 say but little on the synods or councils. These are, as it were, only the external framework for the episcopal conference, which is not legally a council, but must nevertheless be counted as a synodal element of the Church and its modern expression on the diocesan plane.[11]

---

[5] See the heading of *CIC,* book II, title VII (= *CIO,* title IV, pars I): "De suprema potestate deque iis qui eiusdem sunt ecclesiastico (canonico) iure participes".

[6] Cf. K. Mörsdorf, "Bishop IV (Canon Law)", in *Sacramentum Mundi,* I (1968).

[7] Cf. F. J. Murphy, *Legislative Powers of the Provincial Council* (1947); E. O. Poblete, *The Plenary Council* (1958); H. Jedin, *Kleine Konziliengeschichte* (1959), pp. 11 ff.; E. Corecco, *La formazione della Chiesa negli Stati Uniti d'America attraverso l'attività sinodale con particolare riguardo al problema dell'amministrazione dei beni ecclesiastici* (canonical thesis, Munich, 1962; not yet published); K. Mörsdorf, "Die hierarchische Verfassung der Kirche, insbesondere der Episkopat", in *AKK* 134 (1965), pp. 91 f.

[8] Cf. constitution *Lumen Gentium,* Artikle 22, para. 2; on this W. Aymans, *Das synodale Element in der Kirchenverfassung,* pp. 289–300.

[9] Cf. constitution *Lumen Gentium,* Article 23: "Collegialis unio etiam in mutuis relationibus singulorum Episcoporum cum particularibus Ecclesiis . . . apparet" (cf. note 8).

[10] The papal supervision is a measure needed for the sake of the unity of the Church. Cf. K. Mörsdorf, *Kirchenrecht,* I, p. 388; H. Eisenhofer, *Die kirchlichen Gesetzgeber, Technik und Form ihrer Gesetzgebung* (1954), pp. 21–25; H. Schmitz, "Erwägungen zur Gesetzgebungstechnik der Bischofskonferenzen", in *Trierer Theologische Zeitschrift* 73 (1964), pp. 285–301.

[11] Cf. K. Mörsdorf, "Das synodale Element der Kirchenverfassung", in *Volk Gottes,* p. 570.

Article 36 treats of the synods of particular Churches. It states that diocesan synods grew from below,[12] from the sense of communion based on the common mission of the apostles through Jesus Christ. Thus synods were not arbitrarily established, but followed from the communion that is of the essence of the Church. The idea of purpose had been too much neglected in the presentation of episcopal collegiality in the constitution on the Church,[13] but was now clearly set forth. Since the purpose of synods is seen in the context of *communio,* they cannot be misrepresented as being without a theological basis and merely serving a practical end. Thus the proper balance is maintained for the theological and legal evaluation of the synodal element in the constitution of the Church.[14] The article is drawn up on rather general lines, but it is significant that not only the common good but also that of the individual Churches is mentioned. This does not go without saying but it is a statement about the union of Churches manifesting itself in each synod and thus about the synod itself. Even though this is an entity in its own right, different from the members which constitute it, its only basis is nevertheless the particular Churches; hence it shares in the statement which is fundamental for the Council's understanding of the Church, namely that the one and only Catholic Church consists in and of the particular Churches.[15] This deserves the greatest attention when legislating for synodal membership and voting rights.

In para. 1 of Article 36 the manifold synodal forms of the Eastern Churches are summarized under the one term *synodi,* while the forms of the Western Church are called provincial councils and plenary councils. The idea of purpose is here given the form of a statement on the function of these ecclesiastical assemblies and referred to the pastoral and teaching office.[16] These are the episcopal functions accessible to collegial action.[17] A collegial association can only have

---

[12] Cf. especially the word *consociaverunt.*

[13] Cf. K. Mörsdorf, "Das synodale Element der Kirchenverfassung", in *Volk Gottes,* pp. 580f; id., "Primat und Kollegialität", in H. Gering, ed., *Über das bischöfliche Amt* (1966), pp. 45f.

[14] Cf. W. Aymans, *Das synodale Element in der Kirchenverfassung,* ch. VI.

[15] Cf. constitution *Lumen Gentium,* Article 23, para. 1.

[16] This resembles the corresponding dogmatic statement on the episcopal college of which the constitution *Lumen Gentium* (Article 22, para. 3) says that it "is the successor to the college of the apostles in teaching authority and pastoral rule" (cf. also Article 3, 1, of our decree). In Article 20, para. 4, of the same constitution it is stated "that by divine institution bishops have succeeded to the place of the apostles as shepherds of the Church". Here, as elsewhere (see comment on Article 2) the word "pastor" is used in a sense combining the teaching, the priestly and the pastoral offices. While the individual bishop participates in all three "offices" (cf. *Lumen Gentium,* Article 21, 2) the college of bishops is restricted to the doctrinal and the pastoral offices. It is also to be noted that the college as such cannot do all that is to be done within these two offices.

[17] Cf. W. Aymans, *Kollegium und kollegialer Akt*; id., *Das synodale Element in der Kirchenverfassung,* pp. 293–6, 380ff. As far as the exercise of sacred power is concerned, only the pastoral functions can here be directly involved. Thus the three offices of Christ and the Church cannot be ascribed to the sacred power in such a way that the office of sanctification is exclusively attributed to the consecrating and those of teaching and direction to the pastoral power (cf. above note 17 on

those rights and duties compatible with its nature; this excludes all those which necessarily presuppose the natural characteristics of man. In contrast to the physical person who can be the bearer of all rights and duties a council, whether it is a juridical person or not, is limited, so that it cannot completely represent the invisible Lord as the hierarchical structure of the new people of God demands.[18] On the other hand the council has that advantage over a natural person that it is subject to natural death and thus can effectively serve the community in those matters which need constant care regardless of changing personalities.

It has sometimes been argued that the diocesan synods are superseded by the new episcopal conference, at least in the Latin Church, and hence should be abolished.[19] But this is opposed to the desire of the Council, expressed in para. 2, that synodal institutions should flourish with new vigour. The history of diocesan synods in the Latin Church is not encouraging;[20] nevertheless their suppression should not be demanded too hastily. It is no exaggeration to say that a new situation has been created by the doctrine of the collegiality of the bishops implying the *communio Ecclesiarum* which has at long last been resurrected. Thus ancient ecclesiastical heritage has once more come to light, calling for juridical evaluation. Even a synodal institution that has been on its deathbed for centuries can be no telling argument against this new consciousness of the Church. But apart from the desire of the Council, other considerations, too, favour the preservation of these synods.[21] The synods of particular Churches have general legislative and other legal powers in their territories, whereas the episcopal conference has so far been given only particular powers of this kind. True, these individual faculties have now become very numerous and it may perhaps be expected that the episcopal conference will receive a general competence in the near future, yet the more solemn synod has certain advantages. For the episcopal conference meets normally several times a year and is in danger of succumbing to routine, because it has to deal with topical questions and a large

ch. I). Sacramental absolution for example can certainly be given collegially and thus synodally, though it is to be classed as belonging to the office of sanctification. But it is not exclusively an act of the consecrating office, but one in which the consecrating and the pastoral powers closely co-operate; cf. K. Mörsdorf, *Kirchenrecht*, II, pp. 62 ff.; id., "Weihe- und Hirtengewalt in Abgrenzung und Bezug", in *Miscelánea Comillas* 16 (1951), pp. 96 ff.; id., "Primat undKollegialität nach dem Konzil", *loc. cit.*, p. 43.

[18] K. Mörsdorf, "Über die Zuordnung des Kollegialitätsprinzips zu dem Prinzip der Einheit von Haupt und Leib in der hierarchischen Struktur der Kirchenverfassung", in *Wahrheit und Verkündigung. Festschrift für M. Schmaus* (1967), pp. 1435–45.

[19] Cf., for example, A. Gommenginger, "Verfassung und Strukturen in einem neuen Kirchenrecht", in *Orientierung* 31 (1967), p. 27.

[20] In the years between the Council of Trent and the publication of the *CIC*, apart from 13 plenary and national councils *c.* 200 provincial councils have been held, which is *c.* two per cent of the provincial councils which ought to have been held according to the law; cf. E. Corecco, *op. cit.;* K. Mörsdorf, "Das synodale Element in der Kirchenverfassung", *loc. cit.*, pp. 568 f.

[21] W. Aymans, *Das synodale Element in der Kirchenverfassung*, pp. 59–61, 88–90.

variety of subjects. The synod, on the other hand, meets at rather long intervals; it needs comprehensive preparation and offers an opportunity for more intensive discussion. Even according to the present canon law the synods of particular Churches have a larger membership, and according to the future law they will more fully represent the people of God in their territory through their advisory members, perhaps after the pattern of the pastoral council, and will thus be able to exercise an important influence on the life and work of the Church. Thus it seems indicated to create also a regional council beside the provincial and plenary councils, which would be responsible for the *regio ecclesiastica,* that is to say, the territory of an episcopal council (see comment on Article 40, n. 3). The plenary council would then be responsible for the sphere beyond the territory of an episcopal council. The revival of the provincial council will largely depend on the future importance of metropolitans. All these questions will have to be decided during the reform of the *CIC.*

Articles 37 and 38 deal with the episcopal conference, which is the real subject of the first part of Chapter III. Without this being actually mentioned, the relevant provisional instructions about the episcopal conference are replaced.[22] These instructions had been issued on the basis of the constitution on the liturgy[23] (Article 22, para. 2) by the motu proprio *Sacram Liturgiam* of 25 January 1964[24] and the subsequent instruction of the congregation of rites of 26 September 1964.[25] These had replaced can. 292 of the *CIC* and defined in greater detail the competences assigned to the episcopal conferences as the territorial authority; but the directions were at once designated as temporary (interim).[26] All these directions are a legal interpretation of the last sentence of Article 23, para. 4, of the constitution *Lumen Gentium,* even though this is rather jejune from the juridical point of view.[27]

Article 37 contains some general remarks preceding the directions to follow rather in the manner of a motivation of a law such as introduces papal laws.[28]

The first sentence explains the necessity of an ever closer co-operation between

[22] Cf. *ibid.,* pp. 6f.

[23] Constitution *Sacrosanctum Concilium* of 4 December 1963: *AAS* 56 (1964), pp. 97–138.

[24] *AAS* 56 (1964), pp. 139–44.

[25] *AAS* 56 (1964), pp. 877–900.

[26] Motu proprio *Sacram Liturgiam,* n. X, instructio nn. 23f.

[27] Constitution *Lumen Gentium,* Article 23, para. 6, final sentence: "In like manner the episcopal bodies of today are in a position to render a manifold and fruitful assistance, so that this collegiate sense may be put into practical application." The term *collegialis affectus* does much less than justice to the nature of the episcopal conference as defined in the present decree, in contrast to the conception of the *CIC.* It goes without saying that the episcopal conference must have "collegial sense"; this was the characteristic of the original conferences, without which they could not have existed at all. The decisive step forward is this, that the collegial sense is no longer left to itself, as it were, but has been legally defined and thus transformed the episcopal conference into a hierarchical institution. Cf. commentary on Article 38, 4.

[28] This is evident from para. 2 of this article, which is an introduction to Article 38 rather than a conclusion of Article 37.

the bishops, especially nowadays.[29] It deserves attention that this co-operation is required in order that bishops may "fulfil their office suitably and fruitfully"; moreover, the ecclesiastical region is not considered by itself but in essential union with the particular Churches which constitute it.

The usefulness of episcopal conferences is proved by the fruitful apostolate of the existing ones, hence the Council desires emphatically that they should be established in every nation or region. This is the decisive statement of Article 37; apart from the provisional directions (according to the Constitution on the Liturgy) mentioned above, the national episcopal conference is here legally recognized for the first time.[30] A region may here mean a territory that is both smaller or larger than that of a nation. The legal recognition of the national episcopal conference is a clear example of how the legitimate custom[31] of a particular Church may become the common practice of the Church. National episcopal conferences have been in existence since the middle of the 19th century;[32] these have developed in different ways,[33] and the modern Church cannot be imagined without them; nevertheless the *CIC* did not take notice of this development and only provides for episcopal conferences within an ecclesiastical province. It should not, however, be overlooked that as early as the end of the 19th century Pope Leo XIII and later also Pius XI have approved of the work of the larger, national or international episcopal conferences.[34]

Article 38 provides the legal framework for the new episcopal conference.[35] Apart from a description the most important principles governing their establishment and activities are laid down in six subdivisions, the first five of which form a unity, while n. 6 deals with the special case of an inter-ritual conference.

N. 1 is meant to be no more than a *notio* or brief description of the episcopal conference. Here the term *antistes* is used, which is rare in present legal ter-

---

[29] A note attached to the *Textus recognitus* (1965), p. 111, a. 1, mentions especially those questions which concern a whole nation, e.g., schools, administration, the responsible use of civil rights *et his similia*; besides, public statements might sometimes be necessary, which would carry greater weight if they were made in the name of all the bishops.

[30] The directions of the motu proprio *Ecclesiae Sanctae*, I, n. 41, para. 1, lay down that the bishops of nations or territories in which an episcopal conference does not yet exist must establish one as soon as possible and draw up statutes to be examined by the Apostolic See. The immediate establishment of episcopal conferences does not, however, refer to Article 38, as stated in the title, but to Article 37.

[31] Cf. K. Mörsdorf, *Kirchenrecht*, I, p. 390; F. Houtart, "Les formes modernes de la collégialité épiscopale", in *L'Épiscopat et l'Église universelle* (1962), p. 503.

[32] On the history of the episcopal conferences cf. P. Leisching, *Die Bischofskonferenz. Beiträge zu ihrer Rechtsgeschichte mit besonderer Berücksichtigung ihrer Entwicklung in Österreich* (1963); R. Lill, *Die ersten deutschen Bischofskonferenzen* (1964).

[33] Cf. Houtart, *op. cit.,* pp. 497–535; R. Hoffmann, "International Episcopal Co-operation", in *Jurist* 23 (1963), pp. 1–33; P. Leisching, "Der Rechtscharakter der Bischofskonferenz", in *Österreichisches Archiv für Kirchenrecht* 16 (1965), pp. 162–82.

[34] *Ibid.*, pp. 162 ff.

[35] Cf. the commentary on the title of the decree.

minology. It meant originally the head of a particular Church[36] and points to the fact that not only bishops belong to the episcopal conference, but also other pastors who, though not consecrated bishops, yet hold a pastoral position equal to that of the diocesan.

As regards the territorial definition[37] of episcopal conferences this passage only takes up the alternative solution suggested in Article 37, but replaces "region" by the equally indeterminate "territory". This again leaves open the two possibilities of welding both smaller and larger territories than national units into one conference. The present decree does not legislate for national conferences, whereas a special number (5) is devoted to international conferences.[38] National and international conferences are governed by different laws (see commentary on n. 3), hence there are two basic types of episcopal conferences. This is important especially because the motu proprio *Ecclesiae Sanctae*, I, n. 41, provides for an enlargement of the episcopal conference beyond the frontiers of a nation without changing its character of a national conference. It says there (para. 3): "The bishops of a nation in which it is difficult to establish a conference, after consulting the Apostolic See, should join that conference whose apostolic needs most closely resemble those of their own nation."[39]

It cannot be doubted that the bishops are to exercise their pastoral office in the episcopal conference *coniunctim*, but this word does not express the characteristics of this exercise of authority. The reason why the Council has here avoided the only appropriate term *collegialiter exercent* seems to be that the majority of the Fathers did not approve of the principle of collegiality for the particular Churches.[40] Nevertheless, the principle of collegiality has been accepted as a formal structural principle (see commentary on n. 4). In the rulings on the right of membership it has become clear why the word *coniunctim* was chosen instead of *collegialiter* (see explanation of n. 2). When considering the formation of the new episcopal conference the Council Fathers laid more stress on its purpose, as is clear from the second part of n. 1, than when they deliberated on the episcopal college which exercised its supreme power practically only in the rare ecumenical councils.[41] Hence the law of membership seems to be

---

[36] *Antistes* corresponds to the Greek προεστώς. In the phrase "sacrorum Antistites" the term is used in the bull of promulgation of the *CIC*, the constitution *Providentissima Mater Ecclesia* of 27 May 1917 (para. 4) for the local bishops. The *CIC* has *Antistita* for the superior of any women's convent (cf. K. Mörsdorf, *Rechtssprache,* pp. 172f., 174). In the Liturgy *antistes* has remained in frequent use (cf. A. Pflieger, *Liturgicae orationis concordantia verbalia,* I [1964], p. 34).

[37] Cf. W. Aymans, "Ritusgebundenheit und territoriale Abgrenzung der Bischofskonferenzen", in *AKK* 135 (1966), pp. 550–2.

[38] On the interrelation of the various possibilities of territorial organization see under n. 5.

[39] If the said bishops attach themselves to an international conference, this will have in any case no importance for the character of the conference.

[40] Cf. K. Mörsdorf, "Primat und Kollegialität nach dem Konzil", *loc. cit.,* p. 47; id., "Das synodale Element der Kirchenverfassung", *loc. cit.,* p. 581.

[41] Cf. *ibid.,* pp. 580f.

influenced by practical rather than by dogmatic considerations, though just the latter point to the right understanding of the principle of collegiality.

N. 2 lays down the necessary legal norms for the right of membership,[42] para. 2 dealing with deliberative and consultative votes.

According to para. 1 *de iure* members are distinguished from others. The former are those to whom membership belongs by law. Ordinary members of the episcopal conference in this sense are, apart from the local ordinaries[43] of whatever rite — with the exception of the vicars general — bishops, co-adjutors, the auxiliary and other titular bishops holding a special mandate from the Apostolic See or from the episcopal conference. The inclusion of bishops who are not local ordinaries shows that the fact that all bishops belong to the episcopal college (see constitution *Lumen Gentium*, Article 22, para. 1) has had its effect on the membership of the episcopal conference, and thus the new esteem of the Council for all consecrated bishops[44] becomes evident. Nevertheless the episcopal commission has occasionally expressed the opinion that membership of the episcopal conference is not analogous to the rights of episcopal collegiality;[45] this is shown particularly by the fact that not all the titular bishops of the territory belong to the conference by right. It is a strictly observed rule that the condition of membership is not merely consecration, but a specific share in the pastoral office of the relevant district. Hence retired local bishops or those who merely reside in the territory of the conference may attend it only as extraordinary members. But even the duties of apostolic nuncios or legates are of a special character, [46] so that in 1965 the alteration proposed by 151 Fathers was finally accepted, according to which these titular bishops, too, were not to be ordinary members of the conferences.[47]

Now just as there are bishops who share so little in the pastoral work of the conference territory that they are refused membership without prejudice to their episcopal dignity, so the others, too, do not all share equally in the pastoral office but in various degrees, and this, too, is expressed in the law of membership. Hence not all ordinary members are given the vote. According to para. 2 only "local ordinaries and coadjutors hold a deliberative vote", the latter probably because they share in the principal responsibility for the particular Church. A proposal according to which every particular Church would only have one vote, hence either the bishop's or the coadjutor's, was refused by the commission on the grounds that the vote is *personale, non autem nomine diocesis seu collegiale*.[48] This

---

[42] Cf. W. Aymans, *Das synodale Element in der Kirchenverfassung*, pp. 46–58.

[43] Cf. *CIC*, can. 198.

[44] W. Aymans, *Das synodale Element in der Kirchenverfassung*, p. 52.

[45] *Modi Ep*, ch. III, *modus* 12.

[46] *Singularis* cannot here mean "excellent", because in this case the sentence could not give the reason *(ob)* but would rather have to be introduced with "though" *(quamquam)*.

[47] Cf. *Modi Ep*, ch. III, *modus* 17.

[48] *Modi Ep*, ch. III, *modus* 9.

reply is hardly satisfactory, for the distribution of rights is very important within the framework of collegial organization.[49] For the same reason all auxiliary bishops might have been given the vote. It is not very clear what the commission meant by a collegial as opposed to a personal vote; as regards the other reason it must certainly be admitted that the bishop does not appear in the name of his diocese; but this does not alter the fact that he represents it. As a consequence of the present ruling those particular Churches which are not in their normal state carry greater weight in the episcopal conference than the others.

All other ordinary members may be accorded the vote "as the statutes of the conference determine". But according to canon law this is always an extra-ordinary vote, since the statutes can only be determined by the votes of those members enjoying the ordinary vote and much scope is left in this matter between the two extremes of granting the vote to, or withholding it from, all the titular bishops in question. Many variations are possible under material and formal law. A material definition of the vote[50] always includes the difficulties of interpretation and thus uncertainty of the law, whereas from the point of view of formal law all possibilities may be left open if the statutes determine: "Decisions on the vote are made from one session to the other (or from one subject to the other)."[51] Hence in every case the question of the vote has to be decided by particular law, hence a clarification in principle is not to be expected.[52] Nevertheless, the ordinary right of membership of the titular bishops should not be underestimated, for deliberation in common is of the greatest importance for forming the collegial will.[53]

The present law of membership, however, raises one fundamental question which is not sufficiently answered either by the council decree or by the motu proprio. This is the question of whether the episcopal conference is restricted to one rite or not.[54] Now the episcopal conference is in the first place meant to be a synodal institution of the Latin Church, though this does not exclude such conferences from the sphere of the Oriental Churches.[55] While in the constitution of the Eastern Churches the collegial element has always been active in their synods, it had been moribund in the West and made a new start only in the episcopal conferences. These have now developed into a hierarchical

---

[49] Cf. W. Aymans, *Kollegium und kollegialer Akt*, cf. p. 114.

[50] If the relevant statute would say, for example: "In all questions of a pastoral nature all members of the Conference have the vote."

[51] It would also be such a formal rule if it said: "All ordinary members are granted the vote, unless the members having the ordinary vote decide with a majority to reserve the vote."

[52] Cf. K. Mörsdorf, "Das synodale Element der Kirchenverfassung", *loc. cit.*, p. 582.

[53] Cf. W. Aymans, *Kollegium und kollegialer Akt;* id., *Das synodale Element in der Kirchenverfassung,* pp. 301–28.

[54] On this question see W. Aymans, "Ritusgebundenheit und territoriale Abgrenzung der Bischofskonferenz", in *AKK* 135 (1966), pp. 543–9.

[55] Cf. also explanation of n. 6.

institution and thus been given the chance for extensive legal activity. The frequent equation between patriarchal synods and episcopal conferences in post-conciliar legislation points to the same tendency.[56] This, together with the special interritual advisory conference mentioned in n. 6, clearly establishes the fact that the episcopal conference as a hierarchical body can only be of one rite; this, by the way, is also required by the undisputed legal autonomy of the rites.

It is all the more surprising that in n. 2, para. 1, *Ordinarii locorum cuiuscumque ritus* should be mentioned and be called ordinary members of the episcopal conference. This means that also bishops of minority rites who reside or exercise their pastoral office within the territory of a conference are to be members of the episcopal conference of the principal rite.[57] Now though interritual conferences are in principle only of consultative character,[58] as regards n. 2 it must be stated that the mere addition of rites to a conference basically of one rite does not make it an interritual and thus a merely consultative one, just as a merely territorial enlargement of a conference beyond the national frontiers does not turn a national into an international conference.[59] Otherwise the second paragraph of the same number could not mention the vote.

This well-meant ruling is founded on the principle of the equality of all rites in the Church[60] which was also strongly emphasized by the Second Vatican Council. Nevertheless it cannot be approved, for in practice it threatens to have exactly the opposite effect of what had been intended. For owing to the collegial organization of the episcopal conference there is the serious danger that the bishops of a minority rite may be in the majority.[61] In such a case the profitable co-existence and co-operation of the rites seems guaranteed only if the bishops of minority rites are merely given hospitality at the episcopal conferences, so that on the one hand they may have the chance to inform and adapt themselves, and on the other to express their own views. Moreover, this will also make it possible for them to preserve their own rite in districts belonging to another and to develop it faithfully within the community of the Church.

N. 3 treats of drafting the statutes for each episcopal conference, at the same time expressing a wish that is to be considered in drawing up the statutes.

The directions laid down in the motu proprio have qualified the introductory

---

[56] Motu proprio *Ecclesiae Sanctae,* I, nn. 2, 5, 8, paras. 1, 43.
[57] This will normally apply to Oriental bishops appointed for the faithful of their own rite in territories of mostly Latin rite.
[58] Cf. commentary on n. 6.
[59] Cf. commentary on n. 1.
[60] Cf., for example, the Decree on Eastern Catholic Churches, Articles 2 and 3.
[61] Certainly this danger does not only exist in the particular Churches, but also in the synodal institutions of the universal Church in which the rites are not always equally balanced; but the *sensus communis* would rather be an efficacious antidote to majorizing tendencies. The nature of particular laws contains endless occasions for interritual tensions and can lead to too many frictions in deciding topical questions.

general request to the bishops' conferences *(quaelibet Conferentia Episcoporum)* to give themselves statutes to be reviewed by the Apostolic See. It is the duty of the bishops of a nation or a smaller territory where episcopal conferences do not yet exist to establish them as soon as possible and to draw up statutes which are to be examined by the Apostolic See.[62] Existing episcopal conferences which do not yet have statutes must draw these up in accordance with the views of the Council and submit them to the Apostolic See.[63] Episcopal conferences of several nations, called international episcopal conferences can only be established with the approval of the Apostolic See; in this case the special norms, which can only mean the statutes, are to be given by the Apostolic See.[64]

These regulations are generally clear; doubts might only arise in the case of existing international conferences. For these must strictly speaking be counted among the *conferentiae episcopales iam constitutae* and hence be treated according to the motu proprio *Ecclesiae Sanctae*, I, n. 41, para. 2. But this strict interpretation would seem to be against the mind of the lawgiver. For it would be unintelligible why episcopal conferences of the same kind should be subject to basically different laws in such an essential point. According to the mind of the lawgiver the Apostolic See should have a greater influence in the more important international matters. This tendency is noticeable also in n. 5 (motu proprio *Ecclesiae Sanctae*, I, n. 41) according to which the Apostolic See is to be informed when episcopal conferences want to combine for the purpose of common international actions or relations.[65]

To sum up, the episcopal conferences of nations or smaller territories are to draw up statutes which have to be approved by the Apostolic See; in the case of international conferences the statutes are drawn up by the Apostolic See.[66]

---

[62] Motu proprio *Ecclesiae Sanctae*, I, n. 41, para. 1. The phrase *Episcopi territoriorum* here used is to be understood only in the sense given above. Though *territorium* is in itself an indefinite term and may be used of large as well as of small parts of a nation, here only the smaller can be meant, because para. 4 gives a special direction for larger territories.

[63] Ibid., para. 2.

[64] Ibid., para. 4.

[65] "Quoties autem actiones aut rationes a Conferentiis ineuntur formam internationalem praeseferentes, Sancta Sedes praemoneatur oportet." The interpretation of the term *rationes* is difficult. It is understandable that international actions of episcopal conferences are to be subject to the Apostolic See. But it can hardly be understood that all international relations such as are elaborated in para. 5 should be subject to the same supervision, especially as it is not a matter of sending copies of documents etc., but only of informing the Holy See in advance of the fact of such relations. So as not to make international relations and close contacts between the episcopal conferences unnecessarily difficult, the words *aut rationes* should be suppressed in the reform of the *CIC* without putting anything else in their place.

[66] The view that all international conferences without exception are treated in the motu proprio *Ecclesiae Sanctae*, I, n. 41, para. 4, is supported also because of the systematic treatment of paras. 1–4: paras. 1 and 2 deal with national or smaller conferences, para. 3 with enlarged national or smaller conferences, and para. 4 with international conferences.

Article 38, n. 3, suggests several means the better to assure the continued efficiency of the conference. Though no minimum is laid down for the number of meetings, the mention of a permanent board of bishops, episcopal commissions and a general secretariat makes it clear that the Council did not want to see the work of the episcopal conferences restricted to rare occasions. In this they differ from the traditional councils and synods which were mainly concerned with legislation.[67] Thus the episcopal conferences will become truly efficient intermediary institutions between the individual bishops and the Apostolic See.

N. 4 is at the centre of the new legislation on the episcopal conference.

The episcopal conference may make decisions which are legally binding for its whole territory. In this the legal character of the episcopal conference differs from the older legislation of the *CIC*. Thus the conference has lost its merely consultative character[68] and become a truly hierarchical institution.[69] This, however, has neither the same content nor the same form as the synods of particular Churches. Apart from the basic statement on the binding force of its decisions, what is said in n. 4 limits its competence and makes the application of the collegial principle more difficult.

The competence of the episcopal conference extends only to those matters assigned to it by canon law or determined by special mandate of the Apostolic See. The latter possibility has the advantage that special local conditions may be taken into account either on the initiative of the Apostolic See or of the episcopal conference in question.[70] On the whole it cannot be overlooked that the present directions aim at limiting the powers of the episcopal conferences as hierarchical institutions.[71] But it is doubtful whether this system can be carried through at all. For the constant increase of individual competences in the post-conciliar legislation which might continue indefinitely can hardly be combined with the modern desire for clear, brief and intelligible legislation. Hence it is to be expected that the reform of canon law will unify the competences of the episcopal conference and make them of more general application. Ac-

---

[67] Cf. W. Aymans, *Das synodale Element in der Kirchenverfassung*, pp. 271–7.

[68] Very hesitant beginnings are to be found in the *CIC*, which accords a legally binding right to make decisions; but the matters are so insignificant that they need only be mentioned here.

[69] Cf. K. Mörsdorf, *Kirchenrecht*, I, p. 391; J. Ratzinger, "Papst, Patriarch, Bischof", in H. C. Hampe, ed., *Ende der Gegenreformation* (1964), pp. 161 f.; W. Onclin, "Collegiality and the Individual Bishop", in *Concilium* 8, no. 1 (1965), pp. 44–9; K. Mörsdorf, "Primat und Kollegialität", *loc. cit.*, p. 48; id., "Das synodale Element der Kirchenverfassung", *loc. cit.*, p. 548; this is not seen rightly by C. Leitmaier, "Bischofskonferenzen", *Österreichisches Archiv für Kirchenrecht* 16 (1965), p. 69.

[70] Within the legal framework it is an important competence of the episcopal conference that it may ask the Apostolic See for further competences by way of a majority decision. According to n. 44 the episcopal conference as such, not the individual bishops may make such an application.

[71] Cf. K. Mörsdorf, "Primat und Kollegialität nach dem Konzil", *loc. cit.*, pp. 57 f.; id., "Das synodale Element der Kirchenverfassung", *loc. cit.*, pp. 581 ff.

cording to the present law it decides by virtue of ordinary power[72] which may be supplemented by delegated faculties.

Even before the episcopal conference developed into a hierarchical institution there were majority decisions. But with the exception of those cases mentioned in can. 1507 and 1909 they were free agreements which were not legally binding on individual members or particular Churches. This remains valid for those spheres in which the episcopal conference has no ordinary or delegated competence. In these there can at the most develop similar diocesan law which practically presupposes unanimous agreements. But it belongs to the character of these decisions that even unanimity does not give them legal force, whereas within the competence of acts of jurisdiction majority decisions are binding.[73]

The manner in which decisions are to be arrived at by a community leaves much legal scope, extending from the requirement of unanimity to the right of one member left (or present) to determine the will of the community. Here two steps of integration are to be observed. The first is based on the *numerus quorum;* this is concerned with the question whether the opinions of those who are absent, abstain or cast an invalid vote should be assigned equally to the validly voting members or only to those voting against a proposal. The required majority must be determined according to the way in which the lawgiver answers this question. In the second step of integration the lawgiver may either mitigate or aggravate the tendency of the first step to make the collegial act more difficult or easier. Both steps together result in the determination of the majority.[74]

In the relevant law for the episcopal conferences the legal provisions for both steps of integration are disproportionately high if compared with the directions of canon law for the synodal system as a whole. For the proper understanding of the first step of integration it should be noted that the words *ad Conferentiam pertinent* are to be understood of the episcopal conference as a concrete institution, not of the concrete assembly. Hence the majority is not determined by the fully competent members present but by the number of those members of the

---

[72] Cf. W. Onclin, *op. cit.,* p. 668; F. R. McManus, "The Judicial power of the Bishop in the Constitution on the Sacred Liturgy," in *Concilium* 2, no. 1 (1965), pp. 18–26; W. Aymans, *Das synodale Element in der Kirchenverfassung*, pp. 353–67, 395–400. In the *Österreichisches Archiv für Kirchenrecht* status and powers of the episcopal conferences have been discussed. The most diverse opinions on these questions have been voiced, but all authors taking part in the discussion are agreed that the episcopal conference decides not by ordinary, but by delegated or "collegial" power; cf. P. Leisching, *Der Rechtscharakter*, pp. 162–82; C. Leitmaier, "Bischofskonferenzen", in *Österreichisches Archiv für Kirchenrecht* 17 (1966), pp. 165–7; P. Leisching, "Bischofskonferenz", in *Österreichisches Archiv für Kirchenrecht* 17 (1966), pp. 80–84; C. Leitmaier, "Bischofskonferenzen, II", *ibid.,* pp. 165–7; I. Gampl, "Zur Diskussion um Status und Gewalt der Bischofskonferenzen", *ibid.,* pp. 388–413.

[73] On these questions cf. W. Aymans, *Kollegium und kollegialer Akt.*

[74] On these legal questions of a theoretical nature cf. *ibid.*

conference who enjoy the vote.[75] Hence the potential votes of those who are not present, of the abstaining members as well as the invalid votes are counted as opposing a proposal. The two-thirds majority required by the second step of integration is also extremely high in view of the first step.[76] Considering that the doctrine of the collegiality of the bishops was meant especially to emphasize the responsibility of all the bishops in the government of the whole Church, a considerable reserve is to be noticed in the sphere of the particular Churches, where the application of the principle of collegiality would necessarily involve the diminution of episcopal power.[77] This reserve has been expressed in material as well as in formal law.

The inclusion of the first para. of n. 5 within the whole structure of Article 38 is awkward, for nn. 2–4 apply equally to international and national episcopal conferences, unless the *peculiares normas* of the motu proprio *Ecclesiae Sanctae*, I, n. 41, § 4, is to be understood not only of the statutes but also of the whole legislation.[78] A relevant norm concerning the differently drawn up statutes of international conferences might easily have been included in n. 3. But our decree is silent on them, and according to *Ecclesiae Sanctae*, I, n. 41, para. 4, they are to be given by the Apostolic See.

The reference to the special circumstances for establishing international episcopal conferences also provides an important point of view from which to consider the national sphere which is the rule. The instruction of the Congregation of Rites, 26 September 1964, n. 23 c, had suggested as an example of such special circumstances *(peculiaria adiuncta)* the small number of bishops in the territory of a nation and had advised that in such a case the bishops of several nations of the same language or civilization should form a conference. The decisive factor in determining the territory of a conference is the achievement of its ecclesial purpose. Even though national conferences are the rule, the political nation should nevertheless not be regarded as the essential element in the constitution of the Church. Political units affect the territorial organization of the Church only because normally the general living conditions are decisively influenced by the political situation, and thus the Church, too, is faced with

[75] It should be noted that this possibly includes not only the local ordinaries and the coadjutors, but also, according to the terms of the statutes, other ordinary members. If the circle of voters is enlarged by material law, it is possible for one and the same meeting to form a quorum in the one question.

[76] On this question of formal law see W. Aymans, *Das synodale Element in der Kirchenverfassung*, pp. 307–28.

[77] Cf. K. Mörsdorf, "Primat und Kollegialität nach dem Konzil", *loc. cit.*, p. 47; id., "Das synodale Element der Kirchenverfassung", *loc. cit.*, p. 581.

[78] N. 5 occupies a strange position. This may be connected with the fact that in n. 23 b of the instruction of the Congregation of Rites of 26 September 1964 (*AAS* 56 [1964], pp. 877–900) the law of membership for international episcopal conferences provided two alternatives, which are no longer mentioned in the present decree; cf. W. Aymans, *Das synodale Element in der Kirchenverfassung*, pp. 40f., 49.

the same tasks within a nation. If, however, the Church's mission is affected by other data, the national sphere is to be abandoned and smaller or larger areas are to be chosen.[79]

Another important question is whether an international conference is to be established only if there are no smaller episcopal conferences in the area, or whether national or smaller episcopal conferences exclude an international conference in their territory. This has not yet been clearly decided by law. The relevant direction of the instruction of the Congregation of Rites evidently regarded the international conference as a substitute for national conferences in its area (n. 23 c, para. 1) but left the way open for a special regulation through the Apostolic See in particular circumstances (n. 23 c, para. 2). The following explanation for the international conferences is added to the directions on membership of the episcopal synod: "constitutis scilicet pro iis nationibus, quae propriam conferentiam non habent . . .".[80] This limitation is necessary, because otherwise there might be double legal titles for membership of the episcopal synod and hence an equal representation of the world episcopate would not be guaranteed.[81] Nevertheless, the decree *Christus Dominus* and the direction in the motu proprio *Ecclesiam Sanctam* do not completely exclude the possibility that several episcopal conferences of different hierarchical standing may exist in the same territory. For in the territory of a national episcopal conference there may be territorial subdivisions, or in the territory of several national conferences there may also exist a comprehensive international episcopal conference. The relations of such conferences to each other may be defined by assigning different competences to them. As long as no special directions are issued, the basic rule must be that the more comprehensive conference is the higher hierarchical body, as is the case for the synods. Special attention must be paid to these questions, because national and smaller episcopal conferences may constitute themselves on the initiative of the bishops belonging to the territory without previous permission of the Apostolic See.[82] This circumstance may easily lead to a division or multiplication of authorities.

Para. 2 of n. 5 is only outwardly connected with para. 1, because both deal with international matters. But international relations between episcopal

[79] Cf. W. Aymans, "Ritusgebundenheit und territoriale Abgrenzung der Bischofskonferenzen", in *AKK* 135 (1966), pp. 550–2; id., *Das synodale Element in der Kirchenverfassung,* pp. 48 f.

[80] Motu proprio *Apostolica Sollicitudo,* n. V. 1 c, of 25 September 1965: *AAS* 57 (1965), pp. 775–80, and *Ordo Synodi Episcoporum celebrandae,* Article 5, para. 1, n. 1 c, of 8 December 1966: *AAS* 59 (1967), pp. 91–103.

[81] Cf. W. Aymans, *Das synodale Element in der Kirchenverfassung,* p. 203, note 591. It cannot be ascertained from the motu proprio *Apostolica Sollicitudo* that episcopal conferences smaller than the national ones also have the right of membership of the episcopal synod. This papal law and the directions of the *Ordo Synodi Episcoporum celebrandae* only distinguish episcopal conferences of one or more nations; cf. W. Aymans, "Ritusgebundenheit und territoriale Abgrenzung der Bischofskonferenzen", in *AKK* 135 (1966), pp. 550–2.

[82] Motu proprio Ecclesiae Sanctae, I, n. 41, §§ 1 and 2.

conferences differ essentially from international episcopal conferences. A false impression is given by the very fact that relations are recommended only between national conferences, as if episcopal conferences of smaller or larger territories were to be excluded from such contacts.[83] If this wish of the Council had to be expressed, this could have been done in a separate last or last but one number of this article. The term *relationes* is clearer than the term *rationes* of the motu proprio, which has too many meanings.[84] The directions give many examples for the international relations that might be furthered, especially through the secretariats of the conferences;[85] these may be summarized as "comprehensive mutual information" (see comment on n. 3).

N. 6 is to be understood in connection with n. 5, para. 2. It would have been more logical to combine these, because both instructions do not deal with the inner structure of the synodal authorities, but with their relations with each other. The relation between superior and inferior authorities is left out and only that between equal or parallel ones is discussed. Strangely enough n. 6 only deals with the Oriental Churches.[86] The reason is that in them different rites are equally represented in one territory far more frequently than in territories of the Latin rite. This is also why n. 2 decreed that local ordinaries of every rite should be members of the episcopal conference, whereas n. 6 gave another solution. The very fact that n. 6 was included shows that n. 2 was unsatisfactory as a norm of interritual law. The various rites have legal autonomy within the universal Church; hence the synod to which they belong is the hierarchical authority for the bishops of every oriental rite within the sphere of the particular Church. True, there is also an interritual synod with the character of a particular Church,[87] but this is closely related to the Pope and directly subject to him, who appoints his legate for convoking and directing it. As the episcopal conferences of the same rite are the hierarchical authorities for a definite territory and should consult with other conferences (n. 5, para. 2), so also the synods of the same rite are the hierarchical authorities for their district having contacts with each other for the sake of the common good of all rites based on the *communio ecclesiarum*, as is suggested in n. 6, namely in episcopal conferences of a consultative nature. This is not quite a new institution for the Oriental Churches, for n. 6 takes up a direction of the Oriental canon law.[88]

---

[83] Hence the — probably unconscious — limitation *diversarum nationum* has rightly been left out in the directions; cf. motu proprio *Ecclesiae Sanctae*, I, n. 41, § 4.

[84] Cf. motu proprio *Ecclesiae Sanctae*, I, n. 41, §§ 4 and 5. The change of meaning in para. 5 is to be noted; in the introduction this means "relations" but in a) "considerations or reasons".

[85] Motu proprio *Ecclesiae Sanctae*, I, n. 41, § 5.

[86] The request addressed to the prelates of the Oriental Churches seems to exclude the resident prelates of the Latin rite from such conferences, though the difficulties in the relations between Latin and Oriental prelates would seem to make the participation of the Latins especially necessary and welcome.

[87] *CIO*, can. 340, § 3.

[88] *CIO:* "Locorum Hierarchae in eodem territorio iurisdictionem obtinentes, collatis consiliis,

If the connection between n. 5, para. 2, and n. 6 is rightly understood, it will be seen that the episcopal conference as a hierarchical authority is principally regarded as an institution of the Latin Church; the synods are its opposite numbers in the Catholic Oriental Churches (see commentary on n. 2 *ad fin.*).

Section II, "The Boundaries of Ecclesiastical Provinces and the Establishment of Ecclesiastical Regions", considers the constitutional foundations for the co-operation of the bishops in the sphere of the particular Churches.

Article 39 begins with the statement that "the welfare of souls requires appropriate boundaries not only for dioceses but also for ecclesiastical provinces". Thus it is recognized that the diocese must not only be considered in its relation to the whole Church but also in its connection with the neighbouring particular Churches and their associations, as has been shown in our comments on Article 22. The care for the welfare of souls, to which all the activities of the Church are devoted, expresses itself differently according to the different spheres with which it is concerned. The diocese is entrusted with the ordinary accomplishment of the saving mission of the Church (see comments on Articles 11 and 30), whereas the ecclesiastical provinces and regions are responsible for those tasks that cannot be accomplished by the dioceses or can be better performed in an association of dioceses. These intermediate hierarchical institutions are at the same time the foundation of an orderly co-operation of the diocesans in the vast sphere between the diocese and the whole Church. The relations between bishops and civil authorities mentioned at the end of the article are a special concern of the associations of the particular Churches.

Article 40 deals with the organization of the particular Churches. N. 1 provides for an early review of the boundaries of ecclesiastical provinces. Despite its general form this direction may be taken to refer only to cases where a change seems indicated. But even the most careful definition of boundaries cannot do justice to the needs of souls nor provide for the proper relations of the bishops with one another unless the tasks of the diocese or of the ecclesiastical province are suitably determined. Hence the demand that "the rights and privileges of metropolitans are to be defined according to new and suitable norms" is of special importance. Since in the Latin Church the office of metropolitan has been almost completely deprived of any significance[89] the direction of the Council undoubtedly means to give it more importance (see comment on Article 11, para. 2). True, there can be no question of restoring the ancient rights of the metropolitan; yet in view of the tradition of the Oriental Churches which has influenced our view of the episcopal office as well as the revival of the collegial element of the Church's constitution, it is only fitting that the office of the metropolitan should be brought up to date. In order to emphasize the spiritual

unitatem actionis inter diversi ritus clericos foveant, et, viribus unitis, communia adiuvent opera, ad bonum religionis expeditius promovendum et cleri disciplinam efficacius tuendam."
[89] Cf. K. Mörsdorf, *Kirchenrecht,* I, pp. 382 ff.

union of neighbouring particular Churches which are joined in the ecclesiastical province the right of consecration, granted to the metropolitans already by the first ecumenical Council of Nicaea (can. 4) should be restored to them, so that they would be responsible for the consecration of bishops in their ecclesiastical province. Since the dioceses differ considerably in size, it will not be easy so to define the duties of the metropolitan that they can be universally applied. Nevertheless even in those ecclesiastical provinces which consist of large, efficient dioceses there will undoubtedly be many tasks which can be better performed by the ecclesiastical province. These will not be matters of legislation, which still belong to the provincial council, but those of jurisdiction and administration.[90] A well-ordered administration of the law requires trained full-time judges, and experience shows that these are not available even in very large dioceses. The ecclesiastical province provides the possibility to establish efficient courts, a measure which is indispensable in view of the revival of ecclesiastical judicature, especially of the planned jurisdiction over the administration. [91] Apart from an examination of the supervisory and supplementary rights of the metropolitan this means that those tasks that cannot be suitably accomplished by the diocese (see comment on Article 22, para. 2) are to be assigned to the ecclesiastical province and entrusted to the metropolitan.

N. 2 rules that "all dioceses and other territorial divisions which are by law equivalent to dioceses should be attached to an ecclesiastical province". This points to the fact that the Council has recognized the great importance of the metropolitan association within the constitution of the Church, which, however, had long been obscured by the establishment of those dioceses and similar territorial divisions which were directly subject to the Apostolic See.[92] Nevertheless, present canon law has retained that bishops and local superiors in a similar position who are not under a metropolitan as well as archbishops without suffragans must always join a neighbouring metropolitan. Consequently these local bishops have the right and the duty to attend the provincial council whose decisions are binding for them and their particular Churches (*CIC*, can. 285), and the metropolitan becomes their court of appeal (cf. *CIC*, can. 1594, § 3). The precepts of the *CIC* have preserved the nucleus of the new rule of law which has abolished on principle any exemption from the metropolitan association. But the new law can hardly be put into practice in the way suggested by the Council as the first possibility, namely by bringing together dioceses directly subject to the Apostolic See in a new ecclesiastical province; for the same

---

[90] On this see id., *Rechtsprechung und Verwaltung im kanonischen Recht* (1941).

[91] Cf. H. Schmitz, "Möglichkeit und Gestalt einer kirchlichen Gerichtsbarkeit über die Verwaltung", in *AKK* 135 (1966), pp. 18–38; id., *Appellatio extraiudicialis. Entwicklungslinien einer kirchlichen Gerichtsbarkeit über Verwaltungsakte im Zeitalter der klassischen Kanonistik, 1140–1348* (1966; not yet published).

[92] This is a partial aspect of the doctrine of the direct papal primacy of jurisdiction, which the Council has not treated on principle; see comment on Article 2.

principle that applies to the diocese must apply to the ecclesiastical province, namely that its territory should be continuous (see Article 23, n. 1). In general hitherto exempt dioceses will be united to a neighbouring metropolitan province.

N. 3 introduces a measure which is new especially in the constitution of the Latin Church and may be attributed to the fact that the episcopal conference, which normally embraces several ecclesiastical provinces, has become an hierarchical institution. In any case, a grouping of several ecclesiastical provinces into an ecclesiastical region makes sense only where there is a corresponding episcopal conference and it is important to give it greater stability. In the course of further developments the ecclesiastical regions might receive the status of juridical persons; for the rest, the current reform of the *CIC* will legislate for the juridical constitution of the ecclesiastical region.

Article 41 recommends that the competent episcopal conferences examine the question of the boundaries and the establishment of regions and submit suitable suggestions to the Apostolic See. The directions of the motu proprio *Ecclesiae Sanctae*, I, n. 42, give the episcopal conferences the relevant mandate, also with regard to proposals for attaching exempt dioceses to existing ecclesiastical provinces. The suggestion that these proposals are to be guided by the norms given for diocesan boundaries (Article 23 and 24) can only be understood in an analogous sense, because the diocese, the ecclesiastical province and the ecclesiastical region have all different objects. Hence the episcopal conferences[93] have a great responsibility, because they are entrusted with taking the initiative in these reforms.

Under the heading "Bishops with an Interdiocesan Office" the third section deals with tasks which cannot very well be accomplished within a single diocese and therefore need special legislation. Quite different questions are treated side by side, namely the performance of individual tasks in the service of all or several dioceses of a certain territory (Article 42) and the establishment of vicariates for the spiritual care of military personnel. Moreover, tasks going beyond the diocese are usually entrusted not to bishops, but to priests (see commentary on Article 29, 2).

Article 42 takes account of this by stating in para. 1 that such supradiocesan "offices can *even* be filled by bishops". These tasks which are to be accomplished for all or several dioceses of a certain territory need legislation both as regards the assignment of duties and their execution. But in order to secure that these supradiocesan projects do not endanger the constitution of the Church, para. 2 demands that the relations between those serving in these offices on the one hand and the diocesan bishops and the episcopal conferences on the other should be

---

[93] In the Oriental Churches the patriarch is responsible for changes in the boundaries of ecclesiastical provinces with the consent of the patriarchal synod or the patriarchal electoral synod, though these must be confirmed by the Apostolic See (cf. *CIO*, can. 248, para. 1, n. 1; for the major archbishop cf. can. 327, para. 1, and for the Catholicus cf. can. 335, para. 1).

defined by canon law. Whether the tasks are allotted by a superior hierarchical authority (e.g., the episcopal conference) or are based on an agreement of the local bishops concerned, they must be clearly defined and it must be determined to whom those entrusted with them are responsible for their execution.

Article 43 is concerned with the spiritual care of military personnel. This used to be normally exempt,[94] but this was changed by the instruction of the consistorial congregation of 23 April 1951.[95] This laid down that the military bishop has the powers of an ordinary for the persons entrusted to him, but without suspending the powers of the local bishop.[96] The directions of the Council presuppose this situation, which involves difficulties due to the cumulative competence of the military bishop and the local ordinary. The harmonious co-operation demanded by the Council can be guaranteed only if the local bishops and parish priests are content with a subsidiary role in the pastoral care of soldiers. The recent practice of entrusting the military to a diocesan bishop can hardly solve the questions of organization which the institution of a special care of souls for the military involves. Nevertheless it is closely connected with the local ordinary because it does not possess its own spiritual home association and hence relies on diocesan and regular priests.

General Directive. The decree concludes with a general directive concerning the revision of the code of canon law and the drawing up of directories.

Concerning the reform of the *CIC*, the Council demands that "suitable laws be drawn up in keeping with the principles stated in this decree". This directive gives the impression that the decree only states principles but is not itself to be regarded as law. On the contrary, it must be stated that this decree has the character of a constitutional law which combines the enunciation of principles with directly applicable legal norms.[97] Even where its rulings do not represent directly applicable law, the decree makes juridical decisions which are binding for the new legislation on the episcopal office. Moreover, "due consideration should also be given to observations made by individual commissions or Fathers of this Council" in the reform of the *CIC*. It goes without saying that this direction does not in the least question the binding force of the Council decree; it is due to the fact that valuable suggestions of commissions and Council Fathers could not be incorporated in the decree because of the necessary limitation of the material before the assembly.

---

[94] See A. Scheuermann, *Die Exemption,* pp. 208 ff.

[95] *AAS* 43 (1951), pp. 563–5.

[96] Cf. K. Mörsdorf, *Kirchenrecht,* I, pp. 341 f.

[97] The motu proprio *De Episcoporum Muneribus* of 15 June 1966 (*AAS* 58 [1966], pp. 467–72), n. I, points out that the *CIC* and subsequent ecclesiastical laws, as far as they have not been revoked, are still in force, if they have not been completely or partially suppressed by the Council or have been quietly changed by a new ordering of legal matter. This makes clear that the Council has also posited directly applicable legal norms. This is especially true of the decree under discussion.

The creation of general and individual directories mentioned in paras. 2 and 3 is due to the same reason. In view of the abundance of the material produced by the preparatory commissions concerned with pastoral questions it was decided to gather all the proposals not included in the decree and unsuitable for the new *CIC* in directories of various kinds. These directories are official helps for pastoral work; they are not laws and must therefore remain within the existing legislation.[98]

[98] The *Directorium ad ea quae a Concilio Vaticano Secundo de re oecumenica promulgata sunt exequenda,* published by the Secretariat for Christian Unity on 14 May 1967 (*AAS* 59 [1967], pp. 574–92), has the concluding formula: "Contrariis quibuslibet minime obstantibus". This gives the erroneous impression as if the ecumenical directory had created a new legal foundation suppressing possible contrary laws. This, however, is quite out of the question.

Decree on the Appropriate Renewal of the Religious Life

by
*Friedrich Wulf**

Introduction

The draft on the religious life produced for the Council by the Preparatory Commission was indeed comprehensive. It contained about two hundred articles. Obviously much careful labour had gone into this work, as the numerous footnotes bear witness; and the work had gone on for a year and a half (November 1960 until April 1962), during which time seventy-eight plenary sessions took place. In spite of this, the result revealed a striking lack of interior unity. In content and scope it was composed of the most unequal parts, linked together in the loosest possible fashion. With good reason, therefore, the *schema*, delivered in eleven fascicles to the Preparatory Central Commission of the Council during the first half year (January – May 1962), bore the thoroughly general title *Quaestiones de Religiosis* — "Questions concerning the (Life of) Religious". Nonetheless, in retrospect the draft is of great value to the extent that it reflects in compressed form the state of these questions at that time, chiefly as they appeared to the Holy See and the Congregation for Religious. The part played by the world-wide Church in the production of this draft was relatively small. The draft bears an unmistakably Roman stamp. As can be seen from the documents cited, from this draft one could reconstruct almost the whole of the teaching of Pius XII on the religious state, and his efforts to adapt this state to modern times,[1] as well as the similar efforts made during the last twenty years[2] by the

* *Translated by Ronald Walls*

[1] On the teaching of Pius XII on the religious life see J. B. Tse, *Perfectio christiana et societas christiana iuxta magisterium Pii Papae XII* (1963), esp. pp. 109–17, 166–73, 229–38. On this Pope's efforts at "appropriate renewal" of the religious life see the article by P. Lombardi in *Civiltà Cattolica,* 19 March 1949. This article was inspired by the Holy See. A useful survey of the chief statements of Pius XII on this problem is to be found in A. Scheuermann, "Die Ordensleute in den Dokumenten des II. Vatikanischen Konzils", in *AKK* 134 (1965), p. 338.

[2] As well as a few instructions by the Congregation for Religious issued during this period, the documents cited are the statutes dated 7 July 1956, concerning the education of the regular clergy, statutes which were appended to the apostolic constitution *Sedes Sapientiae* of 31 May

Congregation for Religious. Its proper title: "The states that aim at perfection", suggested the dominant concept for all ecclesiastically recognized communities, the members of which bind themselves by the evangelical counsels. This was in line with the modern evolution of canon law, according to which the canonical state of perfection includes not only religious but also societies sharing a common life *(Societates vitae communis sine votis)* and secular communities *(Instituta saecularia)*.[3] Such importance was attached to this conclusion of a process of juridical development that the matter was dealt with in great detail and with much juridical precision and distinction at the very beginning of the draft.[4] The reason for this is perhaps not so self-evident as it may have appeared to the canonist-authors of the document, for the topic under discussion was primarily a specifically charismatic state in the Church. The dominance of the juridical outlook in the whole draft is demonstrated by the fact that the doctrine of the states that aim at perfection, which makes up the first part, contained scarcely any theological statements.[5] (The second, more comprehensive part was devoted to practical problems affecting religious life.)[6]

Even if those responsible for the draft can appeal to the fact that the Dogmatic Constitution on the Church provides a special chapter on the theology of the religious life,[7] this lack of genuinely theological-spiritual thought is remarkable in a document expressly purporting to be the Council's doctrine of the states

1956 (*AAS* 48 [1956], pp. 354 ff.), but never published in the *AAS*. According to Article 16, para. 3, 2, of these statutes and Article 92 of the pre-conciliar draft of the Decree on Religious, these statutes were intended to apply by analogy to the education of all religious.

[3] The *CIC* does not use the term *status perfectionis,* a term which, since St. Thomas Aquinas (*Summa Theologica,* II, II, q. 184), had been used of the religious and the episcopal state. The term was re-introduced into official ecclesiastical use only with the canonical erection of the secular institutes (*cf.* apostolic constitution *Provida Mater* of 2 February 1947: *AAS* 39 [1947], p. 116; likewise the motu proprio *Primo Feliciter* of 12 March 1948: *AAS* 40 [1948], pp. 285–6). According to the pre-conciliar draft of the Decree on Religious it was supposed to become the basic concept of the canons in the *CIC* that deal with those who live by the evangelical counsels. According to Article 9 of this draft, can. 487, which defines the *status religiosus,* ought to be modified thus: "Status perfectionis evangelicae adquirendae est stabilis in aliqua societate vivendi modus, ab ecclesiastica auctoritate christianae perfectionis causa constitutis, quo fideles, praeter communia praecepta, evangelica quoque concilia oboedientia castitatis et paupertatis profitentur." Article 3 of the second, abbreviated draft is much the same.

[4] The titles of the first three chapters of draft are: *De Statu perfectionis adquirendae in genere; Tres species Status perfectionis adquirendae; De diversis formis Status perfectionis adquirendae et de erroribus refellendis.*

[5] What few theological statements there were dealt almost exclusively with moral and ascetical matters.

[6] The four sections of the second part were entitled: 1. *De accommodata renovatione vitae religiosae.* 2. *De alumnorum status perfectionis institutione.* 3. *De vocationibus religiosis promovendis et de alumnorum admissione ad professionem et ad ordines.* 4. *De quibusdam quaestionibus particularibus status perfectionis.* Sections 2 and 3 merely repeated on the whole what is contained in the apostolic constitution *Sedes Sapientiae* and in the statutes which explain it (cf. footnote 2).

[7] In the first draft of the Dogmatic Constitution on the Church, Chapter V, was entitled: "The states of evangelical perfection".

of perfection. This reveals — what was to be frequently censured later — the narrowness which has plagued the official ecclesiastical concept of the religious state, especially since the 19th century. It will take a long time for the orders to free themselves from this one-sidedly juridical mode of thinking.[8] In making this comment, it must not be forgotten that it was the Congregation for Religious themselves who started the idea of an *aggiornamento*, of adaptation to a changed world, an *accommodata renovatio*, of appropriate renewal,[9] and repeatedly stressed this need for twenty years. The first draft bore witness to this fact also, and much of what is contained in the draft on this topic found its way, much abbreviated, into the final version of the decree and into the "Norms for Implementation".[10]

The first pre-conciliar draft discussed here, a draft which for the most part was explicitly linked with the schema of a constitution *De Regularibus* of Vatican I,[11] was delivered at the conclusion of the first phase of the Council at the end of 1962 to the members of the Commission for Religious Orders, which meanwhile had been constituted; but it had never been debated, either in the Commission itself or in the Council in St. Peter's. For meanwhile the Co-ordinating Commission appointed by Pope John, invoking the guiding principles governing further work on drafts between the first two sessions of the Council *(Ordo agendorum)*, issued by the Cardinal Secretary Cicognani at the Pope's order, gave instructions that many of the schemata produced by the Preparatory Commissions including the schema on the states of perfection were to be rigorously abbreviated.[12] The abbreviation of the schema on religious was undertaken by the secretary of the Commission for Religious and a few *periti* under the chairmanship of Archbishop P. Philippe, O. P. This commission accepted, by and large, the draft presented to them by Archbishop Philippe. As was to be expected it contained nothing essentially new, in comparison with the pre-conciliar draft; but, in accord with the pastoral orientation meanwhile declared by the Council,

---

[8] In contrast to the one-sided juridical character of the draft, the "Norms for Implementation", published in the motu proprio *Ecclesiae Sanctae* of 6 August 1966: *AAS* 58 [1966], pp. 775–82, stress in Article 12 that the primary thing in the reform of constitutions and rules, etc., is the study of the biblical and theological foundations of the religious life; and in Article 13 we read: "Only when both elements, the spiritual and the juridical, form a unity, do the fundamental documents of a community possess a sure foundation and become moulded by a true spirit and a life-giving norm. The text, therefore, must not be cast in purely juridical or edificatory terms."

[9] Cf., *inter alia*, the decree of the Congregation for Religious, dated 26 March 1956: *AAS* 48 [1956], p. 295, in which much is said about the *accommodata renovatio* of the religious life.

[10] For example, in Articles 3, 4 and 17–24 of the decree and in section VII (Articles 33–38) of the "Norms for Implementation".

[11] Article 5 of the draft appeals to the schema of the Vatican I constitution *De Regularibus (Collectio Lacensis: Acta et Decreta Sacrorum Conciliorum Recentiorum* [1870–90], VII, p. 671).

[12] The Commission for Religious received their instruction on this score on 30 January 1965. It contained concrete suggestions for abbreviation as well as a list of topics which had to be discussed.

all condemnations were avoided.[13] The shortened schema was examined and re-worked in the plenary session of the Commission of 20 February to 1 March 1963 (fifteen of the twenty-five members were present). A sub-commission was given the task of editing the final text. On 9 March this text was handed to the Co-ordinating Commission for approval. In the minutes of its session on 27 March, this commission, with Cardinal Döpfner as *relator,* commended the abbreviation and confirmed that it dealt with the topics which it had issued, but it also made some not inconsiderable criticisms. For one thing they did not like the title of the schema — *De Religiosis* — for this was not applicable to the secular institutes; and they objected to the frequent use of the traditional term *status perfectionis,* which could cause misunderstandings. They also objected to the following three points: 1) There was no biblical and theological enrichment of the customary views about the religious state and about the counsels, and without this no appropriate renewal of the orders was conceivable. In particular too little heed had been paid to the Christological and ecclesiological concept of the state associated with the evangelical counsels. 2) It could hardly be said adequately to fulfil the desire of the Fathers for an unambiguous and concrete set of guiding principles for an appropriate renewal. 3) It was not enough simply to reiterate warnings about the world and the spirit of this world — however much a renunciation of the world and a voluntary self-denial of the world's goods are an essential mark of the religious state, and however much this needs to be stressed today —, for an effective apostolate is possible only if one knows the modern world as it undergoes colossal change, and the correspondingly changing mentality and concepts of the men who live in that world. Many loud complaints were made about the ignorance of the world found among religious, especially female religious. Rethinking was needed on this point. More cognizance ought to be taken of the fact that gradually a more differentiated relationship was beginning to be adopted by Christians to the modern world. Perhaps, therefore, a harder distinction had to be made between the contemplative (monastic) orders on the one hand and the active (apostolic) congregations on the other.

Despite this criticism, which was underlined again in the final sentence of the minutes, the secretary of the Commission for Religious assumed that the Co-ordinating Commission had indicated their approval of the substance of the shortened schema. A few things had to be corrected and supplemented. And so the idea of calling another plenary session — originally planned for May — was dropped. The work still to be done was entrusted to a small commission. No doubt the reason for this procedure was lack of time. The schema had to be presented to the Council Fathers with all possible haste, so that they could send in their comments and requests in good time before the Council re-assembled.

---

[13] The first draft did contain many such condemnations, with explicit reference to Vatican I. The opening speech by Pope John who, in contrast to individual influential cardinals and bishops, frequently on later occasions expressed his displeasure at the numerous condemnations in the schemata. The *Ordo agendorum,* too, automatically forbade the condemnatory style.

Some of the members of the Commission did not approve of this procedure — Bishop Huyghe of Arras, for example —, who sent in fresh proposals to the secretariat of the Commission. In particular he made suggestions about the declaration of the autonomy of the active religious orders which had acquired such unreality as a result of monastic traditions and institutions, and about a courageous *aggiornamento* of the monastic orders, especially of the contemplative orders. Likewise Cardinal Döpfner, in his capacity as *relator* of the Co-ordinating Commission responsible for the schema on religious, made his wishes known to the Roman secretariat of the Commission for Religious Orders. These wishes had already been expressed in the official minutes, but now he made them in the detailed form of specific texts which he suggested be incorporated in the schema. Because of this Cardinal's official status in the Council, these suggestions were given due attention. About half of them were incorporated — in part *verbatim* — into the draft. The omission of the rest of the texts — and, in view of the above-mentioned objections contained in the minutes, these were the most important — was explained in numerous footnotes. By contrast, the proposals made by the Bishop of Arras were not accepted, on juridical grounds, because the text was no longer in the hands of the Commission; but, along with the whole proposal made by Cardinal Döpfner, they were intimated to all members of the Commission. On 22 April 1963 the now rigorously abbreviated draft was published with the Pope's approval by the Cardinal Secretary Cicognani, and sent to all of the Council Fathers. It ran to fifty-one articles contained in nine chapters.

Before going on to describe the next phase in the development of the schema on religious it will pay us to pause and take stock. The task set had not been a light one. This was so not simply because of the complexity of the material, but also because of the diversity of views among the Council Fathers concerning both the nature of religious life and the methods of accomplishing its appropriate renewal.[14] Even within the Commission opinions were at variance. Unanimity was to be found only in the view that the renewal demanded by the Church and recognized as necessary by everyone required a return to origins as well as an accommodation to the needs of the world.[15] This, however, was no more than a formal principle. What did it mean in actuality? How was it to be applied to the concrete case? Was the traditional doctrine of the religious state really as incapable of improvement as most of them tacitly or explicitly assumed,[16] or did it not require rethinking in important points? Did we really know so per-

[14] Cf. my commentary on Chapters V and VI of the Dogmatic Constitution on the Church (in vol. I of the present work, pp. 253 ff.), the preliminary history of which revealed the same party alignments.

[15] The first draft had already made this point (Article 5). The same statement recurred in the second version (Article 11 and footnote 1), and is still to be found in the final text of the conciliar decree (Article 12), so that we might almost speak of a topic that originated in the addresses of Pius XII.

[16] There can be no doubt that all regarded the theology of St. Thomas concerning the religious life as final and normative for all.

fectly, for example, what evangelical poverty and obedience were, so that we needed only shake our heads at anyone who asked about them, or were those right who pointed out that the history of the orders had left many open questions on these points, thus allowing our traditional concepts of the religious life to be re-assessed in terms of the word of God in holy Scripture? In the course of time perhaps very few of those who took part in producing the text of the decree on religious life and in securing the acceptance of this or that proposal were to become sufficiently clearly aware — through an understanding of history and of modern problems — of the deeper problems affecting the religious life, heavy-laden as it is with the weight of so much tradition. The religious themselves were no exception, no doubt because of their very closeness to the situation. As a rule people discussed from fixed doctrinal or institutional presuppositions which were neither questioned nor reflected upon by the participants; thus they often spoke at cross purposes, failing to understand each other, for they spoke different languages and lived in different worlds. And so for a long time, with the best will in the world, and despite the honest solicitude of all for the continuance and renewal of the religious life with reference to the altered circumstances of the times, progress was laborious and slow. Only now, having reviewed the debates and the development of the various drafts, are we able to see more clearly what the issues really were; only now are the problems of the religious life as it has evolved in the course of history, problems that have contributed to the present crisis in that life, beginning to emerge into the full light of day. In what follows we attempt through this retrospective survey to exhibit these problems, or at least some of them, by means of the second version of the schema on religious life of 1963, a version which on the whole simply reproduced in compressed form the essential content of the original, pre-conciliar draft.

The first question is this: can the traditional doctrine of the counsels, which so decisively stamped the self-understanding of the religious orders in the past, still be maintained today? Many Catholic theologians — a growing number of them, what is more — deny this.[17] On the other hand there are those who are more cautious in their verdict; but even those say that this doctrine requires considerable correction, or at least a deeper and more precise exposition.[18] In my opinion the distinction between commandment and counsel finds its deep meaning within New Testament ethics. Whoever knows the Scriptures is constantly meeting the thing that is meant by this distinction — not so much in the isolated sayings that have been cited from time immemorial in support of the distinction (Mt 19:11–12; 17b; 21; 1 Cor 7:25, 40),[19] but in a much more all-

---

[17] Cf. the recent work of B. Schüller, *Gesetz und Freiheit* (1966), pp. 65 ff., esp. p. 71, with reference to J. Fuchs, *Theologia Moralis* I (1960), pp. 53–58, and also with reference to O. Lottin, *Morale Fondamentale* (1954), pp. 458–505.

[18] Thus, for example, B. Häring, *Das Gesetz Christi* (1954), pp. 272 ff., 321 ff.; F. Wulf, "Gebot und Rat", in *Geist und Leben* 39 (1966), pp. 321 ff.

[19] In 1 Cor 7:25, where according to the Vulgate text "commandment" *(praeceptum)* and

embracing way: in all of our Lord's instructions about the conditions and demands of discipleship, about belonging to the kingdom of God, in the moral imperatives of the apostles, which are deduced from the sanctification of the Christian through baptism and the fellowship with Christ that is thereby effected — all of which is summed up in the phrase "a new commandment" (Jn 13:34; 1 Jn 1:7–8) or "the law of Christ" (Gal. 6:2). How much, however, has even this part of the message of Jesus been misunderstood and quite inadmissably over-simplified in the course of being handed down through the centuries? Even in some of the Fathers we can already detect this process at work. In an almost negative way they set commandment and counsel in opposition, so that the impression of a dualistic ethic arises. The commandment is defined purely in terms of duty, of what one *must* do, whereas the counsel is characterized by the freedom that is supported by grace.

Origen writes: "He who does only what he is bound to do, only fulfils the law, that is, is an unprofitable servant . . .; but St. Paul tells us (1 Cor 7:25) what it is that is added to the commandments and that goes beyond mere duty. This work goes further than the commandments."[20] St. Ambrose writes in like manner in several passages: "Commandment is given to subjects, counsel to friends. Where there is commandment there is law, where counsel, grace. Commandment is given in order to direct nature, counsel in order to call forth grace."[21] Without doubt this is a decisive truncation of New Testament preceptory ethics, justifying itself, no doubt, by an appeal to the Pauline view of the Old Testament law, or to the model of human legislation.[22] Must we not always understand what a Christian is commanded in the light of the salvation-history fulfilled in Christ? Is not the law of God a law of grace and of freedom? A further misunderstanding in respect of the relationship between commandment and counsel crept in at an early date: the counsels — like the commandments — were too much severed from the perennial activation of God's loving will, were materialized and regarded as objective moral performances, to some extent as a superstructure above the commandments that bound everyone. Origen already speaks about works that exceed what is commanded.[23] Later on men were to speak of *opera supererogata* (in connection with Lk 10:35, Vulgate), works of

"counsel" *(consilium)* are set in contrast to one another, "counsel", as in 1 Cor 7:40 and 2 Cor 8:10 (cf. 8:8), means the personal counsel of the apostle, which arises from his spiritual experience (in view of the imminent expectation of the parousia), from the gifts of grace bestowed upon him, and which therefore may appeal to the Lord himself. To translate γνώμη = *consilium* by "opinion", as many do, would not do justice to the spiritual depth of the apostolate; on the other hand neither is the word to be translated in the sense put upon it by the traditional theology of the counsels.

[20] Commentary on the Epistle to the Romans, III, 3, in *PG,* IV, col. 933.
[21] *De Viduis,* ch. XII (n. 72), in *PL,* XVI, 256; cf. many similar passages in the index of this volume (col. 1442) under *Consilium.*
[22] B. Schüller supports the latter view, *op. cit.,* pp. 65 ff.
[23] Cf. the saying quoted in footnote 20 above.

supererogation for which a special reward was promised.[24] Included in such works were almsgiving, prayer and fasting — a trio coming from the Old Testament and sanctioned by Christ (Mt 6:1–18) — provided they were performed in a degree that exceeded what was obligatory; but above all, there were the three evangelical counsels of the religious state, and whoever followed these could be sure of the highest reward.[25]

It is true that both among the Fathers and the great theologians of the Middle Ages are to be found plenty of statements that do much more justice to the real purpose of the doctrine of the counsels. St. Thomas Aquinas, principally, sought clarification on this point.[26] Even St. Thomas, who has dominated the theology of works of supererogation and of the counsels down to the present day, in spite of all the breadth of vision that characterizes his perfectly rounded theology, remains contradictory and unsatisfactory on many points. According to him the counsels — "the three universal and perfect counsels" of the religious life from which all "particular counsels can be deduced"[27] — were proclaimed by Christ and "added to the commandments".[28] This was fitting for the "new law", which is a law of freedom.[29] Urged on by grace the Christian should be able freely to choose the better means of reaching the one goal that is set before all: perfection in love.[30] Whoever resolves upon this course[31] and remains faithful to this way arrives at the "peak of perfection",[32] whereas other Christians as a rule never get beyond the grades of "beginners and advanced", that is the lower and intermediate grades of perfection.[33] St. Thomas even makes bold to assert, that the perfection of love, which is the goal of the religious life, occupies a place between the love of the saints in heaven and the love of Christians living in the

[24] We come upon this concept even before its theological systematization by St. Thomas in, for example, the bull of Honorius III approving the Carmelite order (1226). This concludes chapter XVI with these words: "We have written these things to you in compressed form, thus providing you with a plumb-line for your way of life. But if anyone does more than is required (*supererogaverit*), the Lord will reward him at his coming" (*Bullar. Rom.*, III [1858], p. 417).

[25] Jerome, *Ep.* 22, 20: "Why did (St. Paul) not issue a precept concerning virginity? Because that which is not compulsory but is performed voluntarily earns a greater reward" (*PL*, XXII, col. 104).

[26] Protestants, too, admit this. Cf. F. Lau in *RGG*, II, cols. 786f.; B. Lohse, *Mönchtum und Reformation* (1963), pp. 150 ff.

[27] *Summa Theologica*, I–II, q. 108, a. 4 c.

[28] *Ibid.*, q. 107 a. 2 c; q. 108 a. 4 c.

[29] *Ibid.*, q. 108 a. 4 c. Following St. Augustine, St. Thomas prefers the concept of the "new law" (as fulfilment of the "old law") and discusses this in detail in questions 106–8 of I–II.

[30] The emphasis on the instrumental character of the counsels that is so essential for St. Thomas was to be found in ancient monasticism: cf. *Summa Theologica*, II–II, q. 184, a. 3 c.

[31] According to St. Thomas the counsels were intrinsically set before all men by Christ, "but because of the absence of suitable interior disposition they are not demanded of many, because their effort does not lie along these lines" (*Summa Theologica*, I–II, q. 108, a. 4 ad 1).

[32] On this ancient topic of spiritual tradition cf. my commentary on Chapters V and VI of the Constitution on the Church, cited in footnote 14.

[33] *Summa Theologica*, I–II, q. 108, a. 2 c.

world.[34] Here for the first time the whole gravity of the distinction, as St. Thomas sees it, between commandment and counsel becomes plain. Religious, who by following the counsels "keep as far away as they can from earthly things, even those that are permitted",[35] have chosen "that which is quite simply intrinsically and universally better".[36] If they take the duties of their state seriously, they find themselves wholly and constantly orientated towards God, have, as it were, already begun to leave this aeon behind, and are approaching the condition of the blessed, whereas Christians living in the world, content simply to fulfil the law, are "prevented from having their hearts constantly turned towards the Lord" by their manifold attachments to this world's goods.[37]

Today a number of serious objections are being raised to this view of the relation between commandment and counsel, which was clearly expressed in the first draft of the decree on the religious life.[38] In the first place these objections are concerned with the inadequate scriptural exegesis upon which St. Thomas's theology of the counsels is based. His affirmation, that Christ proclaimed the three counsels as concrete renunciations, in excess of what the law commands, and leading to perfection, cannot find scriptural warrant.[39] This is true especially of obedience, and possibly of poverty also. In particular, his frequent exegesis of the passage about the rich young man in its Matthaean version (Mt 19:16–22) is no longer tenable;[40] and upon this he based the distinction, the sharp contrast, we might say, between commandment and counsel. More important, because dealing with the facts themselves, is St. Thomas's predominantly ascetical

---

[34] *Ibid.*, q. 44, a. 4 ad 2 and ad 3. Pope Paul VI quoted this passage in his allocution of 7 March 1967 to the first ever assembly in Rome of representatives of the international union of superiors general of female religious orders, in order to make clear to them the distinguishing characteristic of the religious life in contrast to the normal Christian life (*AAS* 59 [1967]).

[35] *Summa Theologica*, I–II, q. 44, a. 4, ad 2.

[36] *Ibid.*, q. 108, a. 4 ad 2.

[37] *Ibid.*, q. 44, a. 4 ad 3.

[38] In the preface to the first draft of the Decree on the Religious Life we read: "The divine teacher and pattern of all holiness, Christ the Lord, undoubtedly added to the commandments of the spiritual life through which all men are to be led to their appointed goal, the doctrine that those who wanted to follow him more closely must choose and follow the evangelical counsels." This sentence is taken *verbatim* from the apostolic letter of Pius XI, *Unigenitus Dei Filius*, of 19 March 1924 (*AAS* 16 [1924], p. 133). The beginning of chapter V of the first draft of the Constitution on the Church was in the same vein (note 17): "Jesus Christ the Lord, the august shepherd of the sheep (cf. Heb 13:20), has not only protected his Church with sanctifying grace, through attention to which all who believe in him may find salvation (cf. Mt 19:17–19), but has also endowed it with the most holy counsels so that those who desire it may be granted an unimpeded and surer way to the fulfilment of love which is the fulfilment of the law (cf. Rom 13:10)."

[39] Cf. T.-A. Deman's commentary on the *Summa Theologica*, I–II, q. 108, a. 4 ad 1 and ad 3 in the German edition of St. Thomas, vol. XIV, p. 323. He admits that St. Thomas has deduced the threefold counsels logically and systematically in harmony with the doctrine of threefold concupiscence rather than from a pertinent exegesis of Scripture (*ibid.*, p. 322).

[40] On the exegesis of Mt. 19:16–22 cf. S. Légasse, *L'appel du riche. Contribution à l'étude des fondements scripturaires de l'état religieux* (1966).

interpretation of the counsels. This is specially evident in passages where he deals systematically with the counsels.[41] Here the counsels are not regarded as forms of life and perfections of the imitation of Christ, but primarily as ascetic methods of individual sanctification. More precisely: they are a cutting loose from earthly goods so as to be free for a greater love of God (from which love of one's neighbour necessarily follows), and as such — again following a highly systematized exegesis of 1 Jn 2:16[42] — contrasted with three-fold concupiscence.[43] This emphasis on the ascetic character of the counsels, and the presupposition that all of the faithful are invited to follow the counsels,[44] with the consequence that the individual will is entreated magnanimously to choose the better way, not only expose the doctrine to the danger of an individualistic[45] approach to salvation, but also — all unintentionally — open the door to misinterpretation along the lines of an ethic of works.[46] Both of these things have influenced the common understanding of religious life right down to the present day. At all events it can scarcely be denied, that in St. Thomas the character of the counsels as unmerited, individual gifts of grace is not sufficiently evident.

The core of modern criticism of St. Thomas's doctrine of the counsels lies here: this doctor of the Church based the counsels upon the freedom that characterizes the "new law", a freedom which allows the disciples of Jesus Christ to choose the better way that leads to salvation and a perfect life, without being compelled to do so. "From the commandment", says St. Thomas, "comes constraint; but a counsel is left to the choice of him to whom it is offered."[47] But is not — according to St. Thomas himself — the "new law" as such a law of freedom, because of grace, not only enabling those who are redeemed in Christ to perform what the law commands out of love and in the freedom of the children

---

[41] As well as the questions in the *Summa Theologica* already cited the principal text is *De perf. vit. spir.*

[42] Cf. R. Schnackenburg, *Die Johannesbriefe,* Herders Theologischer Kommentar zum NT XIII, 3 (1953), pp. 112f. (English translation in preparation).

[43] *Summa Theologica,* I–II, q. 77, a. 5; q. 108, a. 3 ad 4; q. 108, a. 4 c.

[44] *Ibid.,* q. 108, a. 4 ad 1.

[45] The idea of an individualistic approach to salvation is suggested above all by the way in which St. Thomas distinguishes love of God and love of one's neighbour, self-sanctification and apostolate (e.g., *Summa Theologica,* I–II, q. 4, a. 8 c; II–II, q. 182, a. 2 c; q. 187, a. 2 c; q. 188, a. 2 c; q. 188, a. 8 c).

[46] It is somewhat astonishing to see how some modern exponents of St. Thomas unquestioningly see the counsels chiefly as a moral performance and lay all the stress upon good works. Thus, for example, B.-M. Dietsche, in the German edition of St. Thomas — commentary on *Summa Theologica,* II–II, q. 184, a. 3: "An evangelical counsel in the sense meant here is a good work that is better than its opposite and is proposed to the faithful by Christ in order that they may gain everlasting life." "A commandment attaches to a necessary work which a man is bound by the law to perform. The counsel covers a work that is not obligatory under the law, because it is not necessary in the sense of being an action demanded by the law."

[47] *Summa Theologica,* I–II, q. 108, a. 4 c.

of God,[48] but also for ever sending them out to seek the whole of God's will, and arousing in them a desire for an ever deeper love, for this law is in harmony with the inscrutable mystery of the God who redeems? Must not, therefore, the counsels of necessity be an interior, essential element in the New Testament preceptory ethic itself — because an element in every act of faith, hope and love? The "new law" did not add any new substance concerning the perfection of man as such to the moral law of the Old Testament. Nothing can be added to the supreme commandment of love from which all other commandments are derived and in which all find their unifying and vitalizing centre.[49] What is new in the "law of grace" is rather that Christ by imparting his Spirit, the Spirit of understanding and love, grants us a share in his own fulfilling of the law, both in the substance and in the manner of fulfilling that law, in the sacrifice of his life for men and their salvation and in his love for the Father. Anyone who lives by this imparting of grace knows ultimately how to fulfil but one commandment in all the separate precepts: the commandment to love. This cannot be restricted to specific, fixed, previously recognizable duties, but is in fact without any limits. In all his objective and universal obligation to the moral demands of the second table of the decalogue, in all the exigencies and situations of his life, he knows that he lives under the ever present, personal call of God, a call that lures and leads to love. He is aware of the imperative that manifests itself in this, the commandment to increase constantly in love. How this imperative is best applied to the here and now of each passing hour cannot be deduced solely from rational considerations, however Christian. Allowing for every attention being given to the morally relevant objective demands and personal duties that must always be presupposed, it is the Spirit of living love alone that enables him to apply this imperative, the Spirit of the crucified Christ imparted to him through grace, for this is perfected love.

This is where we find the counsels: in the realm of that love with which God has loved us in his Son, and by which he empowers us, through his Spirit, to live again like Christ and with Christ. The horizon of those who have fallen under the power of the Spirit of love opens up to the Christian — "because God's love has been poured into our hearts through the Holy Spirit who has been given to us" (Rom 5:5). Thus he is no longer subject to the law of mere reason which gives knowledge only of what is morally correct and in accord with prudence, but obeys the message of the foolishness of the cross in the light of which he begins to deny himself against all reason, and to yield up his life. As long as he still lives in this world, unable simply to ignore its ordinances, he cannot immediately determine when and in what manner he may sacrifice legitimate and even necessary personal goods. Only the voice of the Spirit can tell him, for with the desire the Spirit also gives the insight by which he can discern the will

---

[48] *Summa Theologica,* I–II, q. 108, a. 1 ad 2; *In praecepta legis* (Ed. Parm. XV, pp. 97 and 99).

[49] All this is also frequently stressed by St. Thomas in connection with Rom 13:10.

311

of God in the concrete situation.[50] The general commandment which requires every Christian to imitate the Lord by yielding up his life as an act of love, appears to him at first as an individual counsel, as a call of the counselling and impelling Spirit. This explains why we may say that the demands made in the Sermon on the Mount, which apart from grace make too big a demand upon men, are commandment and counsel in one. A discernment of spirits is always required before the general law of discipleship, the obligation to follow the way of the cross as the road to glory, becomes the commandment of the moment;[51] but because this takes place in an act of supra-rational understanding which can never be traced back to precisely analyzible reasons, the Spirit's call to love, which is addressed to the freedom of a loving heart, will always be a counselling love.

From all of this it would appear that we may speak of two ways, a way of precept and a way of counsel, only if we make careful distinctions, otherwise misunderstandings will arise. For there are many counsels, as many as the calls of grace that come to men in the concrete situations of their lives. It is true that the counsels that are perceived through lending an attentive ear to the call of crucified love are of various degrees. "Outstanding among them is that precious gift of divine grace which the Father gives to some men so that by virginity, or celibacy, they can more easily devote their entire selves to God alone with undivided heart."[52] Hence the call to a religious life will always have its special place in Christianity. The three counsels which constitute it are "a divine gift, which the Church has received from her Lord".[53] In the last analysis, however, every Christian life is concerned with exactly the same thing: fulfilling the commandments, in particular the one great command of love, in the spirit of the evangelical counsels, of the alluring and constraining love of the Lord who gave his life for us. Fundamentally this is what St. Thomas, too, was well aware of, for on the one hand he placed the Sermon on the Mount along with the commandments,[54] and, on the other, saw the counsels there as well.[55] If, however, he regarded the counsels as something which, in view of perfection of love as the performance of special and supererogatory works, Christ had added to the

---

[50] What K. Rahner has expounded quite generally concerning the knowledge of the particular will of God in a concrete situation ("Die ignatianische Logik der existentiellen Erkenntnis", in *Ignatius von Loyola* [1956], pp. 345 ff.) applies very specially in the realm of the renunciations involved in following the way of the cross.

[51] Cf. B. Schüller, *op. cit.*, p. 70: "Even if a life of obedience, celibacy and poverty possessed *in concreto* the character of the counsels, to a man trained in Ignatian indifference it would not be felt as mere counsel, but as a spiritual obligation."

[52] Constitution on the Church, Article 42.

[53] *Ibid.*, Article 43.

[54] *Summa Theologica*, I–II, q. 108, a. 3 c.

[55] *Ibid.*, q. 108, a. 4 ad 4; *De perf. vit. spir.*, chapter XIV (on Mt 5:44, 46). Suárez speaks even more plainly: "We can make a long list of counsels; they are to be found in every object of virtue . . . We might even say that the counsels find their place in every virtue within the actions that are commanded in respect of their concrete circumstances" (*De religione*, tract VII, book I, chapter VIII, n. 4: *Vives*, vol. XV, p. 39 a).

commandments, then not only does he seem to contradict his own principle, that Christian action is primarily an interior thing, manifesting itself only secondarily in external works,[56] but also minimizes — against his will — the universal Christian state (than which there can be no more perfect state).[57] So severely does he do this that by his doctrine of the counsels he not only introduces a difference of state among Christians, but a veritable class-distinction,[58] sharply contradicting the statements of the Second Vatican Council concerning the common dignity of all Christians.[59] Such a dichotomy is bound to create the impression that in his doctrine of the counsels the doctor of the Church was proceeding from more than one *a priori.* The first that strikes us is the pronounced class-thinking, which was so characteristic of the medieval social order, and which, *a priori,* granted the religious orders a special place within a clerically determined society. Then there was the contemplative ideal of the *vacare Deo* which required the almost complete renunciation of earthly goods, of all earthly interests and obligations. Traditionally this idea was unchallenged as the model of the highest Christian perfection. Today, on theological and anthropological grounds, we cannot so easily by-pass the world and its values, ordinances and duties, cannot tear asunder the spiritual and the secular, as the monastic tradition and the theology of the religious state have wanted to do right down to the present day.[60] On the contrary, we stress not only the unity of the Christian ideal of perfection, but also the fundamental, essential equality of the Christian way, in so far as all the baptized must exceed the merely obvious ethics of the commandments by remaining open to the infinite call of God, in order to work out their salvation. Seen in this light the two states, that of the evangelical counsels, and that of Christians in the world, draw closer together. Both are entrusted with the one undivided commission of Christ and the Church to the world and for the world; both are able to transfigure the world and present God only in the spirit of the Beatitudes (which have to be made visible and palpable in each situation). This is what the religious state is meant to symbolize clearly on behalf of all Christians, and to testify in an exemplary fashion,[61] this is its charism, its special ministry within the Church. This view did not appear in the first draft of the decree on religious life, and although in later affirmations of the Council it came more and more into prominence, a genuine and completely logical re-casting

---

[56] *Summa Theologica,* I–II, q. 108, a. 1 ad 1; *ibid.,* q. 81, a. 7 c.

[57] *Ibid.,* q. 106, a. 4 c: "Therefore there can be no more perfect state in our present life than the state of the new law." St. Thomas calls this the "evangelical state" (*ibid.,* ad 1).

[58] "The perfection of love, at which the counsels are aimed, holds an intermediate place between the two modes of perfection we have named" — i.e., between "the perfection of our eternal home" (the blessed) and "the perfection of those on the way there" (Christians who live by the commandments). *Summa Theologica,* I–II, q. 44, a. 4 ad 2 and ad 3.

[59] Dogmatic Constitution on the Church, Article 42.

[60] Cf. my commentary on Chapters V and VI of the Dogmatic Constitution on the Church (referred to above in footnote 14).

[61] Dogmatic Constitution on the Church, Article 31.

of a theology of the relation between commandment and counsel and hence of the religious state was never reached.

Alongside the basic problem of the relation between commandment and counsel there was another which had to be discussed: the old and for ever re-appearing problem of the relation between contemplation and apostolic work. This problem is closely linked with the former. Once again the problem is not purely speculative. Its solution has consequences for the concrete shape of religious life.

The third chapter of the draft of 1963 bore the title: "The appropriate renewal of the states of perfection in respect of their double goal". A distinction was made between the chief goal *(finis principalis)* of the religious life and the specific goal *(finis specificus)* of a community,[62] a mode of speech that has come into use, no doubt, as a result of the full integration of modern active societies (with simple vows) into the religious state.[63] In the draft the chief goal of the religious life was described as perfect union with God, from which love of one's neighbour necessarily arises. Mentioned as specific goals were, on the one hand, the purely contemplative life (with strict enclosure, silence, the liturgy, prayer and penance), on the other, apostolic and charitable activities. According to ancient and universal tradition these make up the two basic types of religious life, the model for which has been seen since the time of the Fathers — although not always unambiguously — in the two sisters in the Gospels, Mary and Martha.[64] The draft said nothing about the so-called mixed life, the *vita mixta*,[65] to which as a rule the medieval (male) orders considered themselves to belong. In fact, mention of it was deliberately avoided.

A twofold purpose lay behind the terminology of the double goal.[66] 1) The

[62] Articles 17 and 20 of the draft.

[63] This was effected by the *CIC*, although the development had already been completed, *de facto*, by Pope Leo XIII's *Conditae a Christo* of 8 December 1900 (*AAS* 33 [1900], pp. 341-7). Thereafter the *terminus technicus*, "specific religious goal" is met with, as, for example, in the *Elenchus quaestionum* of 25 March 1922, according to which the congregations taking simple vows must indicate the specific goal *(scopus peculiaris Instituti)* of their institute in their quinquennial report (*AAS* 14 [1922], p. 278).

[64] The exposition of this tradition which has remained current until today is to be found in St. Thomas: *III Sent.* d. 35 q. 1; *Summa Theologica*, II–II, q. 179–82, 188.

[65] We find the expression in Radulfus Ardens (d. 1200 or a little earlier). He uses it to describe the way of life of pastors and preachers, the way of life that Christ himself followed (*Hom.* 31 *pro tempore: PL*, CLV, cols. 1425–6). Augustine acknowledged a third way of life *(tertium vitae genus)* which united contemplation and activity (*De Civ. Dei*, XIX, 2). St. Thomas does not use the expression *vita mixta*, and even denies the existence of a third way of life (*Summa Theologica*, II–II, q. 179, a. 2); but he describes the preaching order as the highest form of religious life because it makes contemplation fruitful for others ("contemplata aliis tradere": *Summa Theologica*, II–II, q. 188, a. 6 c). In *Summa Theologica*, II–II, q. 181, a. 2 ad 3, he speaks of an "intermediate way of life between the active and the contemplative life."

[66] On this see the book by the secretary of the Congregation for Religious, P. Philippe, *Les fins de la vie religieuse selon S. Thomas d'Aquin* (1962).

authors of the draft were primarily intent upon stressing the absolute necessity of contemplation, of the pre-eminence of the interior life over the exterior apostolate, and hence upon countering the danger of activism, the one-sided emphasis upon apostolic engagement, among modern religious orders.[67] Thus the annotations to the draft — often very detailed — also spoke of contemplation as the chief goal of religious life, by which was understood "interior or theological contemplation"[68] as distinct from "the canonical contemplative way of life" of the contemplative orders. 2) This concept of interior theological contemplation, first introduced into official ecclesiastical parlance by Pius XII,[69] would, it was thought, be more in line with the traditional doctrine of contemplation as the specific and ultimate goal of religious life,[70] and also with the central concern of the active congregations, i.e., the unity of their religious ideal with their way of life. Moreover, it seemed specially adapted to demonstrating clearly the interior integration and linking of contemplation and apostolate, of the general and the particular goals of the religious life.

Many, however, did not agree to this interpretation. They complained that "interior theological contemplation" as the chief goal of religious life signified merely the fact that God, who has come to meet us in Christ and who is thus present in the Church, is the conscious centre of Christian life, and hence to be sought before all else and in everything, in the sense of Mt 6:33, so that this goal becomes set before every Christian (as the draft expressly emphasized in article 6 on the contemplative orders, quoting a saying of Pope Pius XII),[71] and cannot therefore be set forth as the specific goal, which distinguishes the religious from the secular state. Or they objected that it made the practice of contemplation so much the primary and authentic substance of religious life — following the *de facto* traditional understanding of religious life[72] — that it did not do justice to the work of most of our present-day religious orders. The interpretation did,

---

[67] Article 17 of the drafts reads: religious "must not fall into the error usually called 'activism', an error that is on the increase with some, and which consists in the neglect of the interior life and the disparagement of the efficacy of prayer, becoming infected by that restless and often fruitless fever of a more apparent than effective activity, as they call it".

[68] This concept is to be found in the draft text itself (Article 16).

[69] The constitution *Sponsa Christi* of 21 November 1950 (*AAS* 43 [1915], pp. 15–16); radio addresses on the contemplative orders for women of 19 and 25 July, and 2 August 1958 (*AAS* 50 [1958], pp. 565–7, 574, 581).

[70] The classic testimony of this doctrine is St. Thomas, *Contra imp. Dei cultum*, c. 2; c. 11; *Quodl.*, IV a. 24 ad 5; *De perf. vit. spir.*, c. 6. Cf. P. Philippe, *op. cit.*, pp. 42 ff.

[71] The constitution *Sponsa Christi: AAS* 43 (1951), p. 15.

[72] In this way, in a letter written in 1900, Leo XIII described quite generally and without finer distinction between contemplative and active orders, the essence of the religious life: "As everyone knows, the orders have their origin and the justification for their existence in the sublime evangelical counsels which our divine Redeemer addressed to all in every age who desire Christian perfection: to all heroic and generous souls who strive, through prayer and contemplation, through sacred austerity and following a specific way of life, to climb up to the highest peak of Christian perfection" (*Acta Leonis XIII*, vol. XX, p. 340).

indeed, result in a kind of parallelism: there was the monastic life dedicated to silence and prayer, and the life of activity; and this parallelism called the unity of the religious life in question. Closer study of the text of the draft reveals that the latter understanding of contemplation remained normative as the chief goal of the religious life — influenced no doubt by the weight of traditional doctrine and the actual appearance of the orders as they have now come to be. A clear distinction is made between the monastic life, the *vita regularis*[73] and the apostolate or exterior activity (Article 20). The former demands, for the sake of union with God which is the chief goal of the religious life, fervent practice of the contemplative life with the various observances this involves, and hence a separation of religious from the world, having as a consequence the restriction of their intercourse with their fellow men (Articles 19 and 25);[74] even the apostolic work undertaken by contemplatives must be limited, so that their monastic life does not suffer (Article 20); but at the same time, apostolic work will be fruitful only in the measure in which it proceeds from contemplation, from the fulness of interior life (Article 18).

This concept of religious life is clearly applicable to the mendicant orders which endeavour to combine the contemplative life (of a monastic style) with apostolic life, and which have more or less become the model for active religious life (especially for women).

The question, however, — and it was one that greatly exercised the Council — is this: is such a model still in harmony with the goal and requirements of the active orders and societies of modern times (and was it really in harmony with them in the past)? The work they do or are supposed to do cannot so easily be compared with their work of former times. It requires not only much more intensive and highly specialized training, but makes totally different demands upon time, energy and interests than in former days. It can no longer be linked with a monastic style of the *vita regularis,* which on the whole was dedicated to the immediate worship of God, characterized by spiritual exercises, and hedged about by observances. Is this not one of the causes for the present crisis in the active religious orders? Thus the question was raised: must we not find a fresh concept of the relation between contemplation and activity, between the life of prayer and the apostolate? Had St. Thomas, whose thought had determined the model worked out in the draft,[75] really said the last word on this problem? Today this is called in

---

[73] Originally "life under a rule", but the expression took on the meaning of "monastic observance.".

[74] Article 25 of the draft quoted a saying from Pius XII's allocution *Haud mediocri* of 11 February 1958 to superiors general concerning the necessary separation of religious from the world: "Whoever strives for evangelical perfection must withdraw from the world and cut himself off from it, in fact in the measure of the calling with which God has called him, but, as far as inclination is concerned, completely" (*AAS* 50 [1958], p. 156). The draft does not add that the Pope in this context was speaking explicitly of the sinful world.

[75] The many citations from St. Thomas in the notes are proof of this.

question, and rightly so.[76] It is true that St. Thomas had sought to make contemplation more fruitful for the apostolate than had the monastic tradition in general.[77] According to him it is a sign of greater love and is more meritorious if a person is ready to forego the joys of contemplation for the sake of another's salvation.[78]

Nonetheless he still regarded contemplation as an unconditionally greater good than acts of love of one's neighbour; for in virtue of its exclusion of all worldly and sensuous distraction it possesses an immediacy of the divine presence which causes one to be directed without obstacle to the perfection of the love of God,[79] whereas external activity even when it can be accounted love of one's neighbour, diverts us from the one thing that is necessary (Lk 10:41).[80] And so it comes about that "St. Thomas, although he set the *religio mixta* above the purely contemplative life, in the end placed the *vita eremitica* above the *vita socialis* because the perfect is sufficient unto itself.[81]

It is no longer possible for us to attach love of God to contemplation and love of our neighbour to action, as simply as St. Thomas did,[82] quite apart from the fact that to us "to be absorbed in contemplation of God" appears to be a "purely private affair" — not to say egoistic.[83] Even the equivalence which St. Thomas strove to establish between contemplation and action, according to which the two alternate with one another and mutually advance one another,[84] appears to

[76] There is a comprehensive exposition by H. U. v. Balthasar of the doctrine of St. Thomas on the relation between action and contemplation in the German edition of St. Thomas, XXIII, pp. 431 ff.; id., "Aktion und Kontemplation, in *Verbum Caro* (1960), pp. 245 ff.

[77] The classic passage for this is *Summa Theologica*, II–II, q. 188, a. 6 c, which portrays the preaching orders as the highest form of the religious life.

[78] "Speaking generally it would seem to prove greater love when by neglecting the consolations he would gain from contemplating God, a man sought the glory of God in the conversion of another" (*Sent.* d. 35 q. 1 a. 4 sol. 2). "There are men who rise to such heights of love that they give up divine contemplation in spite of the great joy they find in it, in order to serve God by working for the salvation of their neighbour" (*De carit.*, Qu. unica, a. 11 ad 6); similarly *Quodl.*, I, a. 14 ad 2; *Summa Theologica*, II–II, q. 182, a. 2 c).

[79] "The contemplative life aims directly *(directe)* and immediately at the love of God" (*Summa Theologica*, II–II, q. 182, a. 2 c). "The contemplative life is orientated not towards this or that love, but towards the perfect love of God" (*Summa Theologica*, II–II, q. 182, a. 4 ad 1).

[80] "Care about exterior actions and their execution . . . hinders the contemplative life" (*Summa Theologica*, II–II, q. 182, a. 3 c; cf. also *ibid.*, a. 1 c).

[81] H. U. u. Balthasar, *op. cit.*, p. 257, with reference to *Summa Theologica*, II–II, q. 188, a. 8 c.

[82] *Summa Theologica*, II–II, q. 182, a. 1 c (7); *ibid.*, a. 2 c; a. 4 ob. 1.

[83] H. U. v. Balthasar, *op. cit.*, p. 257; cf. *Summa Theologica*, II–II, q. 187, a. 2: "This aim of the religious life is the attainment of perfect love. This comprises first, the love of God, and then love of one's neighbour. Hence religious must principally *(praecipae)* strive — for the sake of their own sanctification — to be free to contemplate God *(quod Deo vacent)*."

[84] Thomas compares those who are dedicated to the salvation of souls to the angels upon Jacob's Ladder (Gen 28:12; Jn 1:51), who ascend in contemplation and descend as they care for the salvation of souls (*De carit.* Qu. unica a. 11 ad 6). He speaks of that third way of life "intermediate between the active and the contemplative life, in respect of that to which they devote themselves, for now they are occupied in contemplation, now in external works" (*Summa Theologica*, II–II, q. 181, a. 2 ad 3).

us as inadequate and too idealistic to be fruitful for the world apostolate today. In addition there is this fact: for us the love of God and the love of our neighbour, in the abstract, and in the concrete situations of everyday life, form an indivisible unity.[85] We believe, even, that we are able to encounter God only in the totality of our existence, only in our neighbour, in our brother, in the fellowship of brothers, because HE first became our brother (in his Incarnation) and wants to meet us in his brothers (Mt 25:14). With reference to the ideal of the active religious life this means: the apostolic and charitable work which explains the origin and existence of our modern religious orders, as radical love of one's neighbour in the sense of the gospels, as imitation of Christ, provided it proceeds from a pure motive and from the charity that grace brings, already is the love of God, is the concrete way in which these congregations love God above all things, and by which they seek to put themselves unreservedly at the disposal of his redemptive will. It is not solitary, self-sufficient contemplation[86] but the apostolate which forms the heart of their religious life. Ignatius of Loyola thought thus. Fundamentally it was no order in the traditional sense that he founded. He was not concerned any longer about linking the contemplative and the apostolic life as he found them in the orders of his time, but simply with the apostolate. For him the goal and substance of his "order" was to help souls *(iuvare animas)*. This by no means signified for him a neglect of the contemplative life. On the contrary, it seemed to him to be more necessary than ever. But he interpreted it, in terms of the call he had heard, not as something self-contained and worth seeking on its own, but as the indispensable power behind any fruitful apostolate.[87] No dualism in the forms of life is to be encouraged — spiritual practices on the one hand and exterior works on the other —, in the end everything must be spiritual and hence a prayer. In the midst of work the apostle ought to be a contemplative, a man of prayer, in union with God.[88]

A realization of the unity of Christian contemplation and Christian action, born of the living unity of love of God and love of one's neighbour, has exerted too hesitant an influence upon the Church's official religious ideal. The monastic tradition was too strong. In the 19th century, a period of political and ecclesiastical

---

[85] Cf. K. Rahner, "Über die Einheit von Nächstenliebe und Gottesliebe", in *Schriften zur Theologie*, VI, pp. 277–98.

[86] *Summa Theologica*, II–II, q. 182, a. 1 c (4); q. 188 a. 8 c.

[87] Cf. the Jesuit Constitution, X, 2: "To attain that for which the Society of Jesus strives, i.e., to assist souls to reach their ultimate and supernatural end, the means which unite the instrument with God, putting that instrument at God's disposal so that he can easily direct it, are much more effective than those means which put the instrument at the disposal of men. These means are righteousness and virtue, above all love and the pure intention of serving God, and closeness to God through spiritual exercises of devotion, and upright zeal for souls, for the glory of him who created and redeemed them, and for no other motive."

[88] Jerome Nadal, a close friend of Ignatius and one best acquainted with the Constitutions, expressed the manner of prayer of the founder of the order in these words: "in the midst of activity he was a contemplative" (*Mon. Hict. S. J., Epist, Nadal*, IV, p. 657).

restoration, it revived mightily and gave its stamp to the religious orders down to very recent times. It is here that individual salvationism and the dualism of modern religious life find their habitat, for both are rooted in the monastic view of the relation between contemplation and action. Not until the Council did this relation become a subject of debate. Insight into the social and ecclesial aspects of the religious vocation and hence of the evangelical counsels was slow in coming, and the question about the necessary relationship of this vocation with the world scarcely emerged. The reason for this was not least that at first the traditional doctrine of the precedence of contemplation over exterior activity was not sufficiently worked out in terms of the biblical theology of redemption. This is made plain by the draft of 1963 and the discussion associated with it.

Let us return to the further course of work upon the Decree on the Religious Life. Having received the draft at the end of April 1963, the Council Fathers were asked to send in their comments and proposed alterations by July. Although relatively few of them responded to this request, the comments ran to over 200 pages. These were handed over for study to the members of the Commission for Religious at the beginning of and during the second phase of the Council. The outcome of this expert enquiry was as follows: a series of laudatory statements about the draft as a whole was balanced by severe criticism (from the English and Dutch episcopate and also from some individual bishops). The substance of the criticism was that the draft contained little more than pious platitudes and merely reiterated the much-repeated official statements of the Church on the theme. It did not really grapple with the real problems of present-day religious life. The criticism came down to details on the following points: the title ("On the states that aim at perfection") was disapproved by many; the schema was too juridical and not sufficiently pastoral; a clearer distinction ought to be made between the contemplative and the active religious life, for different goals were bound to lead to a great variety of institutional forms of religious life; a whole series of bishops expressed disappointment that nothing had been said about closer collaboration between the orders and the episcopate; finally objections were made to the Latinized uniformity of religious life in the Church, leaving too little scope for autonomous development in countries with other traditions and cultures (in missionary countries especially). A noteworthy contribution was sent in by the Dutch Bishop Baeten, who had died meanwhile. He expressed concern lest the proposed *aggiornamento* of the religious life founder because of failure to enquire properly into the contemplative convents of women. Bishop Huyghe had already voiced this concern in the Commission. In proof that these orders themselves were not sufficiently aware that the traditional institutions of the female religious required re-thinking in view of the changed world and the altered mentality of women, he enclosed a longish letter from a Dutch convent which expounded very precisely the problems that face a contemplative nun of today, if she happens to be the sort of person who is aware of the way the world is developing, and is conscious of the special function she has to play in the Church and for mankind. These questions were never properly discussed in the Council, and when they did come up, they were treated with extreme caution, for fear lest the contemplative orders, which have always been regarded in the Church as a specially precious fruit of gracious calling, should suffer any damage.

This short review shows that with a few exceptions they were content by and large with relatively general comments on the draft — whether laudatory or critical. Few constructive contributions towards an appropriate renewal of the religious life were put forward. The deeper problems of such a renewal when examined from the theological, anthropological, psychological and sociological angles were never raised. The whole gravity of the crisis in which the traditional religious life now finds itself never became evident. The time was not yet ripe for this. There is no point in worrying about the situation in the Council at that time. During the second session of the Council the Commission for Religious was occupied almost exclusively with the fourth (finally the fifth) chapter of the Constitution on the Church, "On the Call to Holiness in the Church". The abbreviated draft of the decree on religious of 1963 never appeared on the table, not even later. It suffered the same fate as the original draft of the pre-conciliar commission: it was never discussed in the Council hall.

Towards the end of the second phase of the Council it became obvious that the slowness of the proceedings would result in only a very small part of the material being discussed. Discussion on the Constitution of the Church alone had taken a whole month. And so the Co-ordinating Commission, in a letter dated 29 November 1963, announced that the schema (with four other schemata) would have to be abbreviated even more rigorously. Excluding all juridical regulations, which were to be reserved for the coming reform of the *Codex,* the production of the new text was to pay heed first and foremost to the pastoral intention of the Council. More precisely: a letter, dated 23 January 1964, containing instructions, was sent to the commission. This ordered that the schema was to state only the essential points *(puncta essentialia)* of appropriate renewal of the religious life in the form of short guiding principles *(propositiones),* and these were then to be presented to the council fathers in plenary session for approval without previous discussion. This plan was clearly designed to allow the Council to complete its business by the end of the third session. In these circumstances the third stage of work on the decree on religious began. The Commission set about making the required abbreviation in two sessions, 27 January — 4 February, and 4 March — 9 March. The text was cut down, largely re-arranged, and the number of articles reduced from 51 to 19. Now it ran to scarcely four pages.

As requested, the schema, bearing the fresh title *De Religiosis,* was presented to Cardinal Cicognani, and then, on account of lack of time, handed on by the Co-ordinating Commission to the Pope so that it might be printed immediately.

This was in the middle of April. The fascicle sent to the Council Fathers was dated 27 April. The suggestion made by Cardinal Döpfner, *relator* for the schema in the Co-ordinating Commission, had been made known to the Commission for Religious who had passed these on to its members at the beginning of the third session, along with the comments of the council fathers. (Cardinal Döpfner's view in general was that the schema, while containing many good and useful points, also contained much that was self-evident, and by-passed the concrete problems of religious life today.) By reason of these comments the schema was again revised between the end of September and the beginning of October, and a fourth redaction of the text produced. Shortly before public discussion (10 October 1964), which the *praesidium* and the moderators still thought profitable in the case of the abridged schemata, it was circulated to the Council Fathers. Once again the title had been changed. After much argument back and fore the title finally became: "On the Appropriate Renewal of the Religious Life". It has correctly been remarked that this is the one title among the conciliar documents which refers to Pope John's avowed intention for the Council: the renewal of the Church with reference to the needs of the times. Before going on to discuss the course of the debate let us briefly comment on the character of the third and fourth redactions of the decree on religious. We shall observe specially whether these exhibit any definite development, any distinct progress.

The task set the Commission of reducing the schema to short guiding principles was almost impossible to carry out in view of the diversity of opinion in the Commission, and because of the variety of forms of religious order. Thus the attempt was bound to be unsatisfactory, and bound to provoke objections from this or that quarter. This was, indeed, the fate of all of the abbreviated schemata. After heated discussion these were either rejected, so that they had to be completely re-written, or so many proposals for alteration were made, that they had to be largely re-cast and expanded. Looking back we may well ask whether the Co-ordinating Commission's demand for rigorous abbreviation was a wholly beneficial action. On the other hand it would seem that for formal juridical reasons the Commission for Religious was hampered in its work by too many restrictions. They interpreted the task assigned to them in the sense that an abbreviation of the text was all that was required: fresh statements, even if these remained "within the framework of essential points",[89] were to be permitted only to a very limited extent. All the same the third redaction of the schema, in spite of its brevity, in part because of it, represented progress. For one thing, many juridical expressions, many platitudes and pious flourishes had been dropped, as well as the expression of an unmistakable paternalism in the relation between superiors and subjects. It showed progress, too, in the

[89] Cf. the Council documents: Schema Propositionum, *De Religiosis,* Appendix (Typ. polygl. Vat., 1964), Introduction, p. 6; Commissio Conciliaris, *De Religiosis (Folium Officii* of 5 October 1964), preliminary remarks, p. 1.

inclusion of small but important, because symptomatic, additions. A few of these might be mentioned. The supreme rule for appropriate renewal of religious life was said to be the gospel and the imitation of Christ. This was a substantial and essential statement which was to be incorporated in a somewhat amended form in the final text (Article 2a). The *venerabiles traditiones*, the "venerable traditions" of an order, which were to be preserved, was now changed — still with deference to conservatism — to "sanae traditiones", "wholesome traditions" (Article 2). Furthermore, to the many exhortations to strive with all zeal and generosity for the perfect love of God and one's neighbour or for more perfect fulfilment of the vows, etc., was added, at least in one place (Article 4), the statement that in the religious life the primary thing is not one's own efforts, but faith in the love which God has shown to those whom he has called (*cf*. 1 Jn 4:16). Among the interpolations of a concrete kind the following is noteworthy: even the contemplative orders must reform their style of life, e.g., in respect of their monastic practices; the education of younger members in lay congregations must include competent training in apostolic work in the narrower sense of "evangelism".[90] To the outsider all of this may not seem to go very far, but to those who know it reveals how difficult it was to get away from the original texts. These all had a history, and behind them were definite views of the nature of religious life, of its requirements in the present day, and of the dangers to which it is exposed.

The third draft failed to arouse much of an echo from the Council Fathers. Only thirty individual bishops and two episcopal conferences sent in any comments. Were they becoming tired, or in comparison with other schemata did this one seem unimportant to most of the Fathers? Perhaps both things were true. Examining the relatively few proposals for alteration, it is interesting to note that those which criticized the schema as a whole, which in fact rejected it — there were only two —, did so for completely opposite reasons. Archbishop (now Cardinal) Heenan considered that the draft in its truncated form said so little and was so disappointing, that it ought not to be published. The Jesuit General Janssens (died in October 1964) thought that the draft was so loud in its call for an *aggiornamento* that it encouraged a dangerous weakening of the essential elements in religious life of obedience, poverty, chastity and love. Which of the two was right? Each saw the problem from his own perspective. In the proposals sent in concerning separate articles, too, one found the most contradictory judgments. This was true above all of Articles 5 and 6, the former dealing with the contemplative, the latter with the active orders. Those who battled most violently were the monks who, according to their party, urged the cardinals and bishops to support their own particular views. Memoranda and counter-memoranda were circulated, seeking to influence the Commission.

[90] The occasion of this interpolation ("institutio religiosa et apostolica doctrinalis et technica . . . protrahatur") was the well-known book by Cardinal Suenens: *Promotion Apostolique de la religieuse* (1962).

The abbeys and confederations which did not belong to contemplative orders, felt that their legitimate apostolic work in the future was being threatened by the apparently exclusive division of the orders into contemplative and active forms. Hence they pleaded for a few articles which would stress the indivisible unity of contemplation and apostolate, a unity which these orders have to actualize in accord with their special vocation. Others, again, including the abbot general of the Cistercians, the prior general of the Carthusians and the Abbot of Solesme, urgently entreated the Commission to leave this division alone, because otherwise the unique character of the contemplative religious life would no longer be seen and valued.

On the other hand there was dissatisfaction among the modern congregations with the theological characterization of the active religious life in Article 6. At this point the real problem, which we have discussed more fully above, appeared clearly for the first time. It was complained that this article, because conceived in monastic terms, obstructed rather than encouraged the characteristic spirituality of the apostolic religious life. In these orders apostolic work is of the essence of their religious lives, it is their way to holiness. It was then that the superior general of the Missionary Society of Scheut formulated the statement which was to find its way almost *verbatim* into the final text: "Tota vita religiosa spiritu apostolico imbuatur. Tota autem actio apostolica spiritu religioso informetur" — "The whole of the religious life must be permeated with the apostolic spirit, and all apostolic work must be inspired by the spirit of the religious life." Among the comments sent in by the Council Fathers were other proposals which merit attention: the question of poverty, for example (new forms of poverty bearing more the character of witness to our present age; of the work of religious as a sign of true poverty); of the relation of superiors to subjects (education in greater sharing of responsibility and hence the right use of freedom, both indispensable to the sensibility and maturing of modern man); of the corporate celebration of the Eucharist in communities, as a sign and source of brotherhood; of the introduction of the younger members in the concrete milieu in which, later, they are to exercise apostolic, educational or charitable work.

A small commission was appointed to examine the proposals of the Fathers for improving the draft, and to present their verdict to the plenary commission as to what might be accepted and what rejected. Most of the proposals were rejected, partly with justice, but in some cases unjustly: whenever something unaccustomed came up and the hot iron of the modern problem of religious life was really laid hold of, the negative answer was always too ready.

Of some importance were the following additions, all of which found their way into the final text: "Lest the adaptations of religious life to the needs of our time be merely superficial, and lest those who by constitution pursue the external apostolate prove unequal to the fulfilment of their task, religious should be properly instructed, according to the intellectual gifts and personal endowments of each, in the prevailing manners of contemporary social life, and in its characteristic ways of feeling and thinking. If such training is harmoniously co-ordinated it will contribute to integrity of life on the part of religious. Throughout their lives religious should labour earnestly to perfect their spiritual, doctrinal and professional development. As far as possible, superiors should provide them with the opportunity, the resources, and the time to do so" (Article 18 of the decree). "Where the Church has newly taken root, special attention should be given to the establishment and development of fresh forms of religious life. These should take into account the natural endowments and the manners of the people, and also local customs and circumstances" (Article 19). "All communities should participate in the life of the Church and make their own her efforts at renewal, in the biblical, liturgical, social and ecumenical spheres, and should foster these enterprises according to their abilities" (almost *verbatim* in Article 2c). "The missionary spirit should be thoroughly maintained in religious communities, and, according to the character of each one, given a modern expression. In this way the preaching of the gospel among all peoples can be done more successfully" (Article 20).

In addition two fresh articles were presented to the plenary commission as a result of many requests. These concerned obedience and chastity and were meant to supplement the existing articles on these topics. Both had derived from the second draft of 1963 and from a passage taken from an address by Pope Paul VI to religious chapters on 23 May 1964. This demonstrated how reluctant people were to depart from the material produced by the Preparatory Commission, and to open the door to new stimuli and new perceptions. It required the energetic intervention of some of the members of the Commission to change the too negative style at least of the article on chastity, and to introduce a more positive and apostolic horizon, at the same time pointing out the psychological side of education for the free acceptance of celibacy. (The original had been made up mostly of warnings and exhortations.)

With this, the fourth redaction of the decree on the religious life was ready. The effort that had gone into its production, the relatively small, almost closed circle of those who finally edited the text, the difficulty of putting ideas over according to the official rules of Roman grammar (a problem that has long been apparent with official Church documents), the way in which much that was produced was automatically placed *ad acta,* proved that behind it all was an unfavourable atmosphere, and betrayed a certain tension that was not confined to the commission. Moreover, it was precisely during the third year of the Council that memoranda were coming in from religious in all parts of the world, from monastic orders, including contemplative orders, even more perhaps from the active orders; in this period unrest among the religious orders became perfectly obvious, and meanwhile the leaders of the orders stood more or less helpless in face of the malaise, because their attitude was merely defensive. If we consider this fact, we begin to understand why interest in the approaching discussion of the schema, however little time was to be allotted for it, was so great. As with the shortened schemata dealing with the ministry and life of priests and with the missions, which had been debated, a stirring debate was expected. In fact attendance at the discussion, which lasted from 10 November until 12 November — barely two sessions —, was very high. Speeches were made by eight cardinals, eighteen bishops and religious superiors; another thirty-three fathers sent in written interventions. Altogether the interventions ran to 232 pages.

What was accomplished by the discussion in the Council hall? First, it became evident that there was clear awareness everywhere of the seriousness of the situation in the religious orders, of the growing unrest among the younger generation, of their criticism of the existing arrangements, and of their desire for new forms; there was awareness, even, of the uncertainty about the meaning and the biblical-theological justification of the religious ideal in general. But the reaction to this awareness was most varied. Some, with impassioned warnings, expressed their concern lest the religious life be depreciated in our time (even by the clergy), lest there be a dimming of the religious ideal and a slackening of discipline by the influence of the modern world upon the orders, lest the contemplative life decline in favour of a fruitless activism and a turning towards the world. These men demanded a clear exposition of the authentic meaning of religious life, above all of the vows, and also clear regulations for keeping pure the inalienable elements and institutions of religious life. Others, in contrast, put their finger upon the manifest weaknesses in contemporary religious life: inadequately based spirituality, a one-sided attitude to superiors, lack of missionary spirit, out of date forms and practices, being out of touch with the world, too narrow profiles, inadequate education; and they demanded that these weaknesses be frankly admitted and courageously attacked. The number who spoke or intervened on either side was roughly the same. Many spoke in the name of whole groups. On these particular days the collection of signatures required considerable management. Especially noteworthy was the highly temperamental intervention of a few superiors general of modern priestly and missionary societies who not only complained that in comparison with the monastic orders, they had never been given a fair hearing in the Church or in the Council (because the number of abbots in the Council was relatively large, although many of these represented but a few priest-monks, whereas the other orders were represented by their superiors general alone, and then only if they numbered at least 1000 priests), but sought also to make thoroughly obvious the fact that, because of the traditionally monastic concept of religious life and because of the demands of canon law, they had been forced to accept forms and institutions which were still hindering the formation of an independent type of spirituality appropriate to the active orders, thus damaging both their apostolic work and their religious life itself.

To sum up: while some saw the draft as a sufficient basis for further study, even if requiring improvement and expansion on certain points, others categorically rejected it and demanded, often with great passion, a complete revision. The enquiry at the end of the debate as to whether the separate propositions could be put to the vote (which implied the question whether or not the draft could be regarded as a basis for further discussion) yielded the following result:

Present	Yes	No	Yes with reservations	Invalid
2042	1155	882	3	2

This meant that the draft was not thrown out, but the high proportion of disapproving votes made it quite obvious that the text would have to be revised, not just here and there, but in a more fundamental manner. This became even clearer as a result of the voting on the separate propositions. This voting was scheduled for 14 and 16 November, so that the fathers would still have time to work out suggestions for alteration *(modi)*. The result of the voting was as follows:

		Present	Yes	No	Yes with reservations	Invalid
Preface and Articles	1–3	1955	871	77	1005	2
Article	4	1960	1049	64	845	2
	5–6	1949	883	77	987	2
	7–10	1950	907	66	975	2
	11–13	1946	940	56	947	3
	14	1844	1676	65	103	–
	15–17	2122	1833	63	226	–
	18–19	2117	1936	50	131	–
	20	2112	1639	50	419	4

From this we learn that no article was rejected; the Preface and Articles 1–13 were approved only with reservations, that is, the proposed alterations would have to be incorporated by the Commission; Articles 14–20 were approved by a two-thirds majority, and this required only minor emendations. Because Articles 1–13 were the most significant in the draft, everything depended upon the composition of the sub-commission, who had the task of dealing with the *modi*. In view of the tensions within the Commission, and to ensure the objective and open-minded treatment of the *modi*, some members of the Commission requested that the further course of the work be not directed "from above". All of the *periti* on the Commission ought to meet and, under the chairmanship of one of the Commission members, consider how best to share out this work among each other. And that was what happened.

Reference has often been made to the record number of 14,000 *modi* made to the decree on religious life. No other commission had to deal with so many. But this number is deceptive. A large number of fathers — between 350 and 500 — subscribed to almost the same *modi*. These came from two "factories" whose "manufacturers" showed great distrust of one another. One party believed — to put it perhaps too simply — that they were protecting the religious life from threatening forces of modern dissolution; the other party believed that real difficulties had to be met with positive proposals. Still taking small variations into account, the *modi* could be reduced to not more than 600; in fact the number was even smaller.

In February 1965 the *periti* on the Commission met under the chairmanship of Archbishop Philippe, O. P., and began work on the *modi*. After all that had already happened they knew perfectly well how things would go. Quite soon, however, the atmosphere became quite free and relaxed. There was complete frankness in expression of opinions. Three groups were formed, and each group was entrusted with work on a certain number of articles. The task set them was not easy. This was so especially of the first two groups to whom were given the disputed Articles 1–13. It was not easy, because the *modi* advanced by both of the above mentioned parties, and at times supported by many Fathers, were often so contradictory, that it was hard to reduce them to a common denominator. This is one of the reasons why the final text is not all of a piece. Compromises had to be made. We will mention some of these in detail later on. The result of the work of the groups was then discussed by all together and improvements and additions made. In March the draft thus produced was presented to a sub-commission of Fathers under the chairmanship of Bishop Leiprecht of Rottenburg, the elected vice-president of the Commission, for comment and revision. The plenary commission then sat from 27 April until 1 May, again under the chairmanship of Bishop Leiprecht. After further consultation they approved the final text. This was the fifth redaction which was to be voted upon in the fourth and last phase of the council. Looking back upon this truly adventurous Odyssey the Commission could now enjoy a relaxed and reconciliatory mood.

What followed passed off without friction. The revised text, printed parallel to the text of 1964 along with a detailed account of the way in which the *modi* had been dealt with, was handed to the Fathers in good time during the fourth phase of the Council.[91] The account *(relatio)* of the draft was given in the Council by Bishop Compagnone, O. C. D., of Anagni. Then a vote was taken upon 18 of the 25 articles, because these had been so thoroughly rewritten. The decree had now grown to twice its original size and long since abandoned all pretence of being limited to guiding principles. The voting, which took place on 6, 7 and 8 October was as follows:

---

[91] *Textus recognitus et Modi a Commissione conciliari De Religiosis examinati* (Typ. Polygl. Vat., 1965).

		Present	Yes	No	Invalid
Preface and Article	1	2176	2163	9	4
Article	2	2124	2113	9	2
	3	2062	2057	5	–
	4	2064	2057	5	2
	5	2057	2040	15	2
	6	2055	2049	3	3
	7	2140	2133	4	3
	8	2136	2126	7	3
	9	2150	2142	7	1
	10	2148	2088	57	3
	11	2136	2112	22	2
	12	2130	2126	3	1
	13	2097	2089	3	1
	14	2152	2134	16	2
	15	2152	2134	16	2
	16	2141	2127	12	2
	17	2132	2110	20	2
	18–24	2082	2071	9	2
	25	2082	2071	9	2

Thus the draft was accepted by an overwhelming majority — almost unanimously, we might say. The occasional rise in the number of negative votes allows us to draw certain conclusions. Article 5 was disliked by some because its final section attempted to trace the contemplative and active orders back to a common ideal, and this is out of line with the usual tradition. The teaching brothers and their advocates did not seem to agree with the last passage in Article 10 which says that "there is no objection to religious congregations of brothers admitting some members to holy orders, to supply needed priestly ministrations for their own houses, . . ." Articles 14, 16 and 17 on obedience, enclosure and the religious habit, seem to have aroused in some the fear of a weakening of religious discipline. Article 15 on life in community clearly gave offence on account of its demand that class distinction in monastic communities (priests — lay brothers; choir or teaching sisters — working sisters) be done away with to the greatest possible extent. Seen as a whole, however, these opposing voices scarcely weigh in the balance. They become even less important when seen against the general voting on the whole decree on 11 October. Of the 2142 Fathers present 2126 voted for and only 13 against, with 3 invalid votes.

The solemn, juridical and decisive vote was taken on 28 October when 2321 Fathers approved the decree. Four continued to vote against it. And so it could now be officially proclaimed by Pope Paul VI. On the same day the

Pope also proclaimed the Decrees on the Bishops' Pastoral Office, on Priestly Formation, and on Christian Education, as well as the Declaration on the Relationship of the Church to Non-Christian Religions. This was the seventh public session of the Council.[92]

What, then, is the significance of the Decree on the Religious Life, in respect of the pastoral intention of the Council, which was to light new lamps for the Church as the people of God, to illumine her path as she seeks, under fresh impulses, to fulfil her mission in time?[93] Although the dreary, laborious and often violent discussion produced relatively small fruit in the end, for one thing a deeper theological and spiritual self-understanding of the religious state did emerge. This was not a new understanding, but it did lead back to the sources and helped to supersede a style of thinking that was a blend of legalism and asceticism — the one conditioning the other. For another thing, after centuries of sterility in form of life and practices, new styles of community life, of relation with the world and of work are beginning to appear within the religious orders.

People have started, theologically and spiritually, to break away from the over-emphasis on vows (regarded strictly juridically) and even from the evangelical counsels (understood chiefly in the ascetical sense) as the essence of the religious life. These concepts have for long blinded men to a deeper understanding. Once again men are getting down to bedrock in the gospel, to the imitation of Christ, which is at once a sharing in the way and fate of Christ and a sharing in the work of preaching and redemption. It is only in the light of this that celibacy, poverty and obedience are seen in their true light. Imitation of Christ necessarily manifests the mystery of the Church, because Christ is present in the Church, and in her activity his work is perpetuated and made effective throughout time. Never before in the history of the orders has their close, theologically, or rather, Christologically based link with the Church, with her mystery and her mission, come so clearly to light, as in this Council. The Decree on Religious, too, bears witness to this. The religious state is a state within the Church, not just in the sense that it operates within the Church, receives grace from the Church and is legally sanctioned by the Church, but in the sense that it shares in a special way in the mystery of the Church, is one of her organs, through which the Church perfects her own life. If, then, the religious state wishes to remain in harmony with its own essence and function, as these are portrayed in the preface to the decree (Article 1), then by the witness of its life it must manifest the transcendent, eschatological mystery of the Church, and be aware also of its own obligation to participate in the apostolic mission of the Church.

[92] In terms of its length (3189 words) the Decree on the Religious Life comes tenth in the list of sixteen conciliar documents.

[93] Cf. my introduction to the Decree on the Religious Life ("Dekret über die zeitgemäße Erneuerung des Ordenslebens", *Dokumente des Zweiten Vatikanischen Konzils* [1967], pp. 5 ff.).

The theological and spiritual new mentality which the council introduced into the religious orders has forced us to pose anew the question about the structures of religious life. To begin with we must mention the fundamental law which was present at the founding of every religious order, and which has moved into the forefront of Christian thought today in a specially urgent manner: the law of brotherliness. The orders are not primarily communities of superiors and subjects, but of brothers. This is plainly stated in Article 15 of the decree. Their life ought not to be regulated by the notion of superior vis-à-vis subject, but by mutual consideration and love. Only within this framework does a very radical obedience in the imitation of Christ have its legitimate place. In these terms and not simply on account of the rules of the game, which regulate the common life and the common work of a group of men in our times, is a change in the form of leadership and obedience in the religious orders demanded. On this point, too, the decree has a few things to say. The responsible and effective participation in the common good and in the common task in the spirit of brotherhood can no longer be realized in large communities, for by his psychical constitution, modern man feels lost and threatened in the mass, so that the ideals just mentioned can only be realized in communities of manageable size. In the last decades, therefore, wherever new forms of community life have been born in the Church from the idea of the imitation of Christ, they have taken their shape from the team.[94]

A fact of equal importance is this: although these communities have developed the most diverse ways of life and addressed themselves to vastly differing tasks, they have one thing in common. Despite all detachment from worldly ties, which the imitation of Christ demands, they want to live more obviously and more consciously than was possible in the traditional orders, in the midst of the world.[95] They know that today heed is paid only to him who shares the fate of the other man and who has fellowship with him. That which moves those who hear Christ's call today has been impressively expressed by one who stood outside the door of the Church, Simone Weil, in her last letter written before she died in London. "Today an élite will have to kindle the virtue of poverty in spirit among the wretched masses. To do this it is necessary for those who belong to this élite to be poor, not only in spirit, but in reality. Every day of their lives they must suffer the pains and humiliations of wretchedness. We do not need a new Franciscan Order. Monks' habits and cloisters signify separation. The new élite must live among the masses and mix with them; nothing must come between them. And — still more difficult to bear —, they must be entitled to no kind of compensations; in their relationships to the

[94] As well as the Little Brothers and Sisters of Jesus we ought to mention here the Brethren of the Virgin of the Poor; cf. *Au cœur même de l'Église. Une recherche monastique: Les frères de la vierge des Pauvres* (1966). In some measure the secular institutes belong to this category.
[95] Cf. *Brüder in der Welt. Orden und Kommunitäten in unserer Zeit* (1965).

masses about them they must show that same humility which a naturalized subject would show to the citizens of his adopted country."[96]

Despite all the reservations one has to make for such an absolute situational enthusiasm, this idea contains something essential for the situation of the religious orders of the future, if these can but read the signs of the times. These, too, must live more than formerly in the midst of the world — the apostolic orders as well as the contemplatives, however different the modes of their presence in the world.[97] Otherwise they will no longer be effective enough and will radiate no influence. The decree gives some hint of this presence in the world of the religious orders — not just the secular institutes —,[98] although many may think that it says much less than is necessary. What we have already said of Chapter VI of the Constitution on the Church[99] applies to the decree on religious life also. It is a transitional document, a sign of the Church's emerging into a new epoch. This does not mean that it can be interpreted arbitrarily or that its validity will vanish tomorrow. It is rather that in it the Council has intimated its will, which thus becomes a binding directive for all Catholics. But this directive arises out of the present situation and cannot, therefore, provide a ready-made recipe. On the contrary, Article 4 speaks of the "right amount of prudent experimentation" necessary to solve the various problems.

This was underlined once again in the "Norms for Implementation" of the decree which Pope Paul VI published in the apostolic letter *Ecclesiae Sanctae* on 6 August 1966, with effect from 11 October of the same year. This gave the general chapters, which are called to carry out the conciliar resolutions, wide powers to experiment with new methods (Article 6). These "Norms for Implementation" were given as a remit to the post-conciliar commission for religious inaugurated along with four other post-conciliar commissions by Pope Paul VI with his apostolic letter *Finis Concilio* of 3 January 1966. The members of the original commission were members of the post-conciliar commission also. They were assisted by fifteen consultants, two of whom had already served as *periti* on the original commission. Newcomers included the officiating president of the Roman Union of Superiors General *(Unione Romana dei Superiori Generali)*, the general of the Discalced Carmelites, and P. Anastasius of the Most Holy Rosary. The generals of the great orders, having scarcely come into the picture whilst the conciliar decree was being composed, towards the

---

[96] *Écrits de Londres et derrières lettres* (1957).
[97] Such a presence in the world can be manifested by the strictly contemplative orders by, for example, celebrating the liturgy along with the faithful who visit their churches (the Eucharist or a liturgy of the Word), or by undertaking, within the cloister, some work for a contractor, being paid in exactly the same way as ordinary workmen in the world. The knowledge that men or women are praying behind these walls makes no impression on most people nowadays.
[98] For example, in Articles 2 d; 3, 1; 19, 1; 20, 1 and 2.
[99] Vol. I of the present work, p. 260 (end of general introductory remarks) and p. 274 (end of introduction to chapter VI).

end of the last phase of the council had prepared proposals at least for the post-conciliar commission. The first part of the "Norms for Implementation", in particular, the part concerning the special general chapters, their function, rights and procedure, goes back in substance to these proposals. In three sessions — February (for the consultants), March (the sub-commission), April (the plenary commission) — the "Norms" were produced. As the separate articles of the decree were discussed, we will deal with the relevant norms also.[100] Having received the approval of the Co-ordinating Commission, these were sent to the Pope for publication. In this way a work was completed, which had taken more than five years. Not until a later date will it be possible to judge its merits and estimate its fruit.

[100] Cf. my introduction to the "Norms for Implementation" in *Dokumente des Zweiten Vatikanischen Konzils,* pp. 47 ff.

Commentary on the Decree

Title. The many alterations of title have been discussed in the Introduction: "De Statibus perfectionis adquirendae", "De Religiosis", "De accommodata renovatione vitae religiosae". The reason for the changes is also to be found in the Introduction. The present title is to be found in a decree of the Congregation for Religious of 26 March 1956.[1] "Accommodata renovatio" and "appropriate renewal", or in the words of Article 2, "a continuous return to the sources of all Christian life and to the original inspiration behind a given community" and "an adjustment of the community to the changed conditions of the times" mutually condition and interpenetrate one another. In the course of the discussions the tendency to separate renewal and accommodation kept re-appearing. Renewal was seen as a duty of all of the members of a community, whereas the accommodation regarded as necessary was seen as an operation that should be reserved to the superiors. The danger that lay in such a separation is obvious: renewal would be conceived exclusively as religious renewal in the sense of reviving original fervour, whereas accommodation would be limited to more or less external things: customs, laws, etc.

Article 1. This is an extended preface, the central section of which can for the most part be traced to an intervention by Cardinal Bea. Whereas the representatives of the Congregation for Religious repeatedly stressed that the decree had principally to deal with the juridical questions of religious life (*vita ac disciplina* in the words of the article), because the theological questions had already been dealt with in Chapter VI of the Constitution on the Church, the majority of the Fathers thought that the decree ought to be a religious document as well, in view of the mighty tasks which fall to the orders. Hence the stress even in the preface upon the charismatic as well as the Christological and ecclesial character of the religious state.

A problem already emerges, and it is one that is characteristic of the official

---

[1] *AAS* 48 (1956), p. 295.

ecclesiastical self-understanding of the religious state. A too one-sided separation is made of theology from discipline, of spirituality from law, of the spirit of the gospel from standards expressed in rules. Since the 19th century especially, the accent in the relationship between the two realms has been placed upon the juridical and institutional realm, so that the religious life *(vita religiosa)* has been more or less equated with life according to a rule *(vita regularis)*. As the process of legal codification of the religious state developed, a process which helped to empty the religious content from the basic notions associated with that state — *consilia evangelica, status perfectionis adquirendae, vita contemplativa, v. activa*, etc. —, and to turn these concepts into much used but quite technical phrases (we need only glance at the constitutions of modern societies), so in the same measure did the theological-spiritual factor become edificatory and ascetic. On this point the Council inaugurated a distinct change of course. Once again it stressed the unity of spirit (life) and law. It gave precedence to the living spirit, to lively spirituality and theology, before law; not law, but life, comes first; law follows life and has to protect and assure it. Not only is this the tenor of the decree as a whole: the "Norms for Implementation", too, point this out with a clarity that leaves nothing to be desired. In Article 12 we read: "The general legal code of every community ("Constitutions", "Typica", "Rules", or whatever they are called) ought to include the following elements: a. The biblical and theological basis of the life of the order and its unity with the Church... b. The legal regulations that are necessary to determine the peculiarity, the aims and the methods of the community; but these need not be too many and ought to be reformulated frequently." In Article 13: "Only when both elements, the spiritual and the juridical, form a unity, do the fundamental documents of a community possess a sure foundation, and become moulded by a true spirit and a life-giving norm. The text, therefore, must not be cast in purely juridical or edificatory terms."

The following remarks may be added on the separate sections. When the document points out "how the teaching and example of the Divine Master laid the foundation for a pursuit of perfect charity through the exercise of the evangelical counsels", it speaks primarily of this way as a whole, without affirming that the three counsels themselves can be traced in the same way to the "teaching and example" of our Lord. The addendum, that this way "serves as a blazing emblem of the heavenly kingdom", provides that way of life with its profoundest justification. With Christ the ultimate kingdom of God has come. He himself is the blazing sign of this. And thus it comes about that men, who encounter the Lord and listen to his words, experience a call to such a radical and unconditional imitation of his Life, that they are no longer free to marry, and, "for the sake of the kingdom of heaven", or "for the gospel's sake", or "for his sake" (Mt 19:12; Mk 10:29) — the motive is always the same —, leave everything behind. The vocation to the religious life is this kind of thing.

Within this unity the well-known three evangelical counsels appear relatively late — the 12th century. Thus in the second section of this article the phrase "the practice of the evangelical counsels" must not be pressed too far. However, in this article, in harmony with Chapter V of the Constitution on the Church (Article 44), the specific character of the way of the counsels is distinguished from the general calling of the Christian to follow Christ. The way of the counsels is a call to follow the Lord "more freely and . . . more nearly". (The *modus* put forward by more than 400 fathers, and incorporated in Cardinal Bea's intervention, spoke of a "closer imitation of the inexhaustible example of Christ", thus betraying a one-sidedly ascetical manner of thinking.) Less specifically, in contrast, we find life according to the counsels described as a "life dedicated to God". Does this not describe any truly Christian life? The second section brings out the essentially ecclesial aspect of the religious state, having just spoken of its eschatological aspect.

Whereas the second section of this article places the vocation to religious life in a global, historical perspective, and only incidentally describes this life itself, the third section takes up the topic of the call to follow the evangelical counsels and briefly indicates the marks of the life regulated by the counsels. It would seem that this is saying more precisely that it is all a question of a special surrender to the Lord, a surrender that is therefore a surrender to God the Father. (The *modus* already cited spoke of "undivided" devotion.) This phrase was dropped lest it should give rise to the false notion that the devotion or surrender of the non-religious Christian to Christ has to be regarded as divided. The imitation of Christ described in what follows is an imitation of the Redeemer's obedience to the Father in death, while Jesus' virginity and poverty are mentioned only incidentally. (Here, too, an emendation of the above-mentioned *modus* had to be made, for the *modus* spoke of Christ having desired to redeem and sanctify mankind through his poverty, virginity and obedience unto death on the cross, and *that* can scarcely be stated theologically in just those terms.) The final section of this article not only stresses once again (as in the first sentence) the grace-given character of the religious vocation, but emphasizes the interior link between the complete self-surrender of the individual to the Lord, and the life of the Church as a whole, and also the interior link between that individual self-immolation and the fruitfulness of the related apostolate.

In the last section we meet the popular expression used (especially in Romance languages) to describe the religious life: "a life consecrated by a profession of the counsels" ("la vie consacrée'). This will be discussed in greater detail further on, under Article 5. "The specific guiding principles" were set out in the "Norms for Implementation".

Article 2. Very sensibly, the concrete statements of the decree begin with a comprehensive yet most precise and detailed definition of what is meant by "appropriate renewal". First of all it is explicitly noted that *accommodatio* or *aptatio* (adaptation) and *renovatio* (renewal) form an inner unity and can never be separated from one another: "The appropriate renewal of religious life involves two simultaneous processes." Renewal is more than a simple return to the zeal of the first generation, more than an ascetic and religious intensification: it has to do with a "return to the sources of all Christian life", that is, to holy Scripture and to the Church's great spiritual traditions, as well as to the "original inspiration behind a given community", attention being paid to the fact that this inspiration occurred within a specific historical situation. The word "return" must not, however, be allowed to suggest that we have complete knowledge of that to which we must return. Anyone who thought thus would not advance a single step beyond his own historically and circumstantially conditioned horizon of understanding; he would run the risk of reading what he already knows or thinks he knows, and hence what he assumes constitutes renewal, into the Scriptures, into the general spiritual and monastic tradition and into the history of the foundation of his own community. This sort of thing is constantly happening. It is much more to the point to re-appraise Scripture and tradition, using our modern enlarged and sharpened methods of analysis, with reference to the idea of the counsels, the concrete reality of religious life, with its centuries' old institutions, as well as with reference to the charism, the spirituality and the particular aims of a community. Such re-appraisal has become urgent in our time, but it is something which ought to be going on all the time. And so the decree is right to demand "a continuous return" *(continuus reditus)*. In respect of concrete realization the once-and-for-all call to follow our Lord in celibacy, poverty and obedience, and the special vocation or charism of a community are not inseparably tied to their historical origin. The spirit that becomes effective through these things must for ever be incarnated afresh in accord with the changing circumstances and tasks of the times. Otherwise the original spirit would become a dead letter.

For this very reason the adaptation demanded by the Council cannot be something purely external, and it must consist fundamentally of more than mere modifications of things as we know them at present. This adaptation demands a creative act that presupposes knowledge, experience, and breadth of vision. Ultimately, however, it emerges from the spirit. It is significant that the Council stressed the charismatic character not merely of the origin of the communities following the counsels (Article 1), but also the charismatic character of their appropriate renewal. In this process of renewal it falls to the Church (the hierarchy) to judge the charisms and to discern the spirits. This is the key-signature set before the principles which follow in this article.

a) The importance of this first principle will at once be appreciated by anyone who knows something about the way in which countless detailed rules and regulations — especially in modern communities — have narrowed vision, and how moralistic and ascetic viewpoints have determined the nature of instruction about the religious life. Opening up vision of the theological essence of the religious state, of its origin and centre in Christ, reveals at once the "fundamental norm" according to which religious life today must be re-appraised throughout its whole extent; and it is against this same norm that the methods of appropriate renewal, too, must be judged. The decree speaks deliberately of *following,* not of *imitation.* Imitation of Christ in the biblical sense (1 Cor 11:1; 1 Thess 1:6; cf. also Jn 13:15; Phil 2:6; 1 Pet 2:21) has to be interpreted in terms of the more fundamental following of Christ, and not the other way round.

b) This would seem to plead for a sharper definition of the separate communities, their aims, their spirituality, and, correspondingly, their institutionalization. (Throughout the decree the term "community" — *instituta* — has been deliberately chosen so as to include all who follow the counsels: orders, societies, societies of the common life without vows, and the secular institutes.) This interpretation of the first statement in 2b deplores the evening-out of ancient and modern communities, the standardization of their forms of life, the similarity of their work — offering a very limited choice, and mostly originating in the nineteenth century —, and the colourlessness of their spirituality. The more conservative, however, will see in this statement a device for retaining as much as possible of their traditional form of life;[2] for they fear that in the present upheaval men might be too quick to follow the trend of the times, thus losing values and institutions that are essential for the community. Both interpretations will appeal to the second sentence of 2 b, to the "spirit of founders" and their "particular goals", as well as to the "wholesome traditions which constitute the heritage of each community". In spite of the most careful study of the history of one's own community, the result will largely depend upon preconceived notions. Therefore, what is primarily demanded of all responsible people today is that they learn how to become detached from themselves and their own opinions, thus acquiring an open mind and an open ear, the ability to see objective facts without disguise, and to accept the unaccustomed. For the rest, the effort made by many communities, before and since the Council, to thrash out and actualize their individuality, in respect of the task allotted them, their spirituality, and their form of life,[3] has a limit that may not be overlooked. Judging from the immediate phenomenon (dwelling-place, dress, work, style of life), the differences between the orders will steadily recede. This is connected with the development of modern society and with the tendency towards ever more marked evening-out of the style of life as a whole. The religious orders cannot remain unaffected by these things. Even the change-over from the orders to the secular institutes will of necessity become easier. Concerning the deeper structures of a community, however, it must be borne in mind that there have been relatively few founders whose human and spiritual features have been so marked as to

---

[2] In order to avoid an interpretation that was too one-sidedly orientated towards perseverance, the text of this statement was substantially altered in the final revision. Previously it had run: "Fideliter serventur *natura, finis, spiritus proprius* necnon sanae traditiones; quae omnia . . ."

[3] On the revival of the tendency to express the specific aim of the community through a special vow, cf. G. Gerhartz, *"Insuper promitto . . ." Die feierlichen Sondergelübde katholischer Orden* (1966), pp. 120 ff., 306 ff.

leave a stamp, not merely upon their own orders, but upon the future life of the Church as a whole. Only very few religious founders plainly had a mission for the whole Church in all time, a special charism of universal significance.[4]

In contrast, there have been many perfectly genuine vocations which led to the founding of an order, which, however, bear very clearly the marks of their own period. These orders were intended to serve a concrete need (corporal or spiritual), within a specific historical situation — perhaps only in particular countries, like the Trinitarians, whose task was to redeem Christian prisoners from the Moslems. Countless modern orders fall into this category — especially the nineteenth century foundations. They emerged because of some dire need, and their spirituality, as often as not, was moulded by a devotion that is no longer alive in the Church — at least not as it was experienced by the founders of the orders. Ought all such orders to stick loyally to their historical origins, and to carry on the work and devotions of a past epoch, but largely adapted to meet the modern situation, even if this were possible only in a very artificial way that seemed rather like self-deception? For example, ought the Trinitarians, to remain true to the intention of their founder, to take up the cause of the prisoners of our time, the displaced persons? This is hardly realistic. In thrashing out their individ- ualities, the separate communities should be given much more scope for develop- ment. The history of the religious orders provides plenty of examples of true development that was not devised at the conference table, but grew up as a genu- ine response to the call of God in the present moment. A correct interpretation of Article 2 demands that we keep these things in mind. For what the Council meant by an appropriate renewal amounts in many cases to a fresh foundation, controlled in the last analysis by the same conditions as framed the original foundation.

c) Very often in history, the orders, as charismatically founded communities, have sparked off intellectual and spiritual movements on an enormous scale in the Church. They were God's call and command to Christendom in their own age, and the official Church recognized and accepted their mission as such. The orders, however, like all other defined communities, do have a tendency to cut themselves off from their surroundings, in this case from the ordinary life of the Church, and cultivate their own life in a one-sided manner, to be aware only of their own activities, to propagate their own devotions and recognize only their own saints, to gather round themselves a group of patrons and bene- factors or a spiritual clientele — in other words, to form a Church within the Church. There can be no doubt that this sort of thing took place even in the very recent past. We might even say that since the nineteenth century, doctrinally and institutionally, the orders have belonged in general to the most conservative wing of the Church. This implies no reflection whatever upon their spiritual standards or their effectiveness. The reason for this lies not least in the fact that

---

[4] Cf. H. U. von Balthasar, *Therese von Lisieux, Geschichte einer Sendung* (1950), pp. 15 ff., where the distinction between "habitual" and "representative" holiness, and also the concept of mission are worked out. (The latter concept runs like a thread through the whole book.)

these orders were founded or refounded in a period of Catholic restoration. Thus their main forces scarcely took part in the great renewal movements in the Church during recent decades. This provides the living context for Article 2 c.

d) It has been said quite generally of the Church, that in modern times she has become increasingly removed from the world, especially since the nineteenth century, has inhabited her own ghetto, no longer holding any converse with the real, secularized world, thus contributing to that secularism by her very revulsion from it. If that can be said in general, it is true even more pointedly of the religious orders. The cleavage between the sacrosanct life of the cloister with its attendant mentality, and the normal civil world, has become far too great. As a result the orders have lost influence and the power to bear witness, and have forfeited their presence in the world. They have ceased to make their *sign-character* meaningful to modern man. In the measure this became evident, so did the flow of recruits diminish. The long developing crisis in the religious life came to a head in the discussion, initiated by the Council, on the failure of the orders to adapt to the conditions of modern life. It was this situation that gave rise to Article 2 d. This has specially in mind the active orders and societies, which depend for the effectiveness of their work upon immediate contact and exchange with people in the world. The text makes it abundantly plain that there is no question of an uncritical, unenlightened, naively optimistic merging of religious with the world.

e) With all the special knowledge, breadth of vision and prudence, with all the courage and human stature which the work of renewal of the religious life, as envisaged by the Council, demands in those who are to undertake this work, the fundamental precondition of success, however, is *spiritual renewal*. This means more than fervour, spirituality in general, or greater faithfulness in the observance of vows: it means a fresh spiritual impulse which takes hold not only of individuals, but of the community as a whole, recreating all things from the inner core. Common prayer, spiritual conversation among brethren and sisters — things which in fact make them brethren and sisters — alone cause all of their other efforts to bear fruit. The place where spiritual renewal happens is in the small group. The more a community fosters these small groups, the greater the hope that the work of the general chapter will go beyond mere words and regulations, and reach out into real life.

The "Norms for the Implementation" of the decree have further clarified these principles of renewal through a few criteria. Article 15 states quite generally: "The guiding principles and the spirit to which appropriate renewal must conform are to be found not merely in the decree concerning the religious life, but also from the Dogmatic Constitution on the Church, Chapters V and VI." With reference to Article 2 of the decree, Article 16 of the "Norms" specifically states: "Communities are to take heed that the principles laid down in the Decree on the Appropriate Renewal of the Religious Life, do in fact regulate the renewal of that life. It follows, therefore, that:

"1. All members of religious orders, from the novitiate onwards, must be encouraged in the more intensive study of and meditation upon the Gospels and of the whole of holy Scripture. Likewise, care must be taken to ensure that religious share more fully in the mystery and life of the Church.

"2. The doctrine of the religious life must be examined and expounded from several different angles — theological, historical, canonical, etc.

"3. It is precisely for the sake of the well-being of the whole Church that the religious orders are to seek to understand the spirit to which they owe their origins. If, faithful to that spirit, they resolve upon adaptation, religious life will become purged of foreign elements and out-of-date customs."

It is perhaps striking that this commentary provided by the "Norms" has nothing to say about the serious problem, mentioned in Article 2 d of the decree, concerning the new relationship which has to be established between the orders (and the Church as a whole) and the world. This is a sign of the confusion of mind in which we face this problem, and indicates how little thinking we have done so far on the problem. Such silence will result in a much more violent and unrestrained reaction on the part of many religious.

Article 3. This article is one of the most concrete in the whole of the decree. Most of it was to be found in the first draft, and it reflects the efforts of the Congregation for Religious over the past century and a half. With an eye entirely on practical issues, it advocates first of all a greater flexibility in the external structures of religious life in its whole extent ("the manner of living, praying, and working"). This would correspond to the great diversity of requirements both on the part of the members of religious orders themselves — modern man having become highly differentiated and disinclined to submit to a standardized discipline — and of the environment. The missionary territories, which receive special stress, are but the extreme case of the diversity of political, economic, and cultural environmental conditions in the different continents, regions and countries. Were the requirements here mentioned logically carried out, the image of religious life today would soon undergo radical change. This would be true both in respect of the members of orders themselves, of their everyday experience and self-understanding, and in respect of those in the world outside.

The second section of this article, appearing only in the final redaction of the decree, is of the utmost importance. The aim behind this section is revealed in the *modus* of November 1964, signed by 435 Fathers: "The structural constitution of community life, especially of women religious, should be revised with great care, so that the whole community and every individual work together for the common good, in a truly active manner and with the responsibility that befits adult men and women." ("Magna ergo cum cura examini subiicienda est organisatio structuralis vitae communitatum, speciatim in Institutis Religiosarum, ita ut omnes et singuli, modo vere activo et mente adulta, cooperentur ad bonum totius communitatis.") In the background one can see the much mentioned dependence of sisters upon their superior, and the dependence of the superior upon her superior, and so on. This dependence originated in the servile mentality of the nineteenth century, and has become clothed in all the dignity of holy obedience. This attitude must bear much of the blame for the oft-lamented human immaturity of many nuns, which is often reflected in a sense of unworthiness, of frustration, and of not being taken seriously, and which may lead to discontent and bitterness. From the male point of view this may seem a little one-sided, but it must be remembered that the modern female mind, too, has undergone a great change, by reason of woman's changed place in society and the professional opportunities open to her. The monastic life has been too slow to notice these things, and, having noticed them, has done far too little about it. The conciliar text before us takes up this problem, but deals with it very generally and very cautiously. The text is addressed equally to men and women religious.

The final text of the decree is concerned not only with the individual relationship between superior and subject, but with co-operation between those in authority in a community, and the members of that community, above all in the active orders. For us today the primary image is not that of the distinction between superiors and subjects, but of the community as such, which is a brotherhood of equals, bound together in a unity of faith and love by Christ their only Head (cf. Mt 23:8). What has been said of religious communities applies to the Church as a whole. Within this perspective the dominant role of the superior, following Christ's example, is that of a servant who cares for the interior and exterior preservation and growth of the community. Superiors must, therefore, be much more firmly part of their own communities than formerly, and much that is regulated and enacted ought first to be discussed and approved by the community.

The final section of this article merely draws the conclusions concerning the codification of the various canonical books of the religious communities. The "suppression of outmoded regulations" was a phrase added at the request of 400 Fathers. This underlines their serious intention to have these books revised. Meanwhile it has become evident that no one need worry on this score, for as things stand the documents in question will have to be more or less rewritten.

More precise directions are given in the "Norms". We have already noted Articles 12 and 13 of the "Norms" in our commentary on Article 1 of the decree. Articles 14 and 17 run: "Everything that is outmoded or has changed with the customs of the time or that is merely a regional custom must be removed from the fundamental code of a community. Those norms, however, which are in harmony with the present day, and with the corporal and psychological requirements of members of the religious order, and with current circumstances, are to be set out in supplementary books (Directories, Books of Customs, etc.)." "Anything not belonging to the essence and aims of a community, anything that has lost its meaning and power, and no longer contributes to the life of the order, is to be regarded as outmoded. In judging what has to be given up the factor of witness which is proper to the religious state must not be overlooked."

341

This last sentence was added as a safeguard against the conformity of the religious life with the customs of the modern world, with ensuing loss of all power to bear witness. This power of witness, many thought, might well be served by non-conformity (extending to dwelling and dress), even by giving offence.

Article 4. This article takes up in greater detail the relationship between those in positions of leadership, and the communities they direct. "Successful renewal and proper adaptation cannot be achieved unless every member of a community co-operates." This first sentence strongly underlines the necessity of the democratic element in a religious community. This element is founded upon the Christian principle of the fundamental equality of the brethren and sisters, and has always been expressed in the constitutions of the great orders.[5] It is also in line with the development of modern society. Many of the Fathers saw in this the danger of unrestrained individualism, and feared it would mean the death of the obedience that is essential to religious life. A *modus* along these lines was signed by 497 Fathers. Thus they desired that an equally clear stress be laid upon authority and its inalienable rights. This desire was satisfied in the second sentence; but, so as not to recant or make illusory what had been said so emphatically in the first sentence, a third sentence was added — following a *modus* signed by 417 Fathers — laying the obligation upon superiors to consult their communities: "In decisions which involve the future of an institute as a whole, superiors should in appropriate manner consult the members and give them a hearing."

The uncertainty that emerges at this point, betraying incipient developments, the consequences of which cannot as yet be foreseen, appears once again in Article 2 of the "Norms", which is meant to be a commentary on Article 4 of the decree: "Only through the co-operation of all, superiors and members (the word "subjects" is deliberately avoided), can genuine religious life be renewed; this co-operation is also necessary to prepare the spirit of the chapter, to execute its work, and for the faithful observance of the agreed precepts and guiding principles." There is no question here of the genuine co-operation of all in the work of appropriate renewal; this co-operation is limited almost entirely to the clerical religious ("ad vitam religiosam in seipsis sc. in superioribus et sodalibus renovandam", "ad spiritum Capitulorum praeparandum"; "ad leges et normas a Capitulis latas fideliter observandas"). This is to falsify the meaning and intention of the first sentence of Article 4 of the decree. However, this is balanced once again when the "Norms" declare that "the subjects are to play an active part in the election of the chapters *and* councils" ("sodales partem habeant vere efficacem in eorumdem membris seligendis") (Article 18), and general chapters are endowed with wide powers: "The general *council* shall prepare" for the special general *chapter* ordered by the Council, to be "convened within two or at most three years" and "to meet in two sessions, even if it pass this resolution by secret ballot" (Article 3), by carrying out in the most suitable fashion a com-

---

[5] L. Moulin, *Le monde vivant des Religieux, Dominicains, Jésuites, Bénédictins* ... (1964).

prehensive and public enquiry among the members of the order, so collating the results, that the chapter is assisted and guided thereby. To this end, conventual and provincial chapters may be called, commissions appointed, and questionnaires issued (Article 4). "This general chapter has the right to make tentative changes in particular precepts of the constitution or, in the Eastern Church, of the *Typika,* without, however, violating the purpose, nature, and individuality of the community (here again is an infiltration of what the decree, Article 2 b, expresses in a livelier and less scholastic way) . . . Such experiments may be continued until the next statutory general chapter. This may extend the period of experiment, but no longer than until the following chapter" (Article 6).

"In the period between these chapters the general council has the same authority, within the framework of the powers set up by the chapters, and likewise the Easterns in monasteries under their jurisdiction, both of the *Hegumes* and of the little *Synaxe*" (Article 7).

For the revision and possible alteration of the statutes governing convents of nuns, dealt with in the third section of the article, more precise directions are given in Articles 9–11 of the "Norms". The most important is Article 11: "(The general superiors of the male orders or the plenipotentiaries of the Holy See) have to see to it that the constitutions are revised *after consultation with the nuns themselves, and with their assistance.*" It has been very difficult to convince the representatives of the corresponding male orders that in these days the women of the strictly contemplative orders must be allowed to have a say in determining their own lot and way of life. The nuns will have to prove that they know how to make use of their rights.

The concluding sentence of the article aims, as Article 12 b of the "Norms" shows, at the abolition of the multiplicity of rules, which have been such a characteristic feature of religious life in the past. Religious life today, that of active orders in particular, is becoming less and less amenable to detailed regulation. Were the general chapters to promulgate a host of new laws, this would hinder rather than advance the desired renewal. If rules and constitutions — usually concise — are to be a real help in this renewal, in accord with Article 12 a of the "Norms", they will have to provide fresh spiritual impulse, and, in their juridical aspect, will have to be so framed that they can be obeyed by every member, thus making dispensations superfluous, for dispensations always undermine the obligatory character of juridical norms.

Article 5. This article only appeared in the final redaction of the decree. It was designed to give a preliminary indication of a few elements that are common to all of the communities with which the decree was concerned, before going on, in Articles 7–11, to describe the different types of religious life. Unfortunately the article has not been entirely successful, although its purpose was undoubtedly justified. It begins admirably, by saying that the resolve to follow the Lord by way of the evangelical counsels must be preceded by a divine call, so that the vows corresponding to the counsels represent the response of the one called.

This is followed, however, by the traditional (Thomist) account of the way of the counsels, and many today would consider this open to dispute, if set out with insufficient qualification. We have tried to explain all this more fully in the Introduction. Let us, therefore, at this point merely mention briefly those statements which pose problems.

Can we today, without further qualification, say that the Christian religious, by accepting the evangelical counsels, renounces not only the sinful world, but the world in general? Our more differentiated relationship with the world, our new Christian relationship to the world, as expressed by Vatican II, especially in the Pastoral Constitution on the Church, takes exception to this idea. Therefore we can and must expound the statement of the decree by saying that the vow to follow the counsels adds a special, symbolic and charismatically conditioned tangibility and obligation to the renunciation required of every Christian in virtue of his fellowship with the crucified and risen Lord, mediated through baptism (Rom 6:3ff.). For the same reason the statement that the Christian who follows the counsels lives "for God alone" is misleading. It becomes false if one sees a contradiction between the service of God and service in and for the world (for this, in a deep sense, is service of one's neighbour, of humanity), so that service of the world appears as something imperfect, drawing us away from the perfect love of God. The traditional doctrine of the religious state as we find it in St. Thomas gives this very impression. This would explicitly contradict all that Vatican II has been saying about the task of the Christian layman in the world. All service of God is proved genuine only by service of our neighbour and of the world, within the Church and through her mediation. This applies to religious as well. In this sense, therefore, we must expound the statement that religious have handed over their entire lives to God's service and consecrated themselves to him.[6] By doing this they do only what every Christian must do, but they do it through the symbolic tangibility of a life of celibacy, poverty, and obedience, which leaves them completely free in the Church and for the Church, and they do it with the irrevocability of their special vow. When, however, the decree says in addition that this consecration to God and its attendant service, accomplished through these vows, establishes a *wholly special dedication* (or more weakly, a *special dedication*), this seems to be inexact. For it is not the act of consecration that establishes this dedication, for this, in the strict theological sense of *consecratio*, is always the action of God towards man, quite independent of even the most virtuous action of man.

---

[6] The phrase "totam vitam suam Dei famulatui mancipare" originates in the language of St. Thomas. The phrases used by St. Thomas to denote the servitude that is consecrated to God ("servitium et famulatus": *Summa Theologica,* II–II, q. 188, a. 2 ad 1), which, according to the Fathers, involves the greatest possible renunciation of the world (cf. *Summa Theologica,* II–II, q. 188, a. 2 ad 1), run thus: "totam vitam suam divino servitio deputare"; "se totaliter Deo (divinis obsequiis) mancipare (dedicare)": *Summa Theologica,* II–II, q. 186, a. 1 c. and ad 2; q. 188, a. 2 ad 2 and 3; q. 189, a. 3 c and ad 3.

We would, therefore, view the matter thus. The special dedication *(consecratio)* traditionally associated with the evangelical counsels has three constitutive elements: 1) the gracious call of God; 2) man's response through profession; 3) the acceptance of his vows or promises, in whatever form, by the Church. The third element is just as essential as the other two; for it alone makes plain the way in which the vows of profession provide "an ampler manifestation" of the fundamental and unrepeatable consecration of baptism. This is accomplished primarily, not by the candidate ratifying his baptismal consecration with his whole existence through the clarity and irrevocability of his becoming involved in a new way in the mystery of the Church and hence in the redemptive work of Christ. He is drawn into the *charismatic* dimension of the Church, in distinction to the official ministry of the Church as in ordination to the priesthood — which likewise provides baptismal consecration with "an ampler manifestation". Both consecrations (religious profession and ordination to the priesthood) *obligate a person in a special way to the service of the Church*, but each in a different way. This essential viewpoint is not sufficiently clearly expressed in the decree, especially as the statement about the acceptance of the oblation of the candidate by the Church is isolated in a separate paragraph.

The third paragraph of this article: "The fact that they are in God's service . . .", draws the perfectly logical conclusion from what has just been stated, i.e., that the objective consecration, effected by God's grace, must be a stimulus to subjective Christian activity — indeed, it reminds us of the logical relation between the indicative and the imperative in St. Paul's letters; but this paragraph shows, on the other hand, the preoccupation of the article with individual sanctity, leaving the aspect of service in the religious vocation to occupy second place.

The fourth paragraph: "Therefore, in fidelity to their profession . . .", is intended to counter an opinion often found in tradition: the notion that the various vocations within the Church — contemplative, apostolic, or active — can be derived from particular sayings in Scripture. For example, there is the well-known exposition of Lk 10:38–42 which tells of how Mary sat at our Lord's feet listening to him, while Martha got busy with the housework: "Martha, Martha, you are anxious and troubled about many things; one thing is needful. Mary has chosen the good (Vg: best) portion, which shall not be taken away from her." According to ancient, although not unanimous, tradition this has been taken as the warrant for the contemplative life and even for its superiority over the active life.[7] Today this is no longer possible exegetically.[8] This is not to decry the value and significance of contemplative orders. Nor is

---

[7] Cf. D. A. Csányi, *Optima Pars. Die Auslegung von Lk 10: 38–42 bei den Kirchenvätern der ersten vier Jahrhunderte* (1960); also, *Collectanea O. Cist. Ref.* 24 (1962), pp. 94–97; A Kemmer, "Zur Deutungsgeschichte von Lk 10: 38 ff. im alten Mönchtum", in *Erbe und Auftrag* 40 (1964), pp. 355 ff.

[8] A. Baker, "One Thing Necessary", in *Catholic Biblical Quarterly* 27 (1965), pp. 127 ff.

it possible now, on the basis of scriptural exegesis, to read the notion of a vocation to apostolic following into the sayings about following our Lord (e.g., the rich young ruler or Lk 9:57–62), even when following in the original sense is what is meant. With all of these classic passages, which in one form or another are cited in support of the way of the evangelical counsels and of the religious vocation, the real point is the central truth of the New Testament message: with the entry of Jesus into this age, human life and action have received a new centre, Jesus, in whom the Father is present and through whom he acts. Jesus, therefore, is the "one thing needful" for all men; nothing is of greater importance than to possess him, to be in his company, to be concerned about him and his affairs. All must listen to his words, for they are decisive; at his word men must put worldly things aside, must even at times give them up completely. Within this general redemptive situation there are special vocations. Prominent among these is life according to the evangelical counsels. This has evolved in many forms, but all seek to present one and the same mystery of Jesus, and to serve him.

The final paragraph simply draws a concrete conclusion from the immediately preceding paragraph, that is of the utmost importance for the religious orders. To live the mystery of Christ, to represent that mystery and to serve Christ, is, like the Lord himself, to be at once contemplative and apostolic, is to mould the contemplative life apostolically, and to be apostolically active in a contemplative fashion, to give oneself to God and to man simultaneously, for the one is not possible without the other. These things have not always been seen in that light, nor are they always seen thus today. A realization of this basic Christian truth would have important consequences for religious life, affecting even its institutional forms. The introductory statement, that Christians who live by the counsels must "seek God before all things and only Him", if taken in isolation, would be misleading. It is taken from the vocabulary of the ancient monastic contemplative ideal,[9] but must not be understood in this context in an individualistically redemptive sense. What is meant, rather, as the context shows, is that the God who has effected our redemption in Christ, and is present for us now in Christ, also meets us in our brethren. God and the world, God and mankind, can never be separated. The Church is the "presence of God upon earth" (Schlier).

Article 6. This develops in a more concrete way the theme of the previous article, which dealt with the theological and spiritual basis of life according to the counsels, in respect of the consequences which emerge for the individual religious. In order to interpret the first paragraph correctly it has to be read very carefully. As far as we can see, it reflects the traditional theology of the counsels. From the viewpoint of our earlier exposition, which contained a

---

[9] One of the central concepts in this vocabulary is that of *quaerere Deum* — to seek God —, and this was supposed to describe the inner essence of monasticism. For details see commentary on Article 6.

criticism of this theology, it will evoke contradiction from many. We would interpret thus. First, the *vow* attached to the counsels is directed immediately to God; it is an *actus religionis*, an operation of the virtue of worship. The content of the vow, likewise, celibacy, poverty, and obedience, is orientated towards God. The counsels are accepted for the sake of a greater love of God; by the counsels the religious is supposed to "free himself from those obstacles which might draw him away from the fervor of charity and the perfection of divine worship".[10] The counsels foster and make easier "a life hidden with Christ in God". Out of this seeking and loving God above all else, and out of that alone, flows that "love of one's neighbour for the world's salvation and the upbuilding of the Church". In other words, the evangelical counsels, choosing them and vowing to keep them, are regarded primarily from the viewpoint of individual and immediate union with God. Love of one's neighbour, the apostolate, the salvation of the world, the building up of the Church, take second place, even though they are necessary consequences of the love of God and life in God. This is the language of St. Thomas who took up the vocabulary of ancient monasticism,[11] and incorporated it in his own idea of the *contemplata aliis tradere*, but did not advance sufficiently beyond that vocabulary towards the biblical view of the relationship between love of God and love of one's neighbour, of self-abnegation for the sake of the *service of one's neighbour, of the Church, and of the world*, as is implied in following Christ.[12]

The final sentence states that the love of God and of one's neighbour, that are gained through contemplation (the context suggests that *caritas* is meant),

---

[10] Dogmatic Constitution on the Church, Article 44.

[11] We find the classic phrase of ancient monastic spirituality — quaerere Deum — in Article 5. Jean Leclercq, one of the best-acquainted with this spirituality, has described what this phrase means: "To seek God is indeed the sole aim of the monastic life. It is plain to anyone who knows the Rule of St. Benedict that there is no other reason for the monastic life than *quaerere Deum*. In order to attain eternal life, which, for St. Benedict is the only important goal, a man must detach himself from all earthly goals; this means practising prayer and asceticism in silence and in renunciation of the world. All that a monk does, his study and writing even, serves his spiritual life . . . For St. Benedict there is nothing at all utilitarian about the monastic life; it is directed solely towards the salvation of the monk, towards his search for God, and not towards any earthly purpose or social value. These things are never mentioned" (*Wissenschaft und Gottverlangen* [1963], p. 28). Similarly, L. Bouyer points out in his *Introduction to Spirituality* (1964) that the purpose of monastic life, which is the ultimate justification of all renunciation, is, as the Rule of St. Benedict stresses, solely this searching for God, for immediate union with him, by allowing him to draw our whole being to himself, and allowing all else to fall away from us. The monk seeks God in this life — in so far as that is possible — above all creatures, for himself alone.

[12] The great love and high regard St. Thomas had for the ancient monastic ideal, in spite of the high praise he bestows upon the priestly apostolate and his placing first in rank of the mixed life, is shown by his statement that there is a much more expressive sign of true love of God than any sufferings endured for Christ, i.e., "to hold oneself free of all the things of this life in order to find one's whole bliss in the contemplation of God" (*Summa Theologica*, II–II, q. 182, a. 2 ad 1).

will express themselves in the more intensive realization of the evangelical counsels, will give the practice of the counsels "life and direction". Today one would be inclined, without denying the truth of that statement, to place the accent the other way round: the distress of the neighbour who needs our help, the world-wide concerns of the Church, the helplessness of so many nations facing catastrophe, these are things that bring evangelical counsels to mind and reveal afresh their urgent necessity. For it is precisely in these manifold needs that God calls to us in Christ, and by placing ourselves at his disposal we meet him who gave his Son for us. Undoubtedly such a view of life according to the counsels runs the risk of activism, and could become a threat to contemplation (to the "for God alone") in general. This would be a dreadful loss; but, on the other hand, to neglect this viewpoint would be to fail, culpably, to read the signs of the times.[13] And so a more solid spiritual basis is required for the consequences which arise for the concrete life of many communities. A new "face" and an aim that is in line with the times depends upon a new spiritual impulse. This spirituality, however, will have to be quite different in many points from anything we have known hitherto. It will have to gather up all of past tradition, in a sense supersede it, and carry it further. The next two paragraphs have some very good points to make about this spirituality.

Most important of all, they point to the real sources of Christian spirituality: holy Scripture, the liturgy, and in particular the celebration of the Eucharist. The overladen devotional systems, especially characteristic of modern communities, are to be avoided. One of the marks of present-day spirituality is a simplicity and transparence that seeks to return to the essentials. Quantity is not the standard, it dislikes the prayer-*pensum* that only knows a burden, it reduces a proliferation of exercises to one, indispensable basic practice of prayer, that must come alive afresh each day. This consists in placing oneself in the presence of God, in order to see him and be with him, to hear his word and his call. It is this fundamental practice of individual, personal prayer, especially in a meditative form, which the article underlines. As the "Norms" (Article 21) put it, this is bound to foster the proper execution of the liturgy: "In order to make the participation of religious in the sacred mystery of the Eucharist and in the public prayer of the Church more fervent and fruitful, and that their whole spiritual life receive greater nourishment, in place of a multitude of vocal prayers, more space must be allotted to mental prayer, without, however, doing harm to the universally practised devotions of the Church (the Rosary, etc.). In all of this suitable care must be taken to provide members of religious orders with fundamental instruction in the spiritual life." In respect of common liturgical prayer societies are recommended "to say all or part of the Divine Office instead of the Little Office" (Article 20 of the "Norms"). Allowing for

---

[13] Pastoral Constitution on the Church, Articles 4 and 11; Decree on the Apostolate of the Laity, Article 14.

the absolute value of prayer as the praise of God, the final section of this article stresses also the purpose of prayer upon this earth: like the eating of the bread of the Eucharist it nourishes the individual enabling him to face everyday life as a Christian, and perfectly to fulfil the task laid upon him, in union with God: to "bring a brother's love to the members of Christ . . . and spend themselves completely on (the Church's) mission".

Article 7. This deals, not with the contemplative orders in the broad sense (embracing all monastic orders and many communities of women), but with the strictly contemplative orders (*Instituta vitae unice contemplativae*, as they are named in Article 16 of the decree). In order to obviate all misunderstanding, it chooses a phenomenological definition of the communities in question. These include, amongst others, the Carthusians, Cistercians, Camaldolesi, and, of female orders, notably the Carmelites and Poor Clares — some 40,000 in all. From the very start there was a unanimous desire in the Commission — and it was expressed in each successive draft of the decree — to devote a special article to these orders, on account of their special significance for the Church, and because of the threat to which they are exposed in our times. As a result of the obligatory drastic abbreviation of the text in the third and fourth redactions, this led to annoyance that now one article was to be devoted to the exclusively contemplative life, and one to the exclusively active life. As we have explained, this provoked great agitation amongst many monks who follow an apostolic mode of life, for they feared that in future they would be squeezed into a schema that allowed them very little room, if any, for an apostolate. The placing of the contemplative orders within the communities of religious passed through various stages in the course of work on the decree. According to the second draft they had "their special (inalienable) function within the mystical body of Christ *(proprias partes semper habent)*"; later they were said merely to "have *their* functions *(suas partes)*". A *modus,* signed by 500 Fathers, proposed to speak of the "more excellent functions *(potiones partes)*", which the contemplative orders have always had in the Church.[14] The final text speaks of the "distinguished part *(praeclara pars)*" such communities will always have to play, and describes them as "the glory of the Church". In this way it emphasizes the special quality of the contemplative life and the high dignity of the contemplative vocation, a quality and dignity that only faith can see. These things are not to be violated by anyone in the Church. The contemplative orders enjoy universal approbation.

When we come to enquire more precisely into the substance of this vocation,

---

[14] This requirement can point to centuries-old tradition. For modern times cf., chiefly, the apostolic constitution of Pius XI *Umbratilem,* which says: "It is easy to see that those who commit themselves to a life of prayer and penance contribute far more to the growth of the Church and to the salvation of mankind than do those who work actively in the Lord's vineyard" *(AAS* 16 [1924], p. 389). In his statements on this topic (cf. apostolic constitution *Sponsa Christi* and radio addresses to contemplative nuns) Pius XII was much more cautious.

a host of difficult problems emerge for us today. True, it is an ancient monastic ideal to spend one's life "wholly in contemplation", "in solitude and silence, constant in prayer and generous penance, living for God alone". These phrases have remained unaltered for a millennium and a half.[15] But do they still retain their original sense? Can they, in fact, have that same sense for us today? The answer is "No".[16] Originally, the *soli Dei vacare* — to exist for God alone and constantly to live in his presence — most certainly was understood individualistically. The *individual* sought the close presence of God, loving union with him; the road to this led over complete *apatheia*, which included not just the overcoming of all concupiscence, but the abandonment of all earthly things and thoughts. The theoretical reflection upon this ideal in the monastic literature in the ancient Church and even later makes it quite clear, that this theory drew not only upon biblical ideas,[17] but upon Plotinus also: the yearning for the transcendent *One*, the return from the multiplicity and distraction of the material world to the simple *All* of our origin. In the living development of the contemplative ideal within the Christian order, such reflections have played an ever diminishing role; but one thing has persisted: the yearning of the individual for loving union with the one God. In this aspiration, his fellow-being, the salvation of others, the Church's mission for the redemption and perfecting of the world, played scarcely any part. The religious community itself, the monastery, its separation from the world, the common life of the brethren or sisters, were designed primarily to create the conditions for the mystical ascent of the individual towards union with God. It is true that medieval monasticism even in its strictly contemplative form, was always conscious of its representative function within the Church as the mystical body of Christ, in the sense of Rom 12:4 (this passage is correctly cited in the article), but, quite emphatically, the apostolic responsibility of the contemplative life has become popularly accepted only in modern times, chiefly under recent Popes.[18] If this obligation of contemplative monasteries to exercise an apostolate, through example, prayer, and penance, is to be more than a pious thought, and is to "take full possession of the minds and hearts" of those in contemplative monasteries,[19] and if contem-

---

[15] Jean Leclercq, *Études sur le vocabulaire monastique du Moyen Age* (1961), pp. 29 f., 156.

[16] An urgent problem emerges at this point. For centuries the theology of the religious life and of the spirituality associated with that life has used a vocabulary that originated for the most part in ancient monasticism, and that is understood today only by specialists. How are we to do justice to modern insights gained from theology and anthropology? Are we not heading straight for misunderstandings? In fact, modern man is quite beyond the reach of the language of tradiional spirituality.

[17] The phrase *soli Deo vacare* may owe something to Ps 46(45):11, "*Vacate* et videte, quoniam ego sum Dominus", and also to 1 Cor 7:5, ". . . ut *vacatis* oratione".

[18] The most detailed comments we have on the apostolic mission of the contemplative orders are those of Pius XII, especially in *Sponsa Christi*: *AAS* 43 (1951), p. 14, and in the last radio addresses to contemplative nuns, *AAS* 50 (1958), pp. 584–6.

[19] *Ibid.*, p. 586.

plative religious are not only to "cause the people of God to grow through their *secret* apostolic fruitfulness" but also through a visible and direct radiation of heavenly graces, then the constitution of their institutions must be fundamentally revised. This demands that the members of the contemplative orders must be made familiar with the great concerns and needs of Church and world, with the modern human struggle to create a new form of society. Hitherto the program of the contemplative orders has been quite unadapted to fulfil this demand. It is worth recalling St. Theresa of Lisieux's direct link with the missionaries and the human beings entrusted to her. The life of the contemplative must not centre entirely round spiritual things, and be nourished solely upon spiritual ideas. They must preserve a sense of being in the midst of the world. The phrase *eorum a mundo secessus* (their separation from the world) was chosen advisedly; it denotes merely physical separation and not a flight from the world. They must be able to share in the tasks and sufferings of their brethren and sisters, and must never feel that they have left them and escaped into a better world.

There is a second point: the life and work of the contemplative orders must be more public, in an appropriate manner, to those outside — Christians and non-Christians. Otherwise it cannot preserve its power as a sign. Why, for example, do they not celebrate the liturgy in genuine fellowship with those who visit them, without the artificial barrier of railings and screens? Why, for instance, cannot the Carmelites at Dachau, whose Church is visited on certain days by many people from all over the world, because of proximity to the site of the former concentration camp, from time to time hold a suitable service of the Word, even if that meant cutting out certain Hours from the Divine Office? Why cannot people know first-hand how monks and nuns work, and work hard, to earn their living, just like other people — for work is our primary penance?[20] In all of these ways they could once again become a present reality in the world. The last sentence in the article states that "their manner of living should be revised according to the aforementioned principles" (Articles 2–4). This allows them to create a correspondingly new appearance. In spite of all of faith's awareness of the "*secret* apostolic fruitfulness" of their humble and hidden existence, it would be false to exalt this secrecy of their life and activity into a principle.

---

[20] In the "Norms" a special article is devoted (Article 22) to the penance offered by religious. It might appropriately be cited at this point, although it applies to all communities without distinction. "Religious ought to practise works of penance and mortification more than the rest of the faithful. The penitential practices customary in institutions ought to be revised as far as is needful, so that the members really can carry them out. Account must be taken of the traditions of East and West, and also of modern conditions, and new forms of penance should be devised out of the circumstances of modern life." Anyone who is familiar with the facts knows that the so-called "penitential practices" and "work of mortification" in the orders have very largely fallen into disuse. For this reason real works of penance are all the more necessary, and must be built into the life of religious communities. They must be taken from the harshness of modern industrial life.

Article 8. It is not quite clear which communities are being discussed in this article. Is it those which were founded explicitly for apostolic work (priestly, charitable, educational), the basic reason for the existence of which is thus apostolic action? It would seem to be those; otherwise it could hardly be asserted that this activity constituted the specific and deepest essence of *their* religious life. It was for this very assertion that the active orders, especially modern societies, had fought, because they wanted to resolve that parallelism which monastic tradition and practices had imposed upon them. Do we take it, then, that the medieval canons regular, and also the mendicant orders, "which by rule or constitution closely join the apostolic life with choral prayer and monastic observance" (Article 9), are to be excluded from this article? It is not certain whether these are agreed on this point; more precisely, it is certain that there will be controversy on this point in the orders in question. At all events, this article provides an antithesis to the foregoing article on the strictly contemplative orders.

The first important assertion made here is that there are many different charisms. Applied to the religious orders, that means that the history of religious life is not a straight line of development from ancient monasticism onwards, as if this had simply undergone progressive evolution. However much all of the orders have climbed upon the shoulders of older communities which preceded them, notably upon ancient Christian monasticism, they are not simply derived from them; from time to time they have been original and independent creations arising from some illumination and impulse of grace, which are bound to have stamped them with a special charism, and given them an idiosyncrasy that is expressed in their concrete life. Sad to say, because of the preponderance of monastic traditions, this has not always happened. There has been and still is a standard of institution and customs that has been generally accepted as essential to genuine religious life, and hardly anyone has been able to opt out of this standard. But now a change has become possible for the explicitly active orders. Religious life and apostolic work ought to form an indissoluble unity. This must not remain at the theoretical stage, but must affect the whole form of life of the community. The starting point and plumbline of every consideration must always be "the apostolate to which they are dedicated", and for the sake of which the community was founded. Because "the religious life which is committed to apostolic works takes on many forms", a correspondingly wide scope is allowed for their concrete formation. Necessary and wholesome as this last affirmation may be, one cannot disguise a fear that the propositions in the third section of this article might serve an ultra-conservative purpose, if used as a defence of obsolete traditions under the slogan of "sacred heritage and customs".

With the strong stress upon the character of the active communities, which take their stamp from the *apostolate,* and the consequent distinction of these communities from the monastic way of life, spiritual life in these communities becomes a thing of great urgency, especially today. The article is quite right, therefore, to say that "their apostolic activity should be animated by a religious spirit" — that is the spirit of following Christ —, and further, that "their apostolic activity should result from an intimate union with him. In this way it will happen that love for God and neighbour will itself be nurtured." There can be no doubt at all that the survival of the active communities in future depends upon their foundation upon a deep spiritual life, and upon the guarantee of prayer and meditation; for the enormous demands made by the present-day apostolate, in whatever form, upon the whole man and his time, and the circumstances of modern life, are far from conducive to corporate life and prayer.

Article 9. A separate article is devoted to monastic life, not because the prestige of monasticism requires it, but from the realization that neither the two preceding articles, nor the concept of the *vita mixta*, the "mixed life", could do justice to the character of Christian monasticism, which was godparent to the whole of religious life in the Church. Monasticism in its authentic form lacks the precisely defined aims which are so much a mark of modern orders and societies (to which for the most part the medieval orders have become assimilated). This, too, may have something to do with the aversion of monasticism to centralized organization and leadership. The aim of monasticism is very broadly conceived. Perhaps the best description of its aim is, as we have expounded above, *quaerere Deum,* "to seek God". This aim does not necessarily demand an exclusively contemplative life (although this is what monks most desire), but allows of the most varied activities as well. Throughout their history monks have practised the crafts, land reclamation and agriculture, copying books, writing, mission work, and education. A multitude of forms as modifications of the same ideal still characterizes Catholic monasticism, especially in the West. But it is precisely this variety that makes it difficult to make universally valid concrete statements concerning the "appropriate renewal" of monasticism, as this article bears witness. In addition to giving high praise to "the venerable institution of monastic life" — praise that may sound a little forced to the ears of the men of such a technical age as ours —, the article tries to define the core of the monastic ideal. The decree describes the heart of monastic life thus: "to render to the divine Majesty a service at once simple and noble, within the monastic confines". But it allows of other ancillary functions that have been assumed by this or that abbey or confederation in the course of history, as a result of the circumstances of the times. This is an important affirmation, and one which the monks of today will have to argue out for themselves. At all events, according to the decree, the true function of monasticism, however varied the forms in which it is expressed, is performed "within the monastic confines". These confines need not be too narrowly defined, however. The controlling objective of renewal and fresh inspiration of monasticism is chiefly, to ensure that "monasteries will be seedbeds of growth for the Christian people".

The uninitiate can scarcely imagine what a host of particular problems of an anthropological, sociological, and spiritual kind, such an affirmation holds, given the present situation of the Church and the world. The task set monasticism in the post-conciliar age is no easy one, and the decree provides no recipe for its fulfilment.

The appendage to this article on monasticism of a note on the *vita mixta*, the mixed religious life, shows how difficult it has been to integrate this form of life (affecting mostly the medieval orders) into the model we have hitherto known of monastic life, especially in its traditional version. Closer examination reveals that the topic here is not so much appropriate renewal as the preservation of the traditional heritage. Thus this paragraph will create difficulties for many general chapters, depending upon the opinions represented in them.

Article 10. There were two reasons for the inclusion in the decree of a special article on lay orders and societies, although these had already been covered in Article 8. 1) They desired solemnly to underline the full religious status of those modern societies, which for long had created difficulties for the canonists, and had only found a place in the new canon law. In the process, the distinction between orders and societies, between solemn and simple vows, has fallen into the background. Today this distinction is of small significance. 2) They wished to hold out moral assistance by putting the weight of the Council's backing behind those societies have brought incalculable blessings to the Church, especially during the last hundred years, and have helped to mould the features of the modern Church, and which have, for the most part, fallen upon evil days.

The second paragraph takes up a hotly disputed question, affecting chiefly the larger teaching orders, and cautiously seeks a solution that will do justice both to the objective necessities of the situation and to the lay status of these societies. This execution of the proposed solution will require the efforts of the Pope himself, and whether or not it will be a success, time alone can tell.

Article 11. Knowledge of the history of this article helps us understand and assess it. The pre-conciliar draft of the decree contained a separate chapter of several articles on the secular institutes. With the exception of the teaching brothers, they were the only group to be specially discussed. In the case of the teaching brothers, the discussion was provoked by internal difficulties, in the case of the secular institutes it was the canon lawyers who had initiated the discussion. It was proposed to complete the canonical distinction of the secular institutes from the religious orders and societies and the societies of the common life without vows, initiated in two fundamental documents, *Provida Mater* (1947), and *Primo feliciter* (1948), and to accomplish their integration into the so-called states of perfection, and solemnly to ratify these things by the authority of the council. The rest of the many observations of this draft upon the secular institutes were almost entirely canonical in tone — as was, indeed, most of the decree. The second much abbreviated draft of 1963 contained but a single article on the secular institutes. This made an effort, in line with the directions that had meanwhile been issued, to produce a more theological definition of those communities that had recently emerged in, and been recognized by, the Church. Most of the statements made, however, were to be found word for word, scattered throughout the pre-conciliar draft. In the third and fourth drafts, reduced as they were to short guiding principles, even this article was sacrificed, so that in the whole schema, the secular institutes were no longer mentioned, except for a brief remark on the possibility of amalgamation of their ultimate superiors. In practice, therefore, they were no longer among the themes of the Council. Only in the final redaction of the decree was the article re-introduced in a different form, as the result of several interventions.

As the text concerning the secular institutes was taken, in every draft, more or less *verbatim* from the apostolic constitution *Provida Mater* and the motu proprio *Primo Feliciter*, to which reference was constantly made in the footnotes to the earlier drafts, we ought first to examine the doctrine of these documents on the nature and status of the secular institutes in the Church.[21] The literary genre of the documents is significant: a remarkable mixture of edifying argument — the vocabulary of which no longer appeals — and legal definitions, with canonical interest clearly in the foreground. The basic conception behind the doctrine is roughly as follows: the orders and societies *(religiones)*, whose members renounce the world, and confirm this through public vows recognized by the Church, embody completely and in its highest form the canonical state of perfection. The communities of the common life without (public) vows, but which are for the most part related in spirit and institution to the orders and societies, fulfill what is essential to the canonical state of perfection. Their members, too, have visibly renounced the world and lead a common life separated from the world, and have irrevocably bound themselves by the evangelical counsels. Both groups constitute "a special canonical state *in the strict sense* (i.e., bearing all of the outward marks which characterize a public legal state as such), wholly and solely *(unice et ex integro)* dedicated to striving for perfection". Where, then, do the secular institutes fit in? "By their internal constitution *(interna constitutione)*" and "their hierarchically ordered leadership *(hierarchica regiminis ordinatio)*" and "their complete and unconditional devotion *(plena nullisque aliis vinculis limitata deditione)*" and "through the evangelical counsels *(consiliorum evangelicorum professione)*" and "finally, through their principle, which is to serve and exercise an apostolate *(ratione denique ministeria et apostolatum exercendi)*", they stand in essence *(quoad substantiam)* "close to the states of perfection, chiefly to the societies of the common life without vows *(propius accedunt ad status canonicos perfectionis)*, although they do not lead any religious life in common".

So much for *Provida Mater*. Similarly, according to *Primo Feliciter*, "they are

---

[21] On what follows cf. the apostolic constitution *Provida Mater: AAS* 39 (1947), pp. 115–18; motu proprio *Primo Feliciter: AAS* 40 (1948), pp. 286f.

numbered amongst the canonically regulated and tested states of perfection, on account of the total dedication to God and mankind, to which their members are bound with the Church's approval, *despite remaining in the world*". We cannot fail to notice a gradation downwards from orders to secular institutes. Obviously the secular institutes are highly commended as a special fruit of grace in these days. But the fact that their members remain in the world, with no kind of outward distinguishing mark that declares the reason for their existence, and lack any form of common life, which expresses their separation from the world, constitutes an obstacle to their integration, in terms of the traditional doctrine, in the public and canonical state of perfection. If that has happened, then it has been accomplished through the impact of these institutes and the recognition of their necessity for the apostolate in modern society. The theory has emerged *post hoc*, and is not free from contradictions. The interior, religious core of the states of perfection, as these two documents say, is, traditionally, "the complete profession of Christian perfection, that is firmly anchored in the evangelical counsels, and truly regular (equivalent to religious profession) in essence *(quoad substantiam vere religiosa)*". Such a profession can scarcely last indefinitely in the world without the protection of the religious life (cloister, special dress, common life and community rule). Moreover, it requires a very special vocation — this is twice mentioned in *Provida Mater* —;[22] for the world is full of vice and lies in darkness.

These and similar phrases speak of the world almost entirely in a pejorative sense. The world lures away from God and extinguishes early fervour. Such a vocation is to be carefully tested, and communities, too, ought to be subjected to rigorous examination in order to "avoid the dangers of erecting ever new institutes, which are often imprudently and incautiously founded".[23] Such a view of the world necessarily urges us to keep our distance from it. Nonetheless the "special *worldly* character of the institutes" is stressed, especially in *Primo Feliciter*, and the members of the institutes are to "accommodate themselves to the world in so far as this is consonant with the practice of perfection" and to exercise their apostolate "not merely in the world, but, as it were, by means of the world, that is through their professions and orders, and in places and circumstances which must be in harmony with these situations".[24] Quite obviously these requirements have not been adequately thought out, neither theologically nor spiritually. For in the measure in which the Christian religious enters into this world of trade and the professions, of politics, economics, and culture, the more frankly and completely he enters into it — and he must if he

---

[22] *Loc. cit.*, pp. 117 and 118: "Following a special divine vocation, they yet remain in the world". "By reason of a special vocation and assisted by divine grace, even in the world there certainly can be a fully binding and effective consecration to God, that is not merely interior, but in external form almost equivalent to religious consecration."

[23] *Ibid.*, p. 119.

[24] *Loc. cit.*, pp. 284 f.

is to exercise an effective apostolate, "as it were, by means of the world", in the same measure will he have to acquire a positive relationship to the world. He will no longer be able to get by with the ideal of perfection that characterizes the Church's traditional state of perfection. He cannot be active for God, the creator of the world, and for the cause of Christ, as a "purely spiritual man" wearing the mask of this world, quite unaffected by his surroundings and the work that he is doing. To him, too, applies all that Vatican II had to say about the ambivalent relationship of the Church and of Christians to the world. There is little trace of these things in the fundamental documents concerning the secular institutes. They still bear the stamp of the traditional theology of the religious orders. They make no serious attempt to provide a genuine appropriate theology of the secular institutes; the many edifying passages are insufficient to disguise this defect. Had there been any such new concept it would have been bound to react upon the traditional ideal of perfection attached to the religious life, and to animate this, so that even the problem of the outward form of the various styles of religious life would have had to be posed in a fresh way.

It can be shown that the early drafts of the decree were still stamped by this conception of the secular institutes. In the draft of 1963 we read: "The secular institutes require a true and *essentially* complete *(essentialiter completans)* undertaking, approved by the Church, to live by the evangelical counsels, even if *(atsi)* in the world." Again: "This undertaking, *which in essence is religious,* confers upon these men and women living in the world, laymen and clerics, a consecration, *similar to that possessed by those in the states of perfection.*" The last sentence in the article runs thus: "The attainment of such a high ideal demands of the members of the secular institutes that they not only 'keep . . . unstained from the world' (Jas 1:27), but are able to discern which things in this transitory world (cf. 1 Cor 7:31) are inimical to the cross of Christ, and which are consonant with the kingdom of God and foster its growth." In comparison, the final text can show a few substantial improvements. The phrases in italics have been dropped, so that a downward grading from the orders through the societies of the common life to the secular institutes has disappeared. All the statements in the first paragraph about the secular institutes are positive in tone, without implying any comparison in respect of value with other religious communities. Even the parenthetic concluding sentence in the draft of 1963, which still viewed the relationship to the world quite one-sidedly, has been deleted from the final text of the decree. In its place we have a very sober and specific admonition which all will welcome, who know anything about the deficiencies in the training of novices and in the systematic further education of members of the secular institutes. Not least, something very important is said concerning their secular character, the apostolate, "as it were, by means of the world", when it demands training of the members "in matters both human and divine". The reiteration in the introductory phrase of this article of the explicit separation of the secular institutes from the religious orders (already stated in Article 1, last paragraph), was the result of an influential intervention just before the final voting. The importance of this has been very much played up by many, but it would probably turn out to be relatively insignificant if the theology of religious life were to be thought out afresh and the consequences drawn for the institutional expressions of that life. Much more to the point would be the working out of a definition of spirituality, which blended in a deep unity the fact of *being in the world* — which must be actualized by those following this life — and *being not of this world*.[25]

Article 12. The articles on the evangelical counsels, which follow, are all built on the same pattern. There is a short introduction followed by a theological-spiritual substantiation of the counsel in question. Thereafter problems about its concrete actualization are discussed. The sequence of the counsels is that followed in the Dogmatic Constitution on the Church, Articles 42 and 43. Celibacy is taken first, because in the New Testament it is the most clearly attested charism of the three, and the most unambiguous symbol of the religious state.

The first and most important thing said about "celibacy (or chastity) for the kingdom of heaven's sake" applies equally to the other two counsels, even if it is not specially mentioned, and is often too little remembered in connection with them. It is this: they are a gift of grace (fundamentally one and the same gift),[26] which can therefore be recognized, affirmed, and accepted, only by faith. It is intended to "liberate the human heart in a unique way and cause it to burn with greater love for God and all mankind". It does this, however, only if the one called responds to God's call and enters ever more deeply into it, believes the words of the Lord, trusts in God's help rather than in his own resources, practises mortification and the custody of the senses, and does all these things in a unique way. And if the charism of celibacy is given only to a few,[27] yet it is nothing extraordinary, but, within the framework of the divine dispensation of grace, something completely normal. For the whole Church has a charismatic nature, and there are many charisms. Every member of the people of God has his own gift (cf. 1 Cor 7:7).

Moreover, one must not conceive of the charism of celibacy in too mechanical a fashion, as though it were a material gift bestowed as a finished article once and for all. It is something, rather, that is introduced by God into the concrete anthropological and psychological situation of a human life, and so has a history of its own; it is an adventure, the adventure of the believer. In life's ups and

---

[25] On the question as a whole cf. F. Wulf, "Wesen und Aufgabe der Säkularinstitute nach dem Zweiten Vatikanischen Konzil", in *Glaube und Leben* 40, no. 5 (1967).

[26] Thus in the Dogmatic Constitution on the Church, Article 43. This is stated pre-eminently of celibacy: *ibid.*, Article 42; Decree on Priestly Formation, Article 10; Decree on the Ministry and Life of Priests, Article 16.

[27] Dogmatic Constitution on the Church, Article 42.

downs it brings joy to him who is for ever being called anew — the blessed experience of God and of Christ —, and it also becomes his testing — the test of his faith, hope, and love. Wherever a man goes through with this adventure, it becomes — for the one called himself and for the witness of his life — "an outstanding token of heavenly riches, and also a most suitable way for religious to spend themselves readily in God's service and in works of the apostolate". It is also a witness "to all Christ's faithful of that wondrous marriage between the Church and Christ her only spouse". The high Christological, ecclesiological, and eschatological meaning of Christian celibacy and virginity thus embraces all, if they be but true believers. Of all, according to the circumstances of their lives, is required an ear to hear this call.

The decree of the Council does not conceal the fact that the celibacy which is vowed, when seen in all its moral consequences, and as lived within the ethos of divine grace, reaches deep into the development of man's physical and sexually conditioned nature. The human task imposed by celibacy is not light. Today more than ever before we know in great detail about the importance of the body and of sexuality in the development of human personality. Even he who is celibate "for the kingdom of heaven's sake" has to live entirely in the body, in thought and feeling, in sacrifice and in every activity, always bearing the mark of his sexuality. Otherwise he could neither love truly from his heart — not even God — nor radiate any valid sign or witness for others. Only through conscious acceptance and personal transcendence of sexually differentiated corporeality do the renunciations, freely accepted with celibacy, cease to be a hindrance to the human, mental, and religious development of a man, and become sources of new energy, advancing the aim of Christian celibacy, as described in the conciliar text. The gift as such is not a substitute for the slow and laborious work of learning renunciation; it rather precipitates the struggle; but at the same time it provides assistance that far exceeds all human effort. In this work a man — especially a young man — requires guidance and training. There has been far too little of this in the orders hitherto. Perhaps the need has not been seen, perhaps there has been a dearth of competent educators. As a rule, instruction on the duties involved in the vows was thought sufficient, and for the rest, a little instruction about sex was expected to clear away all difficulties. On the variety of forms and phases in the body-soul encounter between man and woman, as well as on the psychology of the celibate life and its peculiar experiences and crises, hardly anything was ever said. On these things education in the religious orders has much lee-way to make up. As far as is possible in a couple of sentences, the Council decree tries to make this point clear. Most worthy of note is the last sentence in the second paragraph of this article: "Chastity has stronger safeguards in a community when true fraternal love thrives among its members." Monastic regulation as formerly practised, especially in female communities, with a one-sided preoccupation with assemblies and silence, with the prevention of particular friendships, etc., was a hindrance rather than a help to brotherly and sisterly encounter, and the growth of true fellowship. A change must come about here also.[28]

Article 13. We are treated here to very scant theological comment upon evangelical poverty. What is said is confined in the main to one Scripture passage (2 Cor 8:9). This in itself is an indication of the difficulty of producing an exact definition of what evangelical poverty really is. The poverty of Christ himself is not entirely unambiguous. His life knew the dire poverty of manger and cross, the poverty of Nazareth, which was that of humble folk, of the "poor of Jahweh",[29] and the poverty imposed by the years of itinerant preaching.[30] The history of the orders displays more variety in forms of poverty. These have been so closely and indissolubly tied up with the economic and social structure of the times in which they originated, that they are of little help to us today. There has been only one constant factor in Christian poverty: it always contains some element of genuine deprivation, which constitutes a sharing in the deprivation of Christ, and is the expression of acceptance of the death to which the world is doomed through sin, acceptance of the destiny of mankind, expelled from paradise to live in tribulation and hunger. The further motivation of Christian poverty as applied to life and its functions in this or that place and time, and which is also an entering into the example of Christ, has been most varied. There has been poverty for the sake of the community: the renunciation of property in order to share it with others. There has been poverty for the sake of solidarity with the poor of this world or for the sake of greater apostolic mobility. In every case he who renounces — as with celibacy — has not primarily his own sanctification in view, but wants to be free to respond to God's call at any hour and for any task in the service of his fellowmen and the salvation of the world.

The forms of poverty are determined by the motive at the particular time and by the personal call of God. Thus they will always be most diverse. Each community, each house, is different from any other. We need only look at the secular institutes. In general, the economic and social structure of the western world has put a great strain upon the credibility and witnessing power of religious poverty, as exemplified today, especially in the active orders. That is the reason for the request made in the decree on religious life that new forms of poverty must be sought out and tested, not just for individuals, but for the community as a whole (the conciliar text speaks of a "corporate witness to . . . poverty"). In the past such forms have only existed where life according to the counsels has been realized within a small group, in the recently emergent fraternities. Hence a re-organization of religious life is required in order to assure its rightful place in the Church to the indispensable witness of poverty. The stimulus given in

[28] On the whole topic cf. F. Wulf, "Zur Anthropologie von Zölibat und Jungfräulichkeit", in *Glaube und Leben* 36 (1963), pp. 352 ff.

[29] Cf. A. Gelin, *Die Armen — Sein Volk* (1957).

[30] Cf. F. Wulf, "Vom Geist der Armut", in *Glaube und Leben* 38 (1965), pp. 135 ff.

this direction by the Council is certainly useful: the allusion to the duty of all to work quietly puts an end to the idea of mendicancy as a means of earning a living; and the emphasis on care of the poor poses the question of where the poor of today are really to be found; the insistence that "every appearance of luxury, of excessive wealth, and accumulation of possessions" are to be avoided, in spite of a lack of precise definition, may be very needful in some cases; but this stimulus is not sufficient to solve the problem of poverty in the modern religious order, for the problem cannot be solved by well-meaning precepts, but must be worked out at the level of real life, a life that has received a fresh impulse from following the poverty of Christ.[31]

The rest of what this article has to say concerns, for the most part, the internal poverty of the order or of the individual. Here, too, this principle applies: even within the order a general rule about poverty is possible only up to a certain degree. Much, even much of decisive importance, because affecting everyday life and one's personal style of life, will in future have to be left to individual responsibility. The greatest importance must be attached, therefore, to education in personal responsibility. The newly created possibility for members of religious communities "to renounce any inheritance which they have acquired or are due to acquire", has been commented upon thus in Article 24 of the "Norms": "The religious communities with simple vows are to be allowed to decide through their general chapters, whether to incorporate this renunciation of inheritance or expected inheritance in their constitutions, and if it is incorporated, whether it should be obligatory or voluntary, and when the renunciation is to be made — before perpetual profession or after some years." The commentary shows that the carrying out of the possibility provided by the Council may not be simple, especially as it still leaves many open questions. For example, in favour of whom is renunciation to be made, or to what extent is declared renunciation equivalent in status to solemn vows, etc.? The opinion could be held, that the text of the decree, moulded by influences emanating from the Congregation for Religious, amounts to very little in respect of the problem of poverty, especially as the law with regard to poverty in the orders — as in canon law in general and in statements as made from time to time — requires fundamental revision in the light of modern economic and social structure. The general chapters envisaged in the "Norms" will in any case have to study the whole matter, and thus help prepare for a revision of canon law.

Article 14. The theme of obedience was tricky from start to finish — with good reason. It touches the very core of religious life, and for years has been the source of growing difficulties within the orders, and a bone of violent contention, affecting both the traditional doctrine of obedience and also the practice of obedience. The first drafts aimed, therefore, at preserving and strengthening

---

[31] On the whole topic cf. K. Rahner, "Die Armut des Ordenslebens in einer veränderten Welt", in *Glaube und Leben* 33 (1960), pp. 262 ff.; also O. von Nell-Breuning, "Armutsidee und Entwicklungshilfe", in *Stimmen der Zeit* 176 (1965), pp. 331 ff.

the authority of superiors, and were directed "against modern erroneous opinions",[32] such as that the relationship between superiors and subjects ought to be more "democratically" organized, and that genuine dialogue ought to be established between them. Only with the utmost reserve and in very cautious statements, did they try to take into account the altered circumstances of our times and the changed mentality of modern man. The draft of 1963 can be taken as an example: "If in our times members of apostolic and active communities, on account of their more difficult tasks, must be allowed greater scope of decision and action,[33] this does not imply approval of the idea that the subject may set aside simple obedience to his superior, and discuss a course of action until both are of the same mind. Should the subject fail to agree with his superior, then, after humble prayer for God's enlightenment, let him put the matter before his superior ('meekly', says the pre-conciliar draft), always prepared to accept what the superior finally decides."[34] Such rights as subjects do possess were not mentioned effectively in any of the drafts. Obviously, this paternalistic view of the office of a superior, who takes upon himself the activities of the community and entrusts them to the subjects,[35] is bound to provoke a corresponding reaction. This happens in every case where account is not taken soon enough of developments arising of necessity out of the actual circumstances of life, and where these are seen merely as a threat to be fought by the uncompromising adherence to what has held in the past. On this score there is a reciprocal challenge.

How much divergence of opinion on obedience there has been in the past, was shown by two *modi,* which were handed in after the debate in the Council hall in November 1964, each signed by about 400 Fathers. The first ran: "At all costs care must be taken that the authentic concept of religious obedience is preserved undiminished. Religious obedience, as it has always been understood in the Church, does not diminish the dignity of an adult person, but helps it towards full maturity, for it is a sublime total offering *(holocaustum),* through which a man subordinates himself and all that he is, for the sake of the kingdom of heaven, wholly to the will of Christ, whose place is taken by the superior." In contrast, the second *modus* ran thus: "Religious ought to observe the obedience they have promised according to the aims and character of their community, in a mature personal atmosphere. Superiors ought so to share responsibility with their subjects, that all members of the community look upon the affairs of the community as their own, and are solicitous for the good of all alike." The final text had to emerge from these two almost contradictory *modi.* There had to be a

---

[32] Thus in the pre-conciliar draft, Part II, Chapter X, n. 14.

[33] This addition (minus the limiting introductory particle) was put forward by the German bishops.

[34] Chapter IV, Article 26. The central part of this section can be traced to an address by Pius XII to the thirtieth general congregation of the Society of Jesus in 1957: *AAS* 49 (1957), pp. 807–8.

[35] *Ibid.,* Chapter III, Article 18.

compromise; and in fact the text we now have clearly bears traces of such a compromise. We do not presume to criticize the text, but merely want to let it show how well it probably reflects the state of opinion in the council at that time.

The first paragraph sets out once again to describe the meaning and nature of obedience, and to cite its biblical foundation. Obedience is vowed directly to God, and the vow embodies the complete and unreserved surrender of the man to God. The intention of the one making the vow endows it with the character of self-immolation. In more precise terms: the aim of this surrender is to achieve a "greater steadiness and security to the saving *will of God*". This goes beyond the static speculative and abstract theology of St. Thomas and arrives at the *historical* event of God's redemptive dispensation. Accordingly, the ultimate source of religious obedience is Christ's obedience to the redemptive commission of his Father. This is where it acquires the form of a servant and this is what illumines its goal in respect of this world: the service of one's brethren. Religious obedience means being a slave to one's brethren, on the model of Christ, and for his sake, who calls men his brothers. This, too, makes the function of the religious superior plain: the superiors, to whom by faith the members of religious orders subject themselves, ought, through the exercise of the authority given them by God through the Church, to help their subjects to recognize more clearly, and fulfil more promptly, the redemptive will of God, to which both superiors and subjects have yielded themselves for the sake of the service of man, as a continuation of the redemptive work of Christ and in union with him, who was *the* Servant of God. This service, performed by superiors and subjects each in their own way, is thus, fundamentally, nothing other than a special sharing in the ministry and mission of the Church, which is the body of Christ.

This is to interpret obedience in a clearly salvation-historical and salvation-theological manner, in terms of its function as service. All of the statements deriving from the traditional theology of obedience, such as the individualistically slanted introductory sentence, or the quasi identification of superiors with God, whose place they take (a concept that has never been precisely analyzed theologically), have been subsumed under this idea of service. Others, however, may interpret this paragraph in the sense of a more strictly *traditional* theology of obedience. That is still possible. We see here how the authors have not been able to work out any concept neatly and logically in this, the fundamental paragraph of this article. The article does, however, represent substantial progress for the Christologically, soteriologically, and ecclesiologically determined theology of obedience. This becomes evident when we compare the final text with the immediately preceding draft of 1964. There we read: "The religious, who has voluntarily sacrificed his whole will to God through the vow of obedience, humbly obeys his superior as God's representative, from love of Christ, in all that is commanded according to the rule and constitution. This sacrifice of himself is expressed by his meek following of his lawful directors *(moderatoribus)*,

363

even if authority must be exercised in love and with regard for the human person, and although today the religious are called upon to do more numerous and more difficult tasks, requiring greater initiative and resourcefulness."[36]

The next two paragraphs on the exercise of authority and the giving of obedience in practice, are addressed, at times separately, first to the subjects, then to the superiors. As far as we know, this is the first time that an official document on obedience has devoted a special section to the exposition of the duties of superiors to their subjects. The paragraph on subjects merely reiterates traditional doctrine, but it gains a certain perspective from the preceding theological arguments. The fact that voluntarily yielded obedience does not diminish a man's personal dignity, but leads "to maturity in consequence of that enlarged freedom which belongs to the sons of God", will be denied in principle by none. But there must be appropriate presuppositions on both sides, and in our times, by general consent, those affecting superiors are the more decisive. The present crisis of obedience, as was said frequently at the council (in the interventions and the sessions of the commissions), is fundamentally a crisis of authority, because, in view of the complex technical problems of our times and the great individual variations found in men today, the proper exercise of authority makes very heavy demands upon those in authority, demands with which as yet few of them can cope. The crisis amongst the religious orders emerges from the same problem, and it had been latent even before the council. Does this paragraph concerning religious superiors draw sufficient attention to the problem? It does, for those who have eyes to see and ears to hear; for it points out that superiors, too, are bound by avowed obedience to God, and must constantly bear this in mind before giving orders.

It should be stressed even more strongly than in the text (which is extremely cautious on the point) that today discussion with subordinates, with the individual, with advisers, and with the community, is an indispensable factor in finding out what the will of God is. The time for one-man rule or the rule of a secret conclave in religious orders is past. A superior who regularly neglected consultation or respected only its outer form would sin against the will of God. As the decree says, he ought also to "give the kind of leadership which will encourage religious to bring an active and responsible obedience to the offices they shoulder and the activities they undertake". What is that if not an appeal for genuine co-operation between superiors and subordinates, indispensable above all in the active orders? And so, both superiors and subordinates, in virtue of the same obedience, are bound by the same task, which is not least the service of one another and of the community, implying a common responsibility. (The text speaks of the superior exercising his office "as one who will render an account for the souls entrusted to him"; but in spite of the reference to Heb 13:17,

---

[36] The conclusion of the last sentence comes from the address of Paul VI on 23 May 1964 to the superiors and chapters of the religious orders. See *AAS* 56 (1964), p. 567.

it thinks of this in a paternalistic and individualistic way.) Once again the last paragraph of this article underlines the affirmation "that all members of the community have a share in the welfare of the whole community and a responsibility for it". This sharing in responsibility is becoming increasingly necessary. Upon it depends, most critically, whether or not the religious orders will find an entry into a new epoch and overcome the difficulties of the coming years.[37]

Article 15. Fraternal community of life is one of the ultimate motifs of Catholic religious life. In the first foundations of coenobitic monasticism by Basil and Pachomius, we find reference to it. The primitive Church of Acts 4:32 has almost become the classic type of foundation in the history of the religious orders. In our times its internal and external symbolic significance (even in the non-Catholic Christian world) has come more to light through newly founded fraternities. Genuine fraternal community, becoming effective in love, and radiating love, is the most impressive witness the modern world can have to the credibility of the Christian message. What is said in the first paragraph of this article requires no further comment, although perhaps it does elicit the remark that the existence of such community cannot be taken for granted in concrete religious life as actually organized. Community as the conciliar text sees it does not come about simply because like-minded people decide to live together under the same rule: it implies a community of life that finds expression in sharing one another's interests, in conversation, in mutual help, and in many other things. All must contribute to this life. There is much in the traditional orders to obstruct such community: the anonymity of the individual, the assumed distance from one another, the customary largeness of communities, overwork, and, not least, the constitution of modern man who on the one hand desires community, on the other withdraws from it, who needs contact and yet is bad at making it, who would like to love, and yet finds it hard to rise above himself. Much institutional change and great educational effort are required, therefore, if the preconditions for the emergence and maturing of true community life in the religious orders are to be created. Basically, each fresh generation must work this out for itself. The decree only briefly hints at the great importance of this for the active orders in particular. The "Norms" take up this hint and underline it specially in Article 25, where we read: "In orders with an apostolic function the community life that is of such importance is to be fostered by all the means that are suited to the vocation of the order in question, so that all the members may experience a revivifying of their fraternal bonds as a family united in Christ." In all the growing diversity of apostolic work, which makes community life increasingly difficult, no doubt many new forms of workable community life must be evolved. In this perhaps the small group will play an ever bigger part, for it provides the best place for conversation or common

[37] On the whole topic cf. H. Krauss, "Der Gehorsam gegenüber Menschen in Ordenssatzungen. Reflexionen zu einer zeitgemässen Anpassung des Ordensgehorsams", in *Glaube und Leben* 39 (1966), pp. 252 ff.

prayer. For the small group, too, it will be easier to find a time when all can meet together.

The authenticity of Christian community — a fellowship of brethren under one Lord (cf. Mt 23:8), finding its highest expression in mutual service (*ibid.,* v. 11) — will be manifest in the measure in which an order or community succeeds in integrating the lay brothers or sisters in the whole community, as the decree demands. In doing this we must both break away from obsolete constitutions and also guard against recklessly removing distinctions based upon function and aptitude. (The last danger is specially stressed with reference to female communities.) There are one or two institutional regulations governing this process of integration,[38] but because this concerns a very human process, the encounter between person and person, which presupposes a gradual change of mentality, it requires organic growth. This takes time. It is doubtful, therefore, whether the present generation will see the renewal of fraternal community, as the conciliar text sees it. The last paragraph of this article has in mind a possibility, not a precept. The question is about having lay choir monks (with corresponding status in chapter) in monastic orders. This would only be a return to primitive monasticism. This question cannot in practice be separated from the revived controversy over the vocation of the priest within the monastic orders in general. We shall have to consider which offices can be given to lay brothers in the mendicant orders and also in the modern priestly orders and societies. In so far as the actual office of superior brings with it ecclesiastical jurisdiction, then that office would not be open to a lay brother. At all events the participation of the brothers in the affairs of the priestly communities will have to be greatly increased, otherwise we will have failed to obey the spirit of what the council has said on this point.

Article 16. The institutional distinction between purely contemplative and apostolically active nuns had already been made in the apostolic constitution *Sponsa Christi.*[39] This article now widens that distinction. "The little enclosure is now abolished", says Articles 32 of the "Norms". "Nuns, therefore, who in accordance with the statutes of their order are dedicated to external works, are to define a special enclosure in their constitutions. Nuns, however, who are contemplative by reason of their statutes, but have taken up work outside their cloister, must, after a reasonable period in which to think the matter over, either give up that outside work and maintain the papal enclosure, or keep their work

---

[38] Suggestions are to be found in Articles 27 and 28 of the "Norms". Article 27: "The general chapters and synaxes are to seek a way whereby the brothers, by whatever name they are called, will gradually acquire an active voice in certain transactions of the community, and in elections, and acquire also eligibility for certain offices. This would give them a real share in the work of the community, and the priests would be released for their own specific work." Article 28: "In monasteries having only one type of sister, the constitution should contain an obligation to choir duties, heed being paid to the differences between the sisters, arising of necessity from their differing tasks and special aptitudes."

[39] Statuta IV: *AAS* 43 (1951), pp. 16 f.

and define a special form of enclosure in their constitutions, without any pre-judice to their status as nuns." "It may be that this is the beginning of a develop-ment by which convents of nuns, whose contemplative life is nominal rather than real, are moving towards the status of congregations. This is a natural development not to be obstructed permanently through mere fictions. If we consider how centuries old enclosed city convents (e.g., Dillingen, Ingolstadt), under pressure of circumstances, have turned into teaching institutes — with obvious blessings — then we will not regard this development as a misfortune."[40]

Purely contemplative convents are required to adapt the pattern of strict (papal) enclosure to "the conditions of time and place", it is true; but at the same time, "real separation from the outside world"[41] is strongly underlined. According to monastic tradition this is associated "pre-eminently with the special vocation of nuns"; it bears the character of sign and witness, and helps protect them.[42] Neither the decree nor the "Norms" has gone into the psycho-logical difficulties for the modern woman arising from rigorous enclosure, especially in small convents. These difficulties cannot be overcome by idealism and a strong will alone. "Special statutes are to be formulated for sisters in contemplative convents, who do outside work. These will take account, on the one hand, of their imperfectly contemplative vocation, and on the other hand, be consonant with the vocation of the nuns with whom they live, although they themselves are not nuns. The superior of the convent has the hard task of looking after them lovingly and conscientiously, and of giving them an appropriate religious training, and of nourishing their sisterly bond with the community of nuns."[43] The future will have to prove that these directions are sufficient to do greater justice, from the human and religious point of view, to the extern sisters and others in a similar category.

Article 17. The most important point made is that a special religious habit is to be retained. The only traditional reason given for the orders having a special habit is that it is a sign of their special consecration. The directions for the appropriate adaptation of the habit are clear enough, and allow of the possibility of more than slight adjustments of ancient fashion. The rapid changes of our times are likely, however, to bring about much greater changes than most people imagine.

Article 18. The subject-matter of this article — the education of young religious — is of quite critical importance for the appropriate renewal of the reli-gious life. It provides a series of important topics that go beyond the results of many years' previous work by the Congregation for Religious. In addition to reli-gious and vocational training — theoretical and practical — *apostolic* education is

---

[40] A. Scheuermann, "Die Ordensleute in den Dokumenten des II. Vatikanischen Konzils", in *AKK* 134 (1965), pp. 348f.

[41] "Norms of Implementation", Article 31.

[42] *Ibid.*, Article 30.

[43] *Ibid.*, Article 29.

required. This bears reference to the exercise of a direct apostolate — especially in the lay societies. Cardinal Suenens made this demand.[44] It is to this topic that the statements made in the second paragraph apply. Whoever wants to be apostolically active must know the world and the men who live in it. In this sense he must be in the world. We welcome the stress laid upon the duty of constant *further* education of religious — especially amongst the lay societies and the brothers in the clerical orders —, for this is indispensable in the rapid developments of our time. The decree also approves the gaining of suitable qualifications. The article is chiefly concerned, however, with the imparting of knowledge. What, in our opinion, is lacking as a means for the appropriate renewal of the religious life in the coming years — and we are beginning to guess just how hard a task this will be — is the specialized education of a new generation of leaders, who will be made familiar with the problems of religious life in our time, and who, we might hope, would soon be able to tackle the serious problems affecting the internal life of the religious orders. The things that are happening today in the various professions must find their conterpart in the religious orders as well, especially in the active orders.

The "Norms" comment and expand the decree in remarkable detail (Articles 33–38). In particular they speak of the place, time, and duration of education. Articles 33 and 37 are the most important. Article 33 runs thus: "The education of members of religious orders, from the novitiate onwards, is not to be regulated in the same way in every order, but must take into account the peculiarities of each. In trying out and adapting them, ample and prudent scope for experiment must be allowed." Thus a more elastic form of novitiate is envisaged, varying with the character and aims of each community. It is doubtful whether, on these terms, a uniform regulation of the novitiate will ever again be possible. Article 37 is most welcome: "If communities are not in a position on their own to provide an adequate theoretical and practical training, the fraternal collaboration of several could make good their deficiency; but each order would still have to preserve its own characteristic form of education. This could be achieved by various steps and ways: through common lectures or courses, through exchange of tutors and possibly even their association into a college, and through the pooling of resources to form an institution that could be attended by the members of several orders." The same co-operation implied here would be most opportune in other fields also, e.g. in apostolic work.

Article 19. At almost every council which has discussed the religious orders it has been customary to make difficulties for new foundations of a non-traditional kind. This is as it should be, for there can be no doubt that it would have been better had many institutions, now scarcely capable of supporting life, never been founded. On the other hand, it cannot be denied that God is for ever awakening men and women to provide the answer to some specific need, and

---

[44] Cf. his book *Nun in World* (1962).

to undertake work that imperiously cries out to be done. Who dares prevent them following God's call? Church history can show plenty of examples of how genuine vocation has triumphed in face of great difficulties over official opposition. There have been tragic cases, too, when short-sighted men have obstructed such divine callings. As far as concerns our times, by reason of the serious crisis assailing religious life, we are unlikely to see new foundations on the former model within the foreseeable future. It might well be, however, that new forms of communities will arise, more in harmony with the mentality and social circumstances of the present time. The past few years have shown that the problem of new foundation specially affects the missionary countries.

Article 20. The substance of this article is thin because it suffered truncation in the final redaction. Originally Article 2b fell under this heading. Even so, more might have been said about the work appropriate to the orders. Must it really be the first concern of a community to retain or restore the special work which it undertook, perhaps in totally different circumstances? Allowing for fidelity to the traditional heritage, ought one not to remain open to the sometimes altered call of God? Is that not a sign of a missionary spirit? For the rest, ought we not at this point to be discussing in addition to the work of the active orders, the work also of many contemplative houses, which is either insufficient for their support, or unsuitable for a religious order (e.g., the distilling of liquor). There is an important allusion at this point to the common needs and demands of the universal Church. On the other hand, there is no mention of the very necessary co-operation of the orders with each other and with the dioceses in the field of the apostolate.

Article 21. Because there has always been something unpleasant about the compulsory abolition of communities or monasteries, and because such abolition can lead to many kinds of injustice, the "Norms" have provided the following supplementary directions. Article 39: "The initiation of any kind of amalgamation of religious communities presupposes a suitable spiritual, psychological, and juridical preparation, in the spirit of the decree on religious. It will often prove advantageous if the communities have the assistance of a competent assessor." Article 40: "In the cases and circumstances cited not only the good of the Church must be kept in mind, but the specific character of each community and the freedom of the individual member must be respected." Article 41: "The criteria chiefly useful in deciding the question of the abolition of a religious order or monastery, having weighed up all the circumstances, are these: the small number of members of the community in relation to its age; the lack of recruits over a number of years; the advancing age of the majority of members. If the abolition of an institution is to be undertaken, the attempt must be made to have it 'absorbed by a more vigorous community or monastery which approximates their own purpose and spirit' (Decree, Article 21). But first of all, the individual members must be heard, and all must be done in love."

Article 22. The stimulus behind this article came from those countries where there are too many small religious orders, often of the same or similar type, for every city or deanery wants to have its own community. On the other hand, a warning is required against too large amalgamations, because the time of the great centralized community seems to be nearing its end. Once again, the movement of our times may force things to happen more quickly than we ever imagined.[45]

Article 23. The conferences of major superiors suggested here have been inaugurated almost everywhere in the last few years. All without doubt have proved useful and even necessary. But in the long run their work will have to become more concrete and more effective. In some countries it has already gone a step further. As far as the international unions of superiors general is concerned, these might fruitfully supplement the work of the Congregation for Religious, were they but given an adequate voice, and if they themselves will seize their opportunity.

Article 24. Spurred on by necessity we must put recruitment to the religious orders (and for the clergy in general) upon a new basis, and carry it out using modern methods. All of these efforts will, however, bear fruit only in the measure in which the orders succeed in becoming more attractive in structure and in their manner of life, to young people today. This does not at all mean that they should relax real demands and subtract anything from the radical following of Christ.

Article 25. The concluding admonition once again sums up the essentials of the religious life and its importance in preaching the message of Christ. It declares the high esteem in which the Church holds the religious life, and pronounces the instructive verdict that there will always be communities of men whose rule and way of life will be based upon the evangelical counsels.

Even today we may say that the Council's Decree on the Appropriate Renewal of the Religious Life, despite its shortness and shortcomings, is a turning point in the history of religious orders, that it will, indeed, initiate that turning, the full sweep of which cannot yet be seen.

---

[45] On the various sorts of amalgamation enumerated in the article cf. A. Scheuermann, *loc. cit.*, pp. 360 f.

Decree on Priestly Formation

by
*Josef Neuner**

The Council was fully aware of the importance of the decree on the seminaries for the renewal of the Church. It is clearly formulated in the introduction to the decree: "The wished-for renewal of the whole Church depends in large measure on a ministry of priests which is vitalized by the spirit of Christ."[1] The new self-understanding of the Church, reflection on the word of God as its origin, the open attitude to the world in which we live, must be realized in the training of a new generation of priests.

The new orientation of seminaries could not be planned without there being tensions. Continuity with existing traditions and the adaptation to present circumstances with their demands had to be harmonized. The starting-point of the reform, therefore, was the existing seminary system that goes back to the 15th and 16th centuries and was solemnly confirmed as the form of education for the clergy on 15 July 1563, in the twenty-third session of the Council of Trent. The connection of the present reform with the seminary decree of Trent was underlined by the four-hundredth anniversary of this very decree, celebrated during the third session on 3 December 1963 in Rome by a ceremony in St. Peter's. The new decree was to be for the Church today what the seminary decree of Trent was for the stormy age of the Reformation.

This raises immediately the problems of the new decree: The Tridentine decree belongs to the age of the Counter-Reformation. It sought to isolate endangered youth from the dangers of the world and protect it, educate it and fortify it within the Church, in this way creating priests who would serve the Church free from the infections of the spirit of the age.[2] The educational programme was

---

* *Translated by William Glen-Doepel*
[1] As in the Decree on the Priesthood, Article 1.
[2] The whole Decree on the Seminaries given by Trent is based on the sheltering of the seminarian. It begins "Cum adolescentium aetas, nisi recte instituatur, prona sit ad mundi voluptates, sequendas, et nisi a teneris annis ad pietatem religiosam informetur, antequam vitiorum habitus totos homines possideat, numquam perfecte ac sine maximo ac singulari propemodum Dei omnipotentis auxilio, in disciplina ecclesiae perseveret synodus statuit, ut singulae cathedrales . . . cer-

directed wholly towards the service of the Church, whereas hardly anything was said about the debate with the movements of the age. This kind of defensive attitude was probably unavoidable, given the general uncertainty of that time, but was not to determine the priestly education of our own time. The old seminary system ensured for the Church a reliable clergy, but it also increased their separation from the people and the growing estrangement of the Church from the new age. It not only educated people to obedience to Church authority, but also to a clerical mentality and closed thinking, and became combined with the one-sided institutional picture of the Church. If the Church at the Council has now overcome the attitude of the Counter-Reformation, has moved out of a defensive attitude towards innovations and burst open clerical isolation, if she now understands herself in a new way as a sign of salvation for the world, in solidarity with the men of all ages, then this new orientation would inevitably affect the principles behind the training of priests.

Thus the whole concern of the Council is reflected in its debate on the decree on the seminaries and in the progressive formulation of the text. The need for a new orientation was recognized from the beginning — it was given already with the summoning of the Council. But in the first drafts the new beginnings were to be found only in modest remarks hidden among conventional statements and hardly noticed. Many were disappointed. Through the criticism that soon began, through the constantly required compression of the text, and through the persistent demand for the new perspectives to be clearly formulated, the decree found its final shape.

From this very connection with the total renewal of the Church follow both the limitations and the merits of the decree. It consciously gives up the idea of the centralization of Church studies that had existed hitherto and recognized how circumstances varied from country to country. It requires of bishops and seminary directors not passive obedience, but obedient initiative. It has also admitted the need of further developments and periodically renewed adaptations. That is why it limits itself to general norms and is not able to offer clear directives, as many wanted. It has been careful not to shut the doors on further developments, but it has created a fixed basis for the various aspects of priestly formation and laid down clear guiding lines.

Because of its orientation towards what is essential, namely God's word as the source of the renewal of the Church, the text was well received in the conciliar debate and in the voting. It was also welcomed by non-Catholic observers. O. Cullmann said in his summing up of the Council at the end of the fourth session at the German press conference on 2 December 1965: "But there is a

---

tum puerorum ipsius civitatis . . . numerum in collegio . . . alere ac religiose educare et ecclesiasticis disciplinis instituere teneantur . . ." The students must be at least 12 years old and have a good preliminary education; preference is to be given to the poor. In order to introduce them better to Church discipline, they are to receive at once the tonsure and clerical dress (*Concilium Tridentinum, sessio XXIII, De Reformatione*, ch. 18).

text that deserves special mention; outside observers have not done it sufficient justice: it is that on priestly formation. It is, in my opinion, perhaps one of the best and most important. Here the study of Scripture is placed right in the foreground. Moreover, this text is more likely than any of the others to affect the future influence of the Council. If the training of priests is to proceed according to these principles from now on, then the advance of the Catholic Church towards thinking in terms of Scripture and salvation history is assured. The whole work of *aggiornamento* will then continue in the sense of a deepened reflection about essentials. Here we can say immediately that our expectations have been surpassed."

The **history of the decree** begins with the request of the papal Central Commission to the Preparatory Commission *De studiis et seminariis* to consider the two questions relating to the furthering of vocations to the Church and to the training of seminarats. Two schemata were prepared: Schema Decreti *de Vocationibus ecclesiasticis fovendis,* and Schema Constitutionis *de Sacrorum alumnis formandis.* In January 1962 both drafts were printed and given to the Central Commission. Already here the different tendencies of the specialist and the Central Commission became apparent, which were to play a great role in the subsequent history of the document. The Seminary Commission had to deal with the concrete details of the many questions involved and because it considered them important it wanted to treat them, whereas the Central Commission, faced with the vast amount of material which was piling up, sought to cut down the length of the decrees. For example, the Central Commission desired first that both schemata should be amalgamated. The schema on vocations became the first chapter of the planned constitution and in its subsequent development remained only one section within the schema on priestly formation. Moreover, the Central Commission desired the text to be considerably shortened. The Preparatory Commission felt unable to fulfil this wish; it considered that the judgment that ought to be omitted from such a text should be left to the actual Conciliar Commission, which could work under the instructions and according to the norms of the Council Fathers. But some other requested alterations were made, and so in 1963 the schema appeared in the fourth volume of the *Schemata Constitutionum et Decretorum,* pp. 209–75. Under the title *De Sacrorum alumnis formandis* it contained the following seven chapters:

1. De vocationibus ecclesiasticis fovendis
2. De seminariorum ordinatione in genere
3. De institutione spirituali
4. De disciplina in seminariis
5. De studiorum ratione in seminariis
6. De institutione pastorali in seminariis
7. De formatione post seminarium perficienda

Even at this preparatory stage some decisions were made which were retained in the final version of the text. The question of the duty of the individual who has felt the call to a priestly vocation to follow it was left open. Further, all questions relating to clerical orders were omitted, as they were to be treated in a separate decree *De Sacramento Ordinis*. This decree, however, was dropped from the list of the schemata to be treated, and thus the relative questions concerning clerical orders were nowhere treated.

During the first session the work on schema passed to the actual Conciliar Commission (Chairman: Cardinal G. Pizzardo; Secretary: A. Mayer, OSB), while the total planning of the text was undertaken by the *Commissio de Concilii laboribus coordinandis*. In the sifting of all the texts to be treated the schema *De Sacrorum alumnis formandis* was, on 30 January 1963, included among the seventeen drafts which were to be discussed, but strict directions were given for its abridgment. In the Commission's session from 21 February to 2 March the text was revised and on 25 March again placed before the Co-ordinating Commission. It was approved and in May 1963 was ordered by the Pope to be sent to all the Council Fathers. The abridgment desired by the Co-ordinating Commission was achieved by making the bishops' conferences responsible for the concrete implementation of the decree, so that it could be better adapted to local circumstances. Also, an appendix was added which contained subjects on which further work was to be done for the Council in a post-conciliar instruction. In a further appendix the alterations and extensions to the canons of the *CIC* concerning priestly formation were briefly outlined.

After this text was propagated many comments were received from bishops' conferences and individual bishops. During the second session of the Council (1963) these suggestions were worked through by the Commission. The title was changed and now read: *De alumnis ad sacerdotium instituendis,* as it was now concerned only with the education of priests, and not with the training of other clerics, e.g., deacons. The most important result of the new version, however, was the strong emphasis on a new orientation in seminary education. Critical voices complained that the seminaries cut off their students from the world. Many argued against retention of the seminaries at all. A more varied adaptation to local circumstances was desired, education to greater personal responsibility, more emphasis on the human qualities of future priests, a fresher and more confident approach to spiritual formation in place of methods which tended to engender a legalistic attitude. These points that the critics had made had already been largely incorporated into the text, but the new accents had not been placed clearly enough. Hence the sections on education to personal responsibility, the orientation of the studies to modern problems, as well as pastoral training, were re-written.

In its attempt to take account, as far as possible, of the wishes of all Council Fathers, the Commission, in December 1963, again asked those bishops' conferences that had not yet commented on the schema to make suggestions for the improvement of the text. On 23 January 1964, however, the instruction came from the Co-ordinating Commission to reduce the whole schema to short *propositiones*. It was sought to bring the Council to an end if possible after the third session, and therefore the texts still outstanding had to be dealt with as quickly as possible. In the Commission's sessions from 3 to 11 March 1964, the schema propositionum *De institutione sacerdotali* was prepared. It was approved on 27 April by the Co-ordinating Commission and sent to the Council Fathers in May. It was a courageous and obedient attempt to sum up briefly and clearly the substance of what had been already worked out and despite the narrow limits that had been set to give the essential new orientations. This meant, of course, that more detailed explanations and some basic reasoning had to be omitted, which led to criticism, so that the text of the *propositiones* was, after intensive pressure from the bishops, again considerably enlarged. But these enlargements now related to those points in which the Council desired renewal and where greater clarity and deeper motivation were necessary.

Even before the conciliar debate the first extensions were made on the basis of the opinions sent in; they were approved by the Co-ordinating Commission. There were new additions: the articles on the junior seminaries (no. 3), on celibacy (no. 10), and on the method of higher studies (no. 17). The articles to be extended were, primarily, those on the vocation of the priesthood, theological studies, and pastoral training. It emerged, however, that even those extensions were not sufficient and further additions became necessary as a result of the conciliar debate.

The conciliar debate finally took place on 12, 14, 16 and 17 November. After the *relatio* of the Bishop of Verona, G. Carraro, there were thirty-two speakers, of whom many represented large groups of bishops. Most speakers took a positive attitude to the schema, and their wishes mainly concerned points which were already present in the text in an undeveloped form, but required further elaboration. Even the Polish bishops — the only ones who desired a complete reworking of the schema — asked, through their speaker, J. Drzazga, for only a more concrete formulation of the new orientation, which should not, they felt, be left to the individual bishops' conferences, because the basic problems were everywhere the same and the conferences required firm and specific norms. There was universal acknowledgment of the urgency of giving concrete answers to the modern problems of a seminary education and the training of priests. But it was in the answer to this that the right balance had to be found. Cardinal Döpfner recognized that "the propositions concerning the training of priests, which has today become a very difficult question, seem to take the right middle path: they hold on to the rules that have been proved over centuries, but they also openly and courageously introduce new laws appropriate to the changed circumstances of the age."

It is not surprising that representatives of tradition regarded the suggested innovations in seminary discipline and courses of study with anxiety (Cardinal

Ruffini, Cardinal Bacci, Archbishop Staffa). Over against them stood the many who desired to see the basic lines of the new orientation made even clearer (Cardinal Suenens, Cardinal Meyer, Cardinal De Barros Câmara, Cardinal Bueno Monreal, Archbishop Colombo, Archbishop Salazar). In detail, their wishes were concerned mainly with the total orientation of priestly formation to the circumstances of the world today; its organic unity: personal maturity, genuine spirituality, scientific education and a pastoral orientation must complement each other; a more exact description of the characteristics of the priestly vocation and the ways of furthering vocations; the role of junior seminaries; the tremendous importance of the directors of seminaries and their appropriate training; the central importance of the mystery of Christ in priestly spirituality; education to the veneration of Mary; training in a Church attitude towards authority and the people of God; education in the positive understanding of celibacy; guidance in achieving personal responsibility and human maturity within the life of the seminary; the introduction of a "novitiate", and the introduction of periods of pastoral activity into the studies in order to obtain spiritual and human maturity; the orientation of philosophical studies to modern questions and to theology; a deepening of the study of theology by going back to the sources, and the need for theology to deal with modern problems; the importance of Scholasticism; a pastoral orientation.

In the voting which followed the discussion each of the sections obtained far more than the requisite two-thirds majority. The *modi* submitted were chiefly concerned with the points mentioned, where a clarification of principles already contained in the schema seemed to be necessary. On 17 November 1964, it was put to the vote whether the schema should be voted for in detail. Of the 2, 117 votes given, 2,076 were for, 41 against. Then in seven ballots the voting was taken on the individual sections. The result was as follows:

	Votes given	Yes	No	*Modi*	Invalid
Introduction and No. 1	1880	1721	10	149	
Nos. 2–3	1880	1721	10	149	
4–7	1966	1808	4	154	
13–15	1943	1618	5	319	1
16–18	1960	1644	8	307	1
19–22	1945	1845	6	93	1

The incorporation of the *modi* in the text was prepared by a sub-commission under the direction of the *relator,* Bishop Carraro, from 29 March to 3 April 1965, and was concluded in the plenary session of the Commission from 26 April to 3 May. The principles of this last revision were stated to the Council Fathers by the *relator* on 11 October. Since all parts of the texts were approved with more than a two-thirds majority, the existing text had to be regarded as accepted and hence basically retained. Stylistic alterations which did not change the sense were incorporated in it. Where extensions of the text were required in order to clarify the meaning of the decree, to make it more concrete or to give more fundamental reasons for a particular point, the appropriate additions were incorporated in it. This meant that the text of many articles was more than doubled in length. In order to be sure that these extensions really conformed to the intention of the Council, a vote was taken separately on each of the texts that had been significantly extended; then a general vote was taken on the treatment of the *modi* in those texts that had been changed only a little; finally the whole text was voted on. These ballots took place on 11 and 12 October with the following result:

	Votes given	Yes	No	Invalid
Revised introduction	2138	2125	11	2
No. 2: Priestly vocations	2139	2119	19	1
3: Junior seminaries	2141	2046	95	
4: The need for seminaries for priests	2127	2038	88	1
5: The directing of seminaries	2057	2054	3	
9: Ecclesial orientation	2024	2020	3	1
10: Education in celibacy	1989	1971	16	2
11: Seminary discipline, human maturity and personal responsibility	1981	1975	6	
12: "Novitiate", pastoral work during studies	2022	2011	11	
13: Preliminary education in the humanities	2179	2164	14	1
14: Philosophical studies	2185	2127	58	
15: Theological studies	2189	2170	16	3
19: Pastoral training	2186	2180	6	
The revised conclusion	2174	2166	6	2
The treatment of the other *modi* in nos. 1, 6, 7, 8, 14, 17, 18, 20, 21, 22	2135	2120	13	2
Voting on the whole decree	2212	2196	15	1

Thus on 28 November 1965 the decree was finally approved in public session and published. The number of votes given was 2,321, of which 2,318 were positive and 3 negative.

Title. The schema of the Preparatory Commission and the original text of the Conciliar Commission had the title *De sacrorum alumnis formandis*. As a result of the written comment that had been received the title was changed to *De alumnis ad sacerdotium instituendis,* as it was not concerned with the education of clerics in general, but only with training for the priesthood. The brief *propositiones* which were sent to the bishops in May 1964 had the title that they were to keep throughout: *De institutione sacerdotali.* According to the Commission, *institutio* covered the whole of the training, spiritual, academic and pastoral.

Preface. Whereas the introduction of the original schema considered the training of priests in the dogmatic context of the priesthood of Christ and his Church, the *propositiones* and the final text placed the subject right from the beginning in the context of the concrete event of the Council: the renewal of the Church must be carried out by a new generation of priests, on whose training the fruits of the Council would largely depend. In the very first sentence the Christocentric nature of priestly service is emphasized: the words "Christi spiritu animato" were added as a *modus*. Three norms are mentioned as having guided the decree: the laws that had proved themselves over long experience, the new orientations that had been won in the Council, and the concrete need of the world today. These three norms composed the field, with all its potential tension, within which discussion took place; it was from their reconciliation that the text emerged.

It was necessary to decide for whom the decree was intended. Cardinal Meyer objected to the original version because it emphasized the unity of the priesthood and claimed general validity. But in that case it would have had to limit itself to very general principles; otherwise, for example, the norms for a pastoral training of those studying in contemplative orders would undoubtedly be rather different. This is why the final version of the text states only that the training of all candidates for the priesthood, for the diocesan clergy, the orders and the different rites, requires renewal. But the *modus* "quae clerum diocesanum directe respiciunt", which was added, makes clear that the decree relates directly to the diocesan clergy — it is a decree about seminaries. The norms given in the decree are, however, to be applied according to the particular needs of any system of priestly training. The words "utriusque cleri", which were added as a *modus*, covered a request made by 55 bishops that religious, who received their training under the guidance of the superiors of their orders, are also to be trained in the spirit of the decree.[3]

---

[3] There is a survey of modern literature on the training of priests and seminary education in the (German) edition of the Decree on Priestly Formation introduced by A. Antweiler (1967). On the post-conciliar discussion, cf. *Herder-Korrespondenz* 21 (1967), pp. 126 ff.; P. Picard – E. Emrich, *Priesterausbildung in der Discussion* (1967).

CHAPTER I: PROGRAMME OF PRIESTLY FORMATION TO BE UNDERTAKEN BY INDIVIDUAL COUNTRIES

Article 1. The text of the decree is divided into seven chapters of greatly varying length. The first chapter consists of a single article, in which variations in the training of priests from country to country are called for, as concrete circumstances and needs require. The individual bishops' conferences are to work out their own seminary and study system, with the help of professional advisors,[4] a system which is to be approved by Rome. This divides the initiative in seminary legislation between the centre, which lays down the basic principles and gives the final approbation, and the periphery, where the details of implementation are settled. The decree does not seek to limit the authority of the individual bishops over their seminaries and hand it over to the bishops' conference; rather the norms, which hitherto came directly from Rome, are now to proceed from the episcopacy of the particular country. This takes account of local requirements and yet preserves a desirable unity with the country. In order, however, that this accommodation of particular needs does not lead to new regional rigidities, the seminary arrangements are to be revised regularly. Decentralization was accepted without any contrary voice and was joyfully welcomed by many bishops (e. g., by Cardinal Jaeger in the name of the German bishops, Cardinal Meyer, Bishop Reuss in the name of the 127 American bishops, for the missions by Archbishop Mark Gopu from India, Bishop Komba from Tanganyika, etc.). It is an essential condition for a healthy separate development of the Churches.

In an important intervention made in the name of 70 Council Fathers by Archbishop Gabriel Garonne of Toulouse, he pointed out the new task that arose for the Congregation for Studies and Seminaries in Rome. His speech is all the more important, as after the Council he was appointed sub-prefect of this congregation: the Roman Congregation must become the centre of fruitful co-operation with the seminaries of all countries. It must therefore be familiar with the situation of priests in the different countries. Further, it must remain in contact with scientific development in our age. Hence the Congregation should draw on representatives of different countries and on experts from the different fields of knowledge to advise it, so that the training of priests might keep abreast of the growing needs of individual countries.[5]

---

[4] In a *modus* submitted by 53 Fathers it was requested that the decree should call for the collaboration of priests and laymen in working out the plan of the seminaries' work in the region. The Commission replied that this kind of consultation was considered to be automatic and therefore did not need to be mentioned specially in the text.

[5] 35 Fathers requested that the reform of the Roman Congregation of Studies should be called for in the decree itself. This request was refused because the reform of the Curia was reserved to the Pope himself.

CHAPTER II: THE INTENSIFIED ENCOURAGEMENT
OF PRIESTLY VOCATIONS

Article 2. The urgent subject of priestly vocations, which had originally had a schema of its own, had been reduced to a few lines in the *propositiones;* but the suggestions and interventions of many bishops required, first, a more detailed description of the priest's vocation, and, secondly, an account of the ways in which it could be developed (Cardinal Bueno Monreal, Cardinal Döpfner, Bishop Drzazga in the name of the Polish bishops, etc.). For this reason the text had to be considerably extended.

The article contains three sections: the responsibility of the whole Christian community for priestly vocations, the nature of the priest's vocation, and ways of developing vocations. At the beginning the principle is stated that priestly vocations grow out of a living Church community, which produces its own leaders. The basic task here falls to the Christian family, "the first seminary, as it were". The whole educational system, schools and organizations, should create an atmosphere in which young men are able to recognize their vocation and joyfully embrace it. Above all, the priests themselves should present their vocation as attractive through their joy in it and through a genuine community with each other. In these efforts to awaken and maintain priestly vocations the bishop has the chief role, for he is the person mainly responsible for the priestly service of his diocese. His task consists primarily in stimulating and co-ordinating efforts to ensure that there are enough new priests and to be ready to help young men who show a vocation towards the achievement of their goal. In all this it is not so much a question of direct recruiting, which can easily put people off, but of giving a genuine account of priestly life and service in which young men can recognize their own call.[6] (Cf. Decree on the Priesthood, Article 11.)

A vocation comes about through the working together of divine grace and the call of the Church.[7] The Church consecrates those who are called by God. This call shows itself not so much in an emotional inclination as in suitability. But this very suitability is described in the decree as grace (at the request of Cardinal Döpfner), so that the grace of the call to the priestly office that is so emphasized in the New Testament is given its right place. It is the business of the Church authority to test this suitability, to convince itself of the serious intention and freedom of choice of the candidate and finally to consecrate him

---

[6] On the first post-conciliar congress of the national directors of vocation institutes in Western Europe under the direction of Archbishop Garonne in Rome (1 to 3 December 1966), cf. M. Schiltz in *Geist und Leben* 40 (1967), pp. 60 ff. The resolutions taken there and the Pope's speech are to be found in *AAS* 59 (1967).

[7] The text follows the *Catechismus Romanus:* "Nec enim quisquam sibi sumat honorem, sed qui vocatur a Deo tamquam Aaron. Vocati autem a Deo dicuntur, qui a legitimis ecclesiae ministris vocantur" (P. II., Cap. VII, *De Ordinis Sacramento,* n. 3; cf. nn. 4 and 5).

for the twin tasks of celebrating Mass and of serving the mission of the Church and of the people of God.[8]

There follows a schematic list of the ways of awakening vocations. First come the means of inner renewal, prayer and penance, through which the Church opens itself to the influence of grace. In a community that lets God work on it in this way there will be no lack of vocations in the service of the Church. Second come the different forms of instruction, in sermon, catechesis, and the ways of modern media: the meaning of priestly service can be understood only by a deeper total understanding of Christian life and Church community. Third come the organizational measures which are presented and recommended in the papal documents cited. Work furthering vocations for the priesthood and the religious life should make use of all modern means of psychology and sociology; it should proceed methodically and persistently on the diocesan, regional, and also national level. Of course zeal is to be tempered with discretion, which means not only sensible moderation, but above all the recognition of the divine origin of the vocation. Human recruiting should not seek to replace grace; it should remove the obstacles in the way of the call of grace and thus unite with this inner call.

The end of the section deals with the urgent theme of the universal nature of the Church in relation to the search for vocations. Seeking vocations can lead to group egoism, whether of the diocese, the religious community, or the rite. If someone is called to service in the Church, he should be free from any narrow private interests, and should invite men to serve the whole Church, so that the necessary strength may be put at its disposal where the need is greatest.[9]

Article 3. The junior seminaries were a controversial subject. As the decree is concerned only with priestly training in the strictest sense, they were completely omitted in the first version of the *propositiones*. But many bishops demanded a general statement on this question, and thus in the extended text that was presented to the Council for debate, Article 3 was included; what it says is taken largely from the earlier schema. The text was further extended through the *modi*.

Many bishops pointed out the risk that early protective segregation of young men would endanger personal maturity, educate them to passivity and possibly adversely affect their freedom in the choice of career (Cardinal Bueno Monreal of Seville, Cardinal Döpfner, Archbishop Colombo of Milan). In normal circumstances the natural milieu of the family is to be preferred; only where a sound upbringing is not possible in the family, should young people be brought up in a junior seminary. Hence, the institution of junior seminaries is not prescribed

---

[8] On the question of the recognition of a priestly vocation cf. R. Hostie, *Kriterien geistlicher Berufung* (1964).

[9] The Roman conference mentioned in note 6 concerned itself primarily with this idea. M. Schlitz *(loc. cit.)* provides cogent illustration that a pastorate of religious vocations must have its place within a vocational pastorate for all priests.

and not even directly recommended[10] (as had been the case in the first draft of the schema). The article contains only norms for junior seminaries in cases where they already exist.

The religious eductional goal is clearly distinguished from that in the priest's seminary. In the junior seminary we do not have direct education for priesthood, but training to Christian maturity. Family life should not alienate youths from the normal life of those of their own age; it should have a fresh and natural spirit; it should also facilitate the experience of human contacts which is necessary for maturity of character, above all in the family circle, with the help of parents. This refers primarily to the encounter with the other sex. The atmosphere should be such that a nascent sense of vocation is able to develop in it and that later a clear and truly free choice is possible.

Against the background of the clear distinction between the goals of the junior and the senior seminaries we are to understand the sentence that was put in as a *modus,* i.e., that what is said in the following about the senior seminaries is also to be applied to the junior seminaries, according to their task and their nature. This means that instruction in liturgical and biblical spirituality, education aiming at unity in the cultivation of spirit and intellect, etc., is to apply also to boys in a junior seminary. This sentence was added because the brief article was not able to cover the new perspectives that are to be applied in the junior seminaries also. This served to satisfy the bishops who desired details on the spiritual training of those at junior seminaries.

As far as studies are concerned, parity of seminary education with that at secular (state) schools is called for, so that seminarists who want to follow another career can continue without difficulty their training at the appropriate secular schools. This request, which was made especially by Archbishop Colombo, is important in order to ensure true freedom in the choice of profession. A boy should not continue on the way to the priesthood simply because after a few years in a seminary his access to other professions is closed.[11]

The second section of the article deals with the remoter preparation for the priesthood in cases where there are no junior seminaries, in general boarding-schools or homes. The main purpose must be to bring a young man to understand through personal guidance the importance of the priestly vocation and to learn to make a free choice when embracing it.

A single sentence deals with late vocations, which are becoming more and more important in our modern conditions. The subject is in no way developed, but special appropriate training in institutes to be set up for this purpose is envisaged.

[10] 54 bishops signed a *modus* against the obligation to set up junior seminaries.
[11] This sentence referred particularly to the situation in Italy and other southern Latin countries.

CHAPTER III: THE PROGRAMMING OF MAJOR SEMINARIES

From now on the decree deals only with the major seminaries. Chapter III gives the general norms for seminary training.

In **Article 4** we find the basic orientation of the training of priests. It starts with a statement on the need for major seminaries, added as a *modus*, at the request of many bishops (e.g., Cardinal De Barros Câmara). It was retained and especially emphasized despite a *modus* present by 52 Fathers in which the desire was expressed for priestly training to be possible outside seminaries also, but, as was especially noted in the *relatio*, the decree does not seek to exclude single terms outside the seminary at a university, still less the temporary interruption of studies for pastoral work, which the decree itself desires (Article 12).

The purpose of the seminaries is no longer primarily to protect those being trained for the priesthood from harmful influences (as in the decree of Trent), but to provide the necessary uniform training for the pastoral work of the priest, as subsequently described. The organic unity of the training, combining spiritual, intellectual and pastoral formation, is probably the most urgent need of modern seminary education (Cardinal Suenens, Archishop Colombo, Archbishop Hurley,[12] Bishop Reuss). The call for this unity, which proceeds from the pastoral goal of the whole training, is placed purposely before the individual details of the training, because it is the precondition of the following articles. The final version of the text is no longer limited (like the original *propositiones*) to the formal demand for unity, but it concretely derives the chief aspects of priestly education from the threefold office of Christ[13] and thus gives to the decree the Christocentric orientation which is characteristic of all the work of the Council: the personality of the priest must be fashioned according to the model of Christ, who is at once teacher, priest and pastor. The seminarians must be trained in this threefold office: to the service of the word of God, which they themselves must assimilate and preach to others; to priestly service, by making divine salvation effective in liturgy, above all in the celebration of the Eucharist, and in true sanctification; and to the pastoral office, in that they realize in themselves Christ's self-sacrifice and through this surrender of self win men for salvation. Here, with the help of scriptural texts, the basic attitude of priestly service is formulated: the priest is not a man of rank or an official, rather he is consecrated in order to realize in service and self-sacrifice the saving mystery of Christ in his community.

---

[12] Archbishop D. E. Hurley of Durban, a member of the Conciliar Commission, gave perhaps the strongest expression to the need of a unified, pastorally orientated training of priests: "Pastoral Emphasis in Seminary Studies", in *The Furrow* 13 (1962), pp. 16–30, especially p. 17.

[13] 59 bishops expressed in a *modus* the wish to formulate explicitly in the decree the Christocentric orientation of the priestly training. If this wish was fulfilled by pointing out the threefold office of Christ, Article 4 of the decree is wholly in the spirit of the other statements of the Council on the priesthood (e.g., Constitution on the Church, Articles 22–28, 34–36; Decree on the Priesthood, Articles 4–6, 13.)

From this comprehensive view of the aim of the training follows the need to combine the unconnected spiritual, intellectual and practical training towards the one goal of making true pastors. Hence it is necessary to have close co-operation between those in charge of the seminary and the staff of professors, under the direction of the bishop.

Article 5. The chief role in seminary education is played by the directors and the professors. In the first original section of this article the importance of the personal factor was emphasized. The demand for careful selection and training of directors of seminaries and professors was made by many bishops (e. g., Archbishop Colombo, Bishop Pavlovski, Bishop Anoverus Ataun) and was again emphasized in the *modi* submitted. Apart from the academic qualifications and those of character, it is particularly necessary to have had pastoral experience and a training suitable for the spiritual and pedagogic tasks involved. (Criticism of seminaries had been directed largely at an education that was too theoretical and legalistic.) The demand to use the best man for the training of priests is an old one, as emerges from the documents quoted. In order to realize this, the decree calls for special institutes for the training of seminary directors. As it will presumably take time to carry this out, the recommendation is made, with practical realism, that there be held courses or conferences for seminary directors.[14]

In order to stress more specifically the influence that those in charge of a seminary have, the second section was added in the *modi*. It requires, first, that all concerned in the training of priests be aware of their responsibility; their way of thinking and acting has a decisive influence on the future priests. Further, they must cultivate close harmony among themselves — in the spirit of the Council's picture of the Church, in which the people of God is more important than the institutional authority — and in relation to the seminarians they should not be primarily people in authority, but members of a community, as Christ wanted; for it is only in a genuine, living community that the seminarians' joy in their vocation is able to grow.[15] The bishop should not leave the direction of the seminary simply to the director, but he should personally take a share in the training of his future priests. In difficult questions and critical situations, as can easily arise in seminaries, especially today, he shouls awaken new trust. Finally, the seminary, as the "heart of the diocese", is to be closely connected with the whole life of the local Church. The whole clergy should feel at home in it and be ready to help it.[16]

Article 6. The genuineness of the vocation of the seminarians must be tested at every stage of the training. Given the complicated nature of personal life and

---

[14] In the words of the *relatio:* "Quam maxime vero refert ut quomodo Concilium Tridentinum meliori alumnorum conformationi providit, Concilium Vaticanum II moderatoribus et magistris Seminariorum peculiari sollicitudine praeparandis consulat."

[15] The emphasis on fraternal collaboration was firmly called for in a *modus* signed by 63 bishops.

[16] Bishop P. J. Schmitt of Metz formulated this point in his intervention: "Nomine ecclesiae sacerdos munus suum exercet. Tota ergo ecclesia responsabilitatem tenet in institutione sacerdotum." From this the need for all the clergy to co-operate is derived.

social circumstances today, this testing is especially urgent and difficult. First the theology student must have the genuine intention of devoting himself truly to the service of the Church; this must be present from the beginning and be clarified and purified in the course of the training. Secondly, the vocation must be chosen in genuine freedom; it is not enough to establish that no kind of external pressure is being exerted on candidates for ordination, but there must be the genuine possibility of choosing another profession; a theology student should not remain in a seminary because of a (perhaps unacknowledged) fear or uncertainty in the face of another career. Finally, part of the vocation is suitability (cf. Article 2). This is established not only by seeing that the candidate has certain qualities, but must also be based on a total evaluation of personality, with personal and spiritual attitudes, intellectual capacities, as well as total psycho-physical constitution. The picture of personality must be seen also in the context of inherited family characteristics — the latter remark was added as a *modus* at the request of several bishops. Thus the attempt must be made to form a comprehensive judgment on the capacity of the candidate to fulfil the personal and pastoral requirements of a priest's life.

The second section of the article opposes the tendency to lower the requirements asked of the candidates for the priesthood because of the existing shortage of priests. The testing should always be strict (the original words "necessaria adhibita severitate" were changed in the *modi* to "animi firmitas", both a moderation and a clarification). The objection that there is a shortage of priests is answered by pointing to the providence of God, who will not desert his Church if it endeavours to obtain worthy priests.

Finally, there is a call to take a serious interest in ex-seminarians — 60 bishops signed a *modus* on this point —, because they frequently find themselves in a very difficult situation: there often attaches to them the stigma of having given up their vocation, and re-orientation in a secular career is often difficult for them. They should be helped to find suitable work; but above all they should be given the spiritual help that saves them from bitterness and encourages them in the life and apostolic work of Christian laymen.

Article 7. Two principles are stated on the organization of seminaries. The first is concerned with regional seminaries. Following the decree of Trent, existing canon law desires that a separate seminary be set up in every diocese (*CIC,* can. 1354 § 1). This is not possible in the case of small dioceses and especially in mission countries. Also, given the progress of studies today, the inadequacies of many seminaries which are not able to provide a full priestly training, is increasingly felt (thus the interventions of Cardinal Döpfner and Bishop Anoveros).[17] The solution of the problem hitherto was that seminarians

---

[17] In the declaration of the *propositiones* which was distributed to the bishops by the Commission: "Abunde quoque constat quanta damna alumnorum institutio de facili patriatur in studiorum sedibus, quibus desunt magistri vere conspicui, congruus alumnorum numerus, opes vel facultates sufficientes."

of small dioceses were sent to neighbouring seminaries or else interdiocesan seminaries were set up (cf. *CIC*, can. 1354, § 3). The latter solution, i.e., the setting up of regional or national seminaries, is recommended by the Council in order to give an improved training to the seminarists; the sole aim of seminaries should be to give a full training to priests. The innovation in the Council's ordinance is that these inter-diocesan seminaries no longer come directly under papal authority as before (cf. *CIC*, can. 1357, § 4). They are to be governed according to statutes drawn up by the particular bishops and to be approved by Rome.

The first section of the article speaks in favour of a growing concentration of the training of priests in large, efficient institutions, but the second section desires to see seminary life broken up into smaller groups in the interests of better personal shaping. The mass levels out one's personal characteristics and forces individuals into a passive attitude of receptivity, in which one's own initiative and self-responsibility cannot be sufficiently developed. But the important thing in the seminary is training men to full responsibility (cf. Article 11). The aims of personal education can be achieved better in smaller groups. This is not a splitting-up into separate communities, but into groups within the one community. The original words "communitates parviores" were changed in the *modi* to "coetus minores". The direction of the seminary and the academic training remain common to all. The concrete way in which these groups are formed and their integration into the life of the seminary is to be achieved by experiment; the Council was able only to set up the general principle. The section was accepted without notable opposition, although many (e.g., Cardinal Ruffini) feared a relaxation of seminary discipline.[18]

CHAPTER IV: THE DEEPENING OF SPIRITUAL FORMATION

Article 8. The chapter on spiritual formation begins with the oft-repeated request (Cardinal Suenens, Cardinal Meyer, Archbishof Hurley) that the spiritual growth of priests cannot take place in monastic seclusion, but must be closely combined with intellectual and pastoral instruction. The goal of seminary training is the whole priestly personality, which combines theological education with human maturity, consecration to God with a pastoral care for one's neighbour. The role of the spiritual director in this is expressly underlined; according to Article 5 he must be specially trained for his job.

In answer to many requests the originally very inadequate section on the content of priestly spirituality was extended before the Council's debate and further considerably enriched by the *modi*. The trinitarian perspective, the relation to the paschal mystery, the mention of the Breviary and contemplation of the word of God, the statement about the veneration of Mary, the finding

---

[18] The seminary "John XXIII" founded in 1963 in Louvain is considered a model for this kind of formation of groups. Many others have, in the meantime, followed its example.

of Christ in the needy, the founding of priestly spirituality not on emotional piety, but on a way of life based on the gospel are among these extensions, so that the final text expresses the essential attitudes of scriptural and Christocentric piety, in accordance with the perspective of the Council.

In the first place stands personal companionship with God the Father through the Son in the Spirit; this companionship is grounded in the close community with Jesus Christ, which receives its special seal in the priesthood. The priest is called to take part in the Easter mystery of the death and resurrection of Christ in such a way that not only does it become a source of salvation for himself, but he is able to communicate it also by the testimony of his words and his life to the people of God entrusted to him. Being one with Christ is not something apart from the work of the priest, but should realize itself in the activities and relationships of his office (as is expressly set out in the Decree on the Priesthood). The priest finds Christ in the word of God, in the constant frequenting of the sacraments, in the sacrifice of the mass and in the Breviary, in the bishop who sends him, and the people of God to whom he is sent. Special emphasis is laid on the work for those in whose service he is most able to realize the self-sacrifice of Christ for us men: He finds Christ more, the more faithfully he makes the pastoral concern of Christ for the poor and the lost his own. In a *modus* introduced at the request of many bishops — the desire was expressed in the interventions of the Brazilian and Polish bishops, and the *modus* was signed by 31 bishops — the special veneration of Mary is recommended. It is based on the connection of Mary with John, established by Jesus himself.

The other concrete forms of Christian and priestly piety, preserved by tradition, are recommended, but they are not specially listed, because the decree seeks only to lay down principles. Only the twin principle is formulated that the priest should cultivate the traditional forms of piety of the Church, but that his piety should not exhaust itself in them, especially when they are devotions that have a predominantly emotional colouring. He should find the source of his spirituality in the gospel and base his life on faith, hope and love, through which he will learn the spirit of prayer and poverty,[19] the strength of his vocation, the virtues and zeal of his priestly life. Thus priestly holiness will grow forth from the mystery of Christ and the mission of the Church.

Article 9. A special article is devoted to education in the spirit of the Church. The picture of the Church in *Lumen Gentium* must be made concrete in the training of priests. In the theology of the Council the Church does not appear primarily as an institution, but as a "mystery", that is, a visible community in whose social structures and activities God's salvation is actively present. Thus the priest is not to see his relation to his ecclesiastical superiors simply as a

---

[19] In the *modi* 56 bishops desired special mention of poverty in connection with priestly spirituality. The Commission replied that this point was already covered by the formula "secundum Evangelium vivere". Thus the relation of the evangelical way of life to poverty is not an arbitrary construction, but is in accordance with the intention of the Council.

relation to authority and the co-operation with other priests simply as team work, but from his place in the hierarchic structure he is to testify to the unity of the mystery of salvation which is present in the Church. From this attitude there follows a loving bond with the Pope (the mention of the Pope in the text came through the *modi*), a relationship of faithful co-operation and loyalty towards the bishop and genuine community with his priestly brethren. Moreover, there follows from it a share in the whole life of the Church, which expresses itself not only in legal norms, but in the Church movements that renew it, because Christ is at work in them. Hence the Augustinian idea that in the life of the Church we have the spirit of Christ.

The ecclesial spirit of the priest reveals itself most in the proper understanding of his office (Cf. *Lumen Gentium*, Articles 18 and 28). The false picture of the priesthood as a privileged class and the dangerous expectation of a career which offers honours must be eliminated from the start, as was done by Jesus himself (Mk 10:35 ff.). The theology student must learn to see the priesthood as service for the people of God.[20] This service does not consist merely in an activity from which the priest could, as it were, exclude himself, but embraces his whole personality and determines his attitude to life. This attitude of service is described by the three words obedience, poverty, self-denial.[21] The priest is to go beyond the legal distinction between what is allowed and what is not, and place himself within the passion of Christ, renouncing his own interest. We can see how much this attitude to poverty and humility meant to the Council from the *modus* submitted by 62 bishops, in which a stronger emphasis on obedient service of the people of God was requested.

All this must be brought home in a concrete way to the candidates for the priesthood in relation to the task for which they are preparing themselves. The last section deals with this and was added as a *modus* at the request of 25 bishops. On the one hand, the seminarians must face with open eyes the tasks and difficulties of their future vocation; but on the other, it would be wrong to present their future work only as a danger for their spiritual life. They must learn that the grace of the priesthood consists precisely in their experiencing for themselves the power of the grace of Christ in genuine service and loyal self-sacrifice for the people of God (cf. Decree on the Ministry and Life of Priests, Article 12).[22]

Article 10. The article on celibacy has a complicated history. The first Conciliar schema (1963) contained a short section on priestly chastity, which was

---

[20] On the image of the priest after Vatican II, cf. F. Wulf, "Stellung und Aufgabe des Priesters nach dem Zweiten Vatikanischen Konzil", in *Geist und Leben* 39 (1966), pp. 45 ff.

[21] Cf. The Decree on the Priesthood, Articles 15–17.

[22] The sanctification of priests through priestly service was one of the main points of the Decree on the Priesthood. In the debate on the training of priests Cardinal Suenens formulated it as follows: "Non independenter enim a suo ministerio sed ex exigentiis eius, i.e., ex servitio Evangelii apud homines, debet erui spiritualitas quae ipsi convenit et formatio adaequata. In et per apostolatum suum ad intimam cum Deo coniunctionem perducitur."

expanded at the request of various bishops. When the schema had to be reduced to mere *propositiones,* the whole section was dropped. There was an immediate protest from the bishops, who expected the decree to give practical directions on urgent problems. In the new version of the *propositiones,* as they were presented to the Council for debate, the text of the earlier schema appeared as a newly added article. In the discussion, however, the request was made for a profounder justification which drew more on Scripture, as well as a more positive orientation in the education for celibacy (Cardinal Döpfner, Bishop Mendes, Bishop Reuss). 60 bishops signed *modi* with the same request. Thus there emerged in the final version a greatly expanded text.

The article begins with the reservation which Cardinal Bea requested on ecumenical grounds that it is valid only for those who are committed to celibacy by their rite. This also means celibacy is not part of the nature of the priesthood, but is a special charism which is, however, closely connected with priestly service. The following text shows the importance of this charism, gives the reasons for it, and points out ways towards its realization.

The description of celibacy is not limited to the negative demand for the renunciation of marriage, but is consciously supported by the statements of Scripture, even if these are only briefly indicated and no attempt at an exegetical analysis is attempted. The words "for the sake of the kingdom of heaven" refer to the full openness to the coming of the Lord in history and eschatology; it consists in cleaving exclusively to Christ (1 Cor 7:34; 2 Cor 11:2) and becomes a testimony for the eschatological perfection which grows beyond the sacramental sign-character of marriage to the full reality of union in God (Lk 20:35f.). Cleaving to Christ in an unmarried state is by no means only a means of individual sanctification, but is the permanent uniting of oneself with God's saving will, and hence the readiness for the total, all-embracing redemptive love of Christ for men; it enables the priest to give himself fully to his office, in which he is to become everything to all men.[23] This view, based on scriptural theology, goes far beyond a mere juridical attitude to celibacy as a prerequisite for priestly ordination; this would be completely inadequate, especially with the growing understanding of the personal values present in the community of two married people. The vocation to celibacy is a grace and as such must be sought, gratefully received and freely and generously made one's own.

These fundamental considerations are followed by practical directions: the theological students must have sufficient insight into the nature and values of marriage and also into its profound spiritual significance as a sign of the communion of Christ with his Church. But they must also understand the significance of chastity: its special value does not depend on a devaluation of marriage, but on the nature of the Church itself, which must visibly present not only the "in the world"

---

[23] Cf. the analogous account of the vow of chastity in *Perfectae Caritatis,* Article 12, and in the Decree on the Priesthood, Article 16.

element of the incarnation, but also the "beyond the world" element of eschato-logical salvation.[24] It is only on the basis of this clear insight that a free and mature choice is possible, which must necessarily precede the permanent bond of celibacy.

Practical education must go hand in hand with insight into the nature of celibacy. The original text spoke only of the necessity of preparing seminarists for the existing dangers, which today are particularly great. The text expanded in the *modi* calls for a positive education for chastity. The "helps, both divine and human" which are mentioned in the text are not listed in detail; but according to the *relatio* what is meant is, for example, progressive, sensible sexual instruction and the communal life of priests as recommended in the Decree on the Priesthood (Article 8). It is very important that celibacy be integrated into the whole of the priest's personality and activity; if the tensions and problems connected with celibacy are not worked out, there are unresolved conflicts and an impoverishment of the person, whereas the consecration of the whole person to God for men should lead the priest to his full maturity.

Article 11. This article deals with education to full human maturity. One of the chief complaints against seminary training was that it did not sufficiently develop human virtues (Bishop Fernández-Conde), that it was cut off from the world (Archbishop Colombo), and that it did not educate men to full maturity (Cardinal Jaeger, Bishop Charue). The *modi* submitted made the same points. Thus this text, which was originally very short, became almost three times as long in its final version.

First of all the application of the general norms of psychology and pedagogy are called for in the seminary.[25] The danger of the closed seminary life consists precisely in imparting to young men a clerical style of life, building up in them an unreal imaginative and intellectual world with separate interests and special forms of life, and thus alienating those becoming priests from their contemporaries. This alienation must be overcome not only for the sake of the future apostolate, but also in order to educate the students properly. In this closed world it is impossible for a sense of responsibility and human maturity to develop fully, which are the most important things for every man and hence are indispensable for a priest also. Thus the supernatural orientation of the priest's training must be supplemented by the development of personal maturity, social justice, reliability, courtesy, approachability,[26] etc. The stronger emphasis on human qualities will not diminish the high calling of the priest, but make his message more credible and acceptable.[27]

A second section is devoted to the practical and difficult problem of seminary

---

[24] Cf. K. Rahner, "Über die evangelischen Räte", in *Schriften zur Theologie*, VII (1966), pp. 404–34.
[25] Cf. H. Stenger, *Wissenschaft und Zeugnis. Die Ausbildung des katholischen Seelsorgeklerus in psycho-logischer Sicht* (1961).
[26] The need of sympathetic understanding was emphasized in many *modi*.
[27] Cardinal Meyer put the point in his intervention as follows: "Priusquam aliquis bonus sacerdos evadere potest, oportet eum esse bonum hominem et bonum Christianum."

discipline and its importance for training. The accent is moved from an authoritatively imposed house-discipline to a common way of life that is personally affirmed by everyone and intelligently ordered. The point of a house-order is not simply the regularity and uniformity of seminary life; rather it is the necessary framework for true community. Further, it is an essential means of self-education, personal maturity and the overcoming of moods. It should lead to an ordered regularity of life, which is necessary for fruitful work in the Church. All this can be achieved only if the seminarist accepts the order from his own inner conviction and sense of responsibility in relation to authority. The self-responsibility of the individual and his share in the administration of the community should increase at every stage of his training and prove itself in greater freedom. The future priest is to learn to find in his personal life and his relation to others the right forms. That there are difficult problems to be overcome here is no secret. The final section does not deal with these individual problems but characterizes the spirit which should animate the community of the seminarists and in which individual problems can be correctly resolved. Reverence, silence and mutual readiness to help are named as characteristic of this spirit. Thus life in the seminary is to prepare the theology students for their priestly life.

Article 12. Four suggestions are made which all aim at an all-round and mature training of the seminarists and are intended to prevent the ordination of immature and inexperienced candidates: 1) a special period of spiritual training within the general course, a kind of novitiate, 2) the interruption of studies by pastoral work, 3) the raising of the age of ordination, 4) the holding of the diaconate for some time before priestly ordination. None of these suggestions is elaborated further, as far as length of time and implementation are concerned (although many bishops called for more definite norms), since they are measures which depend very much on local circumstances. For the same reason the suggestions in the article are not laid down as an obligation — apart from the first one — but only as recommendations.[28] Further, more exact directives are left to the individual bishops, not to the bishops' conferences, since not only regional, but also local circumstances might influence their implementation.[29] Nevertheless, according to the *relatio* the co-operation of bishops in these important questions is desirable.

A special period of spiritual training was generally welcomed, because it is necessary in order to impart full understanding of the priest's vocation and way of life. Hence it will naturally have to come somewhere near the beginning of the general training.

---

[28] The request for more detailed and binding norms was answered by the Council with the words: 'Commissioni autem visum est opportunum, ut Concilium huiusmodi incepta commendans episcopis committeret, ut ipsi pro locorum et gentium adiunctis normas ferrent magis particulares, consideratis etiam experimentis alibi bono cum exitu factis.''

[29] Concerning the age of ordination, the words "coetum episcoporum" were changed to simply "episcoporum".

The interruption of studies for practical work may also consist in a particular period of pastoral training. But the purpose of the interruption is not to educate the seminarist in theory, but to test him in working conditions and in contact with men of all kinds, as he will later find when he is a priest. This should serve to create a counter-balance to the seclusion of seminary life.

Many bishops felt that the age-limit for the higher orders was too low. The minimum age for the sub-diaconate is 21, the diaconate 22, the priesthood 24 (*CIC,* can. 975). Moreover, the candidate for ordination must commit himself to celibacy when he becomes a sub-deacon, at a time when he often lacks the necessary maturity and experience. The Council does not give new norms, but leaves it to the bishops to decide whether this age should be made higher.

The last form of test, the holding of the diaconate for a period before priestly ordination, was added as a *modus*.[30] The deacon already has his full training and thus he is able to do valuable pastoral work in various fields, but he does not yet have full priestly responsibility, especially in relation to the celebration of the Eucharist and the sacrament of penance; in this way he is able to grow slowly into his work. If he should find in his practical work that he is not called to celibacy, he can as a deacon still obtain an easy dispensation from this obligation. Only experience can show if this form of test will prove suitable. In it the diaconate is conceived as a preliminary stage before the priesthood, whereas it has, through the Council, regained its importance as an order in its own right (*Lumen Gentium,* Article 29).

CHAPTER V: THE REVISION OF ECCLESIASTICAL STUDIES

The chapter on the studies follows the conventional order of the training, with the introduction of the so-called basic course (Article 14) as the only innovation. Behind this traditional structure of the course of studies, however, there is a new orientation which might well revolutionize Church studies. The aim of the training is wholly attuned to the general task of the seminary, namely the shaping of the priestly personality. This uniform relation to the vocation is what is meant by the pastoral orientation of the studies. Thus it does not mean a diminution of the academic side, but the orientation of all subjects towards the vocation. Its centre is the word of God; all the disciplines, even the preparatory linguistic studies, are orientated towards this. It is no longer, then, a question of imparting a closed system of knowledge — in concrete terms, the scholastic system —, which too easily separates the intellectual world of the priest from his environment, but of giving a genuine understanding of revelation from its sources, its development in the life and thought of

---

[30] This holding of the diaconate between the conclusion of studies and ordination to the priesthood has since been introduced in some dioceses.

the Church, in which the tradition of Scholasticism retains its legitimate place, and the importance of revelation for the world of today.

Article 13. Four things are called for as a humanistic and scientific basis for Church studies: 1) In general education university matriculation standard is required, however this is determined in the various countries. This ensures a general level of education and at the same time the possibility is held open of changing over to another career, if necessary. 2) As much knowledge of Latin is required to make available to the students the rich and numerous Latin sources of the tradition of many centuries and those theological works that are written in Latin. The requirement to follow lectures in Latin or to write and speak Latin is no longer made. This restriction on the aims of Latin studies corresponds to the primary goal of training for the priestly office. It was accepted without any serious objection. For seminarists of the Latin rite, there is a further norm for the study of Latin, which was added as a *modus*: 3) The study of the liturgical language that is used in the rite of the particular student. A theology student of the Latin rite must therefore be able to use the Latin liturgical books, as the students of other rites the books in their appropriate language. 4) The study of the languages of the Bible and of tradition is recommended. This recommendation, also added as a *modus,* is the reply to a request made by many to include Greek also as an obligatory subject. It did not, however, appear wise to demand Greek everywhere, in areas, for example, where students have to learn a number of other languages. Thus this was left as a general recommendation, which leaves it open to the bishops' conferences to make Greek an obligatory subject in their areas. These norms show that the Council does not desire to train the seminarists in a clerical Latin culture. The same general level of education is required as for all higher professions, as well as the linguistic knowledge necessary for the studies.

Article 14. Before the philosophical and theological studies are treated, this article deals with the principle, often enunciated, of the co-ordination of all the studies towards the one goal, the understanding of the mystery of Christ (Cardinal Suenens, Cardinal Caggiano, Cardinal Jaeger). The two disciplines had been separated in too mechanical a fashion and treated simply one after the other, so that the world appeared to exist, as it were, at two levels, in the natural and rational sphere, which is accessible to philosophy, and in the super-natural revealed order, in which theology moves. This separation does not do justice to consideration of created being as a whole; it does not give the priest a good basis for the unity of his personality and his office, in which God's grace and the world of men must meet. All studies, including philosophy, must aim at the comprehensive understanding of man and the world, that has its centre in the mystery of Christ. It is indicated only in broad lines how in the Christian view of the world Christ appears as the key to the understanding of the history of mankind, how the Church lives from the mystery of Christ, and how the priest is to realize this day by day. The theological student is to make this view of the world his own right from the beginning, in order to be able to work through it in detail in the course of his studies.

The study of individual subjects can be fruitful only if they find a place in this pre-ordained comprehensive picture. That is why the philosophical studies are to be preceded by an introductory course on the mystery of Christ.[31] No details are given on the arrangement of the subject matter or the length of the course — the text says only generally "per congruum tempus". Thus the course might be shaped in various different ways, indeed it should differ according to the intellectual situation and environment from which the theological students come to their studies. The three aims of this course are stated as : 1) Right at the beginning of his training the theology student is to acquire the proper orientation for the subjects to be studied in the comprehensive plan of the course; thus he is not to feel lost in the midst of a mass of material, without grasping its relation to his priestly office. 2) The theology student is to be strengthened in his own life of faith. This second aim, which was added in the *modi*, is particularly important today, because there are a vast number of influences on young people that they have not properly assimilated; it is no easy task to take all the experiences and ideas that a young man brings with him to his studies and organize them around Christ as the centre, illuminate them with his light, and thus make possible a genuine life in faith; but this is absolutely essential for a future priest. 3) The course is to show the significance and the greatness of the priestly vocation and task and thus foster a deeper joy in the vocation, which has been won from personal insight. Because of the close connection of the introductory course with the spiritual forming of the theology students, it is possible and even desirable that it should be combined with a period of spiritual training (cf. Article 12), because in this way the danger is avoided of separating spiritual shaping from intellectual and pastoral training.[32]

---

[31] The original suggestion for this course came from Archbishop Hurley, who called for an introductory year in which the following programme would be undertaken: "The first year of the seminary programme should take the form of a thorough initiation into the mystery of Christ — or rather in view of the fact that the initiation should already have taken place in the parish or at school, of the systematic intensifying of participation in the mystery in its relation to the pastoral ministry for which the seminarian is being prepared. In that first year he should be given a vision capable of illuminating, inspiring and co-ordinating all his subsequent study and personal striving after priestly and pastoral sanctity." ("Pastoral Emphasis in Seminary Training", in *The Furrow* 13 (1922), pp. 20f.) A summary of the suggestions that were made for this course can be found in A. Mayer and G. Galdanza, "Il Rinnovamento degli studi filosofici e teologici nei seminari", in *Scuola Cattolica* (1966), supplement 2, pp. 101–7. The chief contributions are by J. Möller, *Zur wissenschaftlichen Ausbildung der Studenten der katholischen Theologie: Die Ausbildung der Theologiestudenten in den westeuropäischen Ländern. Akten des zweiten Kongresses über die europäische Priesterfrage* (1964), pp. 65–78; K. Rahner, "Über die theoretische Ausbildung künftiger Priester heute", in *Schriften zur Theologie*, VI (1965), pp. 139–67; G. Muschalek, "Zur Frage eines theologischen Grundkurses in der Priesterausbildung", in *Orientierung* 20 (1965), pp. 54–57.
[32] Archbishop Hurley recommends this combining of the introductory course with spiritual formation: "The advantage of this arrangement would be that the spiritual year would consti-

A note on the controversy about the place of St. Thomas in ecclesiastical studies

On the question of the place of Scholasticism, especially of St. Thomas, in philosophical and theological studies there were two sharply opposed views. The controversy was fought out in discussion in the full session of the Council. Some considered that St. Thomas was not accorded a sufficiently important place in the decree, whereas his teaching had been recommended in more than 100 papal documents (Cardinal Ruffini, Cardinal Bacci, Cardinal Caggiano, Archbishop Staffa), while others were against any special mention of St. Thomas (Cardinal Léger). Others again approved the moderate formula of the text (Cardinal Döpfner). The *modi* submitted on Article 15 on philosophy were almost all concerned with the place of St. Thomas. Over 100 Fathers expressed in one form or another the desire that the system of *philosophia perennis,* as developed by St. Thomas, should be taught in the seminaries. Even after the first vote, 31 further requests for this were received up to 31 January 1965, the last official date for the submission of *modi;* after this date another 420 such requests were received.[33] As against this, a *modus* signed by 117 Fathers requested that no particular philosophical system be prescribed; St. Thomas should be taught to such an extent as was still valid today. With Article 16 on the study of theology also over 200 *modi* asked that either the words "Sancto Thoma magistro" be left out of the text, or that it should be weakened by adding "praesertim", or else that other teachers of the Church should be recommended as well.[34]

In view of this conflict of opinions the original text, accepted by more than a two-thirds majority, was, in essentials, retained. It is in fact more than a compromise between two parties; it expresses in broad terms the double duty of ecclesiastical instruction; to remain in the tradition and at the same time to be open to new questions and insights.[35]

tute a real initiation into pastoral spirituality. Unless this aspect is emphasized the tendency would remain of attempting to give a spiritual formation to pastoral priests according to methods better suited to recluses."

[33] While desiring to preserve the important provision of Thomism, a distinction was made between those doctrines that are outmoded and the lasting contribution of this teacher of the Church. Of this latter, the actual philosophy, Archbishop Staffa said in his intervention: "Pars perennis immutabilis, quod omnino certa, constituitur principiis, hoc est doctrinae capitibus, elementis quae systema constituunt, ideoque conclusionibus ex illis principiis logica necessitate profluentibus, quae secus nullis rei principia essent."

[34] Cardinal Jaeger rejected in his intervention any one-sided preference given to a particular school: "non quia opera S. Thomae spernenda sint, sed quia omnino vitari debet exclusivismus immoderatus. Vae homini unius libri! Vae ecclesiae unius doctoris!"

[35] On the change of attitudes in the Order of Preachers, in which the lasting value of Thomism is recognized, cf. M. D. Chenu, *Das Wort des hl. Thomas von Aquin* (1960); O. H. Pesch and D. Schlüter, "Thomismus", in *LTK,* X (1965), cols. 157–67.

Article 15. In the discussion on philosophy it became clear that the orientation of all the studies towards the one goal of priestly formation, the fuller understanding of revelation and towards the modern world, involves new and difficult tasks for the philosophy professors of the seminaries. In order to cover the many questions on the teaching of philosophy, the final text of the article was more than doubled in length.

It is no longer considered desirable that the aim of philosophical instruction should be the teaching of a comprehensive system — this is hardly possible today and would easily lead to superficial simplifications — but rather the development of a solid and coherent understanding of basic positions that are essential to a Christian view of the world. The three focal points are man, the world, and God. Thus the philosophical training should be: 1) essentially anthropology, in order to provide a genuine understanding of man; 2) it should give a philosophically underpinned world picture, as it emerges from modern science; 3) it should lead to the transcendence of the world and man, to the ultimate ground of being. To obtain this goal, instruction should first base itself on the philosophical heritage of scholastic philosophy, but this does not mean that it is to impart a closed system, but to make fruitful the lasting insights of the scholastic heritage.[36] Similarly, though, the theology student must become familiar with the developments and insights of modern philosophy and the scientific view of the world, with special consideration of the culture and environment in which he has to work. Thus the study of philosophy is part of the preparation for the pastoral task that he has to fulfil as a priest.

With this as the aim of the study of philosophy, the history of philosophy acquires a greater role than before. This is why special norms were added in the *modi* for its teaching. Introduction to the history of philosophy must find the appropriate centre between the positivistic collection of intellectual material which would lead to a relativization and historicization of the truth, and an unhistorical dogmatic approach, which has little feeling for the change and growth of the knowledge of truth. It must be a treatment in depth: the student is to acquire not only an external knowledge of the systems of thought and simply assess what is wrong with them, he is to understand them from within, from their own positions, estimate their positive contribution and deal with their inadequacies and errors in terms of their own basic assumptions.

The practical norms for the teaching of philosophy in the third session were also added as *modi*: unlike theology, which starts from obedience to faith, philosophy must seek the truth with man as its starting point. The theologian is not to learn philosophy in the spirit of dogmatic credulity, but is to experience the seriousness and the rigour of investigation, observation and argument. He

---

[36] The words "perennis philosophiae principia" of the original text which suggested too much of a fixed system, were changed at the request of Cardinal Léger to "innixi patrimonio philosophico perenniter valido".

is to realize how difficult it is to give convincing answers, and thus observe completely the limitations of human thought. Further, the teaching should always emphasize the relation of philosophy to the real problems of humanity and to the personal experience of the students. The over-intellectual treatment of out-of-date and abstract problems which no longer have much importance for the life and work of priests is to be done away with. Finally, the teaching should prepare for the study of theology. This does not take place by anticipating the answers of theology, but by introducing the theology student to the anthropological and cosmological postulates of the world of revelation: by his understanding, for example, the meaning of such basic ideas as intellectuality, freedom and history, thus being prepared for the deeper understanding of man that he will meet in revelation. This in no way diminishes the importance of philosophy — even bishops as pastorally minded as Archbishop Hurley have expressly warned against an undervaluing of philosophy — but it is to come out of the isolation into which it has fallen because of its unrelatedness to life and to theology.

The question whether philosophy is to be taught in a separate period of study or whether the philosophical subjects can be co-ordinated with the study of theology and perhaps even completely integrated with it, has been consciously left open, although naturally the sequence of Articles 15 and 16 suggests the order of philosophy and theology. Undoubtedly, however, the orientation of those subjects towards the same goal of priestly formation must bring the two disciplines closer to one another.

Article 16. The article on theological training probably expresses most clearly the spirit of the decree. It first describes the aim of the theological course and then develops its realization in the most important subjects.

Four aspects of this aim are stressed: 1) The theology student must draw doctrines from the sources and is not to be satisfied with derivative formulae. 2) He must fully understand the doctrine, not simply memorize it, as he has to face the problems of the world today. 3) He has to make it fruitful for his own life, as in his theology he is to understand more deeply and embrace more consciously his own vocation and mission. 4) He is to study it for others, so that he is able to communicate it to men of his time and environment in the service of the word. All this must happen in the light of faith, since what we are dealing with is not a secular subject of study, but the deeper understanding of faith, and that under the direction of the Church, because true theology exists only in the living community of the Church, which is assured of the spirit of truth.

It was in the spirit of the Council that the study of Scripture had to be the first of the theological disciplines to be discussed. Scripture is not merely the subject of study, but "the soul of theology". Thus it must be not only its source, but its chief inspiration. The basis of the study of Scripture is the introduction which makes the seminarian familiar with the literary historical and geographical background to the understanding of the text; much of this would already be treated in the preliminary stages to theology. Then follows exegesis proper, in which it is not sufficient to interpret correctly the meaning of individual texts, but where a detailed introduction to the method of exegetical work is required. Without familiarity with exegetical methods[37] the priest would be exposed to varying interpretations, the value of which he was not able to test. He must know how to handle independently the chief source of his spirituality and his preaching. The instruction should not content itself simply with the analysis of texts, but introduce the student to the intellectual and imaginative world of the whole Bible, as it has revealed itself in the course of salvation history. Apart from the actual study of Scripture, biblical thinking should also govern the daily reading of the Scripture, become the personal possession of the student and shape his whole attitude to life.

In dogmatic instruction a fundamental change is required from the systematic approach hitherto predominant to the genetic-historical methods. Revelation is not given to us in a systematic form, but as the history of salvation. The saving truth that is given to us in Christ must be developed and interpreted by the living Church in its own history and in the constant encounter with the world to which it is sent. Consequently, the teaching is not to begin with a series of fixed propositions but with the biblical statements that have been discovered in the study of Scripture or worked out in the dogma classes. In order to appreciate the richness of revelation, the students must pursue it further in the chief phases of the tradition of the Church, in the patristics of the East and West[38] and in Scholasticism. Whereas in patristic theology the main emphasis lay on the handing down and presentation of revelation, the scholastic period led to a speculative penetration and systematic presentation of it. In this theological work it is not only a question of intellectual clarification, but of the growth of the Church itself, which in all changing situations constantly restates itself and its message; this is why the theological tradition is to be presented in the context of the history of the Church. It is only on the basis of tradition that the actual systematic work of theology can begin which seeks to penetrate speculatively the entire content of the revelation that has been handed down and to grasp its inner connections. In this speculative work St. Thomas is recommended as a teacher. He is not only the master who formulated in his time the contents of revelation in the intellectual and linguistic forms of Aristotelianism (which was then modern) and hence became a model of the adaptation of theological research and language to contemporary life and culture — this was conceded by all, and many requested that the council should limit itself to recommending his

[37] Most of the Council Fathers will probably not have had any more detailed idea of what was meant by "the exegetical method". This is perhaps not surprising, for the subject is a difficult one.
[38] The original text mentioned only "Patres". In order to emphasize explicitly the importance of Eastern theology, the text was made more specific through the *modi:* "Patres Ecclesiae Orientis et Occidentis".

method — but he is also a teacher in as much as he arrived at permanent insights which have to be taught in theological instruction.[39]

Revelation, however, is not merely a subject of knowledge, but is part of the life of the Church, expressing itself in its liturgy and revealing itself in its work. Thus future priests must learn to see the liturgy and life of the Church as the expression of the mystery of Christ that is alive and at work in the Church. Finally, they are to be trained to translate theology into the concrete terms of life, and place the problems that they encounter, especially human problems, in the context of the saving mystery of Christ. It is clear that for the theological student as well as for the philosopher the need is emphasized to translate the knowledge acquired into a language that can be understood by modern men.

Originally the text limited itself to this account of the instruction in dogmatic theology, which is naturally to be applied *mutatis mutandis* to other subjects as well. At the request of many, however, particular remarks on various subjects were added in the *modi*: the basic point is made that all disciplines must be placed within the perspective of salvation history. Above all, renewal is called for in the teaching of moral theology, which too frequently rested on principles of natural law and canonical norms and contained too little theology. The decree speaks of the necessity of basing moral theology more on Scripture and of deriving the demands of morality from the sublimity of the Christian vocation and Christian responsibility for the world.[40] Canon law and the history of the Church are to be presented as an expression of Church life; they are to take the picture of the Church contained in the Constitution on the Church and make it concrete within the dimension of history and society. Similarly, liturgical instruction is not to be limited to an historical exposé, but must always point out the connection with Christian life.

Finally, special mention is made of two particular problems: first, the introduction to the knowledge of the separated Christian communities, for the purpose of preparing the future priests for ecumenical work. This general recommendation was made more specific in the *modi* by adding the words "variarum regionum condicionibus opportune consideratis", as obviously the problems of the denominational situation in different countries present different

---

[39] A *modus* submitted by 116 Council Fathers desired that instead of "S. Thoma magistro", the words "Ecclesia Catholica proponit S. Thomam ut magistrum et exemplar omnium eorum, qui scientias theologicas colunt" should be used, i.e., that St. Thomas is the model for theological work, but that nothing is said about the content of his teaching. The reason given was: "Systema vel doctrina S. Thomae non imponatur, sed potius proponatur S. Thomas in sua habitudine scientifica et spirituali ut praeclarum exemplar indagatoris et creatoris in materia theologica, qui sui temporis scientiam ad utilitatem Evangelii convertit." However, the Commision kept to the original formula, which certainly does not make the totalistic system binding, but in addition to pointing out the model nature of his work also emphasizes the importance of the content of his teaching; its validity, however, is to be examined in particular cases.

[40] Cf. V. Redlich, ed., *Moralprobleme im Umbruch der Zeit* (1957); B. Häring, *Moralverkündigung nach dem Konzil* (1966).

demands on the priests. Secondly, instruction in non-Christian religions, especially those which are widespread in the students' future area of activity, is to be included in the curriculum, with the threefold purpose of recognizing the positive elements in these religions and thus make possible a constructive dialogue;[41] to be able to counter errors; and prepare for the proclamation of the gospel. This naturally applies chiefly to mission countries, but today has universal significance also because the encounter with the non-Christian world takes place almost everywhere and because it requires a tremendous effort from theology, an effort which has hardly begun, to deal with the tremendous variety of doctrines, experiences and customs of other religions. A theology must at least acquire the right perspectives in such an undertaking.

Article 17. The first version of the *propositiones* did not contain this article on the method of theological studies, but even before the conciliar debate it had to be included as an essential supplement to the account of the philosophical and theological studies. It was accepted almost without a contrary voice. The norms given inevitably had to remain very general, because they need to be proved practically and to be adapted to changing concrete circumstances. Two points are firmly made: self-reliance in the students must be stimulated: even where there is a question of the assimilation of a certain amount of material, this should take place more through personal work and communal effort than through an extended course of lectures, which educates students to passivity. The second point is that the goal of the training ought to be a limited one, not in order to lower the standard of the training, but to consolidate it. The treatment of out-of-date and abstract problems, merely because they fill many pages in traditional text-books, are of no value in priestly education. Similarly, there must be no attempt to train all priests on an academic, strictly scholarly level, because this is not necessary for all. It can also distract from the concrete aim of priestly education and moreover often lead only to pseudo-education. As in Articles 15 und 16, it is, however, required that the instruction be unified and substantial.

Article 18. Apart from the general training of priests, however, attention should be given to the specialist training of individual priests, both in the actual sacred sciences as well as in the other subjects in which the bishop requires experts. The article does not go into further detail, such as whether this is to take place before or after ordination, because such questions are to be left to the appropriate bishop. In the *modi* submitted 27 bishops requested that the students should complete the normal course of studies in the seminary of their own diocese before they begin special studies elsewhere. Moreover, concern is expressed lest the spiritual training of theological students studying elsewhere should suffer. In order to cover this second point, the words "virtute apti" were

---

[41] Cf. the Declaration on the Relationship of the Church to Non-Christian Religions; Constitution on the Church, Article 17; Decree on the Church's Missionary Activity, Articles 9 and 11. Cf. also J. Ackermann, "Zum Dialog zwischen Christen und Nichtchristen", in *Geist und Leben* 39 (1966), pp. 354 ff.

added in the *modi* as applying to those theological students who are to specialize; this was to be as necessary a qualification as intellectual aptitude. Similarly the final sentence was added, which requires the spiritual guidance of those students studying elsewhere. The first point was covered by the bishops' being made responsible ("episcoporum erit curare") for all the theological students that are studying elsewhere or doing specialist courses; naturally he can keep his theological students in his seminary up to ordination.[42]

CHAPTER VI: THE PROMOTION OF STRICTLY PASTORAL TRAINING

In many interventions the point was made that the whole training must be pastoral (Cardinal Suenens,[43] Cardinal Jaeger, Archbishop Hurley). The mere external addition of pastoral lectures and practical work would be inadequate. However, the main elements of pastoral training are to be indicated in a special chapter.[44]

Article 19 formulates the aim of pastoral training: preparation for pastoral work embraces primarily the serving of the word of God in catechesis and preaching, liturgical worship, works of charity, and concern for those who are outside the Church. This short list was supplemented in the *modi* by three further points: it was strongly felt that when a priest is overburdened with organizational and administrative tasks his actual pastoral work suffers; thus it is urgently necessary to train the theological students in such a way that they are able effectively to help Christians who are deeply aware of their vocation, in their inner life, their apostolate, and in making their professional life fully Christian. Secondly, the students are to be trained to give intelligent guidance to members of religious orders also, especially nuns, who often find very little understanding for their particular vocation, which is so important in the total life of the Church, and for their particular problems and tasks.[45] Finally, it is asked that the future priests should develop their capacity for human relationships, which is essential in modern pastoral work: the capacity of listening to others and meet with understanding human situations. Thus in pastoral training it is not merely a question of learning to organize, nor simply of having the right

---

[42] In the Decree on the Church's Missionary Activity (Article 16) the point was, however, expressly made that theology students should do their normal studies up to ordination as far as possible in their own country and in contact with their own culture; only after this should they be sent to do special studies abroad.

[43] In this intervention Cardinal Suenens pointed out that simply to add a pastoral year here would be inadequate: "Totus cyclus ut sic efformationis et studiorum est, sit venia verbo, pastorizandus."

[44] Cf. the various writings of the Viennese pastoral theologian F. Klostermann (especially in the journal *Der Seelsorger*).

[45] Cf. the similar remark in the Decree on the Priesthood, Article 6.

theology for the mission of a priest, but of the development of the human and spiritual qualities which go to make the true pastor, in which Christ, the shepherd, seeks to encounter modern men.

Article 20. The introduction to the modern methods of pastoral work is part of pastoral training. Good intentions and spiritual zeal are not sufficient if they are unaccompanied by sober psychological and sociological insights. For example, a pastor must know when a psychiatrist should be consulted; he must be aware of the influence that the concrete social situation and environment exert on men. Above all, the future pastor must learn to work together with the laity (Cardinal Döpfner, Cardinal Suenens), because the life of the Church must be sustained by the whole community. He must be informed concerning the structure and working methods of lay organizations and above all concerning the work of education among the laity.[46] In order to give the future priests a better understanding of the situation and the problem of the faithful, it was repeatedly suggested that laymen also should take part in the training of priests. Pastoral work is not to be limited to the narrow circle of one's immediate sphere of activity but must preserve a catholic breadth and look beyond the often dividing barriers of diocese, country, and rite. In the *modi* a missionary orientation and a readiness to give oneself to the missionary task of the Church were especially recommended.[47] This was expressly at the wish of the Brazilian bishops.

Article 21. Pastoral training can only be effective if it is combined with practical work and experience.[48] Here the Council clearly gives a new orientation as against the sheltering tendency hitherto predominant. The seminarist is to get to know his future field of activity and train himself for his work. This work is, of course, only temporary and limited; nevertheless it is to lead to priestly self-responsibility, which can only be learnt in concrete work. It will also give practice in collaboration, which is indispensable in modern pastoral work and in the Conciliar understanding of the Church's office. The idea of collaboration was first introduced into the text by the *modi*.

The text naturally remains unspecific about the implementation of these ideas. The work is to be done during the school year or also during the holidays (the latter is also an addition of the *modi*); thus even the holidays are to be brought into the general plan of the priests' training. Details are to be settled by the bishops and those in charge of the seminary, with the chief problem being the correct interpretation of the words "opportunas exercitationes": it is to be

[46] On the responsibility of training the laity, cf. the Constitution on the Church, Article 37; the Decree on the Apostolate of the Laity, ch. vi; especially on the communication media: Decree on the Instruments of Social Communication, Article 15; on the duty of the clergy: Decree on the Priesthood, Article 14; on the need for teaching to be adapted to contemporary conditions: Pastoral Constitution on the Church in the Modern World, Article 44; on instruction of the laity in the missions: Decree on the Church's Missionary Activity, Article 21.

[47] Cf. Decree on the Church's Missionary Activity, Articles 38 and 39; Decree on the Bishops' Pastoral Office in the Church, Article 6; Decree on the Priesthood, Article 10.

[48] Cf. the essays of F. Klostermann (see note 44).

genuine pastoral work, but must not cause the systematic academic training and the community life of the seminary to suffer, Three practical norms are given: 1) These trial periods of work are to be suited to the age and the maturity of the seminarist; if too much is asked of him it could cause permanent damage. 2) The work is to be undertaken under experienced guidance; it is in no way to be regarded as a hobby, but as an integral part of the course of training. 3) The supernatural spirit of the priestly mission must be cultivated precisely in this practical work. The realism of the practical work is not to appear as a sober contrast to the spiritual atmosphere of the seminary, but should, on the contrary, make the seminarist aware of the seriousness of his consecration to the priestly office.[49]

CHAPTER VII: THE REFINEMENT OF TRAINING AFTER THE COURSE OF STUDY

Article 22. The final chapter, consisting only of a short article, goes beyond seminary training in the strict sense, since it is concerned with the further training of young priests during the critical years when they start their pastoral work.[50] The reference to the need for this further training in today's conditions indicates the heavy burdens which the priest has to accept in the contemporary world, the numerous new problems, the rapid progress in the theological and pastoral sciences, which make necessary continued systematic study. The means for this further training are pastoral institutes, regular meetings, seminaries, courses, etc. All this can be stated in the decree in only a very general way. It is especially noted, however, that institutes are not to work in isolation, but in connection with living parishes. This further training is, like the seminary training itself, not to be concerned with the imparting of mere intellectual information, but to aim at the organic unity of spiritual, intellectual and pastoral shaping. The young clergy are to be offered the necessary aims to enable them to grow into their way of life and their sphere of work. The bishops' conferences are responsible for their further training, not only the individual bishops, as this is an extremely important[51] matter of general concern that must be taken up on a regional level.

[49] On this point, Cardinal Suenens said in his intervention: "Quae pastoralis initiatio nec pietati nec studiis damnum vel detrimentum afferet. E contrario! Pietas magis realistica et authentica eveniet siquidem fides in exercitio ministerii verificatur. Similiter haec initiatio pastoralis promovebit studia scientifica siquidem non scholae sed vitae discimus."

[50] On the further training of priests see the Decree on the Priesthood, Article 19; on the missions: Decree on the Church's Missionary Activity, Article 20; on the duty of the bishops to be concerned with this further training: Decree on the Bishops, Article 16d; Decree on the Priesthood, Article 7.

[51] The importance that is ascribed to the further training of the young priests follows from the parallel that is drawn in the relation between the Council of Trent's concern for the seminarists

CONCLUSION

The conclusion was added only through the *modi,* simply because the document had developed from the brief *propositiones* to a connected decree that required a final summing up. It takes up again the point of the introduction that the hoped-for renewal of the Church and the effectiveness of its work in the world are bound up with the proper training of priests. The Fathers of Trent knew this, and so does Vatican II; hence the directors and professors of seminaries are reminded of their responsibility to shape the future priests of Christ in the spirit of the Council's renewal.

and that of Vatican II priests: "Commissioni ergo cordi fuit hanc curam episcoporum coetibus enixe commendare, ut sicut Concilium Tridentinum primas leges de Seminariis sapientissime promulgavit, ita Concilium Vaticanum II primas normas de Post-Seminariis opportune tradat."

SUBJECT INDEX

Abrogation of pre-conciliar norms 220
Activism 348
Ad Petri Cathedram 42, 89
Africa 67, 135
Aggiornamento 96, 303, 319, 322, 373
America 103, 125, 180, 225
Anglicans 5, 33, 103, 127, 128, 145, 156
Apologetics 8, 82, 89, 90, 112
Apostles 7, 11, 13, 20
— and Peter 67, 79
Apostolate
— hierarchical 235
— of the laity 235
— and the religious 235, 304, 305, 314–19, 352
— and self-immolation 335
— unified action 254
— of unity 28
Apostolica Sollicitudo 203, 214, 215, 254
Apostolicae Curae 145
Apostolic See, *see* Holy See
Apostolic Succession 37, 43, 44, 77, 134, 145, 155
Armenia 125, 141, 142
Art 42
Assumption, *see under* Mary, Mariology
Atheism 10
Authority, ecclesiastical 7, 13, 18, 67
— problem of 15

Baptism 20, 25, 27, 29, 34, 39, 40, 45, 47, 71, 73, 75, 92, 94, 105, 119, 151, 343–5
— the baptized 20, 21, 26, 27
— conditional 152
— and faith 153
Baroque period 96
Basil, Rule of St. 135
Beatitudes, the 312–13
Belgium 1
Benedict, Rule of St. 136, 347
Bible 8, 16, 24, 25, 29, 40, 45, 46, 51, 64, 74, 92, 97, 116, 133, 139, 144, 148, 163, 348, 397
— and dogma 98
— movement 22, 97, 123
— societies 98
Bishops
— coadjutor and auxiliary 166, 176–9, 230, 242–9

— conferences of, *see* Episcopal conferences
— co-operation of 280–5
— diocesan 175–6, 203, 220–9
— ecumenical attitude and action 21, 36, 37, 49, 93
— military 299
— ordinary faculties 168
— pastoral office 187–97
— and priests 233–4
— synod of, *see* Episcopal synod
— and universal Church 171–3, 198, 201, 203, 214
    See also Episcopal conferences, Episcopal consecration, Episcopal office, Episcopal synod
Body of Christ 21, 41, 72–73, 79, 80, 107, 199
Brazil 387
Brotherliness 330, 341, 365–6

Canada 50
Calvinists 145
Canonical mission 207
Canon law 198, 282
— Eastern 9, 10
— Latin 24, 90, 105
— modern evolution of 302
— reform of 291, 299–300, 320
Cardinals, college of 128, 173, 219
Care of souls 13, 18, 170, 185–7, 231, 256, 261, 299
Cathedral Chapter 251, 253   [130, 136, 140
Catholicity 3, 4, 5, 21, 34, 39, 41, 43, 50, 89, 90, 91, 93,
Celibacy 226, 229, 358–60, 375, 376, 388
— anthropological dimension 358
— justification of 389
— practical education 390
— psychological dimension 324
Centralization 136, 239, 370, 372
Charism 79, 80, 91, 313, 336, 352, 389
— of universal significance 338
Charity 21, 25, 43; *see also* Love
China 125
Christ
— Christocentrism 146, 149
— God and Saviour 16, 105, 147
— head of the Church 7, 40, 46, 66–67, 75
— norm of revelation 148
— prayer for unity 2, 103
— revelation of the Love of God 64

INDEX OF NAMES

412

413

414

INDEX OF NAMES

303